Gruhn's Guide To Vintage Guitars

Gruhn's Guide To Vintage Guitars

George Gruhn
and
Walter Carter

GPI BOOKS
Miller Freeman, Inc.
San Francisco, Cupertino, Atlanta, Boston, Chicago, New York, Brussels

GPI BOOKS
Miller Freeman, Inc., 600 Harrison Street, San Francisco, CA 94107
Publishers of *Guitar Player*, *Bass Player*, and *Keyboard* Magazines

ISBN: 0-87930-195-3
Library of Congress Catalog Card Number: 91-61849
Cover Design: Cassandra Chu
Text Design: Chris Ledgerwood
Printed in the United States of America

92 93 94 95   5 4 3 2

Contents

Contents

Contents

Contents

Introduction

Since 1960, interest in vintage instruments—along with values of vintage instruments—has multiplied many times over. With prices for a single instrument ranging from a few hundred dollars to tens of thousands, accurate information is crucial for the instrument buyer or seller. A Martin D-45 made prior to World War II, for example, is worth more than 20 times as much as a recent issue D-45, even though there is relatively little difference in design. A 1966 Fender Stratocaster is almost identical in appearance to its 1964 counterpart, but Fender instruments made after the company's sale to CBS in 1965 are worth significantly less than pre–CBS examples. Obviously, a buyer or seller must know how to tell the difference.

The question asked most often of the staff at Gruhn Guitars is "How much is my instrument worth?" To know the value of an instrument, one must first know what it is, when it was made, and how original its condition is. With literally thousands of models made by major American manufacturers in the twentieth century, simply identifying and dating a model can often be a great mystery.

We have assembled the best information from every available source—original catalogs and literature, information already in print, the knowledge of many fanatical collectors, and the actual instruments we have personally seen in our day to day business. Nevertheless, seldom does a day go by without an instrument coming through our doorway that prompts some revision in the manuscript of this book. We have seen thousands upon thousands of instruments, yet we still frequently come across one unlike any that we have ever seen or heard of before. We occasionally come across a model that we had previously seen only in catalogs. Conversely, we have seen numerous examples of several models for which we still can't uncover model names.

We have incorporated new information into this book right up to press time, and we believe that the information here is the best available. We also know from the experience of compiling this book that more and more information will surface. We will continue to revise and refine this work for future editions, and we welcome any new information.

As the vintage market grows, it becomes increasingly subject to the same factors that influence the commodities market or the stock market: factors such as foreign currency exchange rates, fad

Introduction

buying, or panic selling. Also, the vintage market is still small enough that a few wealthy collectors could exert a profound influence by taking a sudden interest—or sudden lack of interest—in a certain model. Not only the value of some specific models but the vintage market as a whole could change drastically during the time it takes to turn a manuscript into a book. Consequently, we will not attempt to provide market prices for any models, but we do assess the relative merits of various models in the Comments sections.

For some manufacturers, we have drawn heavily from information found in familiar sources, which are listed separately in a bibliography. In addition, we would like to thank these friends for sharing their expertise in the following areas: Dobro: Mike Cass; Epiphone: Hans Moust; Fender: Gary Bohannon, A. R. Duchossoir, Richard Smith, and John Sprung; Gibson: Ray Atwood, Julius Bellson, Gary Burnett, Dave Patrick, J. T. Riboloff, Tim Shaw, and Tom Van Hoose; Gretsch: Mayner Greene, Duke Kramer, Jay Scott, and Danny Thorpe; Larson Brothers: Dennis Watkins; National: Bob Brozman, Mike Newton and Dennis Watkins; Rickenbacker: Richard Smith; pot codes: Hans Moust. A special thanks is due Mike Longworth for his painstaking, line-by-line proofreading of the Martin section. For their valuable input, we would also like to thank the sales staff at Gruhn Guitars: Dan Green, Dan Mills, Hank Sable, David Sebring, and Dennis Watkins.

George Gruhn
Walter Carter
Nashville
Spring 1991

SCOPE

The purpose of this book is to provide information by which to identify, date, and determine the originality of vintage American stringed instruments.

Not all American manufacturers are included. Some that produced great quantity, such as Kay and Harmony, are omitted because the majority of their instruments were cheaply made and those that are still in one piece are generally not of any significance in the vintage and used instrument market. Other makers are omitted simply because we do not yet have enough information to put together a useful identification section.

If an instrument is not in this book, if it does not fit into the key, or if it is not included in the model descriptions, then one of the following explanations probably applies:

1. It varies from catalog descriptions. Catalog photos and descriptions do not always match the actual instruments. In fact, catalog descriptions do not always match the instruments in catalog photos. Manufacturers have been known to use photos as much as 10 years out of date. Non-standard but factory original parts may have been installed as a result of shortages or surpluses at the factory. Some instruments announced and placed in catalogs were never actually produced and sold.

2. It is a custom-order instrument or an obscure standard model that never appeared in a catalog or in literature.

3. It is of too recent vintage to have been listed in this book.

4. It is a non-original instrument. Parts have been changed, it has been refinished, or it has been customized with non-original inlay, electronics, etc.

ORGANIZATION

Instruments are organized by manufacturer. An alphabetical index by manufacturer is also provided at the end of the book.

At the beginning of each manufacturer's chapter is a General Information section detailing design changes that affect most or all models in the line. Protocol in the General Information sections is the same as that of the individual model descriptions (see Model Descriptions, following). Serial number information is included at the end of General Information sections.

Instruments by each manufacturer are grouped according to

How To Use This Book

type and in the following order: acoustic archtop guitars, flat tops, electric archtops, solidbody electrics, electric basses, steels, mandolins, and other instruments.

At the beginning of most of these instrument sub-sections is a model identification key. The key is organized like an outline. Each level is a yes-or-no question. If yes, go to the next level of indent; if no, then proceed on the same level of indent until the answer is yes.

MODEL DESCRIPTIONS

Models within subsections are arranged in a loose chronological order. However, chronological order is not followed whenever it seems more logical to use some other order. For example, the Gibson L-5P, which is a cutaway version of the L-5, is found with the L-5 description and not in its own separate, chronological place. On the other hand, Gibson's ES-125T, a thinbody version of the ES-125 hollowbody electric, is found with other thinlines and not with the ES-125 and other full-depth models.

The following example from the Epiphone Electric Archtops section illustrates the conventions used in model descriptions:

Zephyr De Luxe:[1] 17 3/8" wide, spruce top, 1 PU[2] with slot-head screw poles and oblong housing, PU in bridge position, volume and tone control on 1 shaft with circular *Mastervoicer* control plate, Frequensator[3] tailpiece, 5-ply top and back binding, triple-bound pickguard, bound rosewood fingerboard, cloud inlay,[4] triple-bound peghead, vine peghead inlay, gold-plated metal parts, blond finish, tenor (with metal peghead logo plate) and plectrum models available[5]
Introduced (first listed as **Deluxe Zephyr Spanish Electric**): **Dec. 1, 1941**[6]
PU in neck position, 2 PUs optional, 2 knobs near edge, *Mastervoicer* control plates, slotted switch on 2-PU model, sunburst or natural finish,[7] by[8] **1950**
Knobs on line parallel to strings: **1951**
Discontinued[9] by **1954**

1. Specifications for each model generally follow this protocol: body shape and size, body wood, pickups, knobs, bridge and tailpiece, pickguard, binding, neck and fingerboard, fingerboard inlay,

How To Use This Book

peghead, metal plating, finish.

Thus, the finish color should always be at the end of a description. The bridge and tailpiece specs should always be somewhere in the middle, after the electronics and before the fingerboard inlay.

2. *PU* means pickup.

3. Many tailpieces, pickups, and other parts whose descriptions are not self-explanatory are described in more detail in the manufacturer's General Information section.

4. *Inlay* refers to fingerboard inlay unless specified as peghead inlay, soundhole inlay, and so on.

5. Tenors and other variations of the same instrument have the same ornamentation unless otherwise specified.

6. Introduction date is the earliest appearance, whether in a catalog, in literature, or as evidenced by an actual instrument.

7. Only the specs that change are listed. Inlay, for example, continues to be cloud pattern. Some dates, especially in the General Information sections, signify a range of years, such as 1955–59 or 1973–current, and in those cases the specifications in question apply only within that range of years.

8. *By* in front of a date means that that date is the earliest that a change or an introduction has been documented. Although we believe the "by" dates are accurate within a year or two, the changes could conceivably have been implemented any time after the last listed date.

Where multiple specification changes are listed, those changes may not have all been made at exactly the same time. It was common practice for manufacturers to use up old supplies before instituting new specs. Some "transitional" instruments may have new-style pickups, for example, but still retain the old-style fingerboard inlay. In the case of Gibson's changeover from PAF (patent applied for) humbucking pickups to patent-number pickups, some instruments were fitted with one of each. Changes in Gretsch models are so difficult to pinpoint that collectors say, only half-jokingly, that all Gretsch models are transitional.

9. *Discontinued* usually refers to the year the model was dropped from the company catalog. Where shipping records are available, it may refer to the first year that the model was no longer shipped. In some cases, the total number of instruments shipped over a model's entire production run is indicated. Production figures not specified as *total* are for that year only.

How To Use This Book

COMMENTS

The authors' comments at the end of each section are intended to be a most general guideline for what models may be highly regarded by collectors. The vintage market, like any other market for collectibles, is constantly changing. The models noted as collectible are likely to remain collectible, even though prices may fluctuate. Some models that are not currently considered to be desirable, and thus are not mentioned in Comments, could become collectible in the future.

A FINAL CAUTION

We urge you to use all the information available here and elsewhere, to cross-check model descriptions with serial number lists and general manufacturer's specs and with other similar instruments. No book or catalog can take the place of in-hand experience.

Again, information may be conflicting in some cases. If a serial number was affixed to an instrument at some length of time before the instrument was completed, then the specifications of the instrument may conflict with the year in which a serial number list indicates it was made. Instruments may be numbered before they are finished, as in the case of the 1963 Gibson Flying Vs and Explorers that bear 1958 serial numbers. Instruments may be numbered after they are finished, as in the case of a Gibson mandolin we have seen with a 1952 serial number but with specs indicating that it was almost certainly built in 1949. In addition, accepted serial number lists are not always completely reliable. We have seen, for example, several Gretsch guitars with a sales receipt from a year earlier than the date given in the generally accepted Gretsch serial number list. We have also seen two Gretsch Model 6120s with consecutive serial numbers, but with earlier features on the example with the later number.

So be careful. The information in this book may not keep you from being surprised by something new, but it should keep you from being fooled.

Dobro &
Regal/Dobro

GENERAL INFORMATION

The term *Dobro* is a registered trade name, but it is also used generically to mean any instrument with 1) a resonator cone mounted so that the cone opens toward the top of the instrument and 2) an 8-armed spider assembly supporting the bridge. (On instruments with a "National-type" cone, the cone opens to the back of the instrument and the bridge sits on the peak of the cone.) The majority of Dobros have a resonator coverplate with rectangular holes arranged in four semi-circular patterns.

The Dobro name derives from the *Do*pyera *Bro*thers—John, Rudy, Emil (Ed), Robert, and Louis—who played various roles in the design, manufacture, and financing of Dobro instruments. John Dopyera and his brothers formed the National String Instrument Company in California in 1926 (see National section). The Dopyeras traded their interest in the company for stock in a new National corporation in 1928.

John Dopyera has said in interviews that he split from National and made the first Dobro brand instruments in 1928, and that is the year agreed upon by collectors as the beginning of the Dobro. His official resignation from National was February 19, 1929. Louis and Robert Dopyera retained their interest in National. After a legal dispute, National and Dobro merged in 1932.

Regal, a Chicago-based mail-order company, was licensed to make instruments using a Dobro resonator in 1932 and introduced the first models in June, 1933. Regal gained exclusive rights to market Dobro in 1937, at the time when National-Dobro was moving all production from California to Chicago.

In addition to the Regal brand, Dobro made instruments in California under the house brand Norwood Chimes. Some California-made examples of the Angelus have *Angelus* on the peghead, although it is a standard model in the Dobro lines. Dobro also made instruments in California for other distributors who sold them under their own brands. Brands probably made in California include Rex (distributed by Gretsch), Broman (student models), Montgomery Ward, and Penetro (a lap size model with small mandolin-size resonator). Brands probably made by Regal include Alhambra (metalbody), Bruno, More Harmony (not a brand of the Harmony company), and Orpheum (metalbody and woodbody). Magn-o-tone brand dobros may have been made both in California and by Regal in Chicago.

According to Ed Dopyera, no resonator instruments were made from 1940 until after World War II.

DB Original: From circa 1954–56, Ed and Rudy Dopyera made some dobros with leftover prewar parts. These were marketed under the brand DB Original. From circa 1957–59, Rudy and John Dopyera made some dobros for the Standel company with the DB Original logo. The logo decal is a blue and yellow shield with stars, the letters *D* and *B*, and a diagonal banner with *Original*.

By 1961, Ed, John, and Rudy Dopyera had reacquired the rights to the Dobro brand and begun making woodbody dobros again. The Original was introduced in 1962, available in ash, walnut or maple, all with 14 frets clear of body. The logo decal is a shield with *Original* running vertically between the letters *D* and *B*. Production is estimated at 31 or 32 per month. Serial numbers begin with 001.

In 1964, Ed Dopyera's son Emil and a group of partners were granted a license to manufacture instruments with the Dobro brand.

In 1966, the Dopyeras made a few dobros with a plaque logo plate that reads *Replica 66*.

Mosrite: In 1967, Semie Mosely of Mosrite acquired the rights to the Dobro brand from Emil Dopyera and his partners. Most of the Mosrite-made Dobros date from 1967–69. Characteristics of Mosrite Dobros include: more rounded shape than earlier models, larger upper soundholes, soundhole screen replaced by a metal sieve-like plate with diamond-shaped holes, Dobro or National type cone, round or square neck, 12 or 14 frets clear of body, metal logo plate on peghead. Models include acoustic or electric resonator guitars, 12-strings and banjo-type models (with metal resonator cone and 5-string neck).

Hound Dog/OMI: In 1967, Ed and Rudy Dopyera, their sister Gabriela Lazar, and their nephew Ronald Lazar formed the OMI (Original Music Instrument) company. OMI made dobros under the Hound Dog brand and banjos under the Dopera brand. Early Hound Dog logos are plastic with a hound dog looking over his shoulder. In 1968, the logo changes to a hound dog wearing a red bowtie, looking forward.

In 1970, OMI regained rights to the Dobro brand. OMI-made Dobros have a decal similar to but not exactly like those of the 1930s. The OMI line includes both woodbody and metalbody instruments, some of which are available with either Dobro or National-type resonator. The OMI-made National-type cone is larger than those of the 1930s and does not have the spiral pattern on cone. See Dobro serial number section for OMI serial numbers.

Resonator Coverplates

PAT PEND, low-rise design, 12 screws with

3

General Information

"clock-point" arrangement (directly below fingerboard is 12 o'clock): **1928 only**

PAT PEND, high-rise design, 12 screws with "clock-point" arrangement (directly below fingerboard is 12 o'clock): **1929–31**

PAT PEND, low-rise design, 12 screws with "clock-point" arrangement (directly below fingerboard is 12 o'clock), poinsettia pattern holes, double-cyclops models only: **1932 only**

Pat #1872633, high-rise design, 12 screws with "clock-point" arrangement (directly below fingerboard is 12 o'clock): **1932 only**

Pat #1896484, other patents pending, high-rise design, screws at 11:30 and 12:30 positions (directly below fingerboard is 12 o'clock, no screw at 12 o'clock), California and Regal models: **1933–39**

Some with *Pat #1896484*, high-rise design, poinsettia pattern, Regal only: **1933–39**

Coverplate Patterns

Standard guitar and tenor guitar: 4 semi-circular groups of holes, 17 holes in each group, California-made and Regal models

"Poinsettia": 4 groups of holes, 7 holes in each group arranged in a sunrise-like pattern, California-made and Regal models

Standard Regal metalbody: 4 groups of holes, 2 rows of 4 semi-rectangular holes in each group

Standard mandolin coverplate: 6 semi-circular groups of holes, 13 round holes in each group

Standard uke coverplate: 4 semi-circular groups of holes, 13 round holes in each group

Stars and crescents: holes shaped like stars and crescents, Regals only (some mandolins, ukes and a few guitars)

Body

Wood...

California-made: poplar, birch, magnolia, mahogany, or walnut body

Regals: birch, mahogany, or maple

3 top holes (at end of fingerboard)...

California-made: most with beveled (countersunk) hole edges

Regal-made: square edges on holes

Note: Except for No. 45 (spruce top), most slot-head Regals and almost all solid-head Regals have no small holes in top.

Thick top: California-made student models with 1/2" thick top and no sound well, poplar body, routed "ledge" around top hole for cone, most with neck tongue mounted between 2 V blocks and additional block at opposite end of sound well, some with normal neck block, some with

Martin-type top bracing pattern in upper chamber, no room at end of fingerboard for another fret...

Some No. 27s, serial numbers in 3000s: **1929**

Some "Cyclops" models (see model descriptions): **1930–31**

Depth...

California-made, 2 7/8" at heel, 3 1/8" at endpin: **1928–c. 34**

California-made, 3" at heel, 3 1/4" at endpin: **c. 1935–37**

Regal-made, 3 1/4" at heel, up to 3 1/2" at endpin: **1933–39**

Binding...

California-made, thick body binding: **1928–34**

California-made, thin body binding: **1934–37**

Regal-made, thick body binding: **1933–39**

A few Regals with wood binding: **1933–39**

Necks and Pegheads

Fingerboard...

"Red bean" wood: **1928 only**

No dot at 17th fret: **1928 only**

Dot at 17th fret: **1929 and after**

California-made, most with unbound fingerboard: **after 1934**

Most California-made have room at end of fingerboard for another fret, except for cyclops and thick-top models

All Regal-made have no room at end of fingerboard for another fret, except No. 45

Peghead, California-made...

Sawn slots, ramped (angled), with square slot-ends (except very late No. 37G): **1928–37**

Some No. 37Gs with upper slot-ends that are round (routed) but still ramped: **1937**

Solid peghead on some walnut body models (Model 100 and higher)

Peghead, Regal-made...

Routed slots with rounded slot-ends, upper slot-ends square to top (not ramped): **1933–39**

Dobro decal, many examples (no discernible pattern): **1934–39**

Green oval decal with *Regal* and crown, many examples: **1933–39**

Solid peghead, many examples (no discernible pattern): **1935–39**

Dobro and lyre decal...

Yellow border: **1928 only**

No yellow border, red is bright, all California-made and some Regals: **1929–39**

Similar to 1929, but with browner red color (OMI-made): **1970–72**

Circled *R* (trademark registration symbol): **1972–current**

4

Regal decal, green oval with crown, some
Regal-made examples (no California-
made): **1933-39**
Neck heel...
California-made roundnecks, heel reaches
at least to back binding
Regals, neck-heel does not reach binding

Resonator Cones

Spun aluminum, spin marks barely visible, no
"lugs" (indentions near widest part of cone
to support spider bridge): **prototypes**
Stamped aluminum, no "lugs": **1928-c. 32**
Stamped aluminum, 4 or 8 "lugs" (indentions
near widest part of cone to support spider
bridge), most California-made and virtually
all Regals (after Regals introduced):
1931-39
Spun aluminum, spin marks visible, no "lugs"
(indentions near widest part of cone to
support spider bridge), some California-
made examples with serial number range
8000-9000: **1937**
4 holes near narrowest part of resonator cone:
many examples of all models

Spiders (Bridge Supports)

Long spider, 8 arms rest on edge of cone, flat
middle section and #14 stamp: **1928**
Long spider, 8 arms rest on edge of resonator,
rounded (half-spherical) middle section...
California-made: **1929-30**
Some Regals: **1933-39**
Short spider, 8 arms rest on "lugs" (indentions
near widest part of cone)...
All California-made: **1931-37**
Some Regals: **1933-39**
Short spider, 4-arms: Angelus and mandolin
models only: **1928-39**

*Note: Coverplates, cones, and spiders are
interchangeable. Various players prefer
various combinations of equipment. Most
players prefer cones with the 4 holes at
the narrowest part of the cone, and some
have had these added. A competent metal-
worker can make these newly cut cones
indistinguishable from those that originally
had holes. The only cones that can safely
be assumed to be original are those that
have never been removed from the instrument. These usually bear evidence of small
tacks (similar in size to the 5th-string
"spikes" sometimes installed on banjo fingerboards) and the original glue that held
them in place.*

Sound Well, California-Made

3-ply wood, very thick sound well construction, thick kerfing around top and back
edges (usually thicker around top than
back), 9, 11, or 13 round holes (13-hole
examples have holes very close together;
9-hole examples typically have holes
unevenly spaced with more holes on the
upper side toward the top screen-holes),
hand-bored holes with edges rounder than
Regal-made machine-punched holes: **1928**
Stamped parallelogram-shaped holes: **1929-37**
Some with no kerfing around back edge: **mid
to late 1930s**
A few with triangular-shaped holes:
throughout

Sound Well, Regal-Made

Thin sound well approximately same thickness
as top, 9 round machine-punched holes
with square edges: **1933-39**
Some Regals made for Broman with 1 hole in
sound well for neck tongue; some with
hole for neck tongue plus 2 holes in lower
body area (at 5 and 7 o'clock positions):
mid 1930s
Some Regals with no sound well, routed
"ledge" around top hole for cone: **mid
1930s**
Most Regal models with *f*-holes (instead of
screen holes) have no sound well.
All Regal metalbody guitars have no sound
well.
Most Regal mandolins and ukes have no
sound well.

Peghead of 1928 Dobro. Like almost all California-made Dobros, slots are cut with a saw and have square ends. Slot-ends are also ramped (angled) rather than cut perpendicularly into peghead. Logo decal is one of the very earliest, with yellow border around the edge.

Peghead of 1980s O.M.I. Dobro. Like the Regal-made Dobros, slots on this model are routed, with round ends cut perpendicularly into peghead. The decal has some slight differences from those of 1928–39, including a larger letter B, different black areas of lyre figure, and the presence of the trademark registration symbol.

Neck and body area of 1928 Dobro No. 45. Coverplate screw is at the 12 o'clock position (centered at end of neck), the 3 holes near the neck have beveled, countersunk-looking edges, there is no room at the end of the fingerboard for another fret, and there is no dot inlay at the 17th fret.

Neck and body area of 1980s Dobro. Coverplate screws are in the 11:30 and 12:30 positions, 3 holes near neck are only slightly beveled, there is a dot inlaid at the 17th fret.

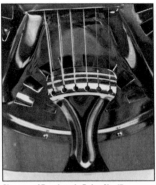

Body of Regal-made Dobro No. 45 from mid-1930s, with standard Dobro coverplate pattern, right-angle edges on 3 holes near neck. Most Regals (except No. 45) have no holes near neck. Most have room for another fret at end of fingerboard.

Close-up of Regal-made Dobro No. 45. Standard Dobro tailpiece, standard Dobro coverplate from mid 1930s with patent #1,896,484 and notice of other patents pending.

Regal-made Dobro mandolin with stars-and-crescents pattern coverplate.

7

SERIAL NUMBERS

California-Made Models, 1928–37

Serial numbers are stamped into the top of the peghead. No factory serial number records are available. This list was compiled by Mike Cass.

Number	Year
900s–1700s	1928
1800s–2000s	1929
3000s	1930–31
no 4000s	
5000s–5500s	1932–33
5700s–7600s	1934–36
8000s–9000s	1937
B###	1931–32 (most cyclops models)

No serial number: possibly a prototype. Dobro made as many as 15 prototypes for some models, identifiable by no serial number and a peghead length of 6" from top to nut (1/4" shorter than production models).

Regal-Made

Most Regals have no serial number. No dating information is available for those Regals that do have a number.

OMI

1970–79: D (#)### # configuration
    D is body type: D=wood; B=metal.
    3 or 4 numerals in center are instrument ranking.
    Single numeral at end is last digit of year.

1980–87: 8 (#)### #D configuration
    8 is decade of manufacture (1980s).
    3 or 4 numerals in center are serial number.
    Numeral before letter is last digit of year.
    D is body type: D=wood; B=metal.

1988–current: A(#) (#)### (S)##D
    First letter (and numeral) is style.
    3 or 4 numerals in center are instrument ranking.
    S denotes squareneck.
    Last 2 numerals are year.
    D is body type (various letters).

ALL MODELS, 1928–1942

Dobro model numbers and specs may be inconsistent. Model information was not stamped on instruments. Models were typically numbered to correspond to retail price, and prices varied from one distributor to another. Some model numbers were used for several different instruments. No. 45, for example, was used at different times in the California-made model series for 3 different models. In the late 1930s, Regal used No. 45 for both a woodbody and metalbody model. Other models had several numbers for the same instrument, such as No. 106 and No. 100.

Two series of Dobro brand models appear in advertisements and literature. Models in the "original" series are from early Dobro advertisements. Later model numbers are from various mail-order catalogs and advertisements. In addition, there seem to be more models in existence than available information indicates.

All guitar models have 3-ply woodbody construction, 2 round screen holes on upper body, and standard coverplate, unless otherwise specified.

SECTION ORGANIZATION

Original California-made Series
Custom Models
California-made "Cyclops" Models
Original Series Regal Woodbody Models
Later Regal Screen-hole Models
Regal _f_-hole Woodbody Models
Regal Metalbody Models
Regal-Dobro Silver Guitars
Dobro Brand Electrics

Original California-made Series

No. 27G: unspecified hardwood body (birch, mahogany, or maple), bound top, unbound back, unbound fingerboard, dot inlay
No. 37G: mahogany body, bound top and back, bound fingerboard, dot inlay
No. 45G: mahogany body, dot inlay, painted mahogany-color coverplate and tailpiece, serial numbers (on Style 45G examples with these specs) range from 1200-1300
In addition to guitar models, 3 tenors, 2 mandolins, and 1 uke available (specs unavailable)
Introduced: **1928**
45G with natural finish spruce top, unpainted chrome-plated coverplate and tailpiece, serial number 1300 and higher: **c. 1930**
37G variation: poplar body, no holes in top at end of fingerboard, bound top, unbound

back and fingerboard, square National-type neck with 12 or 14 frets clear of body, Regal-type fingerboard with no room at end for another fret, slotted peghead with Regal-type routed slots, double-sunburst top finish (sunburst above and below resonator), teardrop sunburst pattern on back, sunburst peghead: **1937**
All discontinued: **1937**

No. 65: sandblasted French scroll design on top, back, and sides, some with sandblasted design on peghead, list price $65
No. 76: poplar or birch body, ivoroid bound top and back, bound ebony fingerboard, pearl dot inlay, 12 frets clear of body, black "piano" finish, list prices $75, $76
No. 86: ribbon tabasco (highly grained) mahogany body, bound top and back, bound rosewood fingerboard, engraved tuner buttons, celluloid peghead inlay, 2-tone reddish brown finish, list price $87.50
All introduced by **late 1928**
All discontinued by **1937**

Angelus: birch body, _f_-holes, 12 large round holes in coverplate, slotted peghead, painted top and back edges to simulate binding, 12 frets clear of body, some with _Angelus_ on peghead, 2-tone walnut finish
Introduced: **c. 1928**
Available as **Regal No. 19**, 12 or 14 frets clear of body, 3-segment _f_-holes, dull walnut finish (later with natural finish or orange-to-brown sunburst finish), by **1934**
Discontinued: **1940**

Custom Models

No. 106 (100): 5-ply burl walnut body with 2-way matched grain, triple-bound top and back, black walnut neck, diamond and arrows fingerboard inlay, bound ebony fingerboard, celluloid inlaid logo, engraved nickel-plated metal parts, list price $100
No. 156 (150): same as No. 106 but with pearl logo, engraved gold-plated metal parts, made for 1928-29 trade show, serial number range 1500-1680
No. 206: same as No. 156 but with spruce top, engraved gold-plated metal parts, list price $200
Walnut body models were introduced at a 1928-29 trade show. All trade show examples have serial numbers below 2000
Introduced: **1928**
No. 106 referred to as **No. 100**, No. 156 referred to as **No. 150**, No. 206 no longer appears in literature: **1934**
Discontinued: **1937**

Tenortrope No. A45: round body of unspecified hardwood, 4 strings (tenor guitar setup), mahogany finish, list price $45
Also available with No. 65 sandblasted finish
Introduced by: **1930**
Discontinued: **1937**

California-Made "Cyclops" Models

No. 27: "silver highlighted" 2-toned Duco finish
No. 45: bound top, back, and neck, rosewood finish
No. 60: bound top and back, sandblasted French scroll design on top, sides and back, ebony 2-tone finish
Variations: some with 1/2"-thick top, some with black finish
Cyclops model: single screen hole, available: **1931 only**
Double-cyclops model: 2 screen holes joined together, some with bound top and fingerboard (no back binding), some with no binding anywhere, available: **1932 only**

Later California-made Models

No. 36: same as original series No. 37G, list price $37.50
No. 36-S: slotted peghead specified, bound fingerboard, list price $47.50
No. 45: later referred to as **Standard** model, unspecified wood, mahogany finish (later walnut finish), list price $45
No. 55: unspecified hardwood, unbound top and back, bound fingerboard, chrome-plated metal parts, walnut finish, list price $55
No. 56: same as No. 55, list price $50
No. 66: same as original series No. 65, sandblasted French scroll design, no body binding, bound fingerboard, list price $62.50 or $65
No. 66B: sames as No. 66 but with bound top and back, list price $72.50
No. 85: also referred to as **Professional** model, same as original series No. 86, mahogany body and neck, engraved coverplate, fleur-de-lis on handrest, bound top and back, bound "Cardinal wood" fingerboard, list price $85
No. 86: same as original series No. 86, list price $87.50
No. 106: same as original series No. 106, 2-way matched burl walnut
No. 125: also referred to as **De Lux** model, 5-ply black walnut construction with 4-way matched burl, *Dobro De Lux* engraved on handrest, triple-bound top and back with black line on side of binding, black walnut neck, triple-bound ebony fingerboard, celluloid inlaid logo, nickel-plated metal parts, natural finish, list price $125

No. 156: same as original series No. 156 (see preceding)
No. 175: referred to as **Special De Luxe** model, spruce top, nickel-plated metal parts, list price $175
No. 206: same as original series No. 206
Mandolin Nos. 5, 7, 10: (specs unavailable) list prices $65, $90, $115.
Tenor Nos. 50, 75, 100: (specs unavailable) list prices $50, $75, $100
Tenortrope (tenor models with round body) **Nos. 40, 45, 60, 75**: (specs unavailable) list prices $45, $45, $60, $75
Uke Nos. 30, 40: (specs unavailable) list prices $30, $40
All introduced by **1932**
All discontinued: **1937**

Original Series Regal Woodbody Models

Regal-Dobros may have 12 or 14 frets clear of body, roundneck or squareneck, slotted or solid peghead, Regal or Dobro decal logo.

Regal No. 27: birch, mahogany, or maple body, bound top, 2-tone walnut finish
Regal No. 37: mahogany body, bound top and back, some with bound fingerboard
Regal No. 45: spruce top, mahogany back and sides, 4-ply top binding, single-bound back, unbound ebonized (black-stain) fingerboard
Regal Tenor Nos. 27 1/2, 37 1/2, 45 1/2: No. 27 1/2 has same specs as guitar model No. 27, etc.
Regal Mandolin Nos. 270, 370, 470: coverplate with 6 hole clusters, No. 270 has same specs as guitar model No. 27, etc.
Regal Uke No. 15: mahogany body and neck, coverplate with 4 hole clusters, rosewood fingerboard
All introduced at: **June 1933**
Discontinued: **1940**

Later Regal Screen-Hole Models

Regal No. 32: mahogany body, 12 or 14 frets clear of body, tenor available
Introduced by **1939**
Discontinued: **1940**

Mandolin No. 210: ebonized fingerboard, 2-tone shaded finish, star and crescent coverplate
Mandolin No. 320: mahogany body (only specs available)
Introduced by **1939**
Discontinued: **1940**

Regal *f*-hole Woodbody Models

All available with roundneck or squareneck

Regal No. 19: 12 large round holes in cover plate, see Dobro Angelus model, preceding

No. 25: bound top and back, 14 frets clear of body, slotted peghead, 2-tone walnut finish
Introduced by **1935**
Regal Mandolin No. 250 and **Regal Tenor No. 25 1/2** available by **late 1930s**
Discontinued: **1940**

Regal No. 5: 8" National-type cone (not 4-armed spider cone), 12 diamond-shaped holes in coverplate, plate tailpiece, blond finish
Introduced by **1939**
Discontinued: **1940**

Regal No. 6: star and crescent coverplate holes, trapeze tailpiece
Introduced by **1939**
Discontinued: **1940**

Regal No. 27: trapeze tailpiece, 12 or 14 frets clear of body, 2-tone walnut finish, tenor available
Introduced by **1939**
Discontinued: **1940**

Regal Metalbody Models

All with violin or fiddle edges (curled edge with top extending slightly over sides), window soundholes (round holes with cross pattern in hole), Dobro or Regal logo

Regal No. 32: sheet metal body, some with *f*-holes, 14 frets clear of body, slotted peghead, yellowish brown sunburst paint finish
Regal No. 46: all-aluminum Dobro-lite or Lumalite body, some with upper *f*-holes, 14 frets clear of body, slotted peghead, silver finish with gold highlights
Regal No. 62: nickel-plated brass body, Spanish dancer/garden scene etched on back, solid peghead
All introduced by **1935**
Discontinued **1940**

Regal No. 35: 3 cutouts in tailpiece, rosewood grain finish
Regal No. 45: clear pickguard, mahogany grain finish
Regal No. 47: some with upper *f*-holes, coverplate with 4 groups of 8 rectangular holes, pickguard, 3 cutouts in tailpiece, mahogany grain finish
Regal No. 65: nickel-plated body, 3 cutouts in

tailpiece
All introduced by **1939**
Discontinued: **1940**

Regal-Dobro Silver Guitars

All with 5-segment *f*-holes, 4 groups of 8 semi-rectangular holes in coverplate, 3 cutouts in tailpiece, 14 frets clear of body, solid peghead, Hawaiian setup (H) optional
Regal Leader (14M or **14H)**: brass body with nickel plating, engraved borders, rosewood fingerboard, pearl logo
Regal Professional (15M or **15H)**: engraved German silver (nickel alloy) body, diagonal banner and Dobro logo across back, white pearloid peghead veneer
Regal Artist (16M or **16H)**: engraved German silver (nickel alloy) body, ebony fingerboard, floral or diamond inlay, more engraving than 15, back engraved with Dobro or (later) Regal logo
model name unknown: like Regal No. 32 metalbody, tortoise-grain plastic pickguard, gold sparkle peghead veneer (some with rhinestones inlaid), Dobro logo, yellow-to-brown sunburst finish
All introduced by **late 1930s**
Discontinued: **1940**

Dobro Brand Electrics

All-Electric: standard mahogany body like original No. 37, bound top and back, bound fingerboard, no holes in coverplate, *Dobro* and lightning bolts etched onto coverplate diagonally under strings, endpin jack
Only appearance in literature: **1933**

Standard Guitar: archtop, *f*-holes, blade PU with oblong housing mounted near bridge, screw-on jack on upper treble side, trapeze tailpiece, pickguard cutout for PU, dot inlay with 3 dots at 7th and 9th frets, bound fingerboard, block letter logo across peghead, sunburst finish
Introduced by **1935**
Renamed **Spanish Electric Guitar**: blade PU with rectangular housing, shorter ebonoid pickguard, bound pickguard, rosewood fingerboard, by **1937**
Discontinued by **1943**

Metalbody Hawaiian: cast aluminum body, large circular lower body with 4 "panels" (cutout sections) on top, no upper *f*-holes, split-blade PU in oblong housing, no knobs on top, large Dobro lyre logo between PU and neck, 20-fret fingerboard, dot inlay, 2 cutouts in peghead, 6 or 7 string
Introduced by **1935**
2 metal PU height-adjustment screws, 2 control knobs, elongated *f*-holes next to neck

(lyre logo and *f*-holes are part of casting
pattern, not cut into body), 26-fret fingerboard optional (fingerboard extends over
lyre logo): **c. 1936**
Discontinued: **c. 1937**

Woodbody Hawaiian: square-end body,
smooth graduation to neck, knobs on
opposite sides, rectangular metal PU cover
extends under knobs, screw-on jack on
bass side, 23" scale, ebonoid fingerboard
and peghead veneer, parallelogram markers with Roman numerals, logo reads
upside down to player, mahogany finish
Introduced by **1937**
Discontinued by **1943**

Electric Mandolin: standard woodbody mandolin construction, arched top, flat back,
blade PU with oblong housing
Introduced by **1935**
Discontinued by **1943**

Post-World War II Dobros: see Dobro General
Information section

COMMENTS

California-made Dobros are the models most
highly regarded by players and collectors,
although several of the best-known musicians play Regal models. Squareneck models bring more than roundnecks. Regal-
made models with a Dobro decal generally
bring more than the same model with a
Regal decal.

Regal woodbody models with *f*-holes are generally not highly regarded by players or
collectors.

Regal metalbody models are not considered by
players to be as good as National metalbody models. Because of their rarity and,
in some cases, their ornate engraving, they
do have some appeal to collectors.

The metalbody Hawaiian lap steel is fairly rare
and collectible. Other electric models are
very rare. All Dobro electric instruments
are of interest primarily to collectors for
historic reasons rather than utility.

Epiphone

GENERAL INFORMATION

Anastasios Stathopoulo, a Greek violin and lute maker, established the House of Stathopoulo in 1873. The company incorporated in 1923 and concentrated on banjos. The Epiphone line was named after Epi Stathopoulo, president of the company and one of the founder's sons. In 1928, the company name was changed to the Epiphone Banjo Corporation.

Epiphone was best known in the 1920s for a line of highly ornamented Recording banjos. In the 1930s, the company changed its emphasis to guitars and became highly successful as a guitar manufacturer—virtually the only banjo company to make a successful switch. Epiphone also made some archtops in the mid 1930s with the Sorrentino and Howard brandnames.

The C. G. Conn Company, primarily a band instrument manufacturer, acquired Epiphone in 1953 and moved production in part to Philadelphia (although labels continued to say New York).

The Stathopoulo family regained control in 1955, but few if any instruments were made from 1956–57.

The Chicago Musical Instrument company, which owned Gibson, acquired Epiphone by 1957, published a brochure in 1958, and began shipping Epiphones from its Kalamazoo, MI, plant in 1959. These are commonly referred to as "Gibson-Epiphones."

The Norlin company purchased CMI (Gibson) in December 1969. Company shipping records show a little over 800 Epiphones shipped from Kalamazoo in 1970. That same year, Gibson moved production of all Epiphones to Japan. Later, Epiphone production was moved to Korea. Many of the imported instruments bear a label with Gibson's Kalamazoo address and no mention of Japan or Korea, which can be misleading. These instruments, however, have model numbers that do not correspond with the model numbers of Kalamazoo-made Epis (listed in this section), and they are quite different in structure from Kalamazoo-made Epi models.

Model Names

In addition to the Zephyr and Zephyr Regent models, Epiphone applied the two terms to other models to signify electric or cutaway models:
Zephyr=electric
Regent=cutaway

Labels

Epiphone Banjo Corporation, Long Island City, N.Y.: **1928–1935**

Masterbilt label, high-end models, several different label styles, all with *Masterbilt* in fancy lettering: **1931–1937**

Silver oval label, *The Epiphone Corp.* on banner, *New York* and *Builders of Art Musical Instruments* below banner: **1932–33**

Rectangular label, white paper with blue or blue-green border and *Epiphone, Inc., New York, N.Y., U.S.A.:* **1935–57**

Gibson-made, rectangular label, blue paper, slashed-*C* (stylized *E*) logo and *Epiphone, Inc., Kalamazoo, Michigan:* **1958–70**

Epi Pickups

Rickenbacker-type horseshoe, magnets wrap over strings: **c. 1937–39**

Oblong shape with bar magnet: **c. 1937–c. 43**

Oblong shape with large slot-head screw poles: **c. 1939–c. 43**

Oblong shape with fat oblong bar magnet: **1940s**

New York: rectangular metal-covered with small slot-head screw poles, poles very close to edge, mounted to top by screws through cream-colored "blocks" or side extensions (some pickups on low-end models have no visible poles and black mounting blocks), dimensions 1 1/8" x 2 13/16" (3 5/8" wide including mounting blocks): **c. 1946–61**

Rectangular metal-covered, larger than New York style, 1 1/2" x 3 1/8", Philips-head screw poles, poles not in center but not as close to edge as New York style, yellow/cream-colored frames: **c. 1950–54**

De Armond, black or white face, 6 evenly-spaced poles, poles adjustable by 6 separate screws (very similar to standard PU on Gretsch models of the period), some Epi examples: **c. 1953**

Gibson-made (see following): **late 1950s–70**

Gibson-Made Epi Pickups

The first Gibson-made electrics were fitted with leftover New York pickups from Epiphone's stock. As these pickups were used up, Gibson began using three different pickups:
1. Mini-humbucking: not used on any Gibson models until 1969 on Les Paul Deluxe, smaller than standard Gibson humbucking pickup, 1 1/8" x 2 5/8", double-coil, rectangular metal-covered, slot-head screw poles close to edge, black plastic frame, slightly smaller than New York style Epi pickups
2. P-90: standard on some Gibson models of

the period, single-coil, poles across center, attached by screws through triangular "ears" extending from each end, some models fitted with a rectangular (no ears) "soapbar" P-90 pickup

3. Melody Maker: standard on some Gibson models of the period, single-coil, narrow oblong shape, plastic covered, no visible poles

Tailpieces

Standard trapeze, all models: **1920s–c. 37**
Heavy trapeze with 4 cutouts, high-end models: **c. 1937– c. 39**
Frequensator tailpiece: allows for a longer string length on the 3 bass strings, shorter string length on the 3 treble strings, sometimes reversed by players to accommodate short strings, high-end models: **1939–70**
Vibrato: flat-arm, strings wrap around metal cylinder of graduated diameter, wooden plate with *E* logo: **1961–70**
Gibson vibratos (see Gibson section): **1961–70**

Truss Rods

No truss rod: **pre-1939**
Truss rod adjustment at body end of neck: **c. 1939–51**
Truss rod adjustment at peghead: **1951–70**
Metal truss rod cover with ridge in center, some models: **1954–61**

Logos

Script: Most Epiphone guitars of the pre-Gibson period have a script logo with a standard script *E*. A few early models have block-letter logos. Gibson continued using New York-made Epiphone necks, with laminated construction and script *E* logo, until all the New York necks were used up.

Slashed-*C*: Epiphone's stylized *E*, which looks like a *C* with a horizontal slash, appeared by 1939 in literature and on metal peghead plates.

Models with inlaid or paint logos made the changeover to Gibson necks and the slashed-*C* logo style circa 1961. On flat tops, the Gibson neck can be distinguished by a wider flare toward the top of the peghead. By the 1963 catalog, all solidbody guitars, all basses, and all flat top guitars, are pictured with the slashed-*C* logo. In the 1965 catalog, all models have the slashed-*C* logo except the Deluxe and Triumph (acoustic) and Emperor and Broadway (electric).

Early Gibson-Made Epiphones

After Gibson bought Epiphone, Epi parts were used up before Gibson parts were utilized. In addition to New York pickups (see preceding), some models—both acoustic and electric—feature a New York neck of laminated construction with more of a *V* shape than Gibson necks. The New York Epi peghead shape is also different from that of later Gibson-made necks. Some New York Epi pegheads have a metal truss rod cover with a ridge in the middle.

New York pickup, standard on most models in the 1950s and for several years after Gibson's acquisition of Epiphone in 1957.

Epiphone metal peghead logo plate. The plate and the slashed-*C* (stylized *E*) were first used on electric models in the late 1930s. The slashed-*C* logo eventually appeared on tuners and pickguards as well as on the modern peghead logo.

Epiphone script logo with script *E*, on a 1948 Blackstone. The vertical oval inlay figure appeared on many later models.

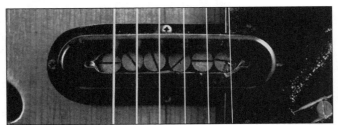

Oblong pickup with large slot-head screws appears on many models from 1939-43.

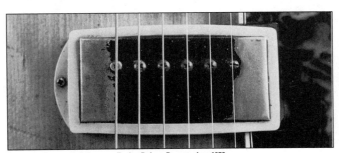

Large metal-covered pickup on a Zephyr Deluxe Regent, circa 1950.

Epiphone

General Information

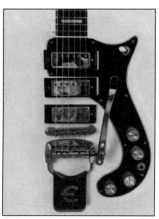

Gibson-made mini-humbucker pickups on a Crestwood Deluxe from the 1960s. This instrument also shows the special Epiphone vibrato that is unlike any vibrato on Gibson models. The vibrato shaft has different diameters for different strings. The rosewood tailpiece insert has the slashed-*C* logo.

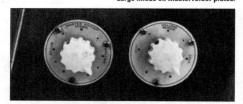

Large knobs on *Mastervoicer* plates.

Frequensator tailpiece. Because some string sets would not reach to the bass side of the tailpiece, some players reversed the Frequensator.

Smaller, 8-sectioned knobs with pointers.

MODEL NUMBERS

Model numbers date from Epiphone's ownership by Conn in 1953 up until Gibson moved Epi production to Japan in 1970.

Letters preceding model numbers: E=electric archtop, A=acoustic archtop, FT=flat top, SB=solidbody, EB=electric bass or Epiphone banjo, EC=Epiphone classical, EM=Epiphone mandolin, BV=bass violin

Letters after numbers: D=double pickup, N=natural finish, T=thinbody, V=vibrato, MV=maestro vibrola, C=cherry or cutaway, E=electric

Model Number	Prefix	Model
7P	EA	Professional
8P	EA	Professional (no specs available)
28	FT	Caballero tenor
30	EC	Madrid
30	FT	Caballero
44	EB	Campus banjo
45	FT	Cortez
66	EM	Venetian mandolin
77	ETB	Tenor banjo
79	FT	Texan
85	FT	Serenader
88	EB	Minstrel banjo
90	EC	Entrada
90	FT	El Dorado
95	FT	Folkster
98	FT	Troubadour
100	EC	Seville
110	FT	Frontier
111, 112	E	Emperor (blond, sunburst)*
111, 112	A	Emperor cutaway (blond, sunburst)*
112	FT	Bard
120	FT	Excellente
121,122	A	Emperor non-cutaway (blond, sunburst)*
150	EC	Classic
188	EB	Plantation banjo
200	EC	Espana
210	FT	Deluxe Cutaway
211, 212	E	Deluxe, c1949–58 (blond, sunburst)*
211, 212	E	Sheraton, 1958–70 (blond, sunburst)*
211, 212	A	Deluxe cutaway (blond, sunburst)*
221, 222	A	Deluxe non-cutaway (blond, sunburst)*
230	E	Casino
231,232	EB	Rivoli (blond, sunburst)*
232	SB	Crestwood Deluxe
251, 252	E	Broadway (blond, sunburst)*
300	EC	Barcelona
311, 312	E	Zephyr cutaway (blond, sunburst)*
311, 312	A	Broadway cutaway (blond, sunburst)*
321, 322	E	Zephyr non-cutaway (blond, sunburst)*
321, 322	A	Broadway non-cutaway (blond, sunburst)*
332	SB	Crestwood Custom
351, 352	E	Windsor (blond, sunburst)*
360	E	Riviera
411, 412	A	Triumph cutaway (blond, sunbust)*
421, 422	A	Triumph non-cutaway (blond, sunburst)*
421, 422	E	Century (blond, sunburst)*
432	SB	Wilshire
444	E	Granada
451, 452	E	Sorrento (blond, sunburst)*
521, 522	A	Devon (blond, sunburst)*
533	SB	Coronet

Model Numbers

621, 622	A	Zenith (blond, sunburst)*
721	SB	Olympic Special
722	SB	Olympic
Caiola		Caiola
EBDL		Embassy Deluxe
EBS		Newport
EBV		Rivoli
HR-SE		Howard Roberts Standard
HR-CE		Howard Roberts Custom

* In 1961, Gibson began using only the even-number model designation for sunburst, blond or any other finish.

SERIAL NUMBERS

1930–57

Serial numbers appear on a label inside the body. During and immediately following World War II, some guitars have numbers on the back of the peghead which do not fit this list.

Number	Year
10,000 series	1930–32
5,000	1932
6,000	1933
7,200	1934
8,000–9,000	1935
10,000	1936
11,000	1937
12,000	1938
13,000	1939–40
14,000	1941–42
18,200	1943
19,000	1944
51,000–52,000	1944
52,000–54,000	1945
54,000–55,000	1946
56,000	1947
57,000	1948
58,000	1949
59,000	1950
60,000–63,000*	1951
64,000	1952
64,000–66,000	1953
68,000	1954
69,000	1955–57

*Many instruments throughout the 1930s have numbers in the 60,000s and 61,000s.

Gibson-made Epis, 1958–61

Hollowbody models: Number is on the label, with *A* preceding the number. The Epi number series is different from the A-series used on Gibson brand instruments of the same period.

Number	Year
A 1000	c. 1958
A 2000	c. 1959
A 3000, A 4000	c. 1960–early 61

Solidbody models: Number is inked on the back of the peghead with the following configurations: ####, ######, or # ####. As with Gibson brand solidbody models of the same period, the first digit corresponds to the last digit of the year. Numbers with #### configuration were used in 1960 only.

Gibson-made Epis, 1961–70

Beginning in 1961, Epiphone serial numbers follow Gibson's number series (see Gibson Serial Numbers section).

ACOUSTIC ARCHTOPS KEY

Upper treble bout with lopped-off appearance, model letter on peghead
  Dot inlay=**Recording A** (flat top)
  Large engraved-block inlay
    Cross engraving on inlay=**Recording D**
    Floral engraving on inlay=**Recording E**
  Small paired-diamond inlay
    Black binding=**Recording B** (flat top)
    Triple binding=**Recording C**
Standard guitar body shape
  Cloud inlay=**De Luxe, 1937–70**
  Block inlay=**Broadway, 1934–58**
  3-piece V-block inlay=**Emperor**
  Slotted-block inlay
    Non-cutaway=**Spartan 1937–54**
    Pointed cutaway
      Vertical oval peghead inlay=**Howard Roberts**
      Vine peghead inlay=**Howard Roberts Custom**
  Single-parallelogram inlay=**Blackstone, 1937–54**
  Oval inlay
    Frequensator tailpiece (17 3/8″ wide)=**Devon**
    Trapeze tailpiece (16 3/8″ wide)=**Zenith, 1958–68**
  Floral and notched-diamond inlay
    Checkered top binding=**De Luxe, 1931–37**
    Triple-bound top=**Tudor**
  Notched-diamond inlay=**Triumph, 1934–70**
  4-point star inlay=**Broadway, 1931–34**
  Small paired-diamond inlay=**Triumph, 1931–34**
  Dot inlay
    Bound fingerboard
      Round hole=**Spartan, 1934–37**
      ƒ-holes
        Maple back and sides=**Blackstone, 1931–34, 1937-50**
        Walnut back and sides=**Royal, c. 1934-35**
        Mahogany back and sides
          Sharply peaked peghead=**Blackstone, 1934-37**
          Rounded peghead=**Royal, 1931-c. 33**
    Unbound fingerboard
      Maple back and sides
        White binding=**Zenith, 1931–34, early 1950s–58**
        Tortoise grain binding=**Ritz**
      Mahogany back and sides
        Rounded peghead
          Archtop=**Olympic**
          Flat top=**Beverly**
        Center-dip peghead=**Byron**
      Walnut back and sides=**Zenith, 1934–early 50**

ACOUSTIC ARCHTOPS

SECTION ORGANIZATION

Recording Series
Masterbilt Series
Later New York-made Models
Gibson-made Models

Recording Series

All with asymmetrical body with cutaway bout appearing to be lopped off, round hole, spruce top, 3-ply figured maple back and sides, moveable bridge on fixed base, trapeze tailpiece, 3 center laminates in neck, 25″ scale; engraved celluloid peghead veneer with *Epiphone* banner across top, *Recording* banner across middle, and ornate letter of model name; banjo tuners, amber-to-red sunburst finish, available in concert or auditorium (larger) size

Variations on Recording models include: flat top, fixed bridge and staggered bridge pins

Recording A: flat top and back, black body binding, rosewood fingerboard, dot inlay

Recording B: flat top, arched back, black body binding, rosewood fingerboard with white binding, small paired-diamond inlay, green leaves engraved on peghead

Recording C: archtop, triple-bound top and back, bound pointed-end ebony fingerboard, small paired-diamond inlay, gold celluloid peghead veneer with black engraving, green leaves engraved on peghead

Recording D: archtop, bound top and back, violin purfling around edges, elevated pickguard follows body contour, bound pointed-end fingerboard, large celluloid block inlay with cross-like engraving

Recording E: archtop, ebony and ivory bridge, elevated black pickguard follows contour of body, bound pointed-end fingerboard, large celluloid block inlay with floral engraving, mother-of-pearl tuner buttons, engraved gold-plated metal parts

Recording series introduced: **mid to late 1920s**

Discontinued by **early 1930s**

Masterbilt Series

All with arched spruce top, f-holes, rosewood fingerboard; some models with Masterbilt peghead: *Epiphone* across top, *Masterbilt* across bottom, model name slanted across center, asymmetrical peghead with dip on treble side

Masterbilt series announced (already in production): **June 1931**

De Luxe: 16 3/8" wide, curly maple back and sides, 3-segment f-holes, trapeze tailpiece, triple-bound top with rope-pattern purfling, triple-bound back, diamonds and triangles inlay, Masterbilt peghead with flowers, bound peghead, gold-plated metal parts, sunburst finish

Introduced: **1931**

Floral and notched-diamond inlay pattern, vine peghead inlay, block letter logo, white pickguard: **1934**

17 3/8" wide, multiple binding, dark pickguard extends below bridge, standard f-holes with single-ply binding, flat-plate tailpiece with 4 cutouts, cloud inlay, script logo, by **1937**

Frequensator tailpiece, center-dip peghead, natural finish optional, by **1939**

Cutaway available, some with flower peghead inlay, by **1949**

Non-cutaway discontinued by **1958**

Gibson-Epi De Luxe (see following): **1958**

Empire: tenor version of Deluxe, 15 1/2" wide, otherwise same specs and changes

Introduced: **1931**

Discontinued by **1939**

Broadway: 16 3/8" wide, walnut back and sides, 3-segment or standard f-holes, trapeze tailpiece, unbound pickguard, triple-bound top and back, bound ebony fingerboard with rounded end, 4-point-star shape inlay, Masterbilt peghead, sunburst finish

Introduced: **1931**

Bound pickguard, large block inlay, no inlay at 1st fret, wandering vine peghead inlay, block letter logo, unbound peghead, gold-plated metal parts: **1934**

17 3/8" wide, bridge extends even with bridge, standard f-holes, flat-plate tailpiece with 4 cutouts, multiple-bound top, inlay at 1st fret, multiple-bound peghead, script logo, gold-plated metal parts, by **1937**

Maple back and sides, Frequensator tailpiece, center-dip peghead, by **1939**

Blond finish optional: **1941**

Flower peghead inlay: **mid 1940s**

Broadway Regent: single cutaway, available by **1951**

Broadway acoustic discontinued (Broadway electric continued in Gibson line, see Hollowbody Electrics): **1958**

Bretton: tenor version of Broadway, 15 1/2" wide, otherwise same specs and changes

Introduced **1931**

Renamed **Broadway Tenor**, plectrum available, by **1937**

Discontinued by **1954**

Tudor: 16 3/8" wide, trapeze tailpiece, triple-bound top and back, single-bound fingerboard, floral and notched-diamond inlay, Masterbilt peghead, gold-plated metal parts

Introduced: **early 1930s**

Maple back and sides, bound pickguard, block letter logo, wandering vine peghead inlay, unbound peghead, by **1934**

Discontinued by **1937**

Triumph: 16 3/8" wide, walnut back and sides, trapeze tailpiece, 3-segment f-holes, paired-diamond inlay, Masterbilt peghead, sunburst finish

Introduced: **1931**

Maple back and sides, unbound pickguard, single-bound fingerboard, notched-diamond inlay, block letter logo, floral ornament with fleur-de-lis design at top inlaid on peghead, unbound rounded-peak peghead, by **1934**

Script logo by **1935**

17 3/8" wide, standard f-holes, triple-bound

Epiphone

Acoustic Archtops

top, single-bound back, bound pickguard extends below bridge, single-bound peghead, flat-plate tailpiece with 4 cutouts, by **1937**

Frequensator tailpiece by **1939**

Center-dip peghead, blond finish optional: **early 1941**

Triumph Regent: single cutaway, available by **1949**

E on pickguard, fat column peghead inlay, by **1949**

Non-cutaway discontinued by **1958**

Gibson-Epi Triumph (see following): **1958**

Hollywood: tenor version of Triumph, otherwise same specs and changes

Introduced by **1934**

Renamed **Triumph Tenor**, plectrum available: **1937**

Discontinued by **1958**

Royal: mahogany back and sides, 3-segment *f*-holes, single-bound top and back, single-bound fingerboard, dot inlay, Masterbilt peghead, sunburst finish

Introduced **1931**

15 1/2" wide, walnut back and sides, rounded-peak peghead, by **1934**

Discontinued: **1935**

Spartan: 16 3/8" wide, maple back and sides, round hole, trapeze tailpiece, bound top and back, bound fingerboard, dot inlay, stickpin peghead inlay, block letter logo, rounded-peak peghead, sunburst finish

Introduced: **1934**

Standard *f*-holes, walnut back and sides, bound top, bound fingerboard, slotted-block inlay, bound peghead, Greek column peghead inlay, script logo, by **1937**

Center-dip peghead: **1939**

Blond finish optional, prima vera wood (white mahogany) back and sides with blond finish: **early 1941**

Discontinued by: **1950**

Regent: tenor companion to Spartan, 15 1/2" wide, mahogany back and sides, standard *f*-holes, bound top and back, trapeze tailpiece, bound fingerboard, dot inlay, block letter logo, stickpin peghead inlay, rounded-peak peghead, sunburst finish

Introduced: **1934**

Regent discontinued; **Spartan Tenor**, same specs and changes as Spartan, plectrum available, introduced: **1937**

Discontinued by **1950**

Blackstone: 14 3/4" wide, maple back and sides, single-bound top and back, bound fingerboard, dot inlay, sunburst finish

Introduced: **1931**

Masterbilt banners on rounded-peak peghead,

sunburst finish on top, back, and sides: **1933**

15 1/2" wide, mahogany back and sides, block letter logo, stickpin peghead inlay, unbound sharp-peaked peghead: **1934**

16 3/8" wide, maple back and sides, standard *f*-holes, trapeze tailpiece, parallelogram inlay, notched elongated diamond peghead inlay, script logo, by **1937**

Tenor and plectrum available: **1937**

Center-dip peghead: **1939**

Blond finish optional: **early 1941**

Abalone vertical oval peghead inlay, abalone logo, by **1945**

Discontinued: **1950**

Zenith: 13 5/8" wide, maple back and sides, 3-segment *f*-holes

Introduced: **1931**

14 3/4" wide, walnut back and sides, trapeze tailpiece, dot inlay, bound top and back, unbound square-end fingerboard, dot inlay, block letter logo, stickpin peghead inlay, rounded-peak peghead, sunburst finish, by **1934**

16 3/8" wide, standard *f*-holes, notched elongated diamond peghead inlay, script logo, by **1937**

Tenor and plectrum available by **1937**

Center-dip peghead: **1942**

Vertical oval peghead inlay, blond finish optional, by **1954**

Gibson-Epi Zenith (see following): **1958**

Melody: tenor companion to Zenith, 13 1/4" wide, walnut back and sides, bound top and back

Introduced: **1931**

Melody does not change size with 1934 Zenith

Melody discontinued; **Zenith Tenor**, same specs as Zenith, plectrum available, introduced: **1937**

Discontinued: **1958**

Olympic: 13" wide, mahogany back and sides, 3-segment *f*-holes, no logo

Introduced: **1931**

13 5/8" wide, trapeze tailpiece, rounded-end fingerboard, dot inlay, rounded non-peaked peghead, sunburst finish, by **1933**

Decal logo with *Epiphone* on banner and *Masterbilt* underneath banner: **1934**

15 1/4" wide, standard *f*-holes, by **1937**

Tenor and plectrum available: **1937**

Script logo with tail underneath: **1942**

Center-dip peghead: **c. 1939**

Discontinued by **1950**

Beverly: 13" wide, flat top, arched back, mahogany back and sides, 3-segment *f*-holes, adjustable bridge, trapeze tailpiece, elevated pickguard, no body binding, dot inlay, rounded-top peghead, brown finish,

tenor available
Introduced: **1931**
Discontinued by **1937**

Later New York-made Models

Emperor: 18 1/2" wide, maple back and sides, plate tailpiece with 4 cutouts and *Epiphone*, elongated pickguard, 7-ply binding on top and back, 3-ply binding on f-holes, single-bound ebony fingerboard with 2 white lines inlaid along edges, 3-segment V-block pearl inlay, triple-bound peghead, vine peghead inlay, dip on treble side of peghead, gold-plated metal parts, sunburst finish
Introduced: **late 1936**
Frequensator tailpiece, abalone wedge in 3-segment V-block inlay, center-dip peghead, natural finish optional: **c. 1939**
Rosewood fingerboard by **1950**
Emperor Cutaway, introduced by **1950**
Non-cutaway discontinued: **mid 1950s**
Gibson-Epi Emperor (see following): **1958**

Byron: 15 3/8" wide, mahogany back and sides, adjustable bridge, trapeze tailpiece, unbound elevated pickguard, single-bound top and back, rosewood fingerboard, dot inlay, script decal logo with tail underneath, center-dip peghead
Available: **c. 1938**

Ritz: 15 1/4" wide, maple back and sides, tortoise grain binding, trapeze tailpiece, dot inlay, center-dip peghead, cherry neck, blond finish, tenor available
Introduced: **early 1941**
Discontinued by **1950**

Devon: 17 3/8" wide, Frequensator tailpiece, single-bound pickguard, triple-bound top, oval inlay, vertical-oval peghead inlay, script logo, sunburst or blond finish
Introduced: **c. 1951**
Discontinued: **1957**

Gibson-made Models

Emperor: 18 1/8" wide, rounded cutaway, Frequensator tailpiece, multiple binding, ebony fingerboard, 3-segment V-block inlay with abalone wedge, vine peghead inlay, gold-plated metal parts, sunburst or natural finish
Introduced (continued from earlier Epi line): **1958**
Available by special order only: **1963**
Discontinued: **1970**

Deluxe: 17 3/8" wide, rounded cutaway, Frequensator tailpiece, single-bound f-holes, multiple-bound top and pickguard, triple-bound back, multiple-bound ebony fingerboard, cloud inlay, triple-bound peghead, vine peghead inlay, gold-plated metal parts, sunburst or natural finish
Introduced (spelling changed, model continued from earlier Epi line): **1958**
Available by special order only: **1965**
Discontinued: **1970**

Triumph: 17 3/8" wide, rounded cutaway, Frequensator tailpiece, bound top and back, rosewood fingerboard, notched-diamond inlay, fat column peghead inlay, sunburst or natural finish
Introduced (continued from earlier Epi line): **1958**
Available by special order only: **1965**
Discontinued: **1970**

Zenith: 16 3/8" wide, non-cutaway, trapeze tailpiece, single-bound top and back, vertical oval peghead inlay, sunburst
Introduced (continued from earlier Epi line): **1958**
Available by special order only: **1965**
Discontinued: **1970**

Howard Roberts and **Howard Roberts Custom**: offered in catalog as acoustic models without PU, cherry or sunburst finish (see Epiphone Electric Archtops): **1965–68**

COMMENTS

Recording models were Epiphone's earliest high quality guitars. They are hard to find in good condition and are more sought after by blues players and collectors than by jazz or folk players.

Pre-1937 Epis are of very high quality and are generally much scarcer than later models. They are of considerable interest to collectors. They have a smaller body and a less modern neck feel than later models, and they are less sought after by players for utility use.

The models that are most highly regarded by collectors are those made from 1937, when body sizes were increased, up to the end of New York production. Most desirable are the professional grade models on which the company built its reputation: the Emperor, De Luxe, Broadway, and Triumph. These models, along with Gibsons, are considered by most collectors and musicians to be the best vintage factory-made archtop guitars ever produced. Low-end models are generally regarded as excellent instruments for serious amateurs.

FLAT TOPS KEY

Flat top and archtop guitars with a non-standard, lopped-off cutaway on the upper treble bout are
Epiphone Recording series models, which are all listed together in the Epiphone Acoustic
Archtops section.

Cloud inlay
    Non-cutaway
        Maple body=**FT De Luxe**
        Rosewood body=**Excellente**
    Cutaway=**FT Deluxe Cutaway**
Slotted-block inlay
    Cutaway=**Zephyr-Regent style**
    Non-cutaway
        12-fret neck=**Madrid, 1930s**
        14-fret neck
            Tortoise grain pickguard
                Maple body=**Frontier (FT 110)**
                Walnut body=**FT 79, 1946–54**
            2 white pickguards=**Troubadour**
Single-parallelogram inlay
    Maple body
        Notched-stickpin peghead inlay=**FT 75**
        Vertical oval peghead inlay=**FT 79, 1954–58**
    Mahogany body
        Pickguard extends below bridge=**El Dorado**
        Pickguard does not extend below bridge=**Texan (FT 79), 1954–70**
Dot inlay
    Mahogany top=**Caballero (FT 30)**
    Mahogany finish spruce top (*f*-holes)=**Beverly**
    Shaded spruce top
        12-fret neck=**Navarre**
        14-fret neck
            Banner logo decal
                Walnut body=**FT 37**
                Mahogany body=**FT 27**
            Script logo=**FT 45**
    Natural spruce top
        Tortoise grain binding=**FT 50**
        Non-tortoise grain binding
            6-string
                12-fret neck=**Folkster**
                14-fret neck=**Cortez (FT 45), 1962–70**
            12-strings
                16 1/4" wide=**Bard**
                14 1/4" wide=**Serenader**
No inlay (classical models)
    Asymmetrical fingerboard with treble-side extension
        Bound fingerboard
            Gold-plated metal parts=**Concert**
            Nickel-plated metal parts=**Alhambra**
        Unbound fingerboard=**Seville, c. 1939**
    Symmetrical fingerboard
        Mahogany back and sides
            Rounded peghead corners=**Classic**
            Pointed peghead corners
                Fan bracing
                    25 1/2" scale=**Seville** or **Seville Electric, 1961–70**
                    22 3/4" scale=**Entrada**
                Non-fan bracing=**Madrid, 1962–70**
        Maple back and sides
            Gold-plated metal parts=**Barcelone**
            Nickel-plated metal parts=**Espana**

FLAT TOPS

SECTION ORGANIZATION
Steel-string Models, 1931–57
Gibson-made Steel-String Models, 1958–70
12-Strings
Epi-made Classicals
Gibson-made Classicals

Steel-String Models, 1931–57

All with round hole unless otherwise specified.

Recording Series: asymmetrical body with lopped-off cutaway on upper treble bout, see Epiphone Acoustic Archtops section

Beverly: 13" wide, spruce top, 3-segment *f*-holes, arched back, mahogany back and sides, adjustable bridge, trapeze tailpiece, elevated pickguard, no body binding, rounded peghead, brown finish, tenor available
Introduced: **1931**
Discontinued: **1937**

Madrid: Hawaiian model, 16 1/2" wide, 4 *f*-holes, maple back and sides, bound top and back, staggered bridge pins, 12 frets clear of body, celluloid frets flush with fingerboard (some with Spanish setup), slotted-block inlay
Introduced: **early 1930s**
Round hole by **1937**
Classical-type bridge with strings through bridge, trapeze tailpiece, center-dip peghead, dark cherry red sunburst finish: **c. 1939**
Discontinued: **1942**
Model name re-introduced as a classical (see following): **1962**

Electar *f*-hole electric flat-top (model name unknown): see Electric Archtops, available: **c. 1938**

Navarre: Hawaiian model, 16 1/2" wide, mahogany back and sides, bound top and back, bound fingerboard, 12 frets clear of body, celluloid frets flush with fingerboard (some with Spanish setup), dot inlay, rounded-peak peghead
Introduced: **early 1930s**
Trapeze tailpiece, center-dip peghead: **c. 1939**
Discontinued: **1942**

FT 75: 16 1/2" wide, maple back and sides, multiple-bound top and back, bound fingerboard, 14 frets clear of body, single-parallelogram inlay, notched-stickpin peghead inlay, script logo, dark cherry sunburst

finish
Introduced by **1935**
Trapeze tailpiece, single-bound top and back, by **1939**
Blond finish optional: **early 1941**
Discontinued: **1942**

FT 37: 15 1/2" wide, walnut back and sides, single-bound top and back, 14 frets clear of body, dot inlay, banner peghead decal, sunburst finish
Introduced by **1935**
Trapeze tailpiece, script logo, natural finish optional: **c. 1939**
Discontinued: **1942**

FT 27 (early example labeled **F.T. No. 1**): 14 1/2" wide, mahogany back and sides, 2 routings in bridge parallel to strings, ebony saddle, bound top, unbound back, 14 frets clear of body , dot inlay, peghead decal with block letter logo on banner arching over *Masterbilt*, sunburst finish
Introduced by **1935**
Trapeze tailpiece, script logo, natural finish optional: **c. 1939**
Discontinued: **1941**

FT De Luxe: 16 1/2" wide, maple back and sides, pickguard, trapeze tailpiece, multiple-bound top and back, maple neck, multiple-bound rosewood fingerboard, cloud inlay, vine peghead inlay, gold-plated metal parts, sunburst or natural finish
Introduced: **c. 1939**
Discontinued: **1942**
De Luxe Cutaway flat top introduced (see following): **early 1950s**

Concert, **Seville**, and **Alhambra**, see Epi-Made Classicals (following)

FT 110: 16" wide, arched maple back, multiple-bound top, fixed bridge with compensating saddle, single-bound fingerboard, cherry neck, slotted-block inlay, enclosed tuners, vertical oval peghead inlay
Introduced: **1942**
Model number continued by Gibson as **Frontier** (see following): **1958**

FT 79: 16" wide, walnut back and sides, triple-bound top, single-bound back and peghead, slotted-block inlay, stickpin peghead inlay
Introduced: **1942**
Maple back and sides, triple-bound top and back specified (some single-bound), single-parallelogram inlay, vertical oval peghead inlay, by **1954**
Model number continued by Gibson as **Texan** (see following): **1958**

Epiphone

Flat Tops

FT 50: 14 1/2" wide, mahogany back and sides, tortoise grain binding on top and back, dot inlay, center-dip peghead, natural top finish
Introduced by **1941**
Discontinued by **1950**

FT 45: 14 1/2" wide, walnut back and sides, bound top and back, dot inlay
Introduced by **1942**
Model number continued by Gibson as **Cortez** (see following): **1958**

FT 30: 14 1/2" wide, mahogany body and top, cherry neck, dot inlay, mahogany finish
Introduced by **1941**
Discontinued by **1954**
Model number continued by Gibson as **Caballero** (see following): **1958**

De Luxe Cutaway (flat top): 17 3/8" wide, single rounded cutaway, multiple-bound top and back, single-bound fingerboard, cloud inlay, flower peghead inlay, natural top (some sunburst)
Introduced: **early 1950s**
Discontinued: **1957**

"Zephyr Cutaway" (model name unknown): 17 3/8" wide, single rounded cutaway, less fancy than De Luxe Cutaway flat top, slotted-block inlay
Introduced: **early 1950s**
Discontinued by **1957**

Gibson-made Steel-String Models, 1958–70

All 16 1/4" wide, with 25 1/2" scale, 14 frets clear of body, unless otherwise specified

Frontier: square-shouldered dreadnought shape, maple back and sides, bound fingerboard, slotted-block inlay, gold-plated metal parts, slashed-*C* logo on pickguard, walnut finish back and sides, natural or sunburst top finish
Model number FT 110 continued from Epi line: **1958**
Vertical oval peghead inlay: **1961**
Adjustable saddle: **1962**
Large pointed pickguard with rope and cactus design: **1963**
Standard teardrop shape pickguard with slashed-*C* logo: **1965**
Discontinued: **1970**

Texan: round-shouldered dreadnought shape, mahogany back and sides, slashed-*C* logo on pickguard, rosewood fingerboard, single-parallelogram inlay, plastic tuner buttons, sunburst or natural top finish
Model number FT 79 continued from Epi line: **1958**
Vertical oval peghead inlay: **1961**
Adjustable rosewood saddle: **1962**
Metal tuner buttons by: **1967**
Discontinued: **1970**

Cortez: 14 1/4" wide, mahogany back and sides, 24 3/4" scale, dot inlay, slashed-*C* logo on pickguard, metal peghead logo plate, sunburst or natural top finish
Model number FT 45 continued from Epi line: **1958**
Sunburst finish only: **1959**
Natural top optional, adjustable saddle on natural top only: **1962**
Discontinued: **1970**

Caballero: 14 1/4" wide, all mahogany, tortoise grain binding, slashed-*C* logo on pickguard, 24 3/4" scale, dot inlay
Model number FT 30 continued from Epi line: **1958**
No logo on pickguard: **1961**
Adjustable saddle: **1963**
Tenor available: **1963–68**
Discontinued: **1970**

Excellente: square-shouldered dreadnought shape, rosewood back and sides, tune-o-matic bridge, large pointed pickguard with eagle, multiple-bound top and back, multiple-bound ebony fingerboard, cloud inlay, large pearl and abalone peghead inlay, single-bound peghead, gold-plated metal parts, natural top finish
Introduced: **1963**
Discontinued: **1970**

El Dorado: square-shouldered dreadnought shape, mahogany back and sides, multiple-bound top and back, bound fingerboard, single-parallelogram inlay, vertical oval peghead inlay, metal tuner buttons
Introduced: **1963**
Adjustable saddle: **1965**
Discontinued: **1970**

Troubadour: square-shouldered dreadnought shape, maple back and sides, 2 white pickguards, multiple-bound top, single-bound back, 12 frets clear of body, classical fingerboard width, 24 3/4" scale, slotted-block inlay, solid peghead, gold-plated metal parts, walnut finish back and sides
Introduced: **1963**
Discontinued: **1970**

Folkster: 14 1/4" wide, mahogany back and sides, 2 white pickguards, 12 frets clear of body, classical fingerboard width, 24 3/4"

scale, dot inlay
Introduced: **1966**
Discontinued: **1970**

12-Strings

Bard: mahogany back and sides (maple back
and sides with walnut finish listed as
option), adjustable saddle, slashed-*C* logo
on pickguard, multiple-bound top and
back, 24 3/4" scale, dot inlay, vertical oval
peghead inlay
Introduced: **1962**
Discontinued: **1970**

Serenader: 14 1/4" wide, mahogany back and
sides (walnut finish), adjustable saddle,
slashed-*C* logo on pickguard, 24 3/4" scale,
dot inlay
Introduced: **1963**
Discontinued: **1970**

Epi-made Classicals

Concert: 16 1/2" wide, maple back and sides,
multiple-bound top and back, rosewood
bridge, 12 frets clear of body, 14-fret neck
optional, asymmetrical bound rosewood
fingerboard extends over soundhole, slotted peghead, gold-plated metal parts
Introduced: **Nov. 1938**
Discontinued: **late 1940s**

Alhambra: 14 3/8" wide, maple back and sides,
bound top and back, fixed rosewood
bridge, 12 frets clear of body, 14-fret neck
optional, asymmetrical bound rosewood
fingerboard extends over soundhole, slotted peghead, nickel-plated metal parts
Introduced: **1938**
14-fret option discontinued: **1941**
Discontinued: **late 1940s**

Seville: 14 3/8" wide, mahogany back and
sides, rosewood bridge, 12 frets clear of
body, 14-fret neck optional, asymmetrical
rosewood fingerboard extends over
soundhole, slotted peghead
Introduced: **1938**
14-fret option discontinued: **1941**
Discontinued: **late 1940s**
Model name re-introduced by Gibson (see following): **1961**

Gibson-made Classicals

All 14 1/4" wide with 25 1/2" scale, fan bracing

Seville and **Seville Electric** (with ceramic PU):
mahogany back and sides, tortoise grain
binding, standard rounded neck heel,
pointed peghead corners

Introduced: **1961**
Electric discontinued: **1964**
French heel with sharp back edge: **1965**
Discontinued: **1970**

Barcelone: maple back and sides, black binding, French heel with sharp back edge,
pearloid tuner buttons, gold-plated metal
parts, rosewood finish on back and sides
Introduced: **1963**
Discontinued: **1969**

Espana: maple back and sides (walnut finish),
black binding, French heel with sharp back
edge
Introduced: **1962**
Discontinued: **1969**

Classic: mahogany back and sides, French
heel with sharp back edge, tortoise grain
binding
Introduced: **1963**
Standard heel: **1965**
Discontinued: **1970**

Entrada: 13 1/4" wide, 22 3/4" scale, standard
rounded neck heel, pointed peghead corners
Introduced: **1963**
Discontinued: **1969**

Madrid: mahogany back and sides, tortoise
shell grain binding, standard rounded neck
heel, ladder bracing, pointed peghead corners
Introduced: **1962**
Discontinued: **1970**

COMMENTS

During the New York era, Epiphone made flat
tops of good quality, but they never
achieved the recognition of Epi archtops or
the flat top guitars made by Gibson and
Martin. Gibson-made Epi flat tops are better known, partly because so many were
sold. They are fully equivalent in quality to
similar Gibson models of the same period.
However, since the 1960s was a period
when Gibson's quality had declined from
Gibson's prime collectible period of the
1940s and 50s, very few Gibson-Epis are
highly sought by collectors today.
Jumbo size models are the most highly regarded, especially those from 1958–c. 61 with
New York-style neck and non-adjustable
saddle. The most desirable of all models is
the Excellente, which is fancier than any
Gibson dreadnought flat top of its time and
rivaled only in the Gibson line by the
jumbo-shaped J-200.

29

ELECTRIC ARCHTOPS KEY

Cloud inlay
    Non-cutaway=**Zephyr De Luxe**
    Cutaway=**Zephyr Deluxe Regent**
V-block 3-piece inlay
    Non-cutaway=**Deluxe Electric**
    Single cutaway
        Full-depth body
            1 or 2 PUs=**Zephyr Deluxe Regent**
            3 PUs=**Zephyr Emperor Regent, Emperor Electric**
        Thinbody=**Emperor**
    Double cutaway=**Sheraton**
Block inlay
    Single cutaway=**Broadway**
    Double cutaway=**Caiola** or **Caiola Custom**
Single-parallelogram inlay
    Knobs into pickguard=**Professional**
    Knobs into top
        Mini-humbucking PUs=**Riviera**
        P-90 PU(s)=**Casino, 1963–70**
Slotted-block inlay
    Non-cutaway=**Zephyr, 1937–58**
    Rounded cutaway
        Full-depth body=**Zephyr Regent (Zephyr Cutaway)**
        Thinbody=**Zephyr, 1958–70**
    Pointed cutaway
        Vertical oval peghead inlay=**Howard Roberts**
        Vine peghead inlay=**Howard Roberts Custom**
Oval inlay
    Gold-plated metal parts=**Windsor**
    Nickel-plated metal parts=**Sorrento, 1962–70**
Dot inlay
    Non-cutaway
        Knobs into pickguard=**Granada**
        Knobs into top
            Horseshoe PU (wraps over strings)=**Electar Spanish**
            Non-horseshoe PU
                Full depth body
                    Mahogany back and sides=**Kent**
                    Maple back and sides
                        13 1/2" wide (flat top)=model name unknown
                        14 3/8" wide=**Coronet**
                        15 1/4" wide=**Harry Volpe**
                        16 3/8" or 15 1/4" wide=**Century, c. 1939–58**
                Thinbody
                    24 3/4" scale=**Century, 1958–70**
                    22" scale=**Century 3/4**
    Pointed cutaway
        24 3/4" scale
            Knobs into top=**Sorrento, 1960–62**
            Knobs mounted on pickguard=**Granada Cutaway**
        22" scale=**Sorrento 3/4**
    Double cutaway
        Knobs into top=**Casino, 1961–62**
        Knobs and switches on arc-shaped plate=**Caiola Standard**

ELECTRIC ARCHTOPS

Epiphone's earliest electrics were introduced by November 1935. Specs are unavailable for these models.

Most pre–World War II Epiphone electrics have a rectangular plate on the back of the peghead with 7 (or more) patent numbers licensed from Miessner Inventions Inc., Millburn, NJ.

SECTION ORGANIZATION

New York-made Models (including electric banjos), 1937–57
Gibson-made Models, 1958–70

New York-made Models, 1937–57

Electar Spanish: 16 3/8" wide, horseshoe PU (wraps over strings), cloth-covered plate on back, height-adjustable bridge, bound *f*-holes, bound top and back, bound fingerboard, dot inlay, *Electar* peghead logo, sunburst finish, tenor available
Introduced by **1937**
Discontinued: **c. 1939**

Electar *f*-hole flat top (model name unknown): 13 1/2" wide, *f*-holes, flat top, blade PU in oblong housing, bound top and back, dot inlay, *Electar* peghead logo plate, sunburst finish.
Available: **c. 1938**

Electar Banjo: maple top, screw-on back, horseshoe PU (wraps over strings), 2 knobs on opposite sides, jack in side, trapeze tailpiece, pickguard covers upper treble quadrant of top, triple-bound top, single-bound back, block inlay, *Electar* peghead logo plate, sunburst finish, tenor or plectrum available
Introduced: **1937**
PU with slot-head screw poles, 2 knobs on bass side, 1 knob and jack on treble side, *Electar* on peghead reads upside down to player: **1938**
Renamed **Zephyr Banjo**, 2 knobs on opposite sides, knobs on large circular *Mastervoicer* plates, metal *Epiphone* peghead logo plate, natural finish: **1939**
Metal PU cover: **1941**
Discontinued by **1954**

Century Banjo: blade PU, metal PU cover, jack on top, trapeze tailpiece, pickguard covers upper treble quadrant of top, block inlay, metal peghead logo plate, natural finish
Introduced: **c. 1939**
Dot inlay: **1942**
Discontinued by **1950**

Zephyr: 16 3/8" wide, maple top, 1 pole PU with oblong housing, PU in bridge position, metal PU cover/handrest, 2 knobs on circular *Mastervoicer* plates, knobs in a line parallel to strings, jack on top, trapeze tailpiece, multiple-bound top, single-bound back and fingerboard, block inlay, metal *Epiphone* peghead logo plate, blond finish, tenor and plectrum available
Introduced by **1939**
No handrest, knobs close to edge, jack on side: **1942**
PU in middle position, single-bound top and back: **mid 1940s**
17 3/8" wide, laminated spruce top, by **late 1940s**
Frequensator tailpiece (although pictured in catalog with trapeze), 1 New York PU in neck position, knobs in line at right angle to strings, sunburst or blond finish, by **1950**

Zephyr Regent: 17 3/8" wide, rounded cutaway, sunburst finish only, introduced by **1950**
De Armond PU, some examples: **1953**
Zephyr and Zephyr Regent cataloged as **Zephyr Electric**, available in non-cutaway or cutaway, cutaway sometimes labeled **Zephyr Cutaway**, tenor available as non-cutaway only, knobs in a line that crosses strings, sunburst or blond finish, by **1953**
Gibson-Epi Zephyr (see following): **1958**

Century: 16 3/8" wide, blade PU with oblong housing, PU in bridge position, metal PU cover/handrest, 2 knobs near edge, jack on top, trapeze tailpiece, single-bound top and back, bound fingerboard, dot inlay, metal peghead logo plate, highlighted walnut finish, 3/4 size available
Introduced: **c. 1939**
15 1/4" wide, no handrest, jack on side: **1942**
16 3/8" wide, oblong PU with fat blade in neck position, square control plates with radial markings, unbound fingerboard: **mid 1940s**
Large rectangular PU with non-adjustable poles in neck position, knobs in a line that crosses strings, *E* logo on pickguard, highlighted mahogany finish, by **1950**
Blond finish available, by **1954**
Rectangular black PU housing with oblong chrome plate: **c. 1954**
Gibson-Epi Century (see following): **1958**

Coronet: 14 3/8" wide, blade PU with oblong housing, PU in bridge position, no handrest, jack on top, knobs in a line parallel to strings, trapeze tailpiece, single-bound top and back, unbound fingerboard, dot inlay, metal peghead logo plate, brown sunburst finish, Spanish or Hawaiian setup
Introduced: **c. 1939**
Knobs close to edge, jack on side: **1942**
Discontinued by **1950**

Epiphone

Electric Archtops

Model name revived (see Electric Solidbodies): **1958**

Zephyr De Luxe: 17 3/8" wide, spruce top, 1 PU with slot-head screw poles and oblong housing, PU in bridge position, volume and tone control on 1 shaft with circular *Mastervoicer* control plate, Frequensator tailpiece, 5-ply top and back binding, triple-bound pickguard, bound rosewood fingerboard, cloud inlay, triple-bound peghead, vine peghead inlay, gold-plated metal parts, blond finish, tenor (with metal peghead logo plate) and plectrum models available
Introduced (first listed as **Deluxe Zephyr Spanish Electric**): **Dec. 1, 1941**
PU in neck position, 2 PUs optional, slotted switch on 2-PU model, 2 knobs near edge, *Mastervoicer* control plates, sunburst or blond finish, by **1950**
Knobs in line parallel to strings: **1951**
Discontinued by **1954**

Zephyr De Luxe Regent: 17 3/4" wide, rounded cutaway, laminated spruce top, 2 large rectangular PUs, 2 knobs near edge, circular *Mastervoicer* control plates, slotted switch, Frequensator tailpiece, 7-ply binding on top and back, triple-bound rosewood fingerboard, 3-piece V-block inlay (some with cloud), triple-bound peghead, vine peghead inlay, gold-plated metal parts, sunburst or blond finish
Introduced by **1949**
2 New York PUs, knobs in line parallel to strings, by **1950**
5-ply top and back binding, triple-bound pickguard: **c. 1951**
Knobs in line that crosses strings, by **1953**
Renamed **Deluxe Electric**, by **1954**
Discontinued: **1958**

Zephyr Emperor Regent: 18 1/2" wide, rounded cutaway, 3 New York PUs, 2 knobs, control plate with 6 small pushbuttons, 7-ply binding on top and back, 3-ply binding on *f*-holes, single-bound rosewood fingerboard with 2 white lines inlaid near edges, 3-piece V-block inlay with abalone wedge, triple-bound peghead, sunburst or blond finish
Introduced by **1952**
Some with De Armond PUs: **1953**
Renamed **Emperor Electric** by **1954**
Gibson-Epi Emperor (see following): **1958**

Kent: 15 1/4" wide, mahogany back and sides, large rectangular PU with non-adjustable poles, PU in bridge position, 2 knobs on a line that crosses strings, trapeze tailpiece, bound top, slashed-*C* logo on pickguard,

dot inlay, metal peghead logo plate, sunburst finish
Introduced by **1950**
Discontinued by **1954**

Harry Volpe: 15 1/4" wide, black rectangular PU, oblong chrome plate in center area of PU, PU in neck position, knobs in a line that crosses strings, slashed-*C* logo on pickguard, trapeze tailpiece, single-bound top and back, dot inlay, metal peghead logo plate, extra-wide string spacing, sunburst finish
Introduced: **March 1955**
Discontinued by **1957**

Gibson-made Models, 1958–70

Emperor: 18 1/2" wide, single rounded cutaway, thinbody, 3 New York PUs, 4 knobs, tune-o-matic tailpiece, Frequensator tailpiece, multiple binding, ebony fingerboard, 25 1/2" scale, 3-piece V-block inlay with abalone wedge, vine peghead inlay, stairstep tuner buttons, gold-plated metal parts, sunburst or natural finish
Model name continued from Epi line: **1958**
Mini-humbucking PUs by **1961**
Available by special order only: **1963**
Sunburst finish only: **1965**
Discontinued (later in Japanese-made line with different specs): **1969**

Sheraton: 16" wide, double rounded cutaway, thin semi-hollow body, 2 New York PUs, tune-o-matic bridge, Frequensator tailpiece, optional Epi vibrato with slashed-*C* logo on tailpiece, multiple-bound top and back, multiple-bound pickguard, 24 3/4" scale, bound fingerboard, V-block inlay, metal tuner buttons (early with New York style tuners), multiple-bound peghead, vine peghead inlay, gold-plated metal parts, sunburst or natural finish
Introduced by **1958**
Mini-humbucking PUs, vibrato standard, by **1961**
Cherry finish optional: **1965**
Discontinued (later in Japanese-made line): **1970**

Broadway: 17 3/8" wide, single rounded cutaway, full-depth body, 2 New York PUs, rosewood bridge, Frequensator tailpiece, single-bound pickguard, 25 1/2" scale, block inlay, fat column peghead inlay, deluxe plastic tuner buttons, sunburst or natural finish
Continued from Epi line: **1958**
Mini-humbucking PUs by **1961**
Tune-o-matic bridge: **1963**
Cherry finish optional, only year shipped: **1967**

Natural finish listed but none shipped: **1968**
Discontinued: **1970**

Century: 16 3/8" wide, non-cutaway, thinbody, 1
New York PU, rosewood bridge, trapeze
tailpiece, unbound tortoise grain pick-
guard, 25 1/2" scale, dot inlay, metal peg-
head logo plate, sunburst finish
Model name continued from Epi line: **1958**
P-90 pickup: **1959**
3/4 size available: **1961**
Royal burgundy finish: **1961**
No peghead plate: **1963**
3/4 size discontinued: **1968**
Sunburst finish only: **1968**
Discontinued (later in Japanese-made line):
1970

Zephyr: 17 3/8" wide, single rounded cutaway,
thinbody, 2 New York PUs, trapeze tailpiece, unbound tortoise grain pickguard,
slotted-block inlay, metal peghead logo
plate, natural or sunburst finish
Model name continued from Epi line: **1958**
No peghead plate: **1960**
Mini-humbucking PUs by **1961**
Discontinued: **1964**

Windsor: 16 3/8" wide, single pointed cutaway,
thinbody, 1 or 2 New York PUs, 1 PU in
neck position, rosewood bridge, trapeze
tailpiece, unbound tortoise grain pickguard, 24 3/4" scale, oval inlay, metal peghead logo plate, gold-plated metal parts,
sunburst or natural finish
Introduced: **1959**
No peghead plate: **1960**
Mini-humbucking PU(s) by **1961**
Discontinued: **1962**

Sorrento: 16 1/4" wide, single pointed cutaway,
thinbody, 1 or 2 mini-humbucking PUs, PU
in neck position on single-PU model, tune-
o-matic bridge, vibrato optional, trapeze
tailpiece, unbound tortoise grain pickguard, 24 3/4" scale, dot inlay, metal peghead logo plate, nickel-plated metal parts,
sunburst, natural, or royal olive finish
Introduced: **1960**
3/4 size, 22" scale, available: **1961–62**
Oval inlay: **1962**
Vibrato discontinued: **1962**
No peghead plate, by **1963**
Cherry or sunburst finish: **1968**
Discontinued: **1970**

Casino: 16" wide, rounded double cutaway,
fully hollow thinbody, 1 P-90 PU in middle
position or 2 P-90 PUs, tune-o-matic
bridge, trapeze tailpiece, vibrato optional,
white 3-ply pickguard with beveled edge,
single-bound top and back, 24 3/4" scale,

16 frets clear of body, single-bound finger-
board, dot inlay, sunburst or royal tan
finish
Introduced: **1961**
Vibrato optional: **1962**
Chrome pickup cover(s), single-parallelogram
inlay, by **1963**
Cherry finish optional: **1967**
Discontinued (later in Japanese-made line):
1970

Granada: 16 1/4" non-cutaway, thinbody, 1 *f*-
hole, 1 Melody Maker PU mounted into
pickguard, rosewood bridge, trapeze tailpiece, controls built into pickguard (like
Gibson ES-120T), pickguard surrounds PU,
24 3/4" scale, dot inlay, sunburst finish
Introduced: **1962**
Granada Cutaway: single pointed cutaway,
introduced: **1965**
Granada and Granada Cutaway discontinued:
1970

Professional: 16" wide, double cutaway, thinbody, 1 mini-humbucking PU, 2 knobs on
treble side, 3 knobs and numerous switches on bass side (companion amplifier had
no control knobs and was controlled from
the guitar), all controls mounted through
symmetrical pickguard, tune-o-matic
bridge, Frequensator tailpiece, single-
bound top and back (catalog specifies multiple), single-parallelogram inlay, multi-
prong jack and standard jack, mahogany
finish
Introduced: **1962**
Discontinued: **1967**

Riviera: 16" wide, double cutaway, thinbody, 2
mini-humbucking PUs, tune-o-matic
bridge, Frequensator tailpiece, single-
bound top and back (catalog specifies multiple binding), single-bound tortoise grain
pickguard, 24 3/4" scale, single-bound fingerboard, single-parallelogram inlay, royal
tan finish
Introduced: **1962**
Riviera 12-string introduced: **1965**
Sunburst finish standard: **1965**
White 3-ply pickguard with beveled edge,
cherry finish optional: **1966**
Vibrato optional (6-string only): **1967**
Discontinued (later in Japanese-made line):
1970

Caiola: 16" wide, double cutaway, thinbody, no
soundholes, 2 mini-humbucking PUs,
ebony adjustable bridge, trapeze tailpiece
with wood center insert, *Caiola Model*
inlaid on trapeze insert, arc-shaped control
plate with 2 knobs and 5 switches plus PU
selector switch, 7-ply top binding, 5-ply

back binding, 5-ply pickguard binding,
Custom on block at body end of neck,
single-bound rosewood fingerboard, zero
fret, 25 1/2" scale, block inlay, single-bound
peghead, fat column peghead logo,
mahogany red (walnut) or royal tan (yellow
sunburst) finish

Introduced: **1963**
Tune-o-matic bridge by **1965**
Renamed **Caiola Custom: 1966**
Walnut finish only: **1968**
Discontinued: **1970**

Caiola Standard: 2 P-90 PUs, same switch system as Caiola Custom, single-bound top
and back, dot inlay, unbound peghead, no
peghead ornament

Introduced: **1966**
Cherry or sunburst finish: **1968**
Discontinued: **1970**

Howard Roberts: 16 1/4" wide, single pointed
cutaway, full-depth body, carved spruce
top, single-bound oval soundhole, no
rosette, 1 floating mini-humbucking PU,
single-bound top and back, plate tailpiece
with 3 raised parallelograms and pointed
ends, white 3-ply pickguard with beveled
edge, rosewood bridge, bound rosewood
fingerboard, slotted-block inlay, vertical
oval peghead inlay, chrome-plated metal
parts, cherry finish

Introduced: **1964**
Triple-bound top: **1965**
Natural or sunburst finish optional: **1965–67**
Natural or sunburst finish standard, cherry not
listed: **1968**
Tune-o-matic bridge: **1967**
Discontinued: **1970**

Howard Roberts Custom: tune-o-matic bridge
(pictured in catalog with adjustable rosewood bridge), triple-bound top, single-
bound back, single-bound pickguard,
single-bound ebony fingerboard, triple-
bound peghead, vine peghead inlay, walnut finish

Introduced: **1965**
Natural finish optional, only year (6 shipped):
1966
Multiple-bound top and pickguard, triple-
bound back, multiple-bound peghead,
black finish optional: **late 1960s**
Discontinued: **1970**
Re-introduced with changes in Gibson line
(see Gibson Electric Archtops): **1974**

COMMENTS

New York-made electric archtops are interesting but generally are not nearly as highly
regarded as equivalent acoustics.
Acoustics are solid carved top and back
whereas electrics are plywood. In addition, the electronics on New York Epis are
not of high quality compared to Gibsons of
the same period or to the later Gibson-
made Epis. Consequently, New York Epi
electrics bring less than Gibsons of the
same period or equivalent Epi acoustics.

Early Gibson Epis with New York PUs are of
interest to collectors. Most hollowbody Epi
electrics bring less than the equivalent
Gibson models.

Double cutaway thinbody electrics are the
most highly sought after. The Emperor
(single cutaway) is the rarest of the thinlines (66 total made) and will command a
high price. The Sheraton, especially the
early version with blond finish, has caught
on with collectors. Some seek Sheratons
with New York PUs, though not for sound.
The Sheraton brings fully as much and
sometimes more than the equivalent
Gibson ES-355 of the same period. The
Riviera, though equal in playability and
sound, is not nearly as sought after and
brings less than the equivalent ES-335. The
Casino brings as much as, or more than,
the equivalent ES-330 because John
Lennon played one.

ELECTRIC SOLIDBODIES KEY

Single cutaway
  2 PUs=**Olympic Double, 1960–62**
  1 PU
    Standard scale=**Olympic, 1960–62**
    3/4 scale=**Olympic 3/4, 1960–62**
Symmetrical double cutaway
  2 PUs
    Gold-plated parts=**Crestwood (Custom), c. 1958–62**
    Nickel-plated parts=**Wilshire, c. 1958–62**
  1 PU
    Poles visible on PU=**Coronet, c. 1958–62**
    No PU poles=**Olympic Special, 1963–65**
Bass-side horn longer than treble-side horn
  Block inlay=**Crestwood Deluxe**
  Oval inlay=**Crestwood Custom, 1963–70**
  Dot inlay
    2 PUs
      Poles visible on PUs=**Wilshire, 1963–70**
      No PU poles=**Olympic Double, 1963–70**
    1 PU
      Poles visible on PUs
        Slashed-*C* on truss rod cover=**Coronet, 1963–70**
        Dwight on truss rod cover or peghead=**Dwight**
      No PU poles
        Some frets not clear of body=**Olympic Special, 1965–70**
        All frets clear of body=**Olympic, 1963–70**

ELECTRIC SOLIDBODIES

All Epiphone solidbody electrics are double cutaway with 24 3/4" scale, unless otherwise specified. All were listed by 1963 as available in the following custom colors: sunset yellow, California coral and Pacific blue.

Crestwood: symmetrical slab body (square body edges), 1 3/4" deep, 2 New York PUs, tune-o-matic bridge, asymmetrical pickguard with slashed-*C* logo, rosewood fingerboard, dot inlay, metal peghead logo plate, gold-plated metal parts, sunburst finish
Introduced by **1958**
1 3/8" deep, rounded body edges, symmetrical pickguard, cherry finish: **c. 1959**
Renamed **Crestwood Custom**: **1959**
2 mini-humbucking PUs, vibrato, oval inlay, no pickguard logo, no peghead plate, pearl logo: **1961**
White finish optional by: **1962**
Asymmetrical body with upper bass horn slightly longer than upper treble, vibrato optional, asymmetrical pickguard, 6-on-a-side tuners, nickel-plated metal parts: **1963**
Vibrato standard: **1965**

Discontinued: **1970**
Crestwood Deluxe: asymmetrical body with bass horn slightly longer than treble, rounded body edges, 1 3/8" deep, 3 mini-humbucking PUs, tune-o-matic bridge, vibrato, asymmetrical pickguard, bound ebony fingerboard, block inlay, triple-bound peghead, 6-on-a-side tuners, cherry or white finish
Introduced: **1963**
Discontinued: **1970**

Coronet: symmetrical slab body (square body edges), 1 3/4" deep, 1 New York PU, asymmetrical pickguard, combination bridge-tailpiece, dot inlay, metal peghead logo plate, sunburst finish (some black)
Introduced: **1958**
P-90 PU: **c. 1959**
1 3/8" deep, rounded body edges, symmetrical pickguard, cherry finish: **c. 1960**
No peghead plate: **1961**
Vibrato optional: **1962**
Asymmetrical body with upper bass horn slightly longer than upper treble, metal covered P-90 PU, 6-on-a-side tuner arrangement, silver fox finish optional: **1963**
Vibrato discontinued: **1966**
Discontinued: **1970**

Wilshire: symmetrical slab body (square body edges), 1 3/4" deep, 2 white soapbar P-90 PUs, symmetrical pickguard, tune-o-matic bridge, vibrato optional, dot inlay, sunburst finish
Introduced: **1959**
1 3/8" deep, rounded body edges, cherry finish: **c. 1960**
Black soapbar P-90 PUs, slashed-*C* logo on pickguard, no vibrato: **1961**
Asymmetrical body with upper bass horn slightly longer than upper treble, 2 mini-humbucking PUs, 6-on-a-side tuners, by **1963**
Maestro vibrato optional: **1963–65**
Red fox finish (cherry stain with yellow fill) optional: **1965**
Wilshire 12-string, center-dip peghead, available: **1966–68**
Discontinued: **1970**

Olympic (1PU), **Olympic Double** (2 PUs), and **Olympic 3/4** (1 PU, 3/4 scale): single cutaway (like Gibson single-cutaway Melody Maker), combination bridge-tailpiece, rosewood fingerboard, dot inlay, sunburst
Introduced: **1960**
Asymmetrical double cutaway with upper bass horn slightly longer than upper treble, logo between PUs: **1963**
Olympic 3/4 discontinued: **1964**
6-on-a-side tuner arrangement: **1964**
Maestro vibrato optional: **1964**
Vibrato standard: **1965**
Cherry finish optional: **1966–69**
Discontinued: **1970**

Olympic Special: symmetrical body with sharper cutaway tips than other Epi models, 1 Melody Maker PU, pickguard extends around PU, vibrato optional, dot inlay, narrow peghead, logo reads upside down to player, sunburst finish
Introduced: **1962**
Maestro vibrato optional: **1964–65**
Asymmetrical body with bass horn slightly longer than treble (still with sharper tips than other Epis), vibrato standard: **1965**
Discontinued: **1970**

Dwight: same specs and model number as Coronet (see preceding) but with *Dwight Model* on truss rod cover or peghead, no Epiphone logo on peghead
75 shipped: **1963**
36 shipped: **1967**

COMMENTS

Some collectors are interested in early solid-body models with New York pickups, but not for their sound. Later solidbodies with mini-humbucking pickups bring less money than their Gibson equivalents with standard humbucking pickups. None are especially valuable, although Epi workmanship and playability is fully equivalent to Gibson brand instruments of the same period.

ELECTRIC BASSES KEY

Solidbody
>Tune-o-matic bridge=**Embassy Deluxe**
>Combination bridge-tailpiece=**Newport**
Hollowbody=**Rivoli**

ELECTRIC BASSES

Rivoli: thin hollowbody, symmetrical double cutaway, *f*-holes, vibrato available (rare), 1 large rectangular PU with poles, dot inlay, banjo tuners, vertical oval peghead inlay, natural or sunburst finish
Introduced: **1959**
Right-angle tuners: **c. 1960**
Discontinued: **1962**
Re-introduced, sunburst finish only: **1963**
Natural finish optional: **1965**
Cherry finish optional: **1966**
Discontinued: **1969**
Re-introduced with 2 PUs: **1970**
Discontinued: **1970**

Newport: solidbody, asymmetrical double cutaway with bass horn longer than treble, 1 large rectangular PU with poles, combination bridge-tailpiece, metal hand rest over strings, 30 1/2" scale, dot inlay, 2-on-a-side tuner arrangement, cherry finish
Introduced: **1961**
2 PUs optional: **1961–63**
Fuzz-tone available: **1962**
6-string model available: **1962–65**
4-on-a-side tuner arrangement: **1963**
Red fox finish (cherry stain with yellow fill) optional: **1965**
Discontinued: **1970**

Embassy Deluxe: solidbody, asymmetrical double cutaway with bass horn longer than treble, 2 PUs with no poles (like Gibson Thunderbird basses), metal hand rest and bridge cover, tune-o-matic bridge, 34" scale, dot inlay, 4-on-a-side tuner arrangement, cherry finish
Introduced: **1963**
Discontinued: **1970**

COMMENTS

Epiphone electric basses are not especially sought after by collectors or players, although their workmanship and playability is fully equivalent to Gibson brand instruments of the same period. The Embassy Deluxe is the Epiphone equivalent to the highly sought after Gibson Thunderbird basses, and it has the potential to gain some of appeal that the Thunderbirds hold for collectors and players.

STEELS KEY

Singleneck
    Guitar-shaped body
        Electar peghead logo=**Electar Hawaiian, Model C**
        Epiphone peghead logo
            White pickguard=**Coronet**
            No pickguard
                Metal handrest=**Kent**
                Metal bridge/PU cover=**Century, 1950–57**
    Straight-line body edges
        Electar peghead logo=**Model M**
        Epiphone peghead logo=**Zephyr**
    Rounded body sides, no guitar waist=**Century, 1939–1950**
    Rectangular body shape
        Pitch changing levers=**Varichord**
        No pitch changing levers=**Solo Console**
Doubleneck
    Rectangular body shape=**Duo Console, Double Console**
    Angled body corners=**Rocco**
Tripleneck=**Console Triple Neck**

STEELS

Electar Hawaiian: guitar shape, amplifier in case
Introduced by **Dec. 1936**
Renamed **Model C**: guitar shape, oblong bar PU, 2 knobs on opposite sides with treble knob mounted through pickguard, bound top, dot markers, *Electar* peghead logo, sunburst finish: **1937**
Discontinued: **1939**

Model M: metalbody, stairstep body shape with art deco ornamentation, horseshoe PU (wraps over strings), 2 knobs on opposite sides, bound rosewood fingerboard, colored dot markers, *Electar* peghead logo, black finish
Introduced: **1937**
PU with large slot-head screw poles, chrome-plated PU cover, blue and black top finish, gray body finish: **c. 1938**
Some with 3 knobs: **c. 1938**
Discontinued: **1939**

Rocco: doubleneck, rectangular body with angled corners, metal top, horseshoe PUs (PU magnets wrap over strings), 2 volume knobs on opposite sides, 1 tone knob between necks (later 2 knobs), jack on top, geometric pattern markers, *Electar* logo plate and *Rocco Model* between necks, string dampers, standard setup with 7-string and 8-string neck, combinations of 6, 7, or 8 strings available by special order
Introduced: **1937**
Discontinued, replaced by Solo and Duo

Console models (see following): **c. 1939**

Zephyr: maple body with square end, metal PU cover/handrest, knobs on opposite sides, black metal fingerboard, fancy markers, metal *Epiphone* peghead logo plate, black body finish, white plastic top, 6, 7, or 8 strings
Introduced: **c. 1939**
Bottom corners scooped out, knobs on same side, metal PU/bridge cover with slashed-*C* logo, varied-color markers, by **1954**
Knobs on rectangular control plate, bound top and back, by **1954**
Discontinued: **1957**

Century: teardrop body shape with rounded bottom edge, 2 knobs on opposite sides, metal PU cover/handrest, plastic pickguard, metal fingerboard, bowtie markers, metal *Epiphone* peghead logo plate, black finish, 6, 7, or 8 strings
Introduced: **c. 1939**
Rounded guitar-like bouts, knobs on same side, metal PU/bridge cover with *E* logo, by **1950**
Bound top and back, by **1954**
Discontinued: **1957**

Coronet: guitar shape, blade PU with oblong housing, knobs on opposite sides, white pickguard, rosewood fingerboard, dot markers, metal peghead logo plate, black finish, 6-string only
Introduced: **1939**
Discontinued by **1950**

Solo Console: rectangular body of prima vera

wood (white mahogany), black binding, removable PU cover, 2 knobs, black metal fingerboard/control plate, bowtie markers, *Electar* logo between neck and pickup, metal peghead logo plate, 6, 7, or 8 strings

Duo Console: doubleneck, rectangular maple body, black celluloid and white mahogany binding, large screwed-down pickup cover, 2 bar-like string dampers, 2 knobs on circular *Mastervoicer* plates between pegheads, metal logo plate at extreme peghead end of body, 2 8-string necks standard, combinations of 12, 13, 14, or 15 strings available by special order
Introduced: **c. 1939**
Duo Console renamed **Double Console**: metal bridge covers with slashed-*C* logo: **1950**
Solo Console discontinued by **1954**

Console Triple-Neck: 3 necks, rounder corners than Duo Console, tortoise grain bridge covers, sunburst or natural finish, available by **1954**
Discontinued: **1958**

Electar Grande: wooden stand (not an instrument) for Solo or Duo Console, prima vera wood (white mahogany), Electar-style script *E* in relief on front panel, wheels, breaks down to 2 luggage-like carrying cases
Introduced: **1939**
Discontinued by **1950**

Varichord: rectangular body of prima vera wood (white mahogany), PU with large slot-head screw poles, wood bridge cover does not extend over PU, 2 knobs on circular *Mastervoicer* plates, 7 strings, 7 pitch-changing levers on top
First sold: **1939**
First appearance in literature: **1941**
Discontinued by **1943**

Kent: guitar shape, maple body, New York PU with no poles and black mounting frames, metal handrest, knobs on same side, no binding, metal peghead logo plate (some with decal script logo with tail underneath)
Introduced by **1950**
Discontinued by **1954**

COMMENTS

Epiphone lap steels were good utility instruments for their time, but their pickups make them less desirable today than some models by Gibson, Rickenbacker, or Valco (National and Supro). The models of greatest interest to collectors are those that are rare, aesthetically appealing, or historically interesting, such as the Model M, the Rocco, and the Varichord.

MANDOLINS

Mandolins pictured in Epiphone catalogs do not change from 3-segment f-holes to standard f-holes until 1939, and that is the date listed in the following model descriptions. However, it is highly possible that Epi mandolins went to standard f-holes at the same time the guitar models did, by 1937.

SECTION ORGANIZATION

Mandolins
Mandolas
Mandocellos
Electric Mandolins
Gibson-made Model

Mandolins

Windsor: symmetrical 2-point body, carved top and back, "curly" maple back and sides, 3-segment f-holes, bound elevated pickguard, triple-bound top and back, maple neck, bound ebony fingerboard, diagonal bowtie inlay, Masterbilt peghead, gold-plated metal parts, sunburst finish
Introduced by **1934**
Style discontinued, name continues on Windsor Special design (see following), by **1937**

Windsor Special: scroll body, carved top and back, "curly" maple back and sides, 3 segment f-holes, unbound elevated pickguard, triple-bound top and back, maple neck, bound ebony fingerboard with treble-side extension, diagonal bowtie inlay, Masterbilt peghead, gold-plated metal parts, sunburst finish
Introduced by **1934**
Renamed **Windsor**, "flame" maple back and sides, by **1937**
Standard f-holes, pickguard dips around bridge, rosewood fingerboard, slotted-block inlay, vine peghead inlay, dip on treble side of peghead: **1939**
Discontinued by **1954**

Strand: symmetrical 2-point body, carved top and back, walnut back and sides, 3-segment f-holes, unbound elevated pickguard, single-bound top and back, mahogany neck, single-bound fingerboard with rounded end, diagonal paired-diamond inlay, Masterbilt peghead, nickel-plated metal parts, sunburst finish
Introduced by **1934**
Triple-bound top, single-bound back, block letter logo, elongated diamond peghead inlay, rounded-peak peghead: **1935**
Standard f-holes, pickguard dips around

bridge, rosewood fingerboard with square end, single-parallelogram inlay, script logo, center-dip peghead, by **1939**
Oval hole, small peghead inlay, by **1954**
Discontinued by **1958**

Artist: same as 1937 Windsor but with "curly" maple back and sides, single-bound top and back, nickel-plated metal parts, sunburst finish
Introduced: **1937**
Standard f-holes, single-parallelogram inlay, wandering vine peghead inlay: **1939**
Discontinued by **1954**

Rivoli: symmetrical A-style body, walnut back and sides, 3-segment f-holes, walnut neck, rosewood fingerboard, dot inlay, rounded-top peghead with 2 banners and model name in center, sunburst top, walnut back and sides finish
Introduced by **1934**
Standard f-holes, pickguard dips around bridge, center-dip peghead, stickpin peghead inlay, script logo, by **1939**
Oval hole, vertical oval peghead inlay, by **1954**
Discontinued by **1958**

Adelphi: symmetrical A-style body, maple back and sides, 3-segment f-holes, unbound elevated pickguard, single-bound top and back, unbound rosewood fingerboard with square end, dot inlay, rounded peghead with 2 banners and model name in center, yellow-to-cherry sunburst top finish, cherry back and sides finish
Introduced by **1934**
Standard f-holes, pickguard dips around bridge, script logo with tail underneath, no other peghead ornamentation, by **1939**
Discontinued by **1954**

Mandolas

Windsor, **Strand**, **Rivoli**, and **Adelphi**, introduced by **1934**
Artist introduced by **1937**
Mandolas discontinued by **1954**

Mandocellos

No. 1: A-style body shape, same wood and ornamentation as Blackstone guitar
No. 2: A-style body shape, same wood and ornamentation as Triumph guitar
No. 3: A-style body shape, same wood and ornamentation as De Luxe guitar
Introduced: **1934**
Mandocellos discontinued by **1954**

Electric Mandolins

Zephyr Mandolin: A-style symmetrical body, *f*-holes, maple top, maple back and sides, 1 PU with slot-head screw poles in oblong housing, 2 white knobs on opposite sides, knobs on circular *Mastervoicer* plates, jack into top, bound fingerboard, block inlay (some with dots), metal peghead logo plate, center-dip peghead, blond finish
Introduced by **1939**
Knobs on same side, no *Mastervoicer* plates, sunburst finish optional, by **1954**
Discontinued: **1958**

Century Mandolin: A-style symmetrical body, *f*-holes, unspecified wood, large oblong blade PU mounted on large rectangular plate, 2 knobs on opposite sides, jack into top, bound top and back, bound rosewood fingerboard, dot inlay, metal peghead logo plate, pointed-top peghead, sunburst
Introduced by **1939**
No plate under PU, center-dip peghead: **1941**
Discontinued by **1950**

Gibson-Made Model

Venetian: similar to Gibson A-50, A-style symmetrical body, maple back and sides, bound fingerboard, dot inlay, sunburst finish
Introduced: **1961**
Electric model available: **1966**
Discontinued: **1970**

COMMENTS

The Windsor, Windsor Special, and Artist mandolins, along with all mandola and mandocello models, are so rare that it is questionable whether they ever existed beyond the prototypes used for catalog pictures. If any of these should turn up, they would certainly be of interest to collectors

Of the other Epi mandolin models, the relatively rare Strand is of the most interest to collectors. The Strand and Rivoli are regarded by players as quality instruments.

ACOUSTIC BASSES

All Epiphone basses have laminated body. All are 3/4 size (standard acoustic bass size) with 42" scale.

B-4: fine-grain spruce top, highly figured maple back and sides, black-white-black binding on top and back, Brazilian rose-wood fingerboard and tailpiece, brass tuner plates and machines, colored (later described as light golden brown) or blond finish

B-3: select spruce top, figured maple back and sides, inlaid purfling, Brazilian rosewood fingerboard and tailpiece, brass tuner plates and machines, Cremona brown sun-burst finish with highlights on top, back, and sides

B-2: spruce top, good figured maple back and sides, Brazilian rosewood fingerboard and tailpiece, nickel-plated metal parts, light cherry sunburst finish

B-1: maple back and sides, ebonized finger-board and tailpiece, dark cherry red sun-burst finish

Models B-1, B-2, B-3, and B-4, introduced: **1940**

B-3 and B-2 switch finishes in catalog descriptions; B-3 has French red finish with yellow highlights, B-2 has Cremona brown sun-burst: **1942**

Metal logo plate on tailpiece, all models: **1942**

B-1, B-2, and B-3, discontinued by **1954**

B-4 continued in Gibson line (see following): **1958**

B-5 Artists Model: fine-grain spruce top, high-ly figured maple back and sides, Brazilian rosewood fingerboard and tailpiece, triple-bound top and back, engraved gold-plated tuner plates, light golden brown or blond finish

Introduced by **Feb. 1941**

Metal logo plate on tailpiece: **1942**

Continued in Gibson line (see following): **1958**

Gibson-Made Models

B5, The Artist: continued from Epi line, Van Eps adjustable bridge, gold-plated metal parts, natural (N) or shaded (S) finish

B4, The Professional: continued from Epi line, Van Eps adjustable bridge, polished brass metal parts, natural (N) or shaded (S) finish

BV, The Studio: student model, shaded finish

Introduced: **1958**

All basses discontinued: **1965**

Total Shipments of Gibson-Epi Basses, 1958–64

B5N	37
B5S	40
B4N	46
B4S	166
BV	355

COMMENTS

Epiphones are considered by players to be among the finest laminated-construction upright basses. It was Epi's bass produc-tion capability that sparked Gibson's initial interest in acquiring Epiphone. Although Gibson shipping records show a fair num-ber of basses produced (644 total), Gibson-made Epi basses are seldom seen.

Fender

GENERAL INFORMATION

Leo Fender and Doc Kauffman began making K&F brand lap steels and amplifiers in Fullerton, CA, in the fall of 1945. Kauffman left in early 1946 and the name of the company was changed to the Fender Electric Instrument Company.

With the introduction of the Esquire and Broadcaster (soon to be Telecaster) in 1950, Fender became the first company to successfully market solidbody electric guitars. The first solidbody bass, the Precision, was introduced in late 1951.

Fender was sold to CBS on January 4, 1965.

In May 1982, Fender and Japanese partners, known as Fender Japan, announced a line of vintage reissues for Japanese and European markets. These were marked with a small *made in Japan* peghead decal. Beginning in October 1983, Japanese-made Fenders were labeled with the Squier designation and marketed in the United States. Not all Japanese-made Fenders have the Squier designation.

CBS sold Fender to a group of private investors in March 1985, and the Fullerton plant was closed. After a short period, during which all Fender instruments were made in Japan, U.S. production was resumed in Corona, CA. Many Fender models are now made in Japan. Squier models are now made in Korea.

Dates on Instruments

From 1950 to March 1962, almost all Fender guitars (except for a few from April 1959 to early 1960) have a date written in pencil at the body end of the neck. From March 1962 to about March 1973, the neck date is rubber stamped. (The number before the month is *not* a part but a neck specification code.) No necks are dated from 1973–81.

On many instruments, dates can be found in body routings (1950–c. 63) or on the bottom of pickups (1964–late 70s). Neck and body dates are usually within 30 days of each other but may be several months apart.

Dates on necks, bodies, pickups, and pots (see Appendix) are dates for that part only. They do not date the finished instrument.

Terms

Bakelite: Bakelite is a trade name for a molded phenolic resin. It has become a generic term used for all similar materials, such as the Phenolite used for black pickguards on early Telecasters and Esquires. Bakelite is most common in black, brown or white. It is somewhat similar in appearance to modern postwar thermal plastics, but is less shiny and more brittle. Although Bakelite should properly be capitalized, the term *bakelite* (lower case) is commonly used in reference to Fenders and is used here to refer to Phenolite and to similar material used on early Stratocasters.

Body

Finish…
   Nitrocellulose finish on non-custom colors: **1950–68**
   Custom colors, any available DuPont Duco color: **1950–60**
   Custom colors standardized, high-end models (see Stratocaster section): **1960–current**
   Polyester finish: **1968–current**
Wire…
   Cloth-covered wire: **1950–68**
   Transition to plastic-covered wire: **1968–69**
   Plastic-covered wire: **1968–current**

Neck and Fingerboard

1-piece maple, no truss rod, no skunk stripe on back, early Esquire: **1950 only**
1-piece maple, walnut skunk stripe on back (to fill truss rod routing): **1950**
Rosewood fingerboard, Jazzmaster only: **mid to late 1958**
"Slab" rosewood fingerboard, flat-milled on back side (maple neck/fingerboard still available as replacement or special order): **Sept. 1959**
"Curved" rosewood fingerboard, thinner than "slab," curved back side: **mid 1962**
Thinner, veneer-like rosewood board: **mid 1963**
Separate maple fingerboard (no skunk stripe) optional on Telecaster, Telecaster Custom, Stratocaster, Jaguar, Esquire, Esquire Custom, Precision Bass, Jazz Bass, all 2-PU Coronado 6-strings, and all Coronado basses: **1967**
1-piece maple neck/fingerboard with skunk stripe, acrylic finish, optional on Telecaster, Telecaster Custom, Stratocaster, Jaguar, Esquire, Esquire Custom, Precision Bass, Jazz Bass, all 2-PU Coronado 6-strings, and all Coronado basses: **1969**
Slab fingerboard (with Biflex truss rod): **1980s**
Neckplate…
   4-screw plate: **1950**
   F on neckplate: **c. Aug. 1965–current**
   3-screw plate…
      Stratocaster, Telecaster Thinline, Custom Telecaster, Telecaster Bass: **1971**

Telecaster Deluxe (from introduction):
1972
Jazz Bass: **1975**
Starcaster (from introduction): **1976–81**
4-screw plate re-introduced...
Anniversary Stratocaster: **1979**
All Stratocasters: **1980**
All other models: **1981**
Truss rod...
Rod adjustment at body end: **1950**
Tilt-neck, allen nut adjustment on peghead,
some models: **1971**
Biflex truss rod: **1980s**
Bound fingerboard introduced...
Strat (very rare): **mid 1965–67**
Jaguar, Jazzmaster, Jazz Bass, Bass VI,
Electric XII: **late 1965–early 66**
Block inlay introduced on Jaguar, Jazzmaster,
Jazz Bass, Bass VI, Electric XII: **mid 1966**

Pegheads

String guides...
Single round guide for E and B strings:
1950
Butterfly clip: **mid 1956**
Metal spacer between clip and peghead:
1959
2 butterfly clips...
Telecaster, Telecaster Deluxe, Custom
Telecaster, Esquire: **1971**
Stratocaster: **c. 1974**
Mustang: **1976**
4 strings through guide, Starcaster (from
introduction): **1976**
2 pin clips, non-vintage Strats and Teles
only: **1983**
Tuners...
"Single line," *Kluson Deluxe* on back,
patent pending notice, button shaft
does not go through gear enclosure:
1950–early 51
Kluson, no writing on tuner cover, button
shaft does not go through gear enclosure: **mid 1951–early to mid 1952.**
No writing on tuner cover, button shaft end
visible through tuner cover: **early to
mid 1952–late 55**
"Single line," *Kluson Deluxe* on back, button shaft goes through gear enclosure:
late 1955–64
"Double line," *Kluson Deluxe* on each line:
1964–67
Fender tuners with *F* logo: **1967–81**
Fender stamped on back: **1981–current**
Peghead matches body color on custom color
Jazzmaster, Jaguar and Jazz Bass models,
except for blond and shoreline gold finish.

Logos

All Fender solidbody guitars have the model-
name on the peghead except for the following: "No-caster" (see Telecaster),

Rosewood Telecaster, Telecaster Thinline
from 1968–71, Swinger, and a few custom
color Jaguars and Jazzmasters.
Montego and LTD archtop models have a pearl
logo rather than the standard decal.
"Spaghetti" logo, gold or silver outlined in
black, unconnected *nde* in *Fender*...
Model name under logo: **1950**
Model name after logo, Stratocaster only:
1954
New models as introduced: **1950s**
"Transition" logo, gold (silver on Precision
only), connected *nde* in *Fender*, model
name after logo...
New models as introduced: **1960–68**
Jazz Bass: **1960**
Jaguar, Precision Bass, by **1962**
All other models except Telecaster and
Esquire: **Jan. 1965**
Telecaster: **1967**
Esquire: **1968**
Black logo...
All models except following: **1968**
Stratocaster: **July 1968**
Telecaster Bass, Mustang: **1972**
Mandolin by **1974**
Musicmaster, Mustang Bass, by **1976**
Musicmaster Bass, by **1978**
Trademark registration symbol, circled-*R* with
logo: **1966**
New transition-type logo, silver (Lead I and II)
or gold (Strat, Precision Bass Special):
1980
New transition-type logo, silver outlined in
black: **1983**
Spaghetti or transition logos on reissue mod-
els: **1982–current**

Other Peghead Decals

Patent numbers on peghead: **1961–76**
Serial number and *Made in USA* on peghead,
no patent numbers: **1976**

Cases for High-End Models

"Thermometer," bulbous peghead area: **1950**
"Contour," 1 edge follows body contour, 1
edge straight: **1953**
Rectangular, center pocket, tweed cover: **mid
1954**
Side pocket, tweed cover, red lining: **mid 1955**
Side pocket, tweed cover, orange lining: **late
1958**
Brown Tolex cover, burnt orange lining: **1960**
Brown Tolex cover, reddish orange lining: **mid
1962**
White or black Tolex cover, black leather
ends, reddish orange lining, logo on case:
late 1962–65
Black Tolex cover, no logo: **1965–67**
Black Tolex cover, logo: **1968 and after**
Tweed cases, some reissues: **1980s**

Slab rosewood fingerboard, used from 1959-62. Maple neck is planed flat, and the line between fingerboard and neck is straight.

Curved rosewood fingerboard, used from 1962-80s. Maple neck surface is curved, fingerboard is uniform width, and the line between fingerboard and neck is curved.

Jazzmaster pickup.

Close-up of Jaguar pickup, with notched pickup frames.

Fender humbucking pickup on a Telecaster Thinline.

Telecaster body, with slab body style.

Jaguar body, with standard Jazzmaster-type tremolo.

Stratocaster body, with rounded body edges.

Musicmaster body with anodized aluminum (gold colored) pickguard.

Spaghetti logo on a 1956 Stratocaster, small Strat peghead.

Transition logo on a 1965 Jazzmaster.

Black logo on a 1979 Stratocaster, large Strat peghead used from late 1965-81, bullet truss rod.

Telecaster peghead with mid 1970s style logo.

SERIAL NUMBERS

Fender guitars have a serial number on the bridgeplate, neckplate, or peghead decal. Serial numbers are not strictly chronological, as is evident by the wide range of overlapping numbers from year to year, but they do fall into rough chronological groups.

Exceptions:

From 1950 into 1954, Telecasters and Esquires have a single series, Precision Basses (beginning in 1951) have their own series, and Stratocasters (1954) have their own series.

LTD guitars, acoustic guitars, mandolins, and lap steels have their own number series.

Most Coronados have numbers in the 500000 and 600000 series.

Most Bass Vs have numbers in the 600000 series.

The serial number list is a summary of numbers and neck dates compiled by James Werner.
The cross-check number list contains information from Fender records.

Number Placement

On bottom end of body or bridgeplate (lap steels): **1946–49**
On bridgeplate near bridge…
    Lap steels: **1950–80**
    Guitars and Precision Bass: **1950–54**
On tremolo plate, Stratocaster only: **1954**
On upper edge of back neckplate: **1954–mid 76**
On lower edge of back neckplate, some examples: **1959–60**
Double-stamped, some examples: **late 1957–early 59**
On peghead decal: **mid 1976–current**
On backplate, reissue models: **1982–current**

Esquire and Broadcaster/No-caster/Telecaster, 1950-54

Number Range	Year
0001–0999	1950–52
1000–5221	1952–54

Precision Bass, 1951–54

Number Range	Year
161–357	1951
0001–0999	1952–53
1000–1897	1953–54

Stratocaster, 1954

Number Range	Year
Under 6000	1954

Electric Models, 1954 and after

General Range	Lowest	Highest	Year of Neck Date	
0001–6000s	0001	09599	late 1954	
7000–8700	6727	10798	1955	(some preceded by 0)
9000–16000	08999	16957	1956	
17000–24000	13438	025919	1957	(some preceded by –)
25000–30000	023384	33687	1958	(some preceded by 0)
30000–39000	022878	51593	1959	
44000–58000	44221	66626	1960	
55000–72000	55531	72827	1961	
71000–93000	70862	96203	1962	
80000–99000	76722	99304	1963–65	

L-Series

L00001–L00400	L00001	L13181	1962	
L01000–L20000	L01153	L24179	1963	

| L25000–L55000 | L20596 | L76159 | 1964 |
| L60000–L99000 | L34983 | L99809 | 1965 |

F-Series, F on Neckplate

100000–110000	100173	147397	1965
120000–200000	115151	215697	1966
180000–210000	180882	230599	1967
220000–250000	213820	262774	1968
220000–280000	224160	290835	1969
290000–300000	293780	304089	1970
300000–330000	295668	331031	1971
340000–370000	315451	375648	1972
380000–520000	362789	588161	1973
500000–580000	538585	615662	1974
600000–650000	608004	717257	1975

Number on Peghead Decal

7600000 (*76* in boldface)			1976–77
800000–870000	801063	910414 late	1979–80
800000–900000	708736	907411	1981
S600000			1976
S700000–S770000	S707125	S770029	1977
S740000–S800000	S745231	S840993	1978
S800000–S870000	S791741	S926549	1979
S880000–S980000	S800470	S996471	1980
S950000–S990000	S836937	S994644	1981
E000000–E100000	E000005	E114479	1980
E100000–E109000	E09717	E960860	1981
E110000–E210000	E100007	E853764	1982
E300000–E310000	E311285	E339028	1983

Cross-Check Number List, F series

400000s	Apr. 1973–Sept. 76
500000s	Sept. 1973–Sept. 76
600000s	Aug. 1974–Aug. 76
700000s	Sept. 1976–Dec. 76

Cross-Check Number List, S or E prefix

Number	Period Used by Fender
S7	Jan. 1977–Apr. 78
S8	Dec. 1977–Dec. 78
S9	Nov. 1978–Aug. 81
E0	June 1979–Dec. 81
E1	Dec. 1980–Jan. 82
E2	Dec. 1981–Jan. 83
E3	Dec. 1982–Jan. 85
E4	Dec. 1983–early 88

Other Fender Numbers

25####=Anniversary Strat: **mid 1979–early 80s**
GO prefix: **early 80s**
Prefix of CA, CB, CC, CD, or CE, collectors series: **Dec. 1981–Dec. 82**
V######=Vintage reissues: **1982 and after**
4-digit decal on back of peghead=custom order: **1987 and after**
JV prefix=Japanese vintage: **1982 and after**
SQ prefix=Squier model: **1983 and after**
A prefix=Japanese-made (Squier) reissues of Telecaster, Stratocaster and Esquire: **1985–86**

ELECTRIC GUITARS, MANDOLIN, AND VIOLIN

SECTION ORGANIZATION

Esquires
Telecaster (including Broadcaster and No-caster)
Telecaster and Esquire Finishes
Other Telecaster Models
Other Solidbody Instruments, Including Mandolin and Violin
Hollowbody Models

Esquires

Esquire: single cutaway, ash body, 1 PU with flush poles, 2 dome knobs (some smooth, some rimmed on top), 2-position toggle switch, white pickguard with slot-head screws, 3 paired-string adjustable brass saddles, strings anchor through body, no truss rod, slot-head neck bolts, round string guide, logo below string guide, black finish

Announced in *Musical Merchandise Review* magazine: **June 1950**

Routed for 2 PUs, no routing channel between PUs, some examples with 2 PUs, short round 3-way tone selector switch, black bakelite pickguard, butterscotch blond finish: **summer 1950**

No Esquires made: **late Sept. 1950–Jan. 1951**

Re-introduced, 1 PU, truss rod, butterscotch blond finish (later finish changes and options listed after Telecaster, following): **Jan. 1951**

Routing channel between PU routings: **late summer 1951**

Phillips-head neck bolts: **early 1952**

Phillips-head pickguard screws: **mid-late 1952**

White plastic pickguard, non-threaded steel saddles: **late 1954**

Staggered PU poles, "top-hat" switch (thin top, rounded base), serial number on neck-plate, butterfly-clip string guide: **late 1955**

Logo above string guide: **July or Aug. 1956**

Threaded steel saddles: **late 1958**

Strings anchor at bridge: **late 1958**

Strings anchor through body: **early 1960**

Laminated pickguard: **1965**

Last produced: **early 1970**

Esquire Custom: same as Esquire but with bound top and back, rosewood fingerboard, sunburst finish

Introduced: **mid 1959**

Discontinued: **early 1970**

Telecaster

The Telecaster was originally named Broadcaster. However, Gretsch had used the name Broadkaster on drums and banjos since the 1920s and 1930s and was still marketing a Broadkaster drum set in 1950. Consequently, Fender dropped the Broadcaster model name after less than 300-500 Broadcasters were made. During a brief transitional period, some instruments were made with no model name on the peghead; these are commonly referred to as No-casters. Neck dates on Broadcasters, No-casters and Telecasters overlap.

Broadcaster/No-caster/Telecaster: same body design as Esquire, single-cutaway, ash body, 2 PUs, flush poles on bridge PU, serial number stamped on housing of bridge PU, no routing channel between PU routings, 2 dome knobs (some smooth, some rimmed on top), short round PU selector switch, black bakelite pickguard with slot-head screws, 3 brass paired-string adjustable saddles, strings anchor through body, truss rod, slot-head neck bolts, round string guide, logo below string guide

Broadcaster introduced: **late 1950**

Broadcaster replaced by No-caster: **Feb. 1951**

No-caster replaced by Telecaster, routing channel between PU routings (a few No-casters routed between PUs): **early 1951**

Philips-head neck bolts: **early 1952**

Philips-head pickguard screws: **mid to late 1952**

White plastic pickguard, non-threaded steel saddles: **late 1954**

Staggered-height poles on bridge PU, "top-hat" switch (thin top, rounded base), serial number on neckplate, butterfly-clip string guide: **late 1955**

Logo above string guide: **July or Aug. 1956**

Threaded steel saddles: **late 1958**

Strings anchor at bridge: **late 1958**

Strings anchor through body: **early 1960**

Laminated pickguard: **1962**

Still in production

Telecaster & Esquire Finishes

"Butterscotch," whitish yellow to show wood grain, tendency to yellow over time: **1950**

"Tele blond," translucent whitish yellow, somewhat gray on heavily figured ash bodies, less yellowing over time: **mid 1955**

More opaque yellow finish, less wood grain visible: **1960—68**

Custom finishes...
  Sunburst, most common custom finish (but still rare) ...

2-tone: **1957 only**
3-tone: **1958–59**
Black, very few (less than 10) Esquires in
1950, later Teles and Esquires: **late
1958–early 59**
Any DuPont Duco paint color: **until 1960**
Standardized custom colors (see
Stratocaster section): **1960 and after**
Pink paisley and blue floral finish optional:
1968-69 only

Other Telecaster Models

Telecaster Custom: alder body (a few ash),
single-bound top and back, rosewood fingerboard, sunburst finish, a few custom
color examples
Introduced: **mid 1959**
Discontinued: **1969**

Thin Line: ash or mahogany body, hollow on
bass side, 1 *f*-hole, no *Thin Line* decal on
peghead, natural finish, sunburst or custom colors available
Introduced: **late 1968**
2 humbucking PUs, *Thin Line* decal on peghead: **1972**
Discontinued: **c. 1978**

Custom Telecaster: (also called Telecaster
Custom in literature) standard Tele bridge
PU, humbucking neck PU, 4 knobs
Introduced: **March 1970**
Discontinued by **1982**

Rosewood: rosewood body, available: **1969, 70,
72**
Japanese-made reissue introduced: **late 1980s**

Deluxe: contoured body, 2 humbucking PUs, 4
knobs
Introduced: **1972**
Discontinued by **1982**

'52 Telecaster: reissue of 1952 Telecaster,
serial number on bridgeplate, black pickguard, maple neck/fingerboard, spaghetti
logo, butterscotch blond finish
Introduced: **1982**
Still in production

Elite: white plastic-covered PUs with no visible poles, active electronics, special
design bridge
Introduced: **1983**
Discontinued: **early 1985**

Other Solidbody Instruments, Including Mandolin & Violin

Stratocaster: see separate Stratocasters section

Duo-Sonic: 3/4 size, 2 straight-mounted PUs,
plastic PU covers, no visible PU poles, 2
slide switches, 3 paired-string adjustable
bridge saddles, anodized aluminum pickguard, 22 1/2" scale, 24" scale optional,
blond finish
Introduced: **mid 1956**
Plastic pickguard by **1962**
Restyled like Mustang, offset body waists, 2
switches, red, white, or blue finish: **1964**
Models with 24" scale designated **Duo-Sonic
II: 1965**
Discontinued: **1969**

Musicmaster: 3/4 size, same body as Duo-
Sonic, 1 slant-mounted PU near neck, plas-
tic PU cover, no visible PU poles, 2 knobs,
3 paired-string adjustable bridge saddles,
anodized aluminum pickguard, 22 1/2"
scale, 24" scale optional, blond finish
Introduced: **mid 1956**
Plastic pickguard: **late 1959**
Restyled like Mustang, offset body waists, red,
white, or blue finish: **1964**
Models with 24" scale designated
Musicmaster II: 1965–late 1969
Discontinued by **1982**

Jazzmaster: contoured body with offset waist
indents, 2 rectangular white-covered PUs,
(a few early with black PU covers), selector switch, volume and tone roller knobs on
bass side of pickguard, 2 white plastic
knobs (early with chrome-plated barrel
knobs) on treble side, chrome-plated control plates, floating tremolo and bridge,
anodized aluminum pickguard, individual
bridge saddles, 25 1/2" scale, rosewood fingerboard, clay dot inlay, large Strat-like
peghead, sunburst finish
Introduced: **mid 1958**
Tortoise grain pickguard: **late 1959**
Bound fingerboard: **late 1965**
Block inlay: **mid 1966**
Discontinued by **1982**

Jaguar: similar body and peghead shape to
Jazzmaster, 2 white oblong Strat-like PUs
with notched metal side plates, 2 knobs
and 3 individual PU on/off switches on treble side, selector switch and 2 roller knobs
on bass side, string mute, Jazzmaster-type
floating tremolo and bridge, 24" scale, sunburst finish
Introduced: **mid 1962**
Bound fingerboard: **late 1965**
Block inlay: **mid 1966**
Discontinued: **1974**

Mustang: 2 slant-mounted PUs, plastic PU covers, no visible PU poles, 2 on/off switches, master tone knob, master volume knob, tremelo, 24" scale (22 1/2" optional but rare), red, white, or blue finish
Introduced: **Aug. 1964**
Competition Mustang: red, burgundy, or orange finish with racing stripes, available: **1969**
Discontinued by **1982**

Marauder: 4 concealed PUs, some with visible PUs and slanted frets, available (very rare): **1965 only**

Electric XII: 12-string, 2 split PUs, dot inlay, sunburst or blond finish standard, custom colors available
Introduced: **mid 1965**
Bound fingerboard: **late 1965**
Block inlay: **mid 1966**
Discontinued: **1969**

Bronco: 1 Strat-like PU slant-mounted near bridge, tremolo, 24" scale, red finish
Introduced by **1968**
Discontinued by **1982**

Musiclander, **Swinger**, **Arrow**: same model under different names, model designed to use up spare parts from other models, body scooped out at strap button, Musicmaster electronics, 24"-scale neck (from Mustang), necks dated 1966-68, dot inlay, 6-on-a-side tuners, pointed peghead with straight edges on treble and bass side, no model name on Swinger peghead
Introduced: **mid 1969**
Discontinued: **1972**

Custom, **Maverick**: same model under different names, model designed to use up spare parts from other models, asymmetrical double cutaway, body pointed at strap button, 2 split PUs (from Electric XII), pointer knob, 4-position switch, tremolo, bound fingerboard, block inlay, Electric XII neck with 3-on-a-side tuner arrangement, necks dated 1966–68, sunburst finish
Introduced: **mid 1969**
Discontinued: **1972**

Mandolin: 4 strings, 1 oblong PU with reddish/brown plastic cover, no visible PU poles, 1-piece maple neck/fingerboard, anodized aluminum pickguard, logo decal (no other decal) on peghead, sunburst or Tele-type translucent blond finish
Introduced: **early 1956**
Tortoise grain pickguard, rosewood fingerboard, *Original contour body* peghead decal: **late 1959**
No *Original contour body* decal by: **1970**

Sunburst only by **1972**
3-ply black pickguard by **1974**
Discontinued: **1976**

Electric Violin: highly exaggerated body waists, maple body, internal PU, 2 knobs, jack on bass side of top, detachable maple neck, ebony fingerboard, peghead shape similar to Fender guitar pegheads but with single slot, enclosed geared tuners all on bass side, decal logo on treble side, sunburst finish
Introduced: **1958**
Discontinued: **1959**
Re-introduced, peghead with center routing for tuners, ebony tuning pegs: **1969**
Discontinued by **1976**

Hollowbody Models

Coronado I: 16 1/8" wide, symmetrical double cutaway, thinbody, 1 rectangular PU with adjustable poles, bridge similar to Gibson tune-o-matic with individually adjustable saddles, tremolo optional, single-bound top and back, some with checkered binding, dot inlay, sunburst or cherry finish
Coronado II (2 PUs) and **Coronado XII** (12-string): tremolo optional, some with checkered binding, bound f-holes, block inlay
Introduced: **Jan. 1966**
Wildwood colors optional (see Acoustic Flat Tops) on Coronado II and XII only: **1966**
Antigua II and **Antigua XII**: silver-to-black sunburst finish, introduced by **early 1968**
All discontinued except Antigua II and Antigua XII, by **1970**
Antigua II and XII discontinued by **1972**

LTD: 17" wide, single cutaway, full-depth body, hand carved top and back, highly figured maple back and sides, 1 floating humbucking PU, 2 knobs mounted on pickguard, multiple-bound top and back, *F* on tailpiece, bolt-on neck, 25 1/2" scale, single-bound fingerboard, outline block inlay, bound peghead, 3 outline heart-pattern peghead inlays, 3-on-a-side tuner arrangment, gold-plated metal parts, 3-tone sunburst finish
Introduced: **1969**
Discontinued by **1976**

Montego I and **Montego II**: 17" wide, single cutaway, full-depth body, 1 or 2 PUs mounted on top, knobs mounted on body, bound f-holes, bolt-on neck, 6-piece vase-like peghead inlay, bound peghead, chrome-plated metal parts, sunburst or natural finish
Introduced: **1969**
Discontinued by **1976**

Starcaster: asymmetrical double cutaway, thin body, 2 humbucking PUs, 5 knobs, 1 switch on upper treble bout, beveled treble-side edge of peghead
Introduced by **1976**
Discontinued by **1982**

COMMENTS

Esquires, Telecasters and Stratocasters played a major role in the popularization of the solidbody electric guitar. From their introduction into the late 1960s, they are highly regarded by players and collectors. Generally, the earlier the example, the more highly sought after, with custom color examples bringing more than standard finish.

Jazzmasters and Jaguars, the mainstays of the Fender line in the 1960s, fell out of favor in the 1970s and 80s. Interest has revived in these models in the 1990s, though not to the level of interest in Teles and Strats.

Low-end Fender solidbodies are not generally highly regarded by collectors or players.

For most collectors and players, pre–CBS instruments (pre–1965) are more desirable than later examples, although the demand for custom color examples has extended into the late 1960s.

Coronados are not highly regarded by players or collectors, although the wildwood models have some aesthetic appeal.

Montego and LTD models are fairly rare and have some appeal to collectors.

STRATOCASTERS

SECTION ORGANIZATION

Stratocaster with detailed specs
Later Stratocaster Models
Selected Signature Series Models

Stratocaster: asymmetrical double cutaway body shape, contoured body on back and on lower bass bout, 3 PUs, jack angled into top, tremolo standard (see following for more detailed specs)
Introduced: **spring 1954**
Referred to in literature as **Standard Stratocaster** (no *Standard* on peghead): **1982**
Note: The term Standard Stratocaster *was used by Fender to distinguish the basic current Stratocaster from variations and reissues. However, among collectors and dealers, the term is commonly used as if it were a separate model designation, referring to the Stratocasters with the following specs:*
2 knobs, jack in 3rd-knob position, 90-degree jack angle, 1-piece tailpiece with drop-in string loading, single-ply white pickguard, black, sienna sunburst, brown sunburst or ivory finish: **1983**
Marblized "bowling ball" finishes available: **late 1984**
Standard Stratocaster discontinued: **Jan. 1985**

Body Parts

Gold-plated metal parts optional: **1956–67**
Back plate (tremolo spring cover)...
 Round string holes: **1954–early 55**
 Oval string holes: **early 1955 and after**
 No back plate (different type tremolo systems), Standard and Elite: **mid 1983–85**
Knobs and PU covers...
 White bakelite knobs and PU covers, some knobs with parallel sides, some with steep-sloped sides: **1954–56**
 White plastic knobs and PU covers (some bakelite PU covers in 1956 and 1957): **1956–76**
 Black knobs and PU covers: **1976–79**
PUs...
 Staggered-height poles: **1954–late 74**
 Flush-pole PUs: **late 1974–current**
Pickguard...
 Single-layer white bakelite, 8 screws: **1954**
 Single-layer white plastic: **1955–59**
 Anodized aluminum, some examples: **1954–1958**
 3-layer celluloid, white-black-white, greenish tint, 11 screws: **1959–65**
 3-layer plastic, no greenish tint: **Aug. or Sept. 1965–75**
 Tortoise grain plastic (rare): **early 1960s**
 3-layer, black-white-black: **1975–79**
Pickguard, middle screw-hole on bass side...
 Screw-hole near middle PU: **1954–59**
 Screw-hole midway between neck PU and middle PU: **1959–mid 63**
 Screw-hole near middle PU: **mid 1963–current**
Shoulder on control cavity routing: **1959 and after**

Finishes

2-tone sunburst, yellow to black (some 2-tone in 1959 and 1960): **1954–58**
Blond and black available as custom colors, any Dupont Duco paint finish available by special order: **1954–58**
3-tone sunburst, yellow to red to black: **mid 1958 and after**
Custom colors standardized...
 Note: some custom colors have sunburst underneath
 Fiesta red, olympic white, shoreline gold metallic, Lake Placid blue metallic, Dakota red, black, desert sand: **March, 1958**
 Daphne blue, surf green, foam green, sonic blue, burgundy mist metallic, Inca silver metallic, candy apple red metallic, shell pink (in addition to 1958 colors): **1960**
 Blue ice, charcoal frost, teal green, firemist gold, ocean turquoise, firemist silver (all metallic): **1965**
 Blond, Lake Placid blue, sonic blue, olympic white, black, candy apple red metallic, firemist gold metallic, ocean turquoise metallic, firemist silver metallic: **April 1970**
Natural finish optional: **1972**

Peghead Size

Small peghead: **1954–late 65**
Enlarged peghead official: **Dec. 19, 1965**
Transition period to larger peghead: **late 1965–early 66**
Small peghead revived: **1981–current**

Decals

Configuration of *Stratocaster with synchronized tremolo*...
 Small letters, straight line: **1954**
 Bold letters, curved line: **July 1968**
 No *with synchronized tremolo*: **1970**
 Small letters: **1980**
Original contour body...
 No patent notice: **1954**
 Pat. Pend added: **1961**
 Patented replaces *Pat. Pend*: **1968**
 Decal discontinued: **1976**
Made in USA: **1976–current**

Numbers on Decal

No number: **1954**
2 PAT numbers, both beginning with 2: **1961**
3 PAT numbers: **spring 1962**
4 PAT numbers: **mid 1964**
5 PAT numbers: **mid 1965**
2 PAT numbers, 1 DES number: **Feb. 1966**
2 PAT numbers, 2nd begins with 3: **mid 1968**
1 PAT number beginning with 2: **mid 1970**
1 PAT number beginning with 3: **mid 1972**
Serial number, no patent number: **1976**

Later Stratocaster Models

Anniversary Strat: bridge cover, 4-bolt neck,
   Sperzel tuners, 6-digit serial number beginning with 25, *Anniversary* on bass horn, silver metallic finish (c. 500 early examples
   with white pearlescent finish)
Available (around 10,000 shipped): **1979–80**

The Strat: hotter bridge PU than standard, 9
   different tone control combinations, heavier brass bridge assembly than standard,
   lock-nut vibrato system optional, 4-bolt
   neck, smaller peghead than Standard Strat
   but unlike original Strat design, gold-plated
   metal parts, candy apple red, Lake Placid
   blue, or Arctic white finish
Available: **1980**
Discontinued: **July 1983**

Gold Stratocaster: standard PUs and pickguard, 1-piece maple neck/fingerboard,
   pearloid tuner buttons, gold-plated metal
   parts, metallic gold finish
Introduced: **1981**
Discontinued: **July 1983**

Walnut Strat: black walnut body and neck,
   ebony fingerboard, pearloid tuner buttons,
   natural finish
Introduced: **1981**
Discontinued: **July 1983**

'57: reissue of 1957 Strat, white single-layer
   pickguard, maple neck/fingerboard, 2-tone
   sunburst finish standard, vintage custom
   colors available (candy apple red, vintage
   white, black, Lake Placid blue, fiesta red),
   serial number beginning with V
Introduced: **Jan. 1982**
Translucent blond finish available (limited edition): **June 1987**
Still in production

'62: reissue of 1962 Strat, 3-ply pickguard,
   rosewood fingerboard, 3-tone sunburst
   finish standard, vintage custom colors
   available (candy apple red, vintage white,
   black, Lake Placid blue, fiesta red), serial
   number beginning with V
Introduced: **Jan. 1982**

Translucent blond finish available (limited edition): **June 1987**
Still in production

Elite: active electronics, white plastic PU covers with no visible poles, jack on side, special design tremolo with piece covering
   adjustment screw-heads, no back cavity
   for tremolo springs, no backplate, snap-on
   tremolo arm, drop-in string loading
Introduced: **May 1983**
Walnut Elite and Gold Elite available by: **mid
   1983**
Discontinued: **1985**

American Standard: 3-ply white pickguard, 2-
   piece vibrato tailpiece with 2 bearing
   points, 1-piece maple neck/fingerboard or
   maple neck with rosewood fingerboard,
   silver transition logo
Introduced: **Nov. 1986**
Still in production

Strat Plus: white plastic PU covers with
   Fender-Lace sensor, graffiti yellow finish
   standard, other finishes available
Introduced: **June 1987**
Still in production

Selected Signature Series Models

Eric Clapton model: similar to '57 reissue,
   Fender-Lace sensor PUs, no tremolo
Introduced: **spring 1988**
Still in production

Yngwie Malmsteen model: DiMarzio vintage
   replacement PUs, American Standard
   Strat bridge and tailpiece, no pickguard,
   scalloped fingerboard between frets
Introduced: **summer 1988**
Still in production

*Note: Most features from any Fender model
   are currently available on a custom order
   basis.*

COMMENTS

Strats from the 1950s and early 1960s are highly regarded by collectors and players, with
   custom colors bringing more than standard
   finish. The demand for custom color models extends past CBS's acquisition of
   Fender, into the late 1960s.
In the late 1980s, vintage Strats became so
   popular that the buying craze was dubbed
   "Strat-mania." After peaking in 1988,
   prices fell by as much as 50 percent. By
   early 1991, Strats were rising steadily and
   approaching 1988 prices.

BASSES

Precision (P-bass): asymmetrical double cut-away, slab (non-beveled) body, black single-coil PU with level pole pieces, 2 knobs, 2 pressed-fiber saddles, strings anchor through body, serial number on bridgeplate, black bakelite pickguard covering both upper bouts of body, slot-head pickguard screws, metal bridge and PU covers, 34" scale, 1-piece maple neck/fingerboard with skunk stripe, dot inlay, slot-head neck bolts, thin Tele-like peghead, blond finish
Introduced: **Nov. 1951**
Phillips-head neck bolts: **early 1952**
Phillips-head pickguard screws: **mid to late 1952**
Beveled body (a few leftover slab bodies as late as 1957): **1954**
2-color sunburst finish with white pickguard standard, blond finish with black pickguard optional: **1954**
Staggered-height PU polepieces, steel saddles: **1955**
Serial number on neckplate: **late 1955**
Custom Duco colors officially offered, white pickguard standard with blond or custom finish: **1956**
Split double-rectangular PU with raised A-string pole, strings anchor at bridge, smaller pickguard of anodized aluminum, wider Strat-like peghead with point on treble side: **mid 1957**
3-tone sunburst standard (some 2-tones in 1959 and 60): **mid 1958**
Level PU polepieces: **late 1958**
Slab rosewood fingerboard: **mid 1959**
Tortoise grain plastic pickguard with standard finishes, laminated white pickguard with custom finishes (some aluminum pickguards into mid 1960): **late 1959**
Curved rosewood fingerboard: **mid 1962**
Thinner veneer-like fingerboard: **mid 1963**
2-piece maple fingerboard and neck (no skunk stripe) optional: **1968**
1-piece maple neck/fingerboard optional: **late 1969**
Fretless fingerboard optional: **1970**
Thumbrest on bass side by: **1976**
Still in production

'57 Precision: reissue of 1957 Precision, threaded bridge saddles, anodized aluminum pickguard, 1-piece maple neck/fingerboard, 2-tone sunburst, vintage custom colors optional (Lake Placid blue, black, candy apple red, fiesta red, vintage white), serial number beginning with V
Introduced: **1982**
Still in production

'62 Precision: reissue of 1962 Precision, laminated tortoise grain pickguard, rosewood fingerboard, 3-tone sunburst, vintage custom colors optional (Lake Placid blue, black, candy apple red, fiesta red, vintage white), serial number beginning with V
Introduced: **1982**
Still in production

Precision Special: active electronics, visible-pole PUs, 3 knobs
Introduced: **1982**
Discontinued: **1983**

Walnut Precision Special: active electronics, visible-pole PUs, 3 knobs, black walnut body
Introduced: **1982**
Discontinued: **1983**

Elite Precision I: active electronics, white plastic-covered split-coil PU with no visible poles, rosewood fingerboard, chrome-plated metal parts
Elite Precision II: active electronics, 2 white plastic-covered split-coil PUs with no visible poles, maple or rosewood fingerboard, chrome-plated metal parts
Walnut Elite Precision I and II: 1 or 2 PUs, black walnut body, ebony fingerboard, gold-plated metal parts
Gold Elite Precision I and II: 1 or 2 PUs, gold-plated metal parts, available in all Elite finishes
Introduced: **1983**
Discontinued: **1985**

Jazz: offset body waist indents, 2 PUs, 2 concentric (stacked) pots with volume and tone control on a single shaft, individual string mutes, 34" scale, slab rosewood fingerboard, tapered fingerboard narrower at nut than Precision, 3-tone sunburst finish
Introduced: **1960**
Blond or custom finishes available: **1962**
Curved rosewood fingerboard: **mid 1962**
3 non-stacked knobs (2 volume and 1 tone): **early 1962**
No mutes by **1963**
Bound fingerboard: **late 1965**
Block inlay: **late 1966**
Maple fingerboard optional with black binding and black block inlay: **1969**
Pearloid blocks and white binding optional on maple fingerboard by **mid 1970s**
3-bolt neck: **1975**
4-bolt neck: **1981**
Still in production

'62 Jazz: reissue of 1962 Jazz, stacked pots, 3-tone sunburst finish, vintage custom colors optional (Lake Placid blue, black, candy

Basses

apple red, fiesta red, vintage white), serial
number beginning with V
Introduced: **1982**
Still in production

Bass VI: 6-string, 3 Strat-like PUs with metal
frames, 3 on/off switches, master volume
and tone knobs, 6 adjustable bridge saddles, removable bridge cover, Jazzmaster-
type floating tremolo, 30" scale, rosewood
fingerboard, dot inlay, sunburst finish
Introduced: **late 1961**
Foam rubber mute, Jaguar-like PUs with
notched metal sidepieces, 4th "strangle
switch" (condenser): **late 1963**
Approximately 300-400 sold, pre-CBS
Bound fingerboard: **late 1965**
Block inlay: **mid 1966**
Discontinued: **1975**

Bass V: 5-string, 1 split PU, 34" scale, unbound
rosewood fingerboard, dot inlay
Introduced: **June 1965**
Bound finger board: **late 1965**
Block inlay: **mid 1966**
Custom colors available by **1969**
Discontinued: **1970**

Mustang Bass: 1 split-coil PU, 30" scale, red,
white, or blue finish
Introduced: **1966**
Offset waist indents: **1969**
Competition red, burgundy, orange, or blue fin-
ishes with racing stripes, or sunburst
finish: **1970**
Sunburst, natural, walnut, black, white, or
blond finish: **1976**
White, black, natural, antigua, wine, or tobac-
co sunburst finish, by **1979**
Discontinued by **1983**

Coronado Bass I: thin hollowbody, double
rounded cutaway, 1 PU, unbound ƒ-holes,
2 finger rests, 34" scale, dot inlay
Introduced: **1966**
Coronado Bass II: thin hollowbody, double
rounded cutaway, 2 PUs, bound ƒ-holes, 2
finger rests, 34" scale, bound fingerboard,
block inlay
Introduced: **1967**
Wildwood finish (dye injected into beechwood,
see Acoustic Flat Tops) optional: **1967**
All Coronado basses discontinued except
Antigua Bass II, silver-to-black sunburst
finish, 2 PUs: **1970**
Antigua Bass II discontinued: **1972**

Telecaster Bass: similar to 1951–53 Precision,
slab body, 1 single-coil (Telecaster guitar-
style) gray PU, white pickguard, finger rest
on treble side, 34" scale, 1-piece maple
neck/fingerboard with skunk stripe, dark

dot inlay, slender Tele-like peghead, peg-
head decal of *Telecaster Bass* in small
block letters below logo, blond finish stan-
dard, custom colors available
Introduced: **1968**
Pink paisley or blue floral finish available:
1968–69
Some examples with peghead decal of
Telecaster in block letters after logo fol-
lowed by *Bass* in script: **1969–70**
Fretless neck optional: **late 1970**
Humbucking PU: **Feb. 1972**
Discontinued: **1979**

Musicmaster Bass: 1 oblong PU with plastic
cover and no visible poles, 30" scale, dot
inlay, red, white, or blue finish
Introduced: **1970**
White or black finish only, by **1976**
Discontinued by **1983**

COMMENTS

The Precision was the first fretted electric
bass and for almost four decades was the
standard by which all other basses were
judged. Early P-basses are highly sought
after by collectors, although they do not
bring as much as Telecasters, Esquires,
and Stratocasters of the same period.
Those with split-coil pickups (mid 1957 and
after) are more highly regarded by players
than those with earlier pickups.
Early Jazz basses with concentric knobs are
highly sought after by collectors.
Into the 1980s, the P-bass sound was more
highly regarded by players than that of the
Jazz. However, by the late 1980s, the
sound of the Jazz bass had become the
preferred sound, and the demand switched
accordingly from P-bass to Jazz.

ACOUSTIC FLAT TOPS

All have 2 screws in pickguard, 6-on-a-side tuner arrangement (except Classic and Folk), bolt-on neck with metal plate on back.

The first 200-300 flat tops were made with no support rod through the body. All later large-body models (King, Shenandoah) and many smaller body models were fitted with a support rod of aluminum aircraft tubing. These are sometimes referred to as broomstick models.

King: 15 5/8" wide, 20" long, dreadnought shape, spruce top, mahogany back and sides; optional back and sides of Brazilian rosewood, Indian rosewood, zebrawood, or vermilion; multiple-bound top and back, adjustable saddles, 25 1/2" scale, 21-fret fingerboard, bound fingerboard, dot inlay, chrome-plated tuner buttons, natural top finish
Introduced: **late 1963**
Renamed **Kingman**, sunburst or natural top: **1966**
Maple, rosewood or vermilion back and sides optional, antigua finish (silver-to-black sunburst) optional, black and custom color finishes optional: **1968**
Discontinued: **1971**

Wildwood: Kingman with dyed beechwood back and sides, 3-ply beveled-edge pickguard, block inlay, peghead color coordinates with wood: green, gold and brown, gold and purple, dark blue, purple-blue, or blue-green
Introduced: **1966**
Discontinued: **1971**

Concert: 15 3/8" wide, 19" long, single-ply pickguard, 20-fret fingerboard, unbound fingerboard, 25 1/2" scale, same options as King
Introduced: **late 1963**
Dot inlay, mahogany, rosewood, vermilion, or zebrawood optional, by **1966**
Sunburst finish optional: **1968**
Discontinued by **1970**

Classic: 19-fret fingerboard, classical strings, classical bridge with loop-anchored strings, slotted peghead, optional back and sides of Indian rosewood, Brazilian rosewood, or maple, no pickguard
Introduced: **late 1963**
Discontinued: **1966**

Folk: similar to Classic, designed for steel strings, tortoise grain pickguard
Introduced: **late 1963**
Discontinued: **1964**

Shenandoah: Kingman 12-string, 15 3/8" wide, mahogany back and sides, 25 1/2" scale, dot inlay
Introduced: **1965**
Antigua finish (silver-to-black sunburst) optional: **1967**
Sunburst or black finish optional: **1968**
Discontinued: **1971**

Malibu: 14 7/8" wide, mahogany back and sides, single-bound top, 25 1/2" scale, dot inlay, sunburst, mahogany, or black finish
Introduced: **1965**
Discontinued: **1971**

Villager: Malibu 12-string, 25 1/2" scale
Introduced: **1965**
Sunburst optional: **1969**
Discontinued: **1971**

Palomino: 15 3/8" wide, triple bound top and back, 25 1/2" scale, dot inlay, plastic tuner buttons, sunburst, mahogany, or black vermilion finish
Introduced: **1968**
Discontinued: **1971**

Newporter: 14 3/8" wide, mahogany finish spruce top, mahogany back and sides, single-bound top, unbound back, 25 1/2" scale, dot inlay
Introduced: **1965**
Mahogany top, 3-ply pickguard, black finish optional by **1968**
Discontinued: **1971**

Redondo: 14 3/8" wide, Newporter with spruce top, mahogany back and sides, 25 1/2" scale
Introduced: **1969**
Discontinued: **1971**

Other Fender Lines

F-series: Japanese made, 3–5 screws in pickguard, standard neck heel, 2 or 4 outline shapes on peghead, 3-on-a-side tuner arrangement, various steel-string and classical models
Introduced by **1969**
No screws in pickguard, Martin-style teardrop pickguard, dip at top center of peghead, Fender script logo by **1972**
Discontinued by **1979**

Harmony-made series: various styles made by Harmony, stenciled logo
Introduced: **early 1970s**
Discontinued: **mid 1970s**

Tarrega Classics: Swedish-made, available: **1963–69**

Current Fender flat tops are made in Korea.

COMMENTS

American-made Fender flat tops are not highly regarded by players, although the Wildwood, Brazilian rosewood, and other exotic wood models have some aesthetic appeal.

STEELS

General Information

Scale length on non-pedal models: 22 1/2",
except some Stringmasters

Patent pending notice on tuner assembly:
pre—1963

Patent number on tuner assembly: **1963 and
after**

Serial numbers: Each model has its own number series.

SECTION ORGANIZATION

Non-pedal Models
Pedal Models

Non-pedal Models

K and F brand: made by Doc Kauffman and Leo
Fender, straight sides, rectangular PU with
patent pending, strings through PU, 2 small
white knobs, symmetrical control plate,
painted dot markers and frets, bone nut,
right-angle tuners, no peghead plate, black
finish

Introduced: **1945**

Large brown knobs, metal nut, *K and F* on peghead plate, gray crinkled finish: **later**

Curved body sides: **later**

Asymmetrical fingerboard, Roman numeral
markers: **later**

Discontinued by **mid 1946**

Organ Button: similar shape to later K&F style,
body bouts join neck at 17th fret, rectangular PU, strings through PU, 2 non-domed
Broadcaster-type knobs, 1 red pushbutton
for organ-like tonal effect, asymmetrical
control plate, asymmetrical fingerboard,
Roman numeral markers, right-angle
tuners, lightning bolt on peghead plate,
most with non-lacquer wax-like finish

Introduced: **1946**

Discontinued: **1948**

Princeton: longer body bouts than Organ
Button, body bouts join neck at 12th fret,
rectangular PU, strings through PU, 1 knob,
cord built into guitar, asymmetrical control
plate, asymmetrical fingerboard, Roman
numeral markers, right-angle tuners, lightning bolt on peghead plate, serial number
begins with *A*

Introduced: **1946**

Discontinued: **1949**

Deluxe: longer body bouts than Organ Button,
body bouts join neck at 12th fret, rectangular PU, strings through PU, 2 knobs, asym-

metrical control plate, asymmetrical fingerboard, Roman numeral markers, lightning bolt on peghead plate, right-angle
tuners, non-lacquer wax-like finish, serial
number on early examples begins with *B*

Introduced: **1946**

Light or dark-stain lacquer finish: **c. 1947**

Trapezoid-shaped PU with bass end wider
than treble end, strings through PU: **late
1948**

Bound top and back (in catalog photo): **1949
only**

Replaced by Deluxe 6 and Deluxe 8: **1950**

Deluxe 6 (6 strings) and **Deluxe 8** (8 strings):
straight-line body sides (no bouts), block
letter logo on metal plate on treble side of
fingerboard, symmetrical fingerboard, dot
and diamond markers, 1-piece drop-in
tuner assembly, top tuners, walnut or
blond finish

Introduced: **1950**

Walnut finish described as dark finish: **1951**

Script logo on plate: **1956**

Stringmaster model features (see following), 2
understring PUs, control knob for PU balance under bridge cover, rectangular
bridge cover, 3 legs optional, by **1957**

Dark (walnut) finish discontinued by **1972**

White or black finish by **1976**

Discontinued by **1981**

Dual 8 Professional and **Dual 6 Professional**: 2
necks, rectangular PUs, strings through
PUs, *Dual Professional* in block letters on
metal plate between necks (no Fender
logo), 2 diamond-shaped plates on front,
Roman numeral markers, 1-piece drop-in
tuner assembly, top tuners, 3 legs optional,
walnut or blond finish, serial number on
early examples begins with *D*

Dual 8 Professional (2 8-string necks) introduced: **1946**

Trapezoid-shaped PUs with bass end longer
than treble end, strings through PUs,
Fender on logo plate: **very late 1948**

Dual 6 Professional (2 6-string necks) introduced: **1950**

Walnut finish replaced by dark finish: **1951**

Dot and diamond markers: **1953**

Script logo on plate: **1956**

Stringmaster features (see following), 2 understring PUs per neck, control knob for PU
balance under bridge cover, rectangular
bridge cover, script logo decal on front,
22 1/2" scale standard, 24 1/2" scale optional, 4 legs optional: **1957**

Dual 8 discontinued: **1957**

Dark (walnut) finish discontinued: **1973**

White or black finish by **1976**

Discontinued by **1981**

Steels

Champion: symmetrical 2-bout body, Telecaster-style flat-pole PU, non-domed Broadcaster-type knobs, symmetrical bridge cover, dot and diamond markers, right-angle tuners, white plastic tuner buttons, peghead narrows toward top, lightning bolt on peghead plate, felt on back, slot-head screws, body covered in yellow or blue pearloid

Note: Blue pearloid models apparently were produced only in occasional runs: in 1949, 1952–53 and possibly at other times. Blue examples may appear to be green as a result of aging. Yellow examples may vary in color as a result of aging and of different batches of pearloid.

Officially introduced: **summer 1949**
First produced: **late 1949**
A few with painted blond finish: **late 1949**
Listed only as Student model, domed Telecaster-type knobs, Phillips-head screws: **1952**
Discontinued, replaced by **Champ** (see following): **mid 1955**

Champ: straight-line body sides, understring PU with black plastic cover, black knobs, bevel from fingerboard to body edges, rectangular markers, script logo decal near fingerboard, 1-piece drop-in tuner assembly, top tuners, black tuner buttons, desert fawn (tan-blond) finish:
Introduced: **mid 1955**
White or black finish by **1976**
Discontinued by **1981**

Studio Deluxe: 1 PU, white PU cover, chrome knobs, script logo decal next to fingerboard, dots and diamonds markers, 1-piece drop-in tuner assembly, top tuners, white tuner buttons, blond finish, 3 legs
Introduced by **Jan. 1956**
Metal logo plate next to fingerboard by **1970**
White or black finish by **1976**
Discontinued by **1981**

Custom: 3 8-string necks, trapezoid-shaped PUs with bass end longer than treble end, strings between PUs, block letter logo on metal plate between necks, 2 diamond-shaped plates on front, Roman numeral markers, 1-piece drop-in tuner assembly, top tuners, 3 legs optional, walnut or blond finish
Introduced: **1949**
Walnut finish replaced by dark finish: **1951**
Dot and diamond markers, no diamond plates on front, script logo decal on front: **1953**
Discontinued by **1958**

Stringmasters: 2, 3, or 4 8-string necks, 2 plastic-covered PUs per neck (early with metal PU covers like Telecaster neck PU), control knob for PU balance under bridge cover, script logo on metal plate, 2 diamond shape plates and logo decal on front, 26" scale standard, block markers, blocks with arrowheads at frets 12 and 24, 1-piece drop-in tuner assembly, dark or blond finish, 4 legs optional
Introduced: **1953**
22 1/2" scale standard, 24 1/2" scale optional: **1955**
Walnut or blond finish by **1973**
White or black finish by **1976**
4-neck Stringmaster discontinued by **1969**
24 1/2" scale standard, 22 1/2" discontinued by **1979**
All Stringmasters discontinued by **1981**

Pedal Models

1000: 2 8-string necks, 8 pedals, 10 pedals by special order, 24 1/2" scale, cable mechanism, aluminum-magnesium frame, natural blond finish
Introduced: **mid 1957**
Black and white finish by **1960**
Sunburst finish: **1963**
Discontinued by **1976**

400: 1 8-string neck, 4–10 pedals, cable mechanism, natural blond finish
Introduced: **spring 1958**
Black and white finish by **1960**
Sunburst finish: **1963**
Discontinued by **1976**

2000: 2 10-string necks, cable mechanism, sunburst finish
Introduced: **1964**
Discontinued by **1976**

800: 1 10-string neck, cable mechanism, sunburst finish
Introduced: **1964**
Discontinued by **1976**

PS 210: 2 10-string necks, 5–8 pedals, 1–4 knee levers, walnut burl finish, 6 prototypes produced
Cataloged but never in production: **1970–76**

Artist Dual 10: 2 10-string necks, 8 pedals, 4 knee levers, rod mechanism, black or mahogany finish
Introduced by **1976**
Discontinued by **1981**

Artist Single 10: 1 10-string neck, 3 pedals, 4 knee levers, rod mechanism, black or mahogany finish
Introduced by **1976**
Discontinued by **1981**

Student Single 10: 1 10-string neck, 3 pedals, 1 knee lever, rod mechanism, black vinyl covering
Introduced by **1976**
Discontinued by **1981**

COMMENTS

Fender and K&F lap steels from pre–1950 are highly regarded by collectors for their historical value. Champion, Studio Deluxe, Deluxe 8, and Stringmasters are the models most highly regarded by players. Multineck models have some historical appeal.

Fender pedal steels were never highly regarded by players, who felt that the cable pitch-changing design was inadequate. Later models with rods instead of cables are more highly regarded by players.

AMPS, GENERAL INFORMATION

Hardwood Cabinet Models

Slot-head screws; cabinet finish dark (stained mahogany, oak or possibly cherry), medium (stained oak), or light (natural maple, some oak); grille cloth colors gold (yellow), red, blue (medium), or mauve (purple); most early examples with *RM* penciled on chassis (initials of co-designer Ray Massie)

Professional, Deluxe Model 26, Princeton (Student): **mid 1946–48**

Early Cabinet Styles

3 chrome strips on front: **mid 1946**

"TV front" with rounded grille corners, no chrome strips (except V-front Super): **1948**

Upper back panel extends almost halfway down to protect tubes: **1951**

Grille corners squared, wide front panels above and below grille, narrow front panels on sides (chrome strip removed from Super): **mid to late 1952**

Upper and lower front panels narrowed, grille enlarged: **mid to late 1954**

Piggyback design (separate amp and speaker), Bassman and Bandmaster: **early 1961**

Cabinet Covers

Tweed airplane luggage linen…
    Vertical tweed lines, fuzzy mohair-like grille cloth…
        Dual Professional (from introduction): **1946**
        All models except Champion (800 or 600), by **1948**
    Diagonal tweed lines…
        All models except Champion 600 (Champ): **early to mid 1949**
        Champion 600 (Champ): **1953**

Brown Tolex…
    Vibrasonic (from introduction): **mid 1959**
        Bandmaster, Concert, Pro, Super, Twin: **1960**
    Princeton, Deluxe, Tremolux, Vibrolux, Vibroverb: **1961**
    (No Champ or Harvard in brown or blond Tolex; Harvard discontinued in 1961)

Blond Tolex, coarse texture…
    Bandmaster and Bassman: **early 1961**
    Showman (from introduction): **1961**
    Vibrolux: **1962**

Blond Tolex, smooth texture…
    Showman, Bandmaster, Bassman, Vibrolux: **1963**

Black Tolex…
    Concert, Deluxe, Princeton, Pro, Super,
    Twin, Vibrolux, Vibroverb: **mid to late 1963**
    All other models: **Aug. 1964**

Logos and Model Names, Tweed-Covered Models

FENDER in block letters, *Fullerton, California* in small letters…
    Deluxe, Pro, Super, Bandmaster, Twin, Bassman: **pre-1955**
    Champ, Princeton: **pre-1956**

Fender in script, no model name, no *Fullerton*…
    Deluxe, Pro, Super, Tremolux: **1955–56**
    Vibrolux: **1956 only**
    Champ, Princeton: **1956, 61–64**

Fender in script, model name, no *Fullerton*…
    Bassman, Bandmaster, Twin: **1955 and after**
    Champ, Princeton: **1957 only**
    All other models: **1957 and after**

Fender in script, no model name, *Fullerton, California* …
    Champ, Princeton: **1958–60**

Fender in script, model name, *Fullerton, California*…
    Deluxe, Tremolux, Vibrolux, Harvard: **1960 and after**

Logos and Model Names, Tolex-Covered Models

Script *Fender* with tail underlining, logo plate attached to grille cloth, brown control plate on models with brown Tolex covering, blackface control plate on blond and black Tolex-covered models, script model name and *-Amp* on control plate (except no-*Amp* on Bandmaster): **1959**

Silver control plate with block letter model name and *-Amp* (except no *-Amp* on Super Reverb): **1968**

No *-Amp* on control faceplate: **1972**

No tail underlining *Fender*: **1976**

Circled *R* (trademark registration symbol) above letter *r* in *Fender, Made in U.S.A.* underneath letters *en*, blackface control plate with script model name (except block letter model name on Harvard): **1982**

Model name on plate attached to grille cloth, some new models: **1983 and after**

Numbers

2-digit code=model code…
    1st digit signifies decade (5=1950s, 6=1960s).
    In early 1960s, 2nd character is *G*.

2-letter code ink-stamped on tube chart…
    1st letter signifies year.
    2nd letter signifies month.

1st Letter		2nd Letter	
A	1951	A	January
B	1952	B	February
C	1953	C	March
D	1954	D	April
E	1955	E	May
F	1956	F	June
G	1957	G	July
H	1958	H	August
I	1959	I	September
J	1960	J	October
K	1961	K	November
L	1962	L	December
M	1963		
N	1964		
O	1965		
P	1966		
Q	1967		

Examples: DG=July, 1954; KB=February, 1961

6-digit code on speaker rim (*not* speaker model code, which begins with a letter) is same code used on potentiometers (see pot-dating section in Appendix):
First 3 digits signify manufacturer:
220=Jensen, 465=Oxford, 328=Utah.
Fourth digit is last digit of year of manufacture: 1=1951 or 1961, 9=1949 or 1959, etc.
Last 2 digits are week of manufacture.
Example: 220122=Jensen from 22nd week of 1951 or 1961

Uncoded date in the 1960s is not a manufacture date but a service date.

AMPS, 1945–1960s

Models Introduced Before 1950

K&F brand: made by Doc Kauffman and Leo Fender, stenciled *K&F* logo or brass nameplate, 3 models available, 8", 10", or 15" speaker
Introduced: **late 1945**
Discontinued: **mid 1946**

Princeton: also referred to as Student model, 8" speaker, wood cabinet, 3 vertical chrome strips on front, no controls, most with no serial number, brown cord, slot-head screws, Jensen speaker (some with Utah)
Introduced: **mid 1946**
Tweed cover, TV front: **1948**
10" speaker: **1961**
Reverb model introduced: **Aug. 1964**

Model 26: 10" speaker, wood cabinet, 3 vertical chrome strips on front, 3 inputs, 3 controls (mic volume, tone, inst. volume), brown cord, gold anodized (possibly painted) Jensen speaker with no writing or markings except for *1001* written vertically on square magnet, tubes hang down, no extra mounting screw for chassis, 6F6 power tubes, tube configurations vary, serial number range 1–c. 285
Introduced: **mid 1946**
Serial number range c. 286–1250, silver Jensen speaker with *Jensen* stenciled on round magnet, speaker code 220632 (a few exceptions), tubes mounted horizontally with base toward front of amp, usual tube configuration (left to right, from back of amp) 6SC7 6N7 6V6 6V6 5Y3, extra top mounting screw on chassis
Model 26 replaced by **Deluxe**: 12" speaker, tweed cover, TV front: **1948**
Reverb model available: **1963**

Professional: 15" speaker, wood cabinet, 3 vertical chrome strips on front
Introduced: **mid 1946**
Renamed **Pro**, tweed cover, TV front: **1948**
Reverb added, 2-10" speakers: **1965**

Dual Professional: V-Front, 2-10" speakers aimed at different angles, 1 chrome strip on front, tweed cover, silver Jensen speakers usually with date code 220632, crude (looks hand-printed) tube chart, 4 inputs (2 inst., 1 mic, lo gain), tube configuration (left to right from back of amp) 5U4 6L6 6L6 6SJ7 6SJ7 6SJ7
Introduced: **mid 1946**

Renamed **Super**: **early 1947**
Speakers in same direction: **early 1952**
Reverb added, 4-10" speakers: **1963**

Champion 800: TV front, 8" speaker, gray linen covering, hammerloid (gray-green) chassis color, 3 tubes, 1 volume control
Introduced (about 100 made): **1948**
Replaced by **Champion 600**: 6" speaker, 2-tone marbled leatherette covering, early examples with *800* crossed out: **1949**
Renamed **Champ**: **early 1950s**
Vibro-Champ: tremolo, introduced: **1964**

Models Introduced in the 1950s and 1960s

Bassman: 15" speaker, introduced: **1951**
4-10" speakers, 2 inputs: **1954**
4 inputs, mid-range control, plastic handle by **mid 1957**
Piggyback design, 1-12" speaker: **1961**
2-12" speakers: **1962**
Single-unit design: **1968**
2-15" speakers: **mid 1969**

Twin: 2-12" speakers, introduced: **1952**
Presence knob: **1955**
Reverb: **1963**

Bandmaster: 15" speaker, introduced: **1954**
3-10" speakers: **1957**
Piggyback design, 1-12" speaker: **1961**
2-12" speakers: **1962**
Single-unit design: **1968**

Tremolux: 12" speaker, tremolo, introduced: **1955**
Piggyback design, 1-10" speaker: **1961**
2-10" speakers: **1962**
Discontinued: **1966**

Vibrolux: 10" speaker, tremolo, introduced: **mid 1956**
1-12" speaker: **1961**
2-10" speakers, reverb: **Aug. 1964**

Harvard: 10" speaker, introduced: **mid 1956**
Discontinued: **1961**

Vibrasonic: 15" speaker, introduced: **late 1959**
Discontinued: **1963**

Concert: 4-10" speakers, introduced: **1960**
Discontinued: **1965**

Showman 12: piggyback design, 12" speaker, introduced: **1961**
Discontinued: **1965**

Showman 15: piggyback design, 15" speaker, introduced: **1961**

Discontinued: **1969**
Double Showman: piggyback design, 2-15"
    speakers, introduced: **Dec. 1962**
Renamed **Dual Showman**: mid 1963
Single-unit design: **1968**
Discontinued: **1970**

Vibroverb: 15" speaker, introduced: **1963**
Discontinued: **1965**

Fender Reverb unit: rough brown Tolex cover,
    leather handle, flat logo, a few early exam-
    ples with grille cover that looks like back
    panel (no grille cloth visible), later with tan
    grille cloth, brownface chassis, brown
    knobs, brown plastic domed switch, 2-
    spring pan, footswitch with 1/4" jack
Introduced: **1961**
Rough white Tolex cover, oxblood grille, some
    with 6V6 instead of 6K6 power tubes: **mid
    1962**
Tan grille, spring handle (plastic strap), white
    knobs, 2- or 3-spring pan (rare): **late 1962**
Smooth white Tolex cover, blackface control
    plate, 3-spring pan: **mid 1963**
Black Tolex cover: **mid 1964**
Silverface control plate, silver/black amp-type
    knobs: **1966**
Discontinued: **1972**

COMMENTS

Tweed-covered and earlier Fender amps are
    among the most highly sought after by col-
    lectors. The more powerful tweed-covered
    models are highly sought by players. The
    tweed Bassman with 4-10" speakers and 4
    inputs (mid 1957-60) is considered by many
    players to be the finest rock and roll guitar
    amp ever made.
Brown Tolex-covered, blond Tolex-covered,
    and blackface models are highly regarded
    by players.
Silverface and later models are regarded as
    fine utility amps.

Gibson

GENERAL INFORMATION

For information on pickups, knobs, and other specs that apply to electrics only, see Gibson Electrics, General Information. For general information on mandolins, see Gibson Mandolins, General Information.

Orville H. Gibson began making instruments in the late 1800s. His innovative concepts included carving rather than bending the top, back, and even the sides of his instruments. He made guitars and mandolins in addition to unusual instruments such as a harp zither, harp guitar, and lyre mandolin. His only patent, granted in 1898, was for a mandolin design in which the sides and neck are carved from one piece of wood.

The Gibson Mandolin-Guitar Manufacturing Company, Limited, was established in Kalamazoo, MI, on October 11, 1902. Orville Gibson consulted, trained workers, and assigned his mandolin patent to the company, but he was not a partner. The Chicago Musical Instrument company (CMI) bought Gibson in 1944 and continued making instruments in Kalamazoo.

CMI bought the Epiphone company by 1957, published a brochure in 1958 and began shipping Epiphone brand instruments made in Gibson's Kalamazoo plant in 1959. Epiphone production was moved to Japan in 1970 and later to Korea. See Epiphone section for information on all American-made Epiphone models.

The Norlin company bought Gibson in December, 1969 and opened a plant in Nashville in 1974. Production was split between Kalamazoo and Nashville until 1984, at which time the Kalamazoo plant was closed.

Gibson was sold to a group headed by Henry Juszkiewicz in January 1985. In May 1987, Gibson acquired the Flatiron company of Bozeman, MT, to make Gibson F-5 mandolins and to continue the Flatiron-brand mandolin line. (Gibson also acquired other brands, including Steinberger and Oberheim.) In 1989 Gibson built a new Flatiron factory and moved production of all Gibson mandolins and flat top guitars, plus some banjo components and Steinberger bass bodies, to Bozeman.

At various times Gibson has made models under its own budget brands, such as Kalamazoo and Oriole, and for distribution by mail-order houses under such brands as Recording King and Ward (both for Montgomery-Ward), Cromwell, Capital, and Kel Kroydon. See Other Brands section for selected model descriptions.

Gibson history by period

Late 1800s–circa 1904: Instruments from this period are referred to as Orville-style, made by or in the style of Orville Gibson. They typically have a very steep peghead angle (20° or greater), large long neck volute, wide paddle-shaped peghead, friction tuning pegs, integral one-piece neck and sides, back carved with a steep angle at the sides and flat across the middle, and pickguard inlaid into the top.

Circa 1905–circa 1909: Instruments undergo a transition from the primitive Orville-style designs to better playability. By circa 1905, Gibsons have modern style back carving, a smaller peghead shape, geared tuners, and (on some models) slotted peghead. From circa 1906–08, the neck-set angle and bridge height gradually increase on both mandolins and guitars. Body shapes and designs become more refined. Neck and sides are separate pieces with a dovetail neck joint. The elevated pickguard is introduced.

Circa 1909–early 1920s: This is the classic mandolin era. Gibson has become a very succesful company, with mandolins the dominant product. Model designs are standardized. The modern artist mandolin is refined, and its development peaks with the introduction of the F-5 in late 1922. The Master Model concept carries over to the guitar line with the introduction of the first *f*-hole archtop, the L-5. Primitive banjo models are introduced in 1917.

Mid 1920s–1933: The mandolin craze subsides and the banjo era begins. Gibson banjo design evolves rapidly from trap-door resonator style to one-piece flange Mastertone models. Guitars continue to have relatively small dimensions. The *f*-hole archtop design is refined, and the first flat top models are introduced.

Late 1934–World War II: As the big band era begins, archtop guitar body widths are "advanced" (increased) by 1 inch to 17", and the 18"-wide Super 400 is introduced in 1934. New and larger flat top designs are introduced with the jumbo (round-shouldered dreadnought) in 1934 and super jumbo in 1937. Electric lap steels are introduced in 1935, followed by electric archtops in 1936. Cutaway archtops and an optional natural finish are introduced in 1939. From 1939–42, Gibson adds a violin, viola, cello and bass to the line.

World War II: Production is limited because of materials shortages and the war effort. No electric guitars or banjos are produced. Acoustic guitars are produced in limited quantities. Many flat tops have no truss rod due to metal shortages.

1950s–1965: The electric guitar dominates. Gibson's first solidbody electric, the Les Paul, is introduced in 1952. New pickup and bridge systems are developed. New designs for hollowbody electrics include the thinline body depth and laminated construction. Semi-hollow electrics with double-cutaway bodies are introduced in 1958.

1966–1969: Quality begins to fall.

1970–1984: In the Norlin era, many new models are introduced. Some are experimental; many are short-lived. The 1970s are perceived as a period of high production with less attention to quality. By the late 1970s, Gibson faces financial problems.

1985–current: Designs are changing rapidly. Quality improves as Gibson works to regain its past reputation. Many of the models considered to be classics are reissued with more attention to original specs than reissue models of earlier periods.

Labels

Note: Many low-end acoustic instruments and all solidbody instruments have no label.

White rectangular label, *O.H. Gibson*, photo of Orville Gibson and lyre-mandolin: **1890s–late 1902**

White rectangular label, *Gibson Mandolin-Guitar Mfg. Co. Ltd.*, photo of Orville Gibson and lyre, 1898 patent date, no serial number or model name: **late 1902–c. 03**

White oval label, photo of Orville Gibson and lyre, *Gibson Mandolin-Guitar Mfg. Co. Ltd., Patent February first, 1898*, serial number, no model name: **c. 1903–c. 08**

White oval label, *Gibson Mandolin-Guitar Co.*, no photo of Orville Gibson or lyre, 1898 and 1906 patent notices…

Serial number and model name hand-inked or penciled: **c. 1908–32**

Serial number hand-written, model name ink-stamped, some examples: **1917–32**

White oval label, *Gibson Inc.* in typeset lettering (no *Mandolin-Guitar Co.*), serial number and model name name ink-stamped, by **1933–55**

Master models: Style 5 and Style TL (mandolute) only…

Label signed and dated by Lloyd Loar (in addition to Master Model label): **June 1, 1922–Dec. 21, 1924**

Master Model label: **1922–27**

Orange oval label, postwar modern *Gibson* logo on label, serial number (beginning c. A 20000) and model name: **early 1955–70**

Rectangular label, *Gibson Inc.*, label divided into 4 triangles; small black-purple-and-white label on archtops, large orange-and-white label on flat tops; model name, no serial number: **early 1970–83**

White oval label…

Thin script logo, serial number and model name: **1983–89**

Gibson U.S.A., block-letter logo, serial number and model name: **1983–89**

Beige oval label: serial number and model name, electrics with *Gibson U.S.A.*, acoustics with *Gibson Guitar Corp., Bozeman, Montana* : **1989–current**

Body Widths of Catalog Styles

Standard	12 1/2"
Concert	13 1/2"
Auditorium	14 3/4"
Grand concert, pre–WWII	16"
Grand concert, post–WWII	14 1/4"
Grand auditorium	16"
Advanced archtop	17"
Jumbo flat top*	16"
Super jumbo flat top*	17"
(no catalog name)	18"

* Collectors' names: *Gibson jumbo shape* commonly refers to the rounded bouts of the 17" J-200 or the 16" J-185 and Everly Brothers models. *Round-shouldered dreadnought* commonly refers to models such as the Advanced Jumbo, pre-1969 J-50 or pre-1963 SJ, with a more squared-off bottom edge, a thicker waist, and upper bouts that appear to be more rounded than the Martin-style dreadnought shape. *Square-shouldered dreadnought* commonly refers to models such as the Hummingbird and post-1963 J-50, with relatively square upper bouts.

Gibson names: Prior to World War II, Gibson used *super jumbo* for the J-200 and *jumbo* for round-shouldered dreadnoughts. By the 1960s, however, Gibson was using *jumbo* not only for the "jumbo-shape" J-200 and Everly Brothers models, but for all 16"-wide flat tops, including round-shouldered dreadnoughts and square-shouldered dreadnoughts.

Archtop Bridges and Tailpieces

Glued down bridge: **1902**

Non-compensating maple bridge, trapeze tailpiece with pins anchored in tortoise grain crosspiece: **c. 1905**

Compensating ebony bridge, all models except Style U harp guitar (maple bridge and ebony saddles on Style U): **1918**

Some compensating bridges with straight underside (so bridge can be turned over

General Information

for Hawaiian playing: **early 1920s**
Height-adjustable bridge…
    Ebony (some with straight non-compensating underside so bridge can be turned over for Hawaiian playing): **fall 1921**
    Rosewood: **1935**
Trapeze tailpiece with no pins, strings loop under tailpiece…
    L-5: **1923**
    L-4, L-3: **1924**
Strings straight through trapeze: **late 1920s**
Wooden crosspiece on trapeze: **WWII only**

Flat Top Bridges and Tailpieces (Except High-End Models)

Pyramid ends…
    All models except Lucas: **1926–28**
    Lucas (from introduction): **1928**
Short, tiered 2-piece construction, straight-bevel ends, slight belly, all models except Lucas and L-2…
    Extra bridge pin in belly area: **1929**
    No extra bridge pin in belly area: **1930**
Trapeze tailpiece, adjustable bridge…
    L-2, most examples: **1929–30, 32–34**
    Lucas, most examples: **1932–33**
Longer 1-piece with modern type bevels…
    L-2: **1931 only**
    Lucas: **1929–31, 34–41**
    All other models: **1931–c. 49**
2 pearl dots in bridge: **early 1940s–60s**
Martin-type belly bridge, some banner-logo examples: **WWII**
Upper belly (above bridge pins): **c. 1950–late 68**
Adjustable bridge saddle…
    J-160E (from introduction): **1954–70**
    Rare option on some other models: **1956–60**
    Standard on many models: **1960–70**
Trapeze tailpiece, glued-down bridge, B-45-12 and B-25-12, all years of production except: **1962–64**
No pearl dots, transitional period: **1960s**
Plastic bridge, all models below SJ: **1965–67**
Lower belly (below bridge pins): **late 1968–84**
Upper belly, most models: **1984–current**

Bindings

Plain (ungrained) plastic: **pre–1909**
Grained ivoroid: **c. 1909–24**
Return to plain (ungrained) plastic…
    L-5 and K-5: **1924 and after**
    All other models: **1925 and after**
Grained ivoroid re-introduced only on F-5L and later longneck mandolins: **1978**

Necks

Truss rod introduced on all models except Jr. (some flat top examples made during WWII have no truss rod; all pre-WWII models made by Gibson under other brands have no truss rod): **late 1922**
High-end models: L-5, L-12, Super 400, J-200, etc.…
    2-piece with 1 laminate stripe, referred to by Gibson as 3-piece: **pre–1961**
    3-piece with 2 laminate stripes, referred to by Gibson as 5-piece: **1961–late 80s**
Mid-line models: L-7, J-50, Les Pauls SGs, ES-335 series, non-reverse Firebirds, etc.…
    1-piece mahogany: **1910s–69**
    Some examples with laminated neck: **WWII only**
    3-piece mahogany, no laminate stripes…
        Les Pauls, ES-335 series: **1969–74**
        SGs, other existing models introduced by 1974: **1969–current**
    3-piece maple, no laminate stripes, Les Pauls, ES-335 series, new models, basses: **Sept. 1974-early 80s**
    Some walnut and walnut-maple necks: **1978 and after**
    Transition period to 1-piece mahogany (current construction), Les Pauls, ES-335 series: **1980–83**
Low-end models: Melody Makers, SG-100s, LGs, etc.…
    1-piece mahogany: **into early 1970s**
    1-piece maple: **early 1970s–current**

Pegheads

Wide "paddle" peghead: **1890s–c. 1903**
Slotted peghead: **c. 1903–c. 07**
Solid peghead, by **1908**
"Snakehead," peghead narrows toward top…
    Introduced **1923**
    Discontinued on all models except L-5: **1927**
    Discontinued on L-5: **1934**
Fiber peghead veneer replaces wood veneer: **late 1970**
Made in the U.S.A. impressed on back of peghead, instruments made for export only: **late1920s–50s**
Made in U.S.A.. .
    Impressed on back of peghead, all models: **1970–mid 75**
    On decal on back of peghead: **mid 1975–mid 77**
    Stamped on back of peghead: **mid 1977–current**
Peghead pitch, non-grafted and non-spliced pegheads…
    Angle of 20° or greater: **1890s–c. 04**
    Angle of less than 20°, eventually to 17°: **c. 1904–late 65**

75

Angle of 14°: **late 1965–73**
Angle of 17°, some models: **1973–current**
Volute on back of peghead...
Introduction period (varies according to model): **late 1969–74**
L-5, L-5CES, Byrdland, Super 400, Super 400CES and Johnny Smith: **Sept. 1974**
Discontinued, all models: **March 1981**
Peghead thickness...
Thickness (depth) of peghead narrows toward top: **until mid 1950**
Uniform thickness: **mid 1950–current**

Logos

No logo, crescent and star inlay: **1890s–c. 1902**
Some with *The Gibson* logo (slanted or straight across), some with no logo: **c. 1903–c. 07**
The Gibson slanted: **c. 1908-late 20s**
The Gibson straight across peghead, all flat tops, some archtops: **late 1920s**
The Gibson straight across peghead, all models, by **c. 1933**
Transition to *Gibson* logo (varies by model): **1928–34**
Script *Gibson*...
Pearl inlaid, high-end models: **1933–42, 46**
White silkscreen, low-end models: **1928–43**
Thicker *Gibson*, Super 400 and other high-end models: **mid 1930s**
Thicker *Gibson*, all models, by: **late 1930s**
Gold script *Gibson*...
All models made during WWII, low-end postwar models: **1943–early 47**
Only a Gibson is good enough on banner, some examples of LG-2, J-45 and SJ: **1943–45**
"Modernized" script with tail on *G* and *N*, low-end models...
Gold silkscreen, closed *b* and *o*: **early 1946–c. 54**
Gold decal: **c. 1954–current**
"Modernized" script with tail on *G*, high-end models, pearl-inlaid...
Transitional period, some examples with modern logo, some with script: **early 1947**
Dot on *i* connected to *G*, open *b* and *o*, lower link between *o* and *n*: **early 1947–51**
Dot on *i* free from *G*, open *b* and *o*, lower link between *o* and *n*: **1951–68**
"Pantograph" logo, large rectangular pearl inlay (pearl is not cut) with paint stencilled around *Gibson* ...
Dot on *i* free from *G*, closed *b* and *o* (some with open *b* and *o* in 1969), lower link between *o* and *n*: **1968 only**
No dot on *i*, lower link between *o* and *n*: **late 1968–late 70**
Smaller, thinner logo, pre-sunk into fiber

peghead veneer...
No dot on *i*, lower link between *o* and *n*: **late 1970–72**
Dot on *i* re-introduced (some without dot through 1981): **1972–current**
Upper link between *o* and *n*: **1981–current**
Pre-WWII script logos re-introduced...
Some banjos, all mandolins: **1970**
Some high-end guitars, Mark series: **1970s**

Finishes, 1902–20s

Orange or ebony top (some old stock still available as late as 1920): **1902–18**
Uniform red mahogany (described as shaded from golden red to mahogany), L-3, L-4, Style O, A-4, F-2, F-4, H-4, and K-4: **1914–17**
Red mahogany sunburst, L-3, L-4, Style O, A-4, F-2, F-4, H-4, and K-4: **1917–late 20s**
Sheraton brown introduced: **1918**
Old ivory (white) top optional, L-3, A-3, H-2, K-2: **1918–22**
Cremona brown sunburst introduced, Style 4 mandolin family: **early 1921**

Lloyd Loar, Master Models, Virzi Tone-Producer

Lloyd Loar joined Gibson as acoustic engineer in 1919. Among the features introduced during his tenure: *f*-hole mandolins and guitars, elevated fingerboards on guitars and mandolins, and a longer neck (not longer scale) on mandolins. The series of instruments with these innovations was named Style 5 and promoted as the Master Model series (the name was later appropriated for the Mastertone banjo line). Loar personally inspected and signed a label on an estimated 250 instruments. A second special label identified these as Master Model instruments.

Many Loar-signed instruments from 1924 were fitted with the Virzi Tone-Producer, an oval-shaped wood sounding board suspended from the top. Many of these have been removed.

Loar left Gibson in December 1924 to pursue the development of electric instruments. In the early 1930s, he formed the Vivi-Tone company to market electric guitars.

Wartime Models

During World War II, from sometime in 1942 until late 1945, Gibson ceased production on all electric instruments and on most acoustic instruments. Limited quantities of the following models were available: L-00, LG-2, J-45, Southerner Jumbo, L-50, and L-7. Some examples of the LG-2, J-45, and SJ have a banner peghead logo which reads *Only a Gibson Is Good Enough.* Many examples have 3-on-a-plate tuners and (on archtops) a wooden crosspiece on the trapeze tailpiece. Early wartime flat tops have no truss rod; archtops do have a truss rod. Some examples have a laminated neck. Due to materials shortages, specifications may vary greatly from standard catalog descriptions on models produced during and immediately after the war.

Model Names

Model names before World War II often signify the list price of the model. For example, the J-200 listed for $200, the Super 400 for $400, and the L-37 for $37.50. Model names did not change when prices increased.

From 1971–76, Gibson added *Artist, Custom,* or *Deluxe* to the model names of many flat tops: J-200 Artist, Dove Custom, J-50 Deluxe, for example. These names, which appear on labels, are *not* different models unless noted as such in the model descriptions.

J-200 from 1990 with body shape referred to by collectors as jumbo.

SJ from circa 1945, with teardrop pickguard (used postwar to circa 1955) and body shape referred to by collectors as round-shouldered dreadnought.

Hummingbird from 1990 with square-shouldered dreadnought body shape.

L-0 from the 1930s, with prewar small-body shape (14 3/4" wide) and prewar pickguard shape.

B-25 from circa 1968, body shape of postwar small-body (14 3/4" wide) flat tops, including LG-series. Large pickguard with point was introduced circa 1955. Bridge is "belly above bridge" design with height-adjustable saddle.

LG-2 3/4, with 3/4-size body shape.

Gibson peghead before mid 1950, with thinner depth towards top.

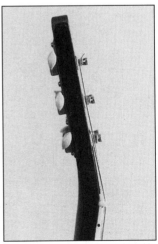

Gibson peghead from mid 1950 and after, with uniform thickness.

SERIAL NUMBERS

Gibson instruments made before 1977 may have a serial number or a factory order number (or code letter), or both, or neither. Due to the various serial number systems employed, some numbers may be duplicated on several instruments.

Gibson instituted a new number system in 1977, after which it is possible to determine the exact day a number was stamped on an instrument.

SECTION ORGANIZATION

Serial Number Configuration and Placement
Factory Order Number Configuration and Placement
Serial Numbers, 1902–47
Factory Order Numbers, 1908–23
Factory Order Numbers and Letter Codes, 1935–41
A-series, 1947–61
Epiphone A-series, 1958–61
Factory Order Code Letters, 1952-61
Serial Numbers, 1961–69
Serial Numbers, early to mid 1970s
Serial Numbers, 1975–77
Serial Numbers, 1977–current

Serial Number Configuration and Placement

Rectangular label, no serial number or model name on label, photo of Orville Gibson and lyre-mandolin on label, date sometimes penciled under top: **1902–c. 04**

Oval label with serial number, no model name, photo of Orville Gibson and lyre-mandolin: **c. 1904–c. 09**

Number and model name on white paper label, number range 1000-99999...

Hand-inked or penciled (some overlap with previous style): **c. 1908–32**

Ink-stamped: **1932–47**

Low-end models with no serial number: **c. 1927 and after**

Hollowbody instruments, 1947–61...

Number preceded by letter *A* on white oval label: **1947–early 55**

Number preceded by letter *A* on orange oval label: **early 1955–61**

Solidbody instruments...

No number: **1952–late 53**

4 digits impressed into top of peghead, space after 1st digit, 1st digit is 3: **late 1953**

Number inked on peghead, 5-digit number with space after first digit or 6-digit number (used late in each year) with no space between digits; first digit of number=last digit of year: **late 1953–early 61**

Number inked on peghead, 4 digits with no space between digits: **1960**

All models, no *Made in USA* on peghead

5 digits impressed into peghead: **1961–63**

6 digits impressed into peghead: **1963–69**

Made in USA on peghead

6 digits impressed into peghead: **1970–75**

Letter followed by 3 digits, custom shop or limited edition models only: **1971–current**

Number on decal: **1975–77**

8 digits impressed into peghead: **1977–current**

Vintage-style numbers ink-stamped on peghead, Heritage and reissue models: **mid 1980s–current**

Number on beige oval (old style) label, hollowbody models: **1989–current**

Factory Order Number Configuration and Placement

Number stamped on neck block inside body: **1908–c. 30**

Number and letter code (A–G) ink-stamped on inside back or on label: **1935–42**

Number and letter code (D–G) impressed into back of peghead: **1938–42**

Number and letter code (Q–Z) ink-stamped on inside back: **1952–61**

Serial Numbers, 1902–47

Note: For the period 1903–10, this list will date instruments as much as two to three years earlier than the generally accepted Gibson serial number list. These revised numbers and dates were compiled by matching actual instruments with documented catalog specs such as elevated pickguard, trapeze-pin bridge, etc.

Series starts with 1000.

Year	Approx. Last Number	Year	Approx. Last Number
1903	1500	1926	83600
1904	2500	1927	85400
1905	3500	1928	87300
1906	5500	1929	89750
1907	8300	1930	90200
1908	9700	1931	90450
1909	10100	1932	90700
1910	10600	1933	91400
1911	10850	1934	92300
1912	13350	1935	92800
1913	16100	1936	94100
1914	20150	1937	95200
1915	25150	1938	95750
1916	32000	1939	96050
1917	39500	1940	96600
1918	47900	1941	97400
1919	53800	1942	97700
1920	63650	1943	97850
1921	69300	1944	98250
1922	71400	1945	98650
1923	74900	1946	99300
1924	81200	1947	99999
1925	82700		

Factory Order Numbers, 1908–23

Numbers consist of a 3- to 5-digit batch number followed by a 1- or 2-digit number (from 1–40) ranking the instrument. This information was compiled by Roger Siminoff.

Year	Selected Batch Numbers
1908	259
1909	309
1910	545, 927
1911	1260, 1295
1912	1408, 1593
1913	1811, 1902
1914	1936, 2152
1915	2209, 3207
1916	2667, 3508
1917	3246, 11010
1918	9839, 11159
1919	11146, 11212
1920	11329, 11367
1921	11375, 11527
1922	11565, 11729
1923	11973

Factory Order Numbers and Letter Codes, 1935–41

Many instruments from 1935–41 have a letter designating the year of production.

1935–37: Letter is between the batch number and the instrument number. Code is ink-stamped on the inside back.

1938–42: 2 or 3 letters precede instrument ranking number. Code is either ink-stamped onto the label or impressed into the back of the peghead (or, on lap steels, impressed into the back of the body near the neck). Second letter indicates brand of instrument: G=Gibson, K=Kalamazoo, W=Recording King (Montgomery Ward). Third letter (if there is one) is E for electric.

Exception: Some high-end models from c. 1939–40 have a serial number consisting of EA followed by 4 digits. The *E* prefix does not denote a 1939 date of manufacture.

Year	1st Letter
1935	A
1936	B
1937	C
1938	D
1939	E (except EA prefix, see preceding)
1940	F
1941	G

A-Series, 1947–61

Series starts Apr. 28, 1947 with A 100. Last number was assigned on Feb. 21, 1961. This information was compiled by A.R. Duchossoir from Gibson records.

Year	Approx. Last Number
1947	A 1304
1948	A 2665
1949	A 4413
1950	A 6597
1951	A 9419
1952	A 12462
1953	A 16101
1954	A 18667
1955	A 21909
1956	A 24755
1957	A 26819
1958	A 28880
1959	A 32284
1960	A 35645
1961	A 36147

Epiphone A-Series, 1958–61

Epiphone models made by Gibson from c. 1958–61 have their own serial number series. After 1961, Gibson and Epi models are numbered in the same series.

Year	Approximate Range
1958	A 1000s
1959	A 2000s
1960–61	A 3000–A 4222

Factory Order Code Letters, 1952–61

Code letter may precede or follow batch number.

Year	Letter	Year	Letter
1952	Z	1957	U
1953	Y	1958	T
1954	X	1959	S
1955	W	1960	R
1956	V	1961	Q

Serial Numbers, 1961–69

Series begins Feb. 1961 with 100. Many numbers are duplicated from 1963–69. This information was originally compiled by A. R. Duchossoir from Gibson records. Some documented numbers and dates have been added.

Number Range	Year
100–42440	1961
42441–61180	1962
61450–64222	1963
64240–70501	1964
71180–96600	1962
96601–99999	1963
000001–099999	1967
100000–106099	1963, 67
106100–106899	1963
109000–109999	1963, 67
110000–111549	1963
111550–115799	1963, 67
115800–118299	1963
118300–120999	1963, 67
121000–139999	1963
140000–140100	1963, 67
140101–144304	1963
144305–144380	1964
144381–149864	1963
149865–149891	1964
149892–152989	1963
152990–174222	1964
174223–176643	1964, 1965
176644–250335	1964
250336–305983	1965
306000–310999	1965, 67
311000–320149	1965
320150–320699	1967
320700–329179	1965
329180–330199	1965, 67
330200–332240	1965, 67, 68
332241–348092	1965
348093–349100	1966
349121–368638	1965
368640–369890	1966
370000–370999	1967

Number Range	Year
380000–385309	1966
390000–390998	1967
400001–400999	1965–68
401000–438922	1966
500000–500999	1965, 66, 68, 69
501009–501600	1965
501601–501702	1968
501703–502706	1965, 68
503010–503109	1968
503405–520955	1965, 68
520956–530056	1968
530061–530850	1966, 68, 69
530851–530993	1968, 69
530994–539999	1969
540000–540795	1966, 69
540796–545009	1969
555000–556909	1966
558012–567400	1969
570099–570755	1966
580000–580999	1969
600000–600999	1966–69
601000–606090	1969
700000–700799	1966, 67
750000–750999	1968, 69
800000–800999	1966–69
801000–812838	1966, 69
812900–819999	1969
820000–820087	1966, 69
820088–823830	1966
824000–824999	1969
828002–847488	1966, 69
847499–858999	1966, 69
859001–895038	1967
895039–896999	1968
897000–898999	1967, 69
899000–972864	1968

Serial Numbers, Early to Mid 1970s

6-digit number, *Made in USA* on back of peghead

Number Range	Year
000000s	1973
100000s	1970–75
200000s	1973–75
300000s	1974–75
400000	1974–75
500000s	1974–75
600000s	1970–72, 1974–75
700000s	1970–72

Number Range	Year
800000s	1973–75
900000s	1970–72
A + 6 digits	1973–75
B + 6 digits	1974–75
C + 6 digits	1974–75
D + 6 digits	1974–75
E + 6 digits	1974–75
F + 6 digits	1974–75

Serial Numbers

Serial Numbers, 1975–77

Number on peghead decal, 2-digit prefix followed by 6-digit number

Year	Prefix
1975	99
1976	00
1977	06

Serial Numbers, 1977–Current

8-digit number impressed into back of peghead: ydddynnn

yy (1st and 5th digits)=year of manufacture

ddd (digits 2–4)=day of the year; 001=Jan. 1, 365=Dec. 31

nnn (digits 6-8)= rank of the instrument that day. All instruments made at the Kalamazoo factory (1977–84) and guitars made at the Bozeman factory (1989–current) are numbered beginning with 001 each day. Instruments made at the Nashville factory are numbered each day beginning with 500. Instruments with a ranking number in the 900s are prototypes, made in either Nashville or Kalamazoo. Beginning in May 1990, some instruments made in Nashville have been given a ranking number in the 300s and 400s.

Examples:

80012005=the 5th instrument made in Kalamazoo on the first day of 1982

82569625=the 125th instrument made in Nashville on the 256th day of 1989

Exceptions:

Some Heritage and vintage reissue models have vintage-style serial numbers. For example, the Les Paul Standard Reissue, a reissue of the 1959 model, has an inked-on serial number beginning with 9.

Mandolins made in Bozeman have a different numbering scheme (see Gibson Mandolins, General Information section).

ACOUSTIC ARCHTOPS KEY

f-holes
- Celluloid peghead veneer=**L-75, 1932–late 34**
- Flowerpot (torch) peghead inlay
    - Non-cutaway=**L-5**
    - Cutaway
        - Full-depth body=**L-5C**
        - Thin body=**L-5CT**
- Double-handled vase peghead inlay=**L-75, late 1934–35**
- 5-piece split-diamond peghead inlay
    - Non-cutaway=**Super 400**
    - Cutaway
        - 18" wide (*Super 400* on tailpiece)=**Super 400C**
        - 17" wide (*Johnny Smith* on tailpiece)=**Johnny Smith**
- 7-piece diamond/star-shaped peghead inlay=**L-12, 1934–41**
- Fleur-de-lis peghead inlay
    - Cloud fingerboard inlay=**Citation**
    - Varied-pattern fingerboard inlay
        - Inlay at first fret=**L-4, 1937–46**
        - No inlay at first fret=**L-7, 1933–mid 34**
- Other ornamental peghead inlay
    - Double-arrow fingerboard inlay=**L-10, 1934–39**
    - Varied-pattern fingerboard inlay
        - Black finish=**L-10, 1934**
        - Sunburst finish
            - Nickel-plated metal parts=**L-7, mid 1934–42**
            - Gold-plated metal parts=**L-12, 1932–34**
    - Double-parallelogram fingerboard inlay
        - Triple-bound peghead=**L-12, 1941–42**
        - Single-bound peghead
            - 17" wide
                - Gold-plated metal parts
                    - Non-cutaway=**L-12, 1947–55**
                    - Cutaway=**L-12C**
                - Nickel-plated metal parts
                    - Non-cutaway=**L-7, 1942–56**
                    - Cutaway=**L-7C**
            - 18" wide
                - Non-cutaway=**Super 300**
                - Cutaway=**Super 300C**
        - Unbound peghead
            - Non-cutaway=**L-4, 1947–56**
            - Cutaway=**L-4C**
- No peghead ornament other than logo
    - 16" wide
        - Black finish
            - Pearl logo=**L-10, 1931–34**
            - Silkscreen logo=**wartime model** (name unknown)
        - Sunburst finish
            - Mahogany sides=**L-48**
            - Maple sides=**L-50, 1935–66**
    - 14 3/4" wide
        - Pearl logo=**L-50, 1934–35**
        - Silkscreen logo
            - Tortoise grain binding=**L-47**
            - White binding
                - Bound pickguard=**L-37**
                - Unbound pickguard=**L-30**

Oval hole
    Symmetrical body
        Black top
            Celluloid top binding
                Unbound back (no pickguard)=**Style 0, 1903–c. 08**
                Bound back
                    Pearl-bordered soundhole ring=**O-1**
                    Diamond pattern soundhole ring=**L-4, 1912–14**
            Pearl and ebony top binding=**O-2**
            Green and white top binding=**O-3**
        Sunburst or orange top
            Herringbone soundhole ring=**L-3, c. 1927–c. 29**
            Non-herringbone soundhole rings=**L-4, 1914–32**
    Scroll body=**Style 0, c. 1908–23**
Round hole
    Single black soundhole binding=**L-Jr.**
    3 white-black-white soundhole rings=**L-50, 1932–34**
    4 thin black soundhole rings=**L-2, 1924–26**
    7-ply white and black soundhole rings
        Maple back and sides=**L-4, 1929–35, 37**
        Mahogany back and sides=**L-75, 1935–39**
    1 colored-wood inlaid soundhole ring=**L**
    2 rope-pattern soundhole rings=**L-1, 1903–c. 1920**
    2 5-ply soundhole rings=**L-1, c. 1920–24**
    3 wood-inlaid soundhole rings
        Unbound fingerboard=**L-2, 1903**
        Bound fingerboard=**L-3, 1903–08**
    Herringbone or checkered soundhole ring=**L-3, 1908–27, 29–33**

ACOUSTIC ARCHTOPS

Some instruments made by Orville Gibson, beginning in 1894 and prior to the formation of the Gibson company, have a star and crescent inlaid on the peghead. Some are dated on the underside of the top.

"Orville-style" instruments, made in the early years of the Gibson company, have a carved back that is flat across the middle.

Note: Even though early Gibson catalogs specify maple back and sides for guitars and mandolins, virtually all pre-1908 instruments (except the F-4 mandolin and some F-2 mandolins) have walnut back and sides. Virtually all instruments (except the F-4) made from 1908 through the mid 1920s have birch back and sides. The L-5 has maple back and sides by 1925. Other models follow the L-5 to maple by circa 1927.

Style 0: oval hole, 2 inlaid wood rings around soundhole, fixed bridge with pyramids at ends, single-bound top, single-bound fingerboard and peghead, dot inlay, solid peghead with large rounded top, peghead veneer with pearl inlay, friction pegs, black top finish, dark mahogany finish back and sides, available in standard, concert, or grand concert size

Variation: catalog picture shows 2 rope-pattern soundhole rings with solid ring between, unbound fingerboard and peghead, plain peghead
Introduced: **1902**
Slotted peghead, pointed-end fingerboard: **1906**
Some examples 18" wide, fixed bridge with pyramids at ends, bound fingerboard, bound peghead, slotted or solid peghead with geared tuners, inlaid peghead ornament or slanted *The Gibson* logo: **c. 1906–07**
Body style commonly referred to by collectors as **Style 0 Artist**: 16" wide, pointed cutaway, carved scroll on upper bass bout, 2 rope-pattern soundhole rings with solid ring between, asymmetrical fingerboard with treble-side extension, trapeze tailpiece with pins anchored in tortoise grain celluloid plate, solid peghead, right-angle tuners, fleur-de-lis inlay at top of peghead: **1908**
First catalog reference to Artist's Model, elevated pickguard with single support, pickguard does not cover entire treble side of soundhole: **1911**
Uniform mahogany (slightly shaded) or golden orange finish: **1914**
Larger pickguard with 2 supports, pickguard covers treble side of soundhole, fleur-de-

lis inlay moved to center of peghead, *The Gibson* logo, red mahogany sunburst finish: **1918**
Discontinued: **1923**

O-1: bound oval soundhole, 2 soundhole rings of fancy wood with pearl border, bound top and back, bound ebony fingerboard, pearl fingerboard inlays and side inlays, peghead veneer with pearl inlay, black top finish, dark mahogany back and sides finish, available in standard, concert, or grand concert size
Only catalog appearance: **1902**

O-2: bound oval soundhole, 2 soundhole rings of fancy colored wood with pearl border, pearl and ebony rope-pattern top binding, mahogany bridge with pearl inlays, inlaid bridge pins, bound ebony fingerboard, pearl dot fingerboard inlays and side inlays, peghead veneer with pearl inlay, pointed peghead with star and crescent, black top finish, dark mahogany back and sides finish, available in standard, concert, or grand concert size
Only catalog appearance: **1902**

O-3: bound oval soundhole, 2 soundhole rings of fancy colored wood with pearl border, mahogany bridge with pearl inlays, green and white rope-pattern top binding with fancy wood purfling, bound ebony fingerboard, pearl fingerboard inlay, peghead veneer with pearl binding, friction tuners with pearl buttons, black top finish, dark mahogany back and sides finish, available in standard, concert, or grand concert size
Only catalog appearance: **1902**

Style L: round soundhole inlaid with fancy colored woods, ebony fingerboard, bound top and back, dot inlay, peghead veneer, orange top finish, dark mahogany back and sides finish, standard size
Only catalog appearance: **1902**

L-1: single-bound round soundhole with 2 rope-pattern soundhole rings, single-bound top, ebony fingerboard, dot inlay, peghead veneer, orange top finish, dark mahogany back and sides finish, standard or concert size
Introduced: **1902**
13 1/2" wide, narrower waist, trapeze tailpiece with pins anchored in tortoise grain celluloid plate, elevated pickguard, 13 frets clear of body, bound fingerboard, standard peghead with slanted *The Gibson* logo: **1908**
No pickguard: **c. 1912**
Pickguard: **1914**

Sheraton brown finish: **1918**
Double 5-ply soundhole rings, by **1920**
Discontinued: **1925**
Reintroduced as flat top (see Gibson flat top section): **1926**

L-2: round hole, 3 inlaid soundhole rings of colored wood, single-bound top, unbound fingerboard, pearl fingerboard inlay, peghead veneer with pearl inlay, orange top finish, dark mahogany back and sides finish, available in standard, concert, or grand concert size
Introduced: **1902**
Discontinued by: **1908**
Re-introduced: 13 1/2" wide, round hole, plain 4-ring soundhole inlay, single-bound top, single-support pickguard, bound back, bound ebony fingerboard, dot inlay, unbound peghead (catalog describes multiple-bound top and single-bound peghead), trapeze tailpiece, amber finish
Introduced: **1924**
Discontinued: **1926**
Model number re-introduced as flat top model (see Flat Tops section): **1929**

L-3: round hole, 3 inlaid soundhole rings of fancy colored wood, bound top, 13 frets clear of body, bound ebony fingerboard, pearl fingerboard inlay and side markers, peghead veneer with pearl inlay, orange top finish, dark mahogany back and sides finish, available in standard, concert, or grand concert size
Introduced: **1902**
13 1/2" wide, herringbone middle soundhole ring, trapeze tailpiece with pins anchored in tortoise grain celluloid plate: **1908**
Floral peghead inlay, pickguard, slanted *The Gibson* logo: **1914**
Red mahogany (slightly shaded) finish: **1914**
Red mahogany sunburst finish standard, ivory finish by special order: **1918**
Trapeze tailpiece with no pins: **1924**
Maple back and sides by **late 1920s**
Oval hole: **c. 1927**
Round hole, checkered pattern on middle soundhole ring: **1929**
Raised fingerboard by: **1932**
Discontinued: **1933**

L-4: 16" wide, oval soundhole, 3-ring soundhole inlay with diamond-pattern middle ring, trapeze tailpiece with pins anchored in tortoise grain celluloid plate, elevated pickguard with 2 supports, bound top and back, 12 frets clear of body, single-bound ebony fingerboard with pointed end, fingerboard extending over soundhole, pearl dot inlay, single-bound peghead, front and back peghead veneers, slanted *The Gibson* logo,

black top finish
Introduced: **1912**
Solid middle ring in soundhole inlay (no diamond pattern), red mahogany (slightly shaded) finish standard, black or orange available by special order: **1914**
Red mahogany sunburst finish: **1918**
Diamond-pattern soundhole ring shown again in catalogs (most examples from 1914–20 have diamond pattern), single pickguard support, straight *The Gibson* logo, by **1920**
Trapeze tailpiece with no pins: **1923**
Checkered outer soundhole rings, solid middle ring: **1927**
Round hole, 7-ply black and white soundhole ring, single-bound top and back, unbound pickguard, single-bound square-end rosewood fingerboard, 14 frets clear of body, dot inlay, unbound peghead, by **early 1928**
Unbound fingerboard, *Gibson* logo: **mid 1928**
Bound fingerboard, diamond peghead inlay, by: **late 1933**
f-holes, raised diamond on trapeze tailpiece, single-bound pickguard, varied-pattern inlay beginning at 1st fret, single-bound peghead, fleur-de-lis peghead inlay, sunburst finish: **1935**
Round hole optional: **1937 only**
Unbound pickguard: **1937**
Natural finish optional: **1940**
Unbound peghead: **1941**
Triple-bound top and back, bound pickguard: **1946**
Double-parallelogram inlay, laminated beveled-edge pickguard: **1947**
Discontinued: **1956**

L-4C: pointed cutaway, pointed-end tailpiece plate with 3 raised parallelograms, laminated pickguard, double-parallelogram inlay, crown peghead inlay, sunburst or natural, introduced by **1949**
Discontinued: **1971**

L-Jr.: budget model of L-1, 13 1/2" wide, round soundhole with single black binding, trapeze tailpiece with pins anchored in tortoise grain celluloid plate, ebony fingerboard, dot inlay, amber top finish specified, most with uniform brown finish on top, back and sides
Introduced: **c. 1919**
Discontinued: **1926**

L-5: 16" wide, birch back, maple sides early with Virzi Tone-Producer standard, trapeze tailpiece, triple-bound top and back, triple-bound pickguard (early with unbound pickguard), pointed-end fingerboard, dot inlay from 5th fret, triple-bound peghead, flowerpot peghead inlay, slanted logo, 3-on-a-plate tuners, snakehead peghead narrow-

er at top, silver-plated metal parts, *The Gibson* logo, Cremona brown sunburst finish all over, *Gibson Master Model* label and Lloyd Loar signature label
Introduced: **late 1922**
Last Loar label: **1924**
Gold-plated metal parts: **1925**
Maple back: **1925**
Dot inlay from 3rd fret, straight *The Gibson* logo, by: **1925**
Last *Master Model* label: **1927**
Block inlay (many pearloid) beginning at 3rd fret, individual tuners: **early 1929**
Square-end fingerboard: **mid 1929**
"Advanced" 17" wide body, X-braced top, 5-ply top binding, triple-bound back, 5-ply pickguard binding, unbound *f*-holes, pointed-end fingerboard with 5-ply binding, flat plate tailpiece with engraved *L-5*, block inlay beginning at 1st fret, wider (non-snakehead) peghead with 5-ply binding: **late 1934**
Bound *f*-holes by: **1936**
Gold-plated tailpiece with silver center insert, 3 engraved diamonds on tailpiece, Grover enclosed tuners with stairstep buttons: **1937**
Wider tailpiece with small hole at bottom center for allen wrench tension adjustment, no hinge on tailpiece, natural finish optional: **1939**
Parallel top bracing: **mid 1939**
Some with white pearloid pickguard: **1939 only**
L-5 Premier: rounded cutaway introduced: **1939**
L-5P renamed **L-5C: 1948**
L-5 non-cutaway discontinued: **1958**
L-5C discontinued: **1982**

L-5 CT: referred to by collectors as George Gobel model, thin body, a few with 2 humbucking PUs, 24 3/4" scale (same scale as 16"-wide models), rounded cutaway, cherry red finish
Introduced: **1959**
Discontinued (43 total shipped): **1961**

L-10: 16" wide, strings loop over trapeze tailpiece, single-bound top and back, single-bound ebony fingerboard, dot inlay, nickel-plated metal parts, black finish
Introduced: **1931**
Single-bound top and pickguard, ornate rectangle-enclosed inlay, single-bound peghead, double-handled vase peghead inlay: **1934**
17" wide, X-braced top, raised diamond on tailpiece, black-and-white checkered binding on top, double-arrow inlay, single-bound peghead, ornate vase and curlicues peghead inlay, red mahogany sunburst finish: **late 1934**

Flat plate tailpiece with cutouts, diamond-and-curlicues peghead inlay: **1935**
Discontinued: **1939**

L-12: 16" wide, trapeze tailpiece, single-bound top and back, single-bound pickguard, single-bound fingerboard, ornate rectangle-enclosed inlay, single-bound peghead, double-handled vase and curlicues peghead inlay, gold-plated metal parts, red mahogany sunburst finish
Introduced: **1932**
17" wide, X-braced top, triple-bound top and pickguard, bound back, double-parallelogram inlay, triple-bound peghead, 7-piece diamond/star-shaped peghead inlay, sunburst finish: **late 1934**
Flat-plate tailpiece with cutouts: **1937**
Parallel top bracing: **mid 1939**
Single-bound pickguard, single-bound peghead, crown peghead inlay, sealed tuners, tulip tuner buttons: **1941**
L-12 Premier: rounded cutaway, introduced: **1947**
L-12P discontinued (some shipped in 1949 and 1950): **1949**
L-12 discontinued: **1955**

L-7: 16" wide, trapeze tailpiece, single-bound top and back, single-bound pickguard, single-bound rosewood fingerboard, varied-pattern inlay beginning at 3rd fret, single-bound peghead, fleur-de-lis peghead inlay, sunburst
Introduced: **1933**
Double-handled vase and curlicues peghead inlay: **mid 1934**
17" wide, X-braced top, ornate rectangle-enclosed inlay: **late 1934**
TG-7: tenor, available: **1934–40**
Tailpiece with pointed ends and raised arrowheads: **1934**
Flat plate tailpiece with cutout (still with pointed ends), some with engraved *L-7* on tailpiece base: **1937**
Natural finish available: **1939**
Parallel top bracing: **mid 1939**
Triple-bound top, double-parallelogram inlay, crown peghead inlay: **1942**
Standard trapeze tailpiece by **1944**
Some with fleur-de-lis peghead inlay: **c. 1944**
Wood crosspiece on tailpiece, 3-on-a-plate tuners, some examples: **1943–46 only**
A few with laminated back: **late 1940s–early 50s**
Laminated beveled-edge pickguard: **1948**
L-7C: cutaway, sunburst or natural, introduced: **1948**
L-7E, L-7ED Pickguard/PU unit (1 or 2 PUs mounted on pickguard, factory-installed or available as an accessory), available by: **1948**

L-7 discontinued: **1956**
Tailpiece with pointed ends and 2 raised diamonds: **1957**
L-7C discontinued: **1972**

L-50: 14 3/4" wide, 17 1/2" long, flat back, round hole (some with *f*-holes), ebony bridge, short trapeze tailpiece, pickguard glued to top, single-bound top and back, dot inlay, pearl *Gibson* logo, dark mahogany sunburst
Introduced: **1932**
19 1/4" long, *f*-holes (some with round hole), standard trapeze tailpiece, elevated pickguard: **1934**
TG-50: tenor, introduced: **1934**
16" wide, arched back: **1935**
Tailpiece with raised diamond: **1936**
Wood crosspiece on tailpiece, 3-on-a-plate tuners, paint or decal logo (at least 1 example with banner logo): **1943–46 only**
Single-bound pickguard, single-bound fingerboard, pearloid trapezoid inlay (tenor remains with dot inlay): **c. 1946**
Laminated beveled-edge pickguard: **1949**
TG-50 discontinued: **1958**
L-50 discontinued: **1971**

L-75: 14 3/4" wide, 17 1/2" long, flat back, mahogany back and sides, short trapeze tailpiece, bound top and back, white pearloid fingerboard and peghead veneer, bound fingerboard, ornate rectangle-enclosed inlay, notched-diamond peghead inlay
Introduced: **1932**
19 1/4" long, standard trapeze tailpiece, single-bound rosewood fingerboard, dot inlay, double-handled vase peghead inlay: **1934**
16" wide, arched back, round hole, elevated pickguard, 3-piece column-like peghead inlay: **1935**
Discontinued: **1939**

Super 400: 18" wide, body shape like c. 1907 Style O with narrow upper bout, X-braced top, figured maple back and sides, adjustable bridge with triangular inlay at each end, tailpiece with Y-shaped center section and model name on crosspiece, 7-ply top binding, triple-bound back, triple-bound *f*-holes, brown pearloid pickguard with 5-ply binding, pointed-end ebony fingerboard, triple-bound fingerboard, 25 1/2" scale, single- and double-split block inlay, 5-ply peghead binding, 5-piece split-diamond peghead inlay, 3-piece split-diamond inlay on back of peghead, model name on heelcap, engraved open-back Grover tuners, gold-plated metal parts, Cremona

brown sunburst finish
Introduced: **1934**
Upper bout widens to 13 5/8": **c. 1936**
Sealed Grover tuners optional, model name on
heelcap: **c. 1937**
Stairstep tuner buttons: **1938**
Super 400 Premier: (later **Super 400C**) rounded
cutaway, introduced by **1939**
Rounded Y shape on tailpiece with hole at bot-
tom center for allen wrench tension
adjustment, no hinge on tailpiece, Kluson
tuners with metal tulip-shaped buttons,
natural finish optional: **1939**
Parallel top bracing: **mid 1939**
Amber plastic tuner buttons: **mid to late 1939**
No model name on heelcap: **1942**
White plastic tuner buttons by: **1947**
Rosewood fingerboard: **1949**
Ebony fingerboard: **1953**
Metal tuner buttons by: **1957**
Super 400, non-cutaway, discontinued: **1955**
Super 400C discontinued: **1983**

L-30: 14 3/4" wide, flat back, adjustable bridge,
elevated unbound pickguard, single-bound
top and back, dot inlay, silkscreen logo,
black finish
Introduced: **1935**
Dark mahogany brown sunburst top,
mahogany finish back and sides: **late 1936**
Discontinued: **1943**

L-37: 14 3/4" wide, flat back, adjustable bridge,
single-bound top and back, single-bound
pickguard, dot inlay, red mahogany sunburst finish
Introduced: **1935**
Brown sunburst top finish, chocolate brown
back and sides: **1937**
Discontinued: **1941**

L-47: 14 3/4" wide, flat back, tortoise grain binding on top and back, white binding on pickguard, natural or sunburst finish
Introduced: **1940**
Discontinued: **1943**

Wartime model (name unknown): 16" wide,
spruce top, maple back and sides, flat
back, trapeze tailpiece, single-bound top
and back, large V-shaped neck, dot inlay,
silkscreen logo, black finish: **c. 1943–c. 46**

L-48: 16" wide, mahogany back and sides,
mahogany top (early with spruce top),
single-bound top and back, dot inlay (a few
early with trapezoid), silkscreen logo, sunburst finish
Introduced: **c. 1946**
Spruce top, maple back, mahogany sides: **1952**
Laminated mahogany top and sides, laminated
maple back specified in catalog but most

with mahogany back, by: **1957**
Discontinued: **1971**

Super 300: 18" wide, triple-bound top and back,
tailpiece with 3 cutouts, laminated
beveled-edge pickguard, single-bound fingerboard with square end, double-parallelogram inlay, single-bound peghead, crown
peghead inlay, sunburst finish
Introduced by **1948**
Super 300C: cutaway, introduced: **1954**
Super 300 discontinued: **1955**
Super 300C discontinued: **1958**

COMMENTS

Gibson invented the concept of archtop guitars and has remained the pre-eminent
maker of archtops. The only models more
sought after by collectors and players are
those by individual makers such as
D'Angelico or Stromberg, whose instruments represent refinements of such
Gibson innovations as carved top and
back, tone bars (and later X-braced top),
fingerboard raised off top, adjustable
bridge, elevated pickguard, large body
size, cutaway body shape, and adjustable
truss rod.
Pre-1910: While of considerable interest to
collectors because of their innovative
design, aesthetic and artistic appeal, and
great rarity, these insturments leave much
to be desired for players.
1910–1923: These are more playable than
those of the earlier period. They are good
for ragtime, blues, and early jazz and blues
styles, but they still do not command as
much interest from players as from collectors.
1924–early 30s: The L-5 is the first Gibson guitar of great interest to collectors. The early
Loar models, although they do not have
such modern characteristics as a large
body, slim neck, cutaway, or high degree
of ornamentation, are nevertheless excep-
tionally fine instruments by modern standards. They are of interest to players of
early jazz as well as collectors. The other
models of the period, all with oval or round
soundhole, are of less interest.
Early 1930s–World War II: This is considered
the classic period of Gibson archtops. The
f-hole, advanced (17" or wider) models
from late 1934 onward defined what an
archtop guitar is today. Except for a Loar-
signed L-5, the prewar Super 400 and
advanced body L-5 are the most sought
after Gibson archtop models by collectors
and players alike, with cutaways bringing
more money than the equivalent non-cut-

aways and natural finish bringing more
than sunburst.

1946–50s: Postwar Gibson archtops are fine
instruments though not as highly regarded
as those of the classic period.

1960s–70s: Instruments from this period, while
still good instruments, are not as highly
regarded by players or collectors as those
of earlier periods.

HARP GUITARS

Note: Although Gibson catalogs specified maple back and sides on all harp guitars, pre-1908 instruments are virtually all made of walnut. Later instruments are made of birch.

Style R: 6 strings on neck, 6 sub-bass strings, 17 7/8" wide, scroll on upper bass bout with pearl in scroll, maple back and sides, oval hole, 2 soundhole rings of fancy colored wood, fixed mahogany bridge with scroll at each end, nickel-plated metal strap tailpiece described in catalog but not in catalog illustration, inlaid bridge pins, single-bound top, 25 1/2" scale, asymmetrical ebony extended fingerboard with treble-side extension, friction keys, veneer peghead piece, orange top finish, dark mahogany back and sides finish
Only catalog appearance: **1902**

Style R-1: 6 strings on neck, 6 sub-bass strings, 17 7/8" wide, scroll on upper bass bout with pearl in scroll, maple back and sides, bound soundhole, 2 soundhole rings of fancy colored wood with pearl border, fixed mahogany bridge with scroll at each end, nickel-plated metal strap tailpiece described in catalog but not in catalog illustration, inlaid bridge pins, pearl and ivory rope-pattern top binding, pearl dot in scroll, 25 1/2" scale, asymmetrical ebony extended fingerboard with treble-side extension, dot inlay, friction keys, scroll on peghead, veneer peghead piece, black top finish, dark mahogany back and sides finish
Only catalog appearance: **1902**

Style U-1: 6 strings on neck, 12 sub-bass strings, 21" wide, scroll on upper bass bout with pearl dot in scroll, maple back and sides, bound soundhole, 2 soundhole rings of fancy colored wood with pearl border, fixed mahogany bridge with scroll at each end, silver-plated metal strap tailpiece, inlaid bridge pins, white and green rope-pattern top binding, 27 1/4" scale, asymmetrical ebony extended fingerboard with treble-side extension, dot inlay, friction keys, scroll on peghead, bound peghead, veneer peghead piece, adjustable extension rod for upright playing, black top finish, dark mahogany back and sides finish
Only catalog appearance: **1902**

Style U: 6 strings on neck, 12 sub-bass strings, 21" wide, scroll on upper bass bout with pearl dot in scroll, maple back and sides, bound soundhole, 2 soundhole rings of fancy colored wood with pearl border, fixed mahogany bridge with scroll at each end, metal strap tailpiece, nickel-plated extension bridge support, inlaid bridge pins, pearl and ivory rope-pattern top binding, pearl in scroll, 27 1/4" scale, asymmetrical ebony extended fingerboard with treble-side extension, dot inlay, friction keys, sub-bass tuners in a 2-2-2-2-2-2 configuration, scroll on peghead, veneer peghead piece, adjustable extension rod for upright playing (described but seldom if ever seen), black top finish, dark mahogany back and sides finish
Introduced: **1902**
6 strings on neck, 10 sub-bass strings, 2 black-and-white rope-pattern soundhole rings with solid ring in between, single-bound top and back, single-bound fingerboard, 25 1/2" scale, slanted *The Gibson* pearl logo, right-angle tuners on guitar neck, sub-bass tuners in 1-2-2-2-2-1 configuration, no extension rod for upright playing: **c. 1906**
18 1/4" wide, moveable 1-piece maple bridge with ebony saddle piece, double-trapeze tailpiece with pins mounted on tortoise grain celluloid plate: **c. 1907**
2 checkered soundhole rings with diamond-pattern ring in between, single-bound top and back, bone saddle piece for 6 strings, 24 3/4" scale, sub-bass tuners in 2-3-3-2 configuration, rounded peghead with scroll on peghead extension: **1908**
Cedar neck specified: **1911**
18 3/4" wide, elevated pickguard with 2 supports, Mexican mahogany neck, dark mahogany top finish: **1913**
Red mahogany sunburst top finish standard, golden orange or ebonized (black) by special order only: **1914**
1 pickguard support, ebony saddle piece: **1915**
Honduras mahogany neck: **1918**
Compensating adjustable bridge for 6 strings, separate bridge for sub-bass strings, no pearl in body scroll, by **early 1920s**
Discontinued from catalog: **1939**

COMMENTS

The Style U with 10 sub-bass strings is the only commonly seen Gibson harp guitar model. Although Gibson carried the Style U in the catalog until 1939, it is unlikely that any were manufactured after circa 1924.

Gibson predicted that the harp guitar would have the same revolutionary effect on music that the piano did. The few musicians playing harp guitars today prefer flat top instruments such as those made with the Dyer brand (see Larson Brothers section). Gibson harp guitars are interesting oddities for aesthetic, artistic, and historical reasons. They are of value primarily because they make great conversation pieces.

FLAT TOPS KEY, 16" or Wider

Dot fingerboard inlay
  Banner logo=**J-45, 1942–46**
  Prewar script logo and model name=**Roy Smeck Stage Deluxe**
  Prewar script logo
    Unbound fingerboard
      White paint logo=**J-35**
      Gold paint logo=**J-45, 1942–47**
      Pearl logo
        Rectangular bridge=**Jumbo**
        Moustache-shaped bridge=**Jumbo Deluxe**
        Asymmetrical fan-shaped bridge
          Rosewood body=**MK-72**
          Maple body=**MK-53**
          Mahogany body
            6-string=**MK-35**
            12-string=**MK-35-12**
    Bound fingerboard
      12 frets clear of body (4 ƒ-holes and round hole)=**HG-24**
      14 frets clear of body
        Square-end fingerboard=**Jumbo 55, 1939–42**
        Pointed-end fingerboard=**Super Jumbo 100**
Postwar block letter logo
  Molded synthetic back and sides=**J-25**
  Maple back and sides
    Dove on peghead=**Gospel**
    No peghead ornament
      Super jumbo (rounded) shape=**J-100**
      Square-shouldered dreadnought shape=**J-35, 1985–87**
  Mahogany back and sides
    12-string
      Natural top
        No peghead ornament=**JG-12**
        2-piece peghead inlay=**B-45-12N**
      Sunburst top=**B-45-12**
    6-string
      Square-shouldered dreadnought
        No-pin bridge=**J-40**
        Arched back=**J-55**
        Unbound back=**JG-0**
        Pin bridge, flat back, bound back
          Belly above bridge=**J-30**
          Belly below bridge
            Sunburst top=**J-45, 1969–81**
            Natural top=**J-50, 1969–81**
      Round-shouldered dreadnought
        Teardrop (Martin style) pickguard
          2 pearl dots on bridge
            Sunburst top=**J-45, 1947–c. 55**
            Natural top=**J-50, 1947–c. 55**
          No dots on bridge=**J-45, 1984–current**
        Non-teardrop pickguard
          Sunburst top=**J-45, c. 1957–69**
          Natural top=**J-50, c. 1957–69**
  Rosewood back and sides
    Ebony fingerboard=**Heritage, 1965–early 70s**
    Rosewood fingerboard
      Non-cutaway
        6-string=**Blue Ridge**
        12-string=**Blue Ridge 12**
      Cutaway=**Les Paul Jumbo**

No fingerboard inlay (cutaway body)=**Bossa Nova**
Custom inlay, fan-shaped bridge, gold-plated metal parts=**Mark 99**
Double-parallelogram fingerboard inlay
   Plain tortoise pickguard
      Dreadnought body shape
         Sunburst=**Southerner Jumbo (SJ)**, 1942–c. 74
         Natural=**Country-Western Jumbo** or **SJN**
      Jumbo (round) body shape=**J-185**
   Dove on pickguard=**Dove**
   Hummingbird on pickguard=**Hummingbird**, 1960–73, c. 80s-current
   2 white pickguards=**Folk Singer Jumbo**
Block fingerboard inlay
   Abalone blocks=**MK 81**
   Pearl or pearloid blocks
      Diamond-and-curlicues peghead inlay=**Heritage, early 1970s–82**
      Crown peghead inlay
         White outer binding=**Hummingbird, 1973-early 80s**
         Black outer binding=**SJ, c. 1974–77**
      No peghead ornament (4 ƒ-holes and round hole)=**HG-24**
Star fingerboard inlay
   Oversized bridge=**Everly Brothers**
   Standard upper belly bridge=**J-180**
Crest fingerboard inlay
   Maple back and sides
      6-string=**J-200, 1946–current**
      12-string=**Artist-12**
   Rosewood back and sides
      Moustache bridge with cutouts=**SJ-200, 1937-42**
      4-point bridge with no cutouts=**J-250R**
Diamond-and-arrowheads fingerboard inlay=**Advanced Jumbo**
Trapezoid fingerboard inlay=**J-160E**
Fancy scroll-type fingerboard inlay
   Dreadnought body shape=**J-45 Celebrity**
   Jumbo body shape=**J-200 Celebrity**
Varied-pattern fingerboard inlay=**Roy Smeck Radio Grande**

FLAT TOPS KEY, 14 3/4" or Narrower

No logo=**GY (Army-Navy)**
Pre–WWII logo or wartime banner logo
   Uniform top finish: natural, amber, or brown-stain
      Mahogany back and sides
         Mahogany top=**L-0, 1928–33**
         Spruce top
            12 frets clear of body
               Round hole=**L-1, 1926–28**
               4 ƒ-holes and round hole=**HG-20**
            14 frets clear of body
               Teardrop (Martin-style) pickguard=**LG-2, 1943–47**
               Pickguard follows body edge=**L-00, 1941–WWII**
      Maple back and sides=**L-0, 1926–28**
      Rosewood back and sides=**L-2, 1932–34**
   Black top
      Unbound back=**L-00, 1932–mid 30s**
      Bound back
         14 frets clear of body=**L-0, 1937–42**
         12 frets clear of body=**HG-0**
   Argentine gray sunburst top (gold sparkle inlay)=**L-2, 1931**

Pre-WWII logo or wartime banner logo (cont.)
    Brown sunburst top
        Varied-pattern fingerboard inlay
            Wood fingerboard=**Nick Lucas Model**
            Celluloid fingerboard
                14 frets clear of body=**Century (L-C)**
                12 frets clear of body=**HG-Century**
        Dot inlay
            Rosewood back and sides=**L-2, 1929–30**
            Mahogany (or maple) back and sides
                No pickguard (Hawaiian setup)
                    Round hole=**HG-00**
                    4 *f*-holes and round hole=**HG-22**
                Teardrop (Martin-style) pickguard shape=**LG-2, 1943–47**
                Pickguard follows contour of body edge
                    Black bridge pins and end pin=**L-00, 1933–45**
                    White bridge pins and end pin=**L-1, 1928–37**
Postwar logo
    Brown sunburst top
        Cutaway
            No pickup=**CF-100**
            Pickup=**CF-100E**
        Non-cutaway
            6-string
                Straight "ladder" bracing
                    14 3/4" wide=**LG-1**
                    12 3/4" wide=**LG-2 3/4, 1949–62**
                X bracing=**LG-2, early 1947–62**
            12-string=**B-25-12**
    Cherry sunburst top
        14 1/4" wide
            6-string
                Upper or lower belly on bridge=**B-25**
                No belly on bridge=**LG-2, 1962**
            12-string=**B-25-12**
        12 3/4" wide
            Upper or lower belly on bridge **B-25 3/4**
            No belly on bridge=**LG-2 3/4, 1962**
Natural spruce top
    Black pickguard
        6-string
            Mahogany back and sides=**Jubilee**
            Rosewood back and sides=**Jubilee Deluxe**
        12-string
            Square-shouldered body shape=**Jubilee-12**
            Round-shouldered body shape=**LG-12**
    Tortoise grain pickguard
        Standard Gibson peghead
            6-string
                14 1/4" wide
                    Upper or lower belly on bridge=**B-25N**
                    No belly on bridge=**LG-3**
                12 3/4" wide=**B-25 3/4**
            12-string=**B-25-12N**
        Narrow (2 1/4" wide) peghead=**B-15**
        2 white pickguards=**F-25**
    Mahogany top=**LG-0**

FLAT TOPS

SECTION ORGANIZATION

*Note: Catalog descriptions of early Gibson flat
    tops in many cases specify slightly arched
    top and/or back. These specs are noted
    here, but there is no easily discernible dif-
    ference between "slightly arched" and the
    later flat specification, except for the
    post–WWII J-55 and the Gospel, which
    have noticeably arched backs.*

Pre-WWII Models,
14 1/2" or Narrower

GY (Army-Navy): 13 1/2" wide, flat top version
of L-Jr. archtop, slightly arched top and
back, maple back and sides, maple bridge,
trapeze tailpiece with pins mounted in tortoise grain celluloid plate, no binding, no
logo, ebony fingerboard, dot inlay,
Sheraton brown finish

Because of the GY's low-budget design,
Gibson ads stated that although the GY is
made by Gibson, it is "not a Gibson." Ads
also recommended that the GY be set up
for Hawaiian playing.
Introduced: **Dec. 1918**
Discontinued (case listed but instrument not
listed): **1921**

L-1 flat top: (earlier archtop, see Gibson archtop section) 13 1/2" wide, round lower body
shape, slightly arched top and back, maple
back and sides, fixed ebony bridge with
pyramids at ends, black pins, 3 evenly
spaced rings around soundhole, bound
soundhole, bound top and back, 12 frets
clear of body, square-end ebony fingerboard, dot inlay at frets 5, 7 and 9, *The
Gibson* paint logo, light amber top finish,
Sheraton brown back and sides
Introduced: **1926**
Mahogany back and sides, short rosewood
bridge with slight belly and straight-bevel

ends, white bridge pins, extra pin below
bridge pins, 1 multiple-ring around soundhole (may vary), triple-bound top and back,
bound rosewood fingerboard, dot inlay to
15th fret, brown sunburst finish, by **1928**
No belly on bridge: **1929**
No extra pin on bridge: **1929**
14 3/4" wide, body more squared at bottom,
longer modern type bridge, unbound fingerboard, by **1931**
Single-bound top and back, 14 frets clear of
body: **1932**
Top and back not specified as slightly arched,
tortoise-grain pickguard, *Gibson* logo: **1933**
Flat top and back specified: **1934**
Discontinued by **1937**
L-1 with 1930 body shape (rounded lower bout)
re-introduced, with cremona brown finish
and other specs different from 1930 version: **1991**

L-0: 13 1/2" wide, round lower body shape,
slightly arched top and back, maple back
and sides, 2-and-1 soundhole ring configuration (may vary), ebony bridge with pyramids at ends, black pins, bound top and
back, 12 frets clear of body, ebonized fingerboard, dot inlay, *The
Gibson* paint logo, amber brown finish all
over
Introduced: **1926**
Mahogany top, mahogany back and sides,
short rosewood bridge with slight belly and
straight-bevel ends, black bridge pins,
extra white pin below bridge pins, ebony
saddle, rosewood fingerboard, dot inlay to
15th fret, ebony nut, amber finish: **1928**
No belly on bridge: **1929**
No extra pin on bridge: **1929**
14 3/4" wide, body more square at bottom,
longer modern type bridge: **1931**
Top and back not specified as slightly arched,
14 frets clear of body, some with *Gibson*
logo: **1932**
L-0 discontinued: **1933**
Re-introduced, spruce top, mahogany back
and sides, bound top and back, black
bridge pins and end pin, tortoise grain
pickguard, some with white pickguard,
black finish: **1937**
HG-0: Hawaiian setup, straight (non-slanted)
saddle, 12 frets clear of body, heavier
bracing, introduced: 1937
L-0 and HG-0 discontinued: **1942**

Nick Lucas Model (Gibson Special): 13 1/2"
wide, deeper (4 1/2" or more at endpin)
than other models, slightly arched top and
back, mahogany back and sides, 2 multi-
ply soundhole rings, rosewood bridge with
pyramids at ends, slight belly on bridge,
extra pin below bridge pins, triple-bound

top and back, triple-bound rosewood fingerboard, small varied-pattern inlay, 12 frets clear of body, *The Gibson* logo, special round Nick Lucas label, sunburst finish
Introduced: **1928**
14 3/4" wide, rosewood back and sides, single 3-ply soundhole ring, modern type bridge (no pyramids), 13 frets clear of body, larger varied-pattern inlay with notched diamond at 3rd fret, fleur-de-lis peghead inlay, *Gibson* logo: **1929**
Pin bridge standard, adjustable bridge and trapeze tailpiece listed as optional (most examples with adjustable bridge and trapeze), most with elevated pickguard (some with pickguard glued to top), ebony fingerboard raised off of top: **1932**
Flat top and back, maple back and sides specified (some with mahogany), pickguard glued to top, 14 frets clear of body, rosewood shade sunburst on back and sides: **1934**
Discontinued from catalog: **1938**
Last shipped (2 instruments): **1941**
Re-introduced with changes: **1991**

L-2 flat top: (earlier archtop, see Acoustic Archtops section) 14 3/4" wide, slightly arched top and back, rosewood back and sides, short bridge with straight-beveled ends specified, most with adjustable bridge and trapeze tailpiece, no pickguard, triple-bound top and back, 13 frets clear of body, bound ebony fingerboard, dot inlay, *The Gibson* logo, sunburst finish specified, most examples with natural top finish
Introduced: **June 1929**
Mahogany back and sides, longer modern type bridge, gold sparkle inlay around top and soundhole borders, 12 frets clear of body, 6-point flame-shaped peghead inlay, Argentine gray sunburst finish, by **1931**
Flat top specified rosewood back and sides, no sparkle trim, adjustable bridge and trapeze tailpiece (listed as optional), elevated pickguard, rosewood fingerboard raised off of top, 13 frets clear of body, *Gibson* logo, natural finish top: **1932**
Pin bridge, no tailpiece, pickguard glued to top: **1933**
14 frets clear of body: **1934**
Discontinued: **1934**

L-00: 14 3/4" wide, mahogany back and sides, bound top, unbound back, black bridge pins and end pin, dot inlay, 14 frets clear of body, *The Gibson* logo, black finish
Introduced: **1932**
Gibson logo, some with white pickguard: **1932**
Tortoise grain pickguard, sunburst top, red mahogany finish back and sides, black finish still available: **1933**

Sunburst finish: **c. 1935**
Bound back, by **1937**
HG-00: Hawaiian setup, straight (non-slanted) saddle, 12 frets clear of body, heavier bracing, introduced: **1937**
Black finish discontinued: **1938**
3/4 size optional (35 total shipped): **1938–39 only**
Natural finish optional: **1941**
Only a Gibson... banner logo (some with white silkscreen logo in 1943), some with no truss rod: **1943**
Discontinued: **1945**

L-C: Century model, 14 3/4" wide, curly maple back and sides, triple-bound top and back, triple-bound fingerboard, white pearloid fingerboard and peghead veneer, notched-diamond inlay within rosewood rectangles (some with hearts-and-flowers or wreath-pattern), 14 frets clear of body (some early with 12 frets clear), notched-diamond peghead inlay, sunburst finish on top, back, and sides
Introduced: **1933**
HG-Century: Hawaiian setup, straight-mounted saddle, 12 frets clear of body, heavier bracing, introduced: **1937**
Single-bound top and back, rosewood peghead veneer, stickpin (elongated diamond) peghead inlay (rare model): **1938**
1 3/4-size model shipped: **1939**
L-C and HG-Century discontinued (3 L-Cs shipped in 1940, 1 L-C shipped in 1941): **1939**

Tenor and Plectrum Models

Tenor scale is 23". Catalog specifies 27" for plectrum, but actual plectrum scale is 26 1/4". Any standard guitar model was available with tenor or plectrum neck by special order.

TG-1: 12 5/8" wide, slightly arched top, mahogany back and sides, short straight-beveled rosewood bridge on large base, extra pin in bridge base, bound top and back, bound rosewood fingerboard with pointed end, dot inlay, 4-point pattern with curlicues peghead inlay, thin *Gibson* logo, sunburst
TG-1 introduced: **1927**
TG-1 discontinued (1 shipped in 1938, 1 in 1940): **1937**

TG-0: all mahogany, slightly arched top, short straight-beveled rosewood bridge, no bridge base, black bridge pins, unbound rosewood fingerboard with pointed end, thin *The Gibson* logo in silver paint, light amber finish

Flat Tops

TG-0 introduced: **1927**
TG-0 discontinued: **1933**
TG-0 re-introduced (see LG-0, following): **1960**

PG-1: plectrum, other specs same as TG-1, introduced: **1928**
14 3/4" wide, longer modern type bridge with no extra pin, *Gibson* logo, no peghead ornament: **1930**
PG-1 discontinued (1 shipped): **1938**

TG-00 and PG-00: black finish, introduced: **1932**
TG-1 and TG-00, unbound fingerboard, sunburst finish, same specs as L-1 and L-00: **1933**
PG-00 discontinued (1 shipped): **1937**
TG-00 discontinued: **1943**

Hawaiian Models

By 1920 Gibson offered steel guitar "equipment"—"nut adjuster," high saddle, steel and picks—to convert any model to Hawaiian setup. Some adjustable bridges in the early 1920s have a saddle with a straight bottom side so that the saddle can be turned over for Hawaiian playing. Any model could also be ordered as a Hawaiian (designated by an *H* after the model name). In addition, the following catalog models were offered.

Note: Contrary to catalog specs for HG-series guitars, virtually all examples are set up for Spanish-style play, with 14-fret neck and standard frets. Roy Smeck models were all originally Hawaiian setup with inlaid fret markers flush with the fingerboard, although many have been converted to Spanish.

HG-24: 16" wide, dreadnought shape, rosewood back and sides, double-wall construction, round hole and 4 *f*-holes, single-bound top and back, 14 frets clear of body, single-bound fingerboard, dot inlay (some with pearloid block inlay), fleur-de-lis peghead inlay, natural top finish (rare model)

HG-22: 14 3/4" wide, maple back and sides, double-wall construction, round hole and 4 *f*-holes, bound top and back, bound fingerboard, 14 frets clear of body, sunburst finish (very rare model)

HG-20: 14 3/4" wide, maple back and sides, double-wall construction, round hole and 4 *f*-holes, 14 frets clear of body, dot inlay, silkscreened logo, brown finish (rare model)

HG series introduced by: **1929**
Only catalog appearance: **1932**

Discontinued: **1933**

Roy Smeck Stage Deluxe: 16" wide, round-shouldered dreadnought shape, mahogany back and sides, single-bound top and back, pickguard follows contour of body edge, 12 frets clear of body, ivoroid frets flush with fingerboard, dot inlay, fingerboard 2 1/4" wide at nut, silkscreened model name and logo on peghead, sunburst finish (see note after Roy Smeck Radio Grand)
Introduced: **1934**
Varied-pattern inlay by: **1939**
Discontinued: **WWII**

Roy Smeck Radio Grande: 16" wide, round-shouldered dreadnought shape, rosewood back and sides, bound top and back, bound fingerboard, 12 frets clear of body, ivoroid frets flush with fingerboard, varied-pattern inlay (like Nick Lucas model) with notched diamond at 3rd fret, fingerboard 2 1/4" wide at nut, silkscreened model name and logo on peghead, natural top
Introduced: **1934**
Discontinued from catalog: **1937**
Last shipped (26 instruments): **1939**

Note: Some Roy Smeck models do not conform to catalog descriptions. Variations include: Stage Deluxe with varied pattern inlay; Radio Grande with mahogany back and sides, sunburst finish. Gibson made at least one guitar with a Smeck body size and L-Century type celluloid fingerboard and peghead veneer.

HG-Century: Hawaiian version of L-C (see preceding)

HG-00: Hawaiian version of L-00 (see preceding)

HG-0: Hawaiian version of L-0 (see preceding)

Jumbo Models, 16" or Wider, Introduced Before WWII

All have 14 frets clear of body.

Jumbo: 16" wide, round-shouldered dreadnought, mahogany back and sides, bound top and back, rectangular bridge, rosewood fingerboard, dot inlay, pearl logo, sunburst finish on top, back, sides, and neck
Introduced: **1934**
Discontinued: **1936**

Jumbo 35: 16" wide, round-shouldered dreadnought, mahogany back and sides, single-
bound top and back, dot inlay, silkscreened logo, sunburst top finish, red
mahogany back and sides finish
Introduced: **1936**
2 pearl dots on bridge by **1937**
Natural finish optional: **1940**
Discontinued: **1943**

Advanced Jumbo: 16" wide, round-shouldered
dreadnought, rosewood back and sides,
single-bound top and back, 25 1/2" scale,
bound fingerboard, diamond-and-arrowheads inlay, vertical diamond-and-arrowheads peghead inlay, sunburst finish
Introduced: **late 1936**
Discontinued (2 shipped): **1940**
Re-introduced: **1990**

Super Jumbo (SJ-200): 16 7/8" wide, jumbo
shape, rosewood back and sides (at least 1
prewar custom-made example with maple
back and sides), large moustache-shaped
ebony bridge with cutouts at bridge ends, 4
semi-rectangular pearl inlays on bridge,
height-adjustable saddle bearings, pickguard with engraved flower motif, multiple-
bound top and back, maple neck, single-
bound ebony fingerboard with pointed end,
crest inlay, triple-bound peghead, crown
peghead inlay, stairstep tuner buttons,
strap-fastening bracket on back of peghead and at endpin, gold-plated metal
parts, sunburst finish
Introduced (none shipped until 1938): **late 1937**
Renamed **Super Jumbo 200,** 17" wide, center-
stripe marquetry on back: **1939**
1-piece saddle, rosewood fingerboard,
pearloid tulip-shaped tuner buttons: **1941**
Cataloged as **J-200** (labeled **SJ-200** into early
1950s), maple back and sides, single-
bound peghead, no strap brackets: **1947**
Natural finish optional: **1948**
At least 1 custom-made with rosewood back
and sides: **mid 1950s**
Adjustable bridge saddle optional: **1960**
Tune-o-matic bridge, 4 pearl inlays replace
bridge cutouts (in addition to previous
inlays): **1961**
Height-adjustable saddle standard by: **1969**
No pearl dots on bridge by: **1970**
Ebony fingerboard by: **1971**
Bridge with points at 4 corners (no moustache
ends) and pearl curlicue inlays below pins,
non-adjustable saddle: **1971**
Rosewood fingerboard: **1979**
Moustache bridge with 1 cutout at each end
and 2 semi-rectangular pearl inlays below
pins, multiple-bound peghead: **1985**
Still in production

J-200 Celebrity: rosewood back and sides,
smaller pickguard with no engraving,
ornate scroll-type inlay, fern peghead
inlay, limited edition of 90, available: **1985
only**

J-250R: same as J-200 but with rosewood back
and sides
Total of 20 shipped: **1972–78**

Jumbo Deluxe: 16" wide, round-shouldered
dreadnought, mahogany back and sides,
moustache-shaped bridge with cutouts at
bridge ends, height-adjustable saddle
bearings, 4 semi-rectangular pearl inlays
and 2 pearl dots on bridge, bound top and
back, unbound fingerboard, dot inlay, sunburst finish
Total of 3 shipped: **1938**

Super Jumbo 100: 17" wide, jumbo shape,
mahogany back and sides, pickguard does
not follow contour of body edge, large
moustache-shaped bridge with cutouts at
bridge ends, adjustable saddle bearings, 2
pearl dots on bridge, wide triple binding on
top, single-bound back, backstrip, maple
neck, bound ebony fingerboard with pointed end, dot inlay, pearl logo, stairstep peghead shape, butterfly tuner buttons, sunburst finish
Introduced: **1939**
Rosewood bridge with beveled edges and 3
pearl dots, 1-piece saddle, standard
Gibson peghead, round tuner buttons: **1941**
Discontinued: **1943**
Re-introduced with different specs (see following): **1985**

Jumbo 55: 16" wide, round-shouldered dreadnought, mahogany back and sides, pickguard does not follow contour of body
edge, moustache-shaped bridge with
cutouts at bridge ends (smaller than SJ-
200 or SJ-100 bridge) and 2 pearl dots, 1-
piece saddle, bound "coffeewood" fingerboard, dot inlay, pearl logo, stairstep peghead shape, sunburst finish
Introduced: **1939**
Rosewood bridge with beveled edges and 3
pearl dots, rosewood fingerboard, standard Gibson peghead shape (non-
stairstep): **1941**
Discontinued: **1943**
Re-introduced with different specs (see following): **1973**

Jumbo Models, 16" or Wider, Introduced WWII–Current

Southerner Jumbo (SJ): 16" wide, round-shouldered dreadnought, first batch (all with factory order batch number 910) with rosewood back and sides, all later with mahogany back and sides (except a few wartime with maple), belly bridge with 2 pearl dots (some with rectangular bridge), multiple-bound top and back, teardrop pickguard, bound rosewood fingerboard, double-parallelogram inlay, *Only a Gibson...* banner peghead logo, sunburst finish

Introduced: **1942**
Some with no truss rod: **1942–43 only**
No banner on peghead: **1946**
Crown peghead inlay: **c. 1947**
Upper belly on bridge by **1949**
Natural finish optional: **1954**
Longer pickguard with point at upper bout: **c. 1955**
Natural finish named **Country-Western Jumbo**: **1956**
Country-Western renamed **SJN**: **1960**
Adjustable saddle: **c. 1961**
SJN renamed **SJN Country Western**: **1962**
Square-shouldered dreadnought shape, 3-point pickguard: **1963**
Belly below bridge: **1969**
Non-adjustable saddle: **1970**
4-ply binding with black outer layer on top and back, black backstripe, 2-ply fingerboard binding with black outer layer, by: **1974**
SJ and SJN Country Western discontinued (4 SJs shipped): **1978**

J-45: 16" wide, round-shouldered dreadnought, mahogany back and sides (some wartime with maple back and sides, some with mahogany top), black bridge pins, 2 pearl dots on bridge, teardrop pickguard, single-bound top and back, dot inlay, *Only a Gibson...* banner logo, sunburst finish
Introduced: **1942**
Some with no truss rod: **1942–43 only**
Standard logo: **c. 1947**
J-50: natural finish version of J-45, introduced: **1947**
Upper belly on bridge, triple-bound top, by **1950**
Longer pickguard with point at upper bout: **c. 1955**
Adjustable bridge saddle optional: **1956**
No dots on bridge: **c. 1961**
Cherry sunburst finish on J-45: **1962**
Belly below bridge: **1968**
Logo on pickguard: **later 1968**
Square-shouldered dreadnought shape, teardrop pickguard with no logo: **1969**

Non-adjustable saddle: **1971**
Longer pickguard with point at upper bout, 4-ply top binding with tortoise grain outer layer, single-layer tortoise grain back binding, by **1975**
White-black-white top binding by **1981**
J-45 and J-50 discontinued: **1982**
J-45 re-introduced: round-shouldered dreadnought, teardrop pickguard, triple-bound top, sunburst, natural, or ebony finish: **1984**
J-45 still in production

J-40: square-shouldered dreadnought, no bridge pins, natural top finish, walnut back and sides finish
Introduced: **1971**
Tortoise grain binding by **1981**
Discontinued: **1982**

J-55: square-shouldered dreadnought, arched back, tortoise grain binding, natural top finish
Introduced: **1973**
White-black-white top binding by **1981**
Discontinued: **1982**

J-45 Celebrity: rosewood back and sides, fancy scroll-type inlay, fern peghed inlay, natural top finish, limited edition of 90, available: **1985**

J-185: 16" wide, jumbo shape, maple back and sides, upper belly on bridge, 2 Maltese-cross inlays on bridge, triple-bound top and back, 24 3/4" scale, single-bound rosewood fingerboard, double-parallelogram inlay, crown peghead inlay, gold-plated metal parts, natural or sunburst finish
Introduced: **1951**
Discontinued (28 natural, 0 sunburst shipped): **1958**
Re-introduced, 25 1/2" scale, shaded mahogany neck on first run only, non-shaded neck finish thereafter on examples with natural finish, chrome-plated metal parts: **1990**

J-160E: 16" wide, round-shouldered dreadnought, laminated spruce top, ladder bracing, mahogany back and sides, ! single-coil adjustable-pole PU at end of fingerboard, straight upper edge of PU, point on lower edge of PU, 2 knobs, upper belly on bridge, adjustable saddle with large adjustment knobs, 2 large dots inlaid on bridge, bound top and back, small pre–WWII style pickguard follows contour of body edge, 15 frets clear of body, bound rosewood fingerboard, trapezoid inlay, crown peghead inlay, sunburst finish
Introduced: **1954**
Smaller saddle adjustment screws by: **1960**

Square-shouldered dreadnought shape, belly below bridge, no dots on bridge, longer pickguard with point at upper treble bout, by **1969**

Non-adjustable saddle: **1970**

Slight extension on upper edge of PU to meet neck, straight lower edge of PU, teardrop pickguard: **early 1970s**

Discontinued: **1979**

Re-introduced: **1991**

Hummingbird: 16 1/4" wide, square-shouldered dreadnought, mahogany back and sides, pickguard with 2 points on upper treble bout and 1 point level with bridge, engraved hummingbird on pickguard, adjustable bridge saddle, upper belly on bridge, multiple-bound top, bound fingerboard, double-parallelogram inlay, crown peghead inlay, cherry sunburst finish

Introduced: **1960**

Some with maple back and sides: **c. 1962–63**

Natural finish top optional: **1963**

Belly below bridge: **1969**

Non-adjustable saddle: **1970**

Block inlay: **1973**

Back to double parallelogram inlay, by **1984**

Still in production

B-45-12: 12-string, 16 1/4" wide, round-shouldered dreadnought, mahogany back and sides, rectangular bridge with adjustable ebony saddle, trapeze tailpiece, long pickguard with point at upper bout, triple-bound top, single-bound fingerboard, dot inlay, vertical double-triangle peghead inlay of pearloid with rounded points, cherry sunburst finish

Introduced: **1961**

Square-shouldered dreadnought , upper belly on bridge, bridge pins, natural top (**B-45-12N**) optional: **c. 1962**

Upper belly on bridge, no bridge pins, no tailpiece: **c. 1963**

Upper belly on bridge, trapeze tailpiece: **c. 1965**

Pearl peghead inlay with pointed ends by: **mid 1960s**

Rectangular bridge, trapeze tailpiece: **1966**

Belly below bridge with pins, no tailpiece: **1970**

Discontinued: **1979**

Everly Brothers: 16 1/4" wide, jumbo shape, maple back and sides, oversized bridge with 3 pearl dots, strings anchor through bridge (no pins), adjustable saddle, double tortoise grain pickguards extend below bridge, single-bound fingerboard, star inlay, star peghead inlay, black finish

Introduced: **late 1962**

Natural top with red back and sides optional (46 shipped): **1963 only**

Natural top standard (no black), walnut stain back and sides, black pickguards, pickguards do not extend below bridge: **1968**

Discontinued: **1972**

Re-introduced as **J-180**, non-adjustable saddle, double oversized pickguards, standard size bridge with belly above bridge, black finish: **1986**

Still in production

Dove: 16 1/4" wide, square-shouldered dreadnought, maple back and sides, tune-o-matic bridge, abstract dove-shaped inlay on bridge ends, pickguard with 2 points toward bridge and 1 toward upper treble bout, pearl dove inlay on pickguard, multiple-bound top and back, bound rosewood fingerboard, double-parallelogram inlay, crown peghead inlay, cherry sunburst or natural finish

Introduced: **1962**

Belly below bridge, adjustable saddle: **1969**

Non-adjustable bridge saddle: **1970**

Ebony fingerboard: **1975**

Still in production

Folk Singer Jumbo (FJN): 16 1/4" wide, square-shouldered dreadnought, mahogany back and sides, straight saddle, double white pickguards, multiple-bound top, 12 frets clear of body, bound fingerboard, fingerboard 2" wide at nut, double-parallelogram inlay, crown peghead inlay, natural top finish, deep red back and sides finish

Introduced: **1963**

Discontinued: **1968**

Heritage: 16 1/4" wide, square-shouldered dreadnought, laminated rosewood back and sides, ebony bridge with upper belly, adjustable ebony saddle, black teardrop pickguard, tortoise grain binding on top and back, ebony fingerboard, dot inlay, no peghead ornament, natural top

Introduced: **1965**

Multiple body binding with white outer layer by **late 1960s**

Heritage-12: 12-string, available: 1968–70

Heritage Deluxe: specs unavailable, 2 shipped: **1968**

Belly below bridge: **1969**

Diamond and curlicues peghead inlay: **1969**

Non-adjustable saddle: **1970**

Large block inlay, large bridge with pointed ends and curlicue inlays: **early 1970s**

Black outer binding by: **1975**

Discontinued: **1982**

Blue Ridge: 16 1/4" wide, square-shouldered dreadnought, laminated back and sides with rosewood outer layer and maple inner, upper belly on bridge, adjustable

rosewood saddle, black teardrop pickguard, bound top and back, rosewood fingerboard, dot inlay, no peghead ornament
Introduced: **1968**
Belly below bridge: **1969**
Blue Ridge-12: 12-string, available **1970–78**
Non-adjustable saddle: **1970**
Oval low-impedance PU optional (1 shipped): **1973**
Discontinued: **1979**

Les Paul Jumbo: 16 1/4" wide, square-shouldered dreadnought with rounded cutaway, rosewood back and sides, oval low-impedance PU, 4 knobs, belly below bridge, backstripe, dot inlay
Introduced: **1969**
Discontinued: **1973**

Artist-12: 17" wide, jumbo shape, maple back and sides, oval hole, belly bridge, elevated pickguard with shape similar to pre–WWII models (follows contour of body edge), maple pickguard with multiple binding, multiple-bound top and back, backstripe marquetry, pearloid heel cap, 5-piece neck, bound rosewood fingerboard with pointed end, J-200 type crest inlay, large crown peghead inlay, sunburst or natural finish
1 instrument shipped: **1970**

JG-0 (6-string) and JG-12 (12-string): 16 1/4" wide, square-shouldered dreadnought, mahogany back and sides, bound top, unbound back, dot inlay, decal logo, natural top
Introduced: **1970**
JG-12 discontinued: **1971**
JG-0 discontinued (17 shipped): **1972**

Bossa Nova: see Classical Models, following

Gospel: 16 1/4" square-shouldered dreadnought, arched back, laminated maple back and sides, ebony bridge, long tortoise grain pickguard with point at upper bout, 4-ply top binding with tortoise grain outer layer, single-layer tortoise grain back binding, ebony fingerboard, dot inlay, dove decal on peghead, chrome-plated metal tuner buttons, natural finish
Introduced: **1973**
Discontinued: **1980**

J-25: 16 1/4" wide, round-shouldered dreadnought, laminated spruce top, molded synthetic back and sides, teardrop pickguard, belly below bridge, dot inlay, natural top finish
Introduced: **1984**
Discontinued: **1987**

J-100: 17" wide, jumbo shape, maple back and sides, teardrop pickguard, maple neck, 25 1/2" scale, unbound rosewood fingerboard, dot inlay, no peghead ornament
Introduced: **1985**
Discontinued: **1991**

J-35: 16 1/4" wide, square shouldered dreadnought, maple back and sides, upper belly on bridge, teardrop pickguard, maple neck, 25 1/2" scale, unbound rosewood fingerboard, dot inlay
Introduced (model name revived from pre–WWII): **1985**
Discontinued: **1987**

J-30: 16 1/4" wide, square-shouldered dreadnought, mahogany back and sides, upper belly on bridge, teardrop pickguard, dot inlay
Introduced: **1985**
Still in production

Mark Series

Mark models were designed by Michael Kasha and Richard Schneider. All are 16 3/16" wide with body shape narrower at the waist than dreadnought models. Special design features include: modified fan-pattern bracing, asymmetrical fan-shape bridge wider on bass end than treble, narrow peghead shape with points at upper corners (similar to snakehead shape of the 1920s), and old-style script logo.

(Mark) MK-99: handcrafted and signed by luthier Richard Schneider, gold-plated metal parts, steel-string or classical, available by special order only

MK-81: rosewood back and sides, removable pickguard, multiple-bound top and back, ebony fingerboard, abalone block inlay, gold-plated metal parts, natural or sunburst finish

MK-72: rosewood back and sides, black binding on top and back, 3-piece ebony-rosewood-ebony fingerboard, dot inlay, nickel-plated metal parts, natural or sunburst finish

MK-53: maple back and sides, multiple-bound top and back, rosewood fingerboard, dot inlay, nickel-plated metal parts, sunburst or natural top finish, walnut-stain back and sides finish

MK-35: mahogany back and sides, black binding on top and back, rosewood fingerboard, dot inlay, nickel-plated metal parts,

natural or sunburst finish
Mark models introduced: **late 1975**
MK-35-12: 12-string MK-35, available (12 shipped): **1977 only**
All discontinued: **1979**

LG Series

All are 14 1/4" wide, with spruce top, mahogany back and sides, dot inlay, silkscreen or decal logo, unless otherwise specified.

LG-2: X-braced top, 2 pearl dots on bridge, black bridge pins, teardrop pickguard, single-bound top and back, some early with *Only a Gibson…* banner logo, sunburst finish
Introduced: **1943**
Some with sunburst mahogany top, some with maple back and sides: **1943–46**
No banner on logo: **1946**
Larger pickguard with point at upper treble bout: **c. 1955**
No pearl dots on bridge: **c. 1961**
White bridge pins, adjustable bridge, cherry sunburst finish: **1962**
Discontinued, replaced by B-25 (see following): **1962**

LG-1: straight-across ladder bracing, black bridge pins, sunburst finish
Introduced: **1947**
Larger pickguard with point at upper treble bout: **c. 1955**
Upper belly on bridge: **1963**
Discontinued (25 shipped): **1968**

LG-3: X-braced top, white bridge pins, triple-bound top, natural finish
Introduced: **1946**
Larger pickguard with point at upper bout: **c. 1955**
Adjustable saddle: **1962**
Discontinued, replaced by B-25N (see following): **1962**

LG-2 3/4: often stamped *LG 3/4*, 12 3/4" wide, straight-across ladder bracing, some with triple-bound top, sunburst top finish
Introduced: **1949**
Larger pickguard with point at upper treble bout: **c. 1955**
No pearl dots on bridge: **c. 1961**
Cherry sunburst finish: **1962**
Discontinued, replaced by B-25 3/4 (see following): **1962**

LG-0: mahogany top, straight-across ladder bracing, black bridge pins, screwed-on teardrop pickguard, dark binding on top and back, natural mahogany finish
Introduced: **1958**
Unbound back by **1967**
LG-0 discontinued: **1970**

TG-0: tenor version of LG-0, mahogany top, introduced: **1960**
White bridge pins: **1962**
Upper belly on bridge: **1963**
TG-0 discontinued (3 shipped): **1974**

LG-12: 12-string, belly bridge, adjustable saddle, long pickguard with point at upper bout, bound top, unbound back, natural top finish, light mahogany finish back and sides
Introduced (does not appear on shipping totals until 1970): **1967**
Non-adjustable saddle, teardrop pickguard: **1970**
Discontinued (2 shipped): **1973**

B-25 Series

All are 14 1/4" wide with spruce top, mahogany back and sides, unless otherwise specified.

B-25: long pickguard with point at upper treble bout, upper belly on bridge, adjustable saddle, triple-bound top, dot inlay, decal logo, cherry sunburst finish or natural top (**B-25N**)
B-25 3/4: 12 3/4" wide, X-braced top (some with straight-across ladder bracing, possibly leftover LG-2 3/4 bodies), adjustable saddle, cherry sunburst finish
TG-25: tenor, adjustable saddle, sunburst finish or natural top (**TG-25N**)
All introduced: **1962**
Plastic bridge: **1965**
B-25 3/4 available with natural top: **1966**
B-25 3/4 discontinued: **1968**
Wood bridge by **1968**
Belly below bridge: **1969**
Non-adjustable saddle: **1970**
TG-25 discontinued: **1971**
B-25 discontinued (6 shipped): **1977**

B-25-12: 12-string, 14 1/4" wide, long pickguard with point at upper bout, oversized pin bridge with upper belly, adjustable saddle, single-bound top and back, cherry sunburst finish or natural top (**B-25-12-N**)
Introduced: **1962**
Upper belly on bridge, no bridge pins, no tailpiece: **c. 1963**
Larger upper-belly bridge, no bridge pins, trapeze tailpiece: **1965**
Rectangular bridge, trapeze tailpiece: **1966**
Belly below bridge, bridge pins, no tailpiece: **1970**

Cherry sunburst finish discontinued: **1970**
Natural top finish only: **1971**
Discontinued (2 shipped): **1977**

Other 14 1/4"-Wide Models Introduced After WWII

All have spruce top, mahogany back and sides, unless otherwise specified.

CF-100: 14 1/8" wide, pointed cutaway, solid spruce top, X-braced top, teardrop pickguard, upper belly on bridge, bound fingerboard, trapezoid inlay, decal logo, sunburst finish
Introduced **1950**
CF-100E: same as CF-100 but with 1 single-coil adjustable-pole PU at end of fingerboard, small prewar type pickguard follows contour of body edge, introduced: **1951**
Pearl logo, crown peghead inlay by **1952**
CF-100 and CF-100E discontinued: **1959**

F-25: Folksinger model, upper belly on bridge, double white pickguards, 12 frets clear of body, dot inlay, fingerboard 2" wide at nut, natural top, walnut back and sides finish
Introduced: **1963**
Discontinued: **1971**

B-15: student model, spruce top, large belly below bridge, adjustable saddle, no body binding, narrow peghead, natural finish: **1967**
Discontinued: **1971**

Jubilee and Jubilee-12 (12-string): similar to square-shouldered body shape but smaller than dreadnought, mahogany back and sides, belly bridge with adjustable rosewood saddle, black teardrop pickguard, single-bound top and back, dot inlay, decal logo, natural top
Jubilee Deluxe: laminated rosewood back and sides, light-colored backstripe, triple-bound top, single-bound back, decal logo, natural top
Introduced: **1970**
Discontinued: **1971**

Classical Models

Unless specified otherwise, all are 14 1/2" wide through 1957. From 1957 on, all are 14 1/4" wide. All post–WWII classicals have slotted peghead unless otherwise noted. GS stands for gut-string.

GS-85: rosewood back and sides, rosewood bridge with rounded ornamental bridge ends and 2 ornamental-shaped pearl inlays, 2 rectangular pearl bridge inlays below strings, multiple-bound top, bound back, ebony fingerboard, solid peghead
GS-35: mahogany back and sides, single-bound top and back, ebony fingerboard, solid peghead
Introduced: **1939**
GS-85 and GS-35 discontinued (total shipments of 27 GS-85s, 39 GS-35s): **1943**

GS-1: mahogany back and sides, black sound-hole rings in groups of 2-3-2, 2 rectangular inlays and 2 Maltese-cross inlays on bridge, triple-bound top, bound back, rosewood fingerboard, bone nut with with lengthwise groove to create zero fret, solid peghead, white tuner shafts, natural top
Introduced: **1950**
Discontinued (1 shipped): **1956**

GS-2: maple top specified, most if not all with spruce top, maple back and sides
Introduced: **1954**
Discontinued: **1960**

Custom Classic (GS-5): rosewood back and sides, 2 Maltese cross inlays on bridge, multiple-bound top and back, engraved tuner plates, decal logo
Introduced: **1954**
Referred to as **C-5** by **1957**
Discontinued: **1960**

C-1: mahogany back and sides, unbound back
Introduced: **1957**
C-1E: ceramic PU built into bridge, introduced: **1960**
C-1S: "petite" size, 13 1/4" wide, introduced: **1961**
Zero fret: **1962**
C-1D: narrow peghead with rounded top, introduced: **1963**
C-1S discontinued: **1967**
C-1E discontinued: **1968**
C-1D and C-1 discontinued: **1971**

C-2: maple back and sides, 3 rings around soundhole, 2 rectangular bridge inlays below pins, bound top and back, rosewood fingerboard, narrow peghead with rounded top, reddish body finish (later walnut)
Introduced: **1960**
Zero fret: **1962**
Discontinued: **1971**

C-6 Custom: Richard Pick model, rosewood back and sides, 3/4"-wide rosewood purfling around soundhole, tortoise grain binding, ebony fingerboard, zero fret, rosewood veneer on peghead, pearloid tuner buttons, gold-plated metal parts
Introduced: **1958**
2 rectangular bridge inlays below strings: **1966**
Discontinued: **1971**

C-0: mahogany back and sides, decal rosette, black top binding, unbound back, rosewood fingerboard, ebony nut, zero fret
Introduced: **1962**
Discontinued: **1971**

C-4: maple back and sides, 2 rectangular bridge inlays below strings, rosewood fingerboard, zero fret, rosewood back and sides finish
Introduced: **1962**
Discontinued: **1968**

C-8: rosewood back and sides, 2 rectangular bridge inlays below strings, ebony fingerboard, zero fret, narrow peghead with rounded top, rosewood peghead veneer, no logo
Introduced: **1962**
Discontinued: **1969**

Flamenco 2: cypress back and sides, thinner body than classicals, 2 rectangular bridge inlays below strings, 2 white pickguards between soundhole and bridge, zero fret
Introduced: **1963**
Discontinued: **1968**

Bossa Nova: classical electric, 16 1/4" wide, dreadnought size and shape, single cutaway, rosewood back and sides, ceramic bridge-mounted PU, adjustable bridge, no inlay, slotted peghead with wriggle-edge top
Introduced: **1971**
Discontinued (7 total sold): **1973**

Models **C-1000** and **C-800**, both with rosewood back and sides, appear in the 1970 catalog only. The entire classical line was replaced in 1971 by the rosewood **C-500** (none shipped), the rosewood **C-400,** and the mahogany **C-300** and **C-200**.
All classicals discontinued: **1973**

COMMENTS

Gibson began as a maker of carved-top instruments only, and early advertising referred to other makers' flat tops as "old style" instruments. When Gibson did introduce flat tops, early models were designed as budget or student instruments (except for the professional quality Lucas model).
In the 1930s Gibson began to develop professional quality flat tops. Some concepts, such as the X-braced top and modified dreadnought body, were appropriated from Martin (the company that developed the American-style flat top guitar). Gibson rapidly developed modern designs of its own, incorporating such features as an

adjustable truss rod, adjustable saddle(s), T-frets (which Gibson had always used), and the super jumbo body shape. Although workmanship in general on prewar Gibsons is not as neat and clean as on Martins of the same period, the Gibsons are very well-designed and lightly constructed so as to have a distinctive tone. Many players prefer Gibsons of this period to all other flat tops. Of the prewar models, those considered to be classics are the Nick Lucas, SJ-200 and all jumbos, especially the Advanced Jumbo.
Flat tops of the late 1940s and 50s are well-made, highly regarded instruments. The most highly sought after models of the 1950s are the J-200 and J-185, with all dreadnoughts highly regarded by players.
Many acoustic players consider the guitars of the 1960s to be inferior in tone due to the adjustable bridges used at the time, although in other respects construction is similar in quality to that of 1950s examples. The Everly Brothers model is highly sought after. The Dove also has some appeal to collectors. Many stage performers who desire an instrument with visual appeal regard the Hummingbird, Dove, Everly Brothers, and J-200 highly enough that these models bring prices rivaling those of 1950s models.
Flat tops from the 1970s are considered to be mediocre by consensus of players, collectors, and even the Gibson company. Workmanship on flat tops of this period was at a low point, and the double-X bracing pattern used at the time was detrimental to tone production.

ELECTRICS, GENERAL INFORMATION

Note: In the first half of 1991, Gibson has planned many changes in pickups, hardware, and general model specifications, with heavy emphasis on reissues plus some new designs. Many specs for 1991 models may differ from earlier issues.

Model Names

Letters usually denote the following: E=electric; S=Spanish; H=Hawaiian; T (before number)=tenor; T (after number)=thinline; D=double pickup; C=cutaway or (at end) cherry finish; N=natural finish

Pre–World War II electric guitar model numbers often refer to the cost of guitar and amp combinations. For example, the ES-150 guitar was originally listed with matching amp (Model EH-150) for $150.

Electric Archtop Bodies

Tops are solid spruce before World War II, laminated maple postwar except for solid spruce tops on L-5, L-5CT (Gobel), Byrdland, Super 400, floating-PU models (Johnny Smith, Citation, Kalamazoo Award), and a few Barney Kessels.

Back and sides are solid maple before World War II, laminated maple postwar, except for solid maple back and sides on L-5, Byrdland, and Super 400. From mid 1960–69, almost all L-5s, Byrdlands, and Super 400s (with pointed cutaway) have a 1- or 2-piece laminated back.

Pickups

"Charlie Christian": (never officially named Charlie Christian), V-ends, black housing, white binding around blade and outer edge of housing, large magnet (not visible) with 3 mounting screws through top...

Note: The following variations apply to guitars only. Early EH-150 lap steels have no binding around outer edge of PU. All 6-string lap steels with Christian PU have Variation #3.

Variation #1: single blade straight across PU: **1935–38**

Variation #2: single blade with notch under B-string: **1938–39**

Variation #3: single blade for 3 bass strings, 3 blades for treble strings: **1939–40**

ES-250 type: 6 non-adjustable blades,

triple-bound: **1938–40**

Christian PU available by custom order: **mid 1950s–60s**

Christian PU standard on ES-175DCC: **1978–80**

ES-100 type: single blade, rectangular white housing, large magnet (not visible) with 3 mounting screws through top: **1938–40**

ES-125 type (prewar): 6 screw poles, metal-covered: **1940–42**

ES-300 type: oblong, adjustable poles, diagonally mounted (large size, then to smaller size within a few months): **1940–42**

ES-125 type (postwar): non-adjustable poles, some with no visible poles, black plastic rectangular cover with extension "ears" to attach to top: **c. 1946–50**

P-90: single coil, adjustable poles, rectangular housing with extension "ears" to attach to top: **1946–current**

"Soapbar": same coil as P-90 but with no "ears," now referred to by Gibson as HP-90: **1952–current**

Finger rest: first cataloged as "conversion" PU, PU and controls integrated into pickguard, available with 1 or 2 non-adjustable-pole PUs for L-7, L-5 and Super 400; units factory-fitted or available as accessory, factory-fitted models designated with E until 1954 (examples: L-7E for single PU, L-7CED for cutaway with 2 PUs): **1948–71**

Alnico V: single-coil, 6 rectangular adjustable magnet-poles (Alnico V is the alloy used for the magnet), extension "ears" to attach to top, used on high-end archtops: **1953–mid 57**

Alnico V small-base version: no extension "ears"...

Les Paul Custom: **1954–mid 57**

Les Paul Custom Reissue (limited edition): **1971 only**

Humbucking: 2 coils, 1 1/2" x 2 3/4", metal cover with 1 visible row of adjustable poles...

Note: The following changes apply to guitars only. Beginning in 1956, some steel guitar models were fitted with different style humbucking PUs—some with 2 visible rows of poles, some with 4-8-4 pole configuration.

No markings on back of PU (not visible without removing PU), brass screw (from introduction): **mid 1957**

Patent-applied-for ("PAF") sticker on back, nickel-plated screw: **1957–62**

Patent number decal (patent granted July 28, 1959) on back: **mid 1962–75**

Transition to patent number decal, many examples with 1 PAF sticker and 1 patent number decal: **mid 1962–early 63**

Patent number stamped onto back (engi-

neering order dated 1974, first appearance 1975): **1975–early 91**
Some with decal on back, some stamped
Gibson USA: **early 1991–current**
Melody Maker: oblong shape, narrow coil,
plastic cover, no visible poles…
7/8" wide: **1959 only**
5/8" wide: **1960–73, 77–81**
Firebird humbucking: smaller than standard
humbucking, metal cover, no visible poles:
1963–69, reissues
Les Paul low-impedance: relatively large,
oblong shape: **1968–c. 73**
Mini-humbucking: 2 coils, 1 1/16" x 2 9/16" (first
introduced on Epiphone models, see
Epiphone section), metal cover, visible
poles: **1969–85**
P-100: same appearance as P-90 (with "ear"
extensions or soapbar) but with stacked
double-coil design: **1990–current**

Gibson embossed on PU covers…
Les Paul Professional, Personal,
Recording, and Signature models; L-5S
(as introduced): **1969-75**
Melody Maker PUs: **late 1970-72**
Some humbucking PUs: **late 1970–72**

Knobs

Smooth rounded top, bumps around top edge,
some with arrow across top, 1 black and 1
brown: **1935–39**
Smooth top, 8-sided, arrow across top, 1 black
and 1 brown: **1936–42**
"Radio," 3 sets of ridges on sides: **1936–42**
"Barrel," 5/8" high, straight-sided…
Clear with no numbers: **1946–49**
Clear with numbers 0–10 visible through
knob: **1949–early 52**
"Speed" knobs, 1/2" high, clear, barrel shape
with numbers visible through knob: mid
1953–mid 55
"Bonnet," flared base…
Plain top, numbers visible through knob:
late 1955–mid 60
Metal *tone* and *volume* caps: **mid 1960–67**
Opaque, numbers imprinted, grooved side,
sharper angle at base: **1967–early 70s**
Reissues of older style knobs: **early 1970s—
current**

Bridges and Tailpieces

Combination trapeze bridge/tailpiece…
Strings loop under bridge, Les Paul Model
only: **mid 1952–53**
Strings loop over bridge, ES-295 and ES-
225 only: **1952–59**
Stud or stop bridge/tailpiece, non-compensat-
ed…
Les Paul Model: **late 1953–55**

Les Paul Jr (from introduction) and other
low-end solidbody models: **mid
1954–62**
Stud bridge/tailpiece, compensating raised
ridge: **1962–71**
Tune-o-matic bridge: individually adjustable
metal saddles, oblong base…
No retaining wire between screw-heads
and base, stamped *ABR-1:* **1954–61**
Retaining wire between screw-heads and
base: **1961–71**
No *ABR-1* stamp: **mid 1960s–91**
Nylon saddles, models with chrome-plated
metal parts, some examples: **1961–71**
Metal saddles, no retaining wire between
screw heads and base: **1971–current**
ABR-1 stamp returns: **1991**
"Nashville" tune-o-matic, large rectangular
base: **1971–82**
TP-6 tailpiece, fine-tuners on tailpiece:
1978–current

Plating

Nickel-plated parts began to be replaced by
chrome-plated in 1965. The changeover
was accomplished faster on the more popular models.

Scales

Archtops 17" wide or wider: 25 1/2" scale,
except Byrdland (23 1/2"), ES-350T from
1955–63 (23 1/2"), Johnny Smith (25"), and
Trini Lopez Custom (24 3/4")
Archtops less than 17" wide: 24 3/4" scale,
except Chet Atkins Tennessean (25 1/2")
Solidbodies: 24 3/4" scale, except Chet Atkins
models, Flying V-90, Explorer-90 (all 25 1/2")
3/4-size models: 22 3/4" scale

Kluson Tuners

Many Gibson models (including Les Paul
Standard, ES-335, ES-345, Explorer, and
Byrdland) fitted with Kluson tuners with
plastic tuner buttons, flared to resemble a
tulip…
Single ring around button base: **1950s–early
60s**
Double ring around button base, introduced…
Models with nickel-plated metal parts:
very late 1960
Models with gold-plated metal parts:
c. 1962

ES-150 style "Charlie Christian" pickup
(installed on an ES-250).

Finger rest pickup unit on an L-7ED.

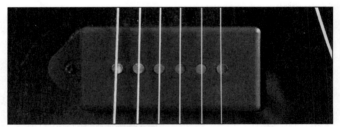

ES-125 type pickup with non-adjustable poles.

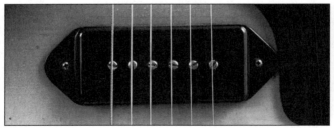

P-90 pickup on a Les Paul Jr.

Metal-covered P-90 pickup on an ES-330.

Soapbar P-90 pickup on a 1952 Les Paul.

Humbucking pickup on a Byrdland.

Mini-humbucking pickup on a Les Paul Deluxe.

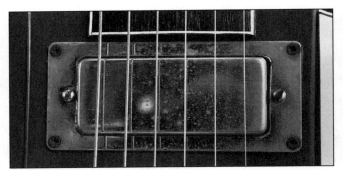

Firebird humbucking pickup.

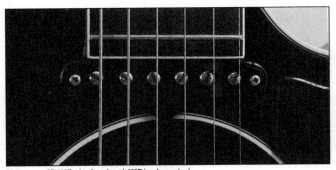

Pickup on a CF-100E, also found on J-160E (early version).

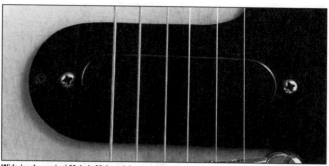

Wide (early version) Melody Maker pickup.

Narrow (later version) Melody Maker pickup.

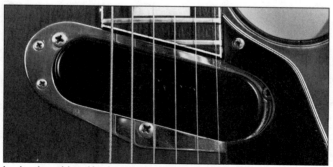

Low-impedance pickup with embossed logo on a Les Paul Recording.

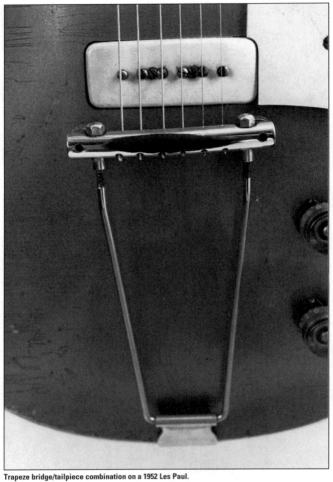

Trapeze bridge/tailpiece combination on a 1952 Les Paul.

Early 1970s-style mini-humbucking pickup with plastic cover, on an SG-II.

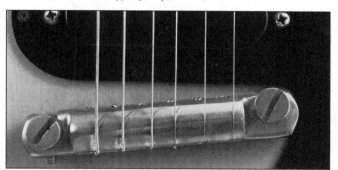

Stud bridge/tailpiece combination on a 1960s Melody Maker.

Tune-o-matic bridge, with no retaining wire between screw-heads and base, and stud tailpiece on a Les Paul Deluxe.

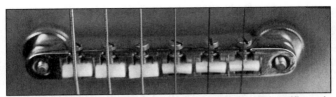

Tune-o-matic bridge, with retaining wire between screw heads and base, and nylon saddles, used on some models from 1961-71.

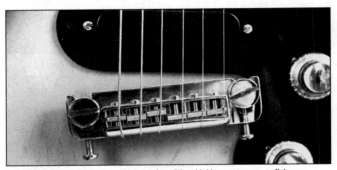

Late 1960s Melody Maker with a replacement (non-Gibson) bridge, a common retrofit item on Gibson models with stud bridge/tailpiece combination.

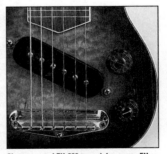

Slant-mounted EH-300 type pickup on an EH-150 from the early 1940s, knobs with rounded top, arrow, and bumps around edges (one of several pre–World War II knob styles used).

Stud bridge with compensating ridges, vibrato system on a 1964 Firebird III.

Lyre-and-logo vibrato cover and *Custom Made* plate on an early 1960s ES-335.

Clear barrel knobs on a late 1940s ES-125.

Barrel knobs with numbers, 5/8" high, on a 1952 Les Paul.

Speed knobs, barrel shape with numbers, 1/2" high, on a 1953 Les Paul.

Clear (gold-backed) bonnet knobs with plain top and numbers visible through knobs, on a late 1950s CF-100E.

Clear bonnet knobs with tone and volume caps on a 1960s ES-335.

Black bonnet knobs on a late 1960s ES-330.

Clear barrel knobs (black-backed) on a late 1970s Les Paul Artisan.

ELECTRIC ARCHTOPS KEY

Non-cutaway
    Full-depth body
        Double-parallelogram, open-book, or fancy varied-pattern inlay
            Oblong PU, slant-mounted=**ES-300, 1940–42**
            Blade PU=**ES-250**
            Pole PU(s) with ears=**ES-300, 1946–52**
        Trapezoid inlay
            Bound fingerboard
                16 1/4" wide=**ES-135**
                17" wide=**ES-150, 1950–57**
            Unbound fingerboard=**ES-125, 1946–50**
        Dot inlay
            14 1/4" wide
                Pole PU=**ES-100/ES-125, 1940–42**
                Blade PU=**ES-100, 1938–40**
            16 1/4" wide
                Prewar script logo=**ES-150, 1936–42**
                Postwar block letter logo=**ES-125, 1950–70**
            17" wide =**ES-150, 1946–50**
    Thinline body
        Melody Maker PU (oblong)=**ES-120T**
        P-90 PU (rectangular with ears)
            16 1/4" wide=**ES-125T**
            12 3/4" wide=**ES-125T 3/4**
Double cutaway, rounded horns
    Winged-*f* peghead inlay=**ES-Artist**
    5-piece split-diamond peghead inlay
        PUs mounted into top=**ES-355TD**
        Floating PUs=**Crest**
    Double-triangle peghead inlay=**ES-335-12**
    Les Paul on peghead=**Les Paul Signature**
    Lucille peghead inlay
        No Vari-Tone=**B. B. King Standard**
        Vari-Tone=**B. B. King Custom** or **B. B. King Lucille**
    Crown peghead inlay
        Small block inlay
            Full-depth body=**ES-150DC**
            Thinline body
                TP-6 tailpiece, brass nut
                    Mono, no master volume=**ES-335TD CRR**
                    Stereo, master volume=**ES-335TD CRS**
                Stop, trapeze, or Bigsby tailpiece; bone nut
                    Tone and volume for each PU=**ES-335TD, 1962–81**
                    Master volume and master mixer=**ES-340TD**
        Large block inlay=**ES-347TD**
        Single parallelogram inlay=**ES-335TD, 1969**
        Double-parallelogram inlay=**ES-345TD**
        Dot inlay
            f-holes
                PU covers
                    Orange oval label=**ES-335TD, 1958–62**
                    Beige or white oval label=**ES-335 DOT**
                Exposed PU coils=**ES-335Pr**
            No *f*-holes=**ES-335 Studio**
    No peghead ornament
        P-90 PU(s)
            1 PU=**ES-330T**
            2 PUs=**ES-330TD**
        Melody Maker PUs=**ES-320TD**
        Mini-humbucking PUs=**ES-325**
        Standard humbucking PUs
            6-on-a-side tuner arrangement=**Trini Lopez Standard**
            3-on-a-side tuner arrangement=**ES-369**

Double cutaway, pointed horns
    Bowtie inlay=**Barney Kessel Custom**
    Double-parallelogram inlay=**Barney Kessel Regular**
    Slashed-diamond inlay=**Trini Lopez Deluxe**
Single cutaway
    Chet Atkins decal on peghead=**Chet Atkins Tennessean**
    Flying bird peghead inlay=**Kalamazoo Award**
    Split-diamond peghead inlay
        PUs mounted in top
            18" wide=**Super 400 CES**
            17" wide=**Super V**
        Floating PU(s)
            1 PU
                Square-end fingerboard=**Johnny Smith**
                Pointed-end fingerboard=**Super V/BJB**
            2 PUs=**Johnny Smith Double**
    Flowerpot peghead inlay
        Wide plate tailpiece=**L-5 CES**
        Tubular tailpiece=**Byrdland**
    Vine peghead inlay
        Rosewood fingerboard=**Howard Roberts Custom**
        Ebony fingerboard=**Howard Roberts Artist**
    Double-crown peghead inlay=**Tal Farlow**
    Fleur-de-lis peghead inlay=**Citation**
    Crown peghead inlay
        Double-parallelogram fingerboard inlay
            Bound peghead
                Full-depth body=**ES-350**
                Thinline body
                    23 1/2" scale=**ES-350T, 1955–63**
                    25 1/2" scale=**ES-350T, 1977–81**
            Unbound peghead
                Gold finish=**ES-295**
                Non-gold finish
                    Full-depth body
                        Spruce top=**L-4CES**
                        Maple top
                            1 adjustable-pole PU=**ES-175**
                            2 adjustable-pole PUs=**ES-175D**
                            1 blade (Christian) PU=**ES-175CC**
                    Thinline body=**ES-175T**
        Pearl block fingerboard inlay
            4 knobs=**ES-5**
            6 knobs=**ES-5 Switchmaster**
        Red blocks on bass side=**Chet Atkins Country Gentleman**
        Dot inlay=**Howard Roberts Fusion**
No peghead ornament
    Full-depth body
        16 1/4" wide
            1 PU=**ES-125C**
            2 PUs=**ES-125CD**
         12 3/4" wide=**ES-140 3/4**
    Thinline body
        Bound fingerboard
            1 PU=**ES-225T**
            2 PUs=**ES-225TD**
        Unbound fingerboard
            16 1/4" wide
                1 PU=**ES-125 TC**
                2 PUs=**ES-125TDC**
            12 3/4" wide=**ES-140 3/4T**

ELECTRIC ARCHTOPS

SECTION ORGANIZATION
Full-depth Models
Thinlines, Non-cutaway
Thinlines, Single Cutaway
Thinlines, Double Cutaway, Semi-hollowbody
Thinlines, Double Cutaway, Fully Hollowbody
Artist Models
Acoustic Archtops With Optional Pickups

Full-depth Models

ES-150: 16 1/4" wide, X-braced top, flat back, slender *f*-holes, Charlie Christian PU with single-bound blade, 3 PU adjustment screws through top, 2 knobs, jack at tail-piece base, trapeze tailpiece with raised diamond, single-bound pickguard, single-bound top and back, single-bound rose-wood fingerboard, dot inlay, pearl logo, sunburst finish

Introduced: **1936**

Notch on PU blade under B-string: **1938**

Single PU blade for bass strings, 3 blades for treble strings: **1939**

Arched back, rectangular metal-covered adjustable-pole PU near bridge, jack on side, unbound fingerboard: **1940**

Production ceased for WWII: **1942**

ES-150 re-introduced, 17" wide, P-90 PU in neck position, jack on side, laminated beveled-edge pickguard, bound top and back, dot inlay, silkscreen logo: **1946**

Trapezoid inlay, bound fingerboard: **1950**

Discontinued (6 shipped): **1956**

EST-150: tenor version of ES-150, 16 1/4" wide, arched back, jack on side

Introduced: **1937**

EST-150 renamed **ETG-150**: **1940**

Production ceased for WWII: **1942**

ETG-150 re-introduced, still 16 1/4" wide (electric version of TG-50), 1 P-90 PU, laminated beveled-edge pickguard, bound fingerboard, dot inlay, no peghead ornament: **1946**

Discontinued: **1971**

Electric Banjo: tenor (**ETB**), 5-string (**ERB**) or plectrum (**EPB**), circular wood body with flat maple top, screwed-on back, Christian PU, 2 knobs on side, Style 7 banjo neck with large bowtie inlay on fingerboard and peghead, sunburst finish

Introduced: **1939**

Discontinued: **1943**

ES-100: 14 1/4" wide, flat back, blade PU with white rectangular housing, PU in neck position, jack on side, some with 2 sound

posts inside, single-bound top and back, rosewood fingerboard, dot inlay, silkscreen logo, no peghead ornament, sunburst finish

Introduced: **1938**

Rectangular metal-covered PU with adjustable poles, PU in bridge position: **1940**

ES-100 renamed **ES-125**: **1941**

Production ceased for WWII: **1942**

ES-125 re-introduced, 16 1/4" wide, black eared PU with 6 non-adjustable poles, some with no visible poles, PU in neck position, tor-toise grain pickguard, trapeze tailpiece with raised diamond, single-bound top and back, unbound fingerboard, pearloid trape-zoid inlay, silkscreened logo, sunburst finish: **1946**

Some all mahogany body and dot inlay: **1946**

Plain tailpiece, dot inlay, by **1950**

Standard P-90 PU : **c. 1951**

ES-125 discontinued: **1970**

ES-125C: 16 1/4" wide, pointed cutaway, 1 P-90 PU

ES-125CD: 2 PUs

Introduced: **1966**

Discontinued: **1971**

ES-125T, ES-125T 3/4: See Thinlines, Non-Cutaway, following

ES-125TC: See Thinlines, Single Cutaway, fol-lowing

ES-250: 17" wide, carved maple back, triple-bound Christian PU with 6 blades, jack at tailpiece base, plate tailpiece with pointed ends and raised diamond and arrows, triple-bound pickguard, wide triple-binding on top and back, single-bound rosewood fingerboard, open-book inlay, carved stairstep peghead, metal tuner buttons, pearl logo, sunburst or natural finish

Variation: single-bound non-stairstep peghead

Variation: double-parallelogram inlay

Variation: fancy rectangular-enclosed inlay (like 1937 L-7)

Variation: postwar logo, P-90 PU (bodies and necks probably leftover prewar stock)

Introduced: **1939**

Discontinued: **1940**

ES-300: 17" wide, large slant-mounted oblong PU with adjustable poles, jack on side, L-5 style plate tailpiece with center insert missing, triple-bound top and back, bound pickguard, maple neck, double-parallelo-gram inlay, single-bound peghead, crown peghead inlay (first Gibson model with crown), pearl logo, sunburst or natural finish

Variation: 7-piece split-diamond peghead inlay

119

Electric Archtops

Introduced: **1940**

Smaller slant-mounted PU, trapeze tailpiece with pointed ends and raised arrows: **1941**

Production ceased for WWII: **1942**

ES-300 re-introduced, P-90 PU in neck position, trapeze tailpiece with pointed ends and 3 raised parallelograms (early with plate tailpiece with 2 *f*-hole cutouts), laminated beveled-edge pickguard (early with bound pickguard), triple-bound top and back, bound peghead and fingerboard, double-parallelogram inlay, crown peghead inlay, sunburst or natural finish: **1946**

2 P-90 PUs, 2 volume knobs on lower treble bout, master tone knob on upper treble bout: **1948**

Discontinued: **1952**

ES-350 (originally **ES-350 Premier**): rounded cutaway version of ES-300, 17" wide, 1 P-90 PU, trapeze tailpiece with pointed ends and 3 raised parallelograms, laminated beveled-edge pickguard (early with bound pickguard), triple-bound top and back, single-bound peghead and fingerboard, double-parallelogram inlay, crown peghead inlay, gold-plated metal parts, sunburst or natural finish

Introduced: **1947**

2 P-90 PUs (single-PU model pictured in ads into 1949 but not offered in catalog), 2 volume knobs on lower treble bout, master tone knob on cutaway bout: **1948**

4 knobs, toggle switch: **1952**

Tune-o-matic bridge: **1956**

Discontinued as full-depth model, replaced by **ES-350T**: see Thinlines, Single Cutaway, following: **1956**

ES-5: 17" wide, rounded cutaway, 3 P-90 PUs, 3 volume controls, 1 master tone knob on cutaway bout, trapeze tailpiece with pointed ends and 3 raised parallelograms, laminated beveled-edge pickguard, triple-bound top and back, bound *f*-holes (a few early with unbound *f*-holes), pointed-end fingerboard with 5-ply binding, large block inlay, single-bound peghead, crown peghead inlay, gold-plated metal parts, sunburst or natural finish

Introduced: **1949**

Tune-o-matic bridge, Alnico V PUs specified (but virtually all with P-90s), 5-ply top and back binding, by **1955**

Renamed **ES-5 Switchmaster**: 3 P-90 PUs, 6 knobs, separate volume and tone controls for each PU, 4-way slotted switch on cutaway bout: **late 1955**

Tubular tailpiece with double-loop design: **1956**

Humbucking PUs: **mid 1957**

Pointed cutaway, most with 1- or 2-piece lami-nated back: **late 1960**

Discontinued: **1962**

ES-175: 16 1/4" wide, pointed cutaway, 1 P-90 PU in neck position, 2 knobs, trapeze tail-piece with pointed ends and 3 raised par-allelograms, laminated beveled-edge pick-guard, triple-bound top, single-bound back, single-bound fingerboard, double-parallel-ogram inlay, crown peghead inlay, sun-burst or natural finish

Introduced: **1949**

ES-175D: 2 PUs, introduced: **1953**

Some with Alnico V PU(s) (rare): **early to mid 1950s**

Tailpiece with T in center and zigzag tubes on sides, on 2-PU model only; pointed-end tailpiece remains on single-PU model: **late 1956**

Humbucking PUs, both models: **mid 1957**

ES-175 (single PU) discontinued: **1971**

Back to original pointed-end tailpiece: **early 1970s**

Tune-o-matic bridge by **1977**

ES-175CC: Charlie Christian PU, 3 screws into top, adjustable rosewood bridge, sunburst or walnut stain finish, available: **1978–79 only**

Mahogany back and sides: **1983**

Maple back and sides: **late 1990**

ES-175D still in production

ES-175T: see Thinlines, Single Cutaway, following

ES-140 (3/4): 12 3/4" wide, pointed cutaway, 1 P-90 PU, trapeze tailpiece, single-bound top and back, 22 3/4" scale, dot inlay, sun-burst finish

Introduced: **1950**

Natural finish optional (rare): **1955**

Discontinued as full-depth model, replaced by **ES-140 3/4T**: see Thinlines, Single Cutaway, following: **1957**

L-5 CES: electric version of L-5C, 17" wide, rounded cutaway, solid carved spruce top, carved maple back, maple sides, 2 P-90 PUs, single-bound *f*-holes, multiple-bound everywhere else, pointed-end ebony fin-gerboard, block inlay, flowerpot peghead inlay, sunburst or natural finish

Introduced: **1951**

Alnico V PUs: **1953**

Humbucking PUs: **1958**

Pointed cutaway, most with 1- or 2-piece lami-nated back: **mid 1960**

Rounded cutaway, solid 2-piece back: **mid to late 1969**

Still in production

L-5S: see Gibson Solidbodies section

120

Super V CES: same as L-5 CES but with Super 400 neck and peghead, 6-finger tailpiece, antique sunburst or natural finish
Introduced: **1978**
Still cataloged

Super V/BJB: same as Super V CES but with 1 floating PU
Introduced: **1978**
Discontinued: **1984**

Super 400 CES: electric version of Super 400C, 18" wide, rounded cutaway, solid carved spruce top, carved maple back, maple sides, 2 P-90 PUs, multiple-bound everywhere including *f*-holes, ebony fingerboard, split-block inlay, 5-piece split-diamond peghead inlay, sunburst or natural finish
Introduced: **1951**
Alnico V PUs: **1953**
Humbucking PUs: **1958**
Pointed cutaway, most with 1- or 2-piece laminated back: **mid 1960**
Rounded cutaway, solid 2-piece back: **mid to late 1969**
Still in catalog

ES-295: ES-175 body and neck, 16 1/4" wide, pointed cutaway, 2 P-90 PUs with white covers, clear pickguard back-painted with white background and gold floral design, trapeze bridge/tailpiece combo with strings looping over bridge, triple-bound top, single-bound back and fingerboard, 19-fret fingerboard, double-parallelogram inlay, crown peghead inlay, gold-plated metal parts, gold finish
Introduced: **1952**
20-fret fingerboard: **1955**
Humbucking PUs: **late 1958**
Last made: **1958**

ES-130: 16 1/4" wide, 1 P-90 PU, trapeze tailpiece with raised diamond, laminated beveled-edge pickguard, single-bound top and back, single-bound fingerboard, trapezoid inlay, no peghead ornament, sunburst finish
Introduced: **1954**
Renamed **ES-135**: **mid 1956**
Discontinued: **1958**

L-4CES: 16 1/4" wide, pointed cutaway, solid spruce top, bound rosewood fingerboard, double-parallelogram inlay, crown peghead inlay
A few with Charlie Christian PU or humbucking PU (no catalog or shipping record): **late 1950s**
9 shipped: **1969**
Re-introduced, carved spruce top, mahogany back and sides, 2 humbucking PUs, 4 knobs, 1 switch on upper bass bout, tune-o-matic bridge, L-5 type plate tailpiece, multiple-bound pickguard, triple-bound top and back, gold-plated metal parts: **1987**
Still in production

ES-150DC: double rounded cutaway, 3" deep, 2 humbucking PUs, 4 knobs on lower treble bout, master volume knob on upper treble bout, triple-bound top, single-bound back, single-bound fingerboard, small block inlay, crown peghead inlay, natural, walnut, or cherry finish
Introduced: **1969**
Discontinued: **1975**

Thinlines, Non-cutaway

ES-125T: thinline ES-125, 16 1/4" wide, P-90 PU, trapeze tailpiece, single-bound top and back, unbound fingerboard, dot inlay, decal logo, sunburst finish
Introduced: **1956**
ES-125T 3/4: 12 3/4" wide, 22 3/4" scale, introduced: **1957**
ES-125TD: 2 PUs, introduced: **1957**
ES-125TD discontinued: **1964**
ES-125T and ES-125T 3/4 discontinued: **1969**

ES-120T: 16 1/4" wide, 1 *f*-hole, Melody Maker PU mounted on pickguard, knobs and jack mounted on pickguard, single-bound top and back, dot inlay, decal logo, sunburst finish
Introduced: **1962**
Discontinued: **1971**

Thinlines, Single Cutaway

ES-225T: 16 1/4" wide, pointed cutaway, P-90 PU in middle position, trapeze bridge/tailpiece combo with strings looping over bridge, laminated beveled-edge pickguard, single-bound top and back, single-bound fingerboard, dot inlay, pearl logo, no peghead ornament, sunburst or natural finish
Introduced: **1955**
ES-225TD: 2 PUs, introduced: **1956**
ES-225T and ES-225TD discontinued: **1959**

Byrdland: named for Billy Byrd and Hank Garland, thinbody short-scale version of L-5CES, 17" wide, rounded cutaway, 2 1/4" deep, carved maple back, 2 Alnico V PUs, triple-loop tubular tailpiece with *Byrdland* engraved on crosspiece, tortoise grain pickguard (a few early with pearloid), 7-ply top binding, triple-bound back, 7-ply pickguard binding, single-bound *f*-holes, ebony fingerboard with pointed end, 5-ply fingerboard binding, 23 1/2" scale, narrow neck, narrow string spacing and narrow PU pole spacing, block inlay, flowerpot peghead

inlay, 7-ply peghead binding, gold-plated metal parts, sunburst or natural finish
Introduced: **1955**
Humbucking PUs: **1958**
A few with humbucking bridge PU and Christian neck PU: **mid 1957–71**
Pointed cutaway, most with 1- or 2-piece lam-inated back: **late 1960**
Stereo and Vari-tone switch (rare): **late 1960–68**
Rounded cutaway, solid 2-piece back: **mid to late 1969**
Still in production

ES-350T (later renamed TD): 17" wide, rounded cutaway, 2 P-90 PUs, tune-o-matic bridge, tailpiece with W-shape tubular design and *ES-350T* on oblong crosspiece, laminated beveled-edge pickguard, triple-bound top and back, neck/body joint at 14th fret, 23 1/2" scale, single-bound fingerboard and peghead, double-parrallelogram inlay, crown peghead inlay, gold-plated metal parts, sunburst or natural finish
Introduced: **1955**
Humbucking PUs: **mid 1957**
Pointed cutaway: **late 1960**
Discontinued: **1963**
Re-introduced: rounded cutaway, 2 humbuck-ing PUs, tune-o-matic bridge, tubular triple-loop tailpiece with *ES-350T*, neck/body joint at 14th fret, 25 1/2" scale, sunburst, fireburst (redder than standard sunburst), or natural finish: **1977**
Fireburst discontinued: **1979**
Discontinued: **1981**

ES-140 3/4T: 12 3/4" wide, pointed cutaway, 1 P-90 PU, single-bound top and back, 22 3/4" scale, dot inlay, no peghead ornament, sunburst or natural finish
Introduced, replacing ES-140 3/4 full-depth model: **1957**
Natural finish discontinued: **1959**
Discontinued: **1968**

L-5 CEST: electric version of L-5CT (see Acoustic Archtops section), rounded cut-away, 2 humbucking PUs, cherry or sun-burst finish
Available: **1959–61**

ES-125TC and **ES-125TCD**: ES-125T with point-ed cutaway, 16 1/4" wide, 1 or 2 P-90 PUs, single-bound top and back, unbound fin-gerboard, decal logo, sunburst finish
Introduced: **1960**
Cherry sunburst finish: **1961**
ES-125TCD renamed **ES-125TDC**: **1961**
ES-125TC (single PU model) discontinued: **1970**
ES-125TDC (2-PU model) discontinued: **1971**

ES-175T: 16" wide, pointed cutaway, 1 7/8" deep, 2 humbucking PUs, 4 knobs on lower treble bout, 1 switch on upper bass bout, laminated beveled-edge pickguard, tune-o-matic bridge, trapeze tailpiece with pointed ends and 3 raised parallelograms, triple-bound top and back, single-bound rosewood fingerboard, double-parallelo-gram inlay, crown peghead inlay, pearl logo, wine red, natural, or sunburst finish
Introduced: **1976**
Discontinued: **1980**

Thinlines, Double Cutaway, Semi-hollowbody

All are 16" wide, 1 5/8" deep, with 24 3/4" scale. All have maple block down middle of body. From Dec. 1972–Aug. 1975 (dates of Gibson engineering orders; dates of implementa-tion may be several months later), maple block extends from tailpiece to endpin only.

ES-335TD: 2 humbucking PUs, 2 tone and 2 vol-ume knobs, 1 switch, tune-o-matic bridge, stop tailpiece, Bigsby vibrato optional (most models fitted with Bigsby have *Custom made* plate covering original tail-piece holes; some without holes or plate), laminated beveled-edge pickguard extends below bridge, single-bound top and back, neck-body joint at 19th fret, single-bound rosewood fingerboard (early with unbound fingerboard), dot inlay, crown peghead inlay, sunburst or natural finish
Introduced: **spring 1958**
Cherry finish optional: **late 1959**
Shorter pickguard does not extend below bridge: **early 1961**
Small pearloid block inlay: **mid 1962**
Trapeze tailpiece (some with stop tailpiece in 1965): **late 1964**
Some with single-parallelogram inlay (very rare), walnut finish optional: **1969**
Coil-tap switch on upper treble bout: **1977**
Discontinued, replaced by ES-335 DOT: **1982**

ES-335 DOT: reissue of 1960 ES-335, 4 knobs, 1 switch, tune-o-matic bridge, stop tailpiece, dot inlay
Introduced: **1982**
Still in production

ES-335-12: 12-string, double-triangle peghead inlay, otherwise same specs and changes as ES-335
Introduced: **1965**
Discontinued: **1971**

ES-335Pro: 2 Dirty Fingers humbucking PUs with exposed coils, tune-o-matic bridge, stop tailpiece, bound fingerboard, dot inlay, antique sunburst or cherry red finish
Introduced: **1979**
Discontinued: **1982**

ES-335TD CRS: Country Rock Stereo model, 2 PUs, stereo electronics, coil-tap switch, master volume control, TP-6 tailpiece, brass nut, country tobacco or Dixie brown (pink-to-brown sunburst) finish
300 instruments made: **1979**

ES-335TD CRR: Country Rock Regular model, 2 Dirty Fingers humbucking PUs with exposed coils, coil-tap switch, brass nut, antique sunburst finish
300 instruments made: **1979**

ES-335 Studio: no ƒ-holes, 2 exposed-coil humbucking PUs, single-bound top and back, unbound rosewood fingerboard, dot inlay, no peghead ornament, decal logo
Introduced: **1987**
Still in production

ES-335S: see Gibson Solidbodies

ES-340TD: identical in appearance to ES-335 except for laminated maple neck (ES-335 has mahogany neck during entire production period of ES-340), 2 humbucking PUs, master volume control and master mixer control, walnut or natural finish
Introduced: **1969**
Discontinued (9 shipped): **1974**

ES-345 TD: 2 humbucking PUs, stereo electronics (separates PUs and necessitates a Y-chord), Vari-tone rotary tone selector, black ring around Vari-tone switch, tune-o-matic bridge, stop tailpiece, laminated beveled-edge pickguard extends below bridge, triple-bound top, bound back, neck/body joint at 19th fret, single-bound rosewood fingerboard, double-parallelo-gram inlay, crown peghead inlay, gold-plated metal parts, sunburst or natural finish
Introduced: **1959**
Cherry finish optional: **late 1959**
Shorter pickguard does note extend below bridge: **early 1961**
Gold ring around Vari-tone switch: **1960**
Last natural finish shipped: **1960**
Trapeze tailpiece with raised diamond: **late 1964**
Walnut finish optional: **1969**
Stop tailpiece: **1982**
Discontinued: **1982**

ES-347TD: 2 humbucking PUs, 4 knobs and 1 PU selector switch on lower treble bout, coil-tap switch on upper treble bout, tune-o-matic bridge, TP-6 tailpiece, laminated beveled-edge pickguard, single-bound top and back, single-bound ebony fingerboard, large block inlay, single-bound peghead, crown peghead inlay, pearl logo
Introduced: **1978**
Multiple-bound peghead by: **1988**
Still in production

ES-355TD: 2 humbucking PUs, mono circuitry, tune-o-matic bridge, Bigsby vibrato (avail-able without vibrato but extremely rare), multiple-bound pickguard extends below bridge, multiple-bound top, triple-bound back, single-bound ƒ-holes, neck/body joint at 19th fret, single-bound ebony fingerboard, large block inlay, multiple-bound peghead, 5-piece split-diamond peghead inlay, Grover Rotomatic tuners, cherry finish
Introduced (a few shipped in 1958): **1959**
Stereo electronics (separates PUs and necessitates a Y-chord) with Vari-tone rotary tone selector (**ES-355 TDSV**) optional but more common than mono, round Vari-tone knob in catalog photos through 1962 but virtually all with pointed knob: **1959**
Shorter pickguard does not extend below bridge: **early 1961**
Vibrato with side-to-side action: **1961**
Kluson tuners: **1961**
Gibson vibrato with lyre on coverplate: **1963**
Grover tuners by **1967**
Walnut finish optional: **1969**
Bigsby vibrato: **1969**
Non-stereo, non-Vari-tone (ES-355TD) discon-tinued: **1970**
Gibson vibrato with lyre on coverplate by **1978**
Discontinued: **1982**

ES-320TD: 2 Melody Maker PUs with embossed logo, oblong metal control plate with 2 knobs and 2 slide switches, tune-o-matic bridge, nickel-plated bridge cover with logo, black plastic pickguard, bound top and back (black-painted edges to sim-ulate binding on natural finish models), rosewood fingerboard, dot inlay, decal logo, natural, walnut, or cherry finish
Introduced: **1971**
Discontinued (10 shipped in 1975): **1974**

ES-325TD: 1 ƒ-hole, semi-circular plastic con-trol plate, 4 knobs, 2 mini-humbucking PUs with no visible poles, tune-o-matic bridge, trapeze tailpiece with pointed ends, single-bound top and back, dot inlay, cherry or walnut finish
Introduced: **1972**

Electric Archtops

Wine red finish optional: **1976**
Discontinued (2 shipped in 1979): **1978**

ES-Artist: 1 3/4" deep, no *f*-holes, 2 humbucking PUs, active electronics, 3 knobs, 1 PU selector switch, 3 mini-toggle switches, tune-o-matic bridge, TP-6 tailpiece, laminated beveled-edge pickguard, multiple-bound top and back, single-bound ebony fingerboard, dot inlay positioned close to bass edge of fingerboard, winged-*f* peghead inlay, pearl logo, gold-plated metal parts
Introduced: **1979**
Discontinued: **1986**

B. B. King Standard: no *f*-holes, 2 humbucking PUs, tune-o-matic bridge, TP-6 tailpiece, stereo electronics with 2 jacks, laminated beveled-edge pickguard, multiple-bound top and back, single-bound rosewood fingerboard, dot inlay, *Lucille* peghead inlay, chrome-plated metal parts, ebony or cherry finish
B. B. King Custom: no *f*-holes, 2 humbucking PUs, Vari-tone rotary tone selector switch, tune-o-matic bridge, TP-6 tailpiece, stereo wiring with 2 jacks, multiple-bound top and back, single-bound pickguard, ebony fingerboard, large block inlay, *Lucille* peghead inlay, gold-plated metal parts, ebony or cherry finish
Introduced: **1980**
B. B. King Standard discontinued: **1985**
B. B. King Custom renamed **B. B. King Lucille**: **1988**
Still in production

ES-369: designed to use up leftover parts, 2 Dirty Fingers PUs with exposed coils, 4 speed knobs, 1 selector switch, 1 mini-toggle coil-tap switch, tune-o-matic bridge, TP-6 tailpiece, single-ply cream-colored pickguard, single-bound top and back, single-bound rosewood fingerboard, pearloid trapezoid inlay, snakehead peghead, old-style script logo
Available: **1982 only**

Thinlines, Double Cutaway, Fully Hollowbody

ES-330T: double rounded cutaway, shorter neck than 335 series, 1 black plastic-covered P-90 PU in middle position, tune-o-matic bridge, trapeze tailpiece, single-bound top and back, bound fingerboard, dot inlay, pearl logo, no peghead ornament, sunburst or natural finish
ES-330TD: 2 black plastic-covered P-90 PUs, sunburst or natural finish
Introduced: **1959**

Cherry finish optional, natural discontinued by **1962**
Block inlay: **mid 1962**
Chrome PU cover(s): **late 1962**
ES-330T (single-PU model) discontinued: **1963**
Sparkling burgundy finish optional: **1967–69**
Walnut finish optional: **1968**
Full length neck (ES-335 type): **1969**
ES-330TD discontinued: **1972**

Crest: double rounded cutaway, flat back (some with arched back), laminated Brazilian rosewood body, 2 floating mini-humbucking PUs, multiple-bound rosewood pickguard, adjustable rosewood bridge, multiple-bound top, triple-bound back, single-bound *f*-holes, backstripe marquetry, neck/body joint at 16th fret 24 3/4" scale, block inlay, multiple-bound peghead, 5-piece split-diamond peghead inlay, Crest Gold with gold-plated metal parts or Crest Silver with silver-plated metal parts
Introduced: **1969**
Discontinued: **1972**

Artist Models

Byrdland: Billy Byrd and Hank Garland model (see Thinlines, Single Cutaway, preceding)

Johnny Smith: 17" wide, 3 1/8" deep (not as deep as L-5), single rounded cutaway, carved spruce top, maple back and sides, X-braced top, 1 (**JS**) or 2 (**JSD**) floating mini-humbucking PUs on pickguard, adjustable ebony bridge, L-5 style tailpiece with model name on center insert, multiple-bound top and back, 25" scale, multiple-bound ebony fingerboard with square end, split-block inlay, multiple-bound peghead, 5-piece split-diamond peghead inlay, gold-plated metal parts, sunburst or natural finish
JS introduced: **1961**
JSD introduced: **1963**
6-finger tailpiece by **1979**
Discontinued: **1989**

Barney Kessel Regular: 17" wide, full-depth body (a few with laminated spruce top), double pointed cutaway, 2 humbucking PUs, tune-o-matic bridge, trapeze tailpiece with raised diamond, model name on wood tailpiece insert, laminated beveled-edge pickguard, triple-bound top and back, 25 1/2" scale, bound rosewood fingerboard, double-parallelogram inlay, bound peghead, crown peghead inlay, nickel-plated metal parts, cherry sunburst finish
Barney Kessel Custom: bowtie inlay, musical note peghead inlay, gold-plated metal

parts
Introduced: **1961**
Both models discontinued: **1974**

Tal Farlow: full-depth body, deep rounded cutaway, binding material inlaid in cutaway to simulate scroll, 2 humbucking PUs, 4-point single-bound pickguard, toggle switch just below pickguard, tune-o-matic bridge, trapeze tailpiece with raised diamond, model name on wood tailpiece insert, triple-bound top, 25 1/2" scale, bound fingerboard, fingerboard inlay like inverted J-200 crest inlay, bound peghead, double-crown peghead inlay, viceroy brown finish
Introduced: **1962**
Discontinued: **1971**

Trini Lopez Standard: ES-335 thinline body, 16" wide, double rounded cutaway, diamond-shaped soundholes, 2 humbucking PUs, tune-o-matic bridge, trapeze tailpiece with raised diamond, model name on wood tailpiece insert, laminated beveled-edge pickguard, single-bound top and back, 24 3/4" scale, bound fingerboard, slashed-diamond inlay, 6-on-a-side tuners, no peghead ornament, decal logo, cherry finish standard, many with sparkling burgundy finish, a few with Pelham blue finish

Trini Lopez Deluxe: full-depth body, double pointed cutaway (like Barney Kessel models), diamond-shaped soundholes, 2 humbucking PUs, 3-way PU selector on treble cutaway bout, standby switch on bass cutaway bout, tune-o-matic bridge, trapeze tailpiece with raised diamond, model name on wood tailpiece insert, bound pickguard, pickguard cutout for switch, triple-bound top and back, bound fingerboard and peghead, slashed-diamond inlay, 6-on-a-side tuner arrangment, no peghead ornament, cherry sunburst finish
Introduced: **1964**
Both models discontinued: **1971**

Les Paul Signature: 16" wide, thin body, asymmetrical double rounded cutaway, 2 oblong low-impedance humbucking PUs with white covers, 2 jacks (1 on top, 1 on side), trapezoid inlay, sunburst or gold finish
Introduced: **1973**
Rectangular PUs: **1975**
High/low impedance humbucking PUs: **1976**
Sunburst finish discontinued: **1976**
Discontinued: **1978**

Howard Roberts Custom: 16" wide, full-depth body, pointed cutaway, laminated maple top, oval hole, 1 floating humbucking PU, height-adjustable ebony bridge, multiple-bound pickguard, multiple-bound top and back, single-bound rosewood fingerboard, slotted-block inlay, multiple-bound peghead, vine-pattern peghead inlay, chrome-plated metal parts, sunburst or cherry finish
Note: Howard Roberts Customs from 1974-76 may have a Howard Roberts Artist *label (see Model Names in General Information section), but the Howard Roberts Artist model did not exist at that time.*
Revived from Epiphone line (with changes): **1974**
Sunburst or wine red finish: **1975**
Discontinued: **1981**

Howard Roberts Artist: same as Howard Roberts Custom but with ebony fingerboard, gold-plated metal parts, sunburst, natural, or wine red finish
Introduced: **1976**
2 PUs optional: **1979**
Discontinued: **1981**

Howard Roberts Fusion: 14 7/8" wide, semi-hollowbody, 2 5/16" deep, cutaway shape similar to Les Paul solidbody models, 2 humbucking PUs, tune-o-matic bridge, TP-6 tailpiece, triple-bound top, bound back, dot inlay, crown peghead inlay, sunburst, fireburst, or ebony finish
Introduced: **1979**
6-finger tailpiece: **1990**
Still in production

B. B. King Custom, B. B. King Standard: see Thinlines, Semi-Hollowbody, preceding

Chet Atkins Country Gentleman: 17" wide, rounded cutaway, thinline semi-hollowbody, 2 humbucking PUs, 3 knobs and 1 switch on lower treble bout, master volume knob on cutaway bout, tune-o-matic bridge, Bigsby vibrato with curved tubular arm, 7-ply top binding, 5-ply back binding, single-bound *f*-holes, laminated maple neck, 25 1/2" scale, unbound ebony fingerboard, red rectangular inlays positioned on bass edge of fingerboard, unbound peghead, crown peghead inlay, metal tuner buttons, gold-plated metal parts, ebony, wine red, or Country Gentleman brown finish
Introduced: **1987**
Sunrise orange finish optional: **1990**
Still in production

Chet Atkins Tennessean: 16 1/4" wide, 1 5/8" deep, single rounded cutaway, laminated maple back and sides, 2 humbucking PUs, tune-o-matic bridge, stop tailpiece, clear

pickguard with silver paint on back and model name stenciled in black, single-bound top and back, 25 1/2" scale, unbound ebony fingerboard, dot inlay positioned closer to bass edge of fingerboard, clear plastic truss rod cover back-painted silver, Chet Atkins signature peghead decal, plastic tuner buttons, orange, wine red, Country Gentleman brown, or ebony finish
Introduced: **1990**
Still in production

Acoustic Archtops With Optional Pickups

Citation: 17" wide, full-depth body, rounded cutaway, solid carved spruce top, solid maple sides, carved maple back, 1 or 2 floating mini-humbucking PUs (some without visible polepieces), wood pickguard with fleur-de-lis inlay, control knob(s) on pickguard, fancy tailpiece, multiple-bound top and back, 25 1/2" scale, bound pointed-end fingerboard, cloud inlay, multiple-bound peghead, fleur-de-lis inlays on front and back of peghead and on bridge, gold-plated metal parts, varnish (non-lacquer) finish in sunburst or natural
Introduced: **1969**
Discontinued: **1971**
Catalogued: **1975**
New series introduced: **1979**
Discontinued: **c. 1981**

Kalamazoo Award: 17" wide, full-depth body, rounded cutaway, solid carved spruce top, solid maple sides, carved maple back, 1 floating mini-humbucking PU (some without visible polepieces), adjustable ebony bridge with pearl inlays, wood pickguard with abalone inlay, knobs mounted on pickguard, multiple-bound top and back, bound f-holes, bound ebony fingerboard, abalone block inlay, multiple-bound peghead, flying bird peghead inlay, gold-plated metal parts, varnish (non-lacquer) finish in antique sunburst or natural
Introduced: **1978**
Discontinued: **1985**

COMMENTS

Prewar: Gibson was the first company to manufacture a commercially viable hollowbody electric. Unlike the earliest efforts of Rickenbacker, Epiphone, or National, the earliest Gibson electrics are still considered to be superb jazz guitars. The ES-150 and ES-250, both of which were used by Charlie Christian, are more highly regarded than any other prewar electric guitar.

Postwar full-depth: Non-cutaway models, except for the early post-war ES-300, were generally designed as student models and do not command high prices. Deluxe models, such as the L-5CES and Super 400CES, are considered by musicians and collectors to be among the finest instruments of their type ever produced. The laminated-body models, originally cheaper than the L-5CES and Super 400CES, are also fine instruments. Early ES-350s and ES-5s (without toggle switch or slide switch) have somewhat less utility than later versions but are fine instruments. The ES-5 Switchmaster, ES-350 (with toggle switch, 1952–56), ES-175 and ES-295 are very highly regarded.

Thinlines, fully hollow, single cutaway: The Byrdland is unsurpassed in quality, but because of its short scale and narrow neck, it brings much less than the extremely rare L-5CEST. The ES-350T was popularized by Chuck Berry, but is also somewhat limited in market appeal by its narrow, short-scale neck. Other single-cutaway thinlines are much less sought after.

Thinlines, double cutaway: The thinline design, double-cutaway body shape and semi-solid construction are Gibson innovations that have been widely copied by other makers. Early ES-335, ES-345, and ES-355 models are highly sought after. The ES-335, which had the lowest list price of the three, brings the highest price. The early version with PAF humbucking pickups, dot inlay, and stop tailpiece is considered one of Gibson's classic models. The Vari-Tone system of the ES-345 and the tremolo that was standard on the ES-355 make them less desirable than the ES-335. Natural finish models bring better prices than sunburst or cherry. Fully hollow thinlines have never had the market appeal of the semi-solid models.

Artist models: All are of fine quality. The Tal Farlow is the most sought after. The Johnny Smith and others with acoustic construction and floating PUs are very highly regarded. Kessel and Lopez models have never had a great market appeal.

The Citation is one of the most modern Gibson models to be revered by collectors, with market prices among the highest for acoustic or electric-acoustic Gibsons from any period. The Kalamazoo Award is also highly regarded.

LES PAULS, SGs, AND MELODY MAKERS KEY

Single cutaway
    3-piece top with walnut center piece=**Les Paul Spotlight Special**
    Carved top
        1 P-90 and 1 Alnico V PU
            Les Paul Custom, 1954–57
            Les Paul Custom '54 (reissue)
        Soapbar PUs
            Ebony fingerboard=**Les Paul Pro-Deluxe**
            Rosewood fingerboard
                Gibson on PU covers=**Les Paul Standard '58** (reissue)
                Plain PU covers
                    Uniform binding depth
                        Les Paul Model, 1952–57
                        Les Paul Reissue Goldtop, 1990-current
                    Deeper cutaway binding=**Les Paul Standard** (reissue 1)
        Oblong low-impedance PUs
            Block inlay
                Guitar jack on top=**Les Paul Recording**
                Mic jack and guitar jack on side=**Les Paul Personal**
            Trapezoid inlay=**Les Paul Professional**
    Humbucking PUs in 5-sided frames=**The Les Paul**
    Standard humbucking PUs
        Hearts-and-flowers inlay=**Les Paul Artisan**
        Slashed-block inlay=**25th Anniversary Les Paul**
        Abalone block inlay=**The Les Paul**
        Pearl block inlay
            Script *LP* peghead inlay=**L.P. Artist**
            5-piece split-diamond peghead inlay
                Contoured back=**Les Paul Custom Lite**
                Flat back
                    Les Paul Custom
                    Les Paul Custom reissue
                    Les Paul Custom/maple fingerboard
                    Les Paul Custom/nickel-plated parts
                    Les Paul Custom/3 pickups
                    Les Paul Custom 35th Anniversary
        Pearl trapezoid inlay
            Exposed-coil PUs=**Les Paul Kalamazoo**
            Covered PUs=**Les Paul 30th Anniversary**
        Pearloid trapezoid inlay
            Unbound top
                No pickguard=**Les Paul Studio Lite, 1991–current**
                Pickguard=**Les Paul Studio, 1990–current**
            Bound top
                No name on truss rod cover
                    Goldtop
                      Les Paul Model, mid 1957–mid 58
                      Les Paul Reissue Goldtop
                  Cherry sunburst top
                    Uniform binding depth
                      Les Paul Standard, mid 1958–60
                      Les Paul Reissue 2nd reissue
                      Guitar Trader and other limited edition reissues
                  Deeper binding in cutaway=**Les Paul CMT**
            Standard on rod cover=**Les Paul Standard, 1976-current**
            Heritage 80 on truss rod cover
                Rosewood fingerboard=**Les Paul Heritage 80**
                Ebony fingerboard=**Les Paul Heritage 80 Elite**
            Classic on truss rod cover=**Les Paul Classic 1960**

Single Cutaway, carved top, humbucking PUs (cont.)
    Dot inlay
        Unbound top
            No coil-tap switch=**Les Paul Studio, 1984–89**
            Coil-tap switch
                Rosewood fingerboard=**L.P. XR-1**
                Ebony fingerboard=**Les Paul Studio Lite, 1988–90**
        Single-bound top
            No coil-tap switch=**Les Paul Studio Standard**
            Coil tap-switch=**L.P. XR-II**
        Multiple-bound top=**Les Paul Studio Custom**
    Mini-humbucking PUs=**Les Paul Deluxe**
Flat top
    1 PU with visible poles
        Standard peghead
            Sunburst or cherry finish
                24 3/4" scale
                    Stud bridge/tailpiece=**Les Paul Jr., 1954–58**
                    Tune-o-matic bridge=**Les Paul Jr.** reissue
                22 3/4" scale=**Les Paul Jr. 3/4**
            Limed mahogany finish=**Les Paul TV**
        Narrow peghead=**Melody Maker** reissue
    1 PU with no visible poles
        24 3/4" scale=**Melody Maker, 1959–60**
         22 3/4"scale=**Melody Maker 3/4, 1959–60**
    2 PUs with visible poles
        Rosewood fingerboard
            Stud bridge/tailpiece=**Les Paul Special**
            Tune-o-matic bridge
                Les Paul Special on peghead
                    Les Paul Special reissue
                    Les Paul Jr. II
                Les Paul Model on peghead=**Les Paul 55**
        Ebony fingerboard
            Walnut body=**The Paul**
            Mahogany body=**The Paul Deluxe**
    2 PUs with no visible poles=**Melody Maker D, 1960**
Double cutaway
    Rounded horns
        1 PU
            Cherry finish
                Stud bridge/tailpiece
                    24 3/4" scale=**Les Paul Jr., mid 1958–early 61**
                    22 3/4" scale=**Les Paul Jr. 3/4, mid 1958–early 61**
                Tune-o-matic bridge=**Les Paul Jr. Double Cutaway**
            Limed mahogany finish
                Les Paul on peghead=**Les Paul TV**
                No *Les Paul* =**SG TV, late 1959–early 61**
        2 PUs
            Les Paul on peghead
                24 3/4" scale
                    Stud bridge/tailpiece=**Les Paul Special**
                    Tune-o-matic bridge=**Special Double Cutaway**
                22 3/4" scale=**Les Paul Special 3/4**
            No *Les Paul* on peghead
                24 3/4" scale=**SG Special, late 1959–early 61**
                22 3/4" scale=**SG Special 3/4, late 1959–early 61**

Double cutaway (cont.)
    Pointed horns, horns point away from neck
        1 PU
            24 3/4" scale=**Melody Maker, 1961–65**
            22 3/4" scale=**Melody Maker 3/4, 1961–65**
        2 PUs
            3-on-a-side tuners
                Stud bridge/tailpiece=**Melody Maker D, 1961–65**
                Tune-o-matic bridge=**Melody Maker Double** reissue
            6-on-a-side tuners=**Les Paul Double Cutaway XPL**
    Pointed horns, horns point into neck
        3 humbucking PUs
            Les Paul plate on body near neck
                SG/Les Paul Custom
                SG Les Paul Custom reissue
            No *Les Paul* on instrument=**SG Custom**
        3 oblong pole-less PUs=**Melody Maker III**
        2 single-coil PUs and 1 humbucking PU=**SG Special 400**
        2 humbucking PUs with covers
            Trapezoid inlay
                Les Paul on peghead=**SG/Les Paul Standard**
                No *Les Paul* on peghead
                    SG Standard
                    SG-62 Reissue
            Block inlay
                2 jacks=**SG Exclusive**
                1 jack
                    Coil tap=**SG Elite**
                    No coil tap
                        Wing pickguard=**SG Deluxe**
                        3-point guard=**SG Standard** reissue
            Dot inlay=**SG Studio**
        2 exposed-coil humbucking PUs
            Walnut body and neck=**The SG (Standard)**
            Mahogany body=**The SG (Deluxe), SG Standard 1981–83**
            Paint finish=**SG Special** reissue, **1987–current**
        1 humbucking PU and 1 single-coil PU=**SG 90 Double**
        2 P-90 PUs
            Knobs mounted into top=**SG Special**
            Knobs on semi-circular control plate=**SG Pro**
        2 oblong PUs with no visible poles
            Controls mounted through pickguard
                6-string=**Melody Maker D, 1966–70**
                12-string=**Melody Maker-12**
            Controls on oblong metal control plate
                1 slide switch=**SG-200**
                2 slide switches=**SG-250**
        2 plastic covered mini-humbucking PUs
            Triangular wing-shaped pickguard
                Cherry or walnut finish=**SG II**
                Cherry sunburst finish=**SG III**
            3-point pickguard=**SG Special** reissue, **1972–87**
        1 P-90 PU
            Les Paul on peghead=**SG/Les Paul Jr.**
            No *Les Paul* on peghead
                Cherry finish=**SG Jr.**
                White finish=**SG TV, 1961–68**
        1 humbucking PU=**SG 90 Single**
        1 plastic-covered mini-humbucking PU=**SG I**
        1 oblong pole-less PU
            Controls into pickguard
                24 3/4" scale=**Melody Maker, 1966–71**
                22 3/4" scale=**Melody Maker 3/4, 1966–70**
            Oblong metal control plate=**SG-100**

129

LES PAULS, SGs, AND MELODY MAKERS

Gibson Names vs. Collectors' Names

Bodies on Les Paul models change to SG-style bodies in early 1961. However, the official changes in model names from Les Paul to SG do not coincide with the body changes. Consequently, collectors may use names other than the official Gibson model names—in particular the term *SG/Les Paul*, which was never used by Gibson—to more clearly identify 1961–63 instruments. For example:

Les Paul on peghead or truss rod cover and Les Paul body shape (single cutaway or double cutaway with rounded horns)=Les Paul

No model name on peghead, double cutaway body with rounded horns (1960 SG Special, for example)=Les Paul

Les Paul on peghead, on truss rod cover, or on body at end of neck, SG body shape=SG/Les Paul

Also, the term *Les Paul Standard* commonly refers to the 1952–58 goldtop (officially called the Les Paul Model) as well as to the cherry sunburst Les Paul Standard of 1958–60.

General Model Descriptions

Although the appearance of an SG is different from a Les Paul, the relationship between models within each series is roughly the same.

Junior: 1 black P-90 PU, stud bridge/tailpiece, unbound rosewood fingerboard, dot inlay, nickel-plated metal parts, decal logo

Special: same body as Jr. of equivalent year, 2 black soapbar P-90 PUs, stud bridge/tailpiece, single-bound rosewood fingerboard, dot inlay, pearl logo, nickel-plated metal parts

Standard: 2 PUs (originally soapbars, then humbucking PUs as soon as available), various bridges/tailpieces (changing as new designs became available), single-bound rosewood fingerboard, pearloid trapezoid inlay, pearl logo, nickel-plated metal parts

Custom: originally with 2 PUs but with 3 as soon as humbuckings available, tune-o-matic bridge, single-bound ebony fingerboard, pearl block inlay, low frets (until 1975), multiple-bound peghead, 5-piece split-diamond peghead inlay, pearl logo, gold-plated metal parts

Note: These differences—number of PUs, type of bridge and style of fingerboard—also generally apply to the four models in the original reverse-body Firebird series: Junior=Firebird I, Special=Firebird III, Standard=Firebird V, Custom=Firebird VII.

Les Paul and SG Body Styles

Les Paul: single cutaway and later (on Jr., Special, and TV) double cutaway with rounded horns; carved top on Standard and Custom, flat "slab" top on Jr. and Special; non-beveled edges on single cutaway models, rounded edges on double cutaway models

SG: double cutaway with pointed horns, beveled body edges

Les Paul Model on Peghead

Les Paul Standard and Deluxe models have *Les Paul Model* on peghead.
Silkscreened *Les Paul Model*: **1952–mid 72**
Decal *Les Paul Model*: **mid 1972–current**

SG Neck/Body Joint

Joint at 22nd fret, smooth joint, immediate bevel (no lip): **1961**

Joint at 22nd fret, smooth joint, straight lip on back of neck at 21st fret: **1962**

Joint at 22nd fret, step around joint, curved lip on back of neck extends to 18th fret: **1962–66**

Joint at 19th fret, step at joint, lip extends to 16th fret: **1967–c. 71**

Joint at 17th fret, step around joint, immediate bevel: **c. 1971–78**

Joint at 18th fret, smooth joint, lip extends to 16th fret: **1979–c. 85**

Joint at 22nd fret, step around joint, lip extends to 20th fret: **c. 1986–current**

SECTION ORGANIZATION

Les Paul Standards

Les Paul Model: carved 3-piece non-matching maple top, mahogany back and neck, 2 soapbar P-90 PUs with cream-colored cover, trapeze bridge/tailpiece combination with strings looping under bridge, single-bound top, single-bound rosewood fingerboard (earliest with unbound fingerboard), trapezoid inlay, pearl logo, Kluson tuners, plastic tulip-shaped tuner buttons with single ring near tuner shaft, yellow silkscreened model name, no serial number, nickel-plated metal parts, goldtop finish, some with gold back and sides
Introduced: **mid 1952**
Serial number on back of peghead: **mid 1953**
Stud bridge/tailpiece: **late 1953**
Tune-o-matic bridge: **mid to late 1955**
Humbucking PUs, a few with all-mahogany body: **mid 1957**
Goldtop discontinued, replaced by **Les Paul Standard:** 2-piece matched-grain maple top, cherry sunburst finish: **mid 1958**
Large size frets: **mid 1959**
Slimmer neck: **1960**
Plastic tuner buttons with double ring near tuner shaft: **very late 1960**
SG body, side-pull Deluxe Gibson vibrato, *Les Paul Model* on peghead, cherry finish: **very late 1960**
Les Paul on truss rod cover, crown peghead inlay, no *Les Paul Model* on peghead, by **early 1961**
A few with pearl-inlaid ebony tailblock: **1962**
Renamed **SG Standard** (see SGs, following): **late 1963**

Les Paul Standard (1st goldtop reissue): soapbar PUs, tune-o-matic bridge, deeper binding inside cutaway on the rest of top (binding is uniform depth on 1950s model), small peghead, goldtop finish
Introduced: **1968**
Wider peghead: **early 1969**
Renamed **Les Paul Deluxe:** 4-piece pancake body (2 layers of mahogany with thin maple layer in middle, maple top), 2 mini-humbucking PUs (some with soapbar PUs), 3-piece neck, rosewood fingerboard, trapezoid inlay, goldtop finish: **1969**
Cherry sunburst finish available: **1971–85**
Cherry finish available: **1971–75**
Walnut finish available: **1971–72**
Tobacco sunburst finish available (some years on left-handed model only): **1972–79**
Standard humbucking PUs optional: **1972–76**
Some with blue or red sparkle top finish: **mid 1970s**
Natural finish optional: **1975**
RR model (specs unavailable): **1975 only**
BB model (specs unavailable): **1975–77**
Wine red finish optional: **1975–85**

2-piece body, solid mahogany with maple top: **1977**
Les Paul Deluxe discontinued: **1985**

Les Paul Pro-Deluxe: 2 soapbar P-90 PUs, tune-o-matic bridge, ebony fingerboard, trapezoid inlay, chrome-plated metal parts, goldtop, ebony, tobacco sunburst, or cherry sunburst finish
Introduced by **1978**
Discontinued: **1982**

Les Paul Standard '58: similar to 1954 Les Paul Standard, 2 soapbar PUs with *Gibson* embossed on covers, stud bridge/tailpiece, 1-piece neck with no volute, goldtop finish
Introduced: **1971**
Discontinued from catalog: **1973**
Last shipped: **1975**

Les Paul Standard: 4-piece pancake body (2 layers of mahogany with thin maple layer in middle, maple top), 3-piece neck, 2 standard humbucking PUs, tune-o-matic bridge, wider binding inside cutaway than on rest of top, *Standard* on truss rod cover, plastic tuner buttons, serial number stamped on back of peghead, wine red, sunburst, cherry sunburst, or natural finish offered in catalog, tobacco sunburst finish also shipped
Introduced (1 tobacco sunburst shipped in 1975): **1976**
2-piece body (solid mahogany with maple top), natural, cherry sunburst, dark sunburst, wine red, ebony, or goldtop finish: **1978**
Goldtop listed as separate model (see following): **1985**
Ebony, heritage sunburst, or vintage sunburst finish: **1989**
TV yellow or honey burst finish optional: **1990**
Note: Some Les Paul Reissues (see following) with less attractive wood-grain top have been downgraded from Reissue to Standard. These have an inked-on serial number and Standard *on the truss rod cover.*
Les Paul Standard still in production

Les Paul Kalamazoo: Les Paul Standard made in Kalamazoo plant, 2-piece top, 2 exposed-coil humbucking PUs with cream-colored coils, speed knobs, large rectangular tune-o-matic bridge, stop tailpiece, examples from first run with *Custom Made* plate nailed onto top below tailpiece, pearl trapezoid inlay, *Les Paul KM* on truss rod cover, antique sunburst, natural, or cherry sunburst finish
Limited edition of 1500 instruments made: **1979**

Custom-order reissues: 1959 Les Paul

Standard reissues for Guitar Trader and others: **1979–early 80s**

Les Paul Heritage 80: reissue of 1959 Les Paul Standard, 2-piece highly flamed maple top, binding inside cutaway same depth as rest of top binding, *Heritage 80* on truss rod cover

Les Paul Heritage 80 Elite: same as Les Paul Heritage 80 but with ebony fingerboard, *Heritage 80 Elite* on truss rod cover
Introduced: **1980**
Discontinued: **1982**

Les Paul 30th Anniversary: copy of 1958 goldtop, pearl trapezoid inlay, *30th Anniversary* engraved on inlay at 15th fret
Introduced: **1982**
Discontinued: **1984**

Les Paul Spotlight Special: 3-piece top with curly maple outer pieces and walnut center piece, 2 humbucking PUs, trapezoid inlay, chrome-plated metal parts
Available: **early to mid 1980s**

Les Paul Reissue: copy of 1959 Les Paul Standard, deep-dish top carving, highly flamed maple top, plastic jack plate, binding inside cutaway same depth as other top binding, plain truss rod cover, inked-on serial number, heritage cherry sunburst or heritage dark sunburst finish
Introduced: **1985**
Still in production

Les Paul Reissue Goldtop (2nd reissue): same as Les Paul Reissue (see preceding) but with goldtop finish
Introduced by **1985**
Soapbar P-100 PUs (same in appearance to P-90 but with humbucking with stacked-coil design): **early to mid 1990**
Still in production

Les Paul CMT: curly maple top, metal jack plate, deeper binding inside cutaway than other top binding, stamped 8-digit serial number
Introduced: **1986**
Discontinued: **mid 1989**

Les Paul Classic: "reissue" of 1960 model, 2 humbucking PUs with exposed coils *1960* on pickguard, binding inside cutaway same depth as other top binding, low profile neck, *Classic* on truss rod cover, inked on 1960-style serial number with 0 as 1st digit, heritage cherry sunburst, bullion gold, vintage sunburst, or honey burst finish
Introduced: **1990**

Last 4-digit number (0 999), later numbers are 5-digit with no space after 0: **late Nov. 1990**
Still in production

Les Paul Customs

Les Paul Custom: 1-piece mahogany body with carved top, Alnico V neck PU, black soapbar P-90 bridge PU, tune-o-matic bridge, stop tailpiece, optional Bigsby (listed as a separate catalog model), multiple-bound top and back, single-bound ebony fingerboard, pearl block inlay, low frets (nicknamed The Fretless Wonder), *Les Paul Custom* on truss rod cover, 5-piece split-diamond peghead inlay, pearl logo, closed-back Kluson tuners, plastic tulip-shaped tuner buttons, gold-plated metal parts, ebony finish (nicknamed The Black Beauty)
Introduced: **1954**
3 humbucking PUs (a few with 2 PUs): **mid 1957**
Grover Rotomatic tuners by **1959**
SG body, 3 humbucking PUs, side-pull Deluxe Vibrato, *Les Paul Custom* on plastic plate between fingerboard and PU, white pickguard, white finish: **early 1961**
Some with pearl-inlaid ebony tailblock (rare): **1962**
Renamed **SG Custom** (see SG section, following): **late 1963**

Les Paul Custom (reissue): carved maple top, 2 humbucking PUs, tune-o-matic bridge, 7-ply top binding, low frets, *Les Paul* on truss rod cover, gold-plated metal parts, black finish
Introduced: **1968**
4-piece pancake body (2 layers of mahogany with thin maple layer in middle, maple top), 3-piece neck: **1969**
Neck volute: **1970**
Cherry or cherry sunburst finish optional: **1971**
3 PUs optional (see separate model listing, following): **1971–73, 76, 78**
Tobacco sunburst finish optional: **1972**
Standard jumbo frets, white or natural finish optional: **1975**
Wine red finish available: **1976**
2-piece body (solid mahogany with maple top): **1977**
Walnut finish optional: **1977–78 only**
No neck volute by **1980**
Alpine white, ebony, heritage sunburst, or vintage sunburst finish: **1988**
Honey burst finish optional: **1990**
Still in production

Les Paul Custom '54: reissue of 1954 Les Paul Custom, Alnico V neck PU, P-90 bridge PU
Introduced: **1972**

Discontinued (3 shipped in 1975, 1 in 1977):
1973

Les Paul Custom 20th Anniversary: same as 1974 Les Paul Custom but with *Twentieth Anniversary* engraved in block letters on inlay at 15th fret, black or white finish
Available: **1974**

Les Paul Custom/maple fingerboard: 4-piece pancake body (2 layers of mahogany with thin maple layer in middle, maple top), carved maple top, 2 humbucking PUs, black pickguard, maple fingerboard, gold-plated metal parts, ebony or natural finish
Introduced: **1976**
Discontinued: **1980**

Les Paul Custom/nickel-plated parts: 4-piece pancake body (2 layers of mahogany with thin maple layer in middle, maple top), ebony or wine red finish
Offered as Special Edition model: **1976 only**
Introduced as catalog model: **1979**
Chrome-plated parts by **1985**
Discontinued: **1987**

Les Paul Custom/3 pickups: 3 PUs available as option on standard (2 PU) Les Paul Custom: **1971–73, 1978**
3 PUs offered as "Special Edition Custom with 3 PUs," natural, ebony, or wine red finish: **1976 only**

Les Paul Custom Lite: 1 3/8" deep (5/8" thinner than Les Paul Custom), contoured back, 2 PUs, 2 volume knobs, master tone knob, coil-tap switch, PU selector switch on upper bass bout, ebony fingerboard, block inlay, Floyd Rose or standard tune-o-matic bridge and tailpiece set, gold-plated metal parts except for chrome-plated tuner buttons
Introduced: **1987**
Discontinued: **1990**

Les Paul Custom 35th Anniversary: 3 humbucking PUs, *35th Anniversary* etched on middle peghead inlay, 1959-style inked-on serial number
Available: **1989 only**

Low-Impedance Les Paul Models

Les Paul low-impedance models have different body dimensions than other Les Paul models.

Model	Width	Length	Depth
Standard	13"..	17 3/8"..	2"
Personal, Professional	14"..	18 1/4"..	2"
Recording	13 1/2"..	17 3/4"..	1 3/4"

Les Paul Personal: single cutaway, carved top, mahogany body, contoured back, 2 oblong low-impedance PUs mounted diagonally, *Gibson* embossed on PU covers, microphone input jack on side of upper bass bout, mic volume control knob and 1 switch on upper bass bout, guitar input jack on side of lower treble bout, 4 knobs and 2 slide switches on lower treble bout, tune-o-matic bridge, Gibson Bigsby vibrato optional, low frets, block inlay, 5-piece split-diamond peghead inlay, gold-plated metal parts, walnut finish
Introduced: **1969**
Discontinued: **1971**
Some sold: **1977-79**

Les Paul Professional: single rounded cutaway, carved top, mahogany body, flat back, 2 oblong low-impedance PUs mounted diagonally, *Gibson* embossed on PU covers, 1 switch on upper bass bout, 4 knobs and 2 slide switches on lower right bout, standard jack, tune-o-matic bridge, Gibson Bigsby tailpiece optional, trapezoid inlay, nickel-plated metal parts, walnut finish
Introduced: **1969**
Discontinued: **1971**

Note: Les Paul Personal and Les Paul Professional models were designed for use with the Les Paul LP-12 amplifier, which is equipped with low- and high-impedance inputs. For use with a standard high-impedance amp, a transformer cord is necessary.

Les Paul Recording: replaces Personal and Professional, 2 oblong low-impedance PUs mounted diagonally, 4 knobs on control plate, high/low impedance selector switch (transformer built into guitar), jack on top into control plate, tune-o-matic bridge, small block inlay, 5-piece split-diamond peghead inlay, walnut finish
Introduced: **1971**
White finish optional: **1975**
Large tune-o-matic bridge, ebony or cherry sunburst finish optional: **1978**
Discontinued: **1980**

Les Paul Signature: See Gibson Electric Archtops section

Later Standard-Related and Custom-Related Les Paul Models

All have carved top and/or humbucking PUs.

The Les Paul: solid maple top on maple back, 2 super humbucking PUs, 5-sided rosewood PU covers, rosewood knobs and switch, rosewood pickguard, rosewood control plates on back, rosewood outer binding, green- and red-stained wood inner bindings, maple neck, 3-piece ebony-rosewood-ebony fingerboard, abalone block inlay, 5-piece split-diamond peghead inlay, pearl tuner buttons, pearl plate on back of peghead with limited edition number, gold-plated metal parts, natural or rosewood finish
Introduced: **1976**
Large tune-o-matic bridge, TP-6 tailpiece, by **1978**
Natural finish only: **1979**
Discontinued: **1980**

Les Paul Artisan: carved maple top, 2 humbucking PUs, 3 PUs optional, tune-o-matic bridge, TP-6 tailpiece, single-bound ebony fingerboard, multiple-bound peghead, hearts-and-flowers inlay, hearts-and-flowers peghead inlay, gold-plated metal parts, walnut, tobacco sunburst, or ebony finish
Introduced: **1976**
3 humbucking PUs standard: **1979**
Large tune-o-matic bridge: **1980**
Discontinued: **1982**

The Paul (Standard): slab walnut body, 2 exposed-coil humbucking PUs, black mounting rings, selector switch near control knobs, tune-o-matic bridge, walnut neck, unbound ebony fingerboard, dot inlay, decal logo
Introduced: **1978**
First shipped: **1979**
Firebrand model, logo burned into peghead: **1980**
Discontinued: **1982**

The Paul Deluxe: slab mahogany body, beveled edges around lower treble bout, 2 exposed-coil humbucking PUs, selector switch below tailpiece, unbound ebony fingerboard, dot inlay, some with *Firebrand* on truss rod cover but not a Firebrand (branded logo) model, natural or antique natural finish
Introduced by **1980**
Ebony or wine red finish: **1985**
Discontinued: **1986**

25th Anniversary Les Paul: limited edition to mark 25th anniversary of model, 50th anniversary of Les Paul's career, carved maple top, 2 humbucking PUs, coil-tap switch, tune-o-matic bridge, TP-6 tailpiece, bound fingerboard and peghead, slashed-block inlay, brass nut, *25* over *50* inlaid on peghead, regular serial number and limited edition number on back of peghead
Available by special order: **1979 only**

L.P. Artist: also referred to as Les Paul Active, 2 humbucking PUs (3 PUs optional), active electronics, 3 knobs, 3 mini-toggle switches, tune-o-matic bridge, TP-6 tailpiece, multiple-bound top, bound ebony fingerboard, large block inlay, brass nut, triple-bound fingerboard, script *LP* peghead inlay, gold-plated metal parts, sunburst finish
Introduced: **1979**
Fireburst or ebony optional: **1980**
Discontinued: **1982**

L.P. XR-1: 2 exposed-coil Dirty Fingers humbucking PUs, coil-tap switch, unbound top, unbound rosewood fingerboard, dot inlay, tobacco sunburst, cherry sunburst, or goldburst finish
Introduced: **1981**
Discontinued by **1983**

L.P. XR-II: figured maple top, 2 Super humbucking PUs with metal covers, *Gibson* embossed on PU covers, coil-tap switch, bound top, unbound rosewood fingerboard, dot inlay, honey sunburst finish
Introduced: **1981**
Discontinued by **1983**

Les Paul Studio: 2 humbucking PUs, tune-o-matic bridge, no binding anywhere, rosewood fingerboard, dot inlay, pearloid tuner buttons, *Studio* on truss rod cover, ebony, white, or wine red finish
Les Paul Studio Standard: same but with cream-colored binding on top and back, sunburst, cherry sunburst, or white finish
Les Paul Studio Custom: same but with multiple-bound top and back, bound fingerboard, gold-plated metal parts, cherry sunburst, sunburst, or ebony finish
Introduced: **1984**
Studio Standard and Studio Custom discontinued: **1987**
Ebony fingerboard: **1987**
Trapezoid inlay: **1990**
Les Paul Studio still in production

Les Paul Double-Cutaway XPL: symmetrical double cutaway, 2 humbucking PUs, vibrato, bound ebony fingerboard, dot inlay, 6-on-a-side tuner configuration, peghead points to treble side

Introduced: **1984**
Discontinued: **1987**

Les Paul Studio Lite: 1 3/8" deep, contoured back, 2 special PUs, 2 knobs, coil-tap switch, tune-o-matic bridge, stop tailpiece, no pickguard, ebony fingerboard, dot inlay, crown peghead inlay, pearl logo
Introduced: **1988**
Flat back, 2 humbucking PUs with exposed coils, standard Les Paul electronics (no coil tap), trapezoid inlay, *Les Paul Model* on peghead (no crown), chrome-plated metal parts, gold-plated (with PU covers) optional: **1991**
Still in production

Les Paul Jr.'s

Les Paul Jr.: flat top, slab mahogany body, single cutaway, 1 black P-90 PU, stud bridge/tailpiece, tortoise grain pickguard, 16 frets clear of body, unbound rosewood fingerboard, dot inlay, yellow silkscreened logo and model name on peghead, nickel-plated metal parts, sunburst finish
Introduced: **mid 1954**
Les Paul Jr. 3/4: same body size and shape as Les Paul Jr., shorter neck, shorter 22 3/4" scale, 14 frets clear of body, introduced: **1956**
Double cutaway with rounded horns, 22 frets clear of body on regular Jr., 15 frets clear on Jr. 3/4, cherry red finish: **mid 1958**
Jr. 3/4 discontinued: **early 1961**
SG body, laminated pickguard, *Les Paul Jr.* on peghead, cherry finish: **early 1961**
Maestro vibrato optional, by **1962**
Renamed **SG Jr.** (see SG section, following): **late 1963**

Les Paul TV: Les Paul Jr. with limed mahogany finish (named TV because it supposedly looked better than sunburst on black-and-white TV); some early examples with maple body, 3/4 size available
Note: Although the Les Paul Special finish (see following) was always officially limed mahogany, the Les Paul TV finish was first described in 1956 as natural in Gibson's price list and as limed oak in the catalog. A few early examples are natural finish mahogany.
First shipped: **1954**
Limed mahogany finish in catalog description: **1957**
Double cutaway with rounded horns: **mid 1958**
Renamed **SG TV**, still with rounded cutaway horns: **late 1959**
SG body shape, white finish (see SG section, following): **early 1961**

Les Paul Jr. (reissue): single cutaway, slab mahogany body, 1 black P-90 PU, tune-o-matic bridge, rosewood fingerboard, dot inlay, model name on peghead, decal logo, metal tuner buttons, chrome-plated metal parts, sunburst finish
Introduced by **1986**
Heritage cherry, pearl white, or tobacco sunburst finish: **1989**
Heritage cherry, tobacco sunburst, or TV yellow finish: **1990**
Still in production

Les Paul Junior II: 2 PUs, same as 1989 Les Paul Special reissue (see following), catalog photo has *Les Paul Special* on peghead, heritage cherry, tobacco sunburst or ebony finish
Introduced: **early 1989**
Discontinued: **late 1989**

Les Paul Jr. Double Cutaway: double cutaway with rounded horns, black P-90 pickup, tune-o-matic bridge, rosewood fingerboard, dot inlay, model name on peghead, decal logo, metal tuner buttons, chrome-plated metal parts, cherry finish
Introduced: **1987**
Plastic tuner buttons, sunburst finish optional: **1989**

Les Paul Specials

Les Paul Special: flat top, slab body, single cutaway, 2 black soapbar P-90 PUs, neck PU next to fingerboard, stud bridge/tailpiece, laminated beveled-edge pickguard, 4 knobs, toggle switch on upper bass bout, single-bound rosewood fingerboard, dot inlay, pearl peghead logo, yellow silkscreen model name, nickel-plated metal parts, limed mahogany finish
Introduced: **1955**
Double cutaway with rounded horns, switch near bridge, 22 frets clear of body, cherry red finish optional: **early 1959**
Space between neck PU and fingerboard, switch farther away from bridge: **mid 1959**
Les Paul Special 3/4: same body shape and size as double cutaway Les Paul Special, shorter 22 3/4" scale, 15 frets clear of body, cherry finish, introduced: **1959**
Renamed **SG Special and SG Special 3/4**: **late 1959**
SG body (see SG section, following): **early 1961**

Les Paul 55: single cutaway, slab mahogany body, 2 black soapbar PUs, tune-o-matic bridge, bound rosewood fingerboard, dot inlay, *Les Paul Model* on peghead, pearl logo, plastic tuner buttons, sunburst or wine red finish

Introduced: **1974**
Sunburst or limed mahogany finish: **1977**
Wine red finish optional: **1979**
Discontinued: **1980**

Special Double Cutaway: double cutaway
with rounded horns, 2 black soapbar PUs,
switch on treble side near bridge, tune-o-
matic bridge, bound rosewood fingerboard, dot inlay, sunburst, cherry, or limed
mahogany finish
Introduced: **1976**
Ebony, tobacco sunburst, sunburst, or wine
red finish: **1978**
Cherry, limed mahogany, or sunburst finish:
1979
Discontinued: **1989**

Les Paul Special (reissue): single cutaway,
slab mahogany body, 2 black soapbar PUs,
tune-o-matic bridge, bound rosewood fingerboard, *Les Paul Special* on peghead,
heritage cherry, tobacco sunburst, or TV
yellow finish
Introduced: **late 1989**
Still in production

SG Standards

SG Standard: Les Paul Standard changes to
SG body shape, side-pull Deluxe Gibson
vibrato, *Les Paul Model* on peghead, cherry finish: **very early 1961**
Les Paul on truss rod cover, by **mid 1961**
Some Les Paul/SG Standards with pearl-inlaid
ebony tailblock (rare): **1962**
Les Paul Standard renamed **SG Standard**:
Maestro vibrato (up-and-down pull) with
lyre and logo on coverplate, no *Les Paul* on
truss rod cover: **late 1963**
Pickguard surrounds PUs, no frames on PUs:
1966
Discontinued, replaced by **SG Deluxe** (see following): **1971**
SG Standard re-introduced (see following):
1972

SG Deluxe: replaces SG Standard, non-
beveled cutaways, 2 humbucking PUs, 4
black bonnet knobs, elevated wing pickguard (like Les Paul Standard), tune-o-
matic bridge, Gibson Bigsby vibrato, semi-
circular control plate, block inlay, natural
cherry or walnut
Introduced: **1971**
Discontinued (SG Standard re-introduced):
1972
16 shipped: **1973–74**
SG Deluxe re-introduced, large tune-o-matic
bridge in rectangular housing, by **1981**
Discontinued: **1985**

SG Standard (reissue): 2 metal-covered humbucking PUs, large tune-o-matic bridge,
old-style 3-point pickguard, 1954-style barrel knobs, 3-way toggle switch, rosewood
fingerboard, small block inlay, crown peghead inlay, metal tuner buttons, chrome-
plated metal parts
Introduced: **late 1972**
Bigsby vibrato standard, stop tailpiece optional, cherry, walnut, white, or tobacco sunburst finish: **1976**
Bigsby optional: **1977**
Discontinued, model name continues with The
SG (Standard) specifications (see following): **1981**
SG Standard re-introduced with above specs,
humbucking PUs, smaller tune-o-matic
bridge, small block inlay, cherry or sunburst finish: **1983**
Discontinued: **1987**
Re-introduced: selector switch near lower
edge of body, jack in side, trapezoid inlay,
metal tuner buttons, ebony or wine red
finish: **1989**
Discontinued: **1990**

The SG (Standard): solid walnut body, 1 standard humbucking PU, 1 Super humbucking
"velvet brick" PU, no PU covers, black
mounting rings, tune-o-matic bridge, speed
knobs, walnut neck, ebony fingerboard, dot
inlay, chrome-plated metal parts, natural
walnut finish
The SG (Deluxe): same as The SG Standard
but with solid mahogany body, antique
mahogany or natural mahogany finish
Introduced: **1979**
The SG (Standard) designated Firebrand
model, burned-in logo: 1980 only
The SG (Standard) renamed **SG Standard** :
1981
SG Standard available with wine red, walnut,
or ivory finish; The SG Deluxe available
with walnut finish only: **1982**
SG Standard specs revert to earlier SG
Standard (see preceding): **1983**
The SG Deluxe available with ebony or wine
red finish only: **1984**
Discontinued: **1985**

SG-62 Reissue: 2 humbucking PUs, tune-o-
matic bridge, stop tailpiece, selector
switch near pickguard, bound rosewood
fingerboard, trapezoid inlay, crown peghead inlay, plastic tuner buttons, nickel-
plated metal parts, cherry finish
Introduced: **1986**
Still in production

SG Customs

SG Custom: Les Paul Custom changes to SG body, 3 humbucking PUs, side-pull Deluxe Vibrato, white laminated pickguard with 3-point shape, *Les Paul Custom* on plastic plate between neck and PU, ebony fingerboard, block inlay, 5-piece split-diamond peghead inlay, white finish: **early 1961**
Some with pearl-inlaid ebony tailblock (rare): **1962**
Les Paul Custom renamed **SG Custom**, no *Les Paul Custom* plate: **late 1963**
Maestro vibrato (up-and-down pull) with lyre and logo on coverplate: **late 1963**
Pickguard surrounds PUs, no PU frames: **1966**
Walnut finish by **1969**
Old-style 3-point pickguard, large tune-o-matic bridge in rectangular housing, no vibrato: **late 1972**
Cherry finish optional: **1972**
White finish or white finish with black binding optional: **1974**
Wine red, white, or walnut: **1975**
Black finish available (7 shipped): **1975 only**
Bigsby vibrato standard, stop tailpiece optional: **1976**
Bigsby optional: **1977**
Tobacco sunburst and cherry finish optional: **1978**
Walnut or white finish standard: **1979**
Discontinued: **1980**
Re-introduced as **SG Les Paul Custom**: small tune-o-matic bridge, antique ivory finish: **1987**
Classic white finish: **1990**
Still in production

SG Jr. and SG TV

SG Jr.: Les Paul Jr. changes to SG body, 1 P-90 PU, laminated pickguard, *Les Paul Junior* on peghead, cherry finish: **early 1961**
Maestro vibrato optional, by **1962**
Les Paul Jr. renamed **SG Jr.**: no model name on peghead: **late 1963**
Vibrato standard: **1965**
Black soapbar PU, pickguard surrounds PU: **1966**
SG Jr. discontinued: **1971**

SG TV: Les Paul TV renamed **SG TV**, double cutaway with rounded horns, 1-P-90 PU, limed mahogany finish: **late 1959**
SG body,: **early 1961**
White finish: **late 1961**
Maestro vibrato optional, by **1962**
Vibrato standard: **1965**
Soapbar PU, pickguard surrounds PU: **1966**
SG TV discontinued: **1968**

SG Specials

SG Special, SG Special 3/4: Les Paul Special and Les Paul Special 3/4 renamed **SG Special** and **SG Special 3/4**: double cutaway with rounded horns, neck PU next to fingerboard, no model name on peghead, cherry or cream (similar to limed finish but more opaque) finish on Special, cherry finish only on Special 3/4: **late 1959**
Space between neck PU and fingerboard: **1960**
SG Special 3/4 discontinued: **early 1961**
SG body, cherry or cream finish: **early 1961**
White finish: **late 1961**
Maestro vibrato optional, by **1962**
Vibrato standard: **1965**
Pickguard surrounds PUs, no frames on PUs: **1966**
Discontinued, replaced by **SG Pro** (see following): **1971**
Re-introduced: **1972**: 2 black mini-humbucking PUs visible poles, old-style 3-point pickguard, 3-way selector switch, large tune-o-matic bridge in rectangular housing, dot inlay, no peghead ornament, cherry or walnut: **late 1972**
Smaller tune-o-matic, small block inlay: **1973**
Discontinued (6 shipped 1978–79): **1978**
Re-introduced as **Special I** (1 PU) and **Special II** (2 PUs), 2 exposed-coil humbucking PUs, rosewood fingerboard, dot inlay, optional vibrato: **early 1984**
Renamed **SG Special**, options include 2 single-coil and 1 Dirty Fingers humbucking PU with coil tap, Kahler vibrato system: **mid 1985**
2 exposed-coil humbucking PUs, tune-o-matic bridge, 3 knobs, 1 toggle switch, no pickguard, ebony fingerboard, dot inlay, *SG* on truss rod cover, plastic tuner buttons: **1987**
Ferrari red or pewter finish: **1989**
Still in production

SG Pro: replaces SG Special, 2 black soapbar P-90 PUs, semi-circular control plate, triangular wing-shaped pickguard, tune-o-matic bridge in large rectangular housing, Gibson Bigsby vibrato, single-bound rosewood fingerboard, pearl logo, cherry, walnut, or natural mahogany finish
Introduced: **late 1971**
Discontinued (SG Special re-introduced): **1972**
25 shipped: **1973–74**

SG Special 400: 2 single-coil PUs, 1 Dirty Fingers exposed-coil humbucking PU, 2 knobs, 3 mini-switches, vibrato, bound rosewood fingerboard, dot inlay, black hardware
Available as special order SG Special: **1985**
Introduced as separate model: **1986**
Discontinued: **1987**

Later SG Models

SG Studio: (similar to SG Special Reissue of 1985) 2 humbucking PUs, 3 knobs, 1 toggle switch, no pickguard, dot inlay, some with satin finish
Available: **1978 only**

SG Exclusive: exposed-coil PUs, control knob for single-coil to humbucking PU adjustment, ebony finish
Available: **1979 only**

SG Elite: 2 humbucking PUs, coil-tap switch, tune-o-matic bridge, TP-6 tailpiece, bound ebony fingerboard, block inlay, locking nut, crown peghead inlay, gold-plated metal parts
Introduced by **1987**
Discontinued: **1989**

SG 90 Single: 1 humbucking PU, pearloid pickguard, strings mounted through body, Floyd Rose tremolo optional, bound ebony fingerboard, 25 1/2" scale, 2-piece split-diamond inlay, crown peghead inlay, alpine white, metallic turquoise, or heritage cherry finish

SG 90 Double: 1 narrow single-coil PU mounted diagonally in neck position, 1 exposed-coil humbucking PU in bridge position, pearloid pickguard surrounds neck PU
Introduced: **1989**
SG 90 Single discontinued: **1990**
SG 90 Double still in production

Melody Makers

Melody Maker: slab body, 1 3/8" deep, single rounded cutaway (Les Paul Jr. shape but 3/8" thinner), 7/8"-wide oblong PU with black plastic cover and no visible poles, stud bridge/tailpiece, pickguard surrounds PUs, knobs mounted into pickguard, unbound rosewood fingerboard, dot inlay, narrow (2 1/4") peghead, decal logo, sunburst finish
MM:1 PU
MM3/4: short scale, 12 frets clear of body
Introduced: **1959**
PU width narrows to 5/8": **1960**
MM-D: 2 PUs, introduced: **1960**
Symmetrical double cutaway with rounded horns, horns point away from neck, slightly rounded body edges: **1961**
Maestro vibrato optional: **1962**
Body edges more rounded, horns point slightly farther away from neck, cherry finish: **1963**
SG body, pointed horns, horns point into neck, white PU covers, enlarged white pickguard covers most of upper body, knobs mounted into top, vibrato standard, fire engine red or Pelham blue finish: **1965**

MM-12: 12-string, 2 PUs, no vibrato, introduced: **1967**
MM-III: 3 PUs, introduced: **1967**
Fire engine red finish discontinued, sparkling burgundy finish optional: **1967**
MM 3/4 discontinued (39 shipped): **1970**
Walnut finish only on MM, MM-D and MM-III, sparkling burgundy and Pelham blue on MM-12, wider peghead: **1970**
Melody Maker line discontinued, replaced by **SG-100, SG-200, SG-250** (see following): **1971**

Melody Maker Double reissue: slab body, double cutaway with rounded horns, horns point away from neck, 2 Melody Maker style PUs, tune-o-matic bridge, switch near tailpiece, jack on top, rosewood fingerboard, dot inlay, narrow peghead, metal tuner buttons, cherry or sunburst finish
Introduced: **early 1977**
Discontinued: **1981**

Melody Maker reissue: single cutaway, slab body, humbucking PU near bridge, tune-o-matic bridge, 2 knobs mounted into pickguard, rosewood fingerboard, dot inlay, narrow peghead, Ferrari red, antique white, or ebony finish
Introduced: **1989**
Still in production

SG-100, SG-200, SG-250: slab body, double pointed cutaways, Melody Maker type PU(s), oblong rectangular control plate, no pickguard, rosewood fingerboard, dot inlay, standard Gibson peghead shape
SG-100: 1 PU, cherry or walnut finish
SG-200: 2 PUs, slide switch, cherry or walnut finish
SG-250: 2 PUs, 2 slide switches, cherry finish
Introduced, replacing Melody Maker series (no SG-250s shipped until 1972): **1971**
SG-100 available with P-90 PU: **1972**
Discontinued, replaced by **SG I, SG II, SG III** (see following): **late 1972**

SG I, SG II, SG III: double pointed cutaway, beveled edges, mahogany body, triangular wing-shaped pickguard, plastic-covered mini-humbucking PU(s) with no visible poles, semi-circular control plate, tune-o-matic bridge, dot inlay, standard Gibson peghead shape
SG I: 1 PU, cherry or walnut
SG II: 2 PUs, 2 slide switches, cherry or walnut
SG III: 2 PUs, cherry sunburst
Introduced: **late 1972**
SG I available with P-90 PU: **1972 only**
All discontinued: **1974**
SG II available with standard humbucking PUs, 61 shipped: **1975**
SG I, SG II, SG III shipped as late as: **1979**

COMMENTS

The Les Paul Standard from 1958–60 (single-cutaway, humbucking pickups, cherry sunburst finish) is, along with the 1958 Flying V and Explorer models, the most sought after solidbody production model on the vintage market. Among goldtops from 1952–58, the latest version (with humbucking pickups) is held in the highest regard by players and collectors, followed in descending order by those with the following features: soapbar PUs and tune-o-matic; stud bridge/tailpiece; and with trapeze bridge/tailpiece. The value of the 1957–61 Standards is illustrated by the premium price that Gibson puts on current reissue models.

Most limited edition models bring prices above those of standard issue from the same period.

Les Paul Customs from the pre-SG period also are highly sought after.

Special, Jr., and TV models from the pre-SG period bring prices on the vintage market several times more than their value as utility instruments, with TV-finish models especially sought by collectors.

Les Paul Recording series models are of some historical interest but are not highly regarded by players.

Les Paul Deluxe models, with smaller mini-humbucking PUs, are regarded strictly as utility instruments.

Early SG/Les Paul models appeal to collectors and players. SG models through 1965 are well regarded, but most collectors do not seek those made after 1965.

Melody Makers, SGs from the early 1970s, and most of the non-Standard and non-Custom models through the 1970s and 1980s have little appeal to collectors.

KORINAS, FIREBIRDS, MISCELLANEOUS SOLIDBODIES & DOUBLENECKS

SECTION ORGANIZATION

Korina Body Modernistic Series,
   Including Reissues and Related Models
   Flying Vs
   Explorers
   Modernes
Firebirds
   Original Reverse Body Series
   Non-reverse Body
   Later Firebirds
Other Solidbody Models
Doublenecks

Flying Vs

Flying V: korina (African limba wood) body, 2 humbucking PUs, 3 knobs in straight line, strings anchor through body, V-shaped string anchor plate, white pickguard (a few black), body shoulders square at neck, all frets clear of body, raised plastic logo, black ridged-rubber strip on side of lower treble bout, triangular peghead with rounded top, gold-plated metal parts, natural finish, brown case with pink or red plush lining
Introduced (3 batches of 40 made): **1958**
Shipping records show 81 in **1958**, 17 in **1959**
Discontinued: **1959**
Models with 1958 body (some with ink-stamped serial numbers, some with oversized stamped serial number), patent-number PUs, nickel-plated metal parts, black case with yellow plush lining: **1962–63**

Flying V (1st reissue): mahogany body, large pickguard surrounds PUs, no frames around PUs, triangular knob configuration, tune-o-matic bridge, stud tailpiece, Gibson vibrato, sloped shoulders, 20 (of 22) frets clear of body, no rubber strip on side, logo embossed on truss rod cover, most with shorter and more rounded peghead than 1958 model, sunburst or cherry finish
Only listing: **1966**
2 shipped in **1965**, 111 in **1966**, 15 in **1969**, 47 in **1970**

Flying V Medallion: limited edition reissue with *LE* medallion on top, same as 1966 model but with even shorter peghead, sunburst or cherry finish
Only year offered, 350 shipped (2 shipped in 1973, 1 in 1974): **1971**

Flying V (2nd reissue): natural mahogany, black, tobacco sunburst, or white finish
Introduced: **1975**
Discontinued: **1980**

Flying V II: walnut or maple top, 5-piece maple/walnut body, beveled top edges, boomerang-shaped PUs, knobs in straight line, ebony fingerboard, dot inlay, stylized *V2* on truss rod cover, gold-plated metal parts, natural finish
Introduced: **1979**
Discontinued: **1982**

Flying V I: specs unavailable, only listing: **1981**

Flying V Heritage: limited edition reissue of 1958 Flying V, korina wood body, V-shape string anchor plate, 2 humbucking PUs, tune-o-matic bridge, bonnet knobs in straight line, rosewood fingerboard, raised peghead logo, pointed peghead, gold-plated metal parts, antique natural, ebony, candy apple red, or white finish, serial number of letter *A* followed by 3 digits
Available: **late 1981–82**
Continues as **Flying V** (3rd reissue): black barrel knobs: **1983**
Discontinued: **1984**

The V: curly maple top, antique sunburst, vintage cherry sunburst, or antique natural finish, available: **1983 only**

Flying V 83: alder body, sloped shoulders, 2 exposed-coil humbucking PUs, triangular knob configuration, several vibrato systems optional, decal logo, chrome-plated metal parts, ebony or ivory finish
Introduced: **1983**
Renamed **Flying V**: 2 Dirty Fingers exposed-coil humbucking PUs, triangular knob configuration, tune-o-matic bridge, vibrato optional, locking-nut system optional, ebony, alpine white, or red finish, custom and designer finishes optional, by June 1984
Flying V Left Hand, available: **June 1984**
Discontinued: **1989**

Flying V CMT: curly maple top, bound top, vibrato optional, some with stylized *V2* on truss rod cover, antique sunburst or vintage cherry sunburst finish
Only listing: **Jan. 1984**

Flying V Black Hardware: Kahler vibrato standard, black hardware, otherwise same specs as Flying V model of June 1984 (see preceding)
Only listing: **early 1985**

Flying V XPL: tune-o-matic bridge/tailpiece, Kahler vibrato optional, scimitar-shaped peghead (like Explorer), 6-on-a-side tuner arrangement, black hardware, night violet or plum winecolor finish
Introduced: **1984**
Discontinued: **1987**

Flying V XPL Black Hardware: Kahler vibrato standard, ebony, alpine white, or red finish, otherwise same specs as Flying V XPL
Only listing: **early 1985**

Flying V 90 Double: 25 1/2" scale, split-diamond inlay
Introduced: **1989**
Still in production

Flying V Reissue: reissue of 1958 Flying V
Introduced: **1990**
Still in production

Explorers

Explorer: korina (African limba wood) body, straight body lines, elongated upper treble bout and lower bass bout, 2 humbucking PUs, knobs in straight line, tune-o-matic bridge, stop tailpiece, white pickguard, scimitar-shape peghead curves to treble side, pearl logo, (a few early with forked peghead and raised plastic logo), rectangular brown case with red or pink plush lining
Introduced (1 batch of 40 made): **1958**
Shipping records do not list Explorer specifically. Records show "Korina (Mod. Gtr)," 19 shipped in **1958**, 3 in **1959**.
Discontinued: **1959**
Models with 1958 body (some with ink-stamped serial number), patent number PUs, nickel-plated metal parts, black case with yellow plush lining, shipped into: **1963**

Explorer reissue: mahogany body, natural, white, or black finish
Introduced: **1975**
Discontinued: **1980**

Explorer II: walnut or maple top, 5-piece walnut and maple body, beveled edges, 2 humbucking PUs with exposed coils, 3 knobs in straight line, TP-6 tailpiece, ebony fingerboard, dot inlay, *E/2* on truss rod cover, gold-plated metal parts, natural finish
Introduced: **1979**
Discontinued: **1984**

Explorer (I): 2 uncovered humbucking PUs, knobs in straight line, tune-o-matic bridge, stop tailpiece, black Kahler Flyer vibrato

with tailpiece fine-tuners, rosewood fingerboard, dot inlay, decal logo
Introduced by **1981**

Explorer Left Hand: available: **June 1984–87**
Triangular knob configuration, no vibrato, ebony fingerboard, by **1987**
Explorer I discontinued: **1989**

Explorer Korina: korina wood body and neck, 2 humbucking PUs, gold speed knobs, metal tuner buttons, candy apple red, ebony, ivory, or antique natural finish
Only listing: **1983**

Explorer Heritage: limited edition reissue of 1958 Explorer, korina wood body and neck (first 8 examples with 1-piece neck), 2 humbucking PUs, black barrel knobs, pearloid tuner buttons, gold-plated metal parts, serial number of single letter followed by 3 digits, antique natural, ebony, or ivory finish
100 made: **1983**

Explorer 83: 2 exposed-coil humbucking PUs, triangular knob configuration, several vibrato systems optional
Introduced: **early 1984**
Referred to as **Explorer**, alder body, custom graphic and original artist finishes optional: **mid 1984**
Discontinued: **1989**

Explorer Black Hardware: Kahler vibrato standard, black hardware
Only listing: **early 1985**

Explorer CMT: bound curly maple top, some with *E/2* on truss rod cover
Only listing: **Jan. 1984**

Explorer III: alder body, 3 soapbar P-90 PUs, 2 knobs, 2 switches, tune-o-matic bridge, rosewood fingerboard, dot inlay, decal logo, chrome-plated metal parts
Introduced: **mid 1984**
Discontinued: **mid 1985**

Explorer III Black Hardware: Kahler vibrato standard, black hardware,
Only listing: **early 1985**

EXP 425: 1 humbucking and 2 single-coil PUs, no PU covers, 2 knobs, 3 mini-toggle switches, Kahler vibrato, ebony fingerboard, black hardware
Available: **1986 only**

XPL Custom: sharply pointed horns, cutout at lower treble horn, 2 Dirty Fingers exposed-coil humbucking PUs, locking nut vibrato system, bound top, dot inlay

Introduced: **1985**
Discontinued: **1987**

Explorer 90 Double: 25 1/2" scale, split-dia-
mond inlay
Introduced: **1989**
Still in production

Explorer Reissue: reissue of 1958 Explorer
Introduced : **1990**
Still in production

Modernes

Moderne: korina (African limba wood) body,
bass side of body like Flying V, treble side
scooped out, asymmetrical peghead
longer on treble side
Gibson shipping records note a total of 22
instruments shipped in 1958 and 1959 as
"Korina (Mod. Gtr.)" The Flying V was listed
separately; the Explorer was not. Both the
Explorer and the Flying V were described
in the 1958 price list as Modernistic
Guitars. The Moderne body style was
patented in 1958, but there is no evidence
that any Modernes were actually produced.

Moderne Heritage: limited edition, issued with
Flying V Heritage and Explorer Heritage
reissues, 2 humbucking PUs, tune-o-matic
bridge, string guides on peghead, serial
number of letter followed by 3 digits
500 made: **1982**

Firebirds, Original Reverse Body Series

All with reverse body, treble horn larger than
bass horn, neck-through-body construction with side wings glued on, raised middle section of body, Firebird humbucking
PUs with nickel-plated covers and metal
mounting rings, 3-ply white-black-white
pickguard with beveled edge, beveled peghead edge, large Kluson banjo-style tuners
all on treble side of peghead with high E-
string nearest nut, sunburst finish
Custom colors available: golden mist, silver
mist, Kerry green, Polaris white, Pelham
blue, frost blue, ember red, Inverness
green, cardinal red, heather
Firebird I: 1 PU, no switch, 2 knobs, stud
bridge/tailpiece, no vibrato, (a few with
Firebird III vibrato), unbound rosewood fingerboard, dot inlay
Firebird III: 2 PUs, 3-way toggle switch, stud
bridge, short flat-arm vibrato, single-bound
fingerboard, dot inlay
Firebird V: 2 PUs, 3-way toggle switch, tune-o-

matic bridge, Deluxe vibrato (tubular lever
arm with plastic end cap, metal tailpiece
cover engraved with Gibson and leaf-and-
lyre), single-bound fingerboard, trapezoid
inlay
Firebird VII: 3 PUs, 3-way toggle switch, tune-
o-matic bridge, Deluxe vibrato (tubular
lever arm with plastic end cap, metal tailpiece cover engraved with Gibson and
leaf-and-lyre decoration), single-bound
ebony fingerboard, block inlay beginning at
1st fret, gold-plated metal parts
Firebird line introduced: **mid 1963**
Peghead reversed, pegs on bass side: **1965**
Variations of Firebird I and Firebird III: non-
beveled peghead, right-angle tuners, black
P-90 PUs: **1965**
Non-beveled peghead standard: **1965**
Discontinued: **May 1965**

Firebirds, Non-reverse Body

All with non-reverse body, body and peghead
shape opposite of original Firebirds, bass
horn larger than treble horn, glued-in neck
with visible joint, black sliding selector
switch, no PU mounting rings, white pickguard surrounding PUs with red Firebird
logo on upper left, unbound rosewood fingerboard, dot inlay, non-beveled peghead
(similar to Fender shape), right-angle
tuners, sunburst finish, custom colors
available
Firebird I: 2 black soapbar P-90 PUs, stud
bridge, short-arm vibrato with tubular lever
and plastic tip
Non-reverse Firebird III: 3 black soapbar P-90
PUs, stud bridge, vibrato with tubular lever
arm and plastic tip
Non-reverse Firebird V: 2 Firebird mini-humbucking PUs, tune-o-matic bridge, Deluxe
vibrato (tubular lever arm with plastic end
cap, metal tailpiece cover engraved with
Gibson and leaf-and-lyre decoration), nickel-plated metal parts
Non-reverse Firebird VII: 3 Firebird mini-humbucking PUs, tune-o-matic bridge, Deluxe
Vibrato (tubular lever arm with plastic end
cap, metal tailpiece cover engraved with
Gibson and leaf-and-lyre decoration), gold-
plated metal parts
Non-reverse Firebird line introduced: **1965**
Firebird V 12 string: available: **1966–67**
Non-reverse Firebirds discontinued: **1969**

Later Firebirds

Firebird V (reissue): *LE* limited edition medallion, logo embossed on PU covers, otherwise exact replica of original reverse-body
Firebird V
366 shipped: **1972–73**

Firebird 76: reverse body, 2 PUs, tune-o-matic bridge, stop tailpiece, dot inlay, gold-plated metal parts, sunburst, mahogany, white, or black finish
Introduced: **1976**
Discontinued: **1979**

Firebird: reverse body slightly different from original reverse body, same specs as 1964 Firebird V but with no vibrato, tune-o-matic bridge, stop tailpiece, tuners on treble side of peghead
Introduced: **1990**
Still in production

Other Solidbody Models

L-5S: 13 1/2" wide, single cutaway, carved maple top, contoured back, 2 large oblong low-impedance PUs with metal covers and embossed logo, 4 knobs, large rectangular tune-o-matic bridge, large L-5 type plate tailpiece with silver center insert, no pickguard, 7-ply top binding and 3-ply back binding with black line on side, 5-ply fingerboard binding with black line on side, 22-fret fingerboard, 17 frets clear of body, 24 3/4" scale, bound ebony fingerboard with pointed end, abalone block inlay, 5-ply peghead binding, flowerpot peghead inlay, gold-plated metal parts, cherry sunburst finish
Introduced: **1972**
First shipped: **1973**
Humbucking PUs: **1974**
Stop tailpiece: **late 1975**
TP-6 tailpiece: **mid 1978**
Discontinued: **1985**

L-6S: 13 1/2" wide, 1 1/8" deep, single cutaway, maple body, 2 humbucking PUs with ceramic magnets and no visible poles, 3 knobs, 6-position rotary tone selector switch, large rectangular tune-o-matic bridge, stop tailpiece, 24-fret fingerboard, 18 frets clear of body, 24 3/4" scale, maple fingerboard with natural finish, ebony fingerboard with tobacco sunburst finish, small block inlay, narrow peghead with similar shape to snakehead L-5 of late 1920s, chrome-plated metal parts, natural or cherry finish
Introduced: **1973**
Dot inlay: **1975**
Renamed L-6S Custom: **1975**
Discontinued: **1980**

L-6S Deluxe: same body shape as L-6S, strings anchor through body, string holes on a line diagonal to strings, rosewood fingerboard, small block inlay
Introduced: **1975**

Discontinued: **1980**

Marauder: 12 3/4" wide, Les Paul-type single cutaway, humbucking PU in neck position, blade-type PU in bridge position, PUs set in clear epoxy, 2 knobs, rotary tone selector switch between knobs, large pickguard covers entire upper body and extends around lower treble bout, bolt-on neck, rosewood fingerboard, triangular peghead with rounded top
Introduced: **1975**
Marauder Custom: same as Marauder but with 3-way selector switch on cutaway bout, bound fingerboard, block inlay, tobacco sunburst finish, available: **1976–77**
Maple fingerboard: **1978**
Some Marauders with selector switch on cutaway bout: **1978**
Marauder discontinued: **1980**

S-1: 12 3/4" wide, Les Paul-shape single cutaway, 3 single-coil PUs with no poles, PUs set in clear epoxy, 2 knobs, 1 switch, large rectangular tune-o-matic bridge, stop tailpiece, large pickguard covers entire upper body and extends around lower treble bout, bolt-on neck, maple fingerboard, dot inlay, triangular peghead with rounded top
Introduced: **1976**
Discontinued: **1980**

RD Standard: double cutaway, upper treble horn longer than upper bass horn, lower bass horn larger than lower treble horn, 2 humbucking PUs, 4 knobs, 1 selector switch, tune-o-matic bridge, 25 1/2" scale, rosewood fingerboard, dot inlay, model name on truss rod cover, decal logo, chrome-plated metal parts, natural, tobacco sunburst or walnut finish
RD Custom: same as RD Standard, but with active electronics, 1 selector switch and 1 mini-switch, large back plate, maple fingerboard, natural or walnut finish
Introduced: **1978**
Discontinued: **1979**

RD Artist/79: double cutaway, upper treble horn longer than upper bass horn, lower bass side larger than lower treble side, active electronics, 2 humbucking PUs, 4 knobs, 1 selector switch, 2 mini-switches, tune-o-matic bridge, TP-6 tailpiece, large backplate, 24 3/4" scale, bound ebony fingerboard, block inlay, multiple-bound peghead, winged-ƒ peghead inlay
Introduced: **1978**
RD Artist/77: 25 1/2" scale, available by special order: **1980**
Listed as **RD**: **1981**
Discontinued: **1982**

GK-55: Les Paul body size and shape, single cutaway, slab mahogany body, 2 Dirty Fingers PUs with exposed coils, 2 knobs, rotary coil-tap control switch, rectangular tune-o-matic bridge, TP-6 tailpiece, no pickguard, single-bound rosewood finger-board, model name on truss rod cover, tobacco sunburst finish
1,000 instruments made: **1979**

335-S Deluxe: double rounded cutaway, solid mahogany body narrower than ES-335, 2 Dirty Fingers exposed-coil humbucking PUs, coil-tap switch, tune-o-matic bridge, TP-6 tailpiece, triangular wing-shaped pickguard, bound ebony fingerboard, dot inlay, brass nut
Introduced: **1980**
335-S Custom: unbound rosewood fingerboard, available: **1981 only**
335-S Deluxe discontinued: **1983**

Sonex-180 Custom: Les Paul body size and shape, single cutaway, molded Masonite body, 2 exposed-coil humbucking PUs, 1 switch, 1 coil-tap switch, tune-o-matic bridge, bolt-on neck, ebony fingerboard, dot inlay, ebony or white finish
Sonex-180 Deluxe: no coil-tap switch, rose-wood fingerboard, ebony finish
Sonex Artist: active electronics, 3 mini-switches, TP-6 tailpiece, rosewood finger-board, candy apple red or ivory finish
Introduced: **1981**
Sonex-180 Custom discontinued: **1982**
Sonex-180 Deluxe Left Hand listed: **1982**
Sonex Deluxe and Sonex Artist discontinued: **1984**

Victory MV-2: asymmetrical double cutaway, extended upper bass horn, 2 humbucking PUs with exposed coils (zebra neck PU, black bridge PU), 2 knobs, 1 coil-tap switch, 1 3-position slide switch, tune-o-matic bridge, single-bound rosewood fin-gerboard, dot inlay positioned near bass edge of fingerboard, 6-on-a-side tuner arrangement, candy apple red or antique firebrust finish
Victory MV-10: 2 humbucking PUs (both zebras) and 1 stacked-coil PU, 1 coil-tap switch, 5-position slide switch, ebony fin-gerboard, antique cherry sunburst, candy apple red, or twilight blue finish
Introduced: **1981**
Discontinued: **1984**

Map-shape: limited edition promotional model, mahogany body shaped like United States, 2 humbucking PUs, 4 knobs, 1 switch, tune-o-matic bridge/tailpiece, 3-piece maple neck, ebony fingerboard, dot inlay, crown peghead inlay, pearl logo, some with Epiphone logo (not made in Japan), metal tuner buttons, natural mahogany finish
Available: **1983 only**

Chet Atkins Standard (CE): classical electric, top cutout to simulate round soundhole, single cutaway, spruce top, mahogany body, transducer PU, knobs recessed into upper bass side, multiple-bound top, 25 1/2" scale, rosewood finger-board, wider fingerboard optional (2" at nut), slotted peghead, antique natural or alpine white finish,
CEC: 2"-wide ebony fingerboard
Introduced: **1982**
Ebony or wine red finish optional: **1990**
Still in production

Chet Atkins SST: steel-string electric, top cutout to simulate round soundhole, trans-ducer PU, 2 knobs on top, 25 1/2" scale, ebony fingerboard, dot inlay, solid peg-head, antique natural, alpine white, or ebony finish
Introduced: **1987**
Wine red finish optional: **1990**
Still in production

Chet Atkins Phasar: asymmetrical double cut-away, 2 stacked-coil humbucking PUs with no visible poles, 1 PU straight-mounted in middle position and 1 PU slant-mounted in bridge position, 2 knobs, rosewood finger-board, 25 1/2" scale, dot inlay, 6-on-a-side tuner arrangement
Introduced: **1987**
Discontinued: **1989**

Futura: neck-through-body construction, cutout along entire bass side of body, cutout on upper treble side, deep cutout from bottom end almost to bridge, 2 hum-bucking PUs with no visible poles, 2 knobs, vibrato optional, TP-6 tailpiece, 6-on-a-side tuners, gold-plated metal parts, ebony, ultra violet or pearl white finish
Introduced: **1983**
Discontinued: **1985**

Corvus I: same specs as Futura except: 1 hum-bucking PU with no visible poles, tune-o-matic bridge/tailpiece, bolt-on neck, chrome-plated metal parts, silver finish standard, other finishes optional
Corvus II: 2 humbucking PUs with no visible poles
Corvus III: 3 single-coil PUs
Introduced: **1983**
Discontinued: **1985**

Challenger I: Les Paul-type single cutaway, 1 humbucking PU with no visible poles, tune-o-matic bridge/tailpiece combination, bolt-on neck, rosewood fingerboard, dot inlay, standard peghead shape

Challenger II: 2 humbucking PUs with no visible poles
Introduced: **1983**
Discontinued: **1985**

Invader: Les Paul-shape single cutaway, beveled bass-side edge, 2 exposed-coil humbucking PUs, tune-o-matic bridge, stop tailpiece, ebony fingerboard, dot inlay
Introduced: **1983**
Discontinued: **1989**

Spirit I: double cutaway with rounded horns, 1 exposed-coil humbucking PU, 2 knobs, tune-o-matic bridge/tailpiece combination, tortoise grain pickguard, rosewood fingerboard, dot inlay

Spirit II: 2 exposed-coil humbucking PUs, 3 knobs, no pickguard, bound top
Introduced: **1983**
Discontinued: **1988**

Spirit II XPL: Kahler tremolo, bound fingerboard, 6-on-a-side tuner arrangement
Introduced: **1985**
Discontinued: **1987**

Q-400: body shape similar to Victory MV series (see preceding), 1 humbucking PU and 2 single-coil PUs, 2 knobs, 3 mini-switches, Kahler vibrato, ebony fingerboard, dot inlay, 6-on-a-side tuner arrangement
Only listing: **1986**

U-2: asymmetrical double cutaway, body shape similar to Fender Stratocaster, basswood body, contoured back, 2 single-coil PUs and 1 humbucking PU, Kahler vibrato, 2 knobs, 3 mini-toggle switches, bound top, rosewood fingerboard, dot inlay, 6-on-a-side tuner arrangement
Introduced: **1987**
Still in production

US-1: double cutaway, body shape similar to Fender Stratocaster, maple top, balsa wood core, 3 humbucking PUs (2 with stacked-coil design) with no visible poles, Kahler locking nut vibrato system, bound top and back, bound ebony fingerboard, slashed-diamond inlay, 6-on-a-side tuner arrangement, natural top finish
Introduced: **1987**
Still in production

SR-71: designed by Wayne Charvel, body shape similar to Fender Stratocaster, 1 humbucking PU and 2 single-coil PUs, locking nut vibrato system
Available: **1989 only**

Doublenecks

EDS-1275 Double 12: 12-string and 6-string necks, double pointed cutaways, hollow maple body with carved spruce top, no soundholes, 2 humbucking PUs for each neck, 2 knobs for each neck, 1 switch on treble side, 1 switch on bass side, 1 switch between bridges, tune-o-matic bridges, triple-bound top and back, 24 3/4" scales, bound rosewood fingerboards, double-parallelogram inlay, no peghead ornament, sunburst, white, or black finish
Introduced (custom order only): **1958**
SG-shape solid mahogany body, double pointed cutaways, beveled edges, 4 knobs on lower treble bout, 1 switch between tailpieces, 1 switch on upper treble bout : **c. 1962**

Discontinued (110 total shipped): **1968**
Re-introduced, sunburst, walnut, or white finish: **1977**
Walnut, white, or cherry sunburst by: **1984**
Cherry finish optional by **1987**
Heritage cherry or alpine white finish: **1990**
Still in production

EMS-1235 Double Mandolin: short 6-string guitar neck (a few with 8-string mandolin neck) and standard 6-string guitar neck, double pointed cutaways, hollow maple body with carved spruce top, no soundholes, 1 humbucking PU for short neck, 2 humbucking PUs for standard neck, height-adjustable bridge for short neck, 15 1/2" scale on short neck (longer than standard mandolin scale), 24 3/4" scale on guitar neck, bound rosewood fingerboards, double-parallelogram inlay, no peghead ornament, sunburst, white, or black finish
Introduced (custom order only): **1958**
SG-shape solid mahogany body, double pointed cutaways, beveled edges, 4 knobs on lower treble bout, 1 switch between tailpieces, 1 switch on upper treble bout: **c. 1962**

Discontinued (61 total shipped): **1968**

EBSF-1250: bass and 6-string, double pointed cutaways, SG-shape solid mahogany body, beveled edges, 2 humbucking PUs for each neck, 4 knobs on lower treble bout, 1 switch between tailpieces, 1 switch on upper treble bout, fuzz-tone on bass, cherry red finish
Introduced (special order only): **1962**
Sunburst, white, or black finish (no cherry): **1963**

Discontinued (22 total shipped): **1968**
*Note: Doublenecks were available in virtually
any combination on a custom order basis.
Several double 6-strings (with 2 standard
6-string necks) exist. At least one early
style (hollowbody) exists with 8-string
mandolin neck and tenor guitar neck.*

COMMENTS

Original 1958–59 Flying Vs and Explorers, as
well as 1962–63 examples with 1958-59
body, are the most highly sought after of
any soldibody Gibson production model.
Due to their extremely high value, they
have been copied by skilled forgers.
Various later versions appeal to players for
aesthetic reasons or for their modern
vibrato systems. Of the later models, only
the Heritage korina wood reissues have
any appeal to collectors.

Original series reverse body Firebirds are very
highly regarded by collectors. Non-reverse
body models bring less but still have some
appeal to collectors.

Of the other solidbody styles in this section,
the L-5S has some appeal to collectors,
and the map-shape promotional model has
some value as a conversation piece. The
Chet Atkins CE is highly regarded by players. In general, all the other models, from
the L-6S through the Q-400 are of interest
primarily in the context of Gibson company
history.

Doublenecks with carved tops are unlike any
other Gibson guitar design and are especially desirable not only for their rarity but
for their sound.

ELECTRIC BASSES KEY

Solidbody
  Explorer guitar body shape=**Explorer**
  Flying V guitar body shape=**Flying V**
  Violin-shaped body
    Brown plastic PU cover, banjo tuners=**EB-1, 1953–58**
    Chrome PU cover, right-angle tuners=**EB-1, 1970–72**
  Firebird body shape
    1 PU
      No *Made in USA* on peghead=**Thunderbird II**
      Made in USA on peghead=**Thunderbird II reissue**
    2 PUs
      Mahogany body
        Handrest and bridge cover
          Thunderbird IV, 1963–69
          Thunderbird 76
          Thunderbird 79
        No handrest or bridge cover=**Thunderbird IV reissue**
      Curly maple top=**Firebird II**
  Single cutaway=**Les Paul Triumph**
  Double cutaway with rounded horns=**EB-0, 1959–early 61**
  Double cutaway with pointed horns (SG-style)
    1 PU with visible poles
      30 1/2" scale
        Crown peghead inlay
          No fuzztone=**EB-0, early 1961–79**
          Fuzztone=**EB-0F**
        No peghead ornament=**EB**
      34 1/2" scale
        3-position slide switch=**EB-4L**
        No slide switch=**EB-0L**
    1 PU with no visible poles
      30 1/2" scale=**SB-300**
      34 1/2" scale=**SB-400**
    2 PUs with visible poles
      6 strings=**EB-6, early 1961–66**
      4 strings
        30 1/2" scale=**EB-3**
        34 1/2" scale=**EB-3L**
    2 PUs with no visible poles
      30 1/2" scale=**SB-350**
      34 1/2" scale=**SB-450**
  Asymmetrical double cutaway, longer bass horn
    Standard Gibson peghead=**Ripper (L9-S)**
    Triangular peghead with rounded top
      Inlay in center of fingerboard
        1 moveable PU=**Grabber**
        3 PUs=**G-3**
      Inlay closer to bass side of fingerboard
        4 strings=**Gibson IV**
        5 strings=**Gibson V**
    Peghead points to bass side (4-on-a-side tuners)
      2 PUs
        Battery pocket on back=**Victory Artist**
        No battery pocket on back=**Victory Custom**
      1 PU=**Victory Standard**
    Peghead points to treble side=**Q-80, Q-90**
  Asymmetrical double cutaway, longer treble horn
    Active electronics=**RD Artist**
    Standard (passive) electronics=**RD Standard**
  Straight-line body edges, 90-degree angles=**20/20**

Semi-hollowbody
    Symmetrical double cutaway
        1 PU
            6 strings=**EB-6, 1960–61**
            4 strings
                Plastic-covered PU=**EB-2, 1958–61**
                Metal-covered PU=**EB-2, 1964–72**
        2 PUs=**EB-2D**
    Asymmetrical double cutaway=**Les Paul Signature**

ELECTRIC BASSES

SECTION ORGANIZATION

Models Introduced 1953–61 and related SG-shape models
Thunderbird (Firebird-style) Models
Les Paul Models
Other Models, 1973 and after: Ripper, Grabber, Victory, Gibson IV, etc.

Models Introduced 1953–61

Gibson Electric Bass (commonly referred to as **EB-1** after introduction of EB-2): violin-shaped mahogany body, carved top, painted-on purfling and f-hole, Alnico magnet PU with poles close to bridge side, brown bakelite PU cover, barrel knobs, elevated pickguard, screw-in endpin, telescopic end pin also provided for upright playing, 30 1/2" scale, Kluson banjo-style tuners, exposed bridge, crown peghead inlay, brown stain finish, brown contoured case with plush pink lining
Introduced: **1953**
Discontinued, 546 total shipped: **1958**
Re-introduced as **EB-1**: humbucking PU with poles across middle, chrome PU cover, chrome bridge cover, black bonnet knobs, standard right-angle tuners, rectangular case: **1970**
Discontinued (4 shipped, 1972–73): **1972**

EB-2 (sunburst) or **EB-2N** (natural finish): ES-335 type semi-hollow body, double rounded cutaway, f-holes, 1 single-coil PU with poles close to bridge side, black plastic PU cover (a few early with brown cover), stud bridge/tailpiece, single-bound top and back, 30 1/2" scale, dot inlay, crown peghead inlay, Kluson banjo-style tuners with large holes through shafts, sunburst or natural finish
Introduced: **spring 1958**
Humbucking PU with poles across center: **mid to late 1958**
Baritone pushbutton control: **1959**
Some with black finish: **May 1959**
Some with cherry finish: **March 1960**

String mute: **1960**
Right-angle Kluson tuners: **late 1960**
Discontinued (32 EB-2 and 7 EB-2N shipped): **1961**
Re-introduced: metal PU cover with poles across middle, string mute, sunburst finish only: **1964**
Cherry finish optional: **late 1965**
EB-2D: 2 humbucking PUs (1 standard bass PU in neck position, smaller PU in bridge position), sunburst or cherry finish, introduced : **1966**
Walnut or burgundy finish optional, by **1969**
EB-2 and EB-2D discontinued: **1972**

EB-0: slab mahogany body, double cutaway with rounded points (like 1959 Les Paul Jr.), 1 black plastic-covered humbucking PU, neck-body joint at 17th fret, 30 1/2" scale, rosewood fingerboard, dot inlay, Kluson banjo-style tuners, cherry red finish
Introduced: **1959**
PU poles across middle of PU: **1960**
SG-style double pointed cutaway, beveled top edges, unbeveled cutaway edges, right-angle tuners: **early 1961**
Metal-covered PU, string mute: **c. 1962**
EB-0F: built-in fuzztone, available: **1962–65**
EB-0L: 34 1/2" scale, introduced: **late 1969**
Walnut finish optional by **1971**
Black finish available (11 shipped): **1971–75**
Natural finish available (5 shipped): **1973**
EB-0 and EB-0L discontinued (6 shipped): **1979**

EB-6: 6 strings, tuned an octave below standard guitar, semi-hollow ES-335 type body, double rounded cutaway, 1 humbucking guitar PU, string spacing like guitar, 30 1/2" scale, crown peghead inlay, right-angle tuners, plastic tulip-shaped tuner buttons, sunburst finish
Introduced: **1959**
Solidbody, SG-style double pointed cutaway, dot inlay, 2 humbucking PUs, larger metal tuning keys, cherry red finish: **late 1961**
Discontinued (135 total shipped): **1966**

EB-3: solid mahogany body, SG-style double pointed cutaway, 2 humbucking PUs (large neck PU, small bridge PU), black plastic cover on neck PU, metal cover on bridge

PU, handrest between PUs, 4-position rotary tone switch with pointer knob, string mute, neck-body joint at 17th fret, 30 1/2" scale, rosewood fingerboard, dot inlay, crown peghead inlay, solid peghead, cherry red finish
Introduced: **1961**
2 metal PU covers: **1962**
No handrest, metal bridge cover, slotted peghead, no crown on peghead: **1969**
EB-3L: 34 1/2" scale, available: **1969–72**
Walnut finish optional by **1971**
Natural finish available on EB-3 (49 total shipped): **1971–73**
Solid peghead, crown peghead inlay: **1972**
White finish available on EB-3 (69 total shipped): **1976–79**
Discontinued: **mid 1979**

EB: solid maple body, SG-style double pointed cutaway, 1 large humbucking PU, 2 knobs, long pickguard extends below bridge, neck-body joint at 15th fret, dot inlay, 30 1/2" scale, decal logo, no peghead ornament
Available: **1970**

EB-4L: solid mahogany body, SG-style double pointed cutaway, 1 large humbucking PU, 2 knobs, 3-position slide switch, string mute, rosewood fingerboard, dot inlay, 34 1/2" scale, cherry or walnut finish
Introduced: **1972**
Discontinued: **1975**
Shipped (including 1 black finish) through: **1979**

SB-400: solid mahogany body, SG-style double pointed cutaway, 1 black plastic-covered mini-humbucking PU, 34 1/2" scale
SB-300: 30 1/2" scale
Introduced by **1971**
Discontinued: **1974**

SB-450: solid mahogany body, SG-style double pointed cutaway, 2 black plastic-covered mini-humbucking PUs, 2 knobs and 2 push switches mounted on control plate, string mute, no pickguard, thumbrest near fingerboard, rosewood fingerboard, dot inlay, 34 1/2" scale, cherry or walnut finish
SB-350: 30 1/2" scale
Introduced by **1972**
Discontinued: **1975**
Shipped through: **1978**

Thunderbird Models

Thunderbird II: companion to Firebird I guitar, reverse body shape, neck-through-body construction, 1 metal-covered PU with no visible poles, 2 knobs, 34" scale, dot inlay, right-angle tuners all on bass side of peghead, sunburst finish standard, custom colors available
Thunderbird IV: companion to Firebird III, same as Thunderbird II but with 2 PUs, 4 knobs
Introduced: **1963**
Non-reverse body, glued-in neck with visible joint: **mid 1965**
Discontinued: **1969**

Thunderbird 76: companion to Firebird 76 guitar, reverse body, 2 PUs, sunburst, natural mahogany, white, or black finish
Available: **1976**

Thunderbird 79: reverse body, 2 PUs, natural mahogany, ebony, or tobacco sunburst finish
500 instruments made: **1979**

Firebird II: reverse body, curly maple top, mahogany body, flat top, glued-in neck
Available: **1982**

Thunderbird II reissue: reverse body, 1 PU
40 instruments made: **1983–84**

Thunderbird IV reissue: reverse body, 2 PUs, 3 knobs, no handrest, no bridge cover
Introduced: **1987**
Still in production

Les Paul Models

Les Paul Bass: solid mahogany body (companion to Les Paul Professional and Les Paul Personal), single rounded cutaway, 2 oblong low-impedance PUs mounted straight across, high/low impedance selector switch, controls on semi-circular control plate, small block inlay, 30 1/2" scale, 5-piece split-diamond peghead inlay, walnut finish
Introduced: **1970**
Renamed **Les Paul Triumph**, white finish optional: **1971**
Discontinued (44 shipped): **1979**

Les Paul Signature: semi-hollow body, asymmetrical double rounded cutaway, 1 oblong low-impedance humbucking PU, trapezoid inlay, sunburst or gold finish
Introduced: **1973**
High impedance PU, gold finish only: **1976**
Discontinued (58 shipped): **1979**

Other Models, 1973 and After

L9-S: solid maple body, asymmetrical double cutaway, 2 humbucking PUs, 3 knobs, 4-position switch, strings anchor through body, 34 1/2" scale, bolt-on maple neck,

maple fingerboard with natural finish,
ebony fingerboard with sunburst finish, dot
inlay, standard Gibson peghead, decal
logo, natural maple or sunburst finish
Introduced: **1973**
Renamed **Ripper**: **1974**
Fretless model (**L9-FS**) introduced, ebony or
tobacco sunburst finish only: **1975**
Sunburst finish discontinued on standard (fretted) Ripper, ebony finish (with ebony fingerboard) optional: **1975**
Discontinued: **1982**

Grabber (G-1): solid maple body, asymmetrical
double cutaway, 1 movable PU with *Gibson*
embossed on plastic cover, 2 knobs, 34 1/2"
scale, bolt-on maple neck, maple fingerboard, dot inlay, triangular peghead with
rounded top, decal logo, wine red or ebony
finish
Introduced: **late 1974**
Natural finish available: **1976**
Discontinued: **1982**

G-3: solid maple body, asymmetrical double
cutaway, 3 single-coil PUs, 2 knobs, 1
switch, transparent PU covers, 34 1/2"
scale, bolt-on maple neck, maple fingerboard, dot inlay, triangular peghead with
rounded top, natural, sunburst, or ebony
finish
Introduced: **1975**
Black PU covers: **1976**
Discontinued: **1982**

RD Standard: asymmetrical double cutaway
with extended treble horn, 2 humbucking
PUs with black covers and no visible poles,
maple fingerboard with natural finish
model, ebony fingerboard with ebony finish
model, no peghead ornament, standard
Gibson peghead, dot inlay, natural or
ebony finish
Introduced: **1979**
Discontinued: **1980**

RD Artist: asymmetrical double cutaway with
extended treble horn, 2 humbucking PUs
with black covers and no visible poles, 4
knobs, 3 switches, active electronics,
strings anchor through body, maple fingerboard with natural finish model, ebony fingerboard with all other finishes, dot inlay,
winged-*f* peghead inlay, standard Gibson
peghead, natural, antique sunburst, ebony
or fireburst finish with ebony fingerboard
Introduced: **1979**
6 RD Artist 6-string models made: **c. 1980**
Discontinued: **1982**

Victory Artist: asymmetrical double cutaway
with extended bass horn, 2 humbucking
PUs, neck PU mounted at slant, 3 knobs, 2
switches, active electronics, battery pocket on back, bolt-on maple neck, rosewood
fingerboard, asymmetrical fingerboard
extension on treble side, fretless fingerboard optional, dot inlay positioned closer
to bass edge of fingerboard, 4-on-a-side
tuners, peghead points to bass side,
antique fireburst or candy apple red finish
Victory Standard: same as Victory Artist but
with 1 slant-mounted PU, 2 knobs, 1
switch, non-active electronics, silver or
candy apple red finish
Introduced: **1981**
Victory Custom: same as Victory Artist but
with passive electronics, no battery pocket
on back, no more than 250 made: **1982–84**
Victory Artist discontinued: **1986**
Victory Standard discontinued: **1987**

Flying V: companion to Flying V guitar
Only listing: **1982**

Explorer: companion to Explorer guitar
Introduced: **1984**
Custom graphics available: **1985 only**
Discontinued: **1987**

Q-80: same body shape as Victory series, 2
PUs, 3 knobs, no pickguard, square-end
rosewood fingerboard, dot inlay in center
of fingerboard, peghead points to treble
side
Introduced: **1986**
Renamed **Q-90**: **1988**
Fretless model available: **1989**
Q-90 still in production

Gibson IV: asymmetrical double cutaway, 2
PUs, 3 knobs in straight line, no pickguard,
ebony fingerboard, dot inlay positioned
closer to bass side of fingerboard, peghead narrows toward top
Gibson V: 5-string
Introduced: **1987**
Discontinued: **1989**

20/20: designed by Ned Steinberger, straight-line body edges with 90-degree angles,
extended bass horn, 2 PUs, 3 knobs, ebony
fingerboard, dot inlay, small rectangular
peghead, 2-on-a-side tuners with offset
configuration, black hardware
Introduced: **1987**
Discontinued: **1989**

WRC I and **WRC II**: companions to SR-71 guitar, designed by Wayne Charvel
Listed but never in production: **1988**

COMMENTS

Reverse-body Thunderbird basses are the most highly sought after of all Gibson basses. They are considered to be the finest electric basses ever made by Gibson.

The early version of the violin-shaped bass (later named EB-1) is highly regarded by collectors. Early versions of the EB-2, EB-0 and EB-3 have some appeal to collectors. The EB-6 is very rare and considered to be of high quality.

In general, Gibson basses never achieved the market recognition or success of Fender models. Virtually all Gibson basses from the mid-1960s onward are generally regarded as having no more than average utility value.

Steels

STEELS KEY

No pedals
    Singleneck
        Symmetrical body, 2 rounded bouts (guitar shape)
            No control plate (knobs into top)
                Green and gray bridge/PU cover=**model name unknown**
                No PU cover
                    Shoulders angle into neck
                        Metalbody=**Metalbody** (no model name)
                        Woodbody=**Woodbody** (no model name)
                    Shoulders taper into neck
                        Hexagonal or oblong PU=**EH-150**
                        Rectangular white PU=**EH-100, 1936–40**
            Metal plate extends under fingerboard to form peghead
                Sunburst finish=**EH-185**
                Natural finish=**EH-275**
            5-sided metal control plate
                Natural mahogany finish=**EH-100, 1940–41**
                Sunburst finish=**EH-125**
            Gold plastic control plate and bridge/PU cover
                Curlicue design on PU cover=**BR-4**
                Plain PU cover=**BR-6, 1949–60**
            White control plate and bridge cover=**BR-6, 1947–49**
        Symmetrical body with points on upper bouts=**Royaltone**
        Symmetrical 3-bout body=**BR-9**
        Symmetrical square-end body (1 bout)=**Century, 1966–67**
        Straight-line body on bass side
            Bittersweet (salmon) finish=**Century, 1949–65**
            Black finish
                10 strings=**Century 10**
                6 strings=**Ultratone**
            Any other paint finish=**Ultratone**
            Natural finish korina wood
                Custom Deluxe on peghead=**Skylark Deluxe**
                No *Custom Deluxe* on peghead=**Skylark**
    Doubleneck
        Rosewood fingerboards
            Rectangular body=**Console Grand, 1939–42**
            Guitar-shaped body=**EH-150 doubleneck**
        Silver back-painted plastic fingerboards
            Sunburst=**Console Grand, 1946–66**
            Natural=**CGN**
        Black back-painted plastic fingerboards=**CG 520**
        Korina wood fingerboards and body=**Consolette**
        Maple fingerboards and body=**CG 530**
    Tripleneck
        Sunburst=**CGT**
        Natural=**CGTN**
4 pedals
    Maple body, contoured top=**Eletraharp, 1949–56; EH-630 1956–67**
    "Limed oak" butcher block body=**EH-610**
6 pedals
    Maple and walnut cabinet=**Electraharp, 1939–42**
    No cabinet
        Doubleneck=**EH-620**
        Tripleneck=**Multiharp**
8 pedals
    Singleneck=**EH-810**
    Doubleneck=**EH-820**

152

STEELS

All singleneck lap steels prior to World War II are of hollowbody construction. All post-war singlenecks are solidbody.

SECTION ORGANIZATION

Lap Models Introduced Before WWII
Lap Models Introduced After WWII
Console Models (with legs) and Pedal Models

Lap Models
Introduced Before WWII

Metalbody (no model name): cast aluminum body, guitar-shaped body with shoulders angled into neck (at a sharper angle than EH-150 and all later models), Charlie Christian PU with bound blade, 2 knobs on opposite sides, black paint logo
98 instruments shipped: **Oct. 1, 1935-Mar. 9, 1936**

Woodbody (no model name): similar to EH-150 (see following) but with shape of metal-body model, shoulders angled into neck (at a sharper angle than all later models), Charlie Christian PU
Some shipped: **1935**

Electric Hawaiian EH-150: guitar shape, shoulders taper into neck more gradually than earlier models, maple top, screwed-on back, Charlie Christian PU, bound PU blade, unbound outer edge of PU, 2 knobs on opposite sides, triple-bound top (early with single-bound top), bound rosewood fingerboard with V-end, pearl dot markers, pearl logo, no peghead ornament, sunburst finish, 6 or 7 strings (later 8, 9, or 10 strings optional; at least 1 with 13 strings)
Introduced: **Jan. 1, 1936**
Glued-on back, bound outer edge of PU, knobs on same side, triple-bound top and back, 4-piece diamond peghead inlay: **1937**
Doubleneck Electric Hawaiian, 2 necks, available: **1937-38**
Chrome-plated bridge cover by **1939**
ES-300 type oblong PU mounted at a slant: **1940**
Fleur-de-lis peghead inlay: **late 1940**
Square-end metal fingerboard, fancy markers: **1941**
Discontinued: **1942**

Roy Smeck Special: guitar-shaped body, shoulders taper into neck, Charlie Christian PU with no binding, 2 knobs on opposite sides, dark binding, V-end fingerboard, dot inlay, model name on peghead, natural finish

1 instrument made and shipped to Roy Smeck: **Mar. 6, 1936**

EH-100: guitar-shaped body, shoulders taper into neck, maple top, ES-100 type blade PU with white rectangular housing, 1 knob on treble side, bound top, rosewood fingerboard with square end, dot inlay, silkscreened logo, black finish, 6 or 7 strings
Introduced: **1936**
2 knobs on opposite sides: **c. 1936**
2 knobs on treble side, sunburst finish by **1937**
Mahogany body, metal-covered PU, 5-sided control plate surrounds knobs and PU, knobs on opposite sides, no body binding, square-end metal fingerboard with fancy markers (some with rosewood fingerboard and pearl dot inlay), point at top of peghead like Kalamazoo models, silkscreened logo, natural mahogany finish: **1940**
Discontinued: **1941**

EH-125: guitar-shaped body, shoulders taper into neck, metal-covered PU, 5-sided metal control plate, metal bridge cover, bound top and back, metal fingerboard, fancy markers, fleur-de-lis peghead inlay, pearl logo, sunburst finish
Introduced: **1939**
Discontinued: **1942**

EH-185: guitar-shaped body, shoulders taper into neck, curly maple top, Charlie Christian PU, 1-piece metal plate extends from peghead to pickguard (under fingerboard) covering most of lower bout, peghead is part of metal plate, wood neckpiece bolts onto back of metal plate, bound rosewood fingerboard with V-end, dot inlay, slotted peghead, top tuners, sunburst finish
Introduced: **1939**
ES-300 type pole PU mounted at a slant: **1940**
Discontinued: **1942**

EH-275: guitar-shaped curly maple body, shoulders taper into neck, Charlie Christian PU, 1-piece metal plate extends from peghead to pickguard (under fingerboard) covering most of lower bout, peghead is part of metal plate, wood neckpiece bolts onto back of metal plate, tortoise grain binding on top and back, rosewood fingerboard with V-end, white fingerboard binding, white and yellow inlay (some with dot inlay), slotted peghead, top tuners, natural finish
Introduced: **1940**
ES-300 type pole PU mouted at a slant: **1941**
Discontinued: **1941**

153

Lap Models
Introduced After WWII

BR-4: guitar-shaped mahogany body, PU with
non-adjustable poles, knobs on opposite
sides, large gold plate covers lower
bouts, curlicue design on PU cover, binding varies (some with none, some with top
only, some with top and back), rounded
neck, sunburst finish
Introduced: **1946**
Discontinued: **1948**

BR-6: guitar-shaped mahogany body, knobs on
opposite sides, plastic control plate back-
painted white, white bridge/PU cover,
square neck, white open-block markers
with numbers, black finish
Introduced: **1946**
Gold plastic control plate and PU cover, string
ends visible, single-bound top and back,
metal fingerboard, gold-painted markers,
round neck, sunburst finish: **1948**
Knobs on same side: **1949**
Discontinued: **1960**

BR-6B: specs unavailable, possibly BR-6 with
black finish, 77 sold: **1956–59**

BR-9: graduated 3-bout body, brown plastic
PU/bridge cover, 2 white radio knobs on
same side, PU with non-adjustable poles,
open-block markers with numbers, beige
finish, brown fingerboard and trim
Introduced by **1947**
Adjustable PU poles: **c. 1950**
Discontinued: **1959**

Ultratone 6 and **Ultratone 7**: straight-line bass
side of body, rounded extension around
knobs on treble side, maple body, PU with
non-adjustable poles, 3 knobs, coral
bridge/PU cover with lyre design and
Ultratone, plastic fingerboard back-painted
silver, fingerboard widens along bass side,
dot markers, coral rectangular tuner buttons, gray and silver peghead cover, white
finish
Introduced: **1947**
Adjustable PU poles: **c. 1950**
No peghead cover, curlicue figure on peghead, peghead points slightly to treble
side, oval tuner buttons, black finish: **early
1950s**
Straight body edge around knobs, flower on
PU cover, fingerboard back-painted blue,
bass edge of fingerboard parallel to
strings, some with *Century* at end of fingerboard, no peghead cover, curlicue peghead ornament, logo straight across peghead, dark blue finish: **c. 1953**
Peghead cover with floral design, seal brown

finish, beige fingerboard, by **1955**
Bound top, clay colored tuner buttons, ivory
top finish, natural mahogany back and
sides finish: **1956**
Ultratone 7 discontinued: **1956**
Humbucking PU, flower design on PU cover:
1958
Ultratone 6 discontinued: **1959**

Century-6: straight-line bass side of body, P-90
soapbar PU matching finish, plastic bridge
cover does not hide PU, 3 knobs, beach
white (beige) fingerboard finish, dot markers, 1-color plastic peghead cover, bitter-
sweet (salmon or clay color) body finish
Introduced: **1948**
Slightly asymmetrical body with square end,
mini-humbucking PU with no poles, rectangular metal PU cover, control plate
extends up neck, dark fingerboard, red and
yellow markers, logo reads upside down to
player, red finish, by **1966**
Discontinued: **1968**

Century 10: 10 strings (possibly intended to be
Gibson version of the Eddie Alkire E-Harp
10-string lap steel), black finish
Introduced: **1948**
Discontinued, total of 90 shipped: **1956**

Royaltone: symmetrical body with points on
upper bouts, maple top, 2-tone dark brown
and black PU cover, natural top finish,
brown back and sides finish
Introduced: **1950**
Discontinued (none shipped 1953–55, 1957–58):
1960

Century Deluxe: specs unavailable, possibly a
2 PU (side by side PUs) version of Century
10
Introduced: **1956**
Discontinued, total of 20 shipped: **1959**

model name unknown: guitar-shaped body,
plastic PU cover, colored dot markers,
olive-mustard finish
Available: **1957**

Skylark (EH-500): korina (African limba wood)
body, square-end body with straight line
on bass side, slant-mounted PU, control
plate has shoulder to include knob, body
beveled around fingerboard, open block
markers with numbers, peghead points
slightly to treble side, raised plastic logo
reads upside down to player, natural finish
Introduced: **1956**
8-string available: **1958**
Discontinued: **1968**

Skylark Deluxe: dot markers, *Custom Deluxe*

stenciled on peghead, otherwise similar to Skylark
No catalog listing, listed as separate model on shipping records, 45 shipped: **1958**
Some made: **1959**

Console and Pedal Models

Console Grand: doubleneck, staggered tiers, Charlie Christian PUs, chrome-plated bridge covers, triple-bound top and back, bound rosewood fingerboards with V-ends, 7- and 8-string combinaton standard, any combination of 6, 7, or 8 strings optional, sunburst finish
Introduced: **1939**
Contoured top, 3 knobs, oblong PUs, plastic fingerboard back-painted silver, double 8-string standard, sunburst or natural (**CGN**) finish: **1948**
4 legs by **1953**
Large humbucking PUs with 4-8-4 pole configuration: **1956**
Discontinued: **1967**

Electraharp: 6-pedals, 8 strings, maple top, maple cabinet with walnut panels, ES-300 type oblong pole PU mounted at a slant, heavy metal bridge and tuner covers (some wood), bound rosewood fingerboard with V-end, dot inlay, tuners at PU end, natural finish
Introduced: **1939**
4 pedals, maple body, top beveled around fingerboard, 4 aluminum legs, pedals anchored on legs, sunburst finish: **1949**
EH-620: 6 pedals, introduced: **1955**
4-pedal model renamed **EH-630**: **1956**
Humbucking PU: **1956**
EH-610: 4 pedals, 6 strings, rectangular "limed oak" butcher block body, non-contoured top, introduced: **1957**
Mute and tone-boost pushbuttons on EH-630 and EH-620: **1960**
EH-820: doubleneck, 8 pedals on rack across front, Vari-Tone rotary tone selector switch, cherry finish, introduced: **1960**
EH-810: singleneck version of EH-820, introduced: **1961**
All Electraharps discontinued: **1967**

Consolette: korina (African limba wood) body, rectangular body shape, 2 8-string necks, staggered tiers, white P-90 PUs, white bridge/PU covers, 2 knobs and switch between necks, natural finish (described in catalog as "mahogany type finish"): **1952**
Discontinued, name continues on laminated maple model C 530 (see following): **1956**
Last korina Consolettes shipped: **1957**

CGT: Console Grand tripleneck, sunburst or natural (**CGTN**) finish, 4 legs

Introduced: **1953**
Renamed **CG 523**, optional legs, oak finish: **1956**
Discontinued: **1957**

CG 520: 2 8-string necks, oak body, PUs with 4-8-4 pole configuration, 2 knobs, 2 push switches, 3-way switch, 4-way tone selector switch on each neck, black binding, black fingerboard, tuners arranged in pairs, raised black logo on front, natural oak finish, 4 non-adjustable legs optional
Introduced: **1956**
Discontinued by **1967**

Console (C 530): listed as Consolette (see preceding), 2 8-string necks, laminated maple body, humbucking PUs with 2 rows of visible poles, mute and tone-boost pushbuttons, maple fingerboards, natural finish, 4 legs optional
Introduced (2 shipped in 1955): **1956**
Listed as Console (C 530): **1957**
Discontinued by **1967**

Multiharp: 3 necks, 6 pedals on middle neck, ebony finish
Introduced: **1957**
Discontinued: **1966**

COMMENTS

Prewar models with the Christian pickup are the most highly regarded by collectors and players. The metalbody model, which is Gibson's first electric instrument and the only metalbody instrument of any kind ever made by the company is very rare and highly sought after.

Prewar models with the oblong slant-mounted pickup are also highly regarded, with the natural finish EH-275 quite rare. Low-end models, especially those with metal-covered pickup, are of considerably less interest.

The Electraharp, which is the first modern, professional quality pedal steel, is quite rare and quite a conversation piece.

Most postwar lap and console models are regarded as fine utility instruments. The Ultratone and Century models are among the most visually appealing of any Gibson instruments in the history of the company. The early Consolette and the Skylark, with korina wood bodies, are sought by collectors who associate them with korina guitars (Explorer and Flying V).

The postwar pedal steels are, ironically, more primitive and cumbersome in design than the prewar Electraharp (due to a patent dispute). As a result these models have limited appeal to collectors or players.

UKULELES

Uke-1: 6" wide, mahogany body, black and white rope-pattern soundhole ring, no body binding, 12-fret ebonized fingerboard with pointed end, all frets clear of body, small dot inlay, ebony nut and saddle, peghead tapers to point at top, *The Gibson* silkscreened logo, black tuner buttons, light amber finish
Introduced: **1927**
17-fret rosewood fingerboard extends to soundhole: **1928**
Gibson logo by **1937**
White-black-white soundhole ring, single-bound top, unbound back, 12-fret fingerboard, larger pearl dot inlay, darker finish: **1937**
Unbound top by **1955**
Discontinued (2 shipped): **1967**

Uke-2: 6" wide, mahogany body, rope-pattern soundhole ring, triple-bound top, single-bound back, 12-fret rosewood fingerboard with pointed end, all frets clear of body, bone nut and saddle, small dot inlay, peghead tapers to point at top, *The Gibson* silkscreened logo, white tuner buttons, light amber finish
Introduced: **1927**
17-fret fingerboard extends to sound hole: **1928**
Discontinued: **1937**

Uke-3: 6" wide, mahogany body, colored-wood rope-pattern soundhole ring, multiple-bound top and back, bound rosewood fingerboard with pointed end, 17-fret fingerboard extends to soundhole, bone nut and saddle, varied-pattern inlay, peghead tapers to point at top, pearl ornamental peghead inlay, *The Gibson* silkscreened logo, black tuner buttons, brown mahogany waxed finish
Introduced: **1927**
Pearl logo, white tuner buttons, (some catalogs specify black buttons and ivoroid saddle): **1928**
Discontinued: **1937**

Custom models: During the late 1920s and early 1930s, virtually any ornamentation was available on a Gibson uke by custom order. Several examples exist with red poinsettia on the top, ivoroid fingerboard, ivoroid peghead veneer, and pearl logo. Other fancy variations exist.

TU: tenor uke, 9" wide, spruce top, mahogany back and sides, tiered belly bridge with sharp-bevel ends and extra pin, white-black-white soundhole ring, single-bound top and back, 18-fret rosewood fingerboard with square end, 12 frets clear of body, small dot inlay, peghead tapers to point at top, *The Gibson* logo, cremona brown finish
Introduced: **1928**
Gibson logo: **1937**
Mahogany top: **1938**
Renamed **TU-1**: **1949**
ETU: electric TU-1, 88 total shipped: **1949–53**
Unbound top and back by **1962**
Discontinued (2 shipped): **1965**

TU-3: specs unavailable, 205 shipped: **1950–55**

BU-1: baritone uke, 10" wide, mahogany body, pin bridge, rosewood fingerboard, dot inlay, truss rod, dip in center of peghead
Introduced: **1961**
Discontinued (4 shipped): **1967**

COMMENTS

Gibson ukes are regarded as excellent instruments. The Style 2 and Style 3 are rare and sought after by collectors.

MANDOLINS, GENERAL INFORMATION

Mandolin Family Styles

A-style: A, C, or D model designation, 10 1/4"
wide, symmetrical rounded body, 13 7/8"
scale

A-style exceptions:

A-1 and A-50: 11 1/4" wide with 14 1/2"
scale, **1937–42 only**

A-5: Florentine 2-point body shape,
1957–71; F-style body shape with lump
scroll, **1971-79**

A-12: F-style with lump scroll body shape,
1971–80 (throughout production)

F-style: F model designation, 10" wide, scroll on
upper bass bout, pre-1910 models with 3
body points, later models with 2 points

Mandola: H model designation, 12" wide **pre-
1908**; 11" wide, **1908 and after**; 15 3/4" scale,
tuned a fifth below mandolin

Mandocello: K model designation, 14" wide, 24
3/4" scale, tuned an octave below mandola

Mandobass: J model designation, 24" wide, 42"
scale, standard bass tuning

General Design Evolution

1890s–late1902: Mandolins made by Orville
Gibson from the 1890s to the formation of
the Gibson company in late 1902: wider
and deeper body than later models, 3-point
body shape on F models, walnut back and
sides, flat back with carved edge, 1-piece
neck heel and sides, pickguard inlaid into
top, pearl dot inlaid in scroll on F models,
long neck volute at peghead, shallow neck
set, large "paddle" peghead on A models,
friction tuners, *O. H. Gibson* on label

Late 1902–c. 04: "Orville-style" early Gibson
company models: same design as Orville
Gibson-made models but with Gibson company label. Although models were cataloged, many examples do not conform to
catalog specs or to each other.

c. 1904–07: carved curved back, low bridge,
neck separate from sides, shallow neck
set, no peghead volute, standard tuners,
The Gibson logo, standard (non-paddle)
peghead on F models

1908–09: birch back and sides except for
maple F-4 and a few maple F-2s, narrower
and shallower body, higher bridge, elevated pickguard, 2 pickguard clamps, no pearl
dot in scroll

1910 and after: 2-point body shape on F models, modern-height bridge, 1 pickguard
clamp

Mid 1922: introduction of Style 5 Master
Models (see Lloyd Loar section in Gibson
General Information), maple back and
sides, many features different from other
F-models (see model descriptions)

c. 1926–27: maple back and sides on all models

By late 1929: lacquer finish, heavier construction

1930s–42: design experimentation beginning in
1937 with larger body on A-1 and A-50,
introduction of electric mandolin EM-150

1942–46: all mandolin production ceased for
World War II

1950s–60s: longneck F-12, larger peghead on F
models, introduction of Florentine solidbody electric model

1970–77: major revamping of F-style in an
attempt to revive older designs, with smaller peghead, new carving pattern, bound
pickguard, fancy fingerboard and peghead
inlay, different style neck joint, pearl or
pearloid tuner buttons

1978–current: modern era begins with intro-
duction of F-5L, production moves from
Kalamazoo to Nashville and finally to
Bozeman (see Gibson General Information)

Contradictions to Catalog Descriptions

Back and sides: Catalogs from 1903 through
the mid 1920s describe all mandolins as
having maple back and sides. However,
the only early models with maple back and
sides are the F-4, F-5, and H-5, plus some
F-2 examples from c. 1906–09. Virtually all
other mandolins, mandolas, and mandocellos have walnut back and sides until c.
1907. From c. 1908 to the mid to late 1920s,
all (except F-4, F-5, and H-5) have birch
back and sides. The K-5 mandocello
changes from birch to maple with the L-5
guitar, by 1925. All other models switch to
maple in the mid to late 1920s. A few later
models are mahogany.

Pickguards: The 1903 catalog describes all A
models as having a tortoise grain pickguard inlaid into the top, with pearl ornament inlaid into the pickguard and pearl
"binding" or border around the pickguard.
The A is pictured, however, with no pickguard; the A-1, A-2, and A-3 are shown
with plain tortoise grain pickguard; only
the A-4 is shown with the pickguard as
described. Many examples from 1903–07
have a pickguard inlaid into the top with
pearl or plastic binding material around the
edge of the pickguard.

Tailpieces: Catalogs as late as 1963 show all
mandolins with clamshell tailpiece. More
accurate dates are provided in this section
and in the model descriptions.

Top Bracing

Oval or round hole models: 1 small transverse brace
f-hole models: 2 lengthwise tone bars

Bridges

1-piece low bridge: **1890s–c. 1907**
Bridge height raised but not to modern height: **1908–09**
Bridge height raised to modern height, moveable saddles: **1910–16**
1-piece compensating bridge (no separate saddle): **1917–early 21**
Height-adjustable...
    Small base, bottom edge flush with top of instrument, 2 extensions on top of base for adjustment screws, adjustable alumimum top, adjustment wheels 3/8" in diameter: **early 1921 only**
    Larger base with 2 feet, 2 extensions on top of base for adjustment screws, no aluminum top, adjustment wheels 3/8" in diameter: **mid 1921–late 30s**
    Larger bridge with 2 feet, 2 extensions on top of base for adjustment screws, adjustment wheels 1/2" in diameter: **late 1930s–42**
    Bottom edge of bridge flush with top of instrument (no feet), flat top of base (no extensions for screws), adjustment wheels 5/8" in diameter: **1946–current**
    1920s style bridges with small adjustment wheels, Style 5 models: **late 1980s–current**

Tailpieces

Top edge with slight points, deep indents on sides near top, engraved *The Gibson*, ornamental pattern above logo: **1902–07**
Wriggle top edge, small indents on sides near top, *The Gibson* ornamental pattern above logo...
    Stamped (or no) ornamentation, all models except Style 5: **1908–42**
    Engraved ornamentation, Style 5 only: **1922–27**
    A few with engraved ornamentation, various models: **early 1930s**
Clamshell shape, no logo...
    A-0 (throughout production): **1927–34**
    A-1: **1941–42**
    A-50: **1942–early 60s**
    A-40 (from introduction): **1948–early 60s**
    EM-150: **1948–early 60s**
Clamshell shape with logo...
    Florentine electric (from introduction): **1954–c. 60**
    A-5 (from introduction): **1957–c. 60**
    F-5, F-12: **1948–late 1950**
Wriggle top edge pattern, modern *Gibson* logo, no ornamental pattern above logo...
    F-5, F-12: **late 1950–70**
    All other models by **1965–70**
Replicas of earlier tailpieces, ornamental pattern above logo, engraved ornamentation: **1970–current**

Pickguards

Inlaid into top: **1890s–1907**
Elevated, 2 clamps around side of body on models with 3-point body shape, 1 clamp on models with 2-point body, spike attachment to bridge, pointed shape at cutout for bridge: **1908–16**
Elevated, no point at bridge cutout: **late 1916–21**
Elevated, right-angle support screwed into side of body, no spike attachment to bridge...
    Style 5 (from introduction): **1922–current**
    All other models (see exceptions, following): **1926–current**
Exceptions: C-1 has painted-on pickguard; oval hole A-00 (1933 only) and A-C (Century model) have pickguard glued to top.

Necks

Cherry neck: **pre-1912**
3-piece mahogany neck: **1912–23**
1-piece mahogany neck, all models except F-5: **1923–1942**
F-5, 1922–42...
    2-piece maple with laminate stripe: **1922**
    1-piece maple: **1923–42**
1-piece mahogany, all models except F-5 and F-12: **1946–70**
F-5 and F-12, 1946–70...
    1-piece mahogany: **1949–early 50s**
    2-piece maple with laminate stripe: **early 1950s–early 60s**
    5-piece maple with 2 laminate stripes: **early 1960s–69**
All models, 1970 and after...
    1-piece maple, longneck models with fingerboard extension support as integral part of neck: **1970–78**
    1-piece maple, fingerboard extension support not part of neck: **1978–current**

The term *longneck* (not longer scale) refers to neck design with more frets clear of body. On longneck models, the body binding meets the neck at approximately the 15th fret. On standard shortneck models, the body binding meets the neck at approximately the 12th fret.

Pegheads

Tuners...

> Friction pegs (most have been replaced by standard tuners): **1890s–c. 1904**
>
> German-made, gear wheel above shaft: **c. 1904–25**
>
> Waverly, gear wheel below shaft: **1926–42**
>
> Kluson Deluxe, 4 on a plate: **1946–c. 71**
>
> Schaller: **c. 1971–current**

Tuner buttons...

> Inlaid on A-3, A-4, all F models, and corresponding mandolas and mandocellos: **pre-1918**
>
> Grained ivoroid, all models except Style 5: **1918–mid 30s**
>
> Plastic, all models except those with pearl buttons (see following): **mid 1930s–current**
>
> Mother-of-pearl tuner buttons: F- 5, **1922–42**; F-5L, A-5L, F-12, **1934–37**

Truss rod (except A-Jr., A-0), introduced: **late 1922**

Tuner plates angling toward each other at top: **1923–27**

Tapered snakehead peghead, A models: **1923–27**

Patent Dates on Parts

Pickguard: **Mar. 30, 1909**
Pickguard clamp: **July 4, 1911**
Adjustable bridge: **Jan. 18, 1921**

Serial Numbers, 1902–87

Mandolins, mandolas and mandocellos have serial numbers in the same series as guitars (see Gibson General Information).

Serial Numbers, 1987-Current

Mandolin-family instruments made in Bozeman, MT, have a different numbering system than the standard 8-digit Gibson system. Each mandolin style has its own series.

Bozeman serial numbers consist of 7 digits: $ynnnmmz$

y=last digit of year of manufacture
nnn=the rank of the instrument within its style series (see note after example)
mm=month of manufacture
z=decade of manufacture

Example: 0280089 was made in August (08), 1990 and is the 280th instrument of its style. For easier interpretation, put the last digit first. The transposed example, 9028008, shows the year (90) followed by the rank (280) followed by the month (08).

Note: The F-5L, Army-Navy, and H-5 models each have their own number series. The A-5G and A-5L are numbered together in a single series. Rankings do not start over at the beginning of each year.

Model A from 1917.

F-4 from 1919 with 2-point scroll body shape, inlaid tuner buttons, long flowerpot peghead inlay. Binding line (hidden by pickguard) meets neck at 12th fret).

F-5L from 1991 with fern peghead inlay. Longneck design, with binding line meeting neck at 15th fret.

Florentine electric from 1969 with carved top, solidbody design.

MANDOLINS

SECTION ORGANIZATION

Symmetrical Body Models (mandolas and mandocellos listed with mandolins of corresponding specs)

Asymmetrical Body Models (mandolas and mandocellos listed with mandolins of corresponding specs)

Other Acoustic Mandolin Family Instruments (mandobass, tenor lute)

Electric Mandolins

Symmetrical Body Models

A: oval hole, colored wood soundhole ring, ebony fingerboard, dot inlay, large rounded paddle-shaped peghead, veneer on peghead, golden orange top finish, reddish back and sides finish
Introduced: **1902**
Smaller non-paddle peghead: **c. 1905**
Single-bound top, by **1906**
Elevated pickguard, no peghead logo, by **1908**
Brown finish standard: **1918**
Snakehead peghead: **1923**
Standard peghead: **1928**
Discontinued: **1933**

H: mandola, same features as Style A mandolin
Only catalog appearance: **1902**

K: mandocello, same features as Style A mandolin
Only catalog appearance: **1902**

A-1: bound oval hole with 2 wood-inlaid rings, pickguard inlaid into top, single-bound top, bound ebony fingerboard, dot inlay, large rounded paddle-shaped peghead, veener on peghead, golden orange top finish, reddish back and sides finish
Introduced: **1902**
Smaller non-paddle peghead, *The Gibson* logo: **c. 1905**
Elevated pickguard: **1908**
Discontinued: **1918**
Re-introduced: 1 ring around soundhole, single-bound top and back, no logo (some with silver paint logo), black top finish, brown back and sides finish: **1922**
Snakehead peghead: **1923**
Discontinued: **1927**
Re-introduced: bound top, straight logo, standard peghead shape, sunburst finish: **1933**
f-holes, bound top and back, white paint logo: **1934**
11 1/4" wide, 14 1/2" scale: **1937**
10 1/4" wide, 13 7/8" scale, clamshell tailpiece cover: **1941**
Discontinued: **1943**

A-2: bound oval hole with 2 wood-inlaid rings, pickguard inlaid into top, single-bound top and back, unbound ebony fingerboard, dot inlay, large rounded paddle-shaped peghead, veneer on peghead, asterisk peghead inlay, golden orange top finish, reddish back and sides finish
Introduced: **1902**
Discontinued by **1908**
Re-introduced, bound oval hole with 2 narrow wood-inlaid rings, elevated pickguard, bound top and back, bound ebony fingerboard, dot inlay, pearl *The Gibson* logo, brown finish: **1918**
Renamed as **A2-Z**: double-bound top, single-bound back, double-bound soundhole, black-white-black soundhole rings, bound fingerboard, amber top finish, brown back and sides finish: **1922**
Snakehead peghead: **1923**
A2-Z renamed **A-2**: **1927**
Discontinued: **1928**

H-1: mandola, same features and changes as A-2 mandolin
Introduced: **1902**
Same features as A-1 mandolin but with treble-side fingerboard extension, bound fingerboard: **1908**
Same features as A-2 mandolin: **1918**
2 wood-inlaid soundhole rings: **1922**
No peghead change (no snakehead shape): **1923–27**
Black top finish: **1925**
Same features as Style A mandolin: **1927**
Discontinued: **1936**

K-1: mandocello, same features and changes as H-1 mandola
Introduced: **1902**
Discontinued (very rare after 1930): **1943**

A-3: bound oval hole with 2 wood-inlaid rings, pickguard inlaid into top, single-bound top and back, bound ebony fingerboard, dot inlay, large rounded paddle-shaped peghead, veneer on peghead, asterisk-like peghead inlay, golden orange top finish, reddish back and sides finish
Introduced: **1902**
Elevated pickguard, smaller non-paddle peghead, ornamental curlicue peghead inlay: **1908**
Wide white soundhole ring between 2 black-white-black rings, ivoroid pickguard, ivory top finish: **1918**
Discontinued: **1922**

A-4: bound oval hole, solid white soundhole ring between 2 ivoroid and wood rope-pattern rings, single-bound top and back, bound ebony fingerboard, dot inlay, asterisk-like peghead inlay, black top

finish, reddish back and sides finish
Introduced: **1902**
Ornamental inlay on pickguard by **1907**
Elevated pickguard with point at bridge cutout, smaller peghead, fleur-de-lis peghead inlay, *The Gibson* logo, front and back peghead veneer, inlaid tuner buttons, by **1908**
Treble-side fingerboard extension: **1912**
Uniform red mahogany finish (slightly shaded) standard, black or orange top finish optional: **1914**
No tuner button inlay: **1918**
Dark mahogany sunburst top finish only, by **1918**
Snakehead peghead: **1923**
Standard peghead: **1928**
Straight *The Gibson* logo: **1928**
Gibson logo, amber red mahogany sunburst top finish: **1928**
Discontinued: **1935**

H-2: mandola, same features and changes as A-4 mandolin
Introduced: **1902**
Ivory finish available by special order: **1918**
Discontinued: **1922**

K-2: mandocello, same features and changes as Style A-4 mandolin and H-2 mandola
Introduced: **1902**
Ivory finish available by special order: **1918**
Discontinued: **1922**

"Artist Model": (no literature or model name available) similar to A-4 except for ornate fingerboard
Introduced: **c. 1904**
Discontinued by **1908**

Alrite, Style D: flat top and back, no body taper at neck, round hole, ebony bridge, elevated pickguard, colored wood inlay around top edge and soundhole, white plastic binding, ebony fingerboard, dot inlay, no peghead logo, special round label with model name, golden orange top finish, reddish back and sides finish
Introduced: **c. 1917**
Discontinued: **1918**

Army and Navy Special, Style DY: flat top and back, round hole, elevated pickguard anchored to bridge, dot inlay, peghead veneer, no logo, special round label with model name, brown stain finish
Introduced: **1918**
Discontinued: **c. 1922**
Reissued as Army-Navy (AN Custom) with different specs (see following): **June, 1988**

A Jr.: oval hole, black binding around hole, elevated pickguard, no body binding, ebony fingerboard, special round Jr. label, dark brown stain finish
Introduced: **c. 1919**
Snakehead peghead: **1923**
Discontinued: **1928**

A-0: oval hole, no binding or hole ornamentation, clamshell tailpiece cover, dot inlay, brown finish
Introduced: **1927**
Discontinued: **1934**

C-1: flat top, oval hole, mahogany back and sides, painted-on pickguard, clamshell tailpiece cover, bound top, unbound back, ebony fingerboard, silkscreened logo, natural top finish
Only catalog appearance: **1932**

A-00: oval hole, carved top, flat back, nonadjustable ebony bridge, pickguard glued to top, bound top, ebony fingerboard, dot inlay, *The Gibson* logo, brown sunburst finish
Introduced: **1933**
f-holes, elevated pickguard, clamshell tailpiece cover, *Gibson* logo: **1934**
Carved back: **1936**
Adjustable bridge, single-bound top and back, sunburst finish: **1939**
Discontinued by **1943**

H-0: mandola, A-style body, *f*-holes, flat back, square-end rosewood fingerboard, dot inlay, sunburst finish
Introduced: **1936**
Discontinued: **1943**

A-50: oval hole, bound top and back, single-bound fingerboard, fingerboard raised off of top, dot inlay *Gibson* logo, dark red mahogany sunburst finish
Introduced: **1933**
f-holes, unbound fingerboard: **1934**
11 1/4" wide, bound pickguard, 14 1/2" scale, bound fingerboard flush with top, varied-pattern inlay, fleur-de-lis peghead inlay (a few with flowerpot), pearl logo, brown sunburst finish, by **1937**
10" wide, 13 7/8" scale, clamshell tailpiece cover, small diamond peghead inlay: **1942**
Yellow silkscreened script logo: **1946**
Modern logo, no peghead ornament: **early 1947**
Laminated beveled-edge pickguard: **late 1947**
Discontinued: **1971**

A-C, Century model: oval hole, flat back, pickguard glued to top, bound top and back, bound pearloid fingerboard, double- and triple-diamond pearl inlay set into rosewood, pearloid peghead veneer, slotted-

diamond pearl peghead inlay set into rosewood
Introduced: **1934**
Discontinued by **1937**

A-75: *f*-holes, bound top and back, fingerboard raised off of top, single-bound fingerboard, dot inlay, 2-handled vase peghead inlay, slanted *Gibson* logo, brown mahogany sunburst finish
Introduced: **1934**
Discontinued by **1937**

A-40: *f*-holes, arched top and back, laminated mahogany back with cross brace, clamshell tailpiece cover, single-bound top, rosewood fingerboard, dot inlay, natural or sunburst finish
Introduced by **1948**
Discontinued: **1971**

A-5: oval hole, Florentine symmetrical 2-point body, maple back and sides, laminated beveled-edge pickguard, clamshell tailpiece cover with *Gibson*, bound rosewood fingerboard with treble-side extension, dot inlay, scroll peghead shape, crown peghead inlay, pearl logo, golden sunburst finish
Introduced: **1957**
Cherry sunburst finish: **early 1960s**
F-style 2-point body shape with lump scroll (no scroll cutout), longneck, fleur-de-lis peghead inlay, script *Gibson* logo: **1971**
Discontinued: **1979**

A-12: F-style 2-point body shape with lump scroll (no scroll cutout), *f*-holes, laminated beveled-edge pickguard, longneck, rosewood extension fingerboard, no peghead ornament, sunburst finish
Introduced: **1971**
Discontinued: **1980**

A-5L: design based on custom-made A-5 signed by Lloyd Loar in 1923, body shape shorter and more rounded than Loar example, same ornamentation and construction as F-5L (see following) but with A-style body, longneck, fingerboard raised off of top, flowerpot peghead inlay (Loar example has fleur-de-lis), snakehead peghead shape, sunburst finish
Introduced: **early 1988**
Still in production

A-5G: same body and neck style as A-5L but with single-bound top, unbound fingerboard, unbound peghead, abalone fleur-de-lis peghead inlay
Introduced: **early 1988**
Still in production

Army-Navy (AN Custom): reissue of Army and Navy Special (see preceding), flat top, flat back, round hole, pearl soundhole ring, non-adjustable ebony bridge, triple-bound top and back, longneck, bound ebony fingerboard with pointed end, ornamental curlicue peghead inlay, script *The Gibson* logo inlaid in pearl
Introduced: **June, 1988**
Still in production

Asymmetrical Body Models

F: 3-point body, oval hole, pearl dot in scroll, bound top, pickguard inlaid into top, pearl inlay in pickguard, ebony fingerboard with treble-side extension, dot inlay, scroll peghead shape, veneer on peghead, friction pegs, golden orange top finish
Only catalog appearance: **1902**

F-2: 3-point body, oval hole, pearl dot in scroll, pickguard inlaid into top, ornate pearl inlay on pickguard, bound soundhole with 2 wood-inlaid rings, pearl and ebony rope-pattern top binding, ebony fingerboard with treble-side extension, dot inlay, scroll peghead shape, star and crescent peghead inlay, front and back peghead veneer, friction pegs, inlaid tuner buttons, black top finish, reddish back and sides finish
Introduced: **1902**
Single-bound top and fingerboard, *The Gibson* peghead inlay, right-angle tuners, tuner plates angle away from each other at top: **c. 1904**
Ivoroid and wood soundhole rings, elevated pickguard with point and 2 clamps, golden orange top finish optional (most examples black): **1908**
2-point body: **1910**
Uniform red mahogany finish (slightly shaded) standard, black or orange top finish optional: **1914**
No inlay on tuner buttons, dark mahogany sunburst finish: **1918**
Truss rod: **late 1922**
1-piece neck, rounded neck heel, arrow-end tuner plates: **1923**
Round-end tuner plates: **1926**
Maple back and sides: **c. 1927**
Discontinued: **1934**

F-3: 3-point body, oval hole, pearl dot in scroll, pearl-bound pickguard inlaid into top, ornate pearl inlay in pickguard, bound soundhole with 2 wood-inlaid rings, white and green rope-pattern top border with pearl binding, ebony fingerboard with treble-side extension, dot inlay, scroll peghead shape, front and back peghead

Mandolins

veneer, friction pegs, inlaid tuner buttons, black top finish, reddish back and sides finish
Only catalog description (no illustration): **1902**

F-4: 3-point body, oval hole, pearl dot in scroll, pearl-bound pickguard inlaid into top, pearl inlay in pickguard, bound soundhole with 2 rope-pattern wood-inlaid rings, white and green rope-pattern top border with pearl binding, bound ebony fingerboard with treble-side extension, dot inlay, scroll peghead shape, pearl peghead binding, front and back peghead veneer, friction pegs, inlaid tuner buttons, black top finish, reddish back and sides finish
Introduced: **1902**
Ivoroid and wood soundhole rings, elevated pickguard with point and 2 clamps, single-bound top and back, pearl nut, ivoroid-bound peghead, ornate long-flowerpot peghead inlay of abalone and wire, no logo, right-angle tuners, notched-end tuner plates angle away from each other at top, black top finish standard, golden orange top finish optional (most examples are golden orange), by **1908**
2-point body: **1910**
Double-flowerpot peghead inlay, slanted *The Gibson* logo: **1911**
Uniform red mahogany finish standard, black or orange finish optional: **1914**
No pickguard at bridge cutout: **1917**
No inlay on tuner buttons, dark mahogany sunburst finish: **1918**
Truss rod, single-flowerpot peghead inlay (some transitional models with truss rod piercing through double-flowerpot inlay): **late 1922**
1-piece neck, rounded neck heel, arrow-end tuner plates: **1923**
Round-end tuner plates: **1926**
Pointed-end fingerboard, unbound peghead, large diamond peghead inlay, yellow-to-brown sunburst top, brown back and sides finish: **1935**
2 checkerboard (black and white plastic) outer sound hole rings with white middle ring: **c. 1936**
Discontinued: **1943**

H-4: mandola, same features and changes as F-4 mandolin
Introduced: **1912**
Last produced: **late 1920s**
Discontinued from catalog: **1940**

K-4: mandocello, same features and changes as F-4 mandolin and H-4 mandola
Introduced: **1912**
Last produced: **late 1920s**
Discontinued from catalog: **1940**

"Artist Model": no literature or model name available, 3-point body, walnut back and sides, oval hole, pickguard inlaid into top, fancy pearl inlay in pickguard, top border of alternating pearl-and-black blocks, pearl and wood soundhole rings, ornate fingerboard inlay similar to F-5 of 1970s, unbound peghead, *The Gibson* logo, no peghead ornament, black top finish
Variations: F-2 body and ornamentation but with ornate fingerboard inlay
Introduced: **c. 1904**
Discontinued by **1908**

F-5: 2-point body, *f*-holes, triple-bound top and back, triple-bound pickguard, pickguard follows body point, right-angle pickguard support screwed into side of body, pickguard support of triple black-and-white binding material, hand-engraved tailpiece cover, truss rod, longneck, 2-piece maple neck with laminate stripe, bound ebony fingerboard with treble-side extension, black line on side of fingerboard binding, dot inlay, bound peghead, black line on side of peghead binding, flowerpot peghead inlay, *The Gibson* logo, notched-end tuner plates, pearl tuner buttons, silver-plated metal parts, Cremona shaded brown (sunburst) finish, *Master Model* and Loar-signature labels
Note: F-5 is first Gibson model with the following features (which would become standard on modern mandolins and modern archtop guitars): parallel top braces, bound pickguard, right-angle pickguard support screwed into side of body, maple neck, fingerboard raised off of top, longer neck (not longer scale) with 15 frets to body binding line.
Introduced: **June 1922**
Narrower 1-piece maple neck, arrow-end tuner plates: **1923**
Some examples with black line on side binding (rather than on top): **1923**
Virzi Tone-Producer (see Gibson General Information), many examples; some examples with fern peghead inlay, most with flowerpot: **1924**
Ivoroid body binding, ungrained fingerboard binding with black line on side, triple-bound peghead, by **mid 1924**
No Virzi Tone-Producer except for 1 example, no Loar label, fern peghead inlay standard, sunburst finish lighter and more golden than Loar-period, gold-plated metal parts: **early 1925**
Metal pickguard bracket, Waverly tuners (rounded ends) with shafts above gear wheels: **early 1927**
No *Master Model* label, stamped (not engraved) *The Gibson* on tailpiece cover,

dot inlay from 3rd fret, darker finish: **c. 1928**
Block inlay from 3rd fret, heavier construction:
late 1929
Gibson logo: **c. 1932**
Block inlay from 1st fret, flowerpot peghead
inlay, by **late 1930s**
A few with fleur-de-lis peghead inlay: **c. 1940**
Discontinued: **1943**
Re-introduced: laminated beveled-edge pickguard, clamshell tailpiece cover with
Gibson, single-bound top and back, triple-
bound fingerboard with black line on side,
1-piece mahogany neck, block inlay from
first fret, triple-bound peghead, flowerpot
peghead inlay, plastic tuner buttons, standard postwar logo, smaller prewar size
peghead: **late 1949**
Wriggle-edge tailpiece with postwar logo,
triple-bound top and back, 2-piece maple
neck with ebony laminate stripe, larger
peghead: **late 1950**
3-piece maple neck with 2 dark laminate
stripes: **early 1960s**
Re-designed: different carving pattern and
structural features, triple-bound pickguard,
1-piece maple neck with integral fingerboard extension support, ornate abalone
fingerboard inlay, flowerpot peghead inlay
like top half of F-4 double-flowerpot from
1911–21 (fancier than Loar-period F-5 flowerpot), script *The Gibson* logo, small peghead, special F-5 label: **1970**
Discontinued: **1980**

H-5: mandola, same features and changes as
F-5 mandolin
Introduced: **1923**
Last made: **late 1920s**
Discontinued from catalog: **1936**

K-5: mandocello, L-5 guitar body, 16" wide,
birch back and sides, asymmetrical fingerboard with treble-side extension, F-5 type
tailpiece mounted onto trapeze tailpiece,
L-5 type peghead, flowerpot peghead inlay,
same ornamentation and changes as L-5
guitar
Introduced: **1924**
Maple back and sides, peghead inlay remains
flowerpot pattern (when F-5 and K-5 go to
fern): **1925**
Last made: **late 1920s**
Discontinued from catalog: **1936**

F-7: 2-point body, *f*-holes, single-bound top
and back, single-bound pickguard, no point
on pickguard at body point, single-bound
square-end fingerboard, fingerboard
raised off of top, varied-pattern inlay,
single-bound peghead, fleur-de-lis peghead inlay or 2-handled vase and curlicues
peghead inlay, sunburst finish

Introduced: **1934**
Discontinued: **1940**

F-10: 2-point body, *f*-holes, single-bound top
and back, single-bound pickguard, no point
on pickguard at body point, single-bound
fingerboard with treble-side extension, fingerboard raised off of top, scroll-pattern
inlay, single-bound peghead, 2-handled
vase and curlicues peghead inlay, ivoroid
tuner buttons, nickel-plated metal parts, all
black finish
Introduced: **1934**
Discontinued by **1937**

F-12: 2-point body, *f*-holes, single-bound top
and back, single-bound pickguard, no point
on pickguard at body point, single-bound
fingerboard with treble-side extension, fingerboard raised off of top, scroll-type inlay,
single-bound peghead, 2-handled vase and
curlicues peghead inlay, pearl tuner buttons, gold-plated metal parts, red
mahogany sunburst top finish, deep red
back and sides finish
Introduced: **1934**
Discontinued by **1937**
Re-introduced: point on pickguard, clamshell
tailpiece cover, mahogany neck, longneck,
bound rosewood fingerboard with square
end, fingerboard flush with top, dot inlay,
unbound peghead, crown peghead inlay,
small prewar size peghead, Cremona
brown sunburst top finish, uniform brown
back and sides finish: **1948**
Wriggle-edge tailpiece cover, fingerboard
raised off of top, larger peghead: **late 1950**
Treble-side fingerboard extension, smaller
peghead, single-bound peghead, fleur-de-
lis peghead inlay, *The Gibson* script logo,
by **1970**
Discontinued: **1980**

F-5L: reissue of Loar F-5 (actually closer to
1925 F-5), fern peghead inlay, gold-plated
metal parts
Introduced: **1978**
Flowerpot peghead and silver-plated metal
parts (F-5L Bill Monroe features) optional:
late 1988–90
Still in production

F-5L Bill Monroe: same as F-5L (preceding) but
with black line on side of body binding
rather than on top, flowerpot peghead
inlay, logo lower on peghead than standard F-5L, silver-plated metal parts, label
signed by Bill Monroe, optional varnish
finish, replica 1923 style case
Introduced: **early 1991**

Mandolins

Other Acoustic Mandolin Family Instruments

Mando-Bass, Style J: 4 strings, A-style body, 24" wide, carved top and back, bound round soundhole, 2 rope-pattern sound-hole rings, maple bridge with 2 slots for individual string saddles, trapeze tailpiece with pins mounted on tortoise grain cellu-loid plate, bound top, unbound back, 42" scale, asymmetrical fingerboard with tre-ble-side extension, dot inlay, elevated arm rest optional, extension support rod from side, pearl *The Gibson* logo, red mahogany sunburst top finish, black or orange top finish optional
Introduced: **1912**
Brown finish: **1918**
Black top finish: **1923**
Adjustable bridge, 1-piece ebony saddle, no arm rest, square-end fingerboard, silver silkscreened logo, black top finish, brown back and sides finish, by **1928**
Last made: **c. 1930**
Discontinued from catalog: **1940**

Tenor Lute, Style TL-1: 4 strings, carved top and back, A-style mandola body, *f*-holes, elevated pickguard, single-bound top, square-end fingerboard raised off of top, 21" scale, dot inlay, banjo type peghead and tuners (a few with 8 strings and man-dolin type tuners), pearl *The Gibson* logo, natural top finish, brown back and sides finish, *Master Model* label
Introduced by **1924**
Discontinued: **c. 1926**

Electric Mandolins

EM-150: A-00 body, 10" wide, carved top and back, Charlie Christian PU with no binding, single-bound pickguard, pickguard cutout for PU, bound top and back, knobs on opposite sides of body, dot inlay, brown sunburst top finish
Introduced: **1936**
Rectangular screw-pole PU, knobs on same side: **1941**
P-90 PU, laminated beveled-edge pickguard, clamshell tailpiece cover, bound finger-board (same specs as postwar A-50): **c. 1949**
Golden sunburst finish, by **1956**
Discontinued: **1971**

EM-100: blade PU with oblong housing (3 screws in top), clamshell tailpiece
Introduced by **1940**
Renamed **EM-125**: **1941**
Discontinued: **1943**

Florentine: solid mahogany body, symmetrical 2-point shape, carved top (similar to Les Paul electric guitar), soapbar P-90 PU, metal saddle, laminated beveled-edge pickguard follows body point, single-bound top, single-bound rosewood fingerboard, dot inlay, scroll peghead shape, crown peghead inlay, gold-plated metal parts, sunburst top finish
Introduced: **1954**
Renamed **EM-200**: **1960**
Renamed **Florentine**: **1962**
Pickguard surrounds PU, by **1966**
Discontinued: **1971**

COMMENTS

Very early mandolins made by or in the style of Orville Gibson generally do not have a very good sound and appeal primarily to collec-tors.

Mandolins from the c. 1904–09 period have a more modern design than those of the ear-lier period. Except for the very late three-point models (with higher bridge and shal-lower body), these still do not have a pow-erful enough sound to appeal to players. They do have some historical appeal and the more ornate models have aesthetic appeal as well.

High-end models from 1910 into the 1920s, in both A and F styles, are considered to be excellent utility instruments for classical, old-timey, or jazz music, but they lack the power of the F-5 design.

The F-5 of the 1920s is considered by players and collectors to be the epitome of man-dolin design. These command some of the highest prices on the vintage market of any production instrument, with Loar-signed examples bringing more than those with-out the Loar label. The Loar F-5 is the stan-dard by which all other mandolins are judged.

By the late 1920s, the mandolin boom had passed, and mandolins had not yet become a major part of country music. Due to the lack of demand for mandolins in general, F-5s of the late 1920s and 1930s are rarer than Loar models, but they are not regarded as having the quality of sound or construction of 1920s models. The F-7, F-10, and F-12 are sought because of their rarity. Because of their shortneck design, they do not bring as much as the F-5.

Postwar models of all styles are generally not highly regarded until the introduction of the F-5L in 1978. The F-5L and the A-5L are both regarded by players as instruments of high quality and are considered to be Gibson's best mandolins since the late

1920s.

Mandolas and mandocellos are not of great appeal to country and bluegrass players. There is an increasing interest in mandolas and mandocellos from players of classical and "new acoustic" music. Gibson models are highly sought for their utility and rarity. With the exception of Loar-signed instruments, mandolas and mandocellos bring prices slightly higher than the equivalent mandolin. The Loar-signed mandolin is so highly sought after that it brings more than Loar-signed mandolas or mandocellos.

The mandobass is rare and has great appeal as a conversation piece.

The tenor lute is rare and is the only non-Style 5 instrument to bear the *Master Model* label, but it is not particularly sought after by collectors or players.

Of the electric mandolins, the EM-150 has some historical appeal (as do all Gibson instruments with the Charlie Christian pick-up). The Florentine has some appeal based on its unusual carved solidbody design.

Gibson mandolins are extremely dominant in the marketplace. While others have made good quality mandolins, Gibsons remain the standard by which all others are judged.

OTHER BRANDS MADE BY GIBSON

Gibson manufactured instruments under other brand names for its own budget lines and for various mail-order houses and distributors.

Many manufacturers made instruments under other brands to bolster sales from the Depression up until World War II. Unlike Martin and Epiphone, whose budget brand models typically have the same construction as regular line models but with different ornamentation, Gibson designed its various budget lines to be less expensive to manufacture and thus different from the models that carry the Gibson brand. Also unlike Martin and Epiphone, Gibson devoted a significant percentage of its production effort to budget brands.

All budget brands were last produced in 1942, when Gibson cut back instrument production because of World War II. Some budget brand parts and features appear on Gibson brand instruments made during the early part of World War II. The Kalamazoo brand was revived from 1965–70.

Some brands are relatively rare and obscure. Some brands included a banjo line, and some of those, such as Kel Kroyden and Studio King, were better known for banjos than for guitars. Gibson also made instruments under other brands for foreign distribution. Undoubtedly, more brands and models exist than are listed in this section.

In addition, Gibson provided guitar bodies and necks to National/Valco (see National/Valco, General Information) from the late 1930s through the 1950s.

Differences Between Gibson Brand and Budget Brand Models

No Gibson budget brands have a Gibson stamp or logo.

No Gibson budget brand models have an adjustable truss rod, except for the postwar Kalamazoo models. Virtually all Gibson brand models during the same period have an adjustable truss rod.

All budget brand archtops have a slightly smaller bridge and shorter *f*-holes than Gibson brand models.

All budget brand flat tops, except for dreadnought-size models, have straight-across ladder top bracing. Budget brand dreadnoughts and Gibson brand flat tops from the same period have X-braced tops.

SECTION ORGANIZATION

Kalamazoo, 1937–42
Kalamazoo, 1965–70
Mastertone
Recording King, Carson Robison, Ward
Cromwell
Fascinator
Capital
Kel Kroyden
Martelle
Washburn

Kalamazoo, 1937–42

Kalamazoo was Gibson's in-house budget brand.

Logos: The prewar Kalamazoo logo is stylized print, almost like script but with unjoined letters. The postwar logo is script with joined letters.

Oriole: The Oriole brand was first used by Gibson in the late 1920s on a budget banjo line, which have *Oriole* on the peghead (no Gibson logo) and no bird decal. The Oriole name was revived in 1940 for a line of Kalamazoo models with tortoise grain binding and natural finish (tan finish on the lap steel). Kalamazoo/Oriole models have *Kalamazoo* and a decal of a bird on the peghead.

Body sizes: Gibson catalogs specify L-0 and L-30 models as 14 3/4" wide. Kalamazoo flyers specify grand concert size as 14 1/2" wide. Unless otherwise specified, they are, in fact, the same body size (14 3/4" wide) and shape as the Gibson equivalent.

Kalamazoo Peghead Shapes, 1937–42

Square top of peghead, KG-11 Spanish: **1938–42**
Top of peghead with straight edges leading to a point...
  All models except KG-11 Spanish, mandolins, mandolas and mandobass: **1937–38**
  Mandolins, mandolas, and mandobass, except Oriole models: **1937–42**
Peghead tapers to a sharp point at the top, except for KG-11, Oriole guitars, all mandolins and mandolas: **1939–41**
Standard Gibson peghead with dip in center, Oriole models only: **1940–42**

Kalamazoo Models, 1937–42

KG-3/4: 3/4-size flat top, 12 3/4" wide, mahogany back and sides, bound top, rosewood fingerboard, dot inlay, sunburst finish
Introduced: **1937**
Renamed **Sport Model**: **1938**

KG-11: flat top, 14 3/4" wide, 17 1/2" long (1 3/4" shorter than 14-fret L-0 body size), mahogany back and sides, L-0 type pickguard with upper part cut off, bound top, unbound back, dot inlay, square top of peghead, sunburst top finish, dark mahogany back and sides finish
KHG-11: Hawaiian, 12 frets clear of body, top of peghead with straight edges to point
Introduced: **1938**

KGN-12: Oriole model flat top, L-0 size, mahogany back and sides specified, most with maple back and sides, L-0 type pickguard with upper part cut off, tortoise grain binding on top and back, unbound fingerboard, dot inlay, bird decal on peghead, natural finish
KHG-12: Hawaiian, 12 frets clear of body
Introduced: **1940**

KG-14: flat top, L-0 size, mahogany back and sides, bound top, L-0 type pickguard with upper part cut off, dot inlay, sunburst finish
KTG-14: tenor
KHG-14: Hawaiian, 12 frets clear of body
Introduced: **1938**

KES-R: electric flat top, L-0 size, 2-segment blade PU in black oval housing, PU mounted on circular plate in soundhole, 2 PU mounting screws through plate, 1 octagonal knob with pointer, rosewood fingerboard, dot inlay, shaded top finish, mahogany back and sides finish
Introduced: **1940**

KG-16: arched top and back, f-holes, L-30 size, adjustable bridge, trapeze tailpiece, unbound pickguard, bound top, unbound back, unbound rosewood fingerboard, dot inlay, mist brown finish
Introduced: **1939**

KG-21: arched top and back, f-holes, L-30 size, adjustable bridge, trapeze tailpiece, unbound pickguard, bound top and back, unbound rosewood fingerboard, dot inlay, sunburst finish
KTG-21: tenor
Introduced: **1938**

KG-22: arched top and back, f-holes, L-50 size, 16" wide, maple back and sides, adjustable bridge, trapeze tailpiece, unbound pickguard, bound top and back, rosewood fingerboard, dot inlay, sunburst finish
Introduced: **1940**

KG-31: arched top and back, f-holes, L-50 size, 16" wide, mahogany back and sides, bound top and back, adjustable bridge, trapeze tailpiece, bound pickguard, bound rosewood fingerboard, dot inlay, sunburst finish, tenor available
Introduced: **1938**

KGN-32: Oriole model, arched top and back, f-holes, L-50 size, 16" wide, spruce top, maple back and sides, adjustable bridge, trapeze tailpiece, single-bound pickguard, tortoise grain binding on top and back, unbound rosewood fingerboard, dot inlay, ebony nut, bird decal on peghead, natural finish
Introduced: **1940**

KEH: lap steel, guitar-shaped maple body, 2-segment blade PU with oval coil, 5-sided control plate, bound top, rosewood fingerboard, dot markers, peghead tapers to point at top, chocolate brown finish
Introduced: **1939**
Renamed **KEH-R**: Oriole model, guitar-shaped mahogany body, no binding, tan finish, bird decal on peghead: **1940**
Metal PU cover, dark-colored metal fingerboard, fancy markers, sunburst finish: **1941**

KM-11: mandolin, A-style body, flat top and back, round hole, mahogany back and sides, clamshell tailpiece cover, pickguard glued to top, bound top, unbound back, bound fingerboard, dot inlay, sunburst top finish, brown back and sides finish
Introduced: **1938**

KM-12N: Oriole model mandolin, A-style body, f-holes, maple back and sides, clamshell tailpiece cover, unbound pickguard, tortoise grain binding on top and back, unbound fingerboard, dot inlay, bird decal on peghead, natural finish
Introduced: **1940**

KM-21: mandolin, A-style body, f-holes, mahogany back and sides, arched top and back, clamshell tailpiece cover, bound top and back, bound pickguard, bound fingerboard, dot inlay, sunburst finish
Introduced: **1938**

KM-22: mandolin, A-style body, f-holes, maple back and sides, clamshell tailpiece cover, bound top and back, bound pickguard, bound fingerboard, dot inlay, sunburst finish
Introduced: **1939**

KH-21: mandola, same trim as KM-21 mandolin, sunburst finish
Introduced: **1938**

KK-31: mandocello, same body and trim as KG-31 guitar, sunburst finish
Introduced: **1938**

KJ: mandobass, A-style body shape, *f*-holes, 24" wide, maple back and sides, bound top, brown sunburst finish
Introduced: **1938**

Kalamazoo, 1965–70

Except for the KG-10 flat top, all Kalamazoo models from 1965–70 are electric solidbodies with the following general specs:
Asymmetrical double cutaway shape similar to many Fender models, Melody Maker PU(s) with white cover, bolt-on neck, rosewood fingerboard, dot inlay, peghead shape similar to Fender, 6-on-a-side tuner arrangement, red, white, or blue finish: **1965–c. 68**
SG-body shape, symmetrical double cutaway with pointed horns, no bevels in cutaways, same peghead shape and tuner arrangement as earlier version: **c. 1968–70**
Note: Kalamazoo solidbody electrics have a 6-digit serial number impressed into the back of the peghead. Although the numbers appear to be standard Gibson numbers, they are inconsistent with numbers on Gibson brand instruments. Some numbers are from series that were used in more than one year; some numbers fall outside of recorded serial number ranges; some numbers have 000 as the first 3 digits, which on the Gibson line indicates a 1973 date of manufacture. These numbers may be from a separate series that applies to Kalamazoos only.

Kalamazoo Models, 1965–70

KG-1: 1 PU, no vibrato
KG-1A: 1 PU, flat-plate vibrato
KG-2: 2 PUs, no vibrato
KG-2A: 2 PUs, flat-plate vibrato
Introduced: **1965**
KG-1, KG-1A, and KG-2 discontinued: **1970**
KG-2A discontinued: **1971**

KB: electric bass, 1 large rectangular PU at neck, metal handrest, dot inlay, 4-on-a-side tuner arrangement, flame red, glacier white, or Las Vegas blue finish
Introduced: **1966**
Discontinued: **1971**

KG-10: flat top, similar to LG-0, all mahogany, narrow peghead 2 1/4" wide (like Melody Maker electric solidbody)
Introduced: **1968**
Discontinued: **1970**

Mastertone

The Mastertone name was introduced in the 1920s on high-end Gibson banjos and continues on current high-end banjos. In 1941, a Mastertone line of electrics was introduced as a budget brand marketed by Gibson. Gibson also marketed a Hawaiian acoustic and possibly other acoustic Mastertone models.

Acoustic Hawaiian: flat top, 14 3/4" wide, 17 1/2" long (1 3/4" shorter than 14-fret L-0 body size), mahogany back and sides, 12 frets clear of body, brown finish
Available: **c. late 1930s**

MESG: electric flat top, all mahogany, metal-covered PU mounted on round plate, plate in soundhole, 1 octagonal knob with pointer, bound top and back, bound fingerboard, dot inlay, *Mastertone Special* on peghead
Introduced: **1941**
Discontinued: **1943**

MEHG: lap steel, mahogany body, no binding, 5-sided control plate, cream-colored metal fingerboard, fancy markers, peghead tapers to point at top, *Mastertone Special* on peghead, tan ripple-spun finish
Introduced: **1941**
Discontinued: **1942**

Recording King

Recording King was a house brand of the Montgomery Ward company. Ward marketed some high-end models made by Gibson and some cheaper models that were not made by Gibson. Some Recording Kings have a Gibson-type serial number stamped onto the back of the peghead or (in the case of lap steels) on the back of the body. These numbers have a 2- or 3-letter prefix, the 2nd letter of which is *W* for Ward. The Recording King crown logo looks like a king's crown and is quite different from the "crown" peghead inlay on later high-end Gibsons.

Ray Whitley: named after country recording star, body similar to Gibson Advanced Jumbo, 16" wide, round-shouldered dreadnought, rosewood back and sides, bridge with points at both ends and at belly (like 1941 Gibson J-55), bridge beveled around edges, bound soundhole, no soundhole ornamentation, tortoise grain pickguard with vine and leaf patterns engraved around edge, 5-piece neck, 24 1/2" scale, single-bound rosewood fingerboard, small-diamonds inlaid on fingerboard in various patterns, no truss rod; peghead ornamen-

tation from top to nut: pearl crown, large pearl rectangle with *Recording King* stenciled in black script, *Ray Whitley* signature stenciled at an angle; peghead tapers to point at top, sunburst finish
Available: **1940-41**

Carson Robison: named after country songwriter, flat top, 14 3/4" wide, 17 1/2" long (1 3/4" shorter than 14-fret L-0 body size), single-bound top, unbound back, triple-bound rosewood fingerboard, dot inlay, square top of peghead, *Carson J. Robison* signature in white paint (no other logo or peghead ornament), sunburst finish, distributed by Montgomery Ward
Introduced by **1936**
L-0 body size and shape, 19 1/4" long, peghead tapers to point at top, stenciled crown on peghead, stenciled *Recording King* and *Carson J. Robison* signature on peghead, Hawaiian model (12 frets clear of body), distributed by Montgomery Ward: **c. 1938**
Discontinued by **1943**

Recording King dreadnought: round-shouldered dreadnought, mahogany back and sides (no other specs available)
Available: **late 1930s**

M-5: *f*-hole archtop, 16" wide, maple back and sides, adjustable rosewood bridge, trapeze tailpiece, checkered top binding, single-bound back, tortoise grain pickguard with checkered binding, 5-piece maple neck (with 2 rosewood laminate stripes), bound rosewood fingerboard with checkered binding on sides, 3-piece pearl inlay of rectangle broken by dot in center, peghead tapers to point at top, single-bound peghead, black front of peghead; pearl peghead inlays (from top to nut): crown with stenciled black ornamentation, large rectangular block with *Recording King* stenciled in black script, vertical rendering of fingerboard inlay pattern, small vertical block with *Model-M5* stenciled in black (some with no model name); metal tuner buttons (some gold-plated), sunburst finish
Variation: some with checkered peghead binding, at least one with script *Gibson* logo stenciled in black on large peghead block inlay and no other stenciling on peghead
Introduced by **1938**
17" wide, 2 pearl diamond inlays on bridge base, trapeze tailpiece with 4 vertical bars and crosspiece in middle, 5-ply top binding, triple-bound back, triple-bound pickguard, single-bound fingerboard, single black line around side of binding on body and fingerboard, large diamond inlay, unbound peghead, rosewood peghead

veneer, same peghead inlay as earlier version except for diamond (fingerboard inlay pattern) instead of broken rectangle, by **1939**

M-3: *f*-hole archtop, 16" wide, adjustable rosewood bridge, 2 inlaid dots on bridge base, single-bound top and back, single-bound tortoise grain pickguard, 5-piece maple neck (with 2 rosewood laminate stripes), single-bound rosewood fingerboard, dot inlay, peghead tapers to point at top, unbound peghead, pearl peghead inlay of crown (with stenciled ornamentation) and rectangular block with *Recording King* stenciled in black script, *Model M-3* stenciled in white block letters above nut, plastic tuner buttons, sunburst finish
Introduced by **1939**

Ward archtop: *f*-holes, 16" wide, maple back and sides, single-bound pickguard, dot inlay, top of peghead with straight edges to point, pearl logo with *WARD* in stylized block letters, round sticker-label inside with *WARDS* framed by stylized *M* and *W*, sunburst finish
Available: **mid to late 1930s**

Ward archtop: *f*-holes, 16" wide, maple back and sides, triple-bound top, single-bound back, single-bound rosewood fingerboard, top of peghead with straight edges to point, narrow rectangular pearl inlay across upper part of peghead (no other peghead ornament or logo), round label inside with *WARDS* framed by stylized *M* and *W*, sunburst finish
Available: **mid to late 1930s**

Roy Smeck AB 104: lap steel, pear-shaped body somewhat like A-style mandolin, blade PU in oval housing, 2 octagonal knobs, no bridge cover, single-bound top, unbound screw-on back, square-end rosewood fingerboard; peghead ornamentation from top to nut: crown stenciled in white, pearl rectangle with *Recording King* stenciled in black script, *Roy Smeck Model-AB104* stenciled in white; sunburst finish
Introduced: **1940**
Wider lower bouts, metal bridge cover, single-bound top and back, bound fingerboard with V-end: **1941**
Discontinued: **1943**

Model D: lap steel, pear-shaped body, blade PU (1 or 2 segments) in oblong black housing, oblong control plate, 2 octagonal knobs on opposite sides, unbound rosewood fingerboard with square end, dot inlay, stenciled crown and logo on peg-

head, top of peghead with straight edges to point, brown finish
Introduced: **1941**
Discontinued: **1943**

Cromwell

Cromwells were distributed by several mail order companies, including Grossman, Richter and Philips, and Continental. They typically have large dots inlaid on the fingerboard, a white line of binding material inlaid down the center of fingerboard, and *Cromwell* in block letters straight across the peghead.
All models discontinued by **1942**

G-2: 14 3/4" wide, flat top, L-0 size, mahogany back and sides, rectangular bridge, white bridge pins, bound top and back, Gibson prewar type pickguard with upper part cut off, rosewood fingerboard, top of peghead with straight edges to point, sunburst finish
GT-2: tenor
Introduced: **1935**
Peghead tapers to point at top, described in Continental catalog as gleaming black finish but pictured with sunburst top: **1938**

G-4: 16" wide, *f*-holes, arched (not carved) top, mahogany back and sides, adjustable bridge, trapeze tailpiece, double-bound top and back, unbound pickguard, unbound rosewood fingerboard, top of peghead with straight edges to point, sunburst top finish, brown back and sides finish
GT-4: tenor
Introduced: **1935**
Peghead tapers to a point at top: **1938**

G-5: 16" wide, *f*-hole archtop, specified as carved top, maple back and sides, adjustable bridge, trapeze tailpiece, bound top and back, single-bound pickguard, single-bound fingerboard, peghead tapers to point at top, sunburst finish
Introduced: **1938**

G-6: 16" wide, *f*-hole archtop, specified as carved top, maple back and sides, adjustable bridge, trapeze tailpiece, double-bound top and back, checkered marquetry around top, elevated pickguard with checkered marquetry around edge, bound rosewood fingerboard with checkered marquetry on sides, pearl logo, top of peghead with straight edges to point, sunburst finish
Introduced: **1935**
Maple back and sides, adjustable bridge, trapeze tailpiece, double-bound top and back, double-bound pickguard, single-

bound fingerboard, double-arrowhead fingerboard inlay (like Gibson L-10 of same period) with center line, peghead tapers to point at top, ornamental peghead inlay, pearl logo, metal tuner buttons, light brown sunburst finish: **1938**

GM-2: mandolin, A-style body, round hole, flat top and back, mahogany back and sides, non-adjustable bridge, clamshell tailpiece cover, triangular pickguard glued to top, single-bound top and back, rosewood fingerboard, top of peghead with straight lines to point, sunburst top finish
Introduced: **1935**

GM-4: mandolin, A-style body, *f*-holes, arched top and back, mahogany back and sides, adjustable bridge, clamshell tailpiece cover, elevated pickguard, bound top and back, rosewood fingerboard, top of peghead with straight lines to point, sunburst top finish
Introduced: **1935**

F-style mandolin (model name unknown): 2-point body with scroll on upper bass bout, *f*-holes, body shape slightly different from Gibson brand F-style mandolins (no other specs available)
Available: **mid 1930s**

Fascinator

The Fascinator line was distributed by the Tonk Bros. Co. of Chicago. Pegheads taper to a sharp point at top. Peghead logo is stenciled on a pearl rectangle with *Fascinator* in block letters diagonally across rectangle. Descriptions and model numbers are from the 1935 Tonk Bros. catalog.

Style 4960: L-0 size flat top, 14 3/4" wide, maple back and sides, bound top and back, rosewood fingerboard, dot inlay, sunburst finish

Style 4970: 16" wide, arched top and back, *f*-holes, mahogany back and sides, adjustable non-compensating bridge, trapeze tailpiece, single-bound traingular pickguard, triple-bound top, single-bound back, rosewood fingerboard specified as bound but pictured without binding, dot inlay, 3 dots at 12th fret

Style 4980: 16" wide, arched top and back, *f*-holes, mahogany back and sides, adjustable non-compensating bridge, trapeze tailpiece, single-bound triangular pickguard, single-bound top and back,

single-bound rosewood fingerboard, varied-pattern inlay with 5-piece cross-like
pattern at 3rd fret, peghead specified as
bound but pictured without binding, V-
shape peghead inlay with small diamond in
V, sunburst finish

Style 5284: A-style mandolin, *f*-holes, arched
top and back, mahogany back and sides,
adjustable non-compensating bridge,
clamshell tailpiece cover, elevated pickguard, single-bound top and back, rosewood fingerboard, dot inlay, sunburst
finish

Capital

Capital may have been a house brand of J.W.
Jenkins Sons Music Co., a Kansas City
mail order house. Those distributed by
Jenkins have the Jenkins name on a small
rectangular paper label.

Flat top: L-0 size, 14 3/4" wide, L-0 type pickguard with upper part cut off, single-bound
soundhole, single-bound top and back,
rosewood fingerboard, large dot inlay at
frets 3, 5, and 7, plus 2 small dots inlaid at
12th fret, line inlaid down center of fingerboard, peghead tapers to a point, script
Capital peghead logo in white paint, sunburst finish, tenor available
Available: **late 1930s**

Kel Kroyden

The Kel Kroyden brand was used on guitar,
mandolin, and banjo models. At least 3 guitar models—the KK-1 and KK-2—2 banjos
and 2 mandolins were available in 1930.

Kel Kroyden guitar: flat top, L-0 size, 14 3/4"
wide, spruce top, mahogany back and
sides, Hawaiian scene stencil-
ed on top (2 volcanos, palm trees, and a
boat), 12 frets clear of body, pearloid fingerboard, art deco markers, *Kel* stenciled
horizontally across top of peghead,
Kroyden stenciled vertically
Available: **early 1930s**

Martelle

Martelle Deluxe: flat top, 16" wide, round-
shouldered dreadnought shape, laminated
maple back and sides, rectangular pin
bridge, elevated pickguard, 3-ply soundhole ring, single-bound top and back, celluloid fingerboard with black binding, rosewood dot inlay, small pearl slotted diamonds inlaid into rosewood dots, wriggle-
top peghead with protrusion in center, cel-

luloid peghead veneer, *Martelle* stenciled
in block letters horizontally across peghead, *Deluxe* stenciled in block letters vertically, gold-plated planetary (banjo-style)
tuners, pearl tuner buttons, sunburst finish
Available: **c. 1934**

Washburn

The Washburn brand was acquired by the
Tonk Bros. Co. of Chicago from Lyon &
Healy in the late 1920s. Although Tonk
Bros. marketed a full line of Washburn
brand guitars, the only Gibson-made model
was the rosewood-body Solo.

Solo: flat top, 15" wide, no equivalent Gibson
brand body, rosewood back and sides,
triple-bound top and back, ebony bridge,
mahogany neck, ebony fingerboard, block
inlay, pearl logo, small protrusion at top of
peghead, natural top finish
Note: Not all Solo models were made by
Gibson. The only distinguishing character-
istic is the workmanship on the inside of
the body, which is better on Gibson-made
examples than on those not made by
Gibson.
Available: **c. 1935**

COMMENTS

Although Kalamazoo was Gibson's budget
brand, the high-end Kalamazoo archtop
models from the prewar period rival the
low-end Gibson brand models for sound
and playability. Kalamazoo flat tops all
have ladder bracing and generally do not
compare favorably to the X-braced Gibson
equivalents. Most Kalamazoo models bring
less on the vintage market than their
Gibson equivalent.

Kalamazoo solidbody electrics are not highly
regarded by players or collectors.

High-end Recording King and Cromwell models are roughly equivalent in construction
and ornamentation to midline Gibsons. The
Ray Whitley and the mahogany dreadnought flat top models (both with X-braced
tops) and the 5-M (with carved top) bring
as much as equivalent Gibson models.
Other models generally do not bring quite
as much as those with the Gibson brand.

In general, all prewar brands made by Gibson
are of historical interest to collectors.
Their values range widely, depending on
the quality of the model.

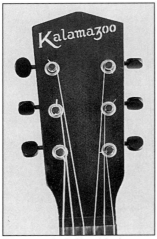

Kalamazoo peghead with straight edges toward top, on a 1938 model.

Kalamazoo peghead tapering to a sharp point, on a 1940 model guitar.

Peghead and logo on a late 1960s Kalamazoo bass.

Peghead of a high-end Recording King model, with crown and logo stenciled over pearl inlay.

Gretsch

GENERAL INFORMATION

The Gretsch company was formed as a tambourine manufacturer in Brooklyn, NY, in 1883, by Friedrich Gretsch, a German immigrant. After the founder's unexpected death in 1895, his son, Fred Gretsch, Sr., headed the company. Fred Gretsch, Sr., retired in 1942, leaving management of the company to his sons. Fred Gretsch, Jr., managed the operation briefly before serving in the Navy. His brother, William Walter (Bill) Gretsch, headed the company from 1942 until his death in 1948. Fred Gretsch, Jr., then assumed the presidency, a position he held until he sold Gretsch to the Baldwin Company in 1967.

The Gretsch line was expanded to include banjos and ukes by 1910 and drums by the 1920s. In 1927, a line of tenor guitars was introduced. In 1930, the company opened a Chicago office for sales and distribution only (no manufacturing). By the mid 1930s, Gretsch was a full-line instrument distributor, offering various brands of stringed instruments, drums, and band instruments.

A full line of Gretsch-American archtop guitars was introduced in the 1933 catalog. Also in the catalog was a wide selection of other instruments and brands, including ukes, banjos, flat top and archtop tenors, Rex brand budget instruments, Kay-Kraft guitars, and Harmony instruments. In 1940, Gretsch acquired the rights to Bacon & Day banjos from the Bacon & Day company.

In the late 1930s and 1940s, Gretsch became known for guitars with fancy trim and design innovations such as cat's eye soundholes on archtops and a triangular soundhole on flat tops. By the mid 1950s, Gretsch's emphasis had shifted to electrics. As with the earlier acoustic models, imaginative finish colors and ornamentation were trademarks of the Gretsch electric line in the 1950s and 1960s. Chet Atkins's endorsement on a line of electric guitars played a major role in the company's success.

In 1967, the Baldwin company of Cincinnati acquired Gretsch. Baldwin proceeded to consolidate Gretsch Guitars, Gretsch Drums, Baldwin guitars, and Ode banjos into one company. Sho-Bro resonator guitars, previously made by the Sho-Bud company of Nashville, were incorporated into the Gretsch guitar line. Sho-Bud pedal steels were distributed by Gretsch.

In 1970, instrument production was moved to Booneville, AR. Administration was moved to Cincinnati in August 1972. Due to two factory fires, few if any Gretsch guitars were made from January 1973 to spring 1974.

Gretsch bought Kustom in 1978. Shortly thereafter, Gretsch was sold to Charlie Roy and administration moved to the Kustom offices in Chanute, KS. By 1982, administration was moved to Gallatin, TN.

The last guitars from the Booneville plant were made in late 1979. Some parts were assembled in Mexico in a plant owned by Baldwin until 1984.

In early 1985, Gretsch was acquired by Fred Gretsch, son of William Walter Gretsch and nephew of Fred Gretsch, Jr. A new line of Japanese-made models was announced in late 1989 and debuted at the NAMM show in early 1990.

Labels

Beginning in the late 1940s, labels have model number and serial number. On flat tops, the label is visible through the soundhole. On open-hole archtops, the label is visible through the bass-side *f*-hole. On solidbodies and closed-hole hollowbodies, the label is on the underside of the control cover plate or in the control cavity.

White rectangular label: *The Fred Gretsch Mfg. Co.—60 Broadway, Brooklyn, N.Y.*, no T-roof logo, serial number in red, model number in blue/black...
Introduced, some models: **1940s**
All models: **c. 1954**
T-roof logo: **1955**
Gray top part, orange background for *The Fred Gretsch Mfg. Co.*, beginning with serial number 25001: **1957–64**
No label, serial number on peghead: **1964–72**
That Great Gretsch Sound across bottom of label, most with 5-digit serial number beginning with 1 or 2: **c. late 1960s**
White label with black border, *Gretsch Guitars*, no address: **1972–c. 83**

Miscellaneous Model Information

Archtop body widths...
Auditorium Special..................16"
Super Auditorium.....................17"
Auditorium Grand....................18"

Synchromatic, inlaid on the peghead of many models, refers to models with "synchronized" stairstep bridge and "chromatic" harp-shaped tailpiece.
Electromatic refers to any Gretsch electric archtop model from 1940 to 1955.

General Information

Model numbers (see separate list for numbers, 1948 and after)…
Number approximating retail price:
1933–48
6000-series: **1948–71**
7000-series (some overlap into 8000 series): **1971–80**
8000-series: **1979 and after**

Pickups

DeArmond: Gretsch Dynasonic, Fidela-tone, single-coil, black face, poles adjustable by a separate set of screws: **1949–57**
Filter 'Tron: double-coil, 2 rows of poles…
No markings on cover, smooth plastic frame: **very late 1957–58**
PAT. APPLIED FOR stamped on cover, ridged plastic frame: **1958–60**
Patent number on cover, ridged plastic frame: **1960–70**
Black face, no cover markings, height adjustable, metal frame, same case as Hi-Lo 'Tron PU: **1970–81**
Project-o-sonic stereo, optional…
Split PUs: each PU with 3 pairs of poles (on 1 side only), bass/treble split…
White Falcon: **1958 only**
Country Club: **1958–59**
4-switch system: 6 pairs of pole screws per PU, 4 switches on upper bass bout, numerous tone combinations possible…
White Falcon: **1959–80**
Country Club: **1960–62**
1 PU per channel, Double Anniversary only: **1960–62**
Hi-Lo 'Tron: single coil, polepieces through black face, low-end models: **1961–80s**
Super 'Tron: 2 metal bars (no screw poles): **1964–80s**
Humbucking: screw poles, metal cover: **1976–80s**

Knobs

Clear plastic, barrel shape: **1949–c. 54**
Plated brass, cross-hatch pattern on sides
Plain top: **1954**
Arrow on top: **early 1955–57**
Arrow through G on top: **1957–mid 67**
Aluminum, parallel ridges on sides, arrow through G on top…
Low-end models: **1966–80s**
High-end models: **mid 1967–80s**
Steel, cross-hatch pattern on sides, arrow through G on top, new models: **1990s**

Bridges

Ebony bridge with bone nut: **1933–late 30s**
"Synchronized," rosewood, extended stairstep on bass side, height-adjustable

(Synchromatic models): **late 1930s–53**
Rosewood height-adjustable (low-end models): **1933–80s**
Melita "Synchrosonic," individually adjustable saddles…
Electric hollowbodies: **1951–late 57**
Electric solidbodies: **1953–59**
Compensating metal, non-height-adjustable (Atkins models): **1954–58**
Metal bar, height-adjustable only, (Atkins and some low-end models): **1958–80s**
Space Control, "roller," individual string rollers: **late 1957–80s**
Floating "tuning fork" bridge, bridge unattached to body, tuning fork extends through hole in top into body, always used with roller bridge: **1965–72**
Adjustamatic, similar to Gibson tune-o-matic, individually adjustable string saddles: **1970–80s**
Terminator…
Similar to Fender Stratocaster bridge, spring-loaded string adjustments, (Committee and Beast): **1975–80s**
Standard Terminator, bridge/tailpiece unit, adjustable saddles: **1976–80s**

Tailpieces

Trapeze: **1933–83**
"Chromatic," harp-shaped (Synchromatic models): **late 1930s–54**
G tailpiece: **1951–83**
Bigsby vibrato, *Bigsby* on base…
Arm does not rotate side-to-side, up-and-down action only: **1955**
Arm rotates side-to-side and up-and-down: **1956–59**
Gretsch Bigsby, *Gretsch* and *Bigsby* on base, V-shaped cutout: **late 1959–80s**
Burns vibrato, 3-sided pyramid protrusion at base: **1963 and after**
Palm vibrato, short arm: **1963–68**

Mutes, Referred to as Mufflers in Gretsch Literature

Single mute with 1 rotary knob, Chet Atkins Hollow Body: **mid 1961–63**
Single mute with 1 small lever-action knob…
Chet Atkins Hollow Body (Nashville): **1963–72**
Some Country Clubs: **1963–65**
All hollowbody basses: **1963–73**
Country Gentleman: **1966–71**
Viking: **1968–69**
Double mute with 2 large rotary knobs…
White Falcon: **1960–early 63**
Country Gentleman: **1961–early 63**
Double mute with 2 small lever-action knobs…
Country Gentleman: **early 1963–66**
White Falcon: **early 1963–c. 72**

Neck and Peghead

Thin "miracle neck" patented: **1949**
Script logo...
    Introduced: **late 1930s**
    Solidbody electrics: **1953–54**
    Last script logos and Synchromatic peg
      heads: **late 1950s**
T-roof logo (top of *T* extends from *G* to *H*)...
    Introduced in literature, on some drum
      models and (with shorter *T*) on
      Broadkaster guitar, by **1933**
    New Yorker (archtop): **mid 1940s**
    Model 6003 (flat top): **1951**
    All models except White Falcon, White
      Penguin, Eldorado and Fleetwood: **1954**
    White Falcon and White Penguin: **1957**
    Eldorado and Fleetwood, by **1959**
Truss rod...
    No truss rod cover or adjustment (non-
      adjustable support rod concealed in
      neck): **1933–c. 51**
    Truss rod adjustment at body end of neck:
      c. 1951–52
    Truss rod adjustment at peghead...
      Small truss rod cover on peghead:
        1953–55
      Larger truss rod cover on peghead:
        1956–70
    No truss rod cover on peghead, (except
      Broadkaster), Burns gearbox with
      cover on neck heel: **1970–80s**
Square metal peghead plate with engraved
    model name (White Falcon and Country
    Gentleman also have serial number on
    plate until 1965)...

Country Gentleman: **1958–70**
Anniversary: **c. 1958-70**
White Falcon: **1959–70**
Tennessean, Nashville, by **1964–70**
Viking, Monkees: **mid 1960s–70**
Van Eps, Roc Jet, Streamliner: **late
    1960s–70**
Made in U.S.A. stamped next to serial number:
    June 1967–73
Zero fret...
    Chet Atkins models: **1959**
    Duo-Jets: **1962**
    White Falcon, Country Club: **1963**
    Sal Salvador, Astro Jet: **1965**
    12-string, Viking, Double Anniversary,
      Rally, Broadkaster (hollow and solid),
      short-scale (single cutaway) basses,
      Rancher, Folk, Sun Valley: **1968**
    No zero fret on Sun Valley: **1975**

Booneville Specs

Several across-the-line design changes were
    made between Gretsch's acquisition by
    Baldwin in 1967 and the move to
    Booneville, AR, in 1970. These changes
    include new wiring schemes, new PU
    styles, the introduction of the adjustamatic
    bridge and a pickguard shape with straight
    lines (as opposed to the rounded, some-
    what-teardrop shape of earlier pick-
    guards). Old parts were used up before
    new ones were implemented, so many
    transitional examples were made during
    1970.

DeArmond pickup with slot-head screws to adjust pole height, 1949–57.

Filter 'Tron pickup with patent-applied-for notice, used on high-end models, 1958–60.

Filter 'Tron pickup with patent number, used on high-end models, 1960–70.

Hi-Lo 'Tron pickup, used on low-end models, 1961–80s.

180

Filter 'Tron pickup with no plates between
poles, 1970–80s.

Metal knobs with plain top, 1954 only.

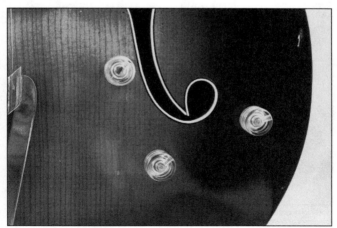

Clear plastic knobs, 1949–circa 54.

Gretsch

General Information

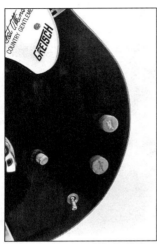

Metal knobs with arrow and *G* on top. Knobs from early 1955–57 have arrow only. Arrow through *G* appears in 1957.

Aluminum knobs with *G* and arrow, introduced on low-end models in 1966, on high-end models in mid-1967.

Synchromatic equipment on a 1952 Model 6192 (forerunner of Country Club): Synchronized bridge with stairstep extensions, Chromatic harp-shape tailpiece.

1961 Chet Atkins Country Gentleman with Gretsch Bigsby tailpiece, straight bar bridge 1/2" in diameter.

1958 Anniversary with Bigsby tailpiece, straight bar bridge 3/8" in diameter.

1955 Duo-Jet with Melita bridge, used on various models from 1951–59, and *G* tailpiece, first used in 1951.

Script logo, introduced in the late 1930s and used on some models into the late 1950s.

Space Control roller bridge, 1957–80s.

T-roof logo, an a few guitar models from the 1940s, on almost all models beginning in 1954.

183

MODEL NUMBERS

Series	Range
Numbers in the 6000s	1948–71
Numbers in the 7000s (some overlap with 8000-series)	1971–80
Numbers in the 8000s	1979–81
Numbers in the 6000s and 7000s, Japanese-made	1989 and after

Number	Model
6000	Classic Hauser, inlaid peghead
6001	Classic Hauser, plain peghead
6002	Folk, sunburst top
6003	Model 6003, 1951–55
	Grand Concert, 1955–59
	Jimmie Rodgers, 1959–63
	Folk Singing, 1963–65
	Folk, natural top, 1965–75
6004	Burl Ives, 1952–55
	Folk, mahogany top, 1970–75
6005	Ozark Soft String
6006	Electro Classic
6007	Synchromatic Sierra
6008	Wayfarer Jumbo
6009	Jumbo Flat Top
6010	Sun Valley
6012	Synchromatic 6012
6014	Synchromatic 100, sunburst, 1948–49
	Synchromatic 6014 (sunburst), 1949–55
	Corsair, sunburst, 1955–59
6015	Synchromatic 100, natural, 1948–49
	Synchromatic 6015 (natural), 1949–55
	Corsair, natural, 1955–59
6016	Corsair, Bordeaux burgundy
6020	12-string flat top
6021	Jumbo Synchromatic (Model 125F), 1948–55
6022	Rancher
6023	Bikini guitar
6024	Bikini bass
6025	Bikini doubleneck
6028	Synchromatic 160, sunburst
6029	Synchromatic 160, natural
6030	Synchromatic 6030 (sunburst), 1951–55
	Constellation, sunburst, 1955–59
	Sho-Bro Spanish, 1969–71
6031	Synchromatic 6031 (natural), 1951–55
	Constellation, natural, 1955–59
	Sho-Bro Hawaiian, 1969–71
6036	Synchromatic 300, sunburst, 1948–51
	Synchromatic 6036 (sunburst), 1951–55
6037	Synchromatic 300, 1948–51
	Synchromatic 6037 (natural), 1951–55
6038	Synchromatic 6038 (sunburst), 1951–55
	Fleetwood, sunburst, 1955–59
	17" Eldorado, sunburst, 1959–68
6039	Synchromatic 6039 (natural), 1951–55
	Fleetwood, natural, 1955–59
	17" Eldorado, natural, 1959–68
6040	Synchromatic 400, sunburst, 1948–51
	Synchromatic 6040 (sunburst), 1951–55
	18" Eldorado sunburst, 1955–70
6041	Synchromatic 400 natural, 1948–51
	Synchromatic 6041 (natural), 1951–55
	18" Eldorado, natural, 1955–70

184

6042	Synchromatic 400F (flat top)
6050	New Yorker
6070	Hollowbody bass, long scale, 1 PU
6071	Hollowbody bass, short scale, 1 PU
6072	Hollowbody bass, long scale, 2 PUs
6073	Hollowbody bass, short scale, 2 PUs
6075	12-string electric, sunburst
6076	12-string electric, natural
6079	Van Eps 7-string, sunburst
6080	Van Eps 7-string, walnut
6081	Van Eps 6–string, sunburst
6082	Van Eps 6-string, walnut
6100	Black Hawk, sunburst
6101	Country Club, stereo, sunburst, 1959–63
	Black Hawk, black, 1968–72
6102	Country Club, stereo, natural, 1959–63
	Streamliner double cutaway, sunburst, 1969–75
6103	Country Club, stereo, Cadillac green, 1959–63
	Streamliner double cutaway, cherry, 1969–75
6104	Rally, green
6105	Rally, bamboo yellow/copper mist
6106	Princess
6111	Double Anniversary, stereo, sunburst
6112	Double Anniversary, stereo, 2-tone smoke green
6115	Rambler
6117	Double Anniversary, sunburst
	also, custom model, cat's eye soundholes, 1965–68
6118	Double Anniversary, 2-tone smoke green
6119	Chet Atkins Tennessean
6120	Chet Atkins Hollowbody (Nashville, 1967–71)
6121	Chet Atkins Solid Body
6122	Chet Atkins Country Gentleman
6124	Anniversary, sunburst
6125	Anniversary, 2–tone smoke green
6126	Astro-Jet
6127	Duo-Jet tenor, 1959
	Roc Jet, Porsche pumpkin, 1969–71
6128	Duo-Jet
6129	Silver Jet
6130	Round Up, 1955–59
	Roc Jet, Mercedes black, 1969–73
6131	Jet Fire Bird
6132	Corvette solidbody, 1 PU, no vibrato
6134	White Penguin, 1955–63
	Corvette solidbody, 1 PU, vibrato, 1963–68
6135	Corvette solidbody, 2 PUs
6136	White Falcon
6137	White Falcon, stereo
6145	Jet Airliner lap steel
6147	Jet Mainliner lap steel
6148	Jet Twin Console lap steel, no legs
6148L	Jet Twin Console lap steel, 4 legs
6152	Electromatic Student lap steel
6156	Electromatic Standard lap steel
6158	Electromatic Console lap steel
6182	Corvette hollowbody, sunburst
6183	Corvette hollowbody, natural
6184	Corvette hollowbody, jaguar tan
6185	Electromatic Spanish, sunburst, 1949–55
	Clipper, 2 PUs, sunburst, c. 1972–74
6185N	Electromatic Spanish, natural
6186	Clipper

6187	Electro II, non-cutaway, sunburst, 1951–55
	Corvette, ivory top, grey mist body, 1957
	Corvette-style, cutaway, ivory top, grey mist body, 1958
	Clipper, natural, 1959–60
	Viking, sunburst, 1967–75
6188	Electro II, non-cutaway, natural, 1951–55
	Viking, natural, 1967–75
6189	16" electric cutaway, 2 PUs, early 1950s–55
	Streamliner single cutaway, bamboo yellow/copper mist, 1955–57
	Viking, Cadillac green, 1967–72
6190	16" electric cutaway, 1 PU, sunburst, early 1950s–55
	Streamliner single cutaway, sunburst, 1955–57
6191	16" electric cutaway, 1 PU, natural, early 1950s–55
	Streamliner single cutaway, natural, 1955–57
6192	Electro II, cutaway, sunburst, 1951–54
	Country Club, sunburst, 1955–71
6193	Electro II, cutaway, natural, 1951–54
	Country Club, natural, 1955–71
6196	Country Club, Cadillac green
6199	Convertible, 1955–58
	Sal Salvador, 1958–68
7176	Southern Belle
7505	Folk, sunburst
7506	Folk, natural
7514	Sun Valley, sunburst
7515	Sun Valley, natural
7525	Rancher
7535	Deluxe
7545	Supreme
7555	Clipper
7560	Double Anniversary, sunburst
7565	Streamliner, sunburst
7566	Streamliner, cherry
7575	Country Club, sunburst
7576	Country Club, natural
7577	Country Club, walnut
7580	Van Eps, 7-string, sunburst
7585	Viking, sunburst
7586	Viking, natural
7593	White Falcon, single cutaway
7594	White Falcon
7595	White Falcon, stereo
7600	Broadkaster solidbody, natural
7601	Broadkaster solidbody, sunburst
7603	Broadkaster hollowbody, Bigsby, natural
7604	Broadkaster hollowbody, Bigsby, sunburst
7605	Broadkaster bass, natural
7606	Broadkaster bass, sunburst
7607	Broadkaster hollowbody, no Bigsby, natural
7608	Broadkaster hollowbody, no Bigsby, sunburst
7609	Broadkaster hollowbody, red
7610	Roc Jet, black, 1971–75
7611	Roc Jet, Porsche pumpkin, 1971–75
	Roc Jet, black, 1975–80
7612	Roc Jet, cherry
7613	Roc Jet, walnut
7615	Solidbody bass
7617	BST 1000, 2 PUs, walnut
7620	Country Roc, 1974–79
	BST 2000, walnut, 1979–80
7621	Roc II
7623	Corvette solidbody, 2 PUs

7624	TK 300, autumn red
7625	TK 300, natural
7626	TK 300 bass, autumn red
7627	TK 300 bass, natural
7628	Committee
7629	Committee bass
7632	Deluxe Corvette
7635	Roc I
7655	Tennessean
7660	Nashville
7667	Streamliner II
7670	Country Gentleman
7680	Deluxe Chet, autumn red, 1973–75
	Atkins Super Axe, red rosewood, 1976–80
7681	Deluxe Chet, walnut, 1973–75
	Atkins Super Axe, ebony, 1976–80
7685	Atkins Axe, ebony
7686	Atkins Axe, red rosewood
7690	Super Chet, autumn red
7691	Super Chet, walnut
7705	Sho-Bro Hawaiian, 6–string
7710	Sho-Bro Hawaiian, 7–string
7715	Sho-Bro Spanish
8210	BST 1000, 1 PU, walnut
8211	BST 1000, 2 PUs, red
8215	BST 1000, 2 PUs, walnut
8216	BST 1000, 1 PU, red
8217	BST 1000, 2 PUs, walnut
8220	BST 2000, walnut
8221	BST 2000, red
8250	BST 5000

Models Announced September 1, 1989, Except as Noted

400	Synchromatic, similar to Synchromatic 400
6010	Sun Valley, triangular soundhole
6020	Crimson Flyer, electric acoustic, cutaway, triangular soundhole
6030	Nightbird, electric acoustic, cutaway, triangular soundhole
6022	Rancher
6119	Tennessee Rose (similar to Tennessean)
6120	The Nashville
6120W	Nashville, Western trim
6121	Round Up
6122S	Country Classic I (similar to Country Gentleman), single cutaway
6122	Country Classic II (similar to Country Gentleman), double cutaway
6128	Duo-Jet
6129	Silver Jet
6131	Jet Firebird
6136	White Falcon I, single cutaway, no vibrato, (mid 1990)
6175	Electric acoustic fretted bass (Jan. 1, 1990)
6176	Electric acoustic fretless bass (Jan. 1, 1990)
7593	White Falcon I, single cutaway, Gretsch Bigsby (mid 1990)
7594	White Falcon II, double cutaway, Gretsch Bigsby (mid 1990)

SERIAL NUMBERS

Synchromatic Serial Numbers, 1940–49

Synchromatic models with cat's eye soundholes have a serial number stamped on the back, visible through the bass-side soundhole. They are numbered in one consecutive series, with approximate range 007–900.

Number placement, 1949–65

Number ink-stamped on inside back: some *f*-hole models: **1949–55**
Number on label: most *f*-hole models (label on inside back), all solidbody models with control plate on back (label in control cavity or on back of control plate): **1949–65**
Number scratched onto control plate: some solidbody examples: **1953–65**
Small numbers impressed into top of peghead or near top of peghead on back: Tennessean, Corvette and some other solidbody models: **1961–64**

Serial Numbers, 1949–65

No Gretsch serial number list for this period is totally reliable. Although all Gretsches during this period are numbered in the same series, the numbers and labels were not necessarily applied in strict chronological and numerical order. Example: Chet Atkins Solid Body models #23453 and #23454. The later-numbered example has humptop block inlay and no zero fret (earlier specs), while the earlier-numbered example has thumbprint inlay and a zero fret—the opposite of what the serial numbers would indicate.

Number	Year
3000s	1949–50
4000s–5000s	1951
5000s–6000s	1952
6000s–8000s	1953
9000s–12000s	1954
12000s–16000s	1955
17000s–21000s	1956
22000s–26000s	1957
27000s–30000s	1958
30000s–34000s	1959
34000s–39000s	1960
39000s–45000s	1961
46000s–52000s	1962
53000s–63000s	1963
63000s–77000s	1964
77000s–84000s	1964–early 65

Serial Numbers, 1965–72

Number on back of peghead, no hyphen:
    First digit or first 2 digits=month (1–12)
    Next digit=last digit of year (1965–72)
    Remaining digits=rank of individual instrument
Examples:
    106347=Oct. 1966, 347th instrument
    72084=July 1972, 84th instrument
    787=July 1968, 7th instrument
MADE IN USA on back of peghead next to serial number: **June 1967–73**

Serial Numbers, 1973–81

Hyphenated number impressed into back of peghead:
    1 or 2 digits before hyphen=month
    First digit after hyphen=last digit of year
    Last 3 digits=rank of instrument
Example: 11-4252=Nov. 1974, 252nd instrument

ACOUSTIC ARCHTOPS KEY

Round hole
    Scroll peghead inlay with vertical lines=**No. 50R**
    Fern peghead inlay=**No. 100R**
f-holes
    Non-cutaway
        Diamond inlay
            Vertical lines and scroll peghead inlay=**No. 50, late 1930s**
            Flowers and scroll peghead inlay=**No. 65**
            Fern peghead inlay=**No. 100F**
        Rectangular inlay
            Artist on peghead=**No. 150**
            Synchromatic on peghead
                Tortoise grain binding=**Synchromatic 115**
                White outer binding
                    Sunburst=**Synchromatic 100 (6014)**, 1946–55
                    Natural=**Synchromatic 6015**
            Banner logo and fern peghead inlay=**Synchromatic 75**
            T-roof logo only on peghead=**Corsair**
            T-roof logo through circle on peghead=model name unknown
        Slashed humptop block inlay
            Sunburst=**Synchromatic 6036**
            Natural=**Synchromatic 6037**
        Varied-pattern or trapezoid inlay
            Musical note on peghead=**No. 250**
            Fern peghead inlay=**Synchromatic 100**, 1940–46
        Dot inlay
            No binding=**No. 25**
            Bound top and back
                New Yorker or T-roof logo on peghead=**New Yorker**
                Pearl scroll logo=**No. 35**
                Bunting and scroll peghead inlay=**No. 50**, 1940–49
    Cutaway
        Rectangular block inlay
            Sunburst=**Synchromatic 6030**
            Natural=**Synchromatic 6031**
        Slashed humptop block inlay
            Sunburst=**Synchromatic 6038**
            Natural=**Synchromatic 6039**
        Humptop block or thumbprint inlay
            18" wide
                Sunburst=**Eldorado 6040**
                Natural=**Eldorado 6041**
            17" wide
                Humptop block inlay
                    Synchromatic on peghead
                        Sunburst=**Fleetwood 6035**
                        Natural=**Fleetwood 6036**
                    No *Synchromatic* on peghead
                        Sunburst=**Constellation 6030**
                        Natural=**Constellation 6031**
                Thumbprint inlay
                    Sunburst=**Eldorado 6038**
                    Natural=**Eldorado 6039**
            16" wide
                Sunburst=**Corsair 6014**, 1959
                Natural=**Corsair 6015**, 1959
                Bordeaux burgundy=**Corsair 6016**, 1959

Cat's eye sound holes
Ebony fingerboard
Gold sparkle binding
Sunburst=**Synchromatic 400 (6040)**
Natural=**Synchromatic 400 (6041)**
Non-sparkle binding
Sunburst=**Synchromatic 300 (6036)**
Natural=**Synchromatic 300 (6037)**
Rosewood fingerboard
Humptop block inlay=**Synchromatic 200**
Rectangular block inlay
Pearl blocks=**Synchromatic 160**
Abalone blocks=**Synchromatic 6012**

ACOUSTIC ARCHTOPS

Synchromatic Model Names

In a 1939 brochure, Gretsch uses the term *Synchromatic* after a model number—for example, No. 400 Synchromatic. In the 1949 catalog, some references to Synchromatic models have *Synchromatic* before the model number—for example, Synchromatic 400. The latter form is the one commonly used by collectors for models of all periods and is used in this section through all periods.

The 1949 catalog uses both Synchromatic model numbers and the 6000-series model numbers. A 1951 brochure uses *Synchromatic* with the 6000-series numbers only (no 100, 400, etc.), even though the 17" and 18" models are shown with a *G* tailpiece rather than the harp tailpiece that was standard equipment on Synchromatic models. In a 1952 brochure, the term *Synchromatic* is not used. It does appear on some pegheads through the 1950s.

SECTION ORGANIZATION

Gretsch American Orchestra Series, (Models Introduced in Late 1933)
16"-wide Models Introduced in 1935 and After
Synchromatic Models and Other 17"- and 18"-wide Models

Gretsch-American Orchestra Series

At introduction, all models are 16" wide with *f*-holes, carved spruce top, arched back, maple back and sides, trapeze tailpiece, black Bakelite pickguard, 3-piece maple neck (2 pieces of maple with rosewood laminate stripe), 14 frets clear of body, 24 1/2" scale, ebony fingerboard with pointed end, rounded-peak peghead. Changes occur as specified.

No. 25: no body binding, non-adjustable ebony bridge, dot inlay, rosewood peghead veneer, pearl scroll logo diagonally across peghead, dark red-to-brown shaded finish
Introduced: **late 1933**
Discontinued by **1939**

No. 35: bound pickguard, non-adjustable ebony bridge, single-bound top and back, pearl dot inlay, rosewood peghead veneer, pearl scroll logo diagonally across peghead, dark red-to-golden amber shaded finish
Introduced: **late 1933**
Adjustable maple bridge with rosewood stain, black plastic peghead veneer: **1936**
3-ply pearloid-black-white top binding, pearloid strip around top border of sides, rosewood fingerboard, scroll logo across top of peghead, tortoise grain plastic tuner buttons, nickel-plated metal parts, brown-to-amber shaded finish, by **1939**
Discontinued by **1949**

No. 65: 4-ply top and back binding, bound pickguard, adjustable ebony bridge, single-bound fingerboard, notched-diamond inlay, rosewood peghead veneer, vertical floral peghead inlay, pearl scroll logo across top of peghead, dark red-to-golden amber shaded finish
Introduced: **late 1933**
Adjustable maple bridge with rosewood stain, black plastic peghead veneer, center-dip peghead: **1936**
Discontinued by **1939**

No. 100F: adjustable ebony bridge, trapeze tailpiece, single-bound pickguard, multiple-bound top and back, small diamond inlay, rosewood peghead veneer, bound peghead, fern peghead inlay, pearl scroll logo across top of peghead, Grover tuners, metal tuner buttons, gold-plated metal parts, dark red-to-golden amber shaded finish
No. 100R: No. 100 with round hole
Introduced: **late 1933**
Tortoise grain pickguard, black plastic peghead veneer, center-dip peghead: **1936**
No. 100R (round hole model) discontinued by **1939**
Renamed **Synchromatic 100**: stairstep bridge, harp tailpiece, pickguard extends below bridge, rosewood fingerboard, varied-pattern inlay, larger fern-pattern peghead inlay, amber-to-brown shaded finish, by **1939**
Double-bound top and back, bound pickguard and *f*-holes, large block inlay, unbound peghead, *Synchromatic* on peghead, rounded top of peghead, sunburst finish: **early 1946**

Single-bound rounded-peak peghead: late **1947**
Synchromatic 100 designated model **6014**, sunburst: **1949**
Model **6015**, natural finish, available by **1951**
No binding on pickguard, *f*-holes, or peghead: **1952**
Renamed **Corsair**: 16" wide, *G* tailpiece, single-bound top and back, adjustable rosewood bridge, tan pickguard with no logo, single-bound peghead, sunburst (**6014**), natural, (**6015**) or Bordeaux burgundy (**6016**) finish: **1955**
Humptop block inlay by **1957**
Single cutaway, ebony bridge, thumbprint inlay, by **1959**
Discontinued: **1960**

16"-wide Models
Introduced in 1935 and After
All are 16" wide with *f*-holes, maple back and sides, unless otherwise specified.

No. 150: multiple-bound top and back, bound tortoise grain pickguard, floral engraving around pickguard borders, 24 1/2" scale, bound ebony fingerboard with pointed end, block inlay, peghead ornament covers most of peghead, *Artist* on peghead, center-dip peghead, engraved tuner buttons, gold-plated metal parts, sunburst finish
Introduced: **1935**
Discontinued by **1939**

No. 50: maple adjustable bridge with rosewood stain finish, trapeze tailpiece, black Bakelite pickguard, bound top and back, 3-piece neck, 24 1/2" scale, bound ebony fingerboard with pointed end, diamond inlay, black plastic peghead veneer, rounded-peak peghead, pearl vertical lines and scroll peghead inlay, tortoise grain tuner buttons, nickel-plated metal parts, brown-to-amber shaded finish
No. 50R: No. 50 with round hole
Introduced: **1936**
Back of avoidire wood (blond mahogany), bound rosewood fingerboard, crosspiece at middle of tailpiece: **late 1930s**
No. 50R (round hole model) discontinued by **1940**
Rosewood fingerboard, dot inlay, by **1940**
No. 50 (*f*-hole model) discontinued by **1949**

No. 250: adjustable ebony bridge, trapeze tailpiece with 4 tubular pieces lengthwise and 1 tubular crosspiece in middle, bound tortoise grain pickguard with 2 pearl-inlaid musical notes, 5-ply binding on top and back, some with bound *f*-holes, 24 1/2" scale, bound ebony fingerboard with pointed end, varied-pat-

tern inlay (later trapezoid and broken trapezoid inlay), single-bound peghead, pearl peghead inlay of 2 large musical notes, peghead indents below E-string tuners, protrusion at top of peghead, pearl tuner buttons, gold-plated metal parts, sunburst finish
Introduced: **1936**
Discontinued by **1939**

No. 240: tenor, adjustable ebony bridge, trapeze tailpiece, single-bound top and back, 23" scale, ebony fingerboard with pointed end, bound top and back, dot inlay, point at top of peghead, pearl scroll logo diagonally across peghead
Note: Any standard model was available in tenor style by special order.
Introduced: **1936**
Discontinued: **1939**

Synchromatic 75: stairstep bridge, trapeze tailpiece, bound pickguard, single-bound top and back, unbound *f*-holes, 3-piece maple neck, 24 1/2" scale, bound pointed-end fingerboard, large block inlay, large floral peghead inlay, scroll logo across top of peghead, black plastic peghead veneer, bound center-dip peghead, metal tuner buttons, nickel-plated metal parts, amber-to-brown shaded finish
Introduced by **1939**
Harp tailpiece, triple-bound tortoise grain pickguard, pickguard extends below bridge, 4-ply top and back binding, unbound peghead, by **1940**
Discontinued by **1949**

No. 30: adjustable maple bridge with rosewood stain, trapeze tailpiece, black Bakelite pickguard, bound top, unbound back, unbound *f*-holes, 24 1/2" scale, rosewood fingerboard, pearl dot inlay, 3-piece maple neck, rosewood peghead veneer, pearl scroll logo diagonally across peghead, rounded-peak peghead, nickel-plated metal parts, dark red-to-brown shaded finish
Introduced by **1939**
Discontinued by **1949**

Synchromatic 115: See Synchromatics, following

16 1/4" archtop (model name unknown): probably made by Harmony, 16 1/4" wide, *f*-holes, laminated top, maple back and sides, wooden tailpiece, 4-ply top binding, single-bound back, single-bound rosewood fingerboard, block inlay, painted T-roof logo slanting through circle, painted stars and rectangles in vertical row under logo, 3-color sunburst top finish, 2-color

sunburst back and sides
Available: **mid to late 1940s**

New Yorker: 16" wide, adjustable rosewood
bridge, trapeze tailpiece, tortoise grain
pickguard, triple-bound top, single-bound
back, bound rosewood fingerboard with
square end, block inlay, stenciled peghead
logo of T-roof *Gretsch* through circle and
New Yorker vertically, rounded top peghead (not peaked) with rounded corners,
sunburst finish
Introduced by **mid 1940s**
Single-bound top and back, unbound fingerboard, dot inlay, T-roof logo, *New Yorker*
and lightning bolt vertically on peghead,
(**6050**), by **1949**
Rounded-peak peghead with sharper corners
by **1955**
Some examples with rectangular (flat top
style) peghead or *Gretsch* plaque on peghead: **late 1960s**
Discontinued: **1970**

Synchromatic Models and Other 17"- and 18"-wide Models

Most Synchromatic models made prior to
World War II have solid maple back and
sides. Most postwar examples are of laminated maple.

Synchromatic 100, Corsair: see Gretsch-
American Series, preceding

Synchromatic 75: see 16"-wide Models
Introduced in 1935 and After, preceding

Synchromatic 160: 17" wide, maple back and
sides, double-bound cat's eye soundholes,
stairstep bridge, harp tailpiece, bound
pickguard almost covers treble soundhole,
triple-bound top and back, 5-piece neck (3
pieces of maple with 2 rosewood laminate
stripes), 26" scale, rosewood fingerboard
with square end, 4-ply fingerboard binding,
large block inlay, black plastic peghead
veneer, script *Gretsch* across top of peghead, *Synchromatic* above E-string posts,
single-bound peghead, peghead indents
above E-string tuners, protrusion on top of
peghead, metal tuner buttons, chrome-
plated metal parts, sunburst finish
Introduced: **1939**
Natural finish with tortoise grain binding
optional: **early 1940s**
Production stopped: **1943**
Re-introduced: some with ebony fingerboard,
no peghead indents, gold-plated metal
parts: **fall 1947**

Sunburst (**6028**) or natural (**6029**): **1948**
Discontinued: **1951**

Synchromatic 200: 17" wide, double-bound
cat's eye soundholes, maple back and
sides, stairstep bridge, harp tailpiece, double-bound pickguard almost covers treble
soundhole, wide multiple binding on top
and back, 26" scale, bound rosewood fingerboard with square end, humptop block
inlay, black plastic peghead veneer, script
Gretsch across top of peghead,
Synchromatic above A- and B-string posts,
peghead indents at E-string tuners, protrusion on top of peghead, engraved metal
tuner buttons, gold-plated metal parts,
amber-to-brown shaded finish or natural
finish
Introduced: **1939**
Discontinued by **1949**

Synchromatic 300: 17" wide, double-bound
cat's eye soundholes, stairstep bridge,
harp tailpiece, bound pickguard almost
covers treble sound hole, multiple-bound
top and back, ebony fingerboard with
square end, 5-ply binding on fingerboard
sides and single-binding on end, 5-piece
maple neck (3 pieces of maple with 2 rosewood laminate stripes), 26" scale, gold-
sparkle slashed humptop block inlay, script
Gretsch across top of peghead,
Synchromatic above A- and B-string posts,
peghead indents at E-string tuners, protrusion on top of peghead, multiple-bound
peghead, enclosed Grover tuners,
stairstep tuner buttons, gold-plated metal
parts, sunburst finish
Introduced: **1939**
Natural finish by **1941**
Sunburst (**6036**) or natural (**6037**) by **1948**
Cataloged as **Synchromatic 6036, 6037**: 17"
wide, double-bound *f*-holes, stairstep
bridge, *G* tailpiece, bound pickguard,
triple-bound top and back, bound fingerboard, slashed humptop block inlay,
Synchromatic on peghead, rounded-peak
peghead, stairstep tuner buttons, gold-
plated metal parts: **1951**
Discontinued by **1955**

Synchromatic 400: 18" wide, double-bound
cat's eye soundholes, stairstep bridge,
harp tailpiece with gold and chrome plating, pickguard with white and gold-sparkle
binding almost covers treble soundhole,
wide multiple binding with gold sparkle on
top and back (some with tortoise grain at
outer edge), 5-piece maple neck (3 pieces
of maple with 2 rosewood laminate
stripes), 26" scale, square-end ebony fingerboard with white and gold sparkle bind-

ing, slashed humptop block inlay, slanted script logo starts between A- and D-string posts, crossed *Synchromatic*-and-tusk peghead ornament, peghead indents at E-string pegs, protrusion at top of peghead, stairstep tuner buttons, gold-plated metal parts, sunburst or natural finish
Variation: triangular soundhole, referred to as Johnny Smith model, at least 2 instruments made
Introduced by **1940**
No crossed peghead ornament, sunburst (**6040**), or natural (**6041**), by **1948**
Cataloged as **Synchromatic 6040, 6041**, *f*-holes, *G* tailpiece, multiple-bound top and back, multiple-bound pickguard and *f*-holes, triple-bound fingerboard and peg-head, crossed peghead ornament returns, no peghead indents, rounded-peak peg-head, available by custom orde: **1951**
Rounded-top peghead by **1952**
Replaced by **Eldorado** (see following) by **1955**

Synchromatic 115: 16" wide, *f*-holes, stairstep bridge, harp tailpiece, tortoise grain pick-guard, tortoise grain top and back binding, tortoise grain fingerboard binding, block inlay, unbound peghead, *Synchromatic* on peghead above A- and B-string posts, translucent blond finish
Introduced by **1946**
Trapeze tailpiece with slanted string-anchor bar: **early 1947**
Synchromatic on peghead below A- and B-string posts: **1947**
Discontinued: **1949**

Synchromatic 6012: similar to Synchromatic 160 (see preceding) but with 4-ply sound-hole binding, abalone block inlay
Available: **c. 1948**

Synchromatic 6030, 6031: 17" wide single cut-away, stairstep bridge, harp tailpiece, bound pickguard, triple-bound top and back, double-bound *f*-holes, bound rose-wood fingerboard, block inlay, *Synchromatic* on peghead, rounded-peak peghead, gold-plated metal parts, sunburst (**6030**) or natural (**6031**) finish
Introduced by **1951**
Renamed **Constellation**: *G* tailpiece, ebony bridge, humptop block inlay, no *Synchromatic* on peghead, by **1955**
Discontinued: **1960**

Synchromatic 6038, 6039: 17" wide, single cut-away, stairstep bridge, *G* tailpiece, double-bound *f*-holes, multiple-bound top and back, bound pickguard, bound fingerboard and peghead, slashed-humptop block inlay, rounded-peak peghead,

Synchromatic on peghead, stairstep tuner buttons, gold-plated metal parts, sunburst (**6038**) or natural (**6039**) finish
Introduced by **1951**
Renamed **Fleetwood** (see following) by **1955**

Eldorado: previously Synchromatic 400, 18" wide, single cutaway, *f*-holes, stairstep bridge, *G* tailpiece, elongated pickguard, triple-bound top and back, trapeze tail-piece, ebony fingerboard, humptop block inlay with black-white-black slash, triple-bound fingerboard and peghead, slanted script logo, crossed *Synchromatic*-and-tusk peghead ornament, rounded-peak peghead, gold-plated metal parts, sunburst (**6040**) or natural (**6041**) finish
Introduced, custom order only, by **1955**
Thumbprint inlay shown in catalog photo (humptop block inlay on some examples through 1960), *Gretsch* only on peghead: **1959**
Natural (6041) discontinued by **1968**
Discontinued by **1970**

Fleetwood: 17" wide, single cutaway, *f*-holes, *Synchromatic* on peghead, otherwise same as Eldorado, sunburst (**6038**) or natu-ral (**6039**) finish
Introduced, custom order only, by **1955**
Renamed **Eldorado 6038** and **6039**, thumbprint inlay, *Gretsch* only on peghead: **1959**
Discontinued by **1968**

COMMENTS

Gretsch's current reputation is based more on electric archtop models than acoustics. Acoustic archtops appeal primarily to Gretsch collectors. The quality of Gretsch workmanship is generally not as high as that of Gibson and Epiphone instruments from the same period. Thus many of the Gretsch models that survive are not in good condition. The high-end models with cat's eye soundholes are visually appeal-ing and rare, and they have been sought for music videos and photo sessions. While these guitars are not equal in sound or playability to Gibson's or Epiphone's top models, they will bring a good price. Other Gretsch archtop acoustics are much less sought after by collectors and musicians.

FLAT TOPS KEY

Triangular hole
    Crossed peghead ornaments=**Synchromatic 400F**
    Script *Synchromatic* on peghead
        Pearloid block inlay=**Jumbo Synchromatic (125F)**
        Slashed humptop block inlay=**Synchromatic 300 flat top**
    75 on peghead=**Synchromatic Sierra (X75F)**
    Gretsch in block letters, no ornament on peghead
        Natural top=**Town and Country**
        Red or orange top=**Rancher**
Round hole
    Round body=**Rhumba**
    Standard guitar shape
        Bridge pickup=**Electro Classic**
        16" wide
            No inlay=**Ozark Soft String**
            Diamond inlay=**No. 40 Hawaiian**
            Dot inlay
                2 dots at 12th fret
                    12-string=**12-string**
                    6-string
                        Natural top=**Wayfarer Jumbo**
                        Sunburst top=**Jumbo Flat Top**
                3 dots at 12th fret
                  Redwood top=**Deluxe**
                  Spruce top=**Supreme**
        15 1/2" wide=**Sun Valley**
        14 1/4" or 14 1/2" wide
            Solid peghead
                Pearloid peghead veneer with *Artist*=**Broadkaster**
                Burl Ives on peghead=**Burl Ives**
                Gretsch only=**Grand Concert (Jimmie Rodgers, Folk)**
            Slotted peghead
                Pin bridge=**Castilian**
                Classical string-loop bridge
                    Wood inlay on back=**Classic Hauser 6000**
                    No wood inlay on back=**Classic Hauser 6001**
Resonator
    Round neck=**Sho Bro Spanish**
    Square neck=**Sho Bro Hawaiian**

FLAT TOPS

Broadkaster: 14 1/2" wide, top and back specified as arched, mahogany top, mahogany
back and sides, ebony pin bridge, no pickguard, mahogany neck, square-end ebony
fingerboard, dot inlay, celluloid peghead
veneer, *Gretsch* in block letters across top
of peghead, *Artist* vertically on peghead,
peghead tapers to point at top, natural
mahogany finish
Introduced by **1933**
Discontinued by **1936**

Castilian: 14 1/2" wide, spruce top, mahogany
back and sides, triple-bound top, rosewood pin bridge, no pickguard, rosewood
fingerboard with square end, dot inlay,
slotted peghead, natural top finish
Introduced by **1933**
Discontinued by **1936**

Rhumba: round body, round hole, maple back
and sides, ebony bridge, short trapeze tailpiece, elevated pickguard with no side
supports, maple neck, ebony fingerboard
with pointed end, dot inlay, rosewood peghead veneer, pearl scroll logo diagonally
across peghead, sunburst finish
Introduced by **1933**
Discontinued by **1936**

No. 40 Hawaiian: 16" wide, spruce top,
mahogany back and sides, round hole,
large bowtie-shape ebony pin bridge, elevated pickguard with no side supports,
double-bound top and back, bound ebony
fingerboard, varied size diamond inlay,
flush frets, 12 frets clear of body, grey
pearloid peghead veneer, pearl peghead
logo, peghead tapers to point at top, tortoise grain tuner buttons, shaded brown
finish
Introduced by **1936**
Discontinued by **1949**

Synchromatic 400F: 18" wide, triangular hole,
arched back, maple back and sides,
stairstep bridge, harp tailpiece, elevated
pickguard, multiple-bound top and back
with tortoise grain outer layer, bound fingerboard, varied size humptop block inlay,
slanted script logo, crossed *Synchromatic*-
and-tusk peghead ornament, peghead
indents below E-string tuners, protrusion
at top of peghead, enclosed Grover tuners,
natural top finish, sunburst back and sides
finish
Introduced by **1947**
Height-adjustable bridge, large triangular
rosewood bridge base, metal string-
anchor piece mounted at a slant, non-ele-

vated pickguard, **(6042)** by **1949**
Discontinued by **1955**

Synchromatic 300 flat top: Buddy Starcher
model, triangular hole, arched back, maple
back and sides, stairstep bridge, harp tailpiece, elevated pickguard, multiple-bound
top and back, bound fingerboard, slashed
humptop block inlay, straight logo,
Synchromatic on peghead above A- and B-
string posts, bound peghead, protrusion at
peghead top and indents below E-string
tuners, natural top finish, dark back and
sides finish
Available by **1947**

Jumbo Synchromatic (Model 125F): 17" wide,
maple back and sides, triangular hole,
arched back, multiple-bound top and back,
height-adjustable bridge, triangular rosewood bridge base, metal string-anchor
plate mounted at a slant, 26" scale, single-
bound rosewood fingerboard, pearloid
block inlay, *Synchromatic* on peghead
above A and B tuners, natural top, sunburst back and sides finish **(6021)**
Variation: translucent white finish, tortoise
grain binding on top, back, soundhole, fingerboard, and peghead
Introduced by **1947**
Replaced by **Town and Country** and **Rancher**
(see following), by **1955**

Synchromatic X75F: 16" wide, triangular hole,
arched back, maple back and sides, trapezoid-shaped bridge, metal string-anchor
plate mounted straight across, rosewood
fingerboard, block inlay, script *Gretsch* and
75 on peghead, sunburst finish
Introduced by **1947**
Renamed **Synchromatic Sierra (6007)**: **1949**
Discontinued by **1955**

Model 6003: 14 1/4" wide, round hole,
mahogany back and sides, pin bridge,
teardrop pickguard, 4-ply top binding,
single-bound back, rosewood fingerboard,
dot inlay, silkscreened T-roof logo within
circle and parallelogram, natural top finish
(6003)
Introduced: **1951**
Named **Grand Concert (6003)**, slanted logo, by
1955
Renamed **Jimmie Rodgers** (endorsed by the
folk-pop star of the 1950s and 60s, not the
country star of the 30s): **1959**
Renamed **Folk Singing**, 14 1/2" wide, 24 1/2"
scale: **1963**
Renamed **Folk**: **1965**
Zero fret, straight-across T-roof logo: **1967**
Sunburst top finish **(6002)** or mahogany top
(6004) optional: **1969**

Flat Tops

Sunburst (6002) and mahogany (6004) models available by special order only: **1972**
Discontinued: **1975**

Burl Ives: 14 1/4" wide, round hole, mahogany back and sides, teardrop pickguard, double-bound top, single-bound back, 9-ply soundhole ring, rosewood fingerboard, dot inlay, black painted peghead front, slanted T-roof logo with *Burl Ives* on peghead and on inside label, natural top (**6004**)
Introduced: **1952**
Discontinued: **1955**

Town and Country: previously Jumbo Synchromatic (see preceding), 17" wide, triangular hole, arched back, maple back and sides, multiple-bound top and back, height-adjustable bridge, triangular rosewood bridge base, metal string-anchor plate mounted at a slant, 25 1/2" scale, bound fingerboard, block inlay (no *Synchromatic* on peghead), natural top (**6021**)
Introduced, replacing Jumbo Synchromatic: **1954**
Discontinued by **1959**

Rancher: 17" wide, Western version of Town and Country, triangular hole, arched back, laminated spruce top, maple back and sides, height adjustable bridge, triangular rosewood bridge base, slant-mounted metal string-anchor plate, *G* brand on bass side of top, longhorn engraved on tortoise grain pickguard, 4-ply top binding, double-bound back, single-bound rosewood fingerboard, 25 1/2" scale, block inlay engraved with cows and cactus, no inlay at first fret, single-bound peghead, peghead inlay of engraved longhorn head, gold-plated metal parts, golden red (orange) finish (**6022**)
Introduced: **1954**
Unengraved block inlay at first fret: **late 1954**
Engraving on first fret inlay: **early 1955**
Gold pickguard, humptop block inlay with no engraving by **1957**
Thumbprint inlay, plain tan pickguard: **1959**
No *G* brand, horseshoe peghead inlay: **1961**
Zero fret: **1969**
Renumbered (**7525**): **1971**
Discontinued by **1973**
Re-introduced, pointed pickguard, *G* brand on treble side, block inlay engraved with cows and cactus, standard pin bridge, horseshoe peghead inlay: **1975**
3-piece saddle, semi-circular bridge pin configuration: **c. 1978**
Discontinued: **1980**

Sun Valley: 15 1/2" wide, mahogany back and

sides, round hole, pin bridge, tortoise grain pickguard, 4-ply top binding, single-bound back, ornamental backstripe, 24 1/2" scale, dot inlay, bound peghead, natural top (**6010**)
Introduced by **1959**
Renumbered (**7515**): **1971**
Sunburst finish optional (**7514**), by **1973**
Discontinued by **1977**

Classic "Hauser Model": 14 1/4" wide, mahogany back and sides, rosewood fingerboard, slotted peghead, back marquetry and peghead inlay (**6000**) or plain back and peghead (**6001**)
Introduced: **1961**
Model 6000 referred to as **Silver Classic**: **1969**
Discontinued, available by special order only: **1972**

Ozark Soft String: 16" wide classical, rosewood back and sides, double-bound top and back, rosewood bridge, rosewood fingerboard, no inlay, slotted peghead, natural finish (**6005**)
Introduced by **1965**
Discontinued by **1968**

Sho Bro Spanish: 16 1/2" wide, dreadnought shape, pointed cutaway, non-cutaway optional, cutaway with thinner body depth than non-cutaway model, spruce top, mahogany back and sides, Dobro-type resonator, screened soundholes in upper bout, multiple-bound top and back, bound rosewood fingerboard, mahogany neck, dot inlay, bound peghead, *Sho Bro* on peghead (no *Gretsch* on peghead), natural top finish (**6030**)

Sho Bro Hawaiian: 16 1/2" wide, dreadnought shape non-cutaway, spruce top, maple back and sides, Dobro-type resonator, screened soundholes in upper bout, multiple-bound top and back, squareneck, bound fingerboard, Lucite fingerboard back-painted white with playing-card markers, bound peghead, *Sho Bro* on peghead (no *Gretsch* on peghead), natural top finish (**6031**)
Introduced: **late 1969**
Spanish renumbered (**7715**), Hawaiian renumbered (**7705**): **1971**
7-string Hawaiian (**7710**) introduced by **1972**
Discontinued by **1978**

Electro Classic: piezo bridge PU system by Baldwin (some amps with separate classical guitar input) (**6006**)
Introduced: **1969**
Renumbered (**7495**): **1971**
Discontinued: **1973**

Wayfarer Jumbo: 16" wide, dreadnought shape, maple back and sides, multiple-bound top, bound back, brown pickguard with model name and ship figure, maple neck, triple-bound fingerboard of ebonized (dyed) rosewood, slashed-block inlay, triple-bound peghead, chrome-plated Grover tuners, natural top finish, cherry finish back and sides (**6008**)
Introduced: **1969**
Discontinued: **1972**

12-string flat top: 16" wide, dreadnought shape, mahogany back and sides, multiple-bound top, bound back, rosewood fingerboard, dot inlay, natural fnish (**6020**)
Introduced: **1969**
Discontinued: **1973**

Jumbo Flat Top: sunburst finish (no other specs available) (**6009**)
Introduced: **1969**
Discontinued: **1972**

Deluxe: 16" wide, redwood top, mahogany back and sides, ebony fingerboard, dot inlay, 3 dots at 12th fret, chrome-plated metal parts (**7535**)
Available: **c. 1978**

Supreme: 16" wide, dreadnought body shape, spruce top, mahogany or rosewood back and sides, 3-piece saddle, ebony fingerboard, dot inlay, 3 dots at 7th and 12th frets, gold-plated metal parts (**7545**)
Available: **c. 1978**

COMMENTS

Gretsch flat tops have never had a reputation for good sound or playability. The orange Rancher with *G* brand and cows-and-cactus inlay is of interest to collectors, primarily as an accessory to the Western-ornamented electric Chet Atkins Hollow Body, Chet Atkins Solid Body, and Round-Up. Triangular-hole models in general bring prices in excess of their intrinsic or utility value. Other Gretsch models, even those that are older and rarer, are less well-known and are of little interest to collectors or players.

ELECTRIC ARCHTOPS KEY

Model numbers change from 6000 series to 7000 series in 1971. See model descriptions for 1970s
model numbers.

Non-cutaway, standard guitar shape
   1 PU
      Zigzag pattern on peghead
         Sunburst=**Electromatic 6185**
         Natural=**Electromatic 6185N**
      No zigzag on peghead
         Sunburst=**Corvette hollowbody 6182**
         Natural=**Corvette hollowbody 6183**
         Jaguar tan=**Corvette hollowbody 6184**
         Ivory top=**Corvette hollowbody 6187**
   2 PUs
      Sunburst=**Electromatic 6187**
      Natural=**Electromatic 6188**
Single pointed cutaway=**Rambler 6115, 1957–59**
Single rounded cutaway, bass bout joins neck at right angle
   2 "eared" Filter 'Tron PUs (gold-plated)
      7 strings
         Sunburst=**Van Eps 6079**
         Walnut=**Van Eps 6080**
      6 strings
         Sunburst=**Van Eps 6081**
         Walnut=**Van Eps 6082**
   2 standard PUs
      Red or black finish, cat's eye soundholes=**custom model 6117**
      White finish
         Old-style Filter 'Tron PUs, plates between pole rows
            Knob on cutaway bout=**White Falcon 6136, c. 1955–63**
            Switch on cutaway bout=**White Falcon 6137, 1959–63**
         No plates on PU face=**White Falcon 7593**
      Stain finish: mahogany, walnut, or amber
         DeArmond or Filter 'Tron PUs
            Peghead plate=**Chet Atkins Country Gent, 1958–61**
            No peghead plate=**Chet Atkins 6120, 1954–61**
         Hi-Lo 'Tron PUs=**Chet Atkins Tennessean, 1961–80**
      Sunburst, natural, or green finish
         Gold-plated metal parts
            Electromatic on peghead=**Electromatic 6189**
            No *Electromatic* on peghead
               Standard electronics (non-stereo)
                  Sunburst=**Country Club 6192**
                  Natural=**Country Club 6193**
                  Green=**Country Club 6196**
               Stereo electronics (see General Information)
                  Sunburst=**Country Club 6101**
                  Natural=**Country Club 6102**
                  Green or 2-tone gray=**Country Club 6103**
          Chrome-plated metal parts
            Standard electronics (non-stereo)
               Sunburst
                 Thumbprint inlay=**Double Anniversary 6117**
                 Dot inlay=**Clipper 6185**
               2-tone green=**Double Anniversary 6118**
            Stereo electronics (see General Information)
               Sunburst=**Double Anniversary 6111**
               2-tone green=**Double Anniversary 6112**

1 PU
    Dot inlay in center of fingerboard
        Sunburst finish=**Clipper 6186**
        Ivory top finish=**Model 6187, 1958**
        Natural finish=**Clipper 6187**
    Dot inlay near fingerboard edges=**Chet Atkins Junior**
    Non-dot inlay
        DeArmond PU
            Knobs on pickguard=**Convertible 6199**
            Knobs mounted on top
                Zigzag on peghead
                    Sunburst=**Electromatic 6190**
                    Natural=**Electromatic 6191**
                No zigzag on peghead
                    Yellow top or jaguar tan=**Streamliner 6189**
                    Sunburst=**Streamliner 6190**
                    Natural=**Streamliner 6191**
        Filter 'Tron or Hi-Lo 'Tron PU
            Ivory top finish=**Rambler, 1960**
            Sunburst finish
                Chrome plated=**Anniversary 6124**
                Gold plated=**Sal Salvador 6199**
            2-tone green finish=**Anniversary 6125**
            Orange or red finish=**Tennessean 6119, 1959–60**
Single rounded cutaway, bass bout joins neck at angle toward body
    Fancy abalone inlay
        Autumn red finish
            No Bigsby=**Super Chet 7690**
            Bigsby tremolo=**Super Chet 7690-B**
        Walnut finish
            No Bigsby=**Super Chet 7691**
            Bigsby tremolo=**Super Chet 7691-B**
    Thumbprint inlay
        Autumn red finish=**Deluxe Chet 7680**
        Walnut finish=**Deluxe Chet 7681**
Double cutaway
    Gold-plated metal parts
        White finish
            3 knobs, 3 switches=**White Falcon 6136, 1963–82**
            Any other knobs/switches=**White Falcon 6137, 1963–82**
        Sunburst=**Viking 6187**
        Natural=**Viking 6188**
        Green=**Viking 6189**
        Uniform stain finish
            4-ply binding=**Chet Atkins Country Gentleman 6122, 1962–83**
            2-ply binding=**Chet Atkins 6120 (Nashville), 1961–80s**
    Chrome-plated metal parts
        Triangular inlay=**12-string**
        Double thumbprint inlay=**Monkees**
        Thumbprint inlay
            Super 'Tron PUs
                Roller bridge
                    Sunburst=**Streamliner 6102**
                    Cherry=**Streamliner 6103**
                Floating tuning fork bridge
                    Sunburst=**Black Hawk 6100**
                    Black=**Black Hawk 6101**
             Hi-Lo 'Tron PUs
                G soundholes=**Songbird**
                f-holes
                    Green=**Rally 6104**
                    Yellow top, copper sides=**Rally 6105**
        Dot inlay=**Broadkaster Hollow Body**

ELECTRIC ARCHTOPS

SECTION ORGANIZATION

Electromatic Models (pre-1955) and Later Related Models (Country Club, Corvette, Streamliner)
Chet Atkins Models
Single Cutaway Models, Introduced in 1955 and After (including models that later changed to double cutaway shape)
Double Cutaway Models

Electromatic Models and Later Related Models

Electromatic models do not have specific model names until 1955.

Electromatic Spanish: 17" wide, maple body, 1 PU, 2 knobs, sunburst finish (no other specs available)
Introduced: **1940**
16" wide, non-cutaway (same body as New Yorker 6050 acoustic), *f*-holes, 1 DeArmond PU, 2 knobs on lower treble bout, rosewood bridge, trapeze tailpiece, unbound beveled-edge pickguard, triple-bound top, bound back, unbound rosewood fingerboard, dot inlay, 2-ply peghead veneer with black outer layer and white underlayer, T-roof logo engraved into peghead veneer, *Electromatic* engraved vertically into peghead over zigzag pattern, edges of peghead veneer beveled to simulate binding, peghead tapers to point at top, sunburst finish (**6185**)
Introduced: **1949**
Natural finish (**6185N**) optional by **1951**
Named **Corvette (hollowbody):** double-bound top and back, *Electromatic* on peghead, truss rod cover, no zigzag pattern, rounded peak peghead, sunburst (**6182**), natural (**6183**), or jaguar tan (**6184**) finish: **1955**
Ivory top with grey mist back and sides finish optional with (**6187**), available: **1957**
Rounded cutaway on Model 6187: **late 1957**
All Corvette models discontinued: **1959**
Corvette name re-introduced as an electric solidbody (see Electric Solidbodies)

Electro II non-cutaway: 16" wide, *f*-holes, 2 DeArmond PUs, 3 knobs on lower treble bout, stairstep bridge, trapeze tailpiece, unbound beveled-edge pickguard, triple-bound top, bound back, bound fingerboard, block inlay, 2-ply peghead veneer with black outer layer and white underlayer, T-roof logo engraved into peghead veneer, *Electromatic* engraved vertically into peghead over zigzag pattern, edges of peg-

head veneer beveled to simulate binding, peghead tapers to point at top, sunburst (**6187**) or blond (**6188**)
Introduced: **1951**
Discontinued by **1955**

Electro II cutaway: 17" wide, 3 3/8" deep, *f*-holes, 2 DeArmond PUs, 3 knobs on lower treble bout, stairstep bridge, harp tailpiece, bound tortoise grain pickguard, multiple-bound top, bound back, single-bound fingerboard, block inlay, single-bound rounded-peak peghead, script logo, *Synchromatic* on peghead, gold-plated metal parts, sunburst (**6192**) or natural (**6193**) finish
Introduced: **1951**
3 knobs on lower treble bout, 1 knob on cutaway bout, double-bound *f*-holes, 4-ply top and back binding, 4-ply pickguard binding: **1952**
Melita bridge, truss rod: **1953**
Triple-bound fingerboard and peghead: **c. late 1953**
Named **Country Club:** 1 PU selector switch added on upper bass bout, Melita bridge, *G* tailpiece, unbound pickguard, 4-ply top and back binding, double-bound *f*-holes, 7-ply fingerboard binding, humptop bridge, 4-ply peghead binding, no *Synchromatic* on peghead, T-roof logo, stairstep tuners, gold-plated metal parts, sunburst (**6192**), natural (**6193**), or Cadillac green (**6196**) finish, some with 2-tone gray finish also numbered 6196: **1954**
Filter 'Tron PUs, 2 knobs on lower treble bout, 1 knob on cutaway bout, 2 switches on upper bass bout, roller bridge, triple-bound fingerboard, thumbprint inlay: **1958**
Project-O-Sonic stereo optional, with bass-treble split, Filter 'Tron PUs with only 3 pairs of screw poles, 2 knobs on lower treble bout, 1 switch on cutaway bout, 2 switches on upper bass bout: **1958**
Project-O-Sonic models given separate model numbers, sunburst (**6101**), natural (**6102**), or Cadillac green (**6103**) finish: **1959**
Project-O-Sonic models: PUs identical in outer appearance to standard Filter 'Trons, 4 switches on upper bass bout: **1960**
Body 1 7/8" deep: **1960**
Body 2 7/8" deep: **1963**
Project-O-Sonic Country Clubs (6101, 6102, 6103) discontinued by **1963**
Mute, 2 control knobs, 1 mute knob and 1 switch on lower treble bout, 1 knob on cutaway bout, 2 switches on upper bass bout, zero fret, large non-stairstep tuner buttons, padded back: **1963**
No mute, 2 knobs and 1 switch on lower treble bout: **1965**
Green finish (6196) discontinued: **1968**

Renumbered, sunburst (**7575**), natural (**7576**):
1971

4 knobs on lower treble bout, 1 knob on cutaway bout, 1 switch on upper bass bout,
wooden tailpiece insert with model name,
block inlay: **1974**

Sunburst finish (7575) discontinued, antique
maple finish (**7577**) available: **1977**

Model 7577 described with walnut stain: **1979
only**

Natural (7576) and antique maple (7577) discontinued: **1981**

Electromatic 16" cutaway: 16" wide, laminated
spruce top, 1 or 2 DeArmond PUs, Melita
bridge, single-bound top and back, single-
bound fingerboard, block inlay, 2-ply peghead veneer with black outer layer and
white underlayer, T-roof logo engraved
into peghead veneer, *Electromatic*
engraved vertically into peghead over
zigzag pattern, beveled edges of peghead
veneer to simulate binding, 2 PUs (**6189**), 1
PU sunburst finish (**6190**), or 1 PU natural
finish (**6191**)

Introduced: **1951**

Melita bridge, trapeze tailpiece by **1954**

Named **Streamliner**: maple top, 1 PU, Melita
bridge, *G* tailpiece, 2 knobs on lower treble
bout, double-bound top and back, single-
bound *f*-holes, 25 1/4" scale, single-bound
fingerboard, yellow or sunburst finish pictured in catalog with block inlay (later with
humptop block), natural finish pictured
with humptop block inlay, metal tuner buttons, *Electromatic* on peghead veneer, no
zigzag pattern, chrome-plated metal parts,
bamboo yellow top with copper mist body
(available in jaguar tan by special order)
(**6189**), sunburst (**6190**) or natural finish
(**6191**): **1955**

Double-bound top and back, double-bound *f*-
holes, single-bound fingerboard and peghead, by **1957**

Transition to Anniversary (see following): transitional Model 6189 like 1957 Streamliner
model but with 1 Filter 'Tron PU in neck
position, 1 knob on upper treble bout, 1
switch on upper bass bout, 24 3/4" scale,
unbound peghead, no *Electromatic* on peghead: **1958**

Streamliner last listed: **1959**

Streamliner name re-introduced as thinbody
double cutaway (see following): **1969**

Chet Atkins Models

Chet Atkins Hollow Body: 16" wide (some as
narrow as 15 5/8"), single cutaway, 2 7/8"
deep, maple top, 2 DeArmond PUs, 3 knobs
on lower treble bout, 1 knob on cutaway
bout, 1 switch on upper bass bout, com-

pensating metal bridge, Bigsby vibrato,
signpost and signature on rounded-end
pickguard, bound *f*-holes, *G* brand on top,
double-bound top and back, double-bound
f-holes, 24 3/4" scale, bound rosewood fingerboard, block inlay engraved with cactus and cows except for unengraved block
at 1st fret, metal nut, single-bound peghead, longhorn peghead inlay, gold-plated
metal parts (except nut and Bigsby), amber
red (orange) finish (**6120**), white leather
case with Western motif tooled leather
trim

Introduced (prototype with serial number
13753): **late 1954**

Engraved block at 1st fret: **1955**

Block inlay with no engraving on any block,
horseshoe peghead inlay: **1956**

No *G* brand: **1957**

Humptop block inlay: **c. late 1957**

Ebony fingerboard: **c. early 1958**

Filter 'Tron PUs, 2 switches on upper bass
bout, bar bridge 1/2" in diameter,
thumbprint inlay, interior top and back
braces meet to form soundpost-like structure: **c. mid 1958**

Gretsch Bigsby vibrato, zero fret, bone nut:
1959

2 1/4" deep, 2 knobs and 1 switch on lower treble bout (total of 3 knobs and 3 switches):
early 1961

Double cutaway, simulated (painted-on) *f*-
holes, single mute, mute knob on lower treble bout, signature (no signpost) on pickguard, leather back pad: **mid to late 1961**

Standard Gretsch (non-white) case: **1962**

Named **Nashville**, nameplate on peghead,
pebble grain vinyl backpad: **c. 1964**

Renumbered 7660: **1971**

Adjustamatic bridge, squared pickguard, no
mute, no nameplate: **1972**

Open *f*-holes, red finish: **1973**

Curved tubular-arm Gretsch Bigsby vibrato,
new PU housing: **1975**

Flat-arm vibrato: **c. 1979**

Discontinued: **1980**

Chet Atkins Country Gentleman: 17" wide,
single cutaway, 2" deep (depth varies),
simulated *f*-holes (see note, following), 2
Filter 'Tron PUs, 2 knobs on lower treble
bout, 1 knob on cutaway bout, 2 switches
on upper bass bout, metal bar bridge 1/2" in
diameter, Bigsby vibrato, signature and
signpost on pickguard, 4-ply binding on top
and back, 24 1/2" scale, bound ebony fingerboard, thumbprint inlay, metal nut,
single-bound peghead, stairstep tuner buttons, nameplate with serial number on
peghead, gold-plated metal parts (except
nut and Bigsby), mahogany finish (**6122**)
Note: Soundholes vary on examples from

introduction through 1961. Most early examples have simulated f-holes of inlaid black plastic; most later examples have painted-on f-holes. Some late examples have painted soundhole borders to simulate binding. A very few have been seen with open f-holes (possibly non-original).

Introduced: **late 1957**

No signpost on pickguard, zero fret, bone nut: **1959**

Gretsch Bigsby: **late 1959**

Some with 15 frets clear of body: **c. 1960**

Double mute with 2 large mute knobs on either side of bridge, padded back: **late 1961**

Double cutaway, 1 standby switch added on lower treble bout: **late 1961**

Gold-plated Gretsch Bigsby vibrato by **1962**

Smaller lever-action mute knobs: **early 1963**

1 Super 'Tron and 1 Filter 'Tron PU: **1964**

Non-stairstep tuner buttons, no serial number on nameplate: **1965**

Single mute, 1 mute knob/lever: **1966**

2 Filter 'Tron PUs by **late 1960s**

Renumbered **7670**, adjustamatic bridge, no mute, no nameplate, walnut finish: **1971**

Open f-holes: **1972**

Curved tubular-arm Gretsch Bigsby by **1975**

Flat-arm vibrato: **c. 1979**

Discontinued: **1981**

Late 1970s parts assembled in Mexico, marketed as **Southern Belle (7176)**: **1983**

Chet Atkins Tennessean: specified in catalog as 16" wide, most vary from 15 5/8" to 15 7/8", 2 5/8" deep, single cutaway, open f-holes, 1 Filter 'Tron PU in bridge position, 1 knob on cutaway bout, 1 switch on upper bass bout, metal bar bridge 1/2" in diameter, Bigsby vibrato, black pickguard with white signature signpost and Gretsch logo, double-bound top, single-bound back, ebony fingerboard, 24 1/2" scale, pearl thumbprint inlay, unbound peghead, chrome-plated metal parts, no peghead ornament, metal tuner buttons, cherry finish (**6119**)

Introduced: **1958**

Zero fret: **1959**

Gretsch Bigsby vibrato: **late 1959**

2 1/4" deep, large violin-style simulated (painted-on) f-holes with no white border, 2 Hi-Lo 'Tron PUs, 1 knob on cutaway bout, 2 switches on upper bass bout, 2 knobs on lower treble bout, double-bound top, unbound back, gray pickguard with Gretsch logo only, single-bound rosewood fingerboard, no zero fret, plastic tuner buttons, "dark cherry" walnut finish: **1961**

2" deep, thinner painted-on f-holes, standby switch on lower treble bout, Atkins signature and Gretsch logo on gray pickguard, zero fret, single-bound fingerboard, metal

tuner buttons, mahogany finish (slightly redder than walnut of 1961): **1962**

White paint outline around simulated f-holes, pearloid thumbprint inlay, padded back: **1963**

Walnut top finish (some faded to amber), mahogany back and sides finish: **1964**

Nameplate on peghead: **c. 1964**

Metal bar bridge 3/8" in diameter, aluminum knobs, uniform dark-stain top and body finish: **mid 1967**

Open f-holes, dark cherry stain finish: **1970**

Renumbered **7655**: **1971**

No nameplate, adjustamatic bridge: **1972**

Discontinued: **1980**

Chet Atkins Junior: 12 3/4" wide, single cutaway, 1 Super 'Tron PU mounted near bridge, 2 knobs and 1 switch on lower treble bout, metal bar bridge 3/8" in diameter, Burns vibrato, gray pickguard with logo and signature, unbound open f-holes, double-bound top and back, 23 1/4" scale, single-bound rosewood fingerboard, dot inlay positioned near bass edge of fingerboard on frets 1, 3, 5, 7, and 9, block inlay at 12th fret, dot inlay positioned near treble edge of fingerboard at frets 15, 17, and 19, zero fret, bone nut, unbound peghead, peghead plate with model name, orange stain finish

Available: **1970**

Super Chet: 17" wide, 2 1/2" deep, rounded cutaway, upper bass bout joins neck at an angle toward body, 2 PUs, 5 knobs (master volume plus individual tone and volume) on pickguard, abalone-inlaid tailpiece insert, model name on pickguard, binding material around middle of sides, 24 1/2" scale, fancy abalone inlay on fingerboard and peghead, zero fret, gold-plated metal parts, 25 1/2" scale or wider neck optional, autumn red finish (**7690**), autumn red with Bigsby vibrato (**7690-B**), walnut finish (**7691**), walnut with Bigsby vibrato (**7691-B**)

Introduced: **1973**

Discontinued: **1980**

Deluxe Chet: 17" wide, 2 1/2" deep, rounded cutaway, upper bass bout joins neck at an angle toward body, top-mounted controls, Bigsby, signature (no model name) on pickguard, thumbprint inlay, autumn red (**7680**) or walnut (**7681**)

Introduced: **1973**

Discontinued by **1975**

Single Cutaway Models, Introduced in 1955 and After

White Falcon: 17" wide, single cutaway, 2 7/8" deep, 2 PUs, 3 knobs on lower treble bout, 1 knob on cutaway bout, 1 switch on upper bass bout, Melita bridge, tubular tailpiece with V-shape piece and *G*, Bigsby vibrato optional, falcon on pickguard, 4-ply top and back binding, double-bound *f*-holes; gold paint under clear plastic binding around sides of body, *f*-holes, fingerboard and peghead; 25 1/2" scale, triple-bound ebony fingerboard, engraved humptop block inlay, stairstep tuner buttons, *Gretsch* vertically on peghead in gold sparkle, gold sparkle wing-shaped peghead inlays, gold sparkle truss rod cover, V-top peghead shape, double-bound peghead, gold-plated metal parts, white finish (**6136**), earliest examples with *The White Falcon* on label and no model number
Introduced: **1955**
Transition to gold-sparkle plastic binding, some examples with some gold leaf and some gold sparkle (peghead logo is last part to get gold sparkle): **1955**
Filter 'Tron PUs, roller bridge, thumbprint inlay: **1958**
Horizontal logo, nameplate on peghead: **1959**
Project-O-Sonic stereo optional, 3 pairs of poles on each PU, bass-treble split , 2 knobs on lower treble bout, 1 switch on upper treble bout, 2 switches on upper bass bout (**6137**): **1958**
Project-O-Sonic model: PUs identical in outward appearance to standard Filter 'Trons, 4 switches on upper bass bout, 1 switch on upper treble bout: **1959**
2" deep, double mute with 2 large mute knobs on either side of bridge, padded back: **1960**
Non-stereo: 2 control knobs and 1 switch on lower treble bout, 1 knob on upper treble bout, 2 switches on upper bass bout: **1960**
Gretsch Bigsby vibrato standard: **1962**
Small lever-action mute knobs: **early 1963**
Double-cutaway, V-shape tailpiece, zero fret: **1962**
Gretsch vibrato with *G* plate and straight tubular arm curving slightly at tip, large non-stairstep tuner buttons: **1964**
Adjustable nut on tremolo arm, T-zone tempered treble-end fingerboard with dot inlay from 15th fret: **1965**
Stereo configuration: 2 large aluminum control knobs and 4 switch knobs on lower treble bout, 1 switch on upper treble bout, 1 switch on lower bass bout, mute knobs on either side of bridge, by **1965**
Tuning fork bridge: **1966–69**
Renumbered: non-stereo **7594**, stereo **7595**: **1971**

Curved tubular-arm Gretsch Bigsby: **1972**
Single cutaway (**7593**) re-introduced: 2 knobs on lower treble bout, 1 knob on cutaway bout, 2 switches on upper bass bout (some examples with stereo wiring, same knob and switch configuration as 1967 stereo model): **early 1970s**
No mute, block inlay by **early 1970s**
No T-zone fingerboard by **1975**
Non-stereo double cutaway (**7594**) and single-cutaway (**7593**) models discontinued, stereo double cutaway model (**7595**) available by special order only: **1980**
Stereo White Falcon (**7595**) discontinued: **1981**

Convertible: 17" wide, single cutaway, 1 DeArmond PU mounted on top, 2 knobs mounted on oversized pickguard, multiple-bound top, triple-bound back, double-bound *f*-holes, *G* tailpiece, adjustable rosewood bridge, multiple-bound rosewood fingerboard, triple-bound peghead, humptop block inlay, stairstep tuner buttons, gold-plated metal parts, lotus ivory top finish with copper mist body finish (**6199**), sunburst finish available by special order
Introduced by **1955**
Ebony fingerboard, thumbprint inlay, bamboo yellow top finish, copper mist back and sides finish: **late 1957**
Renamed **Sal Salvador**: Filter 'Tron PU, triple-bound top and back, triple-bound fingerboard, thumbprint inlay, triple-bound peghead, sunburst finish (**6199**): **1958**
Knobs mounted into top, large block inlay, zero fret: **1965**
Sal Salvador discontinued: **1968**

Rambler: 13" wide, pointed cutaway, 1 DeArmond PU, 2 knobs on lower treble bout, adjustable rosewood bridge, *G* tailpiece, single-bound top and back, 23" scale, rosewood fingerboard, dot inlay, single-bound peghead, ivory top finish, green or black body finish(**6115**)
Introduced by **1957**
Rounded cutaway, Hi-Lo 'Tron PU, red truss rod cover: **1960**
Discontinued by **1961**

Clipper: 16" wide, 1 3/4" deep, 1 PU with slot-head screw poles and oval cutout in PU cover, 2 knobs on lower treble bout, adjustable ebony bridge, trapeze tailpiece, double-bound top and back, 24 1/2" scale, dot inlay, sunburst (**6186**)
Introduced by **1958**
Natural finish (**6187**) available: **1959**
Hi-Lo 'Tron PU: **1960**
Natural finish (6187) discontinued: **1961**
Short-arm "palm" vibrato listed as standard,

but rare: **1963**

No vibrato: **1968**

Renumbered (**7555**): **1971**

Sunburst (6186) discontinued, 2 PU model (**6185**) introduced: **1972**

2 PU Clipper (6185) discontinued: **1975**

Anniversary: named for Gretsch's 75th Anniversary, 16" wide, 2 1/2" deep, 1 Filter 'Tron PU, 1 knob on cutaway bout, 1 switch on upper bass bout, roller bridge, *G* tailpiece, single-bound top and back, 24 1/2" scale, unbound fingerboard, thumbprint inlay, unbound peghead, sunburst (**6124**) or 2-tone smoke green (**6125**)

Double Anniversary: same with 2 PUs, 2 knobs on lower treble bout, 1 knob on cutaway bout, 2 switches on upper bass bout, sunburst (**6117**) or 2-tone smoke green (**6118**) finish

Introduced: **1958**

Nameplate on peghead: **mid 1959**

Hi-Lo 'Tron PUs: **1960**

Stereo (1 PU per channel, *not* Project-O-Sonic) optional on Double Anniversary, sunburst (**6111**) or green (**6112**) finish: **1961**

Short-arm "palm" vibrato listed as standard, but rare: **1963**

Bound fingerboard on Double Anniversary only: **1963**

Stereo models (6111 and 6112) discontinued, models 6118 and 6125 also available in 2-tone tan finish (similar to lotus ivory and copper mist): **1963**

No vibrato, zero fret on Double Anniversary only: **1968**

Sunburst Double Anniversary renumbered 7560: **1971**

Single PU Anniversary (6124, 6125) and 2-tone green Double Anniversary (6118) discontinued: **1972**

Double Anniversary, smaller *f*-holes, adjustamatic bridge, no nameplate, by **1972**

1 switch on upper treble bout, 3 knobs on lower bass bout, trapeze tailpiece: **1973**

Block inlay: **1974**

Double Anniversary discontinued by **1975**

Custom model (name unknown): 16" wide, single cutaway, 2 Hi-Lo 'Tron PUs, cat's eye soundholes, 4 knobs on lower treble bout, 1 switch on upper treble bout, roller bridge, *G* tailpiece, thumbprint inlay, bright red or black finish (**6117**, same model number as standard Double Anniversary)

200 made: **c. 1965–68**

Van Eps: 17" wide, 6 or 7 strings, 2 "eared" Filter 'Tron PUs with extra-heavy covers, *G* tailpiece, roller bridge, floating tuning fork bridge, triple-bound top, triple-bound fingerboard and peghead, 25 1/2" scale,

thumbprint inlay, zero fret, nameplate on peghead, gold-plated metal parts, 7-string sunburst (**6079**) or walnut (**6080**) finish, 6-string sunburst (**6081**) or walnut (**6082**) finish

Introduced: **1968**

Wood bridge, no tuning fork, tailpiece with straight-across string anchors: **1969**

Super 'Tron PUs by **1971**

7-string sunburst renumbered 7580: **1971**

All but 7-string sunburst discontinued: **1972**

7-string sunburst (7580) listed but available by special order only: **1977**

7-string sunburst (7580) no longer listed: **1980**

Double Cutaway Models

White Falcon and **Chet Atkins** double-cutaway models: see Single Cutaway section, preceding

Monkees: 2 Super 'Tron PUs, *Monkees* guitar-shaped logo on pickguard and truss rod cover, bound top and back, double *f*-holes and fingerboard, Gretsch Bigsby, thumbprint inlay along both edges of fingerboard, peghead plate with model name and *Rock 'n' Roll Model*, red finish

Introduced: **1966**

Discontinued: **1969**

Viking: 17" wide, 2" deep, 2 Super 'Tron PUs, 2 control knobs and 1 switch on lower treble bout, 1 knob on upper treble bout, 2 switches on upper bass bout, single mute with 1 small lever knob on lower treble bout, roller bridge, floating tuning fork bridge, model name on pickguard (earliest with name and Viking ship on pickguard), ebony fingerboard, thumbprint inlay, T-zone tempered treble-end fingerboard with dots from 15th fret, zero fret, nameplate on peghead, padded back, gold-plated metal parts, sunburst (**6187**), natural (**6188**), or Cadillac green (**6189**) finish

Introduced: **1964**

Renumbered: sunburst 7585, natural 7586: **1971**

No tuning fork, tubular-arm Gretsch Bigsby, green finish (6189) discontinued: **1972**

Sunburst (7585) and natural (7586) discontinued: **1975**

Rally: 16" wide, 2" deep, 2 Hi-Lo 'Tron PUs, 3 knobs and 1 switch on lower treble bout, 1 knob on upper treble bout, standby and treble booster switches on upper bass bout, bar bridge (some with roller bridge), plate on back for active electronics, Gretsch Bigsby vibrato, rally stripe on pickguard and truss rod cover, double-bound top, single-bound back, single-bound rosewood fingerboard, thumbprint inlay, T-zone tempered treble-end fingerboard with dot inlay from 15th fret, zero fret, green finish (**6104**) or bamboo yellow top finish with 2-tone copper mist body (**6105**)

Songbird: same as Rally but with *G* soundholes and no rally stripe
Introduced: **1967**
Discontinued by **1970**

12 string: 16" wide, 17" wide model optional, 2 Super 'Tron PUs, 2 knobs and 1 switch on lower treble bout, 1 knob on upper treble bout, 2 switches on upper bass bout, *G* tailpiece with straight-across string anchors, large triangular inlay, zero fret, padded back on 17" model only, sunburst (**6075**) or natural (**6076**) finish
Introduced by **1967**
Natural (6076) and sunburst (6075) discontinued, sunburst (6075) available by special order: **1972**

Black Hawk: 16" wide, 2" deep, 2 Super 'Tron PUs, 2 control knobs and 1 switch on lower treble bout, 1 knob on upper treble bout, 2 switches on upper bass bout, roller bridge, floating tuning fork bridge, *G* tailpiece or Gretsch Bigsby vibrato, single-bound top and back, single-bound fingerboard, 24 1/2" scale, thumbprint inlay, T-zone tempered treble-end fingerboard with dot inlay from 15th fret, zero fret, nameplate on peghead, sunburst (**6100**) or black (**6101**) finish
Introduced: **1967**
Sunburst (6100) discontinued: **1970**
Black (6101) discontinued: **1972**

Streamliner double cutaway: 16" wide, 2" deep, 2 Super 'Tron PUs, roller bridge, *G* tailpiece, bound rosewood fingerboard, 24 1/2" scale, thumbprint inlay, T-zone tempered treble-end fingerboard with dot inlay from 15th fret, zero fret, nameplate on peghead, sunburst (**6102**) or cherry (**6103**) finish
Introduced: **1969**
No nameplate, no T-zone, by **1972**
Sunburst (6102) discontinued: **1973**
Cherry (6103) discontinued: **1975**

Broadkaster hollowbody: 16" wide, 2 Super 'Tron PUs, 4 knobs on lower treble bout, 1 knob on upper treble bout, 1 switch on upper bass bout, dot inlay, zero fret, with *G* tailpiece natural (**7607**) or sunburst (**7608**) finish, with Gretsch Bigsby vibrato natural (**7603**) or sunburst (**7604**) finish
Introduced: **1975**
Humbucking PUs, terminator bridge/tailpiece: **1976**
Red finish (**7609**) standard, all other Broadkasters (7603, 7604, 7607, 7608) dis-

continued: **1977**
Red finish (7609) discontinued: **1980**

COMMENTS

The collector's market for Gretsch instruments is based largely on hollowbody electric models made from the mid 1950s through the mid 1960s. This market has been fueled at various times by the use of Gretsch models by such notable players as Chet Atkins, George Harrison, Neil Young and Stephen Stills (with Crosby, Stills, Nash, and Young), and Brian Setzer (of the Stray Cats).

Gretsch guitars tend to be either loved or hated. Gibson and Fender players feel that Gretsches are inferior in workmanship. Binding material and the resin glue used for necksets tend to deteriorate with age, frequently necessitating repair work to put an instrument in playing order. In addition, the Gretsch switch systems and the pick-ups are not generally considered to be as versatile as those of other makes. Despite the drawbacks, Gretsches have a visual appeal—particularly the Atkins models (and other related Western trim models) and the White Falcon—which is quite unlike that of any other maker. Many players of rockabilly and early rock and roll music feel that the DeArmond pickups as well as the later Filter 'Trons have a distinctive twang and tone that is perfect for that type of music.

Models most highly regarded by collectors: single-cutaway versions (up to early 1961) of the Chet Atkins Hollow Body (6120), Chet Atkins Country Gentleman, and White Falcon. The 1963 Chet Atkins Country Gentleman (double cutaway) is highly sought after because of its association with George Harrison.

Models from the 1960s generally bring more than their 1970s equivalents.

New Japanese-made models are generally not true reissues, but combine features from various years. Structurally they are quite good.

ELECTRIC SOLIDBODIES KEY

Non-standard body shape
    Rectangular body=**Bo Diddley**
    Abstract square-ish body=**Jupiter**
    Absract body more curved than Jupiter=**Thunderbird**
    Abstract body, lower bass bout like auto tail fin=**Cadillac**
Single cutaway, standard body shape
    Dot inlay
        1 PU
            Walnut stain=**BST 1000 (8210)**
            Red stain=**BST 1000 (8216)**
        2 PUs
            Walnut stain=**BST 1000 (7617, 8215 or 8217)**
            Red stain=**BST 1000 (8211)**
    Large block, humptop block, or thumbprint inlay
        Flat top=**Roc II**
        Carved top
            3 or 4 knobs
                Black top finish
                    6 strings=**Duo-Jet, 1953–61**
                    4 strings=**Duo-Jet Tenor**
                Stained maple or knotty pine top
                    Belt buckle tailpiece=**Round-Up**
                    Bigsby vibrato=**Chet Atkins Solid Body 6121**
                Red top, black body=**Jet Firebird, c. 1955–61**
                Silver sparkle top=**Silver Jet, c. 1955–61**
                White finish=**White Penguin**
                Green finish=**custom-order Duo-Jet**
                Sparkle finish (except silver)=**custom-order Duo-Jet**
            5 knobs
                Thumbprint inlay=**Roc Jet**
                Western inlay=**Country Roc**
Symmetrical double cutaway
    Dot inlay
        Maple-and-walnut neck through body=**Committee**
        Solid mahogany body
            Walnut stain=**BST 2000 (7620 or 8220)**
            Red stain=**BST 2000 (8221)**
    Thumbprint inlay
        Black top=**Duo-Jet, c. 1961–71**
        Silver sparkle top=**Silver Jet, c. 1961–63**
        Red top=**Jet Fire Bird, c. 1961–71**
        Sparkle top (except silver)=**custom-order Duo-Jet**
Pointed treble-side cutaway, slight cutaway on bass side
    Black control plate=**Super Axe**
    No control plate=**Atkins Axe**
Asymmetrical double cutaway
    No fingerboard inlay=**TK 300**
    Thumbprint inlay=**Astro-Jet**
    Dot inlay
        Maple-and-walnut neck through body=**BST 5000**
        Glue-in or bolt-on neck
            Vibrato
                22 1/2" scale=**Princess**
                24 1/2" scale
                    1 PU=**Corvette 6134**
                    2 PUs=**Corvette 6135**
            No vibrato
                Natural maple finish=**Broadkaster**
                Mahogany or cherry finish=**Corvette 6132**
                Platinum grey finish=**Corvette 6133**

Hinged body sides
    Guitar=**Bikini 6023**
    Bass=**Bikini 6024**
Doubleneck bass/guitar (detachable bodies)=**Bikini 6025**

Specs unavailable:
Roc I
Deluxe Corvette

ELECTRIC SOLIDBODIES

Duo-Jet and Roc-Jet models (including Chet Atkins Solid Body and White Penguin) from the 1950s and 1960s are not actually solid, but are heavily routed underneath the top. Beginning in 1970, all solidbody models are fully solid.

SECTION ORGANIZATION

Original Duo-Jet Series (including Chet Atkins Solid Body and White Penguin)
Later Single Cutaway Duo-Jet Style Models (Roc series)
Bo Diddley Models
Other Models
BST "Beast" Models

Original Duo-Jet Series

Duo-Jet: 13 1/4" wide, 2" deep, single cutaway, mahogany body, 2 DeArmond PUs, 3 knobs (master tone and 2 individual volume) on lower treble bout, 1 master volume knob on cutaway bout, 1 PU selector switch on upper bass bout, Melita bridge, *G* tailpiece, gray plastic pickguard, triple-bound top, single-bound fingerboard and peghead, 24 1/2" scale, block inlay, script logo, chrome-plated metal parts, black top finish (**6128**), a few custom-order green finish (all with gold-plated metal parts), sparkle finishes available (see following)
Introduced at: **mid 1953**
T-roof logo: **1955**
Humptop block inlay: **late 1956**
Roller bridge, thumbprint inlay: **early 1958**
13 1/2" wide, Filter 'Tron PUs, 2 knobs on lower treble bout, 1 knob on cutaway bout, 2 switches on upper bass bout: **1958**
Zero fret: **1959**
Duo-Jet Tenor (**6127**) available: **1959–60 only**
Symmetrical double cutaway body shape: **1961**
Standby switch on lower treble bout, bent flat-arm Burns vibrato, gold plastic pickguard, gold-plated metal parts: **1962**
Sparkle finishes (see Silver Jet, following) listed as custom Duo-Jet finishes: **1963**

Sparkle finishes discontinued: **1966**
Super 'Tron PUs, treble booster switch, Gretsch Bigsby vibrato: **1968**
Discontinued, available by special order only: **1971**

Silver Jet: same specs and changes as Duo-Jet, silver sparkle top finish (**6129**)
Introduced by **1955**
Optional sparkle finishes listed: gold, champagne, burgundy, or tangerine; all sparkle finishes available on Gretsch drums available on Duo-Jet guitar: **1962**
Silver Jet discontinued as separate model, all finishes listed as custom Duo-Jet finishes: **1963**
Discontinued: **1971**

Jet Fire Bird: black pickguard, a few with no logo on pickguard, red top finish, ebony finish back and sides (**6131**), same specs and changes as Duo-Jet
Introduced by **1955**
Discontinued, available by special order only: **1971**

Round-Up: Duo-Jet body shape, maple top, some with knotty pine top, some with mahogany top, 2 DeArmond PUs, 3 knobs (master tone and 2 individual volume) on lower treble bout, 1 master volume knob on cutaway bout, 1 PU selector switch on upper bass bout, Melita bridge, *G* tailpiece, string anchors covered by rectangular "belt-buckle" with Western scene, *G* brand on top, 4-ply top binding, unbound back, sides covered with Western-motif tooled leather, bound fingerboard, block inlay engraved with cows and cactus, no inlay at 1st fret, longhorn head etched on pickguard and inlaid on peghead, bound peghead, gold-plated metal parts, orange-stain top finish (**6130**), tweed case
Introduced: **1954**
Inlay at 1st fret with no engraving: **early 1955**
Engraving on 1st fret inlay: **mid 1955**
Triple-bound top: **1956**
Appears on price list but not in catalog: **1959**
Discontinued: **1960**

Chet Atkins Solid Body: Duo-Jet body shape, maple top, some with knotty pine top, 2 DeArmond PUs, 2 knobs on lower treble

bout, 1 knob on cutaway bout, 1 switch on upper bass bout, height-adjustable metal compensating bridge, Bigsby vibrato, pickguard with signpost and Chet Atkins signature, G brand on top, 4-ply top binding, unbound back, sides covered with Western-motif tooled leather, bound rosewood fingerboard, block inlay engraved with Western scenes, single-bound peghead, longhorn peghead inlay, metal nut, gold-plated metal parts (except for Bigsby), "brown mahogany" orange finish (**6121**), white case with tooled leather trim
Introduced by **1955**

3-ply top binding: **late 1955**

3 knobs on lower treble bout, no leather side covering, triple-bound top and back, ebony fingerboard, unengraved humptop block inlay: **1957**

Straight bar bridge 1/2" in diameter, 4-ply top and back binding: **early 1958**

Filter 'Tron PUs, 2 knobs on lower treble bout, 1 knob on cutaway bout, 2 switches on upper bass bout, thumbprint inlay, horseshoe peghead inlay: **1958**

Gretsch Bigsby: **1959**

Zero fret, bone nut: **late 1959**

Bound top and back: **1960**

Symmetrical double cutaway body shape, 4-ply top and back binding, orange top finish: **1961**

Standby switch added to lower treble bout, standard Gretsch case: **1962**

Discontinued: **1963**

White Penguin: same ornamentation as White Falcon, 2 DeArmond PUs, tubular tailpiece with V-shaped piece and G, penguin on pickguard; gold-sparkle binding on sides of body, fingerboard and peghead; ebony fingerboard, engraved humptop block inlay, white finish (**6134**), (a few early examples with black and white finish, a few with gold sparkle top)
Introduced: **1955**

Filter 'Tron PUs, stereo optional, roller bridge, thumbprint inlay: **1958**

Horizontal logo, nameplate on peghead: **1959**
Symmetrical double cutaway body shape by **1963**

Discontinued (less than 100 total made): **1964**

Later Single Cutaway Duo-Jet Style Models

Roc Jet: Super 'Tron PUs, adjustamatic bridge, Porsche pumpkin (**6127**) or Mercedes black (**6130**)
Introduced: **late 1969**

Porsche pumpkin renumbered (**7611**), Mercedes black renumbered (**7610**)
Red (**7612**) or walnut-stained mahogany (**7613**)

finish optional: **1971**

Porsche pumpkin (7611) discontinued, model number 7611 assigned to black finish, by **1975**

Red (7612) discontinued by **1977**

Humbucking PUs: **1978**

Discontinued: **1980**

Country Roc: Western style Roc-Jet, G brand, block inlay with engraved Western scenes, horseshoe inlaid on peghead, tooled leather side trim (**7620**)
Introduced: **1974**

Discontinued: **1979**

Roc I: specs unavailable (**7635**): **mid 1970s**

Roc II: solid mahogany body, flat top, 2 humbucking PUs, elliptical control plate with 4 knobs and 1 switch and jack, bound top and back, bound ebony fingerboard, thumbprint inlay (**7621**)
Introduced: **1974**

Discontinued: **mid 1977**

Bo Diddley Models

Bo Diddley: rectangular body shape, 2 DeArmond PUs, Melita bridge, G tailpiece, bound fingerboard, thumbprint inlay, red top finish, black back and sides finish, 4 instruments made for singer Bo Diddley
First instrument made: **1958**

Second instrument made: **1960**

Third and fourth instruments made: **1962**

Jupiter, Thunderbird, and **Cadillac**: custom models made for Bo Diddley, Jupiter with abstract square-ish body shape, Thunderbird with more curved body shape, Cadillac with lower bass bout resembling an automobile tail fin, all with 2 Filter 'Tron PUs, Jupiter and Thunderbird with red top finish and black back and sides finish, Cadillac with orange top finish and black back and sides finish
2 Cadillacs made: **1961**

2 Jupiters and 2 Thunderbirds made: **c. 1961**

Other Models

Bikini: removable neck-body shaft and foldup "butterfly" back and wings, Hi-Lo 'Tron PUs, dot inlay, black finish, guitar only (**6023**), bass only (**6024**), or doubleneck (**6025**)
Introduced: **1961**

Discontinued: **1963**

Corvette solidbody: 13 1/2" wide, asymmetrical double cutaway with bass horn slightly longer, slab body, 1 Hi-Lo 'Tron PU, 2

knobs, rosewood bridge, trapeze tailpiece, rectangular plate next to neck, no binding, 24 1/2" scale, dot inlay, narrow peghead, mahogany (**6132**) or platinum grey (**6133**)
Introduced: **1961**

Platinum grey finish (6133) discontinued: **1963**
Beveled body edges, sharper cutaway points, bar bridge 3/8" in diameter, larger pickguard covers routing for metal plate, cherry red finish, 1 PU and no vibrato (**6132**), 1 PU with flat-arm vibrato (**6134**), or 2 PUs with Burns flat-arm vibrato (**6135**): **1963**
2 tuners on bass side, 4 on treble side: **1964**
Silver Duke with glittered silver finish, Gold Duke with glittered gold finish, a few made: **c. 1966**
1 PU models (6132 and 6134) discontinued by **1968**
Bigsby, Super 'Tron PUs: **1968**
2 PU model (6135) discontinued, available by special order only: **1972**
2 PU model re-listed, humbucking PUs (**7623**): **1976**
Deluxe Corvette: specs unavailable (**7632**), available: **early 1977 only**
Discontinued: **1978**

Princess: Corvette-style double cutaway with beveled body edges, 1 Hi-Lo 'Tron PU, 2 knobs, bar bridge 3/8" in diameter, short-arm palm vibrato, trapeze tailpiece, padded back, 22 1/2" scale, dot inlay, gold-plated metal parts (**6106**), optional body/pickguard colors: white/grape (lavender), blue/white, pink/white, white/gold
Available: **1963**

Astro-Jet: asymmetrical double cutaway, pointed horns, beveled body edges, 2 Super 'Tron PUs, 3 knobs, 3 switches, roller bridge, Burns straight-arm vibrato, thumbprint inlay, 4 tuners on bass side, 2 on treble side, red top finish, black back and sides finish (**6126**)
Introduced: **1965**
Discontinued by **1968**

Broadkaster solidbody: 13 1/2" wide, double cutaway similar to Fender Stratocaster shape, rounded horns, bass horn longer than treble horn, maple body, 2 Super 'Tron PUs, 2 knobs, 2 toggle switches, adjustamatic bridge, strings anchor on metal plate tailpiece (tailpiece screwed into top), bolt-on maple neck, maple fingerboard, black dot inlay, no peghead veneer, natural (**7600**) or sunburst (**7601**) finish
Introduced: **1975**
Discontinued: **c. 1979**

Committee: 12 1/2" wide, symmetrical double cutaway, 5-piece walnut and maple body,

neck-through-body construction, 2 humbucking PUs, clear symmetrical pickguard, single-bound rosewood fingerboard, dot inlay, bound peghead, walnut grain peghead veneer, natural finish (**7628**)
Introduced by **1975**
Discontinued: **1981**

TK 300: 12" wide, asymmetrical double cutaway, maple body, slight cutout at endpin, 2 humbucking PUs, bridge PU slant-mounted, 2 knobs, white pickguard, bolt-on neck, no fingerboard inlay, peghead shape similar to hockey stick blade, 6-on-a-side tuner arrangement, vertical block letter logo reads upside down to player, natural (**7625**) or autumn red stain (**7624**) finish
Introduced by **1975**
Discontinued: **1981**

Atkins Super Axe: pointed cutaway, upper bass bout joins neck at angle toward body, 2 humbucking PUs, phaser and compressor electronics, black elliptical control plate, 5 knobs, small square inlay, red rosewood stain (**7680**) or ebony stain (**7681**) finish
Appears in ads as un-named model played by Roy Clark (later Clark prototypes have asymmetrical rounded double cutaway design, no control plate, knobs and switches in elliptical pattern)
Introduced as Atkins Super Axe: **1976**
Discontinued: **1981**

Atkins Axe: pointed cutaway, upper bass bout joins neck at angle toward body, 2 humbucking PUs, standard electronics, 4 knobs on lower treble bout, 1 switch on upper bass bout, small square inlay, ebony stain (**7685**) or red rosewood stain (**7686**) finish
Introduced: **1976**
Discontinued: **1981**

BST "Beast" Models

BST 1000: single cutaway, mahogany body, bolt-on neck, dot inlay, T-roof logo reads upside down to player
1 humbucking PU: walnut stain (**8210**) or red stain (**8216**) finish
2 humbucking PUs with exposed coils: walnut stain (numbered **7617**, **8215**, or **8217**) or red stain (**8211**) finish
Introduced: **1979**
Discontinued: **1981**

BST 2000: symmetrical double cutaway, mahogany body, 2 humbucking PUs, bolt-on neck, dot inlay, T-roof logo reads upside down to player, walnut stain (numbered **7620** or **8220**) or red stain (**8221**) finish

Electric Solidbodies

Introduced by **1979**
Discontinued: **1980**

BST 5000: asymmetrical double cutaway body shape, neck-through-body construction, 5-piece walnut and maple construction, some with no separate fingerboard, 2 humbucking PUs, stud tailpiece, dot inlay, T-roof logo reads upside down to player, natural walnut/maple finish (**8250**)
Introduced: **1979**
Discontinued: **1981**

COMMENTS

The appeal of solidbody Gretsch guitars is primarily aesthetic rather than for playing characteristics. The models of greatest appeal to collectors are those with ornamentation closely related to that of the most desirable hollowbody models. The rare White Penguin is one of the most highly sought after of all vintage electric guitars. The Round-Up and Chet Atkins Solid Body are highly sought after. The Duo-Jet, which has no hollowbody equivalent, is also highly regarded, with custom color and sparkle top models bringing more than standard black top models.

Double cutaway models from the 1960s—especially sparkle top models—are sought by collectors and players but bring less than their single cutaway equivalents.

Later solidbody models are of little interest to collectors.

BASSES

SECTION ORGANIZATION
Hollowbody Models
Solidbody Models

Hollowbody Models

Model 6070: 17" double cutaway, painted *f*-holes, extension endpin, 1 PU, roller bridge, mute, padded back, 34" scale, asymmetrical peghead, 2-on-a-side tuner arrangement, gold-plated metal parts, sunburst finish
Introduced by **1963**
Model 6072: same as Model 6070 but with 2 PUs, introduced: **1968**
No extension endpin: **1965**
Discontinued, available by special order only: **1972**

Model 6071: 16" single cutaway, 29" scale, painted *f*-holes, 1 PU, roller bridge, mute, padded back, zero fret, 4-on-a-side tuner arrangement, red mahogany finish
Model 6073: same as Model 6071 with 2 PUs
Introduced by **1968**
Discontinued, available by special order only: **1972**

Solidbody Models

Solid Body Bass: double cutaway, mahogany body, cutout through upper bass bout, 2 Super 'Tron PUs, 3 knobs, 1 switch, large rosewood grain pickguard with beveled edges, 2 finger rests, bound rosewood fingerboard, dot inlay, asymmetrical peghead with point at top on bass side, 2-on-a-side tuner arrangement, natural mahogany finish (**7615**)
Introduced by **1972**
Discontinued by **1975**

Broadkaster Bass: asymmetrical double cutaway, similar shape to Fender Stratocaster, rounded horns, bass horn longer than treble, 1 Super 'Tron PU, 2 knobs, bolt-on maple neck, maple fingerboard, black dot inlay, no peghead veneer, natural (**7605**) or sunburst (**7606**) finish
Introduced by **1975**
Discontinued: **1979**

Committee Bass: 13" wide, symmetrical double cutaway, 5-piece walnut and maple body, neck-through-body construction, 1 Super 'Tron PU, clear pickguard, metal bridge cover, bound rosewood fingerboard, dot inlay, walnut grain peghead veneer, bound peghead, natural finish (**7629**)

Introduced by **1977**
Discontinued: **1981**

TK 300 Bass: asymmetrical double cutaway, slight cutout at endpin area, 1 Super 'Tron PU, 2 knobs, white pickguard, bolt-on neck, no fingerboard inlay, block letter logo reads upside down to player, 4-on-a-side tuner arrangement, peghead shape similar to hockey stick blade, natural (**7627**) or autumn red stain (**7626**) finish
Introduced by **1977**
Natural (7627) discontinued: **1980**
Autumn red (7626) discontinued: **1981**

COMMENTS

Gretsch hollowbody basses have some visual appeal but are sought by very few players as utility instruments. Solidbody models have little appeal.

STEELS

With the exception of the Electromatic Hawaiian model, all Gretsch steel guitars were made by Valco. Like Valco-made National and Supro models, Gretsch lap steels typically have a small metal serial number plate nailed onto the back of the neck at the peghead. Serial numbers on Valco-made Gretsch lap steels and amps are part of the overall Valco number series (see National/Valco, Serial Numbers).

Electromatic Hawaiian Guitar: mahogany body, symmetrical guitar shape, knobs on opposite sides, wood pickup cover, rope-pattern top binding, wood fingerboard, dot markers, 6-on-a-side Staufer-style tuner arrangement with high E-string shaft longer then low E-string shaft, *Gretsch* and *Electromatic* diagonally across peghead, musical note ornament above logo, natural finish
Introduced in: **1940**
Discontinued: **1943**

Electromatic Standard Guitar: symmetrical body with two points near neck and belly below bridge (like Supro Supreme), square control plate, 1 round knob, 1 pointer knob, bound fingerboard, geometric shape markers, 6-on-a-side tuner arrangement, peghead wider at top than at nut, brown pearloid covering (**6156**)
Introduced by **1949**
Discontinued by **1955**

Electromatic Student Guitar: straight-line body sides, square bottom, beveled from fingerboard to body edges, square control plate, 1 round knob, 1 pointer knob, geometric shape markers, peghead narrower at top than at nut, pearloid covering (**6152**)
Introduced by **1949**
Discontinued by **1955**

Electromatic Console Guitar: 2 6-string necks, straight-line body edges with wedge between necks, body beveled around fingerboard, 2 square PU/control plate units, each plate with 1 round knob and 1 pointer knob, bound fingerboards, geometric shape markers, 6-on-a-side tuner arrangement, brown pearloid covering (**6158**)
Introduced by **1949**
Discontinued by **1955**

Jet Twin Console: 2 6-string necks, asymmetrical bodies joined together, staggered tiers, heavy metal bridge covers with *Gretsch* and *Electromatic*, 2 metal knobs on front neck, 1 knob on rear neck, clear plastic fingerboards back-painted white, geometric shape markers, 6-on-a-side tuner arrangement, black finish (**6148**), 4 legs optional (**6148L**)
Introduced by **1955**
Discontinued: **1963**

Jet Mainliner: 6 strings, asymmetrical body, 2 metal knobs, heavy metal bridge cover with *Gretsch* and *Electromatic*, clear plastic fingerboard back-painted white, geometric shape markers, 3-on-a-side tuner arrangement, asymmetrical peghead longer on treble side, black finish (**6147**)
Introduced by **1955**
Discontinued: **1963**

Jet Airliner: 6 strings, symmetrical body, 2 knobs on opposite sides, control plates shaped like rocket fins (similar to National Rocket 110), plastic bridge/PU cover, painted-on fingerboard, geometric markers, symmetrical peghead, 3-on-a-side tuners, black finish (**6145**)
Introduced by **1955**
Discontinued: **1963**

COMMENTS

The Electromatic Hawaiian of the early 1940s and the Jet series of the 1950s have some aesthetic appeal for collectors.

Unlike Gretsch electric guitars, the postwar lap steels have Valco electronics, which are sought by some players for blues-related music.

Guild

SERIAL NUMBERS

Guild guitars are numbered in one consecutive series from 1952–65 and from 1970–79. From 1965–69 most guitars are numbered with a 2-letter prefix and a separate number series for each model. A few (approximately 89) from 1966–69 are numbered using the original series. Beginning November 1, 1970, all models return to the system with a separate prefix and series for each model.

Numbers for 1952–58 were compiled by Hans Moust. Numbers from 1959–86 are from Guild records. *Note: Not all Guild models are included in these lists.*

Year	Approx. Last Number	Year	Approx. Last Number
1952	350	1966	46608
1953	840	1967	46637
1954	1526	1968	46656
1955	2468	1969	46695
1956	3830	1970	50978
1957	5712	1971	61463
1958	8348	1972	75602
1959	12035	1973	95496
1960	14713	1974	112803
1961	18419	1975	130304
1962	22722	1976	149625
1963	28943	1977	169867
1964	38636	1978	195067
1965	46606	1979	211877

1965–69

Models are arranged alphabetically by prefix. Numbers are last number for that year. All series start with 101.

Model	Prefix	1965	1966	1967	1968	1969
Artist Award	AA	101	113	139	157	167
A-50	AB	136	162	203	240	
D-44	AC	166	318	435	488	570
F-50	AD	119	190	291	355	418
A-500	AF		102	none	115	
F-20	AG	316	1534	2499	2793	2822
F-30	AI	351	1142	1855	2270	2554
A-150	AI				108	113
D-40	AJ	333	1136	2244	2825	3218
F-47	AK	128	218	418	488	583
D-50	AL	192	301	513	584	698
F-212	AN	228	810	1558	2009	2271
F-312	AS	141	230	335	376	497
SF-Bass	BA	177	654	1696	1946	2043
M-85	BB			109	194	241
Mark I	CA	316	996	1973	2156	
Mark II	CB	247	967	1173	2018	
Mark III	CC	252	666	992	1203	
Mark IV	CD	128	292	491	541	
Mark V	CE	120	137	195		
Mark VI	CF		128	175	197	
X-500	DA	106	138	180	235	244
SF-6	DB	101	174	274	329	339
SF-12	DC		586	896	897	910
M-75	DD			138	237	395
X-50	EA	202	326	491	502	506
T-50	EB	196	391	558	607	652
M-65 3/4	EC	182	267	322	334	
M-65	ED	160	194	270	335	414
T-100	EE	601	1939	2794	3003	3109

Model	Prefix	1965	1966	1967	1968	1969
CE-100	EF	211	396	649	719	760
X-175	EG	107	160	239	322	346
DE-400	EH	126	233	275	301	
DE-500	EI	107	116	136	none	141
SF-2/SF-3	EK	387	2098	2819	3028	3098
SF-4	EL	276	1167	1840	2223	2272
SF-5	EN	194	927	1807	2141	2278
ST ES				275	318	
F-112	0A				511	695
F-412	0B				110	114
F-512	0C	(starts with 201)		206	223	
A-350	0D				109	112
M-20 3/4	0E					102
George Barnes	0F					104
D-25	0G				192	233
CA-100	0H				113	114
D-55	0I				105	113
D-35	0J				1003	1592
S-50	SA	201	490	584		
S-100	SB	169	220	251	269	
S-20	SC	101	153	166	191	
Jet Star Bass	SD	108	327	343		

1979–86

Numbering by separate model series resumes on October 1, 1979. Numbers are last number for that year.

Model	Prefix	1979	1980	1981	1982	1983	1984	1985	1986
D-212	AA			101085	101529	101895	102114	102395	102796
S-250	AB			100154	100236	100250			
S-25	AC			100159	100293	100339			
X-79	AD			100304	101342	101509	101705	101790	
SB-201/202	AE				100109	100452			
S-275	AF					100110			
DE-500	AG					100019	100148	100153	100169
D-15	AH					100617	100924	101371	101815
S-26	AJ					100002			
Ashbury Bass	AJ								23
S-260	AK					100030			
D-17	AL						100092	100402	100575
B-50	BA	100002	100012	100168	100212	100249	100269	100306	100326
B-301/302 mah	BB	100400	100846						
B-301/302 ash	BC	100061	100196	100235					
B401/402	BD		100212	100335					
SB-600/602/603	BE					100050	100456	100135	101726
FS-46CE Bass	BF					100008			
SB-608	BG						100068	100116	
SB-604	BH					100226	100616		
Bluesbird	BJ							100060	100215
SB-605	BK								100177
Nightbird	BL							100104	100324
Mark II	CA	100005	100246	100424	100510	100570	100657	100689	100733
Mark III	CB	100014	100163	100283	100305	100367	100406	100425	100461
Mark IV	CC	100017	100101	100199	100218	100232	100253	100270	
Mark V	CD	100021	100064	100089	100124	100137	100156	100176	100184
MKS-10CE	CE						100046	100056	
D-25	DA	100914	105752	109433	111910	112936	113675	114523	115528
D-35	DB	100503	102097	103268	103743	104078	104288	104477	104697
D-40	DC	100247	101105	101638	101782	101889	101972	102066	102190
D-50	DD	100212	100944	101382	101588	101737	101789	101878	101928

Model	Prefix	1979	1980	1981	1982	1983	1984	1985	1986
D-55	DE	100236	100661	101058	101186	101247	101298	101374	101406
G-37	DF	100052	100814	101339	101579	101774	101890	101990	102135
D-40C	DG			100542	100818	100959	101002	101032	101068
G-212	DH	100035	100248	100398	100419	100436			
G-312	DJ	100014	100164	100235	100263	100281	100287		
D-44M	DK								
D-46	DL		100131	100622	?	100839	100887		
S-300 mah	EA	100054	100112	100468	100470				
S-300 ash	EB	100023	100039	100229	100230				
S-60D	EC	100019	100169	100207					
S-60/65	ED	100050	100349	100499	100500				
S-70	EE	100019	100104	100246					
D-70	EF			100151	100208	100250	100263	100280	
D-80	EG	100014	100017	100019					
D-25C	EH						100098	100101	
FS-46CE	EJ					100205	100306	100370	100401
D-52	EK					100034	100054		
D-15-12	EL					100064	100144	100211	
F-20	FA	100051	100244	100394	100490	100524	100545	100595	100663
F-30	FB	100073	100235	100382	100440	100472	100509	100527	
F-40	FC	100015	100197	100381	100393				
F-50	FD	100018	100286	100424	100484	100535	100600	100650	100693
F-50R	FE	100025	100261	100340	100426	100431	100462	100479	100505
F-112	FF	100199	100277	100286	100294				
F-212	FG	100014	100194	100308	100324	100342	100358	100382	
F-212C	FH	100001	100056	100424					
F-212XL	FJ		100233	100401	100486	100525	100545	100567	
F-412	FK	100045	100221	100342	100385	100405	100445	100476	100506
F-512	FL	100040	100225	100362	100440	100477	100519	100543	100569
SF-4	GA	100051	100439	100686	100713	100842	100898	100911	100982
F-45CE	GB				100006	100409	100533	100683	100839
D-17-12	GC						100026		
G-45	GD				100002	100050	100053	100080	
D-47CE	GE					100026	100047	100049	
DS-48CE	GF					100024	100026		
F-30R	GG		100123	100174	100203	100207			
FS-46CE-12	GH					100005	100027		
F-45C-12	GJ						100030		
S-285	GK								100011
Studio 24	GL								100030
M-80	HA		100003	100229	100339	100350			
T-50	HB				100019				
S-280/281	HC					100050	100481	101039	101493
X-80	HD					100023	100129	100172	
S-282	HE						100047		
X-88	HF						100285	100457	
S-284	JG						100101	100435	100637
X-92	HH						129		
X-100	HJ						100004	100095	
T-250	HK								100123
X-170	HL							100014	100076
Artist Award	JA	100012	100043	100067	100097	100107	100122	100127	100133
X-500	JB	100036	100082	100136	100144	100148	100165	100178	100194
X-175	JC	100013	100114	100177	100184	100205	100217		
X-701/702	JD				100174	100234	100235		
SB-902	JE								
X-82	JF			100107	100311	100430	100460		
CE-100	KA	100015	100077	100136	100159	100169	100175		
D-62	KB						100046	100060	
D-64	KC						100030	100050	100193
D-66	KD						100110	100162	100208

Serial Numbers

Model	Prefix	1979	1980	1981	1982	1983	1984	1985	1986
F-42	KG						100036	100065	
F-44	KH						100078	100186	100249
F-46	KJ						100029	100089	100121
Prototypes	LL		100031	100108	100147	100198	100228	100234	100237
Brian May	BHM						150	286	316

Kay

ACOUSTIC BASSES

The Kay company of Chicago began as the Groeschel Company in 1890, making bowl-back mandolins. In 1918 the name was changed to the Stromberg-Voisenet Company, which made the Mayflower line of guitars and banjos. Henry Kay Kuhrmeyer bought the company in 1928 and changed the name to Kay Musical Instruments in 1931. Marketing instruments under its own name and for mail-order house brands, Kay claimed a production of almost 100,000 instruments per year by the mid 1930s.

Basses were introduced in the Kay line in 1937 and also marketed through others under the K. Meyer brand. According to company literature, Kay captured one-fifth of the U.S. bass market in its first year.

Kay was sold to a group headed by Sydney Katz, formerly of Harmony, in 1955. Many Silvertone brand guitars, sold through Sears, were made by Kay during this period. The Seeburg company, a jukebox manufacturer, bought Kay in 1965. In 1967, the company was sold to Robert Engelhardt, who also owned Valco (see National/Valco). Shortly thereafter, Kay went out of business and the name was acquired by an import instrument distributor.

All Kay basses have a laminated spruce top, laminated maple back and sides.

Letters in Model Names

M=Maestro, originally top of the line, later midline and finally a student model
S=(chronologically) Slap, Swingmaster, or Supreme
C=Concert, always a grade below Maestro

Sizes

Regulation or 3/4-size: 72" overall length, body depth 6 3/4"–7 3/4", 42" scale
Junior or 1/4-size (also referred to as 1/2-size): 62 1/4" overall length, 35 1/4" scale
Half-size: no specs available
Slap or Swingmaster: regulation size except for 2" thinner body depth, described as "quick in response to slapping, easy to twirl"

Pre–World War II Models

M-1: Maestro model, 2 black lines inlaid around top and back edges, ebony fingerboard and tailpiece, engraved brass tuner plates, shaded finish
Introduced: **1937**
Blond finish optional by **1939**
M-4: M-1 with blond finish, named by **1941**

Concert: purfling on top and back, 2-piece back, rosewood fingerboard and tailpiece, brass tuner plates, shaded finish
Introduced: **1937**
Blond finish optional by **1941**

Orchestra: ebonized fingerboard and tailpiece, shaded finish
Introduced: **1937**
Blond finish optional by **1941**

S-1: Slap model, thin body, Orchestra model specs
S-3: thin body, Concert model specs
S-4: thin body, Maestro model specs
All introduced: **1939**

S-5: Swingmaster dance band model, ebony fingerboard, purfling on top and back, bound *f*-holes, blond finish, full-depth body optional
S-6: same as S-5 with shaded finish, full-depth body optional
Introduced: **1940**

Post–World War II Models

S-51: Chubby Jackson model, 5 strings, bound top and back, bound *f*-holes, ebony fingerboard and tailpiece, side position dots, nickel-plated tuning heads, shaded finish
S-51B: same but with blond finish
Introduced: **late 1945**

M-1: Maestro "School Model," rosewood fingerboard and tailpiece with ebonized finish, shaded finish
M-1B: same with blond finish
M-5: 5 strings, rosewood fingerboard and tailpiece, side position dots, brass tuning heads, shaded finish
M-5B: same with blond finish
H-10: 1/4-size M-1 (64" overall length), shaded finish
C-1: Concert, rosewood fingerboard and tailpiece with natural finish, shaded finish
S-8: Supreme, purfling of 2 thin black lines around top and back, 2 thin black lines around *f*-holes, ebony fingerboard and tailpiece, nickel-plated metal parts, shaded finish
S-9: Swingmaster, thin body, inlaid purfling, nickel gears, ebony fingerboard and tailpiece, blond finish
S-10: Swingmaster Mighty Midget, 1/3 smaller than S-9
All introduced by **1952**

M-7 Selmer Kay: black-white-black purfling on top and back, triple-bound *f*-holes, ebony fingerboard and tailpiece, gold-plated tuner plates engraved with *Selmer-Kay*,

Acoustic Basses

golden brown finish
Available: **early 1950s**

TV1: burnished gold finish
TV21: two-tone copper and white finish
Introduced by **1955**

H-10 replaced by M-2 or M-3
M-2: 1/2 size M-1, rosewood fingerboard and
tailpiece, violin brown finish
M-3: 1/4 size M-1, single black line inlaid
around top and back edges
S-8 renamed **S-1**
S-2: 1/2 size S-1, ebony fingerboard and tail-
piece, golden brown finish
S-3: 1/4 size S-1
*Note: Dimensions of 1/2 size and 1/4 size are
unavailable*
Introduced by **1958**
M-2 and S-2 discontinued: **1960**

All models discontinued by **late 1960s**

COMMENTS

Kay acoustic basses were the most popular
brand of laminated construction basses.
They are highly regarded by players of
popular music styles.

Larson

Prairie State
Guitars

GENERAL INFORMATION

Carl and August Larson were born in Sweden and immigrated to Chicago in the 1880s. By the late 1890s they were building instruments for Robert Maurer. Maurer, a music teacher and instrument retailer, began production of Champion and other brand instruments between 1882 and 1894. In 1897, he put the Maurer brand on all instruments.

In 1900, Maurer sold his shop to August Larson and others. Carl Larson later replaced all the other partners. They had essentially a two-man operation, with all other employees working only on a part-time basis. By circa 1904, the Larsons were making guitars, tiples, ukuleles, and bowlback mandolins for various distributors, including Wack, Stahl and Dyer. Also circa 1904, the Larsons advertised a catalog of Maurer brand instruments. They added the Prairie State brand to their line, probably in the late 1920s. In the mid 1930s, they discontinued the Maurer brand, replacing it with the Euphonon brand. Many instruments were custom-ordered. Some were made for performers on the WLS "Barn Dance" radio program in Chicago. Instruments with a Larson brand are extremely rare.

August Larson died in 1944. Carl Larson retired in 1940 and died in 1946.

Total production of instruments made by Carl and August Larson is estimated at 11,000 to 12,000.

General Characteristics

From the beginning Larson Brothers flat tops were designed for steel strings, pre-dating Martin and Gibson steel-string flat top designs by more than 20 years. To support the top, the Larsons used an expanded version of Martin's X-pattern, often with laminated braces—spruce with rosewood or ebony center laminate. Instruments made for Wack and Dyer typically have solid maple braces. Some Stahls have laminated braces; some have solid maple braces. The laminated bracing design was patented by August Larson in 1904.

All tops and backs are "built under tension" and slightly arched.

Guitars have 12 frets clear of body until the early 1930s, 14 frets clear thereafter.

Ebony fingerboard, bridge and peghead veneer are standard on all models.

Virtually no Larson Brothers models have a brand logo on the peghead. (At least one example exists with *Advance Music* on the peghead.) Maurer, Euphonon, and Prairie State logos are stamped on the center backstrip. About half of the Stahl brand instruments have a logo stamped on the inside backstrip; the others have a paper label. Except for the stamped Stahls, distributor brand instruments typically have a paper label on the inside back.

The Larsons had more variability in their model designs than any other major maker. They had a larger percentage of instruments that were unlabeled or bore misleading labels than any other highly respected maker.

Maurer

General features: 18 frets, 12 frets clear of body until early 1930s, 14 frets clear from the early 1930s onward.

The Maurer brand was discontinued in the mid 1930s when the Euphonon brand was introduced.

Maurer Model Characteristics

Student models: 487, 489, 491, 493; lower quality woods and tuners; oak back and sides, ladder bracing on lower models; mahogany on higher models

Intermediate models: (in order of ornamentation) 494, 525, 498, 495, 541, 551; X-braced top; mahogany back and sides on lower models, rosewood on higher; laminated necks and braces on higher models

Top of the line models: 585, 587, 590, 593, 340, 440, 350, 450; many with Brazilian rosewood back and sides, some with walnut

Euphonon

The Euphonon brand replaced the Maurer brand in the mid 1930s.

General features: 20 frets, 14 frets clear of body, solid peghead

Euphonon Model Characteristics

Student models: 13 3/4" wide, mahogany back and sides, ladder bracing, single-bound body and fingerboard, ebony bridge and fingerboard, backstripe

Intermediate models: 15" and 16" wide, mahogany or rosewood, X-bracing usually laminated, some with black and white binding, back stripe

Top of the line models: 15" or larger, some with dreadnought shape, rosewood or maple back and sides, pearl soundhole inlay, recessed pickguard, some with pearl around top

General Information

Prairie State

The Prairie State brand was used on guitars only. The first Prairie State models were probably made circa 1927, the year August Larson filed a patent application for an adjustable stabilizing tube. All Prairie State brand instruments have the steel support rod; some instruments with the Maurer or Euphonon brand have the support tube through the body.

The only *f*-hole models the Larson Brothers made were Prairie State models. The tops are arched—not carved—with about the same degree of arch as typical Larson roundhole models. Prairie State *f*-hole models vary in size from 15" to 21" and in ornamentation. The Larsons made at least one cutaway *f*-hole model.

Prairie State models are similar to Maurer and Euphonon models, but with the following added specs: steel stabilizing tube running lengthwise through the body, adjustable neck rod either at the back of neck or inside the body at the neck, laminated neck.

12-fret body sizes: 13 1/2" concert, 14" grand concert, and 15" auditorium

14-fret body sizes: 16" and 17" most common, some examples up to 21" wide

Stahl

The Wm. C. Stahl company of Milwaukee was marketing Stahl brand guitars made by the Larson Brothers by circa 1904. Stahl labels and stamps typically read *Stahl—Maker, Milwaukee*, although there is no evidence that Stahl actually made any instruments. Virtually all Stahls with the logo stamped on the inside backstrip are made by the Larson Brothers. Some models with paper labels were made by the Larson Brothers; some were made by Regal or others.

Some Larson-made Stahl models have laminated braces; some have solid maple braces.

Stahl's mandolin orchestra models, made by the Larsons, have maple back and sides with rosewood grain stain finish.

Wack

The Wack Sales Co., located in Milwaukee, marketed Maurer, Prairie State, and some unlabeled instruments made by the Larson Brothers from 1930 to 1944. Some instruments, particularly large-bodied guitars, were custom-ordered. Most, if not all, instruments sold by Wack have no label.

Dyer

W.J. Dyer & Bro., located in St. Paul, marketed Dyer brand instruments made by the Larson Brothers by circa 1904. Dyer labels typically identify Dyer as the maker, although there is no evidence Dyer actually made any instruments. Dyer also marketed Stetson brand guitars and guitars and mandolins made by Lyon and Healy, Harmony and others.

Most Larson-made Dyer guitars have mahogany back and sides. Most Larson-made Dyer mandolins have rosewood back and sides.

A special line of flat top harp instruments—mandolin, mandola, mandocello and guitar—was made for the Dyer line. Initially (beginning by 1912), Dyer marketed harp instruments designed and built by Chris Knutsen. Knutsen's instruments were redesigned and produced by the Larson Brothers begining circa 1917. Knutsen instruments typically have dot inlay on the fingerboard; most Larson-made instruments have small ornamental fingerboard inlays, including snowflakes and diamonds, or more ornate tree-of-life patterns. Larson-made Dyer harp instruments have solid maple braces.

226

MAURER AND PRAIRIE STATE

The Larson Brothers published very few catalogs. The following models appear in a catalog of Maurer and Prairie State models published in the early 1930s.

All models have ebony bridge, ebony fingerboard, and mahogany neck.

All guitar models have an inlaid backstripe, which is fancier on the more highly ornamented models.

Sizes	Width	Scale
Standard	12 3/4"	24 5/8"
Concert	13 1/2"	25"
Grand Concert	14"	25 3/8"
Auditorium	15"	25 3/8"

Maurer Models From Early 1930s Catalog

487: size unspecified, oak back and sides, ladder bracing, multiple-bound top, "colored veneer" inlay around soundhole and edges, dot inlay

489: mahogany back and sides, otherwise same as Model 487

491: grand concert size, mahogany back and sides, multiple-bound top, colored wood inlaid around soundhole, dot inlay

493: auditorium size, otherwise same as Model 491

494: size unspecified, rosewood back and sides, multiple-bound top, colored wood and celluloid inlaid around soundhole, dot inlay

525: 3/4 size, otherwise same as Model 494

498: rosewood back and sides, multiple-bound top, bound back, colored wood inlaid around soundhole, dot inlay

495: curly maple back and sides, otherwise same as Model 498

541: concert size, rosewood back and sides, elaborate colored wood purfling around soundhole and top edges, bound top and back, bound fingerboard, ornamental inlay, pearl ornamental peghead inlay

551: auditorium size, otherwise same as Model 541

562: standard size, rosewood back and sides, pearl and colored wood purfling around soundhole and top edges, bound top and back, bound fingerboard, ornamental inlay, pearl ornamental peghead inlay

562 1/2: concert size, otherwise same as Model 562

564: auditorium size, otherwise same as Model 562

585: grand concert size, rosewood back and sides, pearl and colored wood purfling around soundhole and top edges, pearl border on top around fingerboard, bound top and back, bound fingerboard, tree-of-life inlay, pearl ornamental peghead inlay, ivoroid tuner buttons

587: pearl tuner buttons, otherwise same as Model 585

585: auditorium size, ivoroid tuner buttons, otherwise same as Model 585

593: auditorium size, pearl tuner buttons, otherwise same as Model 585

15: mandolin, symmetrical pear shape, oval hole, bent top, flat back, maple back and sides, colored wood and celluloid inlaid around soundhole and top edges, rosewood-grain stain finish

30: mandolin, symmetrical pear shape, oval hole, bent top, flat back, rosewood back and sides, ebony bridge with bone saddle, symmetrical pickguard under strings, pearl inlay around soundhole and in pickguard, fancy wood and celluloid inlay around top edges, ornamental fingerboard inlay, pearl peghead ornament

40: tenor mandola, symmetrical pear shape, oval hole, bent top, flat back, maple back and sides, ebony bridge with bone saddle, pickguard on treble side with pearl inlay, fancy wood inlay around top edges, bound top and back, ornamental fingerboard inlay, pearl peghead ornament, rosewood-grain stain finish

45: octave mandola, same ornamentation as Model 40 but larger

50: mandocello, same ornamentation as Model 40

Prairie State Models From Early 1930s Catalog

All models have support tube through body.

225: concert size, rosewood back and sides, fancy colored wood inlay around soundhole and top edges, bound top and back, bound fingerboard, elaborate fingerboard inlay, pearl peghead ornament

425: auditorium size, otherwise same as Model 225

426: auditorium size, high nut for steel playing, otherwise same as Model 225

427: auditorium size, "gear pegs," reinforced neck, otherwise same as Model 225

227

428: auditorium size, "gear pegs," reinforced neck, high nut for steel playing, otherwise same as Model 225

235: concert size, rosewood back and sides, pearl and colored wood purfling around soundhole and top edges, bound top and back, bound fingerboard, ornamental inlay, pearl peghead ornament, ivoroid tuner buttons

335: grand concert size, otherwise same as Model 235

435: auditorium size, otherwise same as Model 235

340: grand concert size, rosewood back and sides, pearl and colored wood purfling around soundhole and top edges, pearl border on top around fingerboard, bound top and back, bound fingerboard, tree-of-life inlay, pearl peghead ornament, ivoroid tuner buttons

350: pearl tuner buttons, otherwise same as Model 340

440: auditorium size, ivoroid tuner buttons, otherwise same as Model 340

450: auditorium size, pearl tuner buttons, otherwise same as Model 340

COMMENTS

The Larsons' reputation today is based primarily on their round-hole flat top (actually slightly arched) models, although their mandolins and *f*-hole archtops are also well made. Workmanship, especially on later models, may be cruder than that of Martin or Gibson, and later bodies are frequently asymmetrical.

In the 1930s, Larson flat tops are rivaled by only by Martin and Gibson. The high-end guitar models are regarded as excellent instruments by players and are highly sought after by collectors.

Harp-style guitars and mandolin family instruments are highly sought after by collectors, in part because of their aesthetic appeal. Most modern harp guitar players prefer the flat top design to the Gibson archtop harp guitar, and the Larson-Dyer models are considered by many players to be the finest harp guitars ever made.

Martin

GENERAL INFORMATION

Christian Frederick Martin, son of a German instrument maker, immigrated to the United States and established the C. F. Martin company in New York in 1833 as a guitar manufacturing company and full-line music store. The company moved to Nazareth, PA in 1839 but continued to use New York on labels and stamps until 1898. Thus all Martin guitars made prior to 1898 are commonly referred to as New York Martins.

Martin formed a company with New York guitar teacher John Coupa in 1840, probably for Coupa to sell guitars through his shop. He also had business associations with Charles Bruno and Henry Schatz. The names of Coupa, Bruno, and Schatz appear with Martin's on some labels from this period.

Martin became the first American guitar manufacture of real repute, and the company continues to be the most famous and respected maker of flat tops. The dreadnought body has become Martin's most popular flat top body style and has been widely imitated by numerous other makers.

Company ownership remains in the Martin family. C. F. (Chris) Martin IV, great-great-great-grandson of the founder, is currently Chairman of the Board and CEO.

Periods

See comments at end of model descriptions for further breakdown and analysis.

1833–1840s: Guitars influenced by Martin's former employer, Staufer of Vienna, Austria. Typical Germanic features include hourglass body shape, some examples through the 1850s with laminated rosewood (outer) and spruce (inner) back and sides, pin bridge, separate neck heel in the shape of an ice cream cone, neck angle adjustable near heel by means of a "clock key," 6-on-a-side tuners with high E-string shaft longer then low E-string shaft. Some examples from late 1840s and early 1850s have purfling around the middle of the sides.

Late 1840s–50s: Development of a new American-style guitar, with body shapes, bracing pattern and ornamentation that define the modern flat top guitar.

Late 1850s–1927: Standardization of sizes and styles.

1928–late 34: Rapid development of steel string guitars and introduction of the dreadnought body style into the Martin line (see Dreadnoughts, following).

1930–76: Relatively stable period for model designs; some transition immediately fol-lowing World War II; gradual increase in production into the 1970s. (For more detailed analysis of this period, see Comments at end of Martin Guitars.)

1976–current: Re-introduction of many old features; introduction of many new features and new models; many custom and limited edition models.

Model Names

Model names of all Martin guitars and some mandolins consist of a body designation and a style designation, separated by a hyphen. Since October 1930 the model name is stamped along with the serial number on the neck block.

Body Designation

By 1852, Martin offered flat tops in sizes (from largest to smallest) 1, 2, 2 1/2, and 3. Sizes 0 and 5 were added in 1854. Size 4 was first recorded in 1857. As larger models were introduced, they continued within the system: size 00 in 1877, size 000 in 1902.

Exceptions to Standard Body Designations

D: In 1916, Martin made a body size larger than 000—the D or dreadnought size, named after the largest class of battleships at the time. The D was initially available only on guitars made for the Ditson company. It first appeared in the Martin line in 1931.

OM: Orchestra Model, 000-size body, 14-fret neck, 25.4" scale

7 or 7/8: dimensions approximately 7/8 of D-size

Other exceptions in the flat top line include C (cutaway), H preceding a body size (herringbone binding), J, Jumbo M (designated by J prefix and M suffix), N (classical), and M.

Archtops and electrics generally do not conform to the size-number system. These prefixes include C, F, E, EB, GT, and R.

Style Designation

The part of a model name after the hyphen refers to the ornamentation and type of wood. The most popular models are, from plainest to fanciest, 15, 17, 18, 21, 28, 35, 42, and 45.

Exceptions to Style Designations

Numeral *2* suffix denotes a koa wood top.
60-series numbers denote maple body models.

4-digit suffix with *32* as last digits denotes a Shenandoah model, a budget line made overseas and finished out at the Martin factory in Nazareth, PA.

Letter suffixes clarify certain styles. These include: A (ash), B (Brazilian rosewood), C (classical), E (electric), G (gut-string classical) H (Hawaiian), K (koa wood), LE (limited edition), M (mahogany), M with J prefix (Jumbo M body size), P (pre–WWII, plectrum), P (1985–current, low profile neck), S (pre–WWII, "special" custom order), S (1967-current, 12-fret neck, slotted peghead), SE (signature edition), T (tenor), V (vintage specs).

Size	Width (Inches)	Scale	Depth (Lower)	Length
early 1/4	6 3/16	17	2 7/8	12
later 1/4	8 15/16	17	3 9/16	12 1/16
1/2	10 1/8	20 7/8	3 3/8	15 1/16
7 (7/8-D)	13 11/16	23	4 3/8	17 1/2
5, pre–c. 1924	11 1/4	21.4	3 7/8	16
5, c. 1924 and after	11 1/4	22	3/78	16
5T, pre–1929	11 1/4	22 5/8	3 7/8	16
5T, 1929 and after	11 1/4	23	3 7/8	16
4	11 1/2	22	3 3/4	16
3 1/2	10 11/16	22	3 7/8	16 7/8
3	11 1/4	23 7/8	3 13/16	17 3/8
2 1/2	11 5/8	24.5	3 7/8	17 7/8
2	12	24.5	4	18 1/4
1	12 3/4	24.9	4 3/16	18 7/8
0, 12-fret	13 1/2	24.9	4 3/16	19 1/8
0, 14-fret	13 1/2	24.9	4 1/4	18 3/8
00, 12-fret	14 1/8	24.9	4 1/16	19 5/8
00, 14-fret	14 5/16	24.9	4 1/8	18 7/8
000, pre-c. 1924, 12-fret	15	24.9	4 1/16	20 7/16
000, c. 1924–34, 12-fret	15	25.4	4 1/16	20 7/16
000, 14-fret	15	24.9*	4 1/8	19 3/8
OM	15	25.4	4 1/8	19 3/8
D, 12-fret	15 5/8	25.4	4 3/4	20 15/16
D, 14-fret	15 5/8	25.4	4 7/8	20
M	16	25.4	4 1/8	20 1/8
J-##M	16	25.4	4 7/8	20 1/8
N	14 7/16	26 3/8**	4 1/8	19 1/8
R	14 5/8	24.9	4 1/4	18 7/8
C	15	24.9	4 3/16	19 3/8
F acoustic	16	24.9	4 1/8	20 1/8
F electric	16	24.9	2	20 1/8
GT-70	16	24.9	2	19 3/4
GT-75	16	24.9	2	16 7/8

* Some 14-fret 000-18s and 000-28s from early 1934 (probably overlaps from the discontinued OM-18 and OM-28 designation) have a 25.4" scale.

** Early N-size guitars (1969) have 25.4" scale; from 1970 onward, N scale is 26 3/8".

Labels and Stamps

Paper labels...
Christian Frederick Martin or *C. F. Martin*: **1833–1840s**
Some with *MARTIN & COUPA*: **1840s**
Some with *C. F. Martin and Bruno*: **May–Nov. 1838**
Some with *Martin & Schatz*: **c. 1836**

Stamps...
C.F. MARTIN, New York on back of peghead, inside body on center backstrip and on neckblock; "ice-cream cone" heel (see neck section) guitars often stamped on outside of back by heel (not on back of peghead): **1830s–67**

C.F. MARTIN, New York on back of peghead, *C.F. MARTIN, New York* inside body on center backstrip and on neckblock—models with 2-piece neck: **1867–98**

C.F. MARTIN, New York on back of body near neck, *C.F. MARTIN & Co, New York* inside body on center backstrip and on neckblock—models with "ice-cream cone" heel: **1867–90s**

C.F. MARTIN & Co, Nazareth, Pa on back of peghead and on inside center backstrip: **1898–1935**

C.F. MARTIN & Co, Nazareth, Pa on inside center backstrip (no stamp on back of peghead): **1935–63**

Made in USA added to brand: **1963–current**
Serial number impressed into neck block
(some 1898–1902 impressed into top of
peghead): **1898–current**
Model impressed into neck block: **Oct. 1930**

Tops

Adirondack spruce: **pre–1946**
Sitka spruce (darker than Adirondack):
1946–current
Occasional Adirondack tops: **1950s–60s**
Some with Engelman spruce, Engelman avail-
able on request: **current**
German Alpine spruce, Style 41 and 45 only:
late 1960s–early 1970s

Back and Sides

Brazilian rosewood replaced by Indian; most
Brazilian is redder (vs. brown or purplish)
and more figured than Indian...
D-size (some D-35s with combination of
Indian and Brazilian rosewood into
1970): **late 1969**
000s and 00s: **early 1970**

Bracing

Scalloped X-bracing introduced by **late 1840s**
X-bracing on all models (except later G, C and
N classicals and a few other examples):
1900
Non-scalloped braces: **late 1944**
Scalloped braces re-introduced...
HD-28: **1976**
HD-35, M series, JM series, from introduc-
tion
D-45: **late 1985**
D-41: **1987**
Position of X on D models...
High X, X positioned 1" from soundhole:
before mid 1939
X moved farther from soundhole (distance
varies): **early 1939**
High X re-introduced, Style 16, Special and
Custom models: **late 1980s**
Bridgeplate...
Maple: **pre–1968**
Rosewood, all models except scallop-
braced: **1968–88**
Maple, models with scalloped bracing
only: **1976–88**
Maple, all models: **1988–current**

Bridges

Ornamental with points at ends, metal fretwire
saddle: **1830s and 40s**
Point at bottom center, ivory saddle, some with
separate ivory and pearl ornament: **1830s
and 40s**

Rectangular ebony pin bridge, some with pyramids at ends, introduced: **late 1840s**
Rectangular bridge with no pyramids, Style 21
and lower (Style 28 and higher stay with
pyramid ends), by **1920s**
Belly bridge...
Long rectangular saddle slot, Style18 and
higher: **1929**
Shorter bridge slot: **1965**

Pickguards

Tortoise grain plastic (a few early with gen-
uine tortoise shell) optional: **late 1929**
Black plastic: **1966**

Binding

First herringbone: **late 1860s**
Elephant ivory, Style 28 and higher: **pre–1918**
Ivoroid, Style 28 and higher: **1918–66**
Black plastic replaces wood on Style 18 and
21: **1934**
Tortoise grain, Style 18 and 21: **1936–66**
Black plastic reinstated, Style 18 and 21:
1966–current
White non-grained plastic, Style 28 and higher:
1966–current
Wood purfling on abalone-trim models:
pre–WWII
Plastic purfling on abalone-trim models:
1968–current
Black-white plastic binding replaces herring-
bone purfling, Style 21 and 28: **early 1947**

Neck

3-piece neck, peghead grafted on with V-joint
and no volute, separate "ice cream cone"
neck heel and clock key mechanism, some
models: **into 1890s**
2-piece cedar neck with grafted-on peghead
and neck volute (much overlap with earlier
style, depending on model): **late
1840s–1916**
1-piece mahogany neck, volute on Style 28 and
higher models only: **1916–current**
14-fret neck introduced with OM-28: **1929**
C-2 and C-3 archtops introduced with 14-fret
neck: **1931**
14-fret neck on 0-17, 0-18: **1932**
14-fret neck on all D's and all 000s, 14-fret neck
on mahogany body 00s and 0s, 12-fret neck
continues on rosewood body 00s and 0s: **1934**
T-frets replace bar frets: **late 1934**
Neck reinforcement...
Ebony bar introduced: **mid 1920s**
Steel T-bar: **late 1934**
Ebony bar (due to wartime metal shortage):
1942
Back to steel T-bar: **1946**
Square steel tube: **1967**

Adjustable truss rod with allen wrench
adjustment inside body: **1985**
Neck width at nut...
12-fret models (size 2 1/2 and larger), 1 7/8":
throughout
14-fret models, 1 3/4": **before mid 1939**
14-fret models, 1 11/16": **after mid 1939**

Tuners

*Note: Models with slotted peghead have 3-on-
a-plate tuners except in the 1930s, when
they have individual Grover tuners slightly
modified from solid-peghead style tuners.
Models with solid peghead have individual
tuners.*

Staufer-style, 6-on-a-side with bass E-string
shaft longer than treble E-string shaft:
1833–1840s
Slotted peghead, 3-on-a-side tuners introduced (some still with Staufer-style
tuners): **c. 1840**
Many examples with 2-piece neck, solid peghead and ivory friction pegs: **1850s–early
1900s**
German-built tuners with gear wheel above
worm gear: **into 1916**
American-built tuners with gear wheel above
worm gear and ivoroid buttons: **1916–c. 25**
Gear wheel below worm gear: **c. 1925**
Grover planetary banjo tuners, Style OM only:
1929-c. 31
Open-back Grover tuners with rivet, thin metal
buttons with seam in middle of button: **1931**
Open-back Grover tuners with adjustment
screw, heavy metal buttons with no visible
seam: **1935**
Sealed-back Grover tuners, heavy metal but-
tons with no visible seam, high-end models
only: **mid 1939–mid 40**
Open-back Kluson tuners, no adjustment
screw, plastic buttons, no peghead bush-
ings: **1942–44 only**
Open-back Kluson tuners, adjustment screw,
metal buttons, peghead bushings
1945–46
Kluson Deluxe tuners, all D models, all Style
28s: **1947**
Open-back Grover Sta-tites, 0, 00, and 000
below Style 28: **1947**
Kluson sealed-back tuners, Style 28: **1949**
Grover Rotomatic tuners...
Style 28: **1958**
All D sizes: **1965**
All styles: **1967**
Sperzel, Schaller, Grover, some stamped with
Martin: **1970s**

Logo on Front of Peghead

Vertical *CF Martin* inlay...
Introduced on C-2, C-3: **1931**
Style 45s with solid peghead: **1934**

F-7 and F-9 (from introduction): **1935**
CF MARTIN & Co, Est. 1833 decal (early with
no black border around letters): **mid 1932**

Finish

French polish: **pre-1900**
Thin shellac: **1900**
Semi-gloss (thin shellac dulled by sanding):
1919
"Satin," high-gloss shellac, varnish top coat
on back and sides: **1923**
Clear nitrocellulose lacquer, some models:
1926
Nitrocellulose, most models: **1929**

Dreadnoughts

Ditson models: made by Martin for Oliver
Ditson company, with Ditson name and
serial numbers, all with brown-stain
spruce top, mahogany back and sides
(some custom-made with rosewood), 19
frets, fan-pattern bracing (on early series)
Model 111: plain, Style 18 trim except for no
back trim
Model 222: plastic binding, plastic heel cap,
inlaid ebony bridge pins
Model 333: pearl inlaid bridge, bound finger-
board and soundhole, German silver tuners
Ditson dreadnoughts introduced: **1916**
Martin serial numbers used after Ditson #571:
1921
Ditson dreadnoughts discontinued: **1921**
Ditson dreadnought Model 111 re-introduced,
X-bracing: **1923**
Ditson Model 111 discontinued (19 made,
1923–30): **1930**
Martin models introduced, mahogany body D-1
(becomes D-18) and rosewood body D-2
(becomes D-28), 12 frets clear of body:
1931
D-18 and D-28 introduced: **later 1931**
First D-45 produced (12-fret): **1933**
14 frets clear of body (except for approximately 16 D-18s, 24 D-28s and 2 D-45s, all with
12 frets clear of body): **1934**
2 wide-body (16 1/4") D-45s (stamped D-45S):
1936
D-45 cataloged: **1938**
D-45 discontinued: **1942**
12-fret neck available but not cataloged: **1954**
D-21 introduced: **1955**
D-28SW (Special Wurlitzer), 12-fret neck, slotted peghead, available from E. U. Wurlitzer:
1962
D12-20, 12-fret neck, introduced: **1964**
D-35 introduced (but not cataloged), D-12-35
introduced: **1965**
D-35 cataloged: **1966**
12-fret S models introduced in Martin line:
1967
D-45 re-introduced: **1968**

Indian rosewood replaces Brazilian: **late 1969**
D-12-41 introduced: **1970**
D-12-18 introduced: **1973**
D-76, HD-28, D-19 introduced: **1976**
HD-35 introduced: **1978**
D-25K, D-25K2, D-37K, D-37K2, D-19M introduced: **1980**
DC-28 introduced: **1981**
HD-37K2 introduced (1 shipped): **1982**
Shenandoah line introduced: **1983**
Custom D-28B and D-35B introduced: **1985**
HD-28B, HD-35B, D-41B, D-45B, D-16K, D-16M introduced: **1986**
HD-28BSE (Brazilian rosewood signature edition), D-45LE (limited edition), prototype D-62 (maple), D-16A (ash), and D-16W (walnut) introduced: **1987**

OMs

Style OM: 000 body, 14 frets clear of body, pyramid bridge, no pickguard, 25.4" scale, inlays consistent with other instruments of same style and year, banjo tuning pegs, no decal, solid peghead
Introduced, Style 28: **1929**
Small pickguard: **late 1929**
Belly bridge: **1930**
Styles 18, 42, 45, and 45 DLX (snowflake inlays on bridge, abalone inlay on pickguard, engraved gold-plated tuners, pearl tuner buttons) introduced (only year for OM-42 and OM 45 DLX): **1930**
Large pickguard: **early 1931**
Standard tuners: **1931**
Decal logo, Styles 18 and 28: **1932**
OM discontinued: **1934**
SOM-28 (reissue of OM-28) available: **1969 only**
SOM-45 (reissue of OM-45) introduced: **1977**
OM-28 and OM-45 still available by special order

Production Ranges for Selected Models, 1898 and After

The following table provides only a rough general guide for production periods. "Major" production denotes periods of continuous production with more than 5 instruments per year in most years of the period. "Sparse" production denotes periods when model production was 5 or less per year (including zero in some years). Models with very small total production spread over several years are not included.

Style	Major Production	Sparse Production
OM-18	1930–33	
OM-28	1929–33, 1969	
OM-45	1930–33, 1977–82	1982–88
OM-45 DLX	1930	
000-17	1952	
000-18	1923–current	1911–22
000-21	1938–59, 79,	1902–23
000-28	1924–current	1902–23
000-28C	1962–66	
000-42	1938–43	1918–25
000-45	1924–42, 76, 81	1906–23, 71–85,
00-16C	1962–75	1976–81
00-17	1930–60, 82–83	1908–17, 86–87
00-18	1898–1981	1981–87
00-18G	1936–62	
00-18C	1962–76	1977–current
00-18K	1918–25	
00-21	1898–current	
00-28	1898–1936	1939–41
00-28G	1936–62	1936–37
00-28C	1966–76	1977–current
00-28K	1919–21	1926–33
00-30	1899–1921	
00-34	1898	1899
00-40		1913–17
00-40H	1928–39	
00-42	1898–1942	1935–38
00-45	1919–29, 70–80	1904–18, 81–current
0-15	1940–61	1935
0-15T	1960–63	
0-16NY	1961–current	

Style	Major Production	Sparse Production
0-17	1929–48	1966, 68
0-17H	1930–40	
0-17T	1933–60	1932
0-18	1898–1983	1985–current
0-18K	1918–35	
0-18T	1929–current	
0-21	1898–1948	
0-21K	1920–26	1927–29
0-28	1898–1931	1937
0-28K	1921–31	1917
0-28T	1931–32	
0-42	1898–1930	
0-45	1919–30	1904–18
1-17	1906–17, 31–34	
1-17P	1928–31	
1-18	1899–1927	
1-18K	1917–19	
1-28P	1928–30	
1-21	1898–1926	
1-27		1989–1900
1-28	1898–1923	
1-30	1900–04, 17	1906–16
1-34	1898–1900	
1-42	1898–1904	1911–19
1-45		1904–19
2-17	1910–36	1937–38
#25	1929–30	
2-18	1898–1900, 29, 38	1902–25
2-21	1898–1929	
2-27	1898–1907	
2-30	1902–10	
2-45	1925–27	
2 1/2-17	1909–14	
2 1/2-18	1898–1923	
2 1/2-21	1909–21	
2 1/2-28		1909–23
2 1/2-30		1901–14
5-15T	1949–62	1963
5-16	1962–63	
5-17	1937–43	1912–36
5-17T	1927–49	
5-18	1919–37, 40–81	1898–1917, 83–87
5-21	1927	1902–20
5-21T	1927–28	
5-28		1901–39, 68-81

Instruments Made by Martin for Other Companies

Since 1900, Martin has made instruments for many different companies and guitar teachers. Not all are included here.

Ditson: from 1917–21 and 1923–30, made for the Ditson Company in Boston in 3 sizes (standard, concert, and dreadnought) and in 3 different styles, plus other instruments in standard Martin styles. Early examples have only a Ditson stamp, later have both Martin and Ditson. Instruments made from 1923–30 have Martin serial numbers. A total of 483 guitars with Ditson numbers have been documented through January 3, 1921.

Foden: 1912–17, made for concert guitarist William Foden, similar to standard Martin models but with different ornamentations. All have soundhole rings grouped into a single band. Foden specified a 20-fret fingerboard, prompting Martin to switch all models from 19 to 20 frets. Foden Special models were made in 0 or 00 size and five different styles: Style A (similar to Martin

Style 18), Style B (Style 21), Style C (Style 28), Style D (Style 30), and Style E (combination of Styles 40, 42, and 45). Only 27 instruments have been documented, but the frequency with which they turn up suggests that more may have been produced.

Olcott-Bickford: 32 instruments made for concert guitarist Vahdah Olcott-Bickford. See Style 44 in model descriptions.

Paramount: c. 1930, resonator guitars, some 4-string, some 6-string; size 2 rosewood body, most with no soundhole, small round soundholes around lip of resonator, rosewood resonator, 14 frets clear of body, rosewood fingerboard, dot inlay to 15th fret, rounded-peak peghead, banjo-style tuners. About 36 were made.

Schoenberg: Soloist model designed by Eric Schoenberg and Dana Bourgeois; most specs taken from 1929 OM-28, some 12-fret 000 models, some limited edition OM-45 Deluxes, some dreadnoughts. Prior to 1991, instruments were assembled at Martin

from wood (excluding necks) supplied by Schoenberg. Schoenberg's luthier (Dana Bourgeois from 1986 to mid 1990, T.J. Thompson thereafter) then did the voicing and inlay. As of mid 1991, Schoenberg supplies necks, bends the sides, braces the tops, inlays the backstripes and does some binding, in addition to previous contributions. All have a special metal plate on the neckblock with a Martin serial number. Sometime in 1991 Schoenberg plans to switch to a brand/stamp instead of the metal plate. As of January 1991, 120 instruments had been produced.

Southern California Music Co. (Rolando): 1916–18, crest on peghead, standard koa wood styles, 261 total guitars consecutively numbered from #1, later examples with Martin serial numbers.

Wurlitzer: 1922–24, standard Martin models but with soundhole rings grouped into a single band, Wurlitzer model number and Wurlitzer stamp on the back of the peghead, 297 total guitars.

Martin flat top body sizes. All photos are shot from the same distance.

1989 M-36.

1939 D-28, 14 frets clear of body, herringbone trim around top edges, slotted diamond fingerboard inlay.

1964 D-28SW, 12 frets clear of body, special-order model for the E.U. Wurlitzer company (courtesy Hank Sable).

1937 000-45.

1969 N-20.

1938 00-28G, with custom-ordered 14-fret neck. Standard models have this body shape with 12 frets clear of body.

1967 00-21, 12 frets clear of body (courtesy Hank Sable).

1938 0-17H, straight-mounted bridge for Hawaiian playing.

1929 1-17P, plectrum.

1930 2-44, Olcott-Bickford model, pyramid bridge.

1930 2 1/2-17.

1929 5-17T, tenor.

1936 T-28, tiple with pickguard added.

240

SERIAL NUMBERS

All Martin guitars (except solidbody electrics from the 1970s), basses, and tiples made since 1898 are numbered in one consecutive series. Mandolins and a few early ukes have their own number series. Solidbody electrics, ukuleles, and many instruments made for sale under other brands do not have Martin numbers.

The serial number is stamped on the neck block inside the instrument, except for some very early examples, which have the number stamped on the top of the peghead.

The guitar series begins with #8000, which was Martin's estimate of the total number of instruments made before 1898.

Year	Last Number
1898	8349
1899	8716
1900	9128
1901	9310
1902	9528
1903	9810
1904	9988
1905	10120
1906	10329
1907	10727
1908	10883
1909	11018
1910	11203
1911	11413
1912	11565
1913	11821
1914	12047
1915	12209
1916	12390
1917	12988
1918	13450
1919	14512
1920	15848
1921	16758
1922	17839
1923	19891
1924	22008
1925	24116
1926	28689
1927	34435
1928	37568
1929	40843
1930	45317
1931	49589
1932	52590
1933	55084
1934	58679
1935	61947
1936	65176
1937	68865
1938	71866
1939	74061
1940	76734
1941	80013
1942	83107
1943	86724
1944	90149

Year	Last Number
1945	93623
1946	98158
1947	103468
1948	108269
1948	112961
1950	117961
1951	122799
1952	128436
1953	134501
1954	141345
1955	147328
1956	152775
1957	159061
1958	165576
1959	171047
1960	175689
1961	181297
1962	187384
1963	193327
1964	199626
1965	207030
1966	217215
1967	230095
1968	241925
1969	256003
1970	271633
1971	294270
1972	313302
1973	333873
1974	353387
1975	371828
1976	388800
1977	399625
1978	407800
1979	419900
1980	430300
1981	436474
1982	439627
1983	446101
1984	453300
1985	460575
1986	468175
1987	476216
1988	483952
1989	493279
1990	503309

Martin

Guitars

FLAT TOPS KEY, 1898–1930

Martin guitars from 1898 and after have *Nazareth, Pa.* on the inside back brand.
Beginning in October 1930 Martin guitars have the model name stamped on the neck block.

Mahogany back and sides
    No back binding=**Style 17, 1909–39**
    Back binding=**Style 18, 1917–30**
Rosewood back and sides
    Plain (rosewood or celluloid) top binding
        Bound fingerboard=**Style 44**
        Unbound fingerboard
            Rope-pattern soundhole inlay=**Style 18, 1898–c. 1901**
            Herringbone soundhole inlay=**Style 21**
            Soundhole rings in groups of 5-9-5=**Style 28**
            Soundhole rings in groups of 1-9-1=**Style 18, c. 1901–17**
            Simpler soundhole ornamentation=**Style 17, 1898–1908**
    Multi-colored wood around top border (abalone soundhole inlay)
        German silver tuners
            Ebony bridge=**Style 30**
            Ivory bridge=**Style 34**
        Brass tuners=**Style 27**
    Abalone top border
        No abalone on top around edge of fingerboard=**Style 40**
        Abalone inlay on top around edge of fingerboard
            Abalone borders around sides and back=**Style 45**
            No abalone borders around sides or back=**Style 42**
Koa back and sides
    Herringbone top trim=**Style 28K**
    No herringbone top trim=**Style 18K**

ARCHTOPS KEY

All roundhole archtop models have model name stamped on neckblock. All acoustic *f*-hole archtop models have model name stamped on back center seam. All electrics have model name stamped on back below soundhole.

Acoustic
    Dot inlay
        14 5/16" or less wide
            Spruce top=**R-18**
            Mahogany top=**R-17**
        15" wide=**C-1**
        16" wide=**F-1**
    Slotted-diamond inlay=**C-2, 1932–39**
    Snowflake inlay=**C-3**
    Hexagonal inlay
        Unbound peghead
            15" wide=**C-2, 1939–41**
            16" wide=**F-2**
        Bound peghead
            Inlay at 6 frets=**F-7**
            Inlay at 8 frets=**F-9**
Electric
    Single cutaway
        1 PU=**F-50**
        2 PUs
            No tremelo=**F-55**
            Tremelo=**GT-70**

Double cutaway
  Sunburst finish=**F-65**
    Burgundy or black finish
      6-string=**GT-75**
      12-string=**GT-75-12**

GUITARS

"Introduced" is the year first sold—not necessarily the first catalog listing.

SECTION ORGANIZATION

Flat Top Styles
Hawaiian and Early Koa Models
12-strings
Tenors and Plectrums
Classicals
Electric Flat Tops
Acoustic Archtops
Electric Archtops
Electric Solidbodies

Flat Top Styles

Style 15: mahogany top, sides and back, no binding, rosewood bridge and fingerboard, semi-gloss finish
Introduced, early examples with maple or birch bodies: **1935**
Mahogany body standard: **1940**
Discontinued: **1944**
Re-introduced: **1948**
Last 0-15, Style 15 available in tenor only: **1961**
Discontinued: **1963**

Style 16: mahogany back and sides, multiple-bound top with dark outer binding, unbound back, dot inlay, non-gloss finish
0-16 and 0-16NY (no pickguard, no fingerboard inlay), introduced: **1961**
5-16 (no pickguard, no fingerboard inlay) available: **1962–63 only**
D-size introduced, single-bound top and back, koa and mahogany offered at separate times in limited runs: **1986**
D-models in ash or walnut added in limited-run offerings: **1987**
000-16 and 000C-16 (cutaway) models introduced: **1990**
Still in production

Style 17: rosewood back and sides, no back binding
Introduced: **1856**
Green-and-white rope-pattern soundhole ring, 4- or 5-layer top binding, by **1870s**
Soundhole rings with no rope pattern by **1898**
Small dot inlay at frets 5, 7 and 9: **1901**
Mahogany back and sides, 3-layer top binding of black line, light wood line and (outer layer) rosewood, rosewood fingerboard and bridge: **1909**
Mahogany top, made for steel strings (Martin's first): **1922**
5-ply soundhole ring on all Style 17 models, no body binding on 5-17T: **1927**
2-17 changed to drop list price to $25, new plainer version referred to as #25: no binding: **1929**
Rosewood back binding on old-style 2-17 only: **1929**
Old-style 2-17 (with binding) last produced: **1930**
No binding, all Style 17 models, by **1930**
Last listed: **1957**
Last 00-17: **1960**
00-17 available by special order only: **1982–87**
Discontinued: **Apr. 1988**

Style 18: early specs not recorded
Introduced: **1857**
Rosewood back and sides, ebony bridge, colored-wood rope-pattern soundhole inlay, rosewood-bound top, ebony fingerboard: **1898**
Soundhole inlay of black-and-white rings in groups of 1-9-1, small dot inlay at frets 5, 7, and 9: **1901**
Mahogany back and sides: **1917**
Rosewood binding on top and back by **1918**
Dark top optional: **1920**
D-size introduced: **1931**
5-ply top binding with black plastic outer layer, single-ply black plastic back binding, small graduated size dot inlay through 15th fret, 2 inlays at 12th fret only: **early 1932**
Shaded top optional: **1934**
Tortoise grain outer binding by **1936**
Some non-dreadnought examples with rosewood fingerboard and bridge: **1935**
Rosewood fingerboard and bridge standard on non-dreadnought models: **1940**
Inlay to 17th fret: **late 1944**
Large uniform-size dot inlay: **1946**
Large graduated-size dot inlay: **1947**
Rosewood fingerboard, D models: **1947**
Black plastic binding: **1966**
Still in production

Style 19: mahogany back and sides, rosewood bridge, Style 28 soundhole ring, 5-ply top binding with black outer layer, 3-ply back binding, rosewood fingerboard, dot inlay, dark-stained spruce top
2 prototypes made: **1976**

Introduced: **1977**
Mahogany top optional: **1980**
Discontinued (last listed): **April 1988**

Style 20: obscure style, rosewood back and sides, herringbone soundhole inlay of red, white, and green, colored-wood herringbone backstripe, available: **mid 1800s**

D12-20: see 12-strings, following

Style 21: rosewood back and sides, rosewood outer binding with 2 additional rosewood lines around top and back, colored wood herringbone-pattern soundhole inlay with 2 rosewood lines on either side, colored-wood herringbone backstripe (fancier than style 20), diamond-pattern inlay on end-piece, ebony fingerboard
Introduced by **1869**
Black and white herringbone inlay, ebony end-piece, by **1898**
Slotted-diamond inlay at frets 5, 7 (2 inlays), and 9: **1901**
Inlays from 5th to 15th fret, 2 inlays at frets 7 and 12: **early 1932**
Black plastic binding: **mid 1932**
Tortoise grain binding by **1936**
Small graduated-size dot inlay to 17th fret: **late 1944**
Large uniform-size dot inlay: **1946**
Large graduated-size dot inlay: **1947**
No herringbone soundhole ring, rosewood fingerboard: **1947**
No herringbone backstripe: **early 1948**
Last D-21: **1969**
00-21 still in production

Styles 22, 23, and 24: obscure styles, available: **mid to late 1800s**

Style 25K: stained amber spruce (**25K**) or koa top (**25K2**), koa back and sides, 2 piece back, rosewood bridge, black pins with white dots, Style 28 soundhole ring, 5-ply top binding, rosewood fingerboard, dot inlay
Introduced, D and 00 size: **Jan. 1, 1980**
Discontinued: **1988**

Style 26: same as Style 28, but with half-herringbone purfling around edge of top,
Available: **mid to late 1800s**

Style 27: fancier than Style 28, rosewood back and sides, ebony bridge, abalone sound-hole ring, multi-colored wood inlay on top border, ivory-bound top and back, ivory-bound ebony fingerboard, brass tuners
Available: **1857–1907**

Style 28: rosewood back and sides, ivory

bound top and back, herringbone purfling around top edges, zipper-pattern back-stripe
Introduced: **1870**
Soundhole inlay of black and white rings in groups of 5-9-5, by **1890s**
Slotted-diamond inlay, 2 inlays at 5th fret, 1 at 7th, 2 at 9th: **1901**
White celluloid binding: **1919**
D size introduced: **1931**
Inlays from 5th to 15th fret, 2 inlays at frets 7 and 12: **early 1932**
Shaded top optional: **1935**
Small graduated-size dot inlay to 17th fret: **late 1944**
Large uniform-size dot inlay: **1946**
Large graduated-size dot inlay: **1947**
Black-and-white binding with white outer layer, no herringbone trim: **early 1947**
Narrow checkered backstripe: **early 1947**
Wider checkered backstripe: **1948**
Grover Rotomatic tuners: **1958**
Indian rosewood replaces Brazilian, D-size: **late 1969**
Indian rosewood replaces Brazilian, all other sizes: **early 1970**
Still in production

Style 30: similar to 27 but with wider wood purfling on top, abalone soundhole ring, ebony fingerboard, diamond-and-wedges inlay at frets 5 and 9, Maltese cross-type inlay at 7th fret, German silver tuners
Available: **1874–1921**

Style 33: obscure style, available: **mid 1800s**

Style 34: similar to Style 30 but with ivory bridge, available: **1860s–1907**

Style 35: Brazilian rosewood back and sides, 3-piece back with marquetry between sections, ebony bridge, side binding of 2 black-and-white lines, bound ebony fingerboard, mitered corners on fingerboard binding, dot inlay
Introduced, D-size only: **1965**
1-piece fingerboard binding: **1968**
Transition to Indian rosewood, various combinations of Indian and Brazilian: **late 1969–70**
Indian rosewood replaces Brazilian: **1970**
Still in production

Style 36: M-size body, same as Style 35 except for rosewood bridge, scalloped braces
Introduced: **1978**
Still in production

Style 37K: stained amber spruce (**37K**) or koa top (**37K2**), flame-grained koa back and sides, ebony bridge, white pins with black

dots, multiple-bound top, ebony finger-board, diamond-and-wedges inlay at frets 5 and 9, Maltese cross-type inlay at 7th fret (same inlay as style 30)
Introduced, D-size only: **1980**
Discontinued: **1989**

Style 38: M-size body, rosewood back and sides, rosewood bridge, abalone sound-hole ring, 7-ply top binding, 3-ply back binding, white body binding around neck heel, triple-bound ebony fingerboard, dot inlay, bound peghead, decal logo, stained top
Introduced: **1977**
Still in production

Style 40: rosewood back and sides, ebony bridge, abalone inlay around top edge and soundhole (not on top around fingerboard), only early listing: **1874**
Sporadic examples: **1909–17**
Re-introduced, Style 45 backstripe, ebony fin-gerboard, inlay at 5 frets, most in style 00-40H: **1928**
Last listed: **1941**

Style 41: rosewood back and sides, abalone inlay around top edge and soundhole (not on top around fingerboard), Style 45 back-stripe, bound fingerboard, Style 45 hexago-nal abalone inlay from 3rd to 15th fret, triple-bound peghead, vertical pearl-inlaid logo
Introduced, D-size only: **1969**
Smaller hexagonal inlay from 1st to 17th fret, scalloped braces: **1987**
Still in production

Style 42: rosewood back and sides, abalone inlay, ivory bridge, screw-adjustable neck, bound ebony fingerboard
First listed: **1874**
Inlaid bridge pins, ivory-bound top and back, abalone soundhole inlay, abalone inlay on top around edge of fingerboard, Style 45 backstripe, snowflake inlay on 3 frets, non-adjustable neck: **1898**
5 frets inlaid: **1901**
Celluloid binding, ebony bridge: **1919**
Pearl inlay around top, no binding or inlay on peghead
Last made: **1942**

Style 44: made for soloist Vahdah Olcott-Bickford, rosewood back and sides, multi-ple-bound top (similar to post-WWII Style 28), backstripe of multiple white and black lines, bound fingerboard and peghead, some pegheads with *Soloist* inlaid
Available: **1913–39**

Style 45: rosewood back and sides, ivory bridge, inlaid bridge pins, ivory-bound top, back, fingerboard and peghead; abalone inlay with wood purfling on top, back, sides, by endpin, around end of finger-board, and around soundhole; fancy back-stripe, ebony fingerboard, snowflake inlay at 5 frets, scroll peghead inlay
First listed: **1904**
Snowflake-pattern inlay at 8 frets, torch or flowerpot peghead inlay: **1914**
Ebony bridge, ivoroid binding: **1919**
C. F. Martin inlaid in pearl on peghead, 14-fret models only: **1934**
Hexagonal inlay on D-size, by **1939**
Last listed: **1941**
Discontinued: **1942**
Re-introduced, black-and-white plastic pur-fling bordering abalone top and side inlay, hexagonal abalone inlay (all sizes), D-size has "boxed" endpiece with abalone border (double abalone border where endpiece meets top and back): **1968**
Old-style endpiece with abalone mitered into side-border abalone: **early 1970**
Scalloped bracing: **1988**
Still in production

Style 64: maple back and sides, 6-ply top bind-ing with tortoise grain on outer edge, Style 28 soundhole binding, Style 45 backstripe, unbound ebony fingerboard, dot inlay, nat-ural top finish
Introduced by **1985**
Still in production

Style 65: Jumbo M size, flame-grained maple back and sides, ebony bridge, tortoise grain pickguard, tortoise grain outer bind-ing on top and back, Style 28 soundhole ring, Style 45 backstripe, ebony finger-board with tortoise grain outer binding, dot inlay
Introduced: **1985**
Still in production

Style 68: maple back and sides, Style 28 checkered backstripe, bound fingerboard, abalone dot inlay, bound peghead, Style 45 vertical peghead logo, carved diamond volute on back of peghead
Introduced with MC body, single cutaway, oval soundhole: **1985**
Still in production

Style 76: D-76 Bicentennial limited edition, rosewood back and sides, 3-piece back with herringbone backstripes, ebony bridge, white bridge pins with black dots, black pickguard, D-28 bindings, herring-bone soundhole ring, ebony fingerboard, pearl star inlay, engraved pearl eagle peg-

head inlay, brass plate on neck block with series and serial numbers
200 made: **1975**
1,776 made (plus 98 for employees stamped D-76E): **1976**

Hawaiian and Early Koa Models

Most Hawaiians have frets flush with fingerboard, bridge saddle mounted straight (no compensation slant) across body. H after model name signifies Hawaiian, K signifies koa wood construction. All H models have 12 frets clear of body.

2-17H: 1927–31
0-17H: 1930–40
0-18K (most are Hawaiian setup): **1918–35**
0-28K (most are Hawaiian setup), 1 in **1935**: **1917–31**
00-18H: 1935–41
00-40H: 1928–39

12-Strings

D12-20: mahogany back and sides, tortoise grain binding, Style 28 checkered back-stripe, 12 frets clear of body, black pins with white dots, slotted peghead
Introduced: **1964**
Black binding and pickguard: **1967**
Still in production

D12-18: 14 frets clear of body, solid peghead: **1973–current**
D12-28: 14 frets clear of body, solid peghead: **1970–current**
D12-35: 12 frets clear of body, slotted peghead: **1965–current**
D12-41: available: **1970–current**
D12-45: 12 frets clear of body, slotted peghead: **1969–current**
J12-40M: 14 frets clear of body, solid peghead: **1985–current**
J12-65M: 14 frets clear of body, solid peghead: **1986–current**
Note: As of mid 1991, only the 28, 40, and 65 were catalog model 12-strings. All other 12-strings were available by special order only.

Tenors and Plectrums

Tenor and plectrum models are designated by T or P after model name. The first recorded Martin tenor was a 5-17 in 1927. Many models have been available as tenors, with scale lengths of 22 1/2" before 1929, 23" from 1929 onward, and as plectrums with scale length of 27". The 0-size tenor body is 17 1/8" long, which is 1 1/4" shorter than the

14-fret 0-size guitar body.

Classicals

Prior to 1928, most Martin guitars were made for gut strings but were not given classical model designations. The G series models were the first attempt by Martin to make a classical guitar that would appeal to players of Spanish style instruments.

00-18G: Style 18 wood and trim, fan-pattern bracing, string-loop bridge, same body shape as 14-fret 00 but only 12 frets clear of body, ebony fingerboard, fingerboard 2" wide at nut, slotted peghead
Introduced: **1936**
Rosewood fingerboard: **c. 1940**
Last made: **1962**

00-28G: Style 28 wood and trim (same changes as Style 28), otherwise same specs as 00-18G
Introduced: **1936**
Last made: **1962**

00-16C: same body shape as 12-fret 00, bound top, Style 18 soundhole ring, Style 18 top binding, no back binding, 25 1/4" scale, non-gloss finish
00-18C: Style 18 wood and trim
000-28C: same body shape as 12-fret 000, Style 28 wood and trim
C series introduced: **1962**
000-28C last listed: **1965**
00-28C introduced: **1966**
Last 000-28C made: **1969**
26 3/8" scale: **1970**
00-16C, 00-18C and 00-28C still in production

N-10: Spanish-style body shape, mahogany back and sides, multiple top binding with black outer binding, white-black-white backstripe, Spanish classical style soundhole rosette, 25.4" scale
N-20: rosewood back and sides, mutliple top and back binding
Introduced: **1968**
26 3/8" scale, rounded peak peghead: **1970**
N-10 last produced: **1985**
N-20 still in production, N-10 still available by special order

Electric Flat Tops

00-18E: 00-18 with 1 DeArmond PU at end of fingerboard, 2 knobs, X-bracing
Introduced: **1959**
Last year made: **1964**

D-18E: D-18 with 2 DeArmond PUs, 3 knobs, toggle switch on upper treble bout, ladder bracing

1 instrument produced: **1958**
301 produced : **1959**

D-28E: D-28 with 2 DeArmond PUs, 4 knobs,
  toggle switch, ladder bracing
Introduced: **1959**
Last year made: **1964**

Pickups: Since the mid 1970s, Martin has
  offered Frap, Barcus-Berry, and Fishman-
  made pickups, installed under the soundhole, with or without pre-amp, and with or
  without tone and volume knobs on the
  upper bass side bout (near heel joint).
  Martin Thinline (made by Fishman) is a
  current option, with or without pre-amp,
  and is standard (with no pre-amp or knobs)
  on all Shenandoah models.

Acoustic Archtops

All *f*-hole archtops have serial number and
model number stamped on the inside center backstripe.

C-1: 000-size body, 15" wide, carved top, back
  arched by braces (not carved), round hole,
  mahogany back and sides, Style 18 trim,
  trapeze tailpiece, earliest with inlaid vertical *Martin* peghead logo (no *C. F.* on logo),
  sunburst top finish
C-2: roughly similar to 000-28, inlaid vertical
  peghead logo, sunburst top finish
C-3: ebony fingerboard, Style 45 pattern
  snowflake inlay, inlaid vertical peghead
  logo, gold-plated metal parts, sunburst top
  finish
Introduced: **1931**
f-holes (some examples): **1932**
Last round holes produced: **1933**
White binding on C-1: **1935**
C-3 last made: **1934**
Bound fingerboard on C-2: **1935**
Hexagonal inlay on C-2, inlay on 6 frets: **1939**
C-1 and C-2 discontinued: **1942**

R-18: 12-fret 00-size, 14 1/8" wide, arched
  spruce top, round hole, back arched by
  braces (not carved), 4-ply top binding with
  black outer layer, sunburst top finish
Introduced stamped 00-18S: **1932**
Stamped R-18: **1933**
14-fret 00-size body, 14 5/16" wide, round hole:
  1933
3-piece *f*-holes: **late 1933**
R-17: arched mahogany top, 3-piece *f*-holes,
  introduced: **1934**
Carved top on R-18, 1-piece *f*-holes: **1937**
R-17 and R-18 last listed: **1941**
R-17 and R-18 last made: **1942**

F-7: 16" wide, carved top, back arched by

braces (not carved), rosewood back and
  sides, *f*-holes, Style 45 backstripe, bound
  ebony fingerboard, 2 white lines inlaid
  down length of fingerboard, hexagonal
  inlay (some ivoroid, some pearloid) on 6
  frets, inlaid vertical peghead logo, sunburst top finish
F-9: rosewood back and sides, bound ebony
  fingerboard, 2 white-black-white lines
  inlaid down length of fingerboard, Style 45
  backstripe, abalone hexagonal inlays (a
  few parloid) on 8 frets (from 1st to 17th),
  inlaid vertical peghead logo, gold-plated
  metal parts, sunburst top finish
Introduced: **1935**
Discontinued: **1942**

F-1: 16" wide, carved top, similar trim to C-1,
  mahogany back and sides, *f*-holes, sun-
  burst top finish
F-2: 16" wide, similar to C-2, *f*-holes
Introduced: **1940**
Discontinued: **1942**

Electric Archtops

F-50: thin hollowbody of plywood, single cutaway, 1 DeArmond PU, 2 knobs, adjustable
  plexiglass bridge, standard Martin shape
  peghead, sunburst
F-55: single cutaway, 2 PUs, 4 knobs, toggle
  switch
F-65: double cutaway, 2 PUs, 4 knobs, toggle
  switch, tremolo
F-series electric models introduced: **1961**
Last made (replaced by **GT** series): **1965**

GT-70: single cutaway, 2 PUs, 4 knobs, tremolo, white pickguard, adjustable truss rod
  with truss rod cover on peghead, larger
  peghead than standard Martin with pointed corners, single-bound peghead, burgundy or black finish
GT-75: double cutaway
GT models introduced: **1965**
Last listed: **1968**

Electric Solidbodies

E-18: maple body with rosewood or walnut
  laminates, 2 Di Marzio PUs with 1 row of
  poles visible, rosewood fingerboard, asymmetrical peghead with *CFM* monogram
  logo
EM-18: same body as E-18, 2 exposed-coil
  humbucking PUs, coil tap switch
EB-18: electric bass, 1 PU
Introduced, serial numbers beginning with
  1000: **1979**
Discontinued: **1983**

E-28: mahogany body, 2 exposed-coil humbucking PUs, ebony fingerboard, asymmetrical peghead with *CFM* monogram logo, shaded finish

EB-28: electric bass, 2 PUs
Introduced: **1980**
Discontinued: **1983**

COMMENTS

Martin has been the premier maker of flat top acoustic guitars since the mid 1800s. Martin's other styles are interesting and in many cases quite rare, but they have not achieved the reputation, collector's appeal or market value of the flat top steel-string guitars.

Classicals are equal in workmanship to steel string models, but the sound and feel is not such that they appeal to most serious classical players. They do not have the market or collector's appeal of equivalent steel-string models.

Acoustic archtops do not have the traditional look, feel and sound of instruments by other makers with carved maple backs. They have the workmanship equivalent to flat top models and they are rare, but they have not achieved the market recognition or value of equivalent flat top models.

On flat top electrics the DeArmond pickup system interferes with the acoustic sound, and the magnetic PUs do not produce a faithful acoustic sound. These models are historically interesting but not sought after.

Archtop electrics are interesting primarily because they were made by Martin. Their designs and electronics were outdated at the time they were introduced. They are of little interest to players or collectors.

Solidbody electrics are not sought after and are interesting primarily as a footnote in Martin history.

Flat tops (by period):

Staufer-style flat tops display extremely fine workmanship. They have considerable appeal to collectors but are not sought after as utility instruments. Prices vary depending on condition and ornamentation but these models generally sell for less money than prime examples from the 1929–44 period.

Models from the 1840s to the early 1900s represent the earliest appearances of modern flat top designs. They exhibit superb workmanship, but they have relatively small bodies designed for gut strings only. These models do not appeal to steel string players due to the gut string design; they do not appeal to classical players because the body and neck dimensions differ from those of modern classicals. They appeal primarily to collectors, and despite their historical appeal, current market values are less than for later steel string models.

Twelve-fret steel-string models and 14-fret models from the mid 1920s to 1944 are characterized by superb workmanship and extremely fine sound and playability. They are of great interest to collectors and musicians. Some musicians prefer the sound and feel of the 12-fret neck, and these are equal in value to 14-fret guitars of the same general period. The 14-fret models are considered by most collectors and musicians to represent the golden era of the flat top Martin. D-45s bring some of the highest prices of any vintage instruments. All high-end styles, all Ds, and all OMs from this period are highly sought after.

Flat tops from late 1944–46 represent the transition from prewar style to postwar. They bring prices lower than prewar models but higher than post-war models.

Flat tops from 1947–69 are regarded as instruments of good quality and playability, although they are not as sought after as those of earlier periods. Rosewood models are of Brazilian rosewood, which is in greater demand than Indian rosewood. D sizes in particular command good prices and are highly respected by musicians.

The 1970–76 period was Martin's period of greatest annual production. Guitars from this period are considered to be excellent utility instruments but are of little interest to collectors.

From 1976 to the present, Martin has been undergoing considerable changes, with numerous reissues, new models, limited editions, new features, specification changes, and a large number of custom-made guitars. Many new model names do not fit into the traditional model numbering system, so that higher style numbers no longer necessarily mean higher grade wood or ornamentation. Workmanship is generally superior to that of the previous period. While not currently regarded as collector's items, these instruments have the workmanship, playability, and sound to be potential future collectibles.

UKULELES, TIPLES, TAROPATCHES, AND BANJOS

General Information

The first Martin ukuleles, built in the first half of 1916, have serial numbers, with numbers ranging from 1 to less than 200. Ukuleles made after mid 1916 do not have a serial number and must be dated by specification changes.

Ukuleles have the Martin stamp on the back of the peghead until 1935.

Peghead decals on ukuleles do not appear in catalog photos until after World War II.

All Martin ukuleles and tiples listed as still in production are available only by special order.

SECTION ORGANIZATION

Standard (Soprano) Ukuleles
Other Ukulele Sizes (including Taropatch)
Tiples
Tenor Banjo
Vega Banjos

Standard (Soprano) Ukuleles

All are 6 3/8" wide with 13 5/8" scale.

Style 0: mahogany body, no body binding, 12-fret rosewood fingerboard, small dot inlay, wood friction pegs
Introduced: **1922**
Ebony nut, nickel patent pegs: **1927**
Still in production (available in koa)

Style 1: mahogany body, rosewood outer binding with black and white wood binding around top, 12-fret rosewood fingerboard, small dot inlay, wood friction pegs
Introduced: **1918**
Koa wood **1K** available: **1920**
Patent pegs: **1927**
Dark plastic binding: **1934**
Style 1K last listed: **1942**
Style 1 last listed: **1965**

Style 2: mahogany body, triple-bound top with ivoroid outer binding, single-bound back, 12-fret fingerboard, small dot inlay
Introduced: **1918**
Koa wood **2K** available: **1920**
Nickel patent pegs: **1923**
Style 2K last listed: **1933**
Style 2 last listed: **1965**

Style 3: mahogany body, 7-ply top binding, 3-ply back binding, 5-ply soundhole ring, celluloid (or bone) ornament lower edge of top, 17-fret ebony fingerboard extends to sound hole, small pearl paired-diamond inlay at frets 5, 7, and 9, diamonds joined at 7th fret, 3 lines inlaid down center of fingerboard, nut of 3-ply plastic, 4-point celluloid (or bone) peghead ornament, friction pegs
Introduced: **1918**
Koa wood **3K** available: **1920**
Unjoined diamond inlay at 7th fret, no peghead ornament, nickel patent pegs: **1923**
Style 3K last listed: **1939**
No celluloid ornament at lower edge of top: **late 1940s**
Style 3 still in production (koa available)

Style 5K: koa wood body, ivoroid-bound top and back with abalone pearl and black-and-white wood around soundhole, ivoroid-bound ebony fingerboard, 17-fret fingerboard extends to soundhole, snowflake inlay, koa peghead veneer with pearl-inlaid flowerpot, patent pegs
Introduced: **1922**
Abalone on sides: **1925**
No abalone on sides: **1927**
Last listed: **1940**

Style 5: mahogany body, same trim as Style 5K
Introduced: **1941**
Last listed: **1942**

Other Ukulele Sizes

Taropatch: 8 strings arranged in pairs, 7 5/8" wide, 14 7/8" scale
Introduced in Styles 1, 2, and 3: **1918**
Koa wood taropatches, Styles 1K, 2K, and 3K, introduced: **1922**
All discontinued except 1 and 2K: **1930**
Styles 1 and 2K discontinued: **1932**

1-C: concert ukulele, 7 5/8" wide (same body as taropatch), 14 3/4" scale, trimmed like Style 1 ukulele
Introduced: **1925**
Last listed: **1965**

1-T: tenor ukulele, 8 15/16" wide, 17" scale, mahogany body, rosewood fingerboard and bridge, ebony nut, ivory saddle, pin bridge, rosewood binding, 12 frets clear of body
Introduced: **1928**
Black plastic binding: **1934**
Tortoise grain binding: **1936**
Black plastic binding: **1966**
Still in production

Style 51: baritone ukulele, 10" wide, 20 1/8"

scale, mahogany body, white-black-white
soundhole rings, 2-ply top binding with
dark outer layer, single-ply dark back binding, pin bridge, rosewood fingerboard, 14
frets clear of body
Introduced: **1960**
Still in production

Tiples

All are 8 15/16" wide, with 17" scale, 10 strings
(in groups of 2, 3, 3, 2; tuned like ukulele
but with octaves on 3 lowest groups),
model and serial number on neckblock.
Specs change as equivalent guitar styles
change.

T-15: mahogany, ring of black and white lines
around soundhole
Introduced: **1949**
Last listed: **1966**

T-17: mahogany, black and white ring around
soundhole
Introduced: **1926**
Last listed: **1948**

T-18: like Style 18 guitar
Introduced: **1923**
Still in production

T-28: like Style 28 guitar, rosewood back and
sides
Introduced: **1924**
Still in production

Tenor Banjo

Style 1: 12 1/2" diameter maple rim, 11" diameter head, Grover "hub-cap" metal resonator recessed into rim, 24 brackets, tension hooks through rim, tension nuts
recessed into back, maple neck, 17 frets,
dot inlay
Introduced: **1923**
Last listed (96 total sold): **1926**

Vega Banjos

Martin acquired the Vega Co. of Boston in
1970. In 1971, Vega banjo production was
moved to the Martin factory in Nazareth,
PA. Vega was sold to an Oriental manufacturer in 1979. Martin-made Vegas have a
Martin decal on the back of the peghead
and on the inside of the body.

COMMENTS

Ukuleles were extremely popular from the
1910s into the 1930s, with a strong appeal
carrying into the 1960s. Production quantities during some periods were as great as
for Martin guitars. Martin ukuleles are
considered to be among the finest ever
made for workmanship and sound.
Demand for vintage Martin ukuleles has
increased dramatically in recent years.
The koa wood models bring more than
mahogany models, with fancier styles
bringing more than plain styles. All sizes
are sought after by players and collectors.

Tiples, adaptated from a South American
instrument, achieved some popularity in
the 1930s. Current interest among players
is extremely limited. Although they do have
excellent sound, they appeal primarily to
collectors.

The original Martin banjo model is of interest
only as a historical footnote.

Martin-made Vega banjos are equivalent in
quality of workmanship to Martin guitars of
the same period and are superior in workmanship to the 1960s Boston-made original
Vega banjos. However, most banjo collectors still regard the Boston Vega as the
authentic original and the Martin-made
Vega as a utility instrument.

MANDOLIN SERIAL NUMBERS

Year	Last Number
1895	23
1896	112
1897	155
1898	359
1899	577
1900	800
1901	881
1902	1171
1903	1348
1904	1507
1905	1669
1906	2026
1907	2357
1908	2510
1909	2786
1910	3098
1911	3431
1912	3847
1913	4162
1914	4462
1915	4767
1916	5007
1917	5752
1918	6370
1919	7237
1920	8761
1921	9627
1922	10196
1923	11020
1924	11809
1925	12520
1926	13359
1927	13833
1928	14170
1929	14630
1930	14892
1931	15290
1932	15476
1933	15528
1934	15729
1935	15887
1936	16156
1937	16437
1938	16580
1939	16747
1940	16957
1941	17263
1942	17405

Year	Last Number
1943–45	none
1946	17641
1947	18303
1948	19078
1949	19559
1950	20065
1951	20496
1952	20902
1953	21452
1954	21952
1955	22254
1956	22629
1957	22985
1958	23111
1959	23262
1960	23512
1961	23663
1962	23938
1963	24139
1964	24339
1965	24439
1966	24564
1967	24639
1968	24839
1969	24989
1970	25039
1971	25139
1972	25289
1973	25339
1974	25679
1975	25895
1976*	26045
1977	26101
1978	none
1979	26112
1980	26156
1981	26215
1982	26225
1983	26247
1984	26254
1985	26263
1986	26273
1987	26279
1988	26281
1989	26283
1990	26291

* also in 1976   #259996–#260020

MANDOLINS

All mandolins are rosewood back and sides, unless otherwise specified.

Serial Number and Model Placement

Bowlback: serial number on neck block
Flat back: model letter (1931 and after) and serial number on inside center strip
Carved back: style number (1931 and after) and serial number on inside back

SECTION ORGANIZATION

Bowlback, Bent Top Models
Flat back, Bent Top Models
Carved Top and Back, Oval Hole Models
Carved Top and Back, ƒ-hole Models
Mandolas
Mandocellos

Bowlback, Bent Top Models

All with oval hole, 13" scale

Style G1: 27 ribs, symmetrical pickguard under strings with ornamental inlay, 2 ornamental tuner plates on front of peghead, ornamental peghead cutout
Style G2: symmetrical pickguard under strings with ornamental inlay, ornamental peghead cutout, tuner plates on back of peghead
Style G3: ivory bridge, symmetrical pickguard under strings with ornamental inlay, tuner plate covers peghead
Style G5: ivory bridge, butterfly-shape tortoise shell pickguard under strings with abalone and pearl inlay, pearl fingerboard with abalone inlays, tuner plate covers peghead, point on top of peghead
Only catalog listing: **1896**

Style 1: 18 ribs, ebony bridge and fingerboard, no fingerboard inlay, symmetrical pickguard with ornamental inlay mounted underneath strings, German silver tuners, tuner plates on front of peghead, ornamental peghead cutout
Introduced: **1898**
20 ribs, no inlay on pickguard, dot inlay, tuners installed from back: **1904**
22 ribs: **1909**
Pickguard on treble side: **1917**
Last made: **1924**

Style 2: 26 ribs, fancier soundhole and binding than Style 1, symmetrical pickguard with inlay mounted under strings, colored wood soundhole ring, ornamental peghead cutout
Introduced: **1898**
Light and dark wood binding with rosewood on outer edge: **1901**
Pickguard on treble side: **1917**
Last made: **1924**

Style 3: 26 ribs, symmetrical pickguard with inlay mounted under strings, ivory-bound top with colored-wood purfling, abalone and ivory-bound soundhole, pearl tuner buttons, ornamental peghead cutout
Introduced: **1898**
Ivory tuner buttons: **1901**
Black and white binding with ivory on outer edge, snowflake inlay: **1904**
Last made: **1922**

Style 4: 34 ribs, symmetrical pickguard with inlay mounted under strings, ivory-bound top with abalone border, abalone and ivory soundhole border, ivory-bound fingerboard, German silver peghead plate, pearl tuner buttons, ornamental peghead cutout
Introduced: **1898**
30 ribs, ivory tuner buttons: **1901**
Last made: **1921**

Style 5: 34 ribs, symmetrical pickguard with inlay mounted under strings, alternating pearl and tortoise top binding, ivory-bound fingerboard, vine inlay, ornamental peghead cutout
Introduced: **1898**
Ivory tuner buttons, ornamental peghead inlay: **1901**
Last made: **1920**

Style 6: 42 ribs fluted and joined with ivory, ivory bridge, symmetrical pickguard with inlay mounted under strings, ivory-bound top with abalone border, abalone border on top around fingerboard, ivory-bound fingerboard, vine inlay, ornamental peghead cutout
Introduced: **1898**
Ornamental peghead inlay: **1901**
Ivory-bound side border: **1904**
Snowflake inlay: **1914**
Last made: **1921**

Style 6A: (not cataloged) same as Style 6 but with pickguard on treble side, some with multiple black-and-white top binding and no peghead inlay
Introduced: **1903**
Discontinued: **1921**

Style 7: 42 fluted ribs, symmetrical pickguard with inlay mounted under strings, elaborate pearl inlay on wide border around top and soundhole, ivory- and abalone-bound

side border, vine fingerboard inlay crosses at 7th fret, floral peghead inlay, ornamental peghead cutout
First made: **1899**
Catalogued: **1904**
Last made: **1917**

Style 000: mahogany bowl, 9 ribs, pickguard on treble side extends to edge, dot inlay, solid peghead
Only year cataloged: **1914**

Style 00: 9 ribs, plain symmetrical pickguard mounted under strings, rosewood binding, dot inlay, solid peghead
Introduced: **1908**
Teardrop pickguard on treble side: **1917**
Mahogany bowl, 14 ribs: **1923**
Last made: **1925**

Style 0: 18 ribs, rope-pattern soundhole ring, plain symmetrical pickguard mounted under strings, ivory saddle, rosewood binding, dot inlay, solid peghead
Introduced: **1905**
Teardrop pickguard on treble side: **1917**
Last made: **1925**

Flat Back, Bent Top Models

All with oval hole, 13" scale

Style A: pickguard on treble side with pointed "tail," rosewood-bound top, dot inlay, solid guitar-style peghead
Introduced: **1914**
Mahogany back and sides, ebony bridge, teardrop pickguard, ebony fingerboard, dot inlay: **1917**
Rosewood-bound top and back by **1918**
AK: koa wood body, introduced: **1920**
5-ply top binding with black plastic outer layer, single-ply black plastic back binding: **early 1932**
Tortoise grain outer binding by **1936**
Shaded top optional: **1937**
Style AK last listed: **1937**
Rosewood fingerboard and bridge: **mid 1940s**
Style A still in production, AK available by special order

Style B: herringbone soundhole ring and back-strip, pickguard on treble side with pointed "tail," rosewood-bound top and back, slotted-diamond inlays at frets 5, 7, and 10, ornamental peghead cutout
Introduced: **1914**
Teardrop pickguard: **1917**
Rosewood and white holly binding: **1919**
BK: koa wood body, available: **1921, 25 only**
5-ply top binding with black plastic outer layer, single-ply black plastic back binding: **early 1932**

Tortoise grain outer binding by **1936**
Discontinued: **1946**
Re-introduced: **1981**
Discontinued: **1987**

Style C: colored wood purfling on top, abalone soundhole ring, teardrop pickguard, ivory-bound top and back, Style 42 inlay from 3rd fret to 17th, ornamental peghead cutout
Introduced: **1914**
Abalone border on top: **1917**
Celluloid binding: **1919**
Colored wood around top border: **1921**
Colored wood on back: **1925**
Last made: **1934**

Style D: ebony bridge, pickguard on treble side with pointed "tail," ivory-bound top, abalone border on top, purfling on sides, ivory-bound ebony fingerboard, Style 45 type snowflake inlay from 1st fret to 17th, engraved silver tuners, ornamental peghead cutout
Introduced: **1914**
Discontinued: **1917**

Style E: pickguard on treble side with pointed "tail," ivory bridge, ivory-bound top and back; abalone borders on top, back, and sides; ivory-bound ebony fingerboard, Style 45 snowflake inlay from 1st fret to 17th, ornamental peghead inlay, German silver tuners, inlaid tuner buttons, ornamental peghead cutout
Introduced: **1915**
Teardrop pickguard: **1917**
Celluloid binding: **1919**
Discontinued: **1937**

Carved Top and Back, Oval Hole Models

All with 13" scale

Style 15: maple back and sides, celluloid-bound top and back, ebony fingerboard and bridge, small dot inlay, solid peghead with rounded peak, natural top, antique brown back and sides
Introduced: **1929**
Discontinued: **1942**

Style 20: symmetrical 2-point body shape, maple back and sides, ebony bridge, elevated pickguard follows body point, multiple-bound top and back, ebony fingerboard, dot inlay, ornamental peghead cutout
Introduced: **1929**
Bound fingerboard: **1930**
Decal on peghead: **1935**
Discontinued: **1942**

Mandolins

Carved Top and Back, *f*-hole Models

All with 13 3/4" scale

Style 2-15: maple back and sides, elevated pickguard, triple-bound top, single-bound back, solid peghead with rounded peak, peghead decal, sunburst top finish, brown stain back and sides
Introduced: **1936**
Discontinued: **1965**

Style 2-20: symmetrical 2-point body, maple back and sides, multiple-bound top and back, ebony bridge, single-bound fingerboard, dot inlay, ornamental peghead cutout, peghead decal, shaded top finish
Introduced: **1936**
Discontinued: **1942**

Style 2-30: symmetrical 2-point body, *f*-holes, maple back and sides, single-bound elevated pickguard, multiple-bound top and back, single-bound fingerboard with treble-side extension, slotted-diamond and square inlay, single-bound peghead with ornamental peghead cutout, peghead decal
Introduced: **1937**
Discontinued: **1942**

Mandolas

Style 1: same wood and trim as Style 1 mandolin, available: **1902-14**
Style 2: same wood and trim as Style 2 mandolin, available: **1901 only**
Style AA: same wood and trim as Style A mandolin, available: **1915-31, 35, 41**
Style BB: same wood and trim as Style B mandolin, available: **1917-21, 32-39**

Mandocellos

4 bowlback instruments made: **1909**
2 with C-2 archtop guitar body, 3 with C-1 body: **1932**
2 with C-1 body: **1935**

COMMENTS

Those modern classical mandolinists who prefer the traditional Italian-style bowlback construction regard the Martin bowlbacks as excellent instruments.
Martin's flat back models and carved models have never achieved great recognition from collectors or musicians. They are of interest primarily to Martin collectors and, in the cases of the fancier models, to those who regard them as works of art.

The carved models exhibit excellent workmanship but are not as ornate as the high-end bowlback or flat back models. The carved Styles 20 and 30 are sought by collectors but, despite their workmanship and rarity, do not command prices equivalent to artist model Gibsons.

National/Valco

GENERAL INFORMATION

Dobros: See Dobro and Regal/Dobro section.

John Dopyera registered the National String Instrument Corporation in California on August 16, 1926, to make resonator instruments. Through the years his brothers Rudy, Robert, Louis, and Emil (Ed) would be involved in various financial and manufacturing roles. On January, 26, 1928, the Dopyeras traded their interest for stock in a corporation whose principals included George Beauchamp, Paul Barth, and Ted Kleinmeyer.

John Dopyera resigned on February 19, 1929, and formed the Dobro Manufacturing company with his brothers to make instruments under the Dobro brand. Dobro merged with National to form the National-Dobro company in 1932.

National-Dobro held patents on several styles of resonator instruments that produced greater volume than conventional design acoustic instruments. Both National and Dobro lines include woodbody and metalbody instruments. Most National-brand resonator instruments have 1 or 3 cones, with the cones opening toward the back of the instrument. Single-cone models have a "biscuit bridge" (bridge mounted on a biscuit-size piece of wood) sitting on the peak of the cone. Dobro-brand resonator instruments, including those licensed to Regal, have the resonator cone opening toward the top of the instrument and a 4- or 8-armed "spider" supporting the bridge.

National marketed its first electric instruments in 1935. The Supro brand was introduced in 1936 as a budget electric line. By the late 1930s, emphasis was shifting from acoustic resonator instruments to electric archtops and lap steels. According to Ed Dopyera, no resonator models of any type were made after 1939. The 1942 National catalog still listed several National type models.

National-Dobro began a move from California to Chicago in 1936. By 1942, the company had reorganized in Chicago as the Valco company, named after principals Victor Smith, Al Frost and Louis Dopyera.

In 1941, the Chicago Music Instrument company (which would own Gibson from 1944-69) began distributing Valco instruments. Some National instruments from the late 1930s through the 1950s have bodies or in some cases entire instruments made by Gibson. Some bodies were made by Harmony (also based in Chicago). Gibson bodies can be identified by their distinctive shape, by a work order number ink-stamped on the inside of the body, and by their workmanship.

From the 1940s through the mid 1960s, Valco made instruments and amps under various brands for other companies. The most commonly seen are Gretsch, Oahu, Silvertone (for Sears), and Airline (for Montgomery Ward). Others include Norman English, Dwight, Atlas, and St. Louis Music.

National introduced many innovative designs throughout the company's history, although not all were successful. In addition to resonator instruments, National's innovations include electric archtops with no soundholes, the first double-pickup electric, a magnesium-core neck with no neck heel, double-coil pickups (3 strings per coil), a 6-coil pickup, and guitar bodies of molded fiberglass.

Valco absorbed the Kay company in 1967. Valco announced a new line of acoustic and electric models in 1967. The company went bankrupt and the last instruments were sold at a bankruptcy auction in the summer of 1968.

The National brand name was used in the early to mid 1970s on electric and acoustic instruments made in the Orient and marketed by the Strum and Drum company.

National Resophonic Guitars was formed in San Luis Obispo, CA, in 1988 by Don Young, former plant supervisor for OMI (see Dobro and Regal/Dobro section), and McGregor Gaines, former shop foreman at OMI. All National Resophonic models have the National type cone. The company began producing woodbody instruments in 1989 and plans to introduce metalbody models in 1991. These instruments have a shield decal with *National* and *Resophonic*.

Terms

Ebonoid: black polished plastic
Ebonized: black-stained wood, typically poplar or maple, to simulate ebony
Pearlette or pearloid: plastic with light areas to simulate mother-of-pearl

Guitar Pickups

Blade in oval housing: **1935–37**
Blade in rectangular housing: **1937–39**
Metal-covered, 2 rows of poles, 3 poles per row: **1939–51**
Bridge PU, integrated into bridge (wire coming out of bridge), some models: **1947–65**
Floating, vinyl-covered, 1 row of poles: **1951–55**
Metal-covered, 1 row of poles...
   No mounting ring: **1951–late 1950s**
   Plastic mounting ring, set screws on sides of ring: **1954–57**
   Plastic mounting ring, no set screws on side, height adjustable by Philips-head E-string polepieces: **1958–59**
   Plastic mounting ring, no set screws on

National/Valco

General Information

side, height adjustable by slot-head E-string polepieces: **1960–68**
Silkscreened design on PU: **1962–65**

Steel Guitar Pickups

Strings through PU...
National steels: **early 1940s only**
Supro steels: **1939–68**
Strings over PU, 1 row of 6 poles, National models: **1942–68**

Guitar Pegheads

National...
Square top (slotted), single-cone models: **1928–36**
Tapers to point at top, tri-cone models only: **1927–42**
Rounded top (solid), all acoustics and electrics except tri-cones: **1936–55**
Wavy top edge: **1956–57**
Asymmetrical shape, longer on treble side: **1958–68**
Angular top, 6-on-a-side tuners: **1966–68**
Supro...
Pointed top (Kay shape) or rounded top: **1936–55**
Narrow asymmetrical shape, longer on bass side: **1955–62**
Wider asymmetrical shape, longer on bass side: **1962–68**
Rounded top, 6-on-a-side tuners: **1966–68**
Airline...
Narrow asymmetrical shape, longer on treble side: **1958–63**
Wider asymmetrical shape, longer on treble side (but not as long as Nationals from same period): **1964–65**
Rounded top, 6-on-a-side tuners (like Supro from same period): **1966–68**

National Logos

Shield...
Decal: **1927–40**
Nickeled and enameled plate, black and silver: **1940–51**
Brass plate with light blue enamel: **1951–60**
Script...
Some with silkscreened logo: **1951–55**
Raised metal (plated pot metal): **1956–60**
Molded plastic, most models: **1960–68**
Some low-end models with foil sticker logo, some steels with plated pot-metal logo: **1960–68**

Supro Logo Plates

Black logo on silver field, black border: **1936–47**
Blue logo on gold field, bronze border: **1948–early 60s**

Early 1930s Style O, standard resonator cover-plate with 9 diamond-shape hole clusters (no ribs), straight-cut f-holes, 12 frets clear of body, Dobro-type tailpiece.

Mid 1930s Style O, small diamond-hole pattern resonator cover, edges of f-holes rolled into body, 14 frets clear of body.

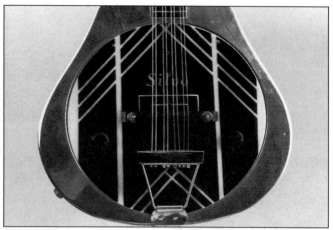

Rectangular pickup with split blade, on a Silvo mandolin, used on Silvo models and other electrics in the late 1930s.

Square control plate, strings-through-pickup design, used on almost all Supro lap steels.

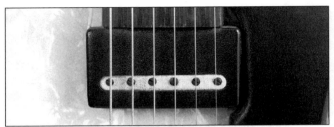

Floating vinyl-covered pickup, used on National and Supro models in the eary 1950s.

Metal-covered pickup with screws in side of mounting ring, used from 1954–57. Earlier models with this pickup have no mounting ring. Later models have no screws in side of mounting ring.

Silkscreened design on pickups, 1962–65.

Shield decal on a 1930s Triolian mandolin.

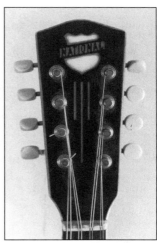

Ebonoid peghead veneer with etched logo, on a late 1930s Silvo mandolin.

NA-10. Supro peghead shape from 1962–68, with plastic logo. Earlier (1955-62) pegheads are narrower. National pegheads from 1958-68 are longer on the treble side.

Metal serial number plate used on all Valco-made instruments and amps from 1941–63.

Foil serial number plate used on Valco-made instruments from 1964-68.

SERIAL NUMBERS

Patents on National Models

Number	Granted	For
1,741,453	Dec. 21, 1929	tri-cone resonator
1,808,756	June 9, 1931	biscuit resonator

Serial Numbers, 1927–35

From 1927–35, National used various serial number series for different models.

On single-cone models, the number is usually stamped onto the top of the peghead, except for Style Os with S-prefix numbers, which are usually stamped into the body by the endpin.

On roundneck tri-cone models, the number is stamped into the body by the endpin up until #2400. On squareneck tri-cone models, the number is stamped into the back of the metal neck near the peg-head up until #2400. After #2400 the number is stamped on the top of the peghead.

Numbers in these tables are arranged by the following priority: all numerals, numerals with letter suf-fix, numerals with letter prefix.

This information and number list was compiled by Bob Brozman.

Number range	Description	Date Range
Tri-Cones		
0100–01002	roundneck	1928–30
100–3323	squareneck	1927–34
S prefix	roundneck	1930–33
Tenors, Styles 1–3		
100–600	tri-cone	1928
600–850	pear-shape, 1 cone	1929
850–1400	guitar-shape, 1 cone	1929–34
Other, Styles 1–3		
100–602	mandolin	1928–34
100–405	uke	1928–34
Triolian		
0100–0202	yellow	1929
1107–1443	woodbody	1928–29 (many with no number)
A223–A1814*	bakelite neck**	1930
1B–87B	green, 12-fret	1933
26P–2249P	yellow, 12-fret	1930–33
2250P–2311P	yellow, 14-fret	1934–35
50W–3173W	brown, 12-fret	1928–35
3174W–3346W	brown, 14-fret	1935–39

* A-prefix numbers are used on other models in 1938 (see following).

** Bakelite necks were extremely prone to warping, and those that survive today are virtually unplayable in Spanish style. As many as half of the approximately 1800 bakelite-neck Triolians were returned to the factory for a wood neck. Renecked examples may have a serial number from a later date than other specs would indicate.

Triolian Tenor		
800–1483		1928–early 30s
W or P suffix		1928–early 30s

Duolian		
2402–7580	14-fret	1936–37
01236–06123	12-fret	1930–35
07919–09464	14-fret	1935–36
C1–C6500*	12-fret, straight *f*-holes	1930–33
C6500–C7500*	12-fret, rolled *f*-holes	1933–34

C7501–C9721*	14-fret, slot-head	1935–36
E7580–E7807	14-fret	1935–36
R60–R572	12-fret, made for Sears	1930–32

* C-prefix numbers are used on other models in 1938 (see following).

Style O

290–5659	14-fret, slot-head	1935
5659–7027	14-fret, solid-head	1936–37
S1–S4400	12-fret, straight *f*-holes	1930–33
S4401–S5401	12-fret, rolled *f*-holes	1933–34
S5401–S6205	14-fret	1934–35

El Trovador

K prefix	1933 only

Trojan

T001–T2025	1934–35

Serial Numbers, 1936–42

From 1936–42, a single series is used for all instruments. The 1936–42 numbers are referred to as Chicago numbers.

Information for 1936–42 numbers was provided by Bob Brozman and Mike Newton.

Letter	Acoustics	Electrics
A prefix*	1937	1935
B prefix	1936	1936–38
C prefix*	1938	1938–40
FS suffix	factory second	
G prefix or suffix	1940–42	1940–42
L prefix	1939	
N prefix		1935

*A and C prefixes are also used in some pre-1936 number series.

Serial Number Plates, 1941–63

Beginning in 1941, Valco put the serial number on a small oblong brass or aluminum plate, nailed onto the back of the neck near the peghead. These plates were also put on amplifiers. All Valco-made instruments and amps—including those made for Sears (Silvertone), Montgomery Ward (Airline), Gretsch, Oahu and others—are numbered in a single series.

This information and number list was compiled by Mike Newton.

Year	Approx. Number Range
1940–42	G suffix
1947	V100–V7500
1948	V7500–V15000
1949	V15000–V25000
1950	V25000–V35000
1951	V35000–V38000
	X100–X7000
1952	X7000–X17000
1953	X17000–X30000
1954	X30000–X43000
1955	X43000–X57000
1956	X57000–X71000
1957	X71000– 85000
1958	X85000–X99000
	T100–T5000
1959	T5000–T25000
1960	T25000–T50000
1961	T50000–T75000

Serial Numbers

1962	T75000–T90000
	G100–G5000
1963	T90000–T99000
	G5000–G15000
1964	G15000–G40000

Serial Number Stickers, 1964–68

In 1964, Valco replaced the metal serial number plate with a rectangular foil sticker. Stickers have numeric prefixes.

Prefix	Range
1	1964–early 68
2	early to mid 1968

1989–Current

Instruments made by National Resophonic Guitars are numbered consecutively. For instruments made in 1989 and 1990, serial numbers are on a paper label on the inside back. In 1991 the company plans to stamp the serial number on the top of the peghead.

Year	Approx. Last Number
1989	12
1990	225

NATIONAL RESONATOR MODELS KEY

Metalbody
    Tri-cone resonator
        Plain nickel-plate finish=**Style 1**
        Wriggly engraving around borders=**"Style 1 1/2"**
        Rose pattern engraving
            No roses on coverplate=**Style 2**
            Roses on coverplate=**"Style 2 1/2"**
        Lily of the Valley engraving =**Style 3**
        Chrysanthemum engraving =**Style 4**
        Musician scene on back=**Style 35**
        Surfer scene on back=**Style 97**
        Maple-grain paint finish=**M-3 (Marino)**
    Single-cone resonator
        Nickel-plated body
            Don on bridge cover
                Plain body=**Don Style 1**
                Sheaf of flowers engraving=**Don Style 2**
                Other elaborate engraving=**Don Style 3**
            No *Don* on bridge cover
                Palm tree etching (8 variations)=**Style O**
                No etching=**Style N**
        Paint finish
            Bound fingerboard=**Triolian**
            Unbound fingerboard
                Gray or brown finish=**Duolian**
                Maple finish=**Collegian**
Woodbody
    Yellow painted body=**Triolian woodbody**
    Magnolia body=**California**
    Mahogany top
        Varied-pattern inlay=**Estralita**
        Dot inlay=**El Trovador**
    Maple top
        Bound fingerboard=**Trojan**
        Unbound fingerboard=**Rosita**
    Spruce top
        Dot inlay=**Havana**
        Double-parallelogram inlay=**Aragon de Luxe**
Plastic-covered solid woodbody
    Cutaway, round neck=**Resophonic (No. 1133)**
    Non-cutaway, square neck=**Resophonic (No. 1033)**
Molded fiberglass hollowbody
    White=**Bluegrass 35**
    Red=**(Supro) Folk Star**
    Black=**(Montgomery Ward) Airline**
    Sunburst=model name unknown

NATIONAL NON-RESONATOR ACOUSTICS KEY

f-holes, archtop
    17" wide
        N-275 (specs unavailable)
        Split half-circle inlay=**N-150** or **1135**
        N-125 (specs unavailable)
    16 1/4" wide
        Gibson L-50 body shape
            Clear pickguard=**N-100** or **1145**
            Opaque pickguard=**1140**
        Harmony or Kay body shape=**N-50** or **NA-35**
    15 1/2" wide=**Cameo**

Round hole, flat top
    No fingerboard inlay=**N-55**
    Dot inlay
        17" wide, Gibson J-200 shape=**N-1111**
        16" wide, Gibson J-45 shape=**N-66** or **1155**
        14 1/4" wide, Gibson LG-1 shape
            Neck heel=**N-33** or **1160**
            No neck heel=**1150**
        13 1/4" wide=**Student model No. 1191**
    Butterfly (diamond enclosed by block) inlay
        Square-shouldered dreadnought=**N-700**
        Rounded bouts=**N-730**
    Block inlay
        12-string=**N-580**
        6-string
            Point on belly of bridge=**N-710**
            Bridge ends shaped like whale fluke=**N-720**

NATIONAL ACOUSTICS

SECTION ORGANIZATION

Tri-plates or "Silvers"
Other Tri-cone Models
Single-cone Resonator, Metalbody, 1928–43
Single-cone Resonator, Woodbody, 1928–43
Single-cone Resonator, 1950s and 60s
Non-resonator Models
    Archtops
    Flat Tops

Tri-plates or "Silvers"

German silver body (solid nickel alloy with nickel plating), tri-cone resonator with 2 cones on bass side and 1 on treble, T-shape bridge cover and handrest, grid-pattern soundholes on upper body, Hawaiian (squareneck) or Spanish (roundneck), 12 frets clear of body, mahogany neck, slotted peghead

Earliest examples: cone configuration offset from the 2 cones on bass side and 1 on treble side arrangement, different shape bridge cover/handrest, grid holes on upper body actually woven with separate pieces of metal soldered to body

Style 1: plain body, early examples with unbound fingerboard, later with bound fingerboard, dot inlay, squareneck model has 1 dot at 12th fret

"Style 1 1/2" (collector's term): many examples of Style 1 with wriggly line engraved around borders

Style 2: Wild Rose or Wild Irish Rose engraving, no engraving on coverplate, dot inlay

"Style 2 1/2" (collector's term): some 1927-28 examples of Style 2 with roses engraved on coverplate as well as on body

Style 3: Lily of the Valley engraving, bound ebony fingerboard, diamond-shaped inlay, some with ebony peghead veneer and pearl logo, some with celluloid peghead veneer and engraved logo

Style 4: Chrysanthemum etching, bound ebony fingerboard, diamond-shape inlay, some with ebony peghead veneer and pearl logo, some with celluloid peghead veneer and engraved logo

Styles 1 and 2, Spanish and Hawaiian, introduced: **1927**

Styles 3 and 4, Spanish and Hawaiian, introduced: **1928**

Style 4, clear pickguard: **1936**

Style 3 referred to as **Artist (S-3)**, with square-neck, dot inlay: **1937**

Style 4, ebonoid peghead veneer, by **1938**

Style 4 discontinued: **1940**

Styles 1, 2, and 3 discontinued: **1943**

Tenor (23" scale) or **plectrum** (26" scale): triangular body shape, tri-cone resonator, no upper body holes, coverplate like guitars, maple neck, straight-through banjo-type tuners, banjo-type peghead

Introduced in Styles 1, 2, and 3 only; no Style 4: **1928**

Pear-shape body, single-cone resonator, by **1930**

Guitar-shape body: **1931**

Styles 1 and 2 discontinued; Style 3 only: **1936**

Clear pickguard: **1937**

Style 3 discontinued by **1939**

Mandolin: triangular body shape, tri-cone resonator, no upper body holes, coverplate

like guitars
Introduced in Styles 1, 2, and 3 only; no Style 4: **1928**

Single-cone resonator: **1928**
Styles 1 and 2 discontinued; Style 3 only: **1936**
Clear pickguard: **1937**
Style 3 discontinued by **1939**

Ukulele: guitar-shaped body, single-cone resonator, no upper body holes, 5 diamond-shaped hole clusters in coverplate
Introduced in Styles 1, 2, and 3 only; no Style 4: **1928**
Smaller body by **1931**
Styles 1 and 2 discontinued; Style 3 only: **1936**
Style 3 discontinued by **1939**

Other Tri-cone Models

Triolian woodbody: earliest examples with round coverplate and 3 cones (see Single-Cone Resonator, Woodbody Models, following)
Available: **late 1928**

Style 35: brass body with nickel plating, etching of Renaissance musician under willow tree on back, airbrushed enamel coloring, maple neck, 12 frets clear of body, bound ebonoid fingerboard on Hawaiian model, bound rosewood fingerboard on Spanish model, dot inlay, solid peghead (tenor and mandolin mentioned in literature but not produced)
Introduced: **1936**
Ebonoid peghead veneer: **1937**
Etched body but with no color by **1939**
Discontinued by **1942**

Style 97: brass body with nickel plating, etching of surf rider on back, airbrushed enamel coloring, 12 frets clear of body, bound ebony fingerboard, mahogany neck, slotted peghead with point at top, ebonoid peghead veneer, shield logo with 3 vertical lines
Tenor: guitar-shape body, single resonator, 4 ribs on coverplate, opaque pickguard, maple neck
Mandolin: triangular body shape, single-cone resonator, 4 ribs on coverplate
Style 97 guitar, tenor, and mandolin introduced: **1936**
Clear pickguard: **1937**
Also referred to as **Marino 97**: **1940**
Discontinued: **1940**

M-3 Hawaii: brass body with nickel plating
Introduced: **c. 1937**
Wood-grain enamel finish by **1942**
Discontinued: **1943**

Single-cone Resonator, Metalbody, 1928–43

All have coverplate with 9 diamond-shape hole clusters, unless otherwise noted. Some coverplates have 4 raised "ribs" radiating from center.

Triolian: woodbody (see Single-Cone Resonator, Woodbody, following)
Introduced: **late 1928**
Triolian metalbody: replaces woodbody, steel body, round shoulders, upper *f*-holes with straight-cut edges, maple or poplar neck, 12 frets clear of body, bound ebonized fingerboard, slotted peghead, brown "2-tone walnut" sunburst finish or yellow finish with stenciled tropical scene on back; tenor, mandolin, and uke available: **1929**
Shaded walnut, "polychrome" maple sunburst, or yellow/green finish, palm tree scene stenciled on back, many yellow/green examples with bakelite neck: **1930**
Square neck available by special order: **1933**
Rolled edges of *f*-holes: **1933**
Shorter body, square shoulders, straight-cut *f*-holes, 14 frets clear of body, 2-tone walnut sunburst finish only, by **1935**
Solid peghead: **1936**
Pickguard with diagonal stripes and letter *N*, rosewood fingerboard, ebonoid peghead veneer, painted mahogany grain finish: **1937**
Discontinued: **1940**

Duolian: steel body, round shoulders, upper *f*-holes with straight-cut edges, unbound fingerboard of ebonized maple, 12 frets clear of body, "frosted duco" paint finish with crystal-like texture, finish varies in color from light gray to greenish gray to black, some with walnut grain finish
Introduced: **1930**
Square neck available by special order: **1933**
Rolled edges on *f*-holes, mahogany neck: **1933**
Shorter body, squared shoulders, straight-cut *f*-holes, rosewood fingerboard, 14 frets clear of body, solid peghead standard (slotted still available), by **1935**
5 hole clusters in coverplate, solid peghead: **1936**
Plain black pickguard (Spanish only), "red bean" fingerboard, unspecified hardwood neck, walnut grain paint finish, by **1937**
Discontinued: **1940**

Style O: brass body with nickel plating, upper *f*-holes with straight-cut edges, Hawaiian scenes sandblasted on front and back, palm trees to right of resonator, canoe on left side of back, "etched" (actually sandblasted) sides, 12 frets clear of body, maple neck, single-bound fingerboard of ebonized maple, dot inlay, slotted peghead, decal logo

Early examples: nickel-plated steel body, front palm trees to bass side of resonator

Introduced: **July 1930**

Tenor, mandolin, and uke available by **1932**

Rolled *f*-hole edges, squareneck available: **1933**

Shorter body, 14 frets clear of body, front palm trees on both sides or resonator, canoe on right side of back, no side etching, by **Dec. 1934**

Small diamond-shaped hole patterns in coverplate: **1935**

Pickguard with flower, bound ebony fingerboard, block inlay, solid peghead with block-letter *National* etched in pearloid block, some with slotted peghead: **1936**

Clear pickguard, unspecified hardwood neck, parallelogram inlay, ebonoid peghead veneer, metal shield logo plate: **1937**

Palm trees etched on sides by **1940**

Uke discontinued by **1942**

All Style 0 models discontinued: **1943**

Style N: plain body version of Style 0, brass body with nickel plating, no etching, 12 frets clear of body, bound ebonized fingerboard, pearloid peghead veneer

Introduced: **1930**

Discontinued: **1932**

Collegian: similar to Duolian, steel body, large round holes in coverplate, clear pickguard, 14 frets clear of body, dot inlay, solid peghead, metal logo plate, maple-yellow finish, round or square neck

Introduced in Supro line: **1938**

Moved to National line, tenor and mandolin available, by **1942**

Discontinued: **1943**

"Don" Silver Guitars: brass body with nickel plating, upper *f*-holes, single-cone resonator, *Don* on bridge cover, 14 frets clear of body, bound fingerboard, slotted peghead

Don Style 1: plain body except for engraved borders, pearl dot inlay, mahogany neck, white pearlette peghead veneer

Don Style 2: "modernistic" body engraving somewhat resembling sheaves of flowers, block inlay specified but some with dot

Don Style 3: same with more elaborate engraving than Don Style 2, described as "conventional" pattern, diamond-shape inlay

Don series introduced by **1934**

Discontinued: **1936**

Single-cone Resonator, Woodbody, 1928–43

California: magnolia body, mahogany neck 14 prototypes made: **1928**

Triolian woodbody: upper *f*-holes, earliest examples with diamond-shape screen holes in coverplate and 3 resonator cones, later with 1 cone and standard single-cone coverplate (transitional examples with screenholes and single cone), 12 frets clear of body, bound ebonized fingerboard specified but most with yellow body finish on fingerboard, yellow finish with red and blue highlights, *PATAPPFOR* on body (not on plate), ocean scene decal on front, Hawaiian girl decal on back, at least one with yellow-to-brown sunburst finish and no decals, tenor available

Introduced: **late 1928**

Discontinued, replaced by Triolian metalbody (see Single-Cone Resonator, Metalbody, 1928–43, preceding): **1929**

Rosita: maple veneer body probably made by Harmony, lyre-shaped holes in upper body, trapeze tailpiece, bound top and back, 14 frets clear of body, ebonized fingerboard, dot inlay, slotted peghead, 2-tone mahogany finish, round or square neck

Introduced: **1933**

f-holes in upper body: **1937**

Discontinued: **1939**

El Trovador: body made by Kay, mahogany top, 2-piece matched mahogany back, upper *f*-holes, triple-bound top and back, trapeze tailpiece, 12 frets clear of body, bound fingerboard, dot inlay, slotted peghead, serial number beginning with *K*

Available for 8 months: **1933**

Trojan: maple veneer body, upper *f*-holes, trapeze tailpiece, bound top, 14 frets clear of body, bound fingerboard, slotted peghead, shaded walnut finish

Introduced: **1934**

Shaded walnut finish, by **1935**

Opaque pickguard: **1936**

Dobro-type tailpiece, ebonoid pickguard with stripes and letter *N* (Spanish only), bound top and back, rosewood fingerboard, solid peghead, bound ebonoid peghead veneer, by **1937**

Discontinued by **1942**

Estralita: mahogany top, 2-piece matched mahogany back, upper *f*-holes, 4-ply binding around coverplate hole, 4-ply binding on top and back, unbound fingerboard, 14 frets clear of body, varied-pattern inlay,

solid peghead, shaded brown finish, tenor, mandolin, and uke available
Introduced by **1934**
Discontinued by **1942**

Havana: spruce top, upper *f*-holes, roundneck or squareneck, bound fingerboard, dot inlay, some with 3 dots at 5th and 9th frets, ebonoid peghead veneer, natural top finish, sunburst back finish
Introduced: **1938**
Clear pickguard by **1939**
Discontinued: **1942**

Aragon de Luxe or **Aragon No. 5**: archtop, spruce top, maple back and sides, bound upper *f*-holes, radial pattern coverplate with semi-rectangular holes in groups of 3, broad plate tailpiece, clear pickguard, triple-bound top and back, bound rosewood fingerboard, double-parallelogram inlay, rosewood peghead veneer, bound peghead, chrome-plated metal parts, light brown sunburst finish, similar in appearance to a fancy Kay guitar (body and neck made by Kay)
Introduced: **1939**
Discontinued: **1943**

Single-cone Resonator, 1950s and 60s

After World War II, National/Valco announced its intent to market the following models: Collegian, Aragon, Style O, M-3, and S-3. However, there is no evidence that these or any other metalbody instruments were made after World War II. None appear on the National price list of February 1948.

No. 1133: 12" wide, Spanish style, semi-solid woodbody, single cutaway, small resonator coverplates on front and back, plastic pickguard on upper bouts, shield logo plate on upper bass bout, Dobro-type tailpiece, 22" scale, dot inlay, shield logo plate on peghead, rounded peghead corners, body covered with black, white, or maroon pearloid

Reso-phonic: white pearloid version of No. 1133 (most examples are black pearloid), model name on plastic plate (upper body)

No. 1033: Hawaiian style, non-cutaway with small upper bouts, small resonator coverplates on front and back, no pickguard on upper bouts, Dobro-type tailpiece, 22" scale, diagonal stairstep markers (like lap steels), shield logo plate on peghead, body covered with black, white, or maroon pearloid
Introduced as "Student Instruments": **1956**

Discontinued from catalogs: **1958**
Sold as late as: **1964**
Note: Some Reso-phonics were assembled from old parts for the bankruptcy auction in 1968. These have no logo plate, a squared-off peghead and a serial number on a foil sticker.

Bluegrass 35: 15" wide, molded Res-o-glas (fiberglass) body, non-cutaway, no upper soundholes, small diamond-shaped holes in coverplate, stickpin logo on upper bass bout, quarter-circle inlay, arctic white
Introduced: **1963**
Discontinued: **1965**

Folk Star: red fiberglass body, Supro logo, see Supro Guitars, Basses, and Mandolins

Airline: black fiberglass body, Airline (Montgomery Ward) model, see Airline section

Sunburst resonator model (name unknown): 15" wide, molded Res-O-Glas (fiberglass) body, 2 screen holes on upper bouts, dot or block inlay, scroll-shape peghead, tortoise grain peghead veneer, sunburst finish sprayed over red fiberglass body
Available: **1960s**

Non-resonator Models

In 1947, National announced three 17"-wide archtops, in natural or sunburst; two 16 1/4"-wide archtops; 3 sizes (unspecified) of flat tops; and 2 mandolins.
The following postwar bodies (and possibly some necks) were made by Gibson through the 1950s, except where noted. Also, some non-catalog examples exist with combinations of National and Gibson specs and ornamentation.
All of National's Spanish style guitars were fitted with the Stylist Hand-Fit neck, a heelless design not made by Gibson, beginning in 1949.

Archtops

N-275: 17" wide, sunburst or blond finish (only specs available)
Only listing: **1947**

N-150: Gibson L-7 body, 17" wide, clear pickguard, triple-bound top and back, bound fingerboard, split half-circle inlay, bound peghead, ebonoid peghead veneer, shield logo, sunburst or blond finish
Introduced: **1947**
Renamed **1135**: **1948**
Triple-bound rosewood peghead veneer: **1951**

Dark pickguard: **c. 1951**
Discontinued: **1954**

N-125: 17" wide, sunburst or blond (only specs
available)
Only listing: **1947**

N-100: Gibson L-50 body, 16 1/4" wide, clear
pickguard, metal endpin, bound top and
back, dot inlay, wide shield logo, sunburst
finish
Introduced: **1947**
Renamed **1145: 1948**
Replaced by **1140**, opaque pickguard: **1951**
Renamed **Cameo**, 15 1/2" wide: **1957**
Discontinued: **1958**

N-50: archtop, 16 1/4" wide, sunburst finish,
probably made by Kay (only specs available)
Only listing: **1947**

NA-35: archtop, 16 1/4" wide, sunburst finish,
probably made by Kay (only specs available)
Only listing: **1947**

Flat Tops

N-111: body shape like Gibson SJ-200, 17"
wide, sunburst finish
Only listing: **1947**

N-66: Gibson J-45 body, 16" wide, round-shoul-
dered dreadnought, mahogany back and
sides, triple-bound top, single-bound back,
dot inlay, wide shield logo, sunburst finish
Introduced: **1947**
Renamed **1155: 1948**
Natural finish optional by **1951**
Natural finish standard: **1954**
Factory-installed PU (No. 1155E) with poles
through fingerboard optional (see
Hollowbody Electrics section): **1954**
Discontinued: **1961**

N-33: Gibson LG-1 body, 14 1/4" wide,
mahogany back and sides, dot inlay, shield
logo plate, natural top
Introduced: **1947**
Renamed **1160: 1948**
Replaced by **1150**, rounder body shape more
like 000 Martin, body probably made by
Harmony or Kay, wide shield logo plate
1951
Discontinued: **1958**

Student Model No. 1191: non-Gibson body,
13 1/4" wide, compensating height-
adjustable bridge, Dobro-type tailpiece,
dot inlay, wide shield logo, sunburst finish
Introduced: **1952**

Listed as **Student Trial Guitar: 1954**
Discontinued: **1955**

N-700: 15 1/2" wide, square-shouldered dreadnought, maple back and sides, point on
belly of bridge, butterfly (diamond
enclosed by block) inlay, asymmetrical
peghead
N-730: 15 1/2" side, jumbo shape (rounded
bouts), maple back and sides, point on
belly of bridge, butterfly (diamond
enclosed by block) inlay, asymmetrical
peghead
N-720: 15 1/2" wide, dreadnought shape,
mahogany back and sides, fancy bridge
with whale fluke shape at each end, wide
rosette, block inlay, asymmetrical peghead
N-710: 15 1/2" wide, mahogany back and sides,
point on belly of bridge, block inlay, asymmetrical peghead
N-55: 14" wide, classical, rectangular bridge,
wide rosette, no inlay, symmetrical slotted
peghead, no peghead logo
N-580: 15 3/4" wide, 12-string, trapeze tailpiece,
block inlay, symmetrical peghead, sun-
burst finish
All introduced: **1967**
Discontinued: **1968**

Mandolins

N-51: carved top, sunburst or blond finish (only
specs available)
N-31: carved top, sunburst finish (only specs
available)
Only listing: **1947**

COMMENTS

National's resonator instruments produced
significantly more volume than conventional design acoustic guitars and were highly
popular in the late 1920s and early 1930s,
with tri-cone models appealing to
Hawaiian-style performers and the single-
cone models appealing to blues players.
Tri-cones: All of the tri-cone models are highly
sought after by collectors, with the rarer,
more ornate Styles 2, 3, and 4 bringing
more than plainer models. Roundneck tri-
cones are rarer than squarenecks and
bring much higher prices. Squareneck tri-
cone models are highly sought after by
those Hawaiian-style players who play
metalbody instruments. (Hawaiian-style
players who play woodbody guitars prefer
Dobro models.)
Single-cone metalbody models: The Style O is
the most sought after by collectors. The
Triolian and the plainer Duolian are very
highly regarded by blues players, many of
whom feel that their sound has yet to be

surpassed for Delta blues music. The Don
models are so rare that it is difficult to estimate their appeal, but they should equal or
exceed the Style O in value.

Woodbody resonator models have some
appeal to collectors but generally do not
bring as much as a Duolian in equivalent
condition, except for the early woodbody
Triolian.

Postwar resonator models, with semi-solid
wood or hollow fiberglass construction,
have some appeal to collectors and players because of their unique design and
funky sound, but they bring less than
woodbody resonator models from the prewar period.

Some of the archtop models are interesting for
historic and aesthetic reasons, but they
are not highly regarded by collectors or
players.

Flat top models with Gibson bodies have some
appeal, primarily due to their Gibson connection.

NATIONAL ELECTRIC HOLLOWBODIES KEY

Metalbody=**Silvo**
Flat top woodbody=**1155E**
Archtop
    Pointed cutaway=**Bel-Aire**
    Rounded cutaway
        Dot inlay=**Debonaire**
        Large block inlay=**Club Combo, 1959–60**
        Butterfly (diamond enlcosed by block) inlay=**Del-Mar**
    Non-cutaway
        1 PU with poles
            Block inlay
                PU in neck position=**California**
                PU near bridge=**Princess**
            Dot inlay
                No soundholes=**Chicago**
                f-holes
                    Natural finish, 16 1/4" wide=**New Yorker, 1947–58**
                    Sunburst finish, 15 1/4" wide=**Dynamic**
            Parallelogram inlay=**New Yorker Spanish, 1939–47**
        1 blade PU
            Dot inlay=**Electric Spanish, 1935–36**
            Block inlay
                No soundholes=**Electric Spanish, 1937–38**
                f-holes=**Aristocrat, c. 1941–42**
        1 standard PU and 1 bridge PU=**Aristocrat, 1942–53**
        2 standard PUs=**Sonora**
        2 floating PUs=**Club Combo, 1952–55**

NATIONAL ELECTRIC HOLLOWBODIES

All National archtop electrics have the Stylist heel-less neck by 1949.

Some models from the 1950s have bodies made by Gibson, some are by Harmony. Gibson bodies can be identified by their distinctive shape, the presence of an ink-stamped work order number inside the body, and workmanship.

SECTION ORGANIZATION

Archtops
Flat tops
Other Electric Instruments (except steel guitars)

Archtops

Electric Spanish: spruce top, maple body, 3-segment *f*-holes, blade PU in oblong housing, PU in bridge position, jack on lower bass side, trapeze tailpiece, 3-piece neck, dot inlay, 2-tone dark mahogany finish
Introduced: **1935**
No soundholes, 2 knobs to adjust PU height: **1936**
Blade PU in rectangular housing, 2 control knobs on lower treble bout, ebonoid pick-

guard with stripes and letter *N*, triple-bound top, 7-ply neck, ebony fingerboard, block inlay, *National* diagonally across peghead with 3 vertical lines: **1937**
Renamed **New Yorker Spanish**: 15 1/2" wide rectangular PU with 2 rows of 3 poles (6 separate coils), PU in neck position, ebony bridge, bound ebonoid pickguard, triple-bound top and back, 1-piece neck, bound ebony fingerboard, single-parallelogram inlay, single-bound peghead with ebonoid veneer, shield logo plate, natural or sunburst finish: **1939**
16 1/4" wide, *f*-holes, rectangular PU with 6 poles in a single line, scalloped-edge pickguard with 2 knobs, trapeze tailpiece, double-bound top and back, dot inlay, wide shield logo plate, natural finish: **1947**
Designated No. 1120: **1954**
2 knobs into top, script logo, natural finish: **1955**
Model name on pickguard: **1956**
Discontinued: **1958**

Electric Tenor: like Electric Spanish, preceding, but with dot inlay, logo straight across peghead, floral peghead ornament under logo
Introduced by **1936**
Discontinued by **1942**

Sonora: *f*-holes, blade PU in neck position,

rectangular PU in bridge position, 2 knobs, screw-on jack on lower bass side, flat plate tailpiece, clear pickguard, bound fingerboard, double-parallelogram inlay, bound peghead, enclosed tuners, sunburst finish
Introduced: **1939**
Discontinued by **1942**

Chicago: spruce top, no soundholes, rectangular PU with 2 rows of 3 poles, PU near bridge, jack on lower bass side, Dobro-type tailpiece, dark pickguard, dark binding on top and back, dot inlay, natural finish
Introduced by **1942**
Discontinued: **1943**

Princess: 15" wide, ƒ-holes, rectangular PU near bridge, 2 knobs, jack on upper bass side, trapeze tailpiece, tortoise grain pickguard, triple-bound top and back, rosewood fingerboard, block inlay, tortoise grain peghead veneer, natural finish
Introduced by **1942**
Sunburst or natural finish: **1947**
Discontinued: **1948**

Aristocrat: 17" wide, spruce top, rectangular PU near bridge, screw-on jack on lower bass side, double-bound top and back, brown pickguard, trapeze tailpiece, unbound rosewood fingerboard, large block inlay, bound peghead, natural top finish
Introduced by **1941**
Bound fingerboard, split half-circle inlay: **1942**
Large bridge/PU assembly with 2 knobs on opposite sides of bridge (1 PU only), jack into bridge, clear pickguard, triple-parallelogram inlay, logo with *National* through shield, 3 vertical lines below logo, appears in advertisement but with no model name: **early 1947**
Advertised as Aristocrat: maple top, 1 standard PU in neck position and 1 PU integrated into bridge, 1 round black knob and 1 black pointer knob on lower treble bout, knobs on square plates, screw-in jack on lower treble side, plate tailpiece with ƒ-hole cutout, clear pickguard, triple-parallelogram inlay, 3 vertical lines through peghead logo, natural or sunburst finish: **1947**
Designated No. 1111, no plates under knobs, sunburst finish only: **1948**
Body made by Kay, white knobs, dark pickguard with wavy edge extends below bridge, block inlay, stickpin figure below logo: **1951**
Discontinued: **1954**

California (No. 1100): body made by Kay, 17" wide, laminated spruce top, laminated

maple back and sides, 1 PU with 6 poles in a line, PU in neck position, controls in pickguard with screw-on jack, trapeze tailpiece, bound ƒ-holes, double-bound top and back (some triple-bound), block inlay, wide logo plate, natural finish
Introduced: **1949**
Black plastic-covered floating PU, script logo: **1953**
Discontinued: **1955**

Dynamic (No. 1125): 15 1/4" wide, metal-covered PU in neck position, straight-edge pickguard with 2 knobs, trapeze tailpiece, single-bound top and back, single-bound ƒ-holes, dot inlay, ebonoid peghead veneer, wide logo plate, sunburst finish
Introduced: **1951**
2 knobs into top, jack on side, script logo: **1955**
Model name on pickguard: **1956**
Discontinued by **1959**

Club Combo (No. 1170): 16 1/4" wide, non-cutaway, 2 plastic-covered floating PUs, 4 knobs and 1 lever switch mounted in pickguard, short trapeze bridge, bound top, large block inlay, script logo, sunburst finish
Introduced: **1952**
Discontinued: **1955**
Re-introduced (No. 1185): rounded cutaway tapered ƒ-holes with smooth lines and no curl at ends, 2 PUs mounted into top, 2 knobs on lower treble bout, 1 lever switch on cutaway bout, asymmetrical plate tailpiece, blond finish: **1959**
Discontinued: **1961**

Debonaire (No. 1107): rounded cutaway, 1 PU, 2 knobs on cutaway bout, trapeze tailpiece, bound top and back, bound ƒ-holes, dot inlay, script logo, sunburst finish
Introduced: **1953**
Discontinued: **1961**

Bel-Aire (No. 1109): Gibson ES-175 body, 16 1/4" wide, pointed cutaway, 2 PUs, 3 knobs on bass side, lever switch on cutaway bout, master tone knob and jack on lower treble bout, trapeze tailpiece, bound top and back, block inlay, script logo, sunburst finish
Introduced: **1953**
Model name on pickguard: **1956**
Renumbered 1198, 3 PUs, 4 knobs and jack on lower treble bout, 3-way slotted switch on cutaway bout, 3 knobs on upper bass bout, plate tailpiece with stairstep edges, metal tuner buttons: **1958**
Discontinued: **1961**

Del-Mar (No. 1103): 17" wide, rounded cut-

away, 2 metal-covered PUs, 2 knobs and jack on lower treble bout, 1 lever switch on cutaway bout, adjustable bridge, plate tailpiece with 2 *f*-shaped cutouts, bound top and back, butterfly (diamond enclosed by block) inlay, butterfly tuner buttons, peghead logo plate, stickpin figure below logo, sunburst finish
Introduced: **1954**
Discontinued: **1958**

Flat Tops

Silvo: nickel-plated metal body, upper *f*-holes, round ebonoid coverplate, *Silvo* on coverplate, squareneck, 23" scale, ebonoid fingerboard and peghead plate, Roman numeral parallelogram markers
Tenor and mandolin available, both with Dobro-type tailpiece, both roundneck
Note: Ebonoid coverplate and electronics were available as optional equipment or replacement part for all National singlecone resonator guitars.
Introduced by **1937**
Discontinued by **1942**

Jumbo Flat Top Electric Spanish (No. 1155E): same body as Gibson J-45, 16" wide, round-shouldered dreadnought shape, mahogany back and sides, PU poles through fingerboard, knobs mounted into side near neck, bridge tapers to small point below pins, triple-bound top, single-bound back, natural top finish
Introduced: **1954**
Discontinued: **1961**

Other Electric Instruments

Violelectric: violin, 1 knob on top
Introduced by **1936**
Discontinued by **1942**

Mandolin: A-style body shape, 1 knob mounted on top, Dobro-type tailpiece, bound fingerboard
Introduced by **1936**
Renamed **New Yorker**, rectangular PU cover, 2 knobs, shield logo, by **1938**
Discontinued: **1942**

Banjo: tenor neck, round body, spruce top, maple sides, arched back, 2 knobs, Dobrotype tailpiece, parallelogram inlay, shield logo
Introduced by **1936**
Renamed **New Yorker** by **1938**
Discontinued: **1942**

COMMENTS

In general, National electric archtops have never been highly regarded by players. Some models with innovative designs, such as archtops with no *f*-holes, are sought after by collectors for historic and aesthetic reasons.
The metalbody Silvo model is highly sought after by collectors.
Models with Gibson-made bodies have some appeal primarily due to the Gibon connection.

NATIONAL ELECTRIC SOLIDBODIES KEY

Map-shape body
    Butterfly (diamond enclosed by block) inlay (fiberglass body)
        Red finish (2 PUs)=**Glenwood 95**
        White finish (2 PUs & bridge PU)
            Black neck finish=**Glenwood 98**
            White neck finish=**Glenwood 99, 1962**
        Sea foam green (2 PUs & bridge PU)=**Glenwood 99, 1963–65**
    Block inlay (woodbody)
        1 PU (blonde or cherry finish)=**Westwood 72**
        1 PU & bridge PU (black-cherry sunburst)=**Westwood 75**
        2 PUs & bridge PU (cherry finish)=**Westwood 77**
    Quarter-circle inlay (fiberglass body)
        Rounded upper treble horn
            Red finish (1 PU)=**Val-Pro 82**
            White finish (1 PU & bridge PU)=**Val-Pro 84**
            Black finish (2 PUs & bridge PU)=**Val-Pro 88**
        Pointed upper treble horn
            Red finish (1 PU)=**Newport 82**
            Sea foam green finish (1 PU & bridge PU)=**Newport 84**
            Black finish (2 PUs & bridge PU)=**Newport 88**
Non-map body shape
    Parallelogram inlay=**Town and Country**
    Butterfly (diamond enclosed by block) inlay
        Slight cutaway on bass side=**Val-Trol Custom**
        No cutaway on bass side
            Lever tone selector switch=**Glendwood, 1954–57**
            Slotted tone selector switch=**Glenwood Deluxe**
    Block inlay
        Slight cutaway on bass side=**Val-Trol Baron**
        No cutaway on bass side
            Controls in pickguard=**No. 1124**
            Knobs into top
                2 knobs=**Avalon**
                4 knobs=**Stylist**
    Dot inlay
        Fiberglass body=**Studio 66**
        Woodbody
            Non-cutaway=**No. 1122 (Cosmopolitan)**
            Single cutaway
                PU in neck position
                    Vinyl-covered PU=**No.1123**
                      Metal-covered PU=**Bolero**
                PU in bridge position=**Westwood**
        Single cutaway, slight cutaway on bass side=**Val-Trol Jr.**

NATIONAL ELECTRIC SOLIDBODIES

SECTION ORGANIZATION

Non-map Body Shape
Map-shaped Models

Non-map Body Shape

Solid Body Electric Spanish (No. 1122): 11 1/4" wide, non-cutaway, 1 vinyl-covered floating PU in neck position, 2 knobs mounted on pickguard, adjustable rosewood bridge, short trapeze tailpiece, 24 3/4" scale, unbound fingerboard, dot inlay, symmetrical peghead, script logo, sunburst finish

Cutaway model (No. 1123): single cutaway, otherwise same as Solid Body Electric Spanish

Double PU cutaway model (No. 1124): 2 vinyl-covered floating PUs, 4 knobs and 1 lever switch mounted on pickguard, block inlay

Introduced: 1952

Non-cutaway (No.1122) renamed **Cosmopolitan: 1954**

Double PU cutaway (No. 1124) available with blond finish (No. 1124B): **1954**

Cosmopolitan (No. 1122) discontinued: **1956**

Models 1123 and 1124 discontinued, replaced by Bolero (No. 1132) and Avalon (No. 1134) (see following): **1956**

Town and Country (No. 1104): 12 1/4" wide, rounded cutaway, 2 metal-covered PUs, 6 knobs in single line on bass side, 1 lever switch on treble side, adjustable bridge, trapeze tailpiece, single-parallelogram inlay, butterfly tuner buttons, script logo, natural top finish, black sides finish, white plastic backplate
Introduced: **1954**

13 5/8" wide, pointed cutaway on treble side, shallower pointed cutaway on bass side, 3 PUs, 6 knobs on bass side, 1 knob and 3-way slotted switch on treble side, asymmetrical plate tailpiece, sunburst finish: **1958**

Discontinued by **1961**

Glenwood (No. 1105): 12 1/4" wide, rounded cutaway, white plastic backplate, 2 rectangular PUs, 6 knobs on bass side, 1 lever switch on treble side, some with *Glenwood* on pickguard, adjustable rosewood bridge, plate tailpiece with 2 *f*-shape cutouts, bound top, bound fingerboard, butterfly (diamond enclosed by block) inlay, triple-bound symmetrical peghead, metal stairstep tuner buttons, logo with *National* through shield, stickpin figure below logo, gold-plated metal parts, natural top finish, black sides finish, white plastic backplate
Introduced as No. 1105: **1954**

Small script peghead logo above shield-like ornament, butterfly tuner buttons: **1957**

Renamed **Glenwood Deluxe**, 13 5/8" wide, 6 knobs on bass side, 1 knob and 3-way slotted switch on treble side, bridge with individually adjustable saddles, Bigsby vibrato, metal tuner buttons: **1958**

Discontinued, model name continues on map-shape models (see following): **1961**

Avalon (No. 1134): 12" wide, cutaway with point not as sharp as No. 1124 (see preceding), 2 metal-covered PUs, 2 knobs on lower treble bout, 1 lever switch on cutaway bout, adjustable rosewood bridge, short trapeze tailpiece, bound fingerboard, block inlay, symmetrical rounded-top peghead (necks left over from No. 1124), butterfly tuner buttons, script logo, blond top finish, black finish on back and sides
Introduced: **1956**
Discontinued: **1958**

Bolero (No. 1132): 12" wide, cutaway with point not as sharp as No. 1124 (see preceding), 1 metal-covered PU, 2 knobs mounted on pickguard, adjustable rosewood bridge, short trapeze tailpiece, unbound fingerboard, dot inlay, symmetrical peghead, butterfly tuner buttons, script logo, sunburst top finish, black back and sides finish
Introduced: **1956**
Discontinued: **1958**

Stylist (No. 1102): 13 1/4" wide, single cutaway, 2 PUs, 4 knobs on lower treble bout, lever switch on cutaway bout, asymmetrical plate tailpiece, large block inlay, asymmetrical peghead longer on treble side, black finish
Introduced: **1958**
Discontinued: **1961**

Val-Trol Junior (No. 1122): 13 5/8" wide, rounded cutaway on treble side, shallower cutaway on bass side, beveled-edge wood body, 1 standard PU and 1 bridge PU, 3 knobs on bass side, 1 knob and 3-way slotted switch on treble side, plate tailpiece, 22" scale, dot inlay, butterfly tuner buttons, ivory finish
Introduced: **1958**
Discontinued: **1961**

Westwood (No. 1101): 12" wide, single cutaway, 1 PU in bridge position, 2 knobs, Dobro-type tailpiece, 22" scale, dot inlay, rectangular peghead shape, gold-to-black sunburst finish
Introduced: **1958**
Discontinued, model name continues on map-shape models (see following): **1961**

Val-Trol Custom (No. 1199): 13 3/4" wide, pointed cutaway on treble side, shallower pointed cutaway on bass side, 2 standard PUs and 1 bridge PU, 6 knobs in pairs on bass side (1 pair below bridge), 1 knob and 3-way slotted switch on treble side, model name on pickguard, plate tailpiece with stairstep edges, bound fingerboard, butterfly (diamond enclosed by block) inlay, gold-plated metal parts, black finish
Introduced: **1959**
Discontinued: **1961**

Val-Trol Baron (No. 1106): 13 1/2" wide, cutaway on treble side with rounded horn, shallow pointed cutaway on bass side, 2 standard PUs and 1 bridge PU, 6 knobs in pairs on bass side (1 pair below bridge), 1 knob and 3-way slotted switch on treble side, asymmetrical plate tailpiece, bound fingerboard, large block inlay, black finish
Introduced: **1959**
Discontinued: **1961**

Studio 66: molded Res-o-glas (fiberglass)

body, single cutaway, 1 PU in bridge position, PU covered by black plastic, 2 knobs, trapeze tailpiece, dot inlay, desert buff (beige) finish

Introduced: **1961**

Smaller body, slight cutaway on bass side, metal-covered PU near neck, black finish: **1963**

Listed as **Varsity 66**: **1964**

Discontinued: **1965**

Map-shaped Models

All have molded Res-o-glas (fiberglass) body, except for woodbody Glenwood series. Body is shaped roughly like a map of the U.S. with upper treble bout corresponding to Florida. All have asymmetrical peghead longer on treble side. Any color within a model group was offered in catalog as optional on all models within that group, but few if any variations from standard colors exist. Standard National vibrato has rectangular coverplate and thin tubular arm. Top-mounted Bigsby vibrato is optional. A few examples have Burns vibrato.

Map-shape models appeared in a late 1961 catalog, but no instruments were sold until 1962.

Glenwood 99: pointed treble horn, 2 standard PUs and 1 bridge PU, 3 knobs and 3-way slotted switch on bass side, 3 knobs on treble side, plate tailpiece with stairstep sides, butterfly (diamond enclosed by block) inlay, peghead veneer edges beveled to show wide black line, white finish on back of neck, snow white body finish

Introduced: **1962**

Bigsby, gold-plated metal parts, sea foam green finish: **1963**

Master volume knob added near jack: **1964**

Discontinued: **1965**

Glenwood 95: pointed treble horn, 2 standard PUs, 3 knobs and 3-way slotted switch on bass side, 3 knobs on treble side, plate tailpiece with stairstep sides, butterfly (diamond enclosed by block) inlay, vermilion red finish

Introduced: **1962**

Discontinued: **1965**

Glenwood 98: pointed treble horn, 2 standard PUs and 1 bridge PU, 3 knobs and 3-way slotted switch on bass side, 3 knobs on treble side, Bigsby vibrato, butterfly (diamond enclosed by block) inlay, peghead veneer edges beveled to show white-black-white lines, chrome-plated metal parts, black finish on back of neck, pearl white body finish

Introduced: **1962**

Master volume knob added near jack: **1964**

Discontinued: **1965**

Val-Pro 88: rounded treble horn, 2 standard PUs, 1 bridge PU, 6 knobs and 3-way slotted switch on treble side, quarter-circle inlay, raven black finish

Introduced: **1962**

Renamed **Newport 88**: pointed treble horn, 6 knobs on bass side in groups of 2, vibrato: **1963**

Discontinued (see note after Newport 82): **1965**

Val-Pro 84: rounded upper treble horn, 1 standard PU, 1 bridge PU, 3 knobs and 3-way slotted switch on treble side, quarter-circle inlay, arctic white finish

Introduced: **1962**

Renamed **Newport 84**: pointed treble horn, vibrato, sea foam green finish: **1963**

Discontinued (see note after Newport 82): **1965**

Val-Pro 82: rounded treble horn, 1 PU, 3 knobs and 3-way slotted switch on treble side, quarter-circle inlay, scarlet finish

Introduced: **1962**

Renamed **Newport 82**: pointed treble horn, knobs and switch on bass side, vibrato, pepper red finish: **1963**

Discontinued: **1965**

Note: Some Newport models were assembled from leftover parts (some with Italian hardware) for bankruptcy auction in 1968.

Westwood 77: solid hardwood body heavily routed from back, rounded treble horn, 2 standard PUs and 1 bridge PU, 6 knobs on bass side, 3-way slotted switch and 1 knob on treble side, clear Lucite bridge base, bound fingerboard, block inlay, cherry finish

Westwood 75: 1 standard PU and 1 bridge PU, 3 knobs on bass side, 3-way slotted switch on treble side, block inlay, cherry-to-black sunburst finish

Westwood 72: 1 PU, 3 knobs on treble side, 3-way slotted switch on bass side, block inlay, blond-ivory finish

Westwood series introduced: **1962**

Cherry finish on Westwood 72: **1963**

Discontinued: **1965**

Note: Some Westwood models were assembled from leftover parts (some with Italian hardware) for bankruptcy auction in 1968.

COMMENTS

National electric solidbodies are not highly regarded by players. Some models, especially the map-shaped lines, are sought by collectors for their unique aesthetic appeal.

NATIONAL BASSES KEY

Solidbody
    Map-shaped body
        Rounded upper treble bout=**Val-Pro Bass 85**
        Pointed upper treble bout=**National 85 Bass**
        Symmetrical double cutaway=**National Electric Bass**
Semi-hollowbody=**N-850**

NATIONAL BASSES

Val-Pro 85: molded Res-o-glas (fiberglass) body shaped like map of United States (upper treble bout corresponds to Florida), rounded treble horn, 1 standard PU and 1 bridge PU, 2 knobs, 24 3/4" scale, quarter-circle inlay, snow white finish
Introduced: 1961
Renamed **National 85**: pointed treble horn, ermine white finish: **1963**
Discontinued: **1965**

National Electric Bass: woodbody, double-cutaway, 1 standard PU and 1 bridge PU, 2 knobs, trapeze tailpiece, 2 fin-shaped elevated finger rests, 24 3/4" scale, dot inlay, white plastic peghead veneer, sunburst finish
Introduced: **early 1960s**
Discontinued: **1965**

N-850: semi-hollowbody, double-cutaway, rounded cutaways, modernistic sound-holes, 2 PUs, block inlay, 3-tone sunburst finish
Introduced: **1967**
Discontinued: **1968**

COMMENTS

National basses are not highly regarded by players or collectors. Map-shaped models have some aesthetic appeal.

NATIONAL STEELS

Electric Hawaiian (no other model name): cast aluminum body, round body shape 10 5/8" in diameter, 7 decorative recessed "panels" on top, *National* on body near neck, blade PU, 1 knob and jack on bass side of body near neck, metal bridge cover, square neck, rosewood fingerboard, 20 frets, dot inlay, cutout in center of peghead, clear lacquer finish, 7-string optional
Introduced: **1935**
1 knob and jack in lower top panel on treble side: **late 1935**
Height-adjustable PU, 2 knurled adjustment knobs in top, 2 control knobs, control knobs and adjustment knobs in middle panels, jack recessed in side: **early 1936**
Control knobs in lower panel: **1936**
Optional 26-fret fingerboard extends over *National* on body: **1936**
Discontinued: **1937**

New Yorker: square-end body, stairstep body sides; "sextet" PU arrangement: large PU/bridge combination, bar PU with notch at 3rd string, 2 additional PUs beneath fingerboard extending to 12th fret; 2 control knobs on treble side labeled *Full Treble* and *Master Control*, 2 knobs on bass side labeled *Natural Haw.* and *Full Bass*, screw-on jack on bass side even with 17th fret marker, chrome PU cover attached by 4 screws, 23" scale (25" by special order), ebonoid fingerboard, *Electric* etched into fingerboard between bridge and fret markers, white parallelogram markers with Roman numerals (some without numerals), shield logo etched on ebonoid peghead veneer, metal tuner buttons, white-black-white stairstep finish, 7 or 8 strings available
Introduced as Electric Hawaiian Model (no other name): **1935**
Visible PU with split bar, 2 concealed PUs, white pointer knob on tone control (actually a PU seclector switch) below bridge, *Hawaiian-chimes-harp* tone settings, black volume knob on treble side, no *Electric* on fingerboard: **early 1937**
Some without Roman numerals in markers: **c. 1938**
Named New Yorker, by **1939**
Rectangular PU with poles in straight line, no concealed PUs, tone control potentiometer (not PU selector switch), black-painted wooden handrest/PU cover attached by 2 knurled nuts, metal fingerboard, multi-colored Roman numeral markers, by **1942**
Clear plastic bridge cover, metal logo plate, plastic tuner buttons: **1946**
Lucite fingerboard with back-painted Roman numerals: **1948**
Large square PU, 3-way tone switch with *bass-mellow-brilliant* settings, *New Yorker* below tone switch: **1949**
Rectangular PU: **1951**
Rounded stairstep corners on body, model name and art deco design on PU cover, totem pole markers, stickpin peghead logo, angled (non-stairstep) peghead corners: **1956**
Discontinued: **1967**

Professional Hawaiian: maple body, stairstep body design like New Yorker (preceding), 4 knobs (2 on each side), *The New Yorker* and shield logo on body under strings, parallelogram markers with Roman numerals, *National* diagonally across peghead with 3 vertical lines, natural finish
Introduced: **1936**
Discontinued: **1940**

Silvo: nickel-plated metal guitar body, flat top, upper *f*-holes, round ebonoid coverplate with rectangular PU, *Silvo* on coverplate, square metal neck, 23" scale, ebonoid fingerboard and peghead veneer, Roman numeral parallelogram markers
Introduced by **1937**
Discontinued: **1942**

Console: 2 8-string necks, *Console* on side, 2 white pointer knobs, 2 black round knobs at bridge end, black handrest extends across both necks, pegheads at different angles, ebonoid fingerboard, open parallelogram markers (some with Roman numerals), shield logo between necks near peghead, black top, white sides, 12 to 20 strings optional
Introduced by **1939**
Discontinued by **1942**

Woodbody (model name unknown): symmetrical woodbody, points near neck, rounded bottom end, strings pass through PU, knobs on square plates with radial markings, rosewood fingerboard, inlaid celluloid frets flush with fingerboard, inlaid dot markers, shield logo plate, mahogany stain finish
Introduced: **early 1940s**
Discontinued by **1947**

Dynamic: stairstep body design like New Yorker, knobs on opposite sides mounted on arrow-shaped plates, 23" scale, Roman numeral markers, rounded peghead, white ebonoid top plates, black sides and back, 8 strings optional
Introduced by **1942**
Non-stairstep body side extensions, pointed

control plates, clear plastic PU cover, black-and-white stairstep markers in octave patterns with multi-colored geometric figures: **1947**

Side pieces beveled in toward body, black PU cover, white plastic body covering (some with olive and white), black control plates, by **1951**

Stickpin logo, knobs on same side, body insets for 3 screw-in legs, wine red and white finish, by **1956**

Discontinued: **1964**

Re-introduced, script logo reads upside down to player: **1967**

Discontinued: **1968**

Chicago: square-end body, scooped graduation to neck, strings pass through PU, knobs on opposite sides, knobs mounted on square plates with radial markings, 23" scale, parallelogram outline markers, "iridescent" black pearlette covering

Introduced by **1942**

Large square PU, no control knob plates, stairstep marker pattern with numbers: **c. 1945**

Discontinued: **1948**

Princess: 1-piece stairstep body, strings pass through PU, 1 round knob on treble side, 1 pointer knob below bridge, knobs mounted on square plates with radial design, parallelogram outline markers, white pearlette covering

Introduced by **1942**

Discontinued: **1948**

Waikiki: slightly rounded end, rounded graduation to neck, strings pass through PU, large square control plate with knobs on opposite sides, 23" scale, light colored fingerboard, Roman numeral markers, "blonde walnut" finish

Introduced: **1942**

Discontinued: **1948**

Grand Console: 2 8-string necks, staggered tiers, pegheads at same angle, large square PUs, clear plastic PU covers, logo between necks in center, controls (1 pointer knob, 1 round knob, 1 selector switch) between necks, totem pole markers, wood peghead covers, cream and copper/brown finish

Introduced: **1947**

Non-staggered tiers optional: **1949**

Cream colored plastic PU covers: **1950**

4 legs optional: **1954**

Listed as **Console**: 2 round knobs and 1 selector switch between necks, 1 knob at each bridge, gold-colored control plate and markers, black and white finish, by **1961**

Discontinued: **1967**

Electra-Chord: rectangular body, single center-support stand with 2 pedals; changers, tuners, and PU at same end; clear plastic changer cover, totem pole markers, 6 strings

Introduced: **1948**

Discontinued: **1949**

Special: 8 strings, symmetrical body with side extensions (like Dynamic), large square PU, 1 pointer knob and 1 round knob mounted on pointed plates, clear plastic PU cover, shield logo plate on body extension below string anchors, 23" scale, Lucite fingerboard with back-painted Roman numeral markers, wooden peghead cover, black and white finish

Introduced: **1948**

Replaced by **Console 8**: stairstep extensions on treble side only, totem pole markers, stickpin logo, 3 legs: **1958**

Discontinued: **1961**

Trailblazer: square end with rounded corners, slight body waists, sharp points at neck, metal handrest, 1 pointer knob, 1 round knob, knobs on opposite sides, 23" scale, numbered markers enclosed in hexagonal figures, model name on peghead, black lacquer finish

Introduced: **1948**

Discontinued: **1950**

Chicagoan: metal handrest, 1 pointer knob, 1 round knob, 23" scale, numbered musical-note markers, oyster (gray) pearloid covering

Introduced: **1948**

Discontinued: **1961**

Triplex Chord Changer: asymmetrical stairstep body of maple and walnut, lever-controlled tuning changer, 2 round white knobs, white plastic PU cover, Lucite fingerboard back-painted white, totem pole markers, rounded top peghead, wide shield logo plate, natural finish

Introduced: **1948**

Variation: fingerboard back-painted brown, geometric markers, standard shield logo: **c. 1955 only**

Script logo, shield with V-like sides below logo: **1956**

Discontinued: **1958**

Clipper: elongated guitar-shaped body, white plastic PU cover, 2 knobs, jack into top, bound top and back, black-and-white stairstep markers in octave patterns, peghead wider at top than at nut, shield logo plate, sunburst finish

Introduced: **1952**
Discontinued: **1956**

Triple-neck Hawaiian: 3 8-string necks, staggered tiers, individual PU covers, 2 knobs, 1 selector switch, peghead covers, 4 legs, black and white finish
Introduced: **1953**
Discontinued: **1961**

Rocket One Ten: rocket fin-shaped body side extensions, model name on bridge cover, white body finish, red or black control plates
Introduced by **1956**
Discontinued: **1958**

Studio 76: rounded bottom end, rounded shoulders, 2 knobs on opposite sides, stairstep pattern markers (or black-white diagonally split rectangular markers), stickpin logo, onyx black pearloid finish
Introduced: **1963**
Discontinued: **1964**

Console 16: 2 8-string necks joined by large tubes, large handrest extends over both necks, 1 knob on each neck, 1 switch on handrest, geometric markers, 4 legs
Introduced as a Supro model: **1958**
Discontinued: **1961**
Re-introduced in National line: **1967**
Discontinued: **1968**

COMMENTS

National steels are good utility instruments. However, most players prefer Gibsons, Fenders, or Rickenbackers.
Early aluminum body National (and Supro and Dobro) lap steels are of interest to collectors for historical reasons. Some later high-end models have a strong aesthetic appeal and make excellent wall-hangers.

SUPRO ELECTRIC HOLLOWBODIES KEY

Non-cutaway
  1 PU on square control plate (flat top guitar)=**Rio**
  1 PU in bridge position=**Electric Spanish, Avalon Spanish**
  1 PU in middle position=**El Capitan, 1942–53**
  1 PU in neck position
      Bound fingerboard=**El Capitan, 1953–55**
      Unbound fingerboard=**Ranchero**
  2 PUs=**Del-Mar**
Single cutaway
  1 PU=**Westwood**
  2 PUs
      White finish=**Sierra**
      Natural top, black back and sides=**Coronado, 1960–62**
      2 standard PUs and 1 bridge PU=**Coronado, 1958–60**
Double cutaway
  2 PUs
      No vibrato=**Croydon**
      Vibrato
          Dot inlay=**Clermont**
          Block inlay=**Carlisle**
  3 PUs=**Stratford**

SUPRO SOLIDBODIES KEY

1 floating vinyl-covered PU
    Non-cutaway=**Ozark, 1952–55**
    Cutaway
        White finish=**Ozark Cutaway**
        Black finish=**Ozark Jet**
1 PU with strings-through-PU design
    Ozark on body or pickguard=**Ozark 1958–61**
    60 or no name on body=**Sixty**
1 metal-covered PU (strings pass over PU)
    Single cutaway, no cutaway on bass side
        White finish=**Super, 1958 or 1962**
        Red finish=**Belmont, 1955–61**
        Gold finish=**Special**
        White-to-black sunburst finish=**Super, 1959–61**
    Single cutaway with slight cutaway on bass side
        Fire bronze finish=**Ozark, 1962**
        Red finish=**Belmont 1962–63**
        Sand buff (beige) finish
            Stairstep tailpiece=**Sahara, 1960–62**
            Dobro-type tailpiece=**Kingston**
        Blue finish=**Sahara, 1963–64**
        White finish=**Holiday**
    Asymmetrical double cutaway (similar to Fender Jazzmaster)
        Vibrato=**Lexington S625**
        No vibrato
            3-tone sunburst finish=**Shaded Guitar S525**
            Cherry-to-black sunburst finish=**Normandy S601**
            Cherry finish
                24 3/4" scale=**Normandy S611**
                22" scale=**Colt**
    Full double cutaways
        24 3/4" (standard) scale
            No vibrato=**Ozark, 1963–65**
            Vibrato=**Supersonic (Suprosonic)**
        22" scale=**Super Seven**

1 standard PU and 1 bridge PU=**Rhythm Tone**
2 standard PUs
   White finish=**Dual-Tone**
   Natural finish wood top=**Coronado, 1961**
   Black finish=**Coronado II, 1962–65**
   Red finish
      Slight cutaway on bass side=**Bermuda**
      Double cutaway, similar to Fender Jazzmaster
         No vibrato=**Normandy S612**
         Vibrato=**Normandy S613**
   Blue finish=**Tremo-Lectric**
   Ivory-to-black sunburst finish=**Super Twin**
   Sunburst finish
      Single cutaway: **Super Twin**
      Asymmetrical double cutaway
         Tortoise grain pickguard
            No vibrato=**12-string**
            Large rectangular vibrato base=**Lexington S635**
            Burns vibrato (small pyramid on base)=**Shaded Guitar S535**
         White pickguard=**Normandy S602**
2 standard PUs and 1 bridge PU
   No cutaway on bass side=**Silverwood**
   Slight cutaway on bass side
      Sunburst finish=**Rhythm Master**
      White finish=**Martinique**
   Asymmetrical double cutaway, similar to Fender Jazzmaster
      Butterfly (diamond enclosed by block) inlay
         Sunburst finish=**Arlington S665**
         White finish=**Arlington S655**
      Dot inlay=**Fiberglass Guitar S555**
3 PUs
   Single cutaway=**Triple-Tone**
   Asymmetrical double cutaway, similar to Fender Jazzmaster
      Large rectangular vibrato base=**Lexington S645**
      Burns vibrato (small pyramid on base)=**Shaded Guitar S545**

SUPRO GUITARS, BASSES, AND MANDOLINS

SECTION ORGANIZATION

Acoustic Archtop Models
Acoustic Flat Top Models
Electric Flat Top
Resonator Models
Electric Archtop Models
Thinline Models
Electric Solidbodies
Electric Basses
Acoustic Mandolins
Electric Mandolins

Acoustic Archtop Models

S6835: 15 1/2" wide, laminated maple body, bound top and back, dot inlay, symmetrical peghead, cherry sunburst finish
S6840: 15 1/2" wide, laminated maple body, bound top and back, dot inlay, symmetrical peghead, golden sunburst finish
S8900: 17 1/4" wide, laminated maple body, bound top and back, dot inlay, symmetrical peghead, golden sunburst finish
Only catalog appearance: **1968**

Acoustic Flat Top Models

S700: 15 1/2" wide, dreadnought shape, mahogany back and sides, large bridge with 3 points at each end, 4-point pickguard, wide rosette, wide top and back binding, bound fingerboard, block inlay, asymmetrical peghead longer on bass side
S710: 15 1/2" wide, rounded bouts (similar to Gibson J-185 or Everly Brothers), rectangular bridge, 2 points on pickguard, tortoise grain binding, bound fingerboard, block inlay, asymmetrical peghead longer on bass side
S720: 14" wide, classical, rectangular bridge with string-loop anchoring, wide rosette, unbound rosewood fingerboard, slotted peghead, no logo

283

Supro Guitars, Basses, and Mandolins

All introduced by **1967**
All discontinued: **1968**

S6109: 15 3/4" wide, dreadnought shape, laminated mahogany back and sides, rectangular bridge, double-bound top, single-
bound back, dot inlay, symmetrical peghead

S6102: 15 3/4" wide, dreadnought shape,
mahogany back and sides, rectangular
bridge, double-bound top, single-bound
back, wide rosette, bound fingerboard, dot
inlay, symmetrical peghead

S7008: 14 1/4" wide, classical, laminated
mahogany back and sides, bound top and
back, slotted peghead

S7005: 14 1/4" wide, classical, mahogany back
and sides, bound top and back, wide
rosette, slotted peghead

S5113: 15" wide, rounded lower bout, laminated
mahogany back and sides, rectangular
bridge, tortoise grain binding on top and
back, no rosette, dot inlay, symmetrical
peghead

S6160: 15 3/4" wide, rounded lower bout, laminated mahogany back and sides, triple-
bound top, single-bound back, wide
rosette, rectangular bridge, dot inlay, symmetrical peghead

S6170: 15 3/4" wide, rounded lower bout, laminated mahogany back and sides, bridge
with small point on belly, triple-bound top,
single-bound back, wide rosette, bound
fingerboard, block inlay, symmetrical peghead

S7900: 12-string, 15 3/4" wide, laminated
mahogany back and sides, bridge with 3
points on belly, wide rosette, triple-bound
top, single-bound back, dot inlay, symmetrical peghead

Only catalog appearance: **1968**

Electric Flat Top

Rio: 13" wide, electronics and bridge mounted
on square plate (same plate used on lap
steels), strings pass through PU, 2 knobs
on opposite sides, 12 frets clear of body,
dot inlay, slotted peghead, natural finish
Introduced by **1942**
Discontinued: **1943**

Resonator Models

Collegian: metal body similar to National
Duolian, large round holes in coverplate,
clear pickguard, maple-yellow finish,
roundneck or squareneck
Tenor, mandolin, and uke available
Introduced: **1938**
Moved to National line, no uke available: **1942**

Arcadia: 3-ply birch body, 14 1/4" wide, *f*-
holes, large round holes in coverplate,
black-and-silver painted top edges to simulate binding, 12 frets clear of body, dot
inlay, solid peghead, metal logo plate, sunburst finish
Introduced by **1939**
Discontinued: **1942**

Folk Star: molded Res-o-glas (fiberglass) body,
standard National single-cone resonator
and coverplate, screen holes in upper
body, stairstep tailpiece, dot inlay (some
with block), "gay festival red" finish
Introduced by **1964**
Renamed **Vagabond**: **1967**
Discontinued (some assembled with parts left
over from National Bluegrass 35 and
Airline resonator models, sold at bankruptcy auction): **1968**

Electric Archtop Models

Supro Electric Spanish: 14 3/4" wide, no
soundholes, bar PU with oblong housing
mounted near bridge, ebonoid pickguard,
trapeze tailpiece, 3-piece neck, rosewood
fingerboard, dot inlay, block letter logo
stenciled across top of peghead
Introduced: **1936**
Rectangular PU housing, Dobro-type tailpiece:
1938
Renamed **Avalon Spanish**, by **1939**
Discontinued: **1942**

El Capitan: 15 3/4" wide, spruce top, maple
back and sides, 3-segment *f*-holes, 1 rectangular PU in middle position, 2 knobs,
Dobro-type tailpiece, adjustable bridge,
ebonized fingerboard, black body binding,
pearl dot inlay, natural finish
Introduced by **1942**
15 1/2" wide, trapeze tailpiece, clear pickguard,
single-bound top and back, single-bound
f-holes, single-bound rosewood fingerboard, dot inlay, point at top of peghead,
metal logo plate, sunburst finish: **1948**
Standard *f*-holes, floating vinyl-covered PU in
neck position, knobs mounted on pickguard: **1953**
Discontinued: **1955**

Ranchero: 15 1/2" wide, unspecified hardwood
construction, 3-segment *f*-holes, 1 PU in
neck position, 2 knobs, Dobro-type tailpiece, black pickguard, bound top and
back, dot inlay, rounded-peak peghead,
metal logo plate, sunburst finish
Introduced: **1948**
Standard *f*-holes, floating vinyl-covered PU in
neck position, knobs mounted into white
plastic pickguard, point at top of peghead,

natural finish: **1953**

Metal-covered PU in neck position, controls into top, model name on black pickguard, 3-point pickguard shape, trapeze tailpiece, enclosed tuners, asymmetrical peghead longer on bass side, black peghead veneer, butterfly tuner buttons: **1955**

White 3-point pickguard follows contour of body, sunburst finish: **1958**

Discontinued: **1960**

Sierra: 15 3/8" wide, rounded cutaway, 2 PUs, 2 knobs, lever switch on cutaway bout, stairstep tailpiece, wing-shape pickguard with straight edge on treble side, black binding, block inlay, butterfly tuner buttons, enclosed tuners, asymmetrical peghead longer on bass side, arctic white finish

Introduced: **1955**

Discontinued: **1958**

Westwood: 15 3/8" wide, rounded cutaway, 1 PU in neck position, 2 knobs, bound top and back, bound f-holes, stairstep tailpiece, wing-shaped pickguard with straight edge on treble side, rosewood fingerboard, dot inlay, butterfly tuner buttons, enclosed tuners, asymmetrical peghead longer on bass side, sunburst finish

Introduced: **1955**

Discontinued: **1959**

Coronado: 16" wide, 2 3/4" deep, rounded cutaway, 2 standard PUs and 1 bridge PU, 1 knob near bridge, 3-way slotted switch on cutaway bout, stairstep tailpiece, small beveled-edge pickguard, multiple-bound top and back, large block inlay, asymmetrical peghead longer on bass side, black finish

Introduced: **1958**

15 1/2 wide, 2" deep, deeper cutaway, no bridge PU, 4 knobs, 3-way slotted switch on cutaway bout, natural top finish, black finish on neck, back and sides: **1960**

Discontinued: **1962**

Del-Mar: 15 7/8" wide, non-cutaway, maple back and sides, tapered f-holes with smooth lines and no curl at ends, 2 PUs, 2 knobs on lower treble bout, 3-way slotted switch on upper treble bout, stairstep tailpiece, triple-bound top and back, block inlay, natural finish

Introduced in Supro line (moved from National line): **1959**

Discontinued: **1960**

Thinlines

Stratford: double cutaway, 3 PUs, 6 knobs, 3 rocker switches, vibrato, block inlay, 6-on-

a-side tuner arrangement, sunburst finish

Carlisle: double cutaway, 2 PUs, 4 knobs, 1 toggle switch, vibrato, block inlay, 6-on-a-side tuner arrangement, cherry finish

Clermont: double cutaway, 2 PUs, 4 knobs, 1 toggle switch, vibrato, dot inlay, 6-on-a-side tuner arrangement, cherry finish

Croydon: double cutaway, 2 PUs, 4 knobs, 1 toggle switch, no vibrato, dot inlay, 6-on-a-side tuner arrangement, cherry finish

All introduced: **1967**

Symmetrical peghead, 3-on-a-side tuner arrangement: **1968**

Discontinued: **1968**

Solidbody Models

Ozark: 11 1/4" wide, non-cutaway, floating vinyl-covered PU, 2 knobs mounted into pickguard, rosewood bridge, short trapeze tailpiece, dot inlay, metal logo plate, point at top of peghead (some with plastic logo and rounded-top peghead), white pearloid body covering

Introduced: **1952**

Ozark Cutaway: single cutaway, introduced: 1953

Ozark and Ozark Cutaway discontinued: **1955**

Ozark model name re-introduced on Sixty model (see following), 12" wide, single cutaway, strings pass through PU, PU and controls mounted on plate with rounded corners, model name on body below PU, dot inlay, narrow asymmetrical peghead longer on bass side, butterfly tuner buttons, arctic white finish: **1958**

Model name on pickguard, gold-to-black sunburst finish: **1959**

13 1/3" wide: **1960**

Single cutaway with slight cutaway on bass side, 1 PU in middle position, strings pass over PU, Dobro-type tailpiece, fire bronze finish: **1962**

Double cutaway, beveled body edges, 1 PU, stud tailpiece with metal cover, dot inlay, narrow asymmetrical peghead longer on bass side, poppy red finish: **1963**

Discontinued: **1967**

Ozark Jet: 11 1/4" wide, single cutaway, 1 floating PU with light-colored vinyl covering, 2 knobs mounted into white plastic pickguard, rosewood bridge, short trapeze tailpiece, bound fingerboard, dot inlay, plastic logo, symmetrical peghead, black finish

Introduced: **1952**

Discontinued: **1955**

Dual-Tone: 11 1/4" wide, single cutaway, 2 PUs, 4 knobs in straight line, lever switch on cutaway bout, dark wing-shape pickguard surrounds rhythm PU, elevated fin-

shape finger rest on treble side, rosewood bridge, short trapeze tailpiece, dot inlay, symmetrical peghead, white plastic body covering
Introduced: **1954**
12" wide, reverse stairstep tailpiece with highest step on bass side, model name on black pickguard, large block inlay, butterfly tuner buttons, asymmetrical peghead longer on treble side, black peghead veneer, metal logo plate, arctic white plastic covering: **1955**
13" wide, 3-way slotted switch near neck PU: **1958**
13 1/2" wide: **1960**
Fiberglass body, slight cutaway on bass side, beveled body edges, 1 knob and 3-way slotted switch on treble side, 4 knobs in groups of 2 on bass side, standard stairstep tailpiece, no model name on pickguard, plastic logo, wider peghead with point more toward center: **1962**
Discontinued: **1966**

Belmont: 12" wide, single cutaway, 1 PU in neck position, 2 knobs on treble side mounted into pickguard, elevated fin-shape finger rest on treble side, reverse stairstep tailpiece with highest step on bass side, model name on white pickguard, dot inlay, butterfly tuner buttons, asymmetrical peghead longer on treble side, black peghead plate, gold-plated metal parts, sherry maroon (red) plastic covering
Introduced: **1955**
Beveled top edges, PU near bridge, Dobro-type tailpiece, no elevated finger rest: **1958**
13 1/2" wide: **1960**
Fiberglass body, single cutaway, slight cutaway on bass side, 1 PU in bidge position, 2 knobs, 1 slide switch, Dobro-type tailpiece, optional vibrato with rectangular coverplate and tubular arm, plastic logo, wider peghead with point more toward center, white peghead veneer, cherry red finish: **1962**
Teardrop pickguard: **1963**
Discontinued: **1964**

Sixty: 12 1/4" wide, single cutaway, PU and controls on plate with rounded corners, strings pass through PU, 2 knobs on opposite sides, jack in control plate, black pickguard, dot inlay, asymmetrical peghead longer on bass side, white plastic covering
Introduced by **1955**
Large *60* on lower treble bout, pin-striping on finish: **1957**
Sixty model name discontinued, model continues as Ozark (see preceding): **1958**

Rhythm Tone: 13" wide, single cutaway,

beveled top edges, 1 standard PU and 1 bridge PU, 3 knobs in straight line, 3-way slotted switch on cutaway bout, reverse stairstep tailpiece on bass side, elevated fin-shape finger rest on treble side, dot inlay, asymmetrical peghead longer on bass side, black finish
Introduced: **1958**
Discontinued: **1959**

Rhythm Master: 13 1/2" wide, single cutaway with slight cutaway on bass side, beveled top edges, 2 standard PUs and 1 bridge PU, 1 knob 3-way slotted switch, reverse stairstep tailpiece with highest step on bass side, rosewood fingerboard, block inlay, asymmetrical peghead longer on bass side, butterfly tuner buttons, sunburst finish
Introduced: **1958**
Discontinued: **1960**

Special: 12" wide, single cutaway, 1 PU near neck, 2 knobs, 1 switch, Dobro-type tailpiece, 22" scale, dot inlay, gold finish
Introduced: **1958**
Discontinued: **1960**

Super: 12" wide, single cutaway, 1 PU near bridge, 2 knobs, 1 switch, Dobro-type tailpiece, 22" scale, dot inlay, symmetrical peghead with rounded top edge, metal logo plate, fawn ivory finish
Introduced: **1958**
Rectangular peghead, plastic logo, ivory-to-black sunburst finish: **1960**
Super Twin: 2 PUs, available: **1959-60**
2 knobs, no switch, *Supro* on pickguard, white finish: **1962**
Discontinued: **1964**

Triple-Tone: 13" wide, single cutaway, beveled top edges, 3 PUs, 4 knobs, 3-way slotted switch, reverse stairstep tailpiece with highest step on bass side, elevated fin-shaped finger rest on treble side, block inlay, black finish
Introduced: **1959**
Discontinued: **1960**

Silverwood: 13 1/2" wide, single cutaway, 2 standard PUs and 1 bridge PU, 6 small knobs in pairs on bass side, 1 knob and 3-way slotted switch on treble side, beveled-edge pickguard with *Val Trol*, bound fingerboard, large block inlay, asymmetrical peghead longer on bass side, white peghead veneer, plastic logo, butterfly tuner buttons, blond finish
Introduced: **1960**
Discontinued: **1962**

Supro Guitars, Basses, and Mandolins

Sahara: 13 1/2" wide, single cutaway with slight cutaway on bass side, 1 PU, 3 knobs on treble side, 1 knob and 3-way slotted switch on bass side, reverse stairstep tailpiece with highest step on bass side, dot inlay, asymmetrical peghead longer on bass side, plastic logo, sand buff (beige) finish
Introduced: **1960**
13 3/4" wide, fiberglass body, beveled edges, 2 knobs, Dobro-type tailpiece, model name and palm tree on pickguard, Wedgewood blue finish: **1963**
Renamed **Sahara 70**: **1964**
Discontinued: **1967**

Coronado solidbody: 15 1/2" wide, 2" deep, arched top, single rounded cutaway, spruce top, 2 PUs, 4 knobs on lower treble bout, 3-way slotted switch on cutaway bout, stairstep tailpiece, double-bound top and back, bound fingerboard, block inlay, plastic logo, natural top finish, black finish on back and sides
Introduced: **1961**
Renamed **Coronado II**: fiberglass body, beveled edges, single cutaway, slight cutaway on bass side, 3-way slotted switch on upper bass bout, vibrato, *Coronado* on pickguard, raven black finish: **1962**
Discontinued: **1967**

Bermuda: 15 1/4" wide, single cutaway, slight cutaway on bass side, slab fiberglass body, 2 PUs, 2 knobs, 1 slide switch, tremolo under pickguard operated by toggle switch, stairstep tailpiece, dot inlay, asymmetrical peghead longer on bass side, plastic logo, "polyester cherry" finish
Introduced: **1962**
Discontinued: **1963**

Martinique: single cutaway, slight cutaway on bass side, beveled body edges, 2 standard PUs and 1 bridge PU, 1 knob and 3-way slotted switch on lower treble bout, 6 knobs in pairs on bass side, Bigsby vibrato optional, *Val-Trol* on pickguard, bound fingerboard, block inlay, asymmetrical peghead longer on bass side, plastic logo, butterfly tuner buttons, ermine white finish
Introduced: **1962**
Non-Bigsby vibrato: **1965**
Discontinued: **1967**

Kingston: Res-o-glas (fiberglass) body, single cutaway with slight cutaway on bass side, slab body, 1 PU near bridge, 2 knobs, 1 slide switch, Dobro-type tailpiece, asymmetrical peghead longer on bass side, dot inlay, butterfly tuner buttons, sand buff finish
Introduced: **1962**
Discontinued: **1964**

Super Seven: asymmetrical double rounded cutaway, PU in middle position, *Supro* on PU, stud tailpiece with metal cover, dot inlay, asymmetrical peghead slightly longer on bass side, oval logo, poppy red finish: **1963**
Discontinued: **1967**

Tremo-Lectric: beveled fiberglass body, single cutaway with slight cutaway on bass side, 2 PUs, 4 knobs on control plate, 2 switches near bridge PU, tremolo under pickguard operated by toggle switch, stairstep tailpiece, dot inlay, asymmetrical peghead longer on bass side, Wedgewood blue finish
Introduced: **1963**
Discontinued: **1967**

Supersonic: beveled fiberglass body, symmetrical double cutaway, 1 PU near neck, vibrato, dot inlay, asymmetrical peghead longer on bass side, holly red finish
Introduced: **1963**
Renamed **Suprosonic 30**: **1964**
Discontinued: **1967**

Holiday: beveled fiberglass body, single cutaway with slight cutaway on bass side, 1 PU near bridge, slide switch on bass side, 3 knobs on treble side, vibrato, teardrop pickguard, bound fingerboard, block inlay, asymmetrical peghead longer on bass side, white finish
Introduced: **1963**
Renamed **White Holiday**: **1964**
Discontinued: **1967**

Shaded Guitars (no other model name): asymmetrical double cutaway shape somewhat like Fender Jazzmaster, tortoise grain pickguard, dot inlay, 6-on-a-side tuner arrangement, sunburst finish
S525: 1 PU, 2 knobs
S535: 2 PUs, 4 rocker switches on bass side, Burns vibrato
S545: 3 PUs, 6 rocker switches on bass side, Burns vibrato
Introduced: **1966**
Discontinued: **1967**

Fiberglass Guitar (no other model name) (No. S555): asymmetrical double cutaway shape somewhat like Fender Jazzmaster, 2 standard PUs and 1 bridge PU, 3 knobs on treble side, 6 rocker switches on bass side, Bigsby vibrato, dot inlay, 6-on-a-side tuner arrangement, white finish
Introduced: **1966**

Supro Guitars, Basses, and Mandolins

Discontinued: **1967**

Arlington: asymmetrical double cutaway
shape somewhat like Fender Jazzmaster, 2
standard PUs and 1 bridge PU, Bigsby
vibrato, 6 rocker switches, butterfly (dia-
mond enclosed by rectangle) inlay, 6-on-a-
side tuner arrangement, sunburst (No.
S665) or white (No. S655) finish
*Note: These models were pictured, with large
block inlay, in ads with Bob and Bobbie
Thomas, but they are not the Bobbie
Thomas models (see National Electric
Solidbodies section).*
Introduced: **1967**
Discontinued: **1968**

Lexington series: asymmetrical double cut-
away shape somewhat like Fender
Jazzmaster, individually adjustable bridge
saddles, vibrato with large rectangular
base, tortoise grain pickguard, dot inlay, 6-
on-a-side tuner arrangement, 3-tone sun-
burst finish
S645: 3 PUs, 6 rocker switches, 3 knobs
S635: 2 PUs, 4 rocker switches, 2 knobs
S625: 1 PU, 2 knobs
Introduced: **1967**
Discontinued: **1968**

Normandy series: asymmetrical double cut-
away shape somewhat like Fender
Jazzmaster, black rectangular PU(s) with
oval shape in center, metal height-
adjustable bridge, white pickguard, dot
inlay, 6-on-a-side tuners
S603: 2 PUs, vibrato, cherry-to-black sunburst
finish
S613: 2 PUs, vibrato, cherry finish
S602: 2 PUs, no vibrato, cherry-to-black sun-
burst finish
S612: 2 PUs, no vibrato, cherry finish
S601: 1 PU, cherry-to-black sunburst finish
S611: 1 PU, cherry finish
Introduced: **1967**
Discontinued: **1968**

Colt: asymmetrical double cutaway shape
somewhat like Fender Jazzmaster, black
rectangular PU with oval shape in center,
white pickguard, 22" scale, dot inlay, 6-on-
a-side tuners, red finish
Introduced: **1967**
Discontinued: **1968**

12-string: asymmetrical double cutaway shape
somewhat like Fender Jazzmaster, 2 PUs, 4
rocker switches on bass side, 2 knobs on
treble side, tortoise grain pickguard, dot
inlay, symmetrical peghead, sunburst
finish
Introduced: **1967**
Discontinued: **1968**

Electric Basses

Pocket Bass: 13 1/2" wide, symmetrical double
cutaway, beveled top edges, 1 rectangular
PU in neck position and 1 bridge pickup,
trapeze tailpiece, 1 finger rest bar, 24 3/4"
scale, dot inlay, jet black finish
Introduced: **1960**
2 elevated fin-shaped finger rests: **1961**
No bridge PU, no finger rests, 4-on-a-side
tuners: **1967**
Discontinued: **1968**

Taurus: asymmetrical double cutaway shape
somewhat similar to Fender Jazzmaster, 1
standard PU and 1 bridge PU, 4-on-a-side
tuner arrangement, sunburst finish
Introduced: **1967**
Discontinued: **1968**

Acoustic Mandolins

S464: A-style, arched top, pear-shape body,
laminated maple body, white pickguard,
dot inlay, symmetrical peghead
S345: asymmetrical body, body point on each
upper bout, arched spruce top, laminated
maple back and sides, black pickguard,
block inlay, symmetrical peghead
Only catalog appearance: **1968**

Electric Mandolins

Supro electric mandolin: conventional woodbody construction, symmetrical A-style
body shape, no sound holes, bar PU with
oblong housing mounted near bridge,
Dobro-type tailpiece, bound fingerboard,
dot inlay, block letter logo across peghead
Introduced: **1936**
Discontinued by **1938**

S395: asymmetrical body, body point on each
upper bout, arched spruce top, laminated
maple back and sides, thin bar PU mounted near neck, 2 knobs on lower treble bout,
black pickguard, block inlay, symmetrical
peghead
Only catalog appearance: **1968**

COMMENTS

Supro was National's budget brand, and the
same relation between Supro and National
generally holds true today, with the possible exception of some lap steel models.
Few players have high regard for Supro
electrics. A few models have some collector's appeal but primarily on the basis of
oddity or weirdness.

SUPRO STEELS

All models have strings passing through PU, 23" scale, unless otherwise noted.

Electric Hawaiian (no other model name): cast aluminum body, round body shape 6 7/8" in diameter, blade PU, strings pass over PU, 1 knob on treble side, rosewood fingerboard, dot inlay, cutout in peghead
Introduced: **1936**
Discontinued: **1939**

Hawaiian (no other model name): symmetrical woodbody, wider body than any other Supro model, rounded bottom corners, 2 points near neck, metal handrest, strings pass over PU, round knob mounted on handrest extension, *Supro/Electric* decal between PU and neck, ebonoid fingerboard, small parallelogram markers, numbered frets, mahogany finish
Introduced: **1936**
2 knobs on opposite sides, dot markers: **late 1930s**
Discontinued: **1943**

Avalon Hawaiian: square end, scooped graduation to neck, enameled handrest, 2 knobs mounted on rectangular plates, *Supro* on knob plates, knobs on opposite sides, aluminum fingerboard, parallelogram markers, black finish
Introduced by **1939**
Discontinued: **1943**

No. 20: symmetrical body, strings pass over PU, 1 knob on square plate on treble side, silver pearlette finish
No. 30: same with sunburst mahogany finish
No. 60: guitar/amp-in-case outfit, No. 20 guitar with 110 volt A.C. amp in case
No. 70: guitar/amp-in-case outfit, No. 30 guitar with battery powered amp in case
Introduced by **1939**
Discontinued: **1943**

Baton: square-end woodbody with 2 points near neck, enameled handrest on square metal plate, 21" scale, diamond-shaped markers, grained walnut finish
Introduced by **1942**
Discontinued: **1943**

Irene: square end, sharp points at neck, PU and controls on square plate, 23 1/2" scale, painted-on fingerboard, Roman numeral markers, cream pearlette covering
Introduced by **1942**
Discontinued: **1943**

Clipper: square corners with rounded belly, 2 points near neck, PU and controls on square plate, bound rosewood fingerboard, plastic frets flush with fingerboard, pearl dot inlay, brown pearlette covering
Introduced by **1942**
Replaced by **Supreme**: bound plastic fingerboard top-painted brown, geometric markers, long V-shaped figures on tuner enclosures: **1947**
Lucite fingerboard back-painted brown, Kluson Deluxe tuners: **1948**
Cream-colored plastic PU cover: **1950**
Butterfly tuner buttons, accordion red finish: **1955**
Tulip yellow finish: **1958**
Discontinued: **1960**

Comet: symmetrical body, straight bottom with rounded corners, beveled around fingerboard, PU and controls on square plate, 1 round knob, 1 pointer knob, cord into body (no jack), painted-on black fingerboard, geometric markers, rounded-top peghead narrower at top than at nut, gray pearlette covering
Introduced: **c. 1947**
Standard jack, arctic white plastic covering: **1948**
Black plastic PU cover, brown painted control plate, plastic logo below control plate on treble side: **1952**
Discontinued: **1966**

Varsity: symmetrical body with slight waists, sharp points near neck, wide handrest, rectangular peghead, lacquer finish
Introduced: **1948**
Discontinued: **1952**

Twin: 2 6-string necks, PUs on square control plates, 3 knobs, logo below control plate on neck farthest from player, geometric markers, rounded-top pegheads, pearlette covering
Introduced: **1948**
Renamed **Console**: black bridge covers and control plates, Lucite fingerboards, black-and-silver stairstep markers in octave pattern, arctic white finish, 4 legs, by **1955**
Logo below control plate: **1966**
Discontinued: **1969**

Airline: asymmetrical body with straight edge on bass side, black plastic bridge/PU cover with *Supro* logo, 2 knobs on treble side, black control plate, black fingerboard (some with *Airline* on fingerboard), totem-pole markers, rounded peghead, black plastic covering on main body (some with white fingerboard and gray pearlette main body covering), white plastic on treble-side body extension

Introduced by **1952**
8-string available: **1961**
Renamed **Jet Airliner**: **1962**
Renamed **Airline**: **1963**
Renamed **Jet Airliner**: **1964**
Discontinued: **1965**

Spectator: symmetrical woodbody, rounded points near neck, PU and controls on round-cornered plate, painted-on fingerboard, totem pole markers, rectangular peghead, natural finish
Introduced: **1952**
Discontinued: **1955**

Student De Luxe: straight-line body sides, 1 knob, PU and controls on metal plate, 21" scale, stairstep pattern fingerboard markers, *Student Special* in script near bridge, black and white pearlette covering, wood finish optional
Introduced: **1952**
Renamed **Special**, wine-maroon finish: **1955**
White plastic covering: **1958**
Discontinued by **1962**

Studio: symmetrical body, rounded points at neck, PU and controls on metal plate with rounded corners, 2 knobs on treble side, jack in control plate on bass side, gold plastic fingerboard, totem pole markers, peghead wider at top than at nut, opalescent blue pearlette covering
Introduced by **1955**
Painted-on fingerboard, totem pole markers, ivory-to-black sunburst finish: **1959**
Ivory finish: **1961**
Discontinued: **1964**

De Luxe: straightline body shape, slight bevel around neck, 1 knob, 21" scale, stairstep-pattern fingerboard markers, *Student De Luxe* in script near bridge, mottled red and white finish, no logo, toolbox-type case contains amp
Introduced: **1955**
Discontinued: **1956**

Studio Four: guitar-shaped body, PU and controls in metal plate with rounded corners, black control plate, painted-on black fingerboard, Bermuda red lacquer finish
Introduced by **1960**
Discontinued: **1965**

Console 8: similar to Airline but with 8 strings and 3 legs, asymmetrical body straight on bass side, black plastic PU cover, black control plate, black plastic covering on main body, white covering on treble side extension
Introduced: **1958**
Discontinued: **1961**

Console 16: 2 8-string necks joined by large tubes, large handrest covers both PUs, 1 knob on each neck, switch on handrest, geometric markers, 4 legs
Introduced: **1958**
Discontinued: **1961**
Re-introduced in National line: **1967**
Discontinued: **1968**

12-string Console: 2 6-string necks
Introduced: **1960**
Discontinued: **1964**

COMMENTS

The Supro lap steel pickup—with strings-through-pickup design and separate coils for bass and treble strings—has a dirty sound that appeals to some players of blues and rock music. For that reason, some players prefer Supro models over National models. Most collectors regard National models more highly than Supro models.

AIRLINE MODELS MADE BY VALCO

Airline was a house brand of the Montgomery Ward company. Not all instruments with the Airline logo were made by National/Valco.

SECTION ORGANIZATION

Acoustic Model
Solidbodies, Single Cutaway
Angular Shape Woodbody
Angular Shape Fiberglass Body
Basses
Lap Steels

Acoustic Model

Resonator model: described as "extra volume folk guitar," single-cone resonator, molded Res-o-glas (fiberglass) body, 15" wide, 8 stylized M-shaped holes in resonator coverplate, 2 screen holes or 2 plastic circular-pattern holes in upper bouts, dot inlay (some with block), asymmetrical peghead longer on treble side, plastic logo, white peghead veneer, black finish
Introduced: **1964**
Discontinued by **1968**

Solidbodies, Single Cutaway

All similar to Supro models, single cutaway with slight cutaway on bass side, beveled body edges, 2 fin-shaped finger rests, bound fingerboard, no backplate, white plastic block inlay, asymmetrical peghead longer on treble side, sticker logo, goldoid (lacquered brass) metal parts, models available:
1 PU
2 PUs
3 PUs
3 PU deluxe: blond finish, Bigsby vibrato
All introduced: **1958**
Backplate, plastic logo, chrome-plated metal parts: **1960**
Slightly thinner body, body edges more rounded, most with black PU mounting rings and knobs, most with sunburst finish, some with cream finish: **1962**
Replaced by angular-shape woodbody models: **1963**

Similar model to Supro White Holiday: single cutaway with slight cutaway on bass side, 1 PU, 3 knobs on bass side, 3-way slotted switch on treble side, white finish
Available: **c. 1961**

Angular Shape Woodbody

All with straight-line edges, longer bass horn than treble, 2 fin-shaped finger rests, models available:
1 PU: dot inlay
2 PUs: block inlay
Introduced: **1963**
Replaced by fiberglass models: **1965**

Angular Shape Fiberglass Body

Models with 24 3/4" scale:
3 PUs, 6 knobs and 3-way slotted switch on bass side, Bigsby vibrato, block inlay, white fiberglass, available: **1963–64**
2 PUs: 4 knobs and 3-way slotted switch on treble side, 1 knob on bass side, plate tailpiece, bound fingerboard, block inlay, red finish, available: **1965–68**
1 PU : yellow finish, available: **1965–68**

Models with short 22" scale, amp in case:
1 PU
2 PUs
Available: **c. 1963**

Basses

Model similar to Supro Pocket Bass, double cutaway, 1 standard PU and 1 bridge PU, 2 knobs, 2 fin-shaped finger rests, dot inlay, sunburst finish
Introduced: **1961**
Discontinued: **1966**

Violin-shape basses: body material unavailable, dot inlay, 4-on-a-side tuner arrangement, 2 models available:
1 PU
1 standard PU and 1 bridge PU
Introduced: **1966**
Discontinued: **1968**

Lap Steels

Hawaiian steel: straight-line body sides, controls and PU on plate with rounded corners, strings pass through PU, 2 knobs on bass side, 20" scale, painted-on fingerboard, split black/white parallelogram markers, logo between PU and neck, black finish
Introduced: **1965**
Discontinued: **1968**

Deluxe Pro: similar to National Rocket 110, body shaped like rocket with fin-like side extensions and control plates, white PU cover with *Rocket*, 23" scale, Roman numeral markers, plastic peghead logo, black and white finish

Introduced by **1965**
Discontinued: **1966**

COMMENTS

The fiberglass angular shape Airline guitars have some aesthetic appeal to collectors due to their unique body shape.

The fiberglass resonator model is essentially the same instrument with the same funky sound as the red Supro Folk Star and has the same appeal. (The white National Bluegrass 35 is rarer and more sought after.)

Ovation

SERIAL NUMBERS

Numbers are provided by the Ovation company.

Serial Numbers, 1967–72

Ovation used at least three different number series during this period. No records of these series are available.

General Series, 1972–Current

Number Range	Date
000001–007000	May–Dec. 1972
007001–020000	1973
020001–039000	1974
039001–067000	1975
067001–086000	1976
086001–103001	Jan.–Sept. 1977
103001–126000	Sept. 1977–Apr. 78
126001–157000	Apr.–Dec. 1978
157001–203000	1979
211011–214933	1980
214934–263633	1981
263634–291456	1982
291457–302669	1983
302760–303319	1984, Elites only
315001–339187	May–Dec. 1984, Balladeers only
303320–356000	1985–86
357000–367999	1987
368000–382106	1988
382107–392900	1989
392901–430292	Jan.–Nov. 1990

Adamas Model Serial Numbers

Series starts with 0077 in Sept. 1977.

Year	Last Number
1977	0099
1978	0608
1979	1058
1980	1670
1981	2668
1982	3242
1983	3859
1984	4109
1985	4251
1986	4283
1987	4427
1988	4696
1989	4974
1990	5580

Rickenbacker

GENERAL INFORMATION

Adolph Rickenbacker, a distant cousin of World War I flying ace Eddie Rickenbacker, was born in Switzerland in 1892. He emigrated to America as a child and moved to Los Angeles in 1918. He and two partners formed the Rickenbacker Manufacturing Company, a metal stamping shop, in 1925. He invested in the original National corporation in 1928 and was contracted to provide metal guitar bodies to National.

Rickenbacker, George Beauchamp (an original partner and general manager of the National corporation), and other figures from National formed the Ro-Pat-In Corporation on October 15, 1931, to develop Beauchamp's design for an electric guitar with a horseshoe-shaped pickup. Rickenbacker was president of Ro-Pat-In; Beauchamp was secretary-treasurer. Rickenbacker's metal stamping company continued to supply metal parts to National. Beauchamp was removed from his position at National on November 10, 1931.

Ro-Pat-In's first guitars were electric models, Hawaiian and Spanish, marketed in 1932 under the Electro String Instruments brand. The company name was changed to the Electro String Instrument Corporation in 1934, and the brand name was changed to Rickenbacher with an *h*, which was the original family spelling. The spelling changed to Rickenbacker, with a *k*, in 1950, although a few old decals with the *h* spelling were used through the 1950s.

A bakelite body lap steel was introduced in 1935. The company line was expanded by 1936 to include electric mandolins, bass viols, violins, cellos, and violas—all with a horseshoe pickup. Lap steels accounted for the majority of Rickenbacker's sales in the pre–World War II period.

George Beauchamp left Electro in 1940. In July 1942 the company diverted its production efforts to war-related products. Instrument production resumed in early 1946.

Adolph Rickenbacker sold the company in 1953 to F. C. Hall, founder of the Radio and Television Equipment Company (Radio-Tel), an electronics distributition company that had earlier been the exclusive distributor for Fender products. Hall shifted the emphasis to Spanish electrics, although steel guitars continued to sell well, due in a large part to an endorsement by Jerry Byrd. The guitar line was expanded with the introduction of the solidbody Combo series in 1954. German-born Roger Rossmeisl designed a new solidbody line in 1957 and the hollowbody Capri series in 1958.

The factory was moved to Santa Ana, California in 1962. Radio-Tel, the distribution company, was renamed Rickenbacker, Inc.

Rickenbacker's image was heightened considerably by the Beatles' use of Rickenbackers in the early 1960s. From 1964–69, the company successfully exported some models for sale in Europe by Rose, Morris & Co., Ltd.

By the late 1960s, the company was the premier maker of electric 12-strings. In the 1970s, basses carried the Rickenbacker reputation. Vintage Series reissues, which first appeared in 1984, play a large role in the company's continuing success.

In 1984, F. C. Hall passed control of the company to his son, John C. Hall, who then combined all the manufacturing and distribution under one company name: Rickenbacker International Corporation.

Export Models

From 1964–69, Rickenbacker exported some models to Rose, Morris & Co, Ltd. in England for sale in Europe. Most of the export models have an equivalent U.S. model. Many hollowbody export models have *f*-holes rather than slash holes or no holes. Rickenbacker designated export models with an *S* after the model number. Rose, Morris assigned a different set of numbers. See model descriptions for individual model specs.

Rickenbacker Model	Rose, Morris Model
325	1996
335	1997
336-12	3262
345	1998
360-12	1993
615	1995
4000-4001	1999
4005	3261

Pickups

Horseshoe, magnets wrap over strings, horse-shoe 1 1/2" wide, all models: **1932-43**
Horseshoe, magnets wrap over strings, horse-shoe 1 1/4" wide…
   Guitars: **1946–59**
   Basses…
      U.S. models: **1957–64**
      Export models: **1964–66**
      Vintage reissues: **1984–current**
   Lap steels : **1946–71**
Oblong metal plate in center of PU: **1956–57**
Rectangular metal plate in center of PU: **1957–58**
Metal bar (part of housing) across middle of PU, black metal housing: **early 1957–Oct. 57**

"Chrome bar," same as above but with chrome-plated housing: **Oct. 1957–70**

Rick-O-Sound stereo (extra jack) on deluxe models: **1960–current**

Hi-Gain, exposed polepieces: **1969 only**

Hi-Gain, black polepiece covers: **1970–current**

Humbucking, poles near edge: **1970s–current**

Hybrid, blackface, no visible poles: **1980–current**

Reissue of chrome bar, vintage reissues: **1984–current**

Vibratos and Tailpieces

Kauffman side-to-side, no roller bridges: **1932–57**

Kauffman with roller bridges: **1957–late 60**

Ac'cent vibrato (name on cover plate on early examples), arm attached by slot-head screw, roller bridge, adjustable saddles: **early 1961–75**

Bigsby, some vintage reissues: **1984–current**

Torsion, like Ac'cent but with no rollers or coil springs: **1980s–current**

Bigsby, 325V59 (reissue model): **1984–current**

R tailpiece, some non-vibrato models: **1963–current**

Pickguards

Plastic or metal (see model descriptions): **1954–early 60s**

Gold-backed Lucite, some models: **1958**

White plastic standard...
  Solidbody models: **1962**
  Hollowbody models: **1963**

Split-level design, hollowbody models: **late 1958**

Ornamentation, 1956–Current

Standard trim: dot inlay, no binding

Deluxe trim...
  Bound top and back, bound fingerboard, triangular inlay goes completely across fingerboard: **1957–70**
  Rounded top edges with no binding on Models 360–375 (bound top available as Old Style trim through 1969), bound fingerboard, sparkle "crushed pearl" fingerboard inlay: **1964–70**
  Bound top or rounded edge top with no binding, bound fingerboard, non-sparkle triangular inlay with rounded corners, triangular inlay does not extend across fingerboard: **1970–current**

Checkered binding...
  Rounded-top deluxe examples and Model 381: **late 1950s–64**
  All rounded top (New Style) deluxe guitar models, solidbody bass models: **1964–70**

4002 bass (from introduction): **1981–current**

Some reissue models: **1984–current**

Logo

Rickenbacher is spelled with an *h* instead of *k* on models made from 1934-49. The spelling changed to Rickenbacker, with a *k*, in 1950, although a few old decals with the *h* spelling were used through the 1950s.

Finishes, Mid 1950s–Current

Sunburst, 2-tone brown: **mid to late 1950s**

Fireglo, shaded red with some yellow: **1960–current**

Autumnglo (shaded with red and brown): **1960–80**

Official custom finishes (custom color finishes available from mid 1950s–current, more finishes available than listed)...
  Fireglo, Mapleglo (natural), Azureglo, Jetglo (black), Burgundyglo, by **1968**
  Fireglo, Azureglo, Jetglo, Burgundy (standard); white, walnut brown, Mapleglo, Autumnglo (custom), by **1971**
  Fireglo, Azureglo, Jetglo, Burgundy (standard); Ruby Walnut, Mapleglo, White (custom glossy); Natural, Black brown (custom matte), by **1981**
  Midnight Blue (metallic), Metallic Silver, Ruby (metallic), White, Red, Mapleglo, Fireglo, Jetglo: **late 1980s**

1957 Combo 800, double cutaway with cut-away 4 frets deeper on treble side, 1 double-coil horseshoe pickup (courtesy Shane's Music).

Early 1957 Combo 450, tulip-shape body (courtesy Wagner Swanson).

Early 1960s Combo 900, modified tulip-shape body with deeper treble-side cutaway.

Late 1950s Combo 850, extreme cutaway body shape, non-original vibrato (courtesy Lloyd Chiate).

Model 360, New Style (1964 and after) rounded top edges, deluxe triangular fingerboard inlay.

301

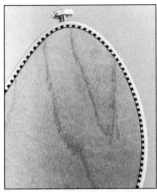

Checkered trim on the back of a New Style Model 360.

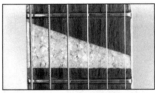

Deluxe triangular inlay from 1964–70, with "crushed pearl" sparkle inlay extending completely across fingerboard.

R tailpiece.

Model 330F with standard trim: unbound body, dot inlay.

Cresting wave body shape on a 4001V63 bass.

Standard Rickenbacker peghead shape.

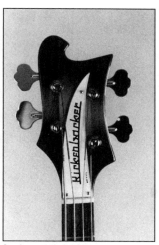

Cresting wave peghead shape.

Split level pickguard.

"Flying saucer" knobs on a bakelite lap steel.

Rickenbacker

General Information

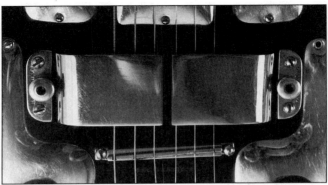

Horseshoe pickup on a late 1930s Electro Spanish (Bakelite roundneck) model, with prewar style pickup magnet (1 1/2" wide).

Postwar horseshoe pickup (1 1/4" wide) on a Bakelite lap steel.

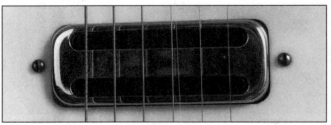

Chrome bar pickup, 1957–70.

SERIAL NUMBERS

Serial Numbers, 1932–54

Serial numbers on early models are unreliable, but patent numbers give the earliest possible date of manufacture (date patent was granted).

Serial Numbers, 1954–Current

Number is stamped on jackplate or bridge.

Solidbodies, 1954–Sept. 59

Number configuration: #(#)C####
Numeral(s) before letter designate model:
4=400 or 425, 6=600, 65=650, 8=800
Letter (represented by C in example) is type of instrument: C=Combo (guitar), B=bass, M=mandolin, V=3/4 size
First numeral after letter is year. Examples:
65C7###=1957 Combo 650, 4C6###=1956 Combo 400
Last 3 numerals are number series. Each model has its own series.
Exceptions:
Model 450s have 4C####A configuration.
3/4 size models have V###, V#### or ####A configuration through Oct. 1960. First numeral is still last digit of year.
Basses have B#### configuration.
Mandolins have M### configuration.
Some examples have #C## configuration and are not dateable by serial number.

Solidbodies (Except 3/4 Sizes) Sept. 1959–Oct. 60

Number configuration: #(#)A###
Only 3 numerals after letter. Numbers do not contain date information.

Hollowbodies, 1958–Oct. 60

Number configuration: #A## (early 1958) or #A###
Numeral before letter is number of PUs (2 or 3).
Letter (denoted by A in configuration example) is V (for vibrato) or T (for standard tailpiece).
1958 range of numbers: V80–3V254
Highest Capri series number in 1959: 2T835
First Capri series number in 1960: 3V706
Series (last 3 numerals) starts over with 001 in Jan. 1960.
Letter R replaces T or V on deluxe models only, June 1960.

All Models, Oct. 1960–86

Configuration: AA## or AA###, letters on jackplate above jack hole, numerals below jack hole
First letter denotes year:
A   1961
B   1962
C   1963
D   1964
E   1965
F   1966
G   1967
H   1968
I   1969
J   1960 or 1970
K   1971
L   1972
M   1973
N   1974
O   1975
P   1976
Q   1977
R   1978
S   1979
T   1980
U   1981
V   1982
W   1983
X   1984
Y   1985
Z   1986

Second letter denotes month:
A   January
B   February
C   March
D   April
E   May
F   June
G   July
H   August
I   September
J   October
K   November
L   December

All Models,1987–Current

Configuration: A### or A####, number on jackplate, letter and 1 numeral above jack, 2 or 3 numerals below jack
Letter denotes month (see preceding table).
Numeral after letter denotes year:
0   1987
1   1988
2   1989
3   1990
4   1991

HOLLOWBODIES KEY

Horseshoe Pickups

All 1932–50 hollowbody models, archtop and flat top, are identifiable by a horseshoe pickup. The only postwar guitar models with horseshoe pickup are solidbody models 650 and 850.

Ornamentation

Standard: unbound body and fingerboard, dot inlay
Deluxe: bound body and fingerboard, triangular inlay
From 1964-68, most double cutaway deluxe models have rounded top edges with no binding. The Old Style trim, with binding on top, is rare from 1968 until the introduction of reissue models in the mid 1980s.

Hollowbody Models With No Soundholes

Most examples in the 310–325 series have no soundholes and the same body shape as solidbody models 650 and 850. Except for a few custom examples, the 650 and 850 have a horseshoe PU; no 310-325 series models have horseshoe PUs. The 650 and 850 have a carved top; the 310-325s do not have a carved top.

Models in parentheses were never in production, although prototypes exist for some models.
Limited edition and vintage reissue models (except for 381-12V69) are not included in this key.

Horseshoe PU
    Archtop
        f-holes on lower bouts=**S-59**
        f-holes on upper bouts=**Rickenbacker Spanish (SP)**
    Flat top
        f-holes on lower bouts=**Ken Roberts Electro Spanish**
        f-holes on upper bouts=**Electro Spanish**
Understring PU(s) or no PU
    Thinbody, single rounded cutaway
        Standard ornamentation
            2 PUs
                No vibrato=**330F**
                Vibrato=**335F**
            3 PUs
                No vibrato=**340F**
                Vibrato=**345F**
        Deluxe ornamentation
            2 PUs
                6-string
                    No vibrato=**360F**
                    Vibrato=**365F**
                12-string=**360F-12**
            3 PUs
                No vibrato=**370F**
                Vibrato=**375F**
    Thinbody, double pointed cutaway
        3/4 size
            2 PUs
                No vibrato=**310**
                Vibrato=**315**
            3 PUs
                No vibrato
                    6-string=**320**
                    12-string=**325-12**
                Vibrato=**325**

Understring PU(s) or no PU
    Thinbody, double pointed cutaway (cont.)
        Full scale
            Standard ornamentation
                2 PUs
                    No vibrato
                        6-string
                            Wood top=**330**
                            Plastic top=**331**
                        12-string
                            6-12 converter=**336-12**
                            No converter=**330-12**
                    Vibrato
                        No soundholes=**355JL**
                        Soundholes=**335**
                3 PUs
                    No vibrato
                        Slash holes=**340**
                        No holes=**350**
                    Vibrato=**345**
             Deluxe ornamentation
                2 PUs
                    6-string
                      No vibrato=**360**
                      Vibrato=**365**
                    12-string
                      6-12 converter=**366-12**
                      No converter=**360-12**
                3 PUs
                  6-string
                    No vibrato=**370**
                    Vibrato=**375**
                  12-string=**370-12**
    Full-depth body, archtop, double cutaway
        No PU=(380)
        2 PUs
            6-string
                No vibrato=**381**
                Vibrato=(382) some sold as 381
            12-string=**381-12V69**
        3 PUs
            No vibrato=(383)
            Vibrato=(384)
    Full-depth body, flat top
        No PU=**385**
        2 PUs
            No vibrato=(386)
            Vibrato=(387)
        3 PUs
            No vibrato=(388)
            Vibrato=(389)
    Full-depth body, archtop, single cutaway
        No PU=(390)
        2 PUs
            No vibrato=(391)
            Vibrato=(392)
        3 PUs
            No vibrato=(393)
            Vibrato=(394)

HOLLOWBODIES

All models from 1958 and after have standard ornamentation—unbound top and back, unbound fingerboard, dot inlay—unless otherwise noted. See General Information for more on ornamentation.

SECTION ORGANIZATION

Pre-1950 models
1958–Current Models
 Capri Series (300 series), Thinbody,
  Double Cutaway
 300-series 12-strings
 Export Models
 Thin Full-body, F-series, Single-cutaway
  Models
 Thick Body Series, Full Depth Body
 Doubleneck Model

Pre–1950 Models

Electro Spanish: flat top, small upper-bout *f*-holes, horseshoe PU, no volume knob, straight bridge, dot inlay, slotted peghead (tenor available with solid peghead), plastic peghead veneer
Introduced: **1932**
Bound top: **1934**
Replaced by Ken Roberts model (see following): **late 1935**

Electro Spanish Guitar (Model B): see Solidbodies section

Ken Roberts Electro Spanish: flat top, 3-ply mahogany body, *f*-holes on lower bouts, horseshoe PU, 1 octagonal knob on treble side near PU, compensating bridge, Kauffman vibrato, bound top and back, 17 frets clear of body, bound fingerboard, dot inlay, rounded-peak peghead, shaded brown finish
Introduced: **late 1935**
Round knob with ridges: **1938**
Discontinued: **1940**

Vibrola Spanish Guitar: see Solidbodies section

S-59: archtop body made by Kay, *f*-holes on lower bouts, horseshoe PU, large screw-on PU unit spans waist to waist (PU also available as accessory), trapeze tailpiece, multiple-bound top and back, alternating 2-dots and single-diamond inlay, point at top of peghead, blond finish
Introduced: **1940**
Discontinued: **1943**

Rickenbacker Spanish (SP): archtop, *f*-holes on upper bouts, horseshoe PU, 2 white knobs, adjustable bridge, triple-bound top, unbound back, bound fingerboard, block inlay, rounded-peak peghead
Introduced: **1946**
Discontinued: **1950**

Capri Series

310-375: thin hollowbody series, double cutaway with pointed horns, both cutaways to 21st fret, bass horn cutaway slightly longer, flat top recessed at tailpiece, top not beveled around bass side like solid-body models with same shape, chrome bar PUs, 4 knobs, brown sunburst or natural finish

	3/4 Scale, Std.	Full Scale, Std.	Full Scale, Dlx.
2 PUs	310	330	360
2 PUs, vibrato	315	335	365
3 PUs	320	340	370
3 PUs, vibrato	325	345	375

310–325 series: 12 3/4" wide, most with no soundholes, standard trim, short scale
Introduced: **Jan. 1958**
Some with *f*-holes: **1961**
5 knobs: **1963**
f-holes standard: **1964**
310 discontinued: **1971**
315 and 325 discontinued: **1975**
Hi-Gain PUs, by **1975**
No soundholes standard, *f*-holes optional: **1979**
310 re-introduced: **1981**
320B, early 1960s style reissue: **late 1982**
325V59: reissue of John Lennon's modified 1959 325, no soundholes, diamond-shape knobs, Bigsby vibrato, Kluson style tuners, introduced: **1984**
325V63: reissue of John Lennon style 1963 325, 5 knobs, Torsion vibrato, Kluson style tuners, introduced: **1984**
310 discontinued: **late 1980s**
John Lennon Special Edition 325 (325JL): Torsion vibrato, chrome bar PUs, signature on pickguard, limited edition, available: **1989–91**
320, 325V59, and 325V63 still in production

330–345 series: 15 1/4" wide, most with slash soundholes, standard trim
Introduced: **early 1958**
Thinner body, 1 1/2" deep: **1961**
5 knobs: **1963**
Some with slanted frets: **late 1969**
345 discontinued: **1975**
335 discontinued: **1978**
340 discontinued: **1985**
330 still in production

331: "Light Show" model, same as Model 330 but with translucent plastic top, colored lights inside body activated by musical tones, external power box provided
Introduced: **1970**
Discontinued: **1975**

350: full-scale version of 320, no soundholes, standard trim
Introduced: **1985**
Still in production

350SH: Susanna Hoffs (of the Bangles) model, 2 chrome bar PUs and 1 humbucking PU, deluxe trim with checkered binding, limited edition of 250
Available: **1988–91**

355JL: full-scale version of John Lennon Special Edition 325JL (preceding)
Introduced: **1989**
Still in production

360–75 series: 15 1/4" wide, slash soundholes, deluxe trim, early natural finish models with brown wood binding
Introduced: **1958**
Rick-O-Sound stereo with 2 output jacks, optional: **1960**
Thinner body, 1 1/2" deep: **1961**
R tailpiece on non-vibrato models: **1963**
New Style: rounded top edges, no top binding, checkered back binding, bound slash holes, introduced: **June 1964**
Rounded top edges, no top binding on almost all examples (Old Style with top binding continues on a few current examples): **1968**
Roller bridge on 365 and 375: **1968**
365 and 375 discontinued: **1975**
365 and 375 re-introduced as **360VB** and **370VB**: Old Style trim (bound top and back), Hi-Gain PUs, *R* tailpiece: **1985**
360VB renamed **360WB**; 370, and 370VB discontinued: **1991**
360V64: Old Style trim (bound top and back), chrome bar PUs, slanted plate tailpiece, introduced: **1991**
360WB and 360V64 still in production

300-Series 12-Strings

360-12 Deluxe: 2 PUs, Rick-O-Sound stereo, double-bound top, bound back, bound slash hole, bound fingerboard, triangular inlay, flat plate tailpiece, fireglo or natural finish
Introduced: **1964**
New Style: rounded top edge and no top binding, checkered back binding, *R* tailpiece: **fall 1964**
Old Style continues with double-bound top, designated 360-12 OS, then 360-12 w/WBBS, then 360-12 WB
Plain back binding on New Style: **early 1970s**
New Style discontinued; Old Style listed as 360-12, Hi-Gain PUs, *R* tailpiece: **1990**

360-12V64: chrome bar PUs, slanted plate tailpiece, introduced: **1985**
360-12 and 360-12V64 still in production

330-12: 12 string version of 330
Introduced: **1965**
Still in production

336-12: 330 with comb-like 6-12 converter, introduced: **1966**
366-12: 360 with comb-like 6-12 converter, introduced: **1966**
336-12 and 366-12 last made: **1974**
Last listed: **1978**

360F-12: thinbody, single cutaway (see Thin Full-Body Series, following)
Introduced by **1973**
Discontinued: **1981**

370-12: Roger McGuinn (of the Byrds) model, limited edition of 1000
Introduced: **1988**

325-12: John Lennon signature model, limited edition
Introduced: **1990**

355-12JL: John Lennon signature model, chrome bar PUs, slanted plate tailpiece, limited edition
Introduced: **1991**

381-12V69: carved top and back (see Thick Body Series, following), deluxe trim, checkered binding, *R* tailpiece
Introduced: **1989**
Still in production

Export Thin Hollowbody Models

Distributed in Europe by Rose, Morris & Co., Ltd.

1996: export version of Model 325 but with *f*-holes
1997: export version of Model 335 but with *f*-holes
1998: export version of Model 345 but with *f*-holes
1993: export version of Model 330-12 but with 1 *f*-hole and double-bound body, some sold in the U.S. and Canada
All introduced with fireglo finish standard: **1964**
Black and autumnglo finishes available: **1965**
Last distributed by Rose, Morris: **1969**

1997VB: *f*-holes, 2 chrome bar PUs, Torsion vibrato

1997: *f*-holes, 2 chrome bar PUs, slanted plate tailpiece
Introduced: **1987**
1997VB discontinued: **1991**
1997 still in production

3262: export version of 336-12
Introduced: **1967**
Last distributed by Rose, Morris: **1969**

Thin Full-Body Series

330F–345F, 360F–375F: 17" wide, thin (2 1/2" deep) hollowbody, single rounded cutaway (most conventional looking body shape in Rickenbacker line), 4 diamond-shaped knobs, 1 switch, controls mounted on split-level pickguard, same trim and feature patterns as regular 330 and 360 series, 14 frets clear of body, sunburst or natural finish

	Standard	Deluxe
2 PUs	330F	360F
2 PUs, vibrato	335F	365F
3 PUs	340F*	370F
2 PUs, vibrato	345F	375F

*No 340Fs appear on shipping totals.

Introduced: **1959**
Last 330Fs shipped (total production 13 instruments), last 335Fs shipped (total production 14 instruments): **1960**
Thinner body (eventually less than 2"): **early 1960s**
Last 345F shipped (total production 11 instruments): **1963**
Controls mounted on top: **late 1960s**
Standard trim models (330F–345F) officially discontinued: **1969**
Deluxe models discontinued by **1973**

360F-12: see 300-Series 12-Strings, preceding

Thick Body Series

All have full depth body and full scale.

380–384: carved top and back, extreme double cutaways, 1 slash hole, triangular inlay
385–389: flat top, dreadnought body shape, round hole, pin bridge
390–394: carved top and back, single cutaway, slash holes
Most of the models in the thick body series never went into production for obvious reasons (Model 389, for example, would have 3 PUs and a vibrato on a flat top acoustic). Only those in boldface were actually production models. Some prototypes exist of non-production models.

	2-Cut Archtop	Flat Top, Round Hole	1-Cut Archtop
No PUs	(380)	**385**	(390)
2 PUs	**381**	(386)	(391)
2 PUs, vibrato	(382)	(387)	(392)
3 PUs	(383)	(388)	(393)
3 PUs, vibrato	(384)	(389)	(394)

381: 2 different prototypes (one with flat back and top), double pointed cutaways, single slash hole, 2 PUs, 2 switches, 2 knobs, 1-piece pickguard shaped like split-level, checkered binding on top and back, dot or triangular inlay, brown sunburst or natural, several variations
Introduced: **1958**
Discontinued: **early 1960s**
Re-introduced, double split-level pickguard, 5 knobs: **late 1960s**
Some examples with vibrato sold as Model 381 (rather than 382): **late 1960s**
Discontinued: **1974**
381V68: introduced: **1987**
Renamed **381V69**: **1991**
Still in production

381JK: John Kay (of Steppenwolf) model, 2 humbucking PUs, active electronics, stereo, limited edition of 250
Available: **1988–91**

381-12V69: see 300-Series 12-Strings, preceding

385: dreadnought body shape, variants include Gibson J-200 body shape (rounded bouts) and classical body shape (**385S**)
Introduced: **1958**
Discontinued: **1972**

Doubleneck Model

362/12: 6-string and 12-string guitar necks, Model 360 features, 2 PUs, stereo electronics, *R* tailpiece, deluxe trim, checkered top binding, standard pegheads
Introduced: **1975**
Discontinued: **1985**

COMMENTS

Rickenbacker was the first company to successfully market electric guitars, but the prewar models most sought after by collectors and players are lap steel models (see Comments at end of Steels section). Spanish models are relatively rare and appeal to collectors for historical reasons.
The most sought after hollowbody models are those from the 1950s and 1960s, particularly those with old-style pickups and fancier ornamentation (checkered binding, sparkle

inlay). The export models are also highly
sought after.

Vintage reissues are among the finest by any
manufacturer in terms of faithfulness to
original designs.

For more on Rickenbackers in general, see
Comments at end of Solidbodies section.

SOLIDBODIES KEY

Ornamentation
Standard: unbound body and fingerboard, dot inlay
Deluxe: bound body and fingerboard, triangular inlay

Understring (non-horseshoe) PU(s)
    Tulip body shape
        Full scale
            1 PU=**400**
            2 PUs=**450, 1957–58**
        3/4 scale
            1 PU
                21 frets=**900, 1957–74***
                18 frets=**1000**
            2 PUs=**950, 1957–74***
    Cresting wave body shape
        1 PU
            Vibrato=**425, 1965–73**
            No vibrato
                Full scale=**425, 1958–64** or **420, 1965-84**
                3/4 scale=**900, 1969–80***
        2 PUs
            Standard ornamentation (dot inlay)
                Boyd vibrato=**450**
                Ac'cent vibrato=**615, 1962-67** or **610VB, 1977–current**
                No vibrato
                    Standard peghead shape
                        Full scale
                            12-string
                              6-12 converter=**456-12**
                              No 6-12 converter=**450-12**
                          6-string
                              4 knobs=**450, 1958–84**
                              5 knobs=**610**
                      3/4 scale=**950, 1969–80***
                  Cresting wave peghead shape=**480**
            Deluxe ornamentation
                Ac'cent vibrato=**625, 1962-67** or **620VB, 1977–current**
                No vibrato
                    12-string
                      Standard trim=**620-12**
                      Deluxe trim=**660/12TP**
                  6-string
                    Standard peghead shape
                        Mono=**460**
                        Stereo=**460, 1961-76** or **620, 1977-current**
                Cresting wave peghead shape=**481**
        3 PUs
            Standard ornamentation=**450****, 1962-77** or **615****
            Deluxe ornamentation
                Standard peghead shape=**460****** or **625****
                Cresting wave peghead shape=**483**
Asymmetrical double cutaway with rounded horns (similar to Fender Strat)
    Bound body=**250**
    Unbound body
        Unbound fingerboard=**430**
        Bound fingerboard=**230**

* Transition from tulip body shape to cresting wave body shape occurs from 1969–74
** 3rd PU optional

Horseshoe PU
Non-cutaway (bakelite body)
4 metal plates on top=**Vibrola Spanish Guitar**
5 metal plates on top=**Electro Spanish Guitar (Model B)**
Cutaway deeper on treble side than bass
1 single-coil PU, 1 switch=**600, 1954–59**
1 double-coil PU, 2 switches=**800, 1954–59**
1 horseshoe PU and 1 bar PU=**800, 1957–59**
Double cutaway with pointed horns
1 single-coil PU, 1 switch=**650, 1957–59**
1 double-coil PU, 2 switches=**850, 1953–57**
1 horseshoe PU and 1 bar PU=**850, 1957–59**

SOLIDBODIES

All post-World War II models have standard
ornamentation—unbound top and back,
unbound fingerboard, dot inlay—unless
otherwise noted.

SECTION ORGANIZATION

Pre-World War II Models (bakelite body)
Cutaway With Slight Cutaway on Bass Side
Tulip Body Shape
Extreme Cutaway Body Shape (both sides to 20th fret)
Cresting Wave Body Shape
Asymmetrical Double Cutaway, Rounded Horns (similar to Fender Stratocaster)
Export Model
Other Brands Made By Rickenbacker (Electro, Ryder, and Contello)

Pre-World War II Models

Electro Spanish Guitar (Model B): black
Bakelite body, horseshoe PU, some with
Kauffman vibrato, 5 decorative chrome
plates, body hollowed out underneath
plates, 1 octagonal knob on lower bass
bout, strings anchor through body, detachable Bakelite neck with integral molded
fret ridges
Tenor available with wood neck and standard
frets
Introduced: mid **1935**
2 round knobs with ridges (some with 1 black
knob, 1 white): **1938**
White enameled plates by **1940**
Named **Model B** by **1941**
Discontinued: **1943**

Vibrola Spanish Guitar: black Bakelite body,
horseshoe PU, 4 decorative chrome plates,
6 small holes on upper treble plate, body
hollowed out underneath plates, motorized
electric vibrola unit, 1 knob on upper bass
bout, 1 knob on lower bass bout, detachable Bakelite neck with integral molded
fret ridges

Introduced: **Dec. 1937**
1 knob on lower bass bout, 1 knob on lower
treble bout, small holes in both upper-bout
plates: **c. 1939**
Discontinued (90 total produced): **1943**

Cutaway With Slight Cutaway on Bass Side

Combo 600: cutaway to 19th fret on treble side,
cutaway to 15th fret on bass side, 1 horseshoe PU, 1 tone switch, 1 chrome volume
knob, knob and switch mounted into body,
small black pickguard does not extend
below PU, square-corner peghead, blond
finish
Combo 800: double-coil horseshoe PU, 1 tone
switch, 1 selector switch
Introduced: **1954**
Black plastic knobs, asymmetrical peghead,
vertical logo: **1955**
Larger pickguard, knobs mounted into pickguard, turquoise blue finish optional: **1957**
1 horseshoe PU and 1 bar PU on Combo 800,
by **late 1957**
Last produced (but still cataloged): **1959**
Offered in catalog with cresting wave cutaway
body shape but none produced: **1964**
Discontinued from price list: **1969**

Tulip Body Shape

Combo 400: symmetrical tulip-shape body,
neck-through-body construction, 1 rectangular PU with oblong metal plate in center,
PU in neck position, 1 tone switch, large
anodized aluminum pickguard covers most
of body but does not completely surround
PU, Cloverfield green (blue-green),
Montezuma brown (golden), or jet black
finish
Introduced: **1956**
Deeper cutaway shape on treble side, 2 knobs
2 switches, pickguard surrounds PU: **1957**
Discontinued, replaced by **425** (see following):
1958

Combo 450: symmetrical tulip-shape body,

neck-through-body construction, 2 rectangular PUs with rectangular metal plate in center, 2 knobs, rotary selector switch with pointed knob on upper treble bout, Cloverfield green, Montezuma brown, or jet black finish
Introduced: **early 1957**
Deeper cutaway shape on treble side: **1957**
2 chrome bar PUs, 2 knobs and 1 selector switch on lower treble bout: **early 1958**
Cresting wave body shape (see following): **Mar. 1958**

Model 900: 3/4-size, tulip-shaped body, neck-through-body construction, 1 rectangular PU with rectangular chrome plate in center, PU in middle position, 2 knobs, 1 toggle switch, 21-fret neck, black finish
Model 950: 2 PUs, 2 knobs, rotary selector switch, 21-fret neck
Model 1000: 1 PU in middle position, 2 knobs, 1 toggle switch, 18-fret neck
Introduced: **1957**
Deeper cutaway shape on treble side, brown, black, gray, or natural finish: **late 1957**
Chrome bar PU(s): **1958**
Fireglo finish optional: **1961**
Rocker bridge: **1968**
900 and 950 to cresting wave cutaway shape (see following), transitional period: **1969–74**
1000 discontinued: **1971**
900 and 950 discontinued: **1980**

Extreme Cutaway Body Shape

Combo 650: double cutaway with pointed horns, both cutaways to 20th fret, top beveled around bass side, some examples with neck-through-body construction, 1 horseshoe PU, natural maple or turquoise finish
Combo 850: 1 double-coil horseshoe PU, 2 knobs, 2 switches
Introduced: **1957**
Chrome-bar PU on 650, 1 horseshoe and 1 chrome bar PU on 850: **late 1957**
Last produced (but still offered): **1959**
650 discontinued from price list: **1960**
850 discontinued from price list: **1967**

Cresting Wave Body Shape

Combo 450: 1 5/8" deep, 2 chrome bar PUs, metal pickguard, sunburst finish
Model name continued from tulip body series (see preceding): **Mar. 1958**
4 knobs, fireglo, black, or natural finish, by **1960**
Thinner body: **1961**
White plastic pickguard: **1962**
Boyd vibrato, a few (if any) examples: **late 1962**
3 PUs optional: **1962–77**

Hi-Gain PUs: **1970**
Discontinued: **1984**

Combo 425: 1 5/8" deep, 1 chrome bar PU, white pickguard, sunburst finish
Introduced: **late 1958**
Thinner body: **1961**
A few with Boyd vibrato (very rare): **1965**
Combo 420: non-vibrato version of 425, introduced: **1965**
425 discontinued: **1973**
420 discontinued: **1984**

Combo 460: 2 chrome bar PUs, 5 knobs (extra mixer control), 1 switch, deluxe trim, black, natural, or fireglo finish: **1961**
Introduced: **late 1961**
Rick-O-Sound stereo standard: **1962**
No stereo: **1968**
Discontinued: **1985**

450-12: 12-string, available: **1964–85**
456-12: 12-string with comb-like converter for 6-string playing, available: **1968–78**

615: top carved out in tailpiece area to accommodate vibrato, 2 PUs, roller bridge, Ac'cent vibrato, fireglo, natural maple or black diamond finish
625: deluxe trim, 2 PUs, roller bridge, vibrato
Introduced: **early 1962**
Adjustable-height pickguard: **late 1963**
Discontinued: **1977**

620: 2 PUs, deluxe trim
Introduced: **1977**
620-12: 12-string, deluxe trim, introduced: **1981**
Standard trim on 620-12: **1989**
620 and 620-12 still in production

610: 2 PUs, 5 knobs, no vibrato
610VB: 2 PUs, 5 knobs, vibrato
Introduced: **1985**
Still in prodution

900: 3/4 scale, 1 PU
950: 3/4 scale, 2 PUs
Model names continued from tulip body series, transition period to cresting wave body shape: **1969–74**
900 and 950 discontinued: **1980**

480: body shape similar to Model 4000 bass with longer bass horn than other cresting wave guitar models, 2 PUs, 3 knobs, bound fingerboard, cresting wave peghead shape
Introduced: **1973**
Discontinued: **1985**

481: body shape similar to Model 4000 bass with longer bass horn than other cresting wave guitar models, 2 humbucking PUs, 3

Rickenbacker

humbucking PUs available by special order, phase reversal switch, deluxe trim, slanted frets, cresting wave peghead shape
Introduced: **1973**
Discontinued: **1984**

660/12TP: Tom Petty model, 12-string, 2 chrome bar PUs, slanted plate tailpiece, deluxe trim, checkered binding, fireglo or jetglo finish, limited edition
Available: **1991**

Asymmetrical Double Cutaway, Rounded Horns (Somewhat Similar to Fender Stratocaster)

430: 2 oblong PUs with plastic covers and no visible poles, 2 knobs, 1 switch, jack into top, laminated beveled-edge pickguard surrounds PUs, detachable neck
Introduced: **1971**
PUs with visible polepieces, 4 knobs, 1 switch, single-ply pickguard does not surround PUs, by **1975**
Discontinued: **1982**

230 Hamburg: 2 shielded single-coil PUs, 4 knobs, 1 switch, jack on side, unbound top and back, bound fingerboard, chrome-plated metal parts
250 El Dorado: 2 shielded single-coil PUs, 4 knobs, 1 switch, jack on side, double-bound top and back, bound fingerboard, gold-plated metal parts
Introduced by **1987**
Still in production

Export Model

Model 1995: distributed in Europe by Rose Morris & Co., same as Model 615, designated Model 615S by Rickenbacker
101 instruments sold (only year): **1964**

Other Brands Made By Rickenbacker

All models sold by Radio-Tel (Rickenbacker's distribution company)

Electro ES-16: 3/4 size, extreme double cutaways with pointed horns, 1 chrome bar PU, 2 knobs, 1 switch, pickguard covers most of body, dot inlay, *Electro* with lightning bolt crossing *t* on peghead, fireglo, black, or natural finish
Introduced: **1964**

Electro ES-17: like Model 425, full scale, cresting wave cutaway shape, 1 chrome bar PU, 2 knobs, 1 switch, pickguard covers most of body, dot inlay, *Electro* with lightning bolt crossing *t* on peghead, fireglo, black, or natural finish
Introduced: **1964**

Ryder: Model 425 with Ryder label, available **1963**

Contello: Model 425 with Contello label, only year: **1962**

Doublenecks

Custom doublenecks available as early as **1961**.

4080: guitar and bass necks, cresting wave body shape, stereo electronics, guitar with Model 480 features, 2 PUs, *R* tailpiece, bass with 4001 features, 2 PUs, deluxe trim, cresting wave pegheads
Introduced: **1975**
Discontinued: **1985**

4080/12: 12-string guitar and 4-string bass necks, cresting wave body shape, 2 PUs per neck, deluxe trim, cresting wave pegheads
Introduced: **late 1970s**
Discontinued: **1985**

COMMENTS

The Bakelite Electro Spanish, which is the first production solidbody electric guitar, and the rare Vibrola Spanish models have considerable historic appeal although they are not regarded as utility instruments.

The most sought after Rickenbacker solidbodies are the early Combo models, particularly those with horseshoe PUs.

Ironically, Rickenbacker was a late entry into the postwar electric guitar market, but its designs for solidbody and hollowbody models were (and still are) unique and distinctive from those of all other makers. The Rickenbacker sound, too, is considered unique. Some players love it; others hate it. Rickenbackers from the 1970s are not highly sought after by collectors but are considered fine utility instruments by those players who prefer the Rickenbacker sound.

Considering Rickenbacker's history and reputation, it has remained a very small company compared to Fender or Gibson. Prior to 1966, the highest yearly sales figure for any model was 266 Model 450s in 1960. Four of the import models sold over 100

315

units in 1964, but no domestic hollowbody model sold over 100 units in a year until 1965. The biggest sales figure for any model in any year (pre-1969) was 1,164 Model 360-12s in 1966. Total sales of all F series models is probably less than 150 instruments. Total sales of all bass models from 1957–68 is probably not more than 800 instruments. Before 1966, which was a boom year for Rickenbacker, almost all models could be called rare in comparison to many Fender and Gibson models.

BASSES

SECTION ORGANIZATION
Solidbody
Hollowbody

Solidbody

4000: cresting wave body shape, horseshoe
PU, 2 knobs, mahogany neck-through-
body, maple side wings, Lucite pickguard
with gold back, rosewood fingerboard, dot
inlay, cresting wave peghead, natural
wood grain or 2-tone brown sunburst finish
Introduced: **June 1957**
Sliding bridge cover plate with string mute:
late 1957
Walnut neck by **1958**
Maple neck with walnut pieces laminated onto
peghead: **1960**
Fireglo finish optional: **1960**
Black or autumnglo finish optional: **early 1960s**
Slimmer, more contoured body: **1961**
Tailpiece with under-string mutes: **1963**
Metal PU cover, non-horseshoe PU: **1964**
Discontinued: **1987**

4001: deluxe version of 4000, 1 horseshoe PU, 1
bar PU, 4 knobs, 1-piece pickguard, checkered body binding, bound rosewood fingerboard, triangular inlay, walnut sides on
peghead, fireglo finish
Introduced: **Nov. 1961**
Metal PU cover, non-horseshoe PU: **1964**
Natural finish optional: **1965**
4001FL: fretless model, available by special
order: **late 1960s**
Some with ebony fingerboard: **late 1960s**
Discontinued: **1986**
4001FL: dot inlay, re-introduced: **1989**

4001S: export model, sold as **Model 1999** in
Europe by Rose, Morris & Co., Ltd., same
as 4001 but with horseshoe PU, dot inlay,
no binding
Export model introduced: **1964**
Metal PU cover, 2 understring (non-horseshoe) PUs: **1967**
Last sold by Rose, Morris: **1969**
Some sold by special order in the U.S.: **early
1970s**
4001S introduced as standard U.S. model: **1980**
4001V63: reissue of 1963 version 4001S, horseshoe PU, introduced: **1984**
4001S discontinued: **1985**
4001V63 still in production

4001CS: Chris Squire model, cresting wave
body shape, 1 horseshoe PU and 1 understring PU, 1-piece peghead and fingerboard of padauk wood (dark), dot inlay,

cresting wave peghead shape, cream
finish, limited edition of 1,000
Available: **1991**

4008: 8 strings, cresting wave body shape,
cresting wave peghead, available by special order only
Introduced: **1970s**
Discontinued: **1984**

3000: double cutaway with rounded horns,
similar shape to Fender Stratocaster, 1
humbucking PU, 2 knobs, 30" scale, standard trim, standard shape peghead
Introduced: **1975**
Discontinued: **1985**

3001: 33 1/2" scale version of 3000, 3 knobs
Introduced: **1975**
Discontinued: **1984**

4003: like 4001 (deluxe trim) but with 2-piece
pickguard and truss rod adjustment at
body end of neck, designed for round-
wound strings, little visible difference from
4001
Introduced: **1979**
4003S: like 4001 but with standard trim, 1-piece
pickguard, truss rod adjustment at peghead, introduced: **1980**
4003S5: 5 strings, introduced: **1987**
4003S8: 8 strings: **1987**
4003 with 1-piece pickguard, truss rod adjustment at peghead: **1985**
All models still in production

Blackstar: Mike Mesaros (of the Smithereens)
model, black fingerboard, pin dot fingerboard inlay, black knobs, limited edition of
200
Available: **1988**

4002: cresting wave body shape, curly maple
top, 2 humbucking PUs, 4 knobs, checkered body binding, bound fingerboard, triangular inlay, cresting wave peghead,
mapleglo or walnut finish, limited edition
Available: **1981**

2030: Hamburg Bass, double cutaway with
rounded horns, body shape somewhat similar to Fender Stratocaster, 2 PUs, 4 knobs,
active circuitry, contoured top, rosewood
fingerboard, dot inlay
Introduced: **1984**
Still in production

2050: El Dorado Bass, double cutaway with
rounded horns, body shape somewhat similar to Fender Stratocaster, 2 PUs, 4 knobs,
active circuitry, bound top, rosewood fingerboard, dot inlay, gold-plated metal parts

Rickenbacker

Basses

Introduced: **1984**
Still in production

Hollowbody

4005 and **4005-6** (6-string model): 360 style
body with New Style rounded top edges,
double cutaway with rounded points, 2
understring PUs, *R* tailpiece, single-bound
rosewood fingerboard, triangular inlay,
cresting wave peghead, fireglo or natural
finish
Introduced: **1965**
4005WB and **4005-6WB**: Old Style, white binding on top and back, introduced: **1966**
4005-8: 8-string model, asymmetrical peghead
longer on bass side (but not cresting wave
shape), available (rare): **late 1960s**
Standard Colorglo finishes optional: **1970s**
4005-6 discontinued: **1978**
All 4005 models discontinued: **1984**

4005S: export model, sold as **Model 3261** in
Europe by Rose, Morris & Co., Ltd.
Available: **1964–69**

4000L: like 331 light show guitar, available:
early 1970s

COMMENTS

Early examples of Models 4000 and 4001, with
horseshoe pickup, are among the most
sought after of all electric basses. They
are far rarer (less than 200 made pre-1964)
than the most sought after Fender models.
Unlike Rickenbacker guitars, the most highly
regarded Rick basses are the solidbody
models. Hollowbody models, although
rarer than solidbodies, are not as sought
after.

STEELS

SECTION ORGANIZATION
Singlenecks (no pedals)
Doublenecks
Console Models
Pedal Models

Singlenecks

Electro Hawaiian Guitar (Frying Pan): circular cast aluminum body, horseshoe PU, magnet 1 1/2" wide, no knobs, dot markers, slotted peghead, metal *Electro* nameplate (engraved logo on early examples)
Model A-25: 25" scale
Model A-22: 22 1/2" scale
Introduced: **1932**
Volume control knob added: **1934**
Rickenbacher added to nameplate: **1934**
Magnet 1/14" wide, chrome tailpiece, Phillips-head PU adjustment screws: **1946**
Discontinued: **1950**
A-22 re-introduced, Bakelite back plate, plastic fingerboard decal on peghead: **1954**
Discontinued: **1958**

Model B: Bakelite body and neck, horseshoe PU, magnet 1 1/2" wide, knurled adjustment nuts on PU, 1 octagonal knob on treble side, strings anchor through body, 5 decorative chrome plates, bolt-on neck with integral molded frets (custom variations include rounded-edge body, silver- or gold-plated parts)
Introduced: **July 1935**
2 round knobs with arrows on top, knobs on opposite sides, frets outlined in white: **1937**
Knobs on same side, frets outlined in white, knobs on same side, 7- and 8-string models available: **1938**
"Flying saucer" knobs with ridged edges by **1940**
10-string model, metal neck, available: **1940**
Black painted plates: **c. 1940**
White painted plates: **1940**
6-string referred to as **Model E** in mail-order literature, 7-string referred to as Model B: **1940 only**
Magnet 1/14" wide, chrome tailpiece, Phillips-head PU adjustment screws, metal insert in neck, T-shaped aluminum logo plate (some transitional examples with some but not all of these features): **1946**
Some with white plastic plates with tone and volume settings molded into plates: **late 1940s**
Some with vertical blade-shape logo plate: c. **1949**
BD: deluxe version, metal peghead cover,

introduced: **Mar. 1949**
Last T-shaped logo plate: **1950**
Model B discontinued by **1955**
Model BD discontinued: **1971**

Silver Hawaiian (pre-WWII model NS, Model No. 100): body stamped from sheet metal (usually brass), chrome-plated body, horseshoe PU, 1 knob, strings attach through holes in top
Introduced: **1937**
1 black knob, 1 white knob, knobs on same side: **1939**
8-string available by **1940**
Discontinued: **1943**

Model 59: body stamped from sheet metal, fixed-height horseshoe PU with 2 screws on each end, 1 knob, ivory or black crinkled paint finish
Introduced: **late 1937**
1 black knob and 1 white knob on opposite sides, shaded gray finish: **1939**
Discontinued: **1943**

Model S or postwar model NS (New Style): body stamped from sheet metal, height-adjustable horseshoe PU, 2 knobs, black dots or open holes for fingerboard markers, decal logo, shaded gray finish, some with slightly crinkled finish, doubleneck available (see following)
Introduced: **1946**
White dot markers, smooth finish, by **1948**
Discontinued: **early 1950s**

Academy: Bakelite body, horseshoe PU, 2 knobs, *Academy* on peghead, brown mahogany, maroon, or white finish
Introduced: **1946**
Discontinued, replaced by Ace (see following), by **1948**

Ace: Bakelite body, non-horseshoe PU, 2 knobs, plastic PU cover, *Ace* on peghead, brown mahogany, maroon, blue, or white finish
Introduced by **1948**
Discontinued: **1953**

Model SD: deluxe version of NS, body stamped from sheet metal, 2 knobs, Lucite fingerboard, peghead cover, 2-tone tan/mahogany enamel finish, 6, 7, or 8 strings
Introduced: **c. 1949**
Discontinued: **late 1953**

Model G (Deluxe Hawaiian): ornate version of Silver Hawaiian, chrome-plated body, Lucite fingerboard back-painted gold, gold-plated peghead cover, gold-plated

metal parts, 6 or 8 strings
Introduced: **late 1940s**
Discontinued: **1957**

Model SW: woodbody, straight-line body sides with bevels around fingerboard, 2 knobs, control plate extends to include knobs, metal fingerboard, block markers, peghead cover, dark or blond finish, 6 or 8 strings, 3 legs optional
Model TW: 10-string, blond finish only
Introduced by **1956**
TW discontinued: **1961**
SW discontinued: **1962**

Model CW: woodbody, 22 1/2" scale, 3 knobs, angled front edge, grille cloth on front edge, 2-tone walnut or maple finish, 3 legs, 6, 7, 8, or 10 strings (**CW-6, CW-7, CW-8, CW-10**)
Introduced: **1957**
25" scale available (**CW-61, CW-71, CW-81, CW-101**): **1958**
22 1/2" scale model renamed **JB** (see following): **1961**
Discontinued: **1971**

Model JB: Jerry Byrd model, woodbody, angled front edge, grille cloth on front with *Jerry Byrd* plate, 22 1/2" scale, 6, 7, 8, or 10 strings, 3 legs
Introduced: **1961**
Discontinued: **1971**

100 series: 6 strings, woodbody, straight-line body sides with bevels around fingerboard, 1-piece triangular control plate for knobs, block markers, no peghead cover
Model 100: light or silver gray finish (early with white speckles on black paint finish)
Model 102: natural finish
Model 100 introduced (listed as S-100) by **1955**
Model 102 introduced: **1957**
Model 105: gray or natural, 3 legs, introduced: **1959**
102 available with fireglo finish: **1961 only**
100, 102, 105 discontinued: **1971**

Model J-6: 6 strings, gray or brown metalbody
Introduced: **1957**
J-6 replaced by **J-8**: 8 strings: **1961**
J-8 discontinued: **1962**

Bronson Model 52: distributed by the Bronson company based in Detroit, Bakelite body, decorative metal plates, peghead cover with horizontal *Bronson* and vertical *Melody King*
Introduced by: **1948**

Doublenecks

Most doublenecks, regardless of body style, were designated by the letter *D* followed by a hyphen, followed by the number of strings. D-12=double 6-string, D-14=double 7-string, D-16=double 8-string. Any combination of 6-, 7-, and 8-string necks was available.

Electro doubleneck: stamped (NS-style) metalbody, Bakelite necks or metal necks
Introduced by **1940**
1 piece cast aluminum body and necks: **1946**
Discontinued by **1953**

Deluxe model: referred to as **DC-12** and **DC-16**, 1 piece cast aluminum body and necks, Lucite fingerboards, peghead covers
Introduced: **c. 1950**
Discontinued by **1953**

Some triplenecks made by custom order before World War II.

Model DW: woodbody, bevels around fingerboard, dark or blond finish, 12 or 16 strings, 3 legs optional
Introduced by **1956**
Discontinued **1961**

Console Models

Console 200 series: walnut or maple body, 22 1/2" scale, metal edge trim, metal tuner covers, blond, natural finish, 4 legs
Console 206: 2 6-string necks
Console 208: 2 8-string necks
Console 208: 8- and 10-string necks
Console 200 series introduced: **1956**
Console 200 series discontinued: **1971**

Console 500 series: walnut or maple, 22 1/2" scale, 3 necks, natural finish, 4 legs
Console 508: 2 8-string necks, 10-string middle neck
Console 518: 3 8-string necks
Console 500 series introduced: **1956**
Console 500 series discontinued: **1971**

Console 700 series: 25" scale, 2 knobs per neck, 1 or 2 pedals optional, walnut or blond finish
Console 706: 2 6-string necks
Console 708: 2 8-string necks
Console 718: 1 8-string and 1 10-string neck
Console 758: 3 8-string necks
Console 768: 2 8-string necks, 10-string middle neck
Console 700 series introduced: **1957**
Console 700 series discontinued: **1971**

Pedal Models

Pedal 780: 25" scale, 8 strings, 6 pedals, natural
finish
Pedal 785: 10 strings, 6 pedals
Pedal 780 and 785 introduced: **1961**
Pedal 790: 2 8-string necks, 6 pedals, intro-
duced: **1962**
All pedal models discontinued: **1971**

COMMENTS

Rickenbacker's prewar (1 1/2" wide) horseshoe
pickup is considered by many players to be
the finest pickup ever made for lap steel
playing. The prewar Frying Pan model, the
first production electric instrument by any
maker, is rare and highly sought after by
collectors. The Bakelite model, especially
the prewar version with wide pickup and
strings anchoring through the body, is not
as rare as the Frying Pan but is one of the
most sought after lap steels by players and
collectors. Models with bodies stamped
from sheet metal are not highly regarded,
except for the chrome-plated Silver
Hawaiian and the more ornate Model G,
which have some aesthetic appeal.
Postwar models are of less interest to collectors although they are considered to be
fine utility instruments, with the Jerry Byrd
model the most sought after.
Rickenbacker's pedal steels are not highly
regarded.

OTHER INSTRUMENTS

Electro Mandolin: flat top and back, oval body shape, body made by Harmony and similar to Harmony Patrician, 10 3/8" wide, 2 5/8" deep at neck, mahogany top, mahogany back and sides, oval hole, horseshoe PU, 5-ply binding above and below horseshoe, 1 knob, low bridge, 4-ply top binding, single-bound back, single-bound asymmetrical fingerboard, dot inlay, pearloid peghead veneer
Introduced: **mid 1930s**
Arched spruce top, maple back and sides: **late 1930s**
Arched back, vibrato available, by **1940**
Discontinued: **1943**

Electric Mandolin: solidbody, wide lower bout, 1 understring PU, shaded walnut finish, 4-string (**Model 5000**), 5-string (**Model 5001**), or 8-string (**Model 5002**)
Introduced: **1958**
Fireglo finish available: **1959**
Last price list appearance: **1961**

Bantar: electric 5-string banjo, round body shape, 2 chrome bar PUs, 4 knobs, *R* tailpiece, large white circular pickguard, deluxe or standard trim (same model number), fireglo or mapleglo finish (**Model 6000**)
Introduced: **1966**
Standard trim model discontinued: **1968**
Deluxe trim model discontinued: **mid 1970s**

Banjoline: endorsed by Eddy Peabody, 360-style body, 6 strings (2 paired, 2 singles), 2 chrome bar PUs, vibrato, plectrum banjo neck, standard (**6005**) or deluxe (**6006**) trim, woodgrain fireglo, woodgrain mapleglo, or solid azureglo finish
Introduced: **1968**
Discontinued: **mid 1970s**

Electro Violin, Viola, Cello: Bakelite body and neck, modified horseshoe PU, tuners below bridge, no peghead
Introduced: **1935**
Tubular aluminum body, conventional peghead, ebony fingerboard, Bakelite chinrest on violin and viola: **1939**
Discontinued: **1941**

Electro Bass Viol: metal body, double-coil horseshoe PU, 1 volume knob, ebony fingerboard, adjustable end pin, amplifier used as support stand
Introduced: **1935**
Tubular aluminum body, volume and tone controls: **1938**
Discontinued: **1941**

COMMENTS

Rickenbacker's pre-World War II instruments are sought after for historical reasons.
The postwar mandolin, along with the Bantar and Banjoline, are regarded as curiosities.

Independent
Makers

BENEDETTO

General Information and Models

Bob Benedetto began making archtop guitars in Clearwater, FL, in 1968. He has made approximately 223 archtop guitars, 150 electric solidbody guitars, 50 electric basses, 45 violins and 5 violas. From 1983-87, he made violins almost exclusively. He currently builds archtop guitars exclusively, making 30–35 instruments a year.

In 1990, Benedetto relocated to Stroudsberg, PA.

Current Models

All models: 16", 17", or 18" wide; single cutaway, spruce top, maple back and sides, floating PU; ebony bridge, tailpiece, fingerboard and pickguard; 25" scale

Cremona: no inlay on tailpiece, string anchor-holes at an angle, narrow pickguard with straight edges, no fingerboard inlay, walnut grain veneer on front and back of peghead, small scroll peghead inlay with engraved model name, ornamental peghead cutout, gold-plated or ebony tuner buttons

Fratello: no inlay on tailpiece, string anchor-holes straight across, unbound pickguard, square-end fingerboard, block inlay, ornamental peghead inlay under logo, center-dip peghead

Manhattan: no inlay on tailpiece, string anchor-holes at an angle, narrow pickguard with straight edges, no fingerboard inlay, small peghead inlay underlining logo, otherwise similar to Fratello

Limelite: ornamental inlay on tailpiece, string-anchor holes at an angle, bound pickguard, pointed-end fingerboard, slashed-block (blocks have slight "waist" indentions) inlay, tied-scroll peghead ornament with model name engraved, ornamental cutout at top of peghead, gold-plated or ebony tuner buttons

7-String: no inlay on tailpiece, string anchor-holes at an angle, narrow pickguard with straight edges, no fingerboard inlay, thin ornamental peghead inlays above and below logo, asymmetrical peghead with point at top, 4 tuners on bass side, 3 tuners on treble side

COMMENTS

Benedetto's craftsmanship is highly regarded and his instruments are played by many noted musicians.

Serial Numbers

All Benedetto archtop guitars are numbered in one series. Electric solidbodies and basses each have their own separate series.

Archtop guitars have a 4- or 5-digit serial number.

Last 2 digits=year.

Digits before last 2 digits=instrument number.

Example: 20189 was made in 1989 and is the 201st archtop made since 1968.

COLLINGS

General Information

Bill Collings began making flat top guitars in Houston, TX, in 1975. He relocated to Austin in 1980. By the late 1980s he had begun making archtops.

Collings has made approximately 350 flat top and 30 archtop guitars in various models.

Labels and Other Markings

No label, signature on inside back strip in green ink: **1975–79**

Light brown oval label, brown ink, *Bill Collings, Luthier*, illustration showing logs floating in river: **1979–84**

Parchment colored oval label (darker than previous label), brown ink, *Bill Collings, Luthier*, illustration showing logs and guitars floating in river: **1984–late 89**

Light brown oval label, black ink, *Collings, Austin, Texas*: **late 1989–current**

Gruhn Series Flat Tops

Collings made a series of flat top guitars designed by George Gruhn, available in dreadnought (D) or jumbo (F) shape, with plain (Style 1) or fancy (Style 2) ornamentation. These have a *Gruhn* logo on the peghead and a Collings label inside. All were made in 1989. They are numbered from 001-020.

Serial Numbers

Collings guitars made from 1975 into 1987 do not have serial numbers. Many have a handwritten date on the underside of the top.

Collings began numbering some (but not all) guitars in 1987.

Flat Tops

In 1988 Collings began numbering all flat top guitars in one consecutive series, beginning with approximately #175. Serial numbers are stamped on the neck block. As of December 12, 1990, flat top numbers had reached #342. Beginning in 1991, archtops are numbered in the same series with flat tops, but with a different number configuration (see following).

Archtops

Prior to 1991, Collings archtops have a separate serial number series. Beginning in 1991, archtops have a 2-part serial number. The first part is the instrument's ranking in the general series (with flat tops); the suffix is the ranking in the separate archtop series.

Example: 343-30 is the 343rd instrument and the 30th archtop.

D'ANGELICO

General Information and Models

John D'Angelico was born in New York City in 1905. At age nine he was apprenticed to a granduncle whose shop made violins, mandolins, and flat top guitars. D'Angelico established his own shop in New York in 1932 to make violins, mandolins, and archtop guitars. He began using model names circa 1934 and standardized his models circa 1937.

Early examples were modeled on Gibson's 16"-wide L-5 (but with 16 1/2"-wide body, different inlay, and no truss rod). Some archtops from the 1940s have a round or oval soundhole.

D'Angelico mandolins were made in two basic styles: a symmetrical pear-shape similar to Gibson's Style A and a two-point shape modeled after Lyon and Healy's Style A. The D'Angelico A has plain to moderate ornamentation. Most D'Angelico two-point models have a violin-type scroll peghead; a few have a peghead like that of the Excel guitar. Both body styles were available with either an oval hole or f-holes.

D'Angelico died September 1, 1964. He built a total of 1,164 guitars, the last 10 of which were finished by his apprentice Jimmy D'Aquisto and bear D'Aquisto's name on the peghead and tailpiece. His total mandolin production is estimated at 300–350.

General Changes

First cutaway model: **May 9, 1947**
f-holes...
    Standard shape: **1932**
    Straight angle rather than point at mid-f: **mid 1930s**
    Standard shape holes except on Excel: **1937**
    Standard shape holes, all models: **late 1930s**
Tailpieces...
    Straight-across string anchor piece: **1932**
    Slanted (but not stairstep) design...
        New Yorker: **mid 1937**
        Excel: **c. 1938**
    Stairstep tailpiece introduced: **c. 1940**
Necks...
    Reinforced but non-adjustable neck (no truss rod cover): **1932–c. 40**
    Adjustable truss rod, truss rod cover, introduced: **c. 1940**
    Some examples with no truss rod as late as **1949**

Models

Model specs vary due to custom orders and to D'Angelico's gradual evolution of designs.

Style A: 17" wide, parallel bracing, a few with X-braced top, smooth edge pickguard, block inlay, some early with dot inlay, rounded peak and 2 small points on top of peghead (some with no points)
Style A-1: specs unavailable
Style B: 17" wide, parallel bracing (a few with X-braced top), block inlay, unbound f-holes, peghead with broken-scroll pediment framing ornamental cupola (button), pointed angles on scroll
Styles A, A-1, and B first specified in D'Angelico's notebook: **1936**
Last A-1 (#1661): **Nov. 20, 1943**
Last Style A (#1690): **Sept. 14, 1945**
Last Style B (#1782): **Feb. 17, 1948**

New Yorker: 18" wide, X-braced top, triple-bound f-holes, black binding lines on body sides and side of fingerboard, split-block inlay, gold-plated metal parts, skyscraper logo, peghead with center dip
First recorded New Yorker: **1936**
Peghead with broken-scroll pediment framing ornamental cupola (button), rounded angles on scroll, some examples: **1937**
Center-dip peghead on some examples as late as: **1958**

Excel: 17" wide, X-braced top, bound f-holes, multiple-bound top and back, single-bound f-holes, block inlay, rounded-top peghead
First recorded Excel: **1936**
Peghead with broken-scroll pediment framing ornamental cupola (button), rounded angles on scroll, by **1937**
Rounded-top peghead on some examples as late as **1939**
Stairstep tailpiece by **1943**

Excel Special: 17" wide, New Yorker trim
First Excel Special (recorded as Small New Yorker): **1943**

G-7: electric hollowbody, plywood body supplied by Code or United (New Jersey-based companies), necks by D'Angelico, no D'Angelico serial number

COMMENTS

Players and collectors consider D'Angelico's Excel and New Yorker models to be among the finest archtop guitars ever made. They are (along with certain Stromberg models) the most sought after and most expensive archtops on the vintage market.

D'Angelico mandolins are extremely fine

instruments, although they have never achieved the recognition of D'Angelico guitars.

Serial Numbers

D'Angelico serial numbers are not strictly chronological. Some overlaps in date ranges occur.

Guitar Numbers	*Approx. Range*
No number	1932–34
1005–1097	1932–34
1105–1235	1936
1234–1317	1937
1318–1385	1938
1388–1456	1939
1457–1508	1940
1509–1562	1941
1563–1621	1942
1622–1658	1943
1659–1681	1944
1682–1702	1945
1703–1740	1946
1738–1781	1947
1782–1804	1948
1805–1831	1949
1832–1855	1950
1856–1885	1951
1886–1908	1952
1909–1936	1953
1933–1962	1954
1961–1988	1955
1989–2017	1956
2018–2040	1957
2041–2067	1958
2068–2098	1959
2099–2122	1960
2123–2164	1961–64
2211–2214	1955–56

Mandolin Numbers	
No number	1932–39
125–135	1940
136–148	1941
149–168	1942–44

D'AQUISTO

General Information and Models

Jimmy D'Aquisto apprenticed to John D'Angelico. After D'Angelico's death in 1964, D'Aquisto opened his own shop. He built his first 10 guitars to D'Angelico specs (but with *D'Aquisto* on the peghead), after which he began implementing his own design concepts. Many of his instruments are custom made, with variations including round holes, oval holes, S-shaped holes, 7-strings, flat tops, and tenors.

Pickguards are in various shapes, with or without stairsteps or points.

The first 16 D'Aquistos have peghead features—including logo, truss rod cover, cutout at top, and ornamental button—similar to those of a D'Angelico New Yorker. The cutout at the top of the peghead evolved from D'Angelico's broken-scroll (inverted-T) shape to a more circular shape.

D'Aquisto-designed guitars have also been manufactured by Hagstrom, beginning in 1968, and by Fender/Japan in the 1980s.

General Changes

Evolution to S-shaped soundholes: **1967–69**
Evolution to circular peghead cutout : **1967–69**
Transition to ebony tailpiece and pickguard: **1970–73**

Archtop Models

New Yorker Special: 17" wide
New Yorker Deluxe: 18" wide
First New Yorker: **May 1965**
Later examples have model name engraved on pearl scroll inlaid on peghead

Excel: 17" wide
First Excel: **Aug. 1965**

New Yorker Classic: 17" or 18" wide, unbound S-holes or oval hole, wood binding, no fingerboard inlay, wood peghead veneer
First New Yorker Classic: **1985**

Avant Garde: unbound elliptical holes, wood binding, wood peghead veneer
First Avant Garde: **1987**

Miscellaneous Models

First solidbody: **1976**
First flat top, 16" wide: **1975**
First hollowbody electric, plywood construction: **1976**

COMMENTS

D'Aquisto is the most highly regarded living builder of archtop guitars. His instruments are so sought after by players and collectors that the waiting list is several years for new instruments. While D'Angelico Excel and New Yorker models bring higher prices than D'Aquisto models, D'Aquisto's reputation is steadily growing, as are the prices of his guitars. His reputation is based on archtops, but all instruments made by him are of value.

Serial Numbers

Standard Archtops

Number Range	Year (Occasional Overlaps)
1001–1005	1965
1006–1014	1966
1015–1022	1967
1023–1029	1968
1030–1036	1969
1037–1043	1970
1044–1050	1971
1051–1063	1972
1064–1073	1973
1074–1084	1974
1085–1094	1975
1095–1102	1976
1103–1112	1977
1113–1125	1978
1126–1133	1979
1134–1142	1980
1143–1151	1981
1152–1160	1982
1161–1164	1983
1166–1175	1984
1176–1183	1985
1185–1192	1986
1193–1202	1987
1201–1210	1988
1211–1217	1989
1218–1228	1990

Other Models

Early solidbody electrics have E### configuration, beginning with E101.
Later solidbody electrics have a 3-digit number, beginning with 111.
Flat tops have their own series from 1973–83, beginning with 101.
Plywood hollowbody electrics are un-numbered through the first 28 instruments (1977–79); numbered examples start in 1982 beginning with 101.
Total production of 3 mandolins: #101, 102, and 103, the last in 1972.

GILCHRIST

General Information

Stephen Gilchrist is an Australian who began making instruments in 1976. He spent 1980 in the United States, refining his designs while working at Gruhn Guitars in Nashville. He is best known for mandolins, mandolas, and mandocellos. His mandolins are modeled after the Gibson F-5. His mandolas are larger than traditional Gibson-size mandolas.

Gilchrist has also made some acoustic and electric guitars. Most of the electric guitars were made from 1987–88. Some do not bear the Gilchrist name anywhere on the instrument, and none has a serial number.

Gilchrist is based in Warrnambool, Victoria, Australia.

COMMENTS

Gilchrist's F-style mandolins and mandolas, as well as his mandocellos, are regarded by players as among the finest by any current maker.

Serial Numbers

From 1978 through 1982, the serial number is preceded by the last 2 digits of the year.

Number Range	Date of Completion
1–9	1976–77
7810–7849	1978
7950–7954	May 1979
7955–7962	June 1979
7963–7965	Aug. 1979
7966–7972	Oct. 1979
7973–7980	Nov. 1979
8081	Mar. 1980
8082	Apr. 1980
8083	June 1980
8084–8087	Aug. 1980
8088–8094	Oct. 1980
8085–8099	Dec. 1980
81100–81101	Apr. 1981
81102	June 1981
81103–81104	July 1981
81105–81108	Sept. 1981
81109–81117	Dec. 1981
82118–82120	May 1982
82121–82122	Mar. 1982
82123	Feb. 1982
82124–82125	Sept. 1982
82126	June 1982
82127–82128	Mar. 1982
82129–82131	Sept. 1982
82132–82144	Dec. 1982
145–152	Dec. 1983
153–160	July 1984
161–170	Jan. 1985
(none made in 1986)	
171–174	July 1987
175	May 1987
176	June 1988
177–183	July 1987
184–185	June 1988
186	May 1989
187–192	Dec. 1989
193	Apr. 1990
194	Dec. 1989
195	July 1989
196–202	July 1990
203–209	Jan. 1991
210–211	Oct. 1990

STROMBERG

General Information and Models

Charles Stromberg opened an instrument business in Boston circa 1905, producing banjos and drums. His son Elmer, born July 14, 1895, joined him in the business in 1910. They began making guitars in the 1930s. Elmer Stromberg died in 1955, a few months after his father's death.

The shop of Chas. Stromberg and Son produced high quality banjos as well as guitars but is best known for the guitars made from the mid 1940s onward. Their great volume made them attractive to players who had to compete with horn sections in jazz bands.

Total production of Stromberg guitars is estimated at about 640 instruments.

Note: Some student-grade instruments from the 1920s and 1930s were marketed under a Chicago-made Stromberg brand that was unrelated to Charles and Elmer Stromberg. Instruments made by Charles and Elmer Stromberg are labeled Chas. Stromberg and Son with a Boston address.

General Changes

16" wide, 3-segment *f*-holes, criss-cross top bracing (2 parallel and 3 ladder braces): **throughout 1930s**

17" wide, 3-segment *f*-holes, 2 parallel braces: **c. 1940**

Standard *f*-holes, 2 parallel braces: **early 1940s**

1 diagonal brace from upper bass bout to lower treble: **mid to late 1940s**

Cutaway available on G-3, DeLuxe, and Master 400 models: **late 1940s**

Adjustable truss rod with adjustment under nut (nut is removable), introduced: **c. late 1940s**

Labels

Stromberg's labels were actually business cards, so instruments can be roughly dated by the telephone numbers on the labels.

Phone Number	Range
Bowdoin 1228R or 1728M	1920–27
Bowdoin 6559W or 1242W	1927–29
Bowdoin 1878R	1929–32
CA 3174	1932–45
CA 7-3174, by	1949–55

Pegheads

Almost all Stromberg guitars have an engraved plastic peghead veneer. Very few examples have a pearl inlaid peghead.

Models

Specs for Deluxe, G-1, and G-3 are for later versions of these models. Specs for all models vary due to custom orders an evolution of designs.

Master 400: 19" wide, non-cutaway (a few cutaways made), heavy tailpiece with 5 cutouts, bound pickguard with stairstep treble side, bound *f*-holes, pointed-end ebony fingerboard, slashed-block inlay (custom patterns optional), plastic peghead veneer, *400* on peghead, gold-plated metal parts, sunburst or natural finish

Master 300: 19" wide, bound stairstep pickguard, block inlay

Deluxe and **Deluxe Cutaway**: 17 3/8" wide, tailpiece with 3 cutouts and Y-shaped center section, bound pickguard with stairstep treble side, bound *f*-holes, bound ebony fingerboard with pointed end, gold-plated metal parts, *Deluxe* on peghead, natural or sunburst finish

G-1 (early **G-100**): tailpiece with 2 horizontal plates and 4 vertical tubes, triple-bound top and back, bound pickguard, notched-diamond or 4-point inlay, bound peghead, nickel-plated metal parts,

G-3 and **G-3 Cutaway**: 17 3/8" wide, bound pickguard with straight edges, ebony fingerboard, slashed-block inlay, gold-plated metal parts, natural or sunburst finish

COMMENTS

Although Stromberg's workmanship is generally regarded as not equal to that of D'Angelico, Stromberg's late model guitars have such superb sound that they bring prices on a par with D'Angelicos. The early models with multiple top braces are not highly regarded by most players but are of interest to collectors because of the Stromberg reputation.

Appendix

Many electric instruments and amplifiers can be dated by the numbers on the potentiometers (pots), speaker rims or other electronic parts. The Electronic Industries Association has a standardized number system, called the "source-date" code, that indicates the company, year, and week of manufacture. Although EIA was formed in 1924, codes on pots and speakers do not appear until after World War II.

The code is a 6- or 7-digit number. On pots it is impressed (except for some ink-stamped in the early 1950s) in various places: straight across the back, arced around the edge of the back, or on the side. On speakers, it is painted on the speaker rim.

The first three digits signify the maker:

    106=Allen-Bradley Corp.
    134=CentraLab
    137=CTS
    140=Clarostat
    220=Jensen (speakers)
    304=Stackpole
    328=Utah/Oxford (speakers)
    381=Bourns Networks
    465=Oxford (speakers)

In a 6-digit code, the fourth digit corresponds to the last digit of the year of manufacturer. In a 7-digit code, the fourth and fifth digits correspond to the year of manufacture. Typically, 6-digit codes were used through 1960 on pots. In 1961 and after, 7 digits are the norm. Most amp speakers did not switch to the 7-digit number but continue with 6 digits.

The last 2 digits signify the week of the year in which the part was made. Obviously, a series of numbers ending with 2 digits greater than 52 can not be a dating code.

Sometimes there is a space after the first 3 digits, sometimes a hyphen, sometimes no space.

Examples:

304-6320 was made by Stackpole in the 20th week of 1963.

1377633 was made by CTS in the 33rd week of 1976.

304731 was made by Stackpole in the 31st week of either 1947 or 1957. The actual date must be determined by the instrument's specs.

The pot must be original, of course, for the date to be of use.

The pot date signifies only the earliest possible date that the instrument could have been made. A pot dated the 50th week of 1952, for example, probably means the instrument wasn't finished until 1953.

Many Fenders from the early 1950s have Clarostat pots with the code stamped in blue ink.

Practically all Fenders from 1966–69 have 1966 pots. (CBS apparently bought a huge supply of pots after acquiring Fender in 1965.)

For Fenders, better-selling models usually have pot dates closer to neck dates than do the less popular models. Lap steels often have pots with dates as far as two years apart.

Gibson began using coded pots in 1953 or 1954.

All Guild electrics from 1979 to current production have 1979 pots.

National used Stackpole pots with source-date codes as early as 1945, although postwar instrument production did not resume until 1946. Up until circa 1955, Stackpole codes are on the back. After that, codes are on the side.

A patent number on an instrument gives the earliest possible date that instrument or part could have been made.

A patent pending notice pre-dates an actual patent number. Patents typically take a year or two from the application to the granting of the patent. Even after a patent has been granted, parts with a patent pending notice may be used up before new parts with a patent number are introduced.

Year	First Number of Year	Year		Year		Year	
1836	1	1880	223,211	1927	1,612,700	1974	3,781,914
1837	110	1881	236,137	1928	1,654,521	1975	3,858,241
1838	546	1882	251,685	1929	1,696,897	1976	3,930,271
1839	1,061	1883	269,820	1930	1,742,181	1977	4,000,520
1840	1,465	1884	291,016	1931	1,787,424	1978	4,065,812
1841	1,923	1885	310,163	1932	1,839,190	1979	4,139,952
1842	2,413	1886	333,494	1933	1,892,663	1980	4,180,867
1846	2,901	1887	355,291	1934	1,941,449	1981	4,242,757
1844	3,395	1888	375,720	1935	1,985,878	1982	4,308,622
1845	3,873	1889	395,305	1936	2,026,516	1983	4,366,579
1846	4,348	1890	418,665	1937	2,066,309	1984	4,423,523
1847	4,914	1891	443,987	1938	2,104,004	1985	4,490,855
1848	5,409	1892	466,315	1939	2,142,080	1986	4,562,596
1849	5,993	1893	488,976	1940	2,185,170	1987	4,633,526
1850	6,981	1894	511,744	1941	2,227,418	1988	4,716,594
1851	7,865	1895	531,619	1942	2,268,540	1989	4,794,652
1852	8,622	1896	552,502	1943	2,307,007		
1853	9,512	1897	574,369	1944	2,338,081		
1854	10,358	1898	596,467	1945	2,366,154		
1855	12,117	1899	616,871	1946	2,391,856		
1856	14,009	1900	640,167	1947	2,413,675		
1857	16,324	1901	664,827	1948	2,433,824		
1858	19,010	1902	690,385	1949	2,457,797		
1859	22,477	1903	717,521	1950	2,492,944		
1860	26,642	1904	748,567	1951	2,563,016		
1861	31,005	1905	778,834	1952	2,580,379		
1862	34,045	1906	808,618	1953	2,624,046		
1863	37,266	1907	839,799	1954	2,664,562		
1864	41,047	1908	875,679	1955	2,698,434		
1865	45,685	1909	908,436	1956	2,728,913		
1866	51,784	1910	945,010	1957	2,775,762		
1867	60,658	1911	980,178	1958	2,818,567		
1868	72,959	1912	1,013,095	1959	2,866,973		
1869	85,503	1913	1,049,326	1960	2,919,443		
1870	98,460	1914	1,083,267	1961	2,966,681		
1871	110,617	1915	1,123,212	1962	3,015,103		
1872	122,304	1916	1,166,419	1963	3,070,801		
1873	134,504	1917	1,210,389	1964	3,116,487		
1874	146,120	1918	1,251,458	1965	3,163,865		
1875	158,350	1919	1,290,027	1966	3,226,729		
1876	171,641	1920	1,326,899	1967	3,295,143		
1877	185,813	1921	1,364,063	1968	3,360,800		
1878	198,733	1922	1,401,948	1969	3,419,907		
1879	211,078	1923	1,440,362	1970	3,487,470		
		1924	1,478,996	1971	3,551,909		
		1925	1,521,590	1972	3,631,539		
		1926	1,568,040	1973	3,707,729		

Recommended Reading

Research on vintage instruments is ongoing, with new discoveries being made almost every day. Some of the books listed here were considered to be thorough, all-encompassing works when they were first published, yet several are now into third editions—an indication that these fields of study are still being expanded, revised, and refined. New books are in progress on a variety of vintage instruments, including Gibson Super 400s by Tom Van Hoose, National metalbody guitars by Bob Brozman, Gretsch guitars by Jay Scott, Fender Telecasters by A. R. Duchossoir, and a Fender company history by Richard Smith.

There are more books available than those listed here, and there is seldom a music-related book, article, or photograph that doesn't hold some useful information.

We feel that the following books are the most accurate and comprehensive on their subjects:

Duchossoir, A. R. *The Fender Stratocaster*. Rev. ed. Milwaukee, WI: Hal Leonard Publishing Corporation (distributor), 1990.

___. *Gibson Electrics, Vol. 1* . Milwaukee, WI: Hal Leonard Publishing Corporation (distributor), 1981.

___. *Guitar Indentification*. 3rd ed. Milwaukee, WI: Hal Leonard Publishing Corporation (distributor), 1990.

Hartman, Robert Carl. *Guitars and Mandolins in America, Featuring the Larsons' Creations*. Rev. ed. Hoffman Estates, IL: Maurer & Co., 1988

Longworth, Mike. *Martin Guitars: A History*. 3rd ed. Nazareth, PA: Mike Longworth, 1988.

Schmidt, Paul William. *Acquired of the Angels: The Lives and Works of Master Guitar Makers John D'Angelico and James D'Aquisto*. Metuchen, NJ: The Scarecrow Press, Inc., 1991.

Smith, Richard. *The Complete History of Rickenbacker Guitars*. Fullerton, CA: Centerstream Publishing, 1987.

Wheeler, Tom. *American Guitars*. New York, NY: HarperPerennial (HarperCollins), 1990.

Model Index

339

Model Index

Model Index

Model Index

Model Index

344

Model Index

Model Index

Model Index

Model Index

349

Model Index

Model Index